Alcoholism

SOURCEBOOK

Fifth Edition

Health Reference Series

Fifth Edition

Alcoholism SOURCEBOOK

Basic Consumer Health Information about Alcohol Use, Abuse, and Addiction, including Facts about the Physical Consequences of Alcohol Abuse, Such as Brain Changes and Problems with Cognitive Functioning, Cirrhosis and Other Liver Diseases, Cardiovascular Disease, Pancreatitis, and Alcoholic Neuropathy, and the Effects of Alcohol on Reproductive Health and Fetal Development, Mental Health Problems Associated with Alcohol Abuse, and Alcohol's Impact on Families, Workplaces, and the Community

Along with Information about Underage Drinking, Alcohol Treatment and Recovery, a Glossary of Related Terms, and Directories of Resources for More Information

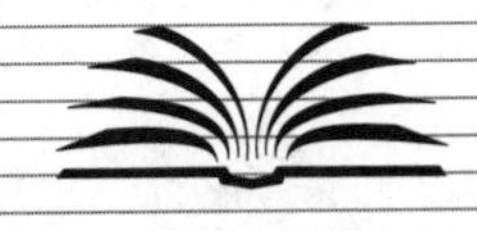

OMNIGRAPHICS

615 Griswold, Ste. 901, Detroit, MI 48226

* * *

OMNIGRAPHICS
Angela L. Williams, *Managing Editor*

***

ISBN 978-0-7808-1624-4
E-ISBN 978-0-7808-1625-1

Library of Congress Cataloging-in-Publication Data

Names: Omnigraphics, Inc., issuing body.

Title: Alcoholism sourcebook: basic consumer health information about alcohol use, abuse, and addiction, including facts about the physical consequences of alcohol abuse, such as brain changes and problems with cognitive functioning, cirrhosis and other liver diseases, cardiovascular disease, pancreatitis, and alcoholic neuropathy, and the effects of alcohol on reproductive health and fetal development, mental health problems associated with alcohol abuse, and alcohol's impact on families, workplaces, and the community; along with information about underage drinking, alcohol treatment and recovery, a glossary of related terms, and directories of resources for more information.

Description: Fifth edition. | Detroit, MI: Omnigraphics, [2018] | Series: Health reference series | Includes bibliographical references and index.

Identifiers: LCCN 2018008018 (print) | LCCN 2018009149 (ebook) | ISBN 9780780816251 (eBook) | ISBN 9780780816244 (hardcover: alk. paper)

Subjects: LCSH: Alcoholism--Popular works. | Consumer education.

Classification: LCC RC565 (ebook) | LCC RC565.A4493 2018 (print) | DDC 362.292/86--dc23

LC record available at https://lccn.loc.gov/2018008018

This book is printed on acid-free paper meeting the ANSI Z39.48 Standard. The infinity symbol that appears above indicates that the paper in this book meets that standard.

Printed in the United States

Table of Contents

Part II: The Problem of Underage Drinking

Part III: The Physical Effects and Consequences of Alcohol Abuse

Part IV: The Effects of Alcohol on Reproductive and Fetal Health

Part V: Mental Health Problems Associated with Alcohol Abuse

Part VI: Alcohol's Impact on Family, Work, and the Community

Part VII: Treatment and Recovery

Part VIII: Additional Help and Information

Preface

About This Book

Excessive alcohol use causes approximately 88,000 deaths each year, making it the third leading lifestyle-related cause of death in the United States. Alcohol affects every organ in the drinker's body. While moderate alcohol use can have some health benefits for adults, heavy alcohol use and binge drinking can harm the body, disrupt relationships, and lead to risky behaviors, injuries, illnesses, or death. Furthermore, alcohol use can cause permanent harm to underage drinkers and to the unborn children of pregnant women.

Alcoholism Sourcebook, Fifth Edition provides readers with updated information about alcohol use, abuse, and dependence. Physical alcohol-related effects on the brain, liver, pancreas, heart, lungs, nerves, and kidneys are described, and mental health issues that often accompany alcohol problems are discussed. A section on the problem of underage drinking looks at the causes and consequences of drinking among adolescents, and another section discusses the effects of alcohol use on reproductive and fetal health. Facts about alcohol's impact on families, workplaces, and communities are included, and guidance is provided for helping someone with an alcohol problem receive appropriate treatment and recovery services. The book concludes with a glossary of terms related to alcohol use and abuse and directories of resources for support and additional information.

How to Use This Book

This book is divided into parts and chapters. Parts focus on broad areas of interest. Chapters are devoted to single topics within a part.

Part I: Understanding Alcohol Use, Abuse, and Dependence reviews guidelines for the safe consumption of alcohol and offers facts about identifying when alcohol use transitions into abuse and may precipitate problems. It explains the course of alcohol dependence and discusses risk factors, including genetic links to addiction vulnerabilities. It further discusses myths about alcohol use.

Part II: The Problem of Underage Drinking describes the overview of underage drinking and also explains the drinking patterns and alcohol-related problems experienced by teens and college students. It discusses alcohol's impact on development, offers prevention strategies for families, schools, and communities, and explains the rationale behind laws establishing a minimum legal drinking age.

Part III: The Physical Effects and Consequences of Alcohol Abuse gives facts about alcohol impairment from various levels of blood alcohol concentration (BAC), alcohol poisoning, and alcohol hangover. It describes how alcohol changes the brain and affects the liver, cardiovascular system, kidneys, lungs, bones, and other organs. Information about alcohol interactions with other disorders and medications are also included. Alcohol-induced organ injury and the role of nutrition are also discussed.

Part IV: The Effects of Alcohol on Reproductive and Fetal Health describes about how excessive alcohol use causes risk to both men and women's reproductive health. It also explains how alcohol use impacts the reproductive organs and how it can lead to life-long impairments among children of women who drink during pregnancy and can also lead to infertility. Detailed information about the effects of alcohol on a fetus is presented along with a discussion of fetal alcohol spectrum disorders (FASD), adopting and fostering children with FASD, and mental illness that co-occur with FASD are also discussed.

Part V: Mental Health Problems Associated with Alcohol Abuse discusses the impact alcohol has on anxiety disorders, and posttraumatic stress disorder (PTSD). Separate chapters describe the connection of alcohol with other addiction disorders and even suicide.

Part VI: Alcohol's Impact on Family, Work, and the Community includes information about children living with alcohol-abusing parents, interpersonal violence related to alcohol, the effects of alcohol-impaired driving, social risks, and alcohol-related fire fatalities.

Part VII: Treatment and Recovery discusses helping strategies, programs, and support groups for families and individuals who decide to change their alcohol consumption habits. It describes alcohol addiction screening and explains the differences between brief interventions and long-term treatments. It also offers facts about the treatment process and explores new treatment options, including information on detoxification, withdrawal, pharmacological treatments, integrated treatments for co-occurring disorders such as drug abuse or mental illness. It also provides information about counseling and long-term support for those with disorders. It discusses about the gaps in clinical prevention and treatment for alcohol use disorders.

Part VIII: Additional Help and Information provides a glossary of terms related to alcohol use and abuse. Resource directories with listings of support groups for alcohol-related concerns, state agencies for substance abuse services, and organizations with additional information about alcohol use and abuse are also included.

Bibliographic Note

This volume contains documents and excerpts from publications issued by the following U.S. government agencies: Centers for Disease Control and Prevention (CDC); Child Welfare Information Gateway; Federal Trade Commission (FTC); Genetic and Rare Diseases Information Center (GARD); National Cancer Institute (NCI); National Heart, Lung, and Blood Institute (NHLBI); National Highway Traffic Safety Administration (NHTSA); National Institute of Arthritis and Musculoskeletal and Skin Diseases (NIAMS); National Institute of Diabetes and Digestive and Kidney Diseases (NIDDK); National Institute of Mental Health (NIMH); National Institute on Aging (NIA); National Institute on Alcohol Abuse and Alcoholism (NIAAA); National Institute on Drug Abuse (NIDA); National Institute on Drug Abuse (NIDA) for Teens; National Institutes of Health (NIH); *NIH News in Health*; Office of Disease Prevention and Health Promotion (ODPHP); Office of Juvenile Justice and Delinquency Prevention (OJJDP); Office of the Surgeon General (OGS); Office on Women's Health (OWH); Substance Abuse and Mental Health Services Administration (SAMHSA); U.S. Coast Guards Boating Safety Division; U.S. Department of Health and Human Services (HHS); U.S. Department of Justice (DOJ);

U.S. Department of the Treasury (USDT); U.S. Department of Veterans Affairs (VA); and U.S. Fire Administration (FA).

It may also contain original material produced by Omnigraphics and reviewed by medical consultants.

About the Health Reference Series

The *Health Reference Series* is designed to provide basic medical information for patients, families, caregivers, and the general public. Each volume takes a particular topic and provides comprehensive coverage. This is especially important for people who may be dealing with a newly diagnosed disease or a chronic disorder in themselves or in a family member. People looking for preventive guidance, information about disease warning signs, medical statistics, and risk factors for health problems will also find answers to their questions in the *Health Reference Series*. The *Series*, however, is not intended to serve as a tool for diagnosing illness, in prescribing treatments, or as a substitute for the physician/patient relationship. All people concerned about medical symptoms or the possibility of disease are encouraged to seek professional care from an appropriate healthcare provider.

A Note about Spelling and Style

Health Reference Series editors use *Stedman's Medical Dictionary* as an authority for questions related to the spelling of medical terms and the *Chicago Manual of Style* for questions related to grammatical structures, punctuation, and other editorial concerns. Consistent adherence is not always possible, however, because the individual volumes within the *Series* include many documents from a wide variety of different producers, and the editor's primary goal is to present material from each source as accurately as is possible. This sometimes means that information in different chapters or sections may follow other guidelines and alternate spelling authorities. For example, occasionally a copyright holder may require that eponymous terms be shown in possessive forms (Crohn's disease vs. Crohn disease) or that British spelling norms be retained (leukaemia vs. leukemia).

Medical Review

Omnigraphics contracts with a team of qualified, senior medical professionals who serve as medical consultants for the *Health Reference*

Series. As necessary, medical consultants review reprinted and originally written material for currency and accuracy. Citations including the phrase, "Reviewed (month, year)" indicate material reviewed by this team. Medical consultation services are provided to the *Health Reference Series* editors by:

Dr. Vijayalakshmi, MBBS, DGO, MD
Dr. Senthil Selvan, MBBS, DCH, MD
Dr. K. Sivanandham, MBBS, DCH, MS (Research), PhD

Our Advisory Board

We would like to thank the following board members for providing initial guidance on the development of this series:

- Dr. Lynda Baker, Associate Professor of Library and Information Science, Wayne State University, Detroit, MI
- Nancy Bulgarelli, William Beaumont Hospital Library, Royal Oak, MI
- Karen Imarisio, Bloomfield Township Public Library, Bloomfield Township, MI
- Karen Morgan, Mardigian Library, University of Michigan-Dearborn, Dearborn, MI
- Rosemary Orlando, St. Clair Shores Public Library, St. Clair Shores, MI

Health Reference Series *Update Policy*

The inaugural book in the *Health Reference Series* was the first edition of *Cancer Sourcebook* published in 1989. Since then, the *Series* has been enthusiastically received by librarians and in the medical community. In order to maintain the standard of providing high-quality health information for the layperson the editorial staff at Omnigraphics felt it was necessary to implement a policy of updating volumes when warranted.

Medical researchers have been making tremendous strides, and it is the purpose of the *Health Reference Series* to stay current with the most recent advances. Each decision to update a volume is made on an individual basis. Some of the considerations include how much new information is available and the feedback we receive from people who use the books. If there is a topic you would like to see added to the update list, or an area of medical concern you feel has not been adequately addressed, please write to:

Managing Editor
Health Reference Series
Omnigraphics
615 Griswold, Ste. 901
Detroit, MI 48226

Part One

Understanding Alcohol Use, Abuse, and Dependence

Chapter 1

Alcohol and Alcohol Use

What Is Alcohol?

Ethyl alcohol, or ethanol, is an intoxicating ingredient found in beer, wine, and liquor. Alcohol is produced by the fermentation of yeast, sugars, and starches.

How Does Alcohol Affect a Person?

Alcohol affects every organ in the body. It is a central nervous system (CNS) depressant that is rapidly absorbed from the stomach and small intestine into the bloodstream. Alcohol is metabolized in the liver by enzymes. However, the liver can only metabolize a small amount of alcohol at a time, leaving the excess alcohol to circulate throughout the body. The intensity of the effect of alcohol on the body is directly related to the amount consumed.

Why Do Some People React Differently to Alcohol than Others?

Individual reactions to alcohol vary, and are influenced by many factors, such as:

- Age
- Sex

This chapter includes text excerpted from "Alcohol and Public Health—Frequently Asked Questions," Centers for Disease Control and Prevention (CDC), March 29, 2018.

- Race or ethnicity
- Physical condition (e.g., weight, fitness level)
- Amount of food consumed before drinking
- How quickly the alcohol was consumed
- Use of drugs or prescription medicines
- Family history of alcohol problems

What Is a Standard Drink in the United States?

A standard drink is equal to 14 grams (0.6 ounce) of pure alcohol. Generally, this amount of pure alcohol is found in:

- 12 ounces of beer (5% alcohol content)
- 8 ounces of malt liquor (7% alcohol content)
- 5 ounces of wine (12% alcohol content)
- 1.5 ounces or a "shot" of 80-proof (40% alcohol content) distilled spirits or liquor (e.g., gin, rum, vodka, whiskey)

Is Beer or Wine Safer to Drink than Liquor?

No. One 12-oz. beer has about the same amount of alcohol as one 5-oz. glass of wine or 1.5-oz. shot of liquor. It is the amount of alcohol consumed that affects a person most, not the type of alcoholic drink.

What Does Moderate Drinking Mean?

According to the *Dietary Guidelines for Americans* (DGA), moderate alcohol consumption is defined as having up to 1 drink per day for women and up to 2 drinks per day for men. This definition refers to the amount consumed on any single day and is not intended as an average over several days. However, the *Dietary Guidelines* do not recommend that people who do not drink alcohol start drinking for any reason.

How Do I Know If It's Okay to Drink?

According to the 2015–2020 DGA, some people should not drink alcoholic beverages at all, including:

- Anyone younger than age 21
- Women who are or may be pregnant

- People who are driving, planning to drive, or are participating in other activities requiring skill, coordination, and alertness
- People taking certain prescription or over-the-counter (OTC) medications that can interact with alcohol
- People with certain medical conditions
- People who are recovering from alcoholism or who are unable to control the amount they drink

The *Dietary Guidelines* also recommend that if alcohol is consumed, it should be in moderation—up to 1 drink per day for women and up to 2 drinks per day for men—and only by adults of legal drinking age. However, the *Guidelines* do not recommend that people who do not drink alcohol start drinking for any reason. By following the *Dietary Guidelines*, you can reduce the risk of harm to yourself or others.

Is It Safe to Drink Alcohol and Drive?

No. Alcohol use slows reaction time and impairs judgment and coordination, which are all skills needed to drive a car safely. The more alcohol consumed, the greater the impairment.

What Does It Mean to Be above the Legal Limit for Drinking?

The legal limit for drinking is the alcohol level above which a person is subject to legal penalties (e.g., arrest and possible loss of a driver's license).

- Legal limits are measured using either a blood alcohol test or a breathalyzer.
- Legal limits are typically defined by state law, and may vary according to individual characteristics, such as age and occupation.

All states in the United States have adopted 0.08 percent (80 mg/dL) as the legal limit for operating a motor vehicle for drivers aged 21 years or older. However, drivers younger than 21 are not allowed to operate a motor vehicle with any level of alcohol in their system.

Legal limits do not define a level below which it is safe to operate a vehicle or engage in some other activity. Impairment due to alcohol use begins to occur at levels well below the legal limit.

What Is Excessive Alcohol Use?

Excessive alcohol use includes binge drinking, heavy drinking, any alcohol use by people under the age 21 minimum legal drinking age, and any alcohol use by pregnant women.

What Is Binge Drinking?

According to the National Institute on Alcohol Abuse and Alcoholism (NIAAA) binge drinking is defined as a pattern of alcohol consumption that brings the blood alcohol concentration (BAC) level to 0.08 percent or more. This pattern of drinking usually corresponds to 5 or more drinks on a single occasion for men or 4 or more drinks on a single occasion for women, generally within about 2 hours.

What Do You Mean by Heavy Drinking?

For men, heavy drinking is typically defined as consuming 15 drinks or more per week. For women, heavy drinking is typically defined as consuming 8 drinks or more per week.

Do All Excessive Drinkers Have an Alcohol Use Disorder?

No. About 90 percent of people who drink excessively would not be expected to meet the clinical diagnostic criteria for having a severe alcohol use disorder. A severe alcohol use disorder, previously known as alcohol dependence or alcoholism, is a chronic disease. Some of the signs and symptoms of a severe alcohol use disorder could include:

- Inability to limit drinking
- Continuing to drink despite personal or professional problems
- Needing to drink more to get the same effect
- Wanting a drink so badly you can't think of anything else

What Does It Mean to Get Drunk?

"Getting drunk" or intoxicated is the result of consuming excessive amounts of alcohol. Binge drinking typically results in acute intoxication.

Alcohol intoxication can be harmful for a variety of reasons, including:

- Impaired brain function resulting in poor judgment, reduced reaction time, loss of balance and motor skills, or slurred speech
- Dilation of blood vessels, causing a feeling of warmth but resulting in rapid loss of body heat
- Increased risk of certain cancers, stroke, and liver diseases (e.g., cirrhosis), particularly when excessive amounts of alcohol are consumed over extended periods of time
- Damage to a developing fetus if consumed by pregnant women
- Increased risk of motor vehicle traffic crashes, violence, and other injuries

Coma and death can occur if alcohol is consumed rapidly and in large amounts.

How Do I Know If I Have a Drinking Problem?

Drinking is a problem if it causes trouble in your relationships, in school, in social activities, or in how you think and feel. If you are concerned that either you or someone in your family might have a drinking problem, consult your personal healthcare provider.

What Can I Do If I or Someone I Know Has a Drinking Problem?

Consult your personal healthcare provider if you feel you or someone you know has a drinking problem. Other resources include the National Drug and Alcohol Treatment Referral Routing Services, available at 800-662-HELP (800-662-4357). This service can provide you with information about treatment programs in your local community and allow you to speak with someone about alcohol problems.

What Health Problems Are Associated with Excessive Alcohol Use?

Excessive drinking both in the form of heavy drinking or binge drinking, is associated with numerous health problems, including:

- Chronic diseases such as liver cirrhosis (damage to liver cells); pancreatitis (inflammation of the pancreas); various cancers, including liver, mouth, throat, larynx (the voice box), and esophagus; high blood pressure; and psychological disorders
- Unintentional injuries, such as motor vehicle traffic crashes, falls, drowning, burns, and firearm injuries
- Violence, such as child maltreatment, homicide, and suicide
- Harm to a developing fetus if a woman drinks while pregnant, such as fetal alcohol spectrum disorders (FASDs)
- Sudden infant death syndrome (SIDS)
- Alcohol use disorders (AUDs)

I'm Young. Is Drinking Bad for My Health?

Yes. Studies have shown that alcohol use by adolescents and young adults increases the risk of both fatal and nonfatal injuries. Research has also shown that people who use alcohol before age 15 are six times more likely to become alcohol dependent than adults who begin drinking at age 21. Other consequences of youth alcohol use include increased risky sexual behaviors, poor school performance, and increased risk of suicide and homicide.

Is It Okay to Drink When Pregnant?

No. There is no known safe level of alcohol use during pregnancy. Women who are pregnant or plan on becoming pregnant should refrain from drinking alcohol. Several conditions, including FASDs, have been linked to alcohol use during pregnancy. Women of childbearing age should also avoid binge drinking to reduce the risk of unintended pregnancy and potential exposure of a developing fetus to alcohol.

Chapter 2

Psychosocial Factors in Alcohol Use and Alcoholism

Chapter Contents

Section 2.1

The Link between Stress and Alcohol

This section includes text excerpted from "Alcohol Alert Number 85—The Link between Stress and Alcohol," National Institute on Alcohol Abuse and Alcoholism (NIAAA), May 16, 2013. Reviewed April 2018.

At present, more and more servicemen and women are leaving active duty and returning to civilian life. That transition can be difficult. The stresses associated with military service are not easily shed. But dealing with stress is not limited to recent Veterans. A new job, a death in the family, moving across the country, a breakup, or getting married—all are situations that can result in psychological and physical symptoms collectively known as "stress."

One way that people may choose to cope with stress is by turning to alcohol. Drinking may lead to positive feelings and relaxation, at least in the short term. Problems arise, however, when stress is ongoing and people continue to try and deal with its effects by drinking alcohol. Instead of "calming your nerves," long-term, heavy drinking can actually work against you, leading to a host of medical and psychological problems and increasing the risk for alcohol dependence.

Common Types of Stress

Most causes of stress can be grouped into four categories: general life stress, catastrophic events, childhood stress, and racial/ethnic minority stress. Each of these factors vary or are influenced in a number of ways by severity, duration, whether the stress is expected or not, the type of threat (emotional or physical), and the individual's mental health status. (For example, does the person suffer from anxiety, co-occurring mental health disorders, or alcoholism?)

General Life Stressors

General life stressors include getting married or divorced, moving, or starting a new job. Problems at home or work, a death in the family, or an illness also can lead to stress. People with an alcohol use disorder

(AUD) may be at particular risk for these types of stresses. For example, drinking may cause problems at work, in personal relationships, or trouble with police.

Catastrophic Events

Studies consistently show that alcohol consumption increases in the first year after a disaster, including both man-made and natural events. As time passes, that relationship is dampened. However, much of this research focuses on drinking only and not on the prevalence of AUDs. In the studies that looked specifically at the development of AUDs, the results are less consistent. In some cases, studies have found no increases in AUDs among survivors after events such as the Oklahoma City bombing, September 11, Hurricane Andrew, or jet crashes. However, other studies of September 11 survivors have found that AUDs increased. This trend was similar in studies of Hurricane Katrina, the Mount St. Helens volcano eruption, and other events. Most of these studies included only adults. Additional studies are needed to better understand how adolescents and young people respond to disasters and whether there is a link to alcohol use.

Childhood Stress

Maltreatment in childhood includes exposure to emotional, sexual, and/or physical abuse or neglect during the first 18 years of life. Although they occur during childhood, these stressors have long-lasting effects, accounting for a significant proportion of all adult psychopathology. Studies typically show that maltreatment in childhood increases the risk for both adolescent and adult alcohol consumption as well as increased adult AUDs. However, childhood maltreatment is more likely to occur among children of alcoholics, who often use poor parenting practices and who also pass along genes to their offspring that increase the risk of AUDs.

Racial and Ethnic Minority Stress

Stress also can arise as a result of a person's minority status, especially as it pertains to prejudice and discrimination. Such stress may range from mild (e.g., hassles such as being followed in a store) to severe (e.g., being the victim of a violent crime). The stress may be emotional (e.g., workplace harassment) or physical (e.g., hate crimes). The relationship of these stress factors to alcohol use is complicated by other risk factors as well, such as drinking patterns and individual differences in how the body breaks down (or metabolizes) alcohol.

Coping with Stress

The ability to cope with stress (known as resilience) reflects how well someone is able to adapt to the psychological and physiological responses involved in the stress response. When challenged by stressful events, the body responds rapidly, shifting normal metabolic processes into high gear. To make this rapid response possible, the body relies on an intricate system—the hypothalamic-pituitary-adrenal (HPA) axis—that involves the brain and key changes in the levels of hormonal messengers in the body. The system targets specific organs, preparing the body either to fight the stress factor (stressor) or to flee from it (i.e., the fight-or-flight response).

The hormone cortisol has a key role in the body's response to stress. One of cortisol's primary effects is to increase available energy by increasing blood sugar (i.e., glucose) levels and mobilizing fat and protein metabolism to increase nutrient supplies to the muscles, preparing the body to respond quickly and efficiently. A healthy stress response is characterized by an initial spike in cortisol levels followed by a rapid fall in those levels as soon as the threat is over.

People are most resilient when they are able to respond quickly to stress, ramping up the health promotion agency (HPA) axis and then quickly shutting it down once the threat or stress has passed. Personality, heredity, and lifestyle all can dictate how well someone handles stress. People who tend to focus on the positive, remain optimistic, and use problem solving and planning to cope with problems are more resilient to stress and its related disorders, including AUDs.

The personality characteristics of resilience are in sharp contrast to the ones associated with an increased risk for substance use disorders (e.g., impulsivity, novelty seeking, negative emotionality, and anxiety). A person with a history of alcoholism in his or her family may have more difficulty dealing with the stress factors that can lead to alcohol use problems. Likewise, having a mother who drank alcohol during pregnancy, experiencing childhood neglect or abuse, and the existence of other mental health issues such as depression can add to that risk.

Alcohol's Role in Stress

To better understand how alcohol interacts with stress, researchers looked at the number of stressors occurring in the past year in a group of men and women in the general population and how those stressors related to alcohol use. They found that both men and women who reported higher levels of stress tended to drink more. Moreover, men tended to turn to alcohol as a means for dealing with stress more often than did women. For example, for those who reported at least six stressful incidents, the percentage of men binge drinking was about 1.5 times that of women, and AUDs among men were 2.5 times higher than women. Veterans who have been in active combat are especially likely to turn to alcohol as a means of relieving stress. Posttraumatic stress disorder (PTSD), which has been found in 14–22 percent of Veterans returning from recent wars in Afghanistan and Iraq, has been linked to increased risk for alcohol abuse and dependence.

Stress and Alcoholism Recovery

The impact of stress does not cease once a patient stops drinking. Newly sober patients often relapse to drinking to alleviate the symptoms of withdrawal, such as alcohol craving, feelings of anxiety, and difficulty sleeping. Many of these symptoms of withdrawal can be traced to the HPA axis, the system at the core of the stress response.

Long-term, heavy drinking can actually alter the brain's chemistry, resetting what is "normal." It causes the release of higher amounts of cortisol and adrenocorticotropic hormone. When this hormonal balance is shifted, it impacts the way the body perceives stress and how it responds to it. For example, a long-term heavy drinker may experience higher levels of anxiety when faced with a stressful situation than someone who never drank or who drank only moderately.

In addition to being associated with negative or unpleasant feelings, cortisol also interacts with the brain's reward or "pleasure" systems. Researchers believe this may contribute to alcohol's reinforcing effects, motivating the drinker to consume higher levels of alcohol in an effort to achieve the same effects.

Cortisol also has a role in cognition, including learning and memory. In particular, it has been found to promote habit-based learning, which fosters the development of habitual drinking and increases the risk of relapse. Cortisol also has been linked to the development of psychiatric disorders (such as depression) and metabolic disorders.

These findings have significant implications for clinical practice. By identifying those patients most at risk of alcohol relapse during early recovery from alcoholism, clinicians can help patients to better address how stress affects their motivation to drink.

Early screening also is vital. For example, Veterans who turn to alcohol to deal with military stress and who have a history of drinking prior to service are especially at risk for developing problems. Screening for a history of alcohol misuse before military personnel are exposed to military trauma may help identify those at risk for developing increasingly severe PTSD symptoms.

Interventions then can be designed to target both the symptoms of PTSD and alcohol dependence. Such interventions include cognitive behavioral therapies (CBT), such as exposure-based therapies, in which the patient confronts the cues that cause feelings of stress but without the risk of danger. Patients then can learn to recognize those cues and to manage the resulting stress. Researchers recommend treating PTSD and alcohol use disorders simultaneously rather than waiting until after patients have been abstinent from alcohol or drugs for a sustained period (e.g., 3 months).

Medications also are currently being investigated for alcoholism that work to stabilize the body's response to stress. Some scientists believe that restoring balance to the stress response system may help alleviate the problems associated with withdrawal and, in turn, aid in recovery. More work is needed to determine the effectiveness of these medications.

Section 2.2

PTSD and Problems with Alcohol Use

This section includes text excerpted from "PTSD and Problems with Alcohol Use," U.S. Department of Veterans Affairs (VA), August 13, 2015.

Posttraumatic stress disorder (PTSD) and alcohol use problems are often found together. This pairing can be big trouble for the trauma survivor and his or her family.

People with PTSD are more likely than others with the same sort of background to have drinking problems. By the same token, people with drinking problems often have PTSD. Those with PTSD have more problems with alcohol both before and after getting PTSD.

Having PTSD increases the risk that you will develop a drinking problem.

Women who go through trauma have more risk for drinking problems. They are at risk for drinking problems even if they do not have PTSD. Women with drinking problems are more likely than other women to have been sexually abused at some time in their lives. Both men and women who have been sexually abused have higher rates of alcohol and drug use problems than others.

Up to three-quarters of those who have survived abusive or violent trauma report drinking problems. Up to a third of those who survive traumatic accidents, illness, or disasters report drinking problems. Alcohol problems are more common for survivors who have ongoing health problems or pain.

Sixty to eighty percent of Vietnam Veterans seeking PTSD treatment have alcohol use problems. War Veterans with PTSD and alcohol problems tend to be binge drinkers. Binges may be in response to memories of trauma. Veterans over the age of 65 with PTSD are at higher risk for a suicide attempt if they also have drinking problems or depression.

Alcohol Use Problems Often Lead to Trauma and Problems in Relationships

If you have a drinking problem, you are more likely than others with your same sort of background to go through a psychological trauma. You may also have problems getting close to others. You may have more conflicts with those people to whom you are close. Problems with alcohol are linked to a confused and disorderly life. This kind of life leads to less closeness and more conflict within a family. The confusion of a life with a drinking problem makes it harder to be a good parent.

Alcohol Can Make PTSD Symptoms Worse

You may drink because using alcohol can distract you from your problems for a short time. You should know, though, that drinking makes it harder to concentrate, be productive, and enjoy all parts of your life.

Using too much alcohol makes it harder to cope with stress and your trauma memories. Alcohol use and intoxication (getting drunk) can increase some PTSD symptoms. Examples of symptoms that can get worse are numbing of your feelings, being cut off from others, anger and irritability, depression, and the feeling of being on guard.

If you have PTSD, you may have trouble falling asleep or problems with waking up during the night. You may "medicate" yourself with alcohol because you think it's helping your sleep. In fact, using too much alcohol can get in the way of restful sleep. Alcohol changes the quality of your sleep and makes it less refreshing.

If you have PTSD, you may have bad dreams or nightmares. You may drink because you think using alcohol will decrease the number of bad dreams or how scary they are. Yet drinking just continues the cycle of avoidance found in PTSD. Avoiding the bad memories and dreams actually prolongs the PTSD. You cannot make as much progress in treatment if you avoid your problems. Alcohol use problems make PTSD treatment less effective. When you suddenly stop drinking, the nightmares often get worse. Working with your doctor on the best way to reduce or stop your drinking makes cutting back on alcohol easier. You will be more likely to have success in your efforts.

Other Mental Health Issues

If you have both PTSD and drinking problems, you are likely to have other mental or physical health problems. Up to half of adults with both PTSD and drinking problems also have one or more of the following serious problems:

- Panic attacks, extreme fears or worries, or compulsions (being driven to do things like checking the door locks over and over)
- Mood problems such as depression
- Attention problems or behaving in ways that harm others
- Addiction to or abuse of street or prescription drugs
- Long-term physical illness such as diabetes, heart disease, or liver disease
- Ongoing physical pain

What Are the Most Effective Treatment Patterns?

Having both PTSD and a drinking problem can make both problems worse. For this reason, alcohol use problems often must be part of the PTSD treatment. If you have PTSD, plus you have, or have had, a problem with alcohol, try to find a therapist who has experience treating both issues.

In any PTSD treatment, several points related to alcohol should be stressed:

- When planning your treatment, you should discuss with your therapist the possible effects of drinking on your PTSD symptoms. As noted above, alcohol can affect sleep, anger and irritability, anxiety, depression, and work or relationship problems.
- Treatment should include education, therapy, and support groups that help you with your drinking problems in a way you can accept.
- Treatment for PTSD and alcohol use problems should be planned in a way that addresses both problems together. You may have to go to separate meetings for each issue, or see providers who work mostly with PTSD or mostly with alcohol problems. In general, though, PTSD issues should be included in alcohol treatment, and alcohol use issues should be included in PTSD treatment.
- Once you become sober (stop drinking entirely), you must learn to cope with your PTSD symptoms in order to prevent relapse (return to drinking). This is important because sometimes the PTSD symptoms seem to get worse or you notice them more right after you stop drinking. Remember that after you have stopped drinking, you have a better chance of making progress in your PTSD treatment. In the long run, you are more likely to have success with both problems.

Chapter 3

When Can Alcohol Be Used Safely?

Chapter Contents

Section 3.1

Drinking Alcohol: Low Risk versus High Risk

This section includes text excerpted from "Rethinking Drinking," National Institute on Alcohol Abuse and Alcoholism (NIAAA), March 10, 2009. Reviewed April 2018.

Do You Enjoy a Drink Now and Then?

Many of us do, often when socializing with friends and family. Drinking can be beneficial or harmful, depending on your age and health status, and, of course, how much you drink.

What's a "Standard" Drink?

Many people are surprised to learn what counts as a drink. In the United States, a "standard" drink is any drink that contains about 0.6 fluid ounces or 14 grams of "pure" alcohol. Although the drinks pictured here are different sizes, each contains approximately the same amount of alcohol and counts as a single standard drink.

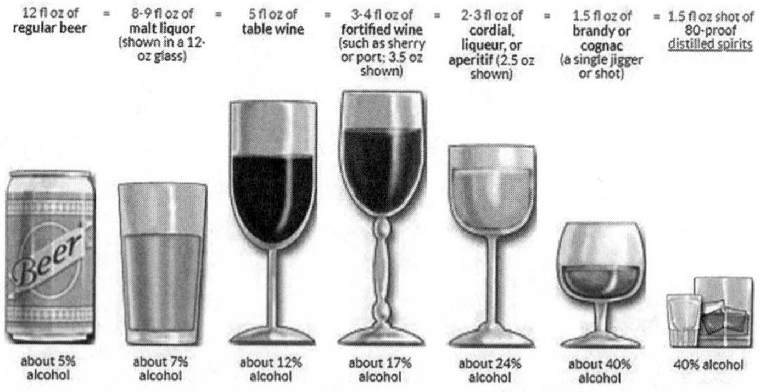

Figure 3.1. *The Percentage of "Pure" Alcohol Expressed in Alcohol by Volume (Alc/Vol)*

The examples above serve as a starting point for comparison. For different types of beer, wine, or malt liquor, the alcohol content can vary greatly. Some differences are smaller than you might expect, however. Many light beers, for example, have almost as much alcohol as regular beer—about 85 percent as much, or 4.2 percent versus 5.0 percent alcohol by volume (alc/vol), on average.

If you want to know the alcohol content of a canned or bottled beverage, start by checking the label. Not all beverages are required to list the alcohol content, so you may need to search online for a reliable source of information, such as the bottler's website.

Although the "standard" drink amounts are helpful for following health guidelines, they may not reflect customary serving sizes. In addition, while the alcohol concentrations listed are "typical," there is considerable variability in alcohol content within each type of beverage (e.g., beer, wine, distilled spirits).

How Many Drinks Are in Common Containers?

In the United States, a "standard" drink is any drink that contains about 0.6 fluid ounces or 14 grams of "pure" alcohol. Below is the approximate number of standard drinks in different sized containers of:

Table 3.1. Number of Standard Drinks in Different Sized Containers

Regular Beer (5% alc/vol)	Malt Liquor (7% alc/vol)	Table Wine (12% alc/vol)	80-Proof Distilled Spirits (40% alc/vol)
12 fl oz. = 1	12 fl oz. = 1½	750 ml (a regular wine bottle) = 5	a shot (1.5-oz. glass/50-ml bottle) = 1
16 fl oz. = 1?	16 fl oz. = 2		a mixed drink or cocktail = 1 or more
22 fl oz. = 2	22 fl oz. = 2½		200 ml (a "half pint") = 4½
40 fl oz. = 3?	40 fl oz. = 4½		375 ml (a "pint" or "half bottle") = 8½
			750 ml (a "fifth") = 17

Although the "standard" drink amounts are helpful for following health guidelines, they may not reflect customary serving sizes. In addition, while the alcohol concentrations listed are "typical," there is considerable variability in alcohol content within each type of beverage (e.g., beer, wine, distilled spirits).

What's "Low-Risk" Drinking?

A major nationwide survey of 43,000 U.S. adults by the National Institutes of Health (NIH) shows that only about 2 in 100 people who drink within both the single-day and weekly limits below have an alcohol use disorder. How do these "low-risk" levels compare with your drinking pattern?

Low-risk drinking limits
MEN
WOMEN
On any single DAY
No more than
4
drinks on any day
No more than
3
drinks on any day
** AND **
** AND **
Per WEEK
No more than
14
drinks per week
No more than
7
drinks per week
To stay low risk, keep within BOTH the single-day AND weekly limits.

Figure 3.2. *Low-Risk Drinking Limits*

"Low risk" is not "no risk." Even within these limits, alcohol can cause problems if people drink too quickly, have health problems, or are older (both men and women over 65 are generally advised to have no more than 3 drinks on any day and 7 per week). Based on your health and how alcohol affects you, you may need to drink less or not at all.

When Is "Low-Risk" Drinking Still Too Much?

It's safest to avoid alcohol altogether if you are:

- Taking medications that interact with alcohol
- Managing a medical condition that can be made worse by drinking
- Underage
- Planning to drive a vehicle or operate machinery
- Pregnant or trying to become pregnant

What's "At-Risk" or "Heavy" Drinking?

For healthy adults in general, drinking more than these single-day or weekly limits is considered "at-risk" or "heavy" drinking:

- **Men:** More than 4 drinks on any day or 14 per week
- **Women:** More than 3 drinks on any day or 7 per week

About 1 in 4 people who exceed these limits already has an alcohol use disorder, and the rest are at greater risk for developing these and other problems. Again, individual risks vary. People can have problems drinking less than these amounts, particularly if they drink too quickly.

Too much + Too often = Too risky

It makes a difference both how much you drink on any day and how often you have a "heavy drinking day," that is, more than 4 drinks on any day for men or more than 3 drinks for women.

Table 3.2. Drinking Pattern and Alcohol Use Disorder

Among People with This Drinking Pattern	This Many Have an Alcohol Use Disorder
1 heavy drinking day a month	2 in 10
1 heavy drinking day a week	3 in 10
2 or more heavy drinking days a week	5 in 10

In short, the more drinks on any day and the more heavy drinking days over time, the greater the risk—not only for an alcohol use disorder, but also for other health and personal problems.

What Are the Risks?

You may have heard that regular light to moderate drinking can be good for the heart. With heavy or at-risk drinking, however, any potential benefits are outweighed by greater risks, including:

- **Injuries.** Drinking too much increases your chances of being injured or even killed. Alcohol is a factor, for example, in about 60 percent of fatal burn injuries, drownings, and homicides; 50 percent of severe trauma injuries and sexual assaults; and 40 percent of fatal motor vehicle crashes, suicides, and fatal falls.
- **Health problems.** People who drink heavily have a greater risk of liver disease, heart disease, sleep disorders, depression, stroke, bleeding from the stomach, sexually transmitted infections (STIs) from unsafe sex, and several types of cancer. They may have problems managing diabetes, high blood pressure, and other conditions.
- **Birth defects.** Drinking during pregnancy can cause brain damage and other serious problems in the baby. Because it is

not yet known whether any amount of alcohol is safe for a developing baby, women who are pregnant or may become pregnant should not drink.

- **Alcohol use disorders.** An alcohol use disorder is a medical condition that doctors can diagnose when a patient's drinking causes distress or harm. In the United States, about 17 million people have an alcohol use disorder.

Beyond these physical and mental health risks, frequent heavy drinking also is linked with personal problems, including losing a driver's license and having relationship troubles.

Section 3.2

Alcohol Dietary Guidelines for Americans

This section contains text excerpted from the following sources: Text in this section begins with excerpts from "Dietary Guidelines 2015-2020—Appendix 9. Alcohol," Office of Disease Prevention and Health Promotion (ODPHP), U.S. Department of Health and Human Services (HHS), December 15, 2015; Text beginning with the heading "Moderate Drinking" is excerpted from "Alcohol and Public Health—Fact Sheets—Moderate Drinking," Centers for Disease Control and Prevention (CDC), October 18, 2016.

If alcohol is consumed, it should be in moderation—up to one drink per day for women and up to two drinks per day for men—and only by adults of legal drinking age. For those who choose to drink, moderate alcohol consumption can be incorporated into the calorie limits of most healthy eating patterns. The *Dietary Guidelines* does not recommend that individuals who do not drink alcohol start drinking for any reason; however, it does recommend that all foods and beverages consumed be accounted for within healthy eating patterns. Alcohol is not a component of the U.S. Department of Agriculture (USDA) Food Patterns. Thus, if alcohol is consumed, the calories from alcohol should be accounted for so that the limits on calories for other uses and total calories are not exceeded.

For the purposes of evaluating amounts of alcohol that may be consumed, the *Dietary Guidelines* includes drink-equivalents. One alcoholic drink-equivalent is described as containing 14 g (0.6 fl oz.) of pure alcohol. The following are reference beverages that are one alcoholic drink-equivalent: 12 fluid ounces of regular beer (5% alcohol), 5 fluid ounces of wine (12% alcohol), or 1.5 fluid ounces of 80 proof distilled spirits (40% alcohol).

Packaged (e.g., canned beer, bottled wine) and mixed beverages (e.g., margarita, rum and soda, mimosa, sangria) vary in alcohol content. For this reason it is important to determine how many alcoholic drink-equivalents are in the beverage and limit intake. The below table lists reference beverages that are one drink-equivalent and provides examples of alcoholic drink-equivalents in other alcoholic beverages.

Table 3.3. Alcoholic Drink-Equivalents of Select Beverages

Drink Description	Drink-Equivalents
Beer, beer coolers, and malt beverages	
12 fl oz. at 4.2% alcohol	0.8
12 fl oz. at 5% alcohol (reference beverage)	1
16 fl oz. at 5% alcohol	1.3
12 fl oz. at 7% alcohol	1.4
12 fl oz. at 9% alcohol	1.8
Wine	
5 fl oz. at 12% alcohol (reference beverage)	1
9 fl oz. at 12% alcohol	1.8
5 fl oz. at 15% alcohol	1.3
5 fl oz. at 17% alcohol	1.4
Distilled spirits	
1.5 fl oz. 80 proof distilled spirits (40% alcohol) (reference beverage)	1
Mixed drink with more than 1.5 fl oz. 80 proof distilled spirits (40% alcohol)	> 1

When determining the number of drink-equivalents in an alcoholic beverage, the variability in alcohol content and portion size must be considered together. As an example, the amount of alcohol in a beer may be higher than 5 percent and, thus, 12 ounces would be greater than one drink-equivalent. In addition to the alcohol content, the portion size may be many times larger than the reference beverage. For example, portion sizes for beer may be higher than 12 ounces and, thus, even if the alcohol content is 5 percent, the beverage would be greater than one drink-equivalent. The same is true for wine and mixed drinks with distilled spirits.

Alcoholic Beverages and Calories

Alcoholic beverages may contain calories from both alcohol and other ingredients. If they are consumed, the contributions from calories from alcohol and other dietary components (e.g., added sugars, solid fats) from alcoholic beverages should be within the various limits of healthy eating patterns. One drink-equivalent contains 14 grams of pure alcohol, which contributes 98 calories to the beverage. The total calories in a beverage may be more than those from alcohol alone, depending on the type, brand, ingredients, and portion size. For example, 12 ounces of regular beer (5% alcohol) may have about 150 calories, 5 ounces of wine (12% alcohol) may have about 120 calories, and 7 ounces of a rum (40% alcohol) and cola may have about 155 calories, each with 98 calories coming from pure alcohol.

Excessive Drinking

In comparison to moderate alcohol consumption, high-risk drinking is the consumption of 4 or more drinks on any day or 8 or more drinks per week for women and 5 or more drinks on any day or 15 or more drinks per week for men. Binge drinking is the consumption within about 2 hours of 4 or more drinks for women and 5 or more drinks for men.

Excessive alcohol consumption—which includes binge drinking (4 or more drinks for women and 5 or more drinks for men within about 2 hours); heavy drinking (8 or more drinks a week for women and 15 or more drinks a week for men); and any drinking by pregnant women or those under 21 years of age—has no benefits. Excessive drinking is responsible for 88,000 deaths in the United States each year, including 1 in 10 deaths among working age adults (age 20–64 years). In 2006, the estimated economic cost to the United States of excessive drinking was $224 billion. Binge drinking accounts for over half of the deaths and three-fourths of the economic costs due to excessive drinking.

Excessive drinking increases the risk of many chronic diseases and violence and, over time, can impair short- and long-term cognitive function. Over 90 percent of U.S. adults who drink excessively report binge drinking, and about 90 percent of the alcohol consumed by youth under 21 years of age in the United States is in the form of binge drinks. Binge drinking is associated with a wide range of health and social problems, including sexually transmitted diseases, unintended pregnancy, accidental injuries, and violent crime.

Those Who Should Not Consume Alcohol

Many individuals should not consume alcohol, including individuals who are taking certain over-the-counter (OTC) or prescription medications or who have certain medical conditions, those who are recovering from alcoholism or are unable to control the amount they drink, and anyone younger than age 21 years. Individuals should not drink if they are driving, planning to drive, or are participating in other activities requiring skill, coordination, and alertness.

Women who are or who may be pregnant should not drink. Drinking during pregnancy, especially in the first few months of pregnancy, may result in negative behavioral or neurological consequences in the offspring. No safe level of alcohol consumption during pregnancy has been established. Women who are breastfeeding should consult with their healthcare provider regarding alcohol consumption.

Alcohol and Caffeine

Mixing alcohol and caffeine is not generally recognized as safe by the U.S. Food and Drug Administration (FDA). People who mix alcohol and caffeine may drink more alcohol and become more intoxicated than they realize, increasing the risk of alcohol-related adverse events. Caffeine does not change blood alcohol content levels, and thus, does not reduce the risk of harms associated with drinking alcohol.

Moderate Drinking

- Alcohol consumption is associated with a variety of short- and long-term health risks, including motor vehicle crashes, violence, sexual risk behaviors, high blood pressure, and various cancers (e.g., breast cancer).
- The risk of these harms increases with the amount of alcohol you drink. For some conditions, like some cancers, the risk increases even at very low levels of alcohol consumption (less than 1 drink).
- To reduce the risk of alcohol-related harms, the 2015–2020 *U.S. Dietary Guidelines for Americans* recommends that if alcohol

is consumed, it should be consumed in moderation—up to one drink per day for women and two drinks per day for men—and only by adults of legal drinking age. This is not intended as an average over several days, but rather the amount consumed on any single day. The *Guidelines* also do not recommend that individuals who do not drink alcohol start drinking for any reason.

- Two in three adult drinkers report drinking above moderate levels at least once a month.

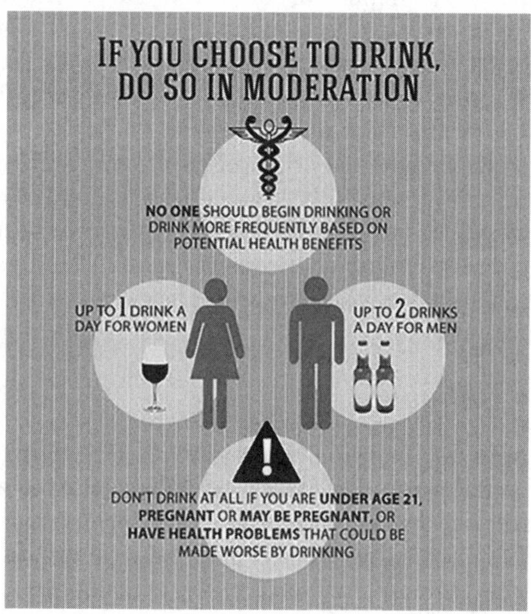

Figure 3.3. *Moderate Levels of Drinking*

Figure 3.4. *Drink Equivalents, as Defined by the 2015–2020 Dietary Guidelines for Americans*

Science around Moderate Alcohol Consumption

- For some conditions, such as certain types of cancer (e.g., breast cancer) and liver disease, there is no known safe level of alcohol consumption
- Although past studies have indicated that moderate alcohol consumption has protective health benefits (e.g., reducing risk of heart disease), recent studies show this may not be true. While some studies have found improved health outcomes among moderate drinkers, it's impossible to conclude whether these improved outcomes are due to moderate alcohol consumption or other differences in behaviors or genetics between people who drink moderately and people who don't.
- Most U.S. adults who drink don't drink every day. That's why it's important to focus on the amount people drink on the days that they drink
- Drinking at levels above the moderate drinking guidelines significantly increases the risk of short-term harms, such as injuries, as well as the risk of long-term chronic health problems, such as some types of cancer

Chapter 4

Ethnicity, Culture, and Alcohol

Racial and ethnic minorities currently make up about a third of the population of the nation and are expected to become a majority by 2050. These diverse communities have unique behavioral health needs and experience different rates of mental and/or substance use disorders and treatment access.

Communities of color tend to experience greater burden of mental and substance use disorders often due to poorer access to care; inappropriate care; and higher social, environmental, and economic risk factors.

African Americans

There are about 44.5 million African Americans in the United States (about 14.2% of the total population). According to data from the National Survey on Drug Use and Health (NSDUH)—2014:

- The rate of binge drinking (drinking five or more drinks on a single occasion for men) among African Americans ages 12 and up was 21.6 percent—compared with the national average of 23 percent.

This chapter includes text excerpted from "Racial and Ethnic Minority Populations," Substance Abuse and Mental Health Services Administration (SAMHSA), January 17, 2018.

- African Americans ages 12–20 in 2014 reported past-month alcohol use at a rate of 17.3 percent, compared with the national average of 22.8 percent. Past-month underage binge drinking was 8.5 percent for African American youth, while the national average was 13.8 percent.
- The rate of illegal drug use in the last month among African Americans ages 12 and up in 2014 was 12.4 percent, compared to the national average of 10.2 percent.

Rates of mental disorders are generally low among African Americans. In 2014, 3.8 percent of African American adults ages 18 and older had a past-year mental illness and a substance use disorder, while the national average was 3.3 percent. The 2014 national average for any mental illness in the past year for adults was 18.1 percent, compared to 16.3 percent for African American adults.

African Americans face higher rates of death from major diseases and higher rates of human immunodeficiency virus (HIV) infection than their Caucasian counterparts. African Americans in 2010 accounted for 44 percent of HIV infection cases in the country.

American Indians and Alaska Natives

There are about 5.2 million American Indians and Alaska Natives in the United States (about 1.7% of the total population). American Indians and Alaska Natives experience some of the highest rates of substance use and mental disorders compared to other U.S. racial or ethnic groups. For instance:

- American Indians and Alaska Natives ages 12–20 in 2014 reported past-month alcohol use at a rate of 21.9 percent, compared with the national average of 22.8 percent.
- Past-month underage binge drinking was 14.3 percent for American Indian and Alaska Native youth, while the national average was 13.8 percent.
- In 2010, Native Americans had the highest rate of drug-induced death (17.1%).
- The rate of illegal drug use in the last month among American Indians and Alaska Natives ages 12 and up in 2014 was 14.9 percent.

Rates of mental disorders in American Indians and Alaska Natives in 2014:

- The percentage of American Indians and Alaska Natives ages 18 and up who reported a past-year mental illness was 21.2 percent.
- The rate of serious mental illness among American Indians and Alaska Natives ages 18 and up in this population was 4 percent.
- In 2014, 8.8 percent of American Indians and Alaska Natives ages 18 and up had co-occurring, past-year mental and substance use disorders, while the national average was 3.3 percent.

In addition, according to a 2015 fact sheet published by the Centers for Disease Control and Prevention (CDC), the suicide rate among American Indian and Alaska Native adolescents and young adults between the ages of 15 and 34 (19.5 per 100,000) is 1.5 times higher than the national average for that age group (12.2 per 100,000). The 2015 NSDUH rate of serious thoughts of suicide among those ages 18 and up was 4.8 percent for American Indians and Alaska Natives, compared with the national average of 3.9 percent.

The Substance Abuse and Mental Health Services Administration (SAMHSA) Office of Tribal Affairs and Policy (OTAP) serves as SAMHSA's primary point of contact for tribal governments, tribal organizations, federal departments and agencies, and other governments and agencies on behavioral health issues facing American Indians and Alaska Natives. OTAP supports SAMHSA's efforts to advance the development and implementation of data-driven policies and innovative practices that promote improved behavioral health for American Indian and Alaska Native communities and populations. OTAP also brings together SAMHSA's tribal affairs, tribal policy, tribal consultation, tribal advisory, and Tribal Law and Order Act (TLOA) responsibilities to improve agency coordination and meaningful progress.

Asian Americans, Native Hawaiians, and Other Pacific Islanders

There are about 18.2 million people who identify themselves as Asian American. There are also 1.4 million Native Hawaiians or Other Pacific Islanders in the United States. According to the 2010 U.S. Census, Asians are the fastest growing racial group in the nation.

In 2014:

- The rate of binge alcohol use was lowest among Asian Americans ages 12 and up (14.5%). The binge alcohol use rate was 18.3 percent among Native Hawaiian or other Pacific Islanders.
- The past-month binge alcohol use rate for youth ages 12–20 was 6.7 percent for Asian Americans, compared with the national average of 13.8 percent.
- The rate of substance dependence or abuse was 4.5 percent for Asian Americans and 10 percent for Native Hawaiians or other Pacific Islanders.
- Among people ages 12 and up, the rate of illegal drug use in the last month was 4.1 percent among Asian Americans and 15.6 percent among Native Hawaiians or other Pacific Islanders.

In 2014, the percentage of Asian Americans ages 18 and up reporting a past-year mental illness was 13.1 percent, and 3.1 percent of Asian Americans and 1.2 percent of Native Hawaiian or other Pacific Islanders ages 18 and older had serious thoughts of suicide, compared to the national average of 3.9 percent.

However, examination of disaggregated data unmasks disparities experienced by groups within the Asian American, Native Hawaiian, and Pacific Islander population. For instance, older Asian American women have the highest suicide rate of all U.S. women over the age of 65. Southeast Asian refugees are also at risk for posttraumatic stress disorder (PTSD) associated with trauma experienced before and after emigration to the United States.

Hispanics or Latinos

There are about 52 million Hispanics or Latinos in the United States (about 16.7% of the total population). By 2050, the number of people in this population group is expected to double to about 132.8 million, making up approximately 30 percent of the total U.S. population.

Regarding substance abuse among Hispanics or Latinos, data from the 2015 NSDUH indicates:

- The rate of binge alcohol use among Hispanics or Latinos within this age group was 24.7 percent. Alcohol use in the last year among people ages 12–17 was 23.9 percent for Hispanic youth.

- The rate of illicit drug use in the past month among Hispanic individuals ages 12 and up was 8.9 percent, while the national average was 10.2 percent.

Rates of mental disorders for Hispanics or Latinos in 2014 include:

- The percentage of people ages 18 and up reporting a past-year mental illness was 15.6 percent.
- About 3.5 percent of adult Hispanics or Latinos had a serious mental illness.
- The percentage of people who reported a major depressive episode was 5.6 percent.
- About 3.3 percent of this population had a co-occurring mental health and substance use disorder.

Chapter 5

Binge Drinking

Binge drinking is a serious but preventable public health problem. Binge drinking is the most common, costly, and deadly pattern of excessive alcohol use in the United States. The National Institute on Alcohol Abuse and Alcoholism (NIAAA) defines binge drinking as a pattern of drinking that brings a person's blood alcohol concentration (BAC) to 0.08 grams percent or above. This typically happens when men consume 5 or more drinks or women consume 4 or more drinks in about 2 hours. Most people who binge drink are not alcohol dependent.

- One in six U.S. adults binge drink about four times a month, consuming about eight drinks per binge.
- Binge drinking is most common among younger adults aged 18–34 years, but is reported across the lifespan.
- The prevalence of binge drinking among men is twice the prevalence among women.
- Binge drinking is more common among people with household incomes of $75,000 or more than among people with lower incomes. However, people with lower incomes binge drink more often and consume more drinks when they do.
- Over 90 percent of U.S. adults who drink excessively report binge drinking in the past 30 days.

This chapter includes text excerpted from "Alcohol and Public Health—Fact Sheets—Binge Drinking," Centers for Disease Control and Prevention (CDC), June 7, 2017.

- Most people younger than age 21 who drink report binge drinking, usually on multiple occasions.

Binge Drinking Has Serious Risks

Binge drinking is associated with many health problems, including the following:

- Unintentional injuries such as car crashes, falls, burns, and alcohol poisoning
- Violence including homicide, suicide, intimate partner violence, and sexual assault
- Sexually transmitted diseases (STDs)
- Unintended pregnancy and poor pregnancy outcomes, including miscarriage and stillbirth
- Fetal alcohol spectrum disorders (FASDs)
- Sudden infant death syndrome (SIDS)
- Chronic diseases such as high blood pressure, stroke, heart disease, and liver disease
- Cancer of the breast, mouth, throat, esophagus, liver, and colon
- Memory and learning problems
- Alcohol dependence

Binge Drinking Costs Everyone

Drinking too much, including binge drinking, cost the United States $249 billion in 2010, or $2.05 a drink. These costs resulted from losses in workplace productivity, healthcare expenditures, criminal justice costs, and other expenses. Binge drinking was responsible for 77 percent of these costs, or $191 billion.

Preventing Binge Drinking

The Community Preventive Services Task Force (CPSTF) recommends evidence-based interventions to prevent binge drinking and related harms. Recommended strategies include:

- Using pricing strategies, including increasing alcohol taxes
- Limiting the number of retail alcohol outlets that sell alcoholic beverages in a given area

- Holding alcohol retailers responsible for the harms caused by illegal alcohol sales to minors or intoxicated patrons (dram shop liability)
- Restricting access to alcohol by maintaining limits on the days and hours of alcohol retail sales
- Consistently enforcing laws against underage drinking and alcohol impaired driving
- Maintaining government controls on alcohol sales (avoiding privatization)
- Screening and counseling for alcohol misuse

Chapter 6

Facts about Alcoholism

Alcohol Use in the United States

- **Prevalence of Drinking:** According to the 2015 National Survey on Drug Use and Health (NSDUH), 86.4 percent of people ages 18 or older reported that they drank alcohol at some point in their lifetime; 70.1 percent reported that they drank in the past year; 56 percent reported that they drank in the past month.
- **Prevalence of Binge Drinking and Heavy Alcohol Use:** In 2015, 26.9 percent of people ages 18 or older reported that they engaged in binge drinking in the past month; 7 percent reported that they engaged in heavy alcohol use in the past month.

Alcohol Use Disorder (AUD) in the United States

- **Adults (ages 18+):** According to the 2015 NSDUH, 15.1 million adults ages 18 and older (6.2% of this age group) had AUD. This includes 9.8 million men (8.4% of men in this age group) and 5.3 million women (4.2% of women in this age group).
    - About 6.7 percent of adults who had AUD in the past year received treatment. This includes 7.4 percent of males and 5.4 percent of females with AUD in this age group.

This chapter includes text excerpted from "Alcohol Facts and Statistics," National Institute on Alcohol Abuse and Alcoholism (NIAAA), June 2017.

- **Youth (ages 12–17):** According to the 2015 NSDUH, an estimated 623,000 adolescents ages 12–17 (2.5% of this age group) had AUD. This number includes 298,000 males (2.3% of males in this age group) and 325,000 females (2.7% of females in this age group).
- About 5.2 percent of youth who had AUD in the past year received treatment. This includes 5.1 percent of males and 5.3 percent of females with AUD in this age group.

Alcohol-Related Deaths

- An estimated 88,000 people (approximately 62,000 men and 26,000 women) die from alcohol-related causes annually, making alcohol the third leading preventable cause of death in the United States. The first is tobacco, and the second is poor diet and physical inactivity.
- In 2014, alcohol-impaired driving fatalities accounted for 9,967 deaths (31 percent of overall driving fatalities).

Economic Burden

- In 2010, alcohol misuse cost the United States $249.0 billion.
- Three quarters of the total cost of alcohol misuse is related to binge drinking.

Global Burden

- In 2012, 3.3 million deaths, or 5.9 percent of all global deaths (7.6% for men and 4% for women), were attributable to alcohol consumption.
- In 2014, the World Health Organization (WHO) reported that alcohol contributed to more than 200 diseases and injury-related health conditions, most notably *Diagnostic and Statistical Manual of Mental Disorders (DSM-IV)* alcohol dependence, liver cirrhosis, cancers, and injuries. In 2012, 5.1 percent of the burden of disease and injury worldwide (139 million disability adjusted life-years) was attributable to alcohol consumption.
- Globally, alcohol misuse was the fifth leading risk factor for premature death and disability in 2010. Among people between the ages of 15 and 49, it is the first. In the age group 20–39 years, approximately 25 percent of the total deaths are alcohol attributable.

Family Consequences

- More than 10 percent of U.S. children live with a parent with alcohol problems, according to a 2012 study.

Underage Drinking

Prevalence of Underage Alcohol Use

- **Prevalence of Drinking:** According to the 2015 NSDUH, 33.1% of 15-year-olds report that they have had at least 1 drink in their lives. About 7.7 million people ages 12–20 (20.3% of this age group) reported drinking alcohol in the past month (19.8% of males and 20.8% of females).
- **Prevalence of Binge Drinking:** According to the 2015 NSDUH, approximately 5.1 million people (about 13.4%) ages 12–20 (13.4% of males and 13.3% of females) reported binge drinking in the past month.
- **Prevalence of Heavy Alcohol Use:** According to the 2015 NSDUH, approximately 1.3 million people (about 3.3%) ages 12–20 (3.6% of males and 3% of females) reported heavy alcohol use in the past month.

Consequences of Underage Alcohol Use

- Research indicates that alcohol use during the teenage years could interfere with normal adolescent brain development and increase the risk of developing AUD. In addition, underage drinking contributes to a range of acute consequences, including injuries, sexual assaults, and even deaths—including those from car crashes.

Alcohol and College Students

Prevalence of Alcohol Use

- **Prevalence of Drinking:** According to the 2015 NSDUH, 58 percent of full-time college students ages 18–22 drank alcohol in the past month compared with 48.2 percent of other persons of the same age.
- **Prevalence of Binge Drinking:** According to the 2015 NSDUH, 37.9 percent of college students ages 18–22 reported

binge drinking in the past month compared with 32.6 percent of other persons of the same age.

- **Prevalence of Heavy Alcohol Use:** According to the 2015 NSDUH, 12.5 percent of college students ages 18–22 reported heavy alcohol use in the past month compared with 8.5 percent of other persons of the same age.

Consequences—Researchers estimate that each year:

- 1,825 college students between the ages of 18 and 24 die from alcohol-related unintentional injuries, including motor-vehicle crashes.
- 696,000 students between the ages of 18 and 24 are assaulted by another student who has been drinking.
- 97,000 students between the ages of 18 and 24 report experiencing alcohol-related sexual assault or date rape.
- Roughly 20 percent of college students meet the criteria for AUD.
- About 1 in 4 college students report academic consequences from drinking, including missing class, falling behind in class, doing poorly on exams or papers, and receiving lower grades overall.

Alcohol and Pregnancy

- The prevalence of fetal alcohol syndrome (FAS) in the United States was estimated by the Institute of Medicine (IOM) in 1996 to be between 0.5 and 3.0 cases per 1,000.
- More reports from specific U.S. sites report the prevalence of FAS to be 2–7 cases per 1,000, and the prevalence of fetal alcohol spectrum disorders (FASDs) to be as high as 20–50 cases per 1,000.

Alcohol and the Human Body

- In 2015, of the 78,529 liver disease deaths among individuals ages 12 and older, 47 percent involved alcohol. Among males, 49,695 liver disease deaths occurred and 49.5 percent involved alcohol. Among females, 28,834 liver disease deaths occurred and 43.5 percent involved alcohol.

- Among all cirrhosis deaths in 2013, 47.9 percent were alcohol related. The proportion of alcohol-related cirrhosis was highest (76.5%) among deaths of persons ages 25–34, followed by deaths of persons ages 35–44, at 70 percent.
- In 2009, alcohol-related liver disease was the primary cause of almost 1 in 3 liver transplants in the United States.
- Drinking alcohol increases the risk of cancers of the mouth, esophagus, pharynx, larynx, liver, and breast.

Health Benefits of Moderate Alcohol Consumption

- Moderate alcohol consumption, according to the *2015–2020 Dietary Guidelines for Americans* (DGA), is up to 1 drink per day for women and up to 2 drinks per day for men.
- Moderate alcohol consumption may have beneficial effects on health. These include decreased risk for heart disease and mortality due to heart disease, decreased risk of ischemic stroke (in which the arteries to the brain become narrowed or blocked, resulting in reduced blood flow), and decreased risk of diabetes.
- In most Western countries where chronic diseases such as coronary heart disease (CHD), cancer, stroke, and diabetes are the primary causes of death, results from large epidemiological studies consistently show that alcohol reduces mortality, especially among middle aged and older men and women—an association that is likely due to the protective effects of moderate alcohol consumption on CHD, diabetes, and ischemic stroke.
- It is estimated that 26,000 deaths were averted in 2005 because of reductions in ischemic heart disease, ischemic stroke, and diabetes from the benefits attributed to moderate alcohol consumption.
- Expanding our understanding of the relationship between moderate alcohol consumption and potential health benefits remains a challenge, and, although there are positive effects, alcohol may not benefit everyone who drinks moderately.

Chapter 7

What Alcohol Does to Your Body

Effects on the Brain

You're chatting with friends at a party and a waitress comes around with glasses of champagne. You drink one, then another, maybe even a few more. Before you realize it, you are laughing more loudly than usual and swaying as you walk. By the end of the evening, you are too slow to move out of the way of a waiter with a dessert tray and have trouble speaking clearly. The next morning, you wake up feeling dizzy and your head hurts. You may have a hard time remembering everything you did the night before.

These reactions illustrate how quickly and dramatically alcohol affects the brain. The brain is an intricate maze of connections that keeps our physical and psychological processes running smoothly. Disruption of any of these connections can affect how the brain works. Alcohol also can have longer-lasting consequences for the brain—changing the way it looks and works and resulting in a range of problems. Most people do not realize how extensively alcohol can affect the brain. But recognizing these potential consequences will help you make better decisions about what amount of alcohol is appropriate for you.

This chapter includes text excerpted from "Beyond Hangovers," National Institute on Alcohol Abuse and Alcoholism (NIAAA), October 2015.

What Happens inside the Brain?

The brain's structure is complex. It includes multiple systems that interact to support all of your body's functions—from thinking to breathing and moving.

These multiple brain systems communicate with each other through about a trillion tiny nerve cells called neurons. Neurons in the brain translate information into electrical and chemical signals the brain can understand. They also send messages from the brain to the rest of the body.

Chemicals called neurotransmitters carry messages between the neurons. Neurotransmitters can be very powerful. Depending on the type and the amount of neurotransmitter, these chemicals can either intensify or minimize your body's responses, your feelings, and your mood. The brain works to balance the neurotransmitters that speed things up with the ones that slow things down to keep your body operating at the right pace.

Alcohol can slow the pace of communication between neurotransmitters in the brain.

Discovering the Brain Changes

There still is much we do not understand about how the brain works and how alcohol affects it. Researchers are constantly discovering more about how alcohol interrupts communication pathways in the brain and changes brain structure, and the resulting effects on behavior and functioning. A variety of research methods broaden our understanding in different ways:

- **Brain imaging:** Various imaging tools, including structural magnetic resonance imaging (MRI), functional magnetic resonance imaging (fMRI), diffusion tensor imaging (DTI), and positron emission tomography (PET), are used to create pictures of the brain. MRI and DTI create images of brain structure, or what the brain looks like. fMRI looks at brain function, or what the brain is doing. It can detect changes in brain activity. PET scans look at changes in neurotransmitter function. All of these imaging techniques are useful to track changes in the alcoholic brain. For example, they can show how an alcoholic brain changes immediately after drinking stops, and again after a long period of sobriety, to check for possible relapses.
- **Psychological tests**: Researchers also use psychological tests to evaluate how alcohol-related brain changes affect mental

functioning. These tests demonstrate how alcohol affects emotions and personality, as well as how it compromises learning and memory skills.

- **Animal studies**: Testing the effect of alcohol on animals' brains helps researchers better understand how alcohol injures the human brain, and how abstinence can reverse this damage

Defining the Brain Changes

Using brain imaging and psychological tests, researchers have identified the regions of the brain most vulnerable to alcohol's effects. These include:

- **Cerebellum:** This area controls motor coordination. Damage to the cerebellum results in a loss of balance and stumbling, and also may affect cognitive functions such as memory and emotional response.
- **Limbic system:** This complex brain system monitors a variety of tasks including memory and emotion. Damage to this area impairs each of these functions.
- **Cerebral cortex:** Our abilities to think, plan, behave intelligently, and interact socially stem from this brain region. In addition, this area connects the brain to the rest of the nervous system. Changes and damage to this area impair the ability to solve problems, remember, and learn.

Alcohol Shrinks and Disturbs Brain Tissue

Heavy alcohol consumption—even on a single occasion—can throw the delicate balance of neurotransmitters off course. Alcohol can cause your neurotransmitters to relay information too slowly, so you feel extremely drowsy. Alcohol-related disruptions to the neurotransmitter balance also can trigger mood and behavioral changes, including depression, agitation, memory loss, and even seizures.

Long-term, heavy drinking causes alterations in the neurons, such as reductions in the size of brain cells. As a result of these and other changes, brain mass shrinks and the brain's inner cavity grows bigger. These changes may affect a wide range of abilities, including motor coordination; temperature regulation; sleep; mood; and various cognitive functions, including learning and memory.

One neurotransmitter particularly susceptible to even small amounts of alcohol is called glutamate. Among other things, glutamate affects memory. Researchers believe that alcohol interferes with glutamate action, and this may be what causes some people to temporarily "blackout," or forget much of what happened during a night of heavy drinking.

Alcohol also causes an increased release of serotonin, another neurotransmitter, which helps regulate emotional expression, and endorphins, which are natural substances that may spark feelings of relaxation and euphoria as intoxication sets in.

Researchers now understand that the brain tries to compensate for these disruptions. Neurotransmitters adapt to create balance in the brain despite the presence of alcohol. But making these adaptations can have negative results, including building alcohol tolerance, developing alcohol dependence, and experiencing alcohol withdrawal symptoms.

What Factors Make a Difference?

Different people react differently to alcohol. That is because a variety of factors can influence your brain's response to alcohol. These factors include:

- **How Much and How Often You Drink**: The more you drink, the more vulnerable your brain is.
- **Your Genetic Background and Family History of Alcoholism**: Certain ethnic populations can have stronger reactions to alcohol, and children of alcoholics are more likely to become alcoholics themselves.
- **Your Physical Health**: If you have liver or nutrition problems, the effects of alcohol will take longer to wear off.

Are Brain Problems Reversible?

Abstaining from alcohol over several months to a year may allow structural brain changes to partially correct. Abstinence also can help reverse negative effects on thinking skills, including problem solving, memory, and attention.

The Alcohol-Related Brain Conditions

Liver Damage That Affects Brain

Not only does alcoholic liver disease affect liver function itself, it also damages the brain. The liver breaks down alcohol—and the toxins it releases. During this process, alcohol's byproducts damage liver cells. These damaged liver cells no longer function as well as they should and allow too much of these toxic substances, ammonia and manganese in particular, to travel to the brain. These substances proceed to damage brain cells, causing a serious and potentially fatal brain disorder known as hepatic encephalopathy.

Hepatic encephalopathy causes a range of problems, from less severe to fatal. These problems can include:

- Sleep disturbances
- Mood and personality changes
- Anxiety
- Depression
- Shortened attention span
- Coordination problems, including asterixis, which results in hand shaking or flapping
- Coma
- Death

Doctors can help treat hepatic encephalopathy with compounds that lower blood ammonia concentrations and with devices that help remove harmful toxins from the blood. In some cases, people suffering from hepatic encephalopathy require a liver transplant, which generally helps improve brain function.

Fetal Alcohol Spectrum Disorders (FASDs)

Alcohol can affect the brain at any stage of development—even before birth. Fetal alcohol spectrum disorders are the full range of physical, learning, and behavioral problems, and other birth defects that result from prenatal alcohol exposure. The most serious of these disorders, fetal alcohol syndrome (FAS), is characterized by abnormal facial features and is usually associated with severe reductions in brain function and overall growth. FAS is the leading preventable birth defect associated with mental and behavioral impairment in the United States. The brains of children with FAS are smaller than normal and contain fewer cells, including neurons. These deficiencies result in lifelong learning and behavioral problems. Current research is investigating whether the brain function of children and adults with FAS can be improved with complex rehabilitative training, dietary supplements, or medications.

Effects on the Heart

Americans know how prevalent heart disease is—about 1 in 12 of us suffer from it. What we don't always recognize are the connections heart disease shares with alcohol. On the one hand, researchers have known for centuries that excessive alcohol consumption can damage the heart. Drinking a lot over a long period of time or drinking too much on a single occasion can put your heart—and your life—at risk. On the other hand, researchers now understand that drinking moderate amounts of alcohol can protect the hearts of some people from the risks of coronary artery disease. Deciding how much, if any, alcohol is right for you can be complicated. To make the best decision for yourself, you need to know the facts and then consult your physician.

Know the Function

Your cardiovascular system consists of your heart, blood vessels, and blood. This system works constantly—every second of your life—delivering oxygen and nutrients to your cells, and carrying away carbon dioxide and other unnecessary material. Your heart drives this process. It is a muscle that contracts and relaxes over and over again, moving the blood along the necessary path. Your heart beats about 100,000 times each day, pumping the equivalent of 2,000 gallons of blood throughout your body.

The two sides, or chambers, of the heart receive blood and pump it back into the body. The right ventricle of the heart pumps blood into the lungs to exchange carbon dioxide from the cells for oxygen. The heart relaxes to allow this blood back into its left chamber. It then pumps the oxygen rich blood to tissues and organs. Blood passing through the kidneys allows the body to get rid of waste products. Electrical signals keep the heart pumping continuously and at the appropriate rate to propel this routine.

Know the Risks

Alcoholic Cardiomyopathy

Long-term heavy drinking weakens the heart muscle, causing a condition called alcoholic cardiomyopathy. A weakened heart droops and stretches and cannot contract effectively. As a result, it cannot pump enough blood to sufficiently nourish the organs. In some cases, this blood flow shortage causes severe damage to organs and tissues. Symptoms of cardiomyopathy include shortness of breath and other breathing difficulties, fatigue, swollen legs and feet, and irregular heartbeat. It can even lead to heart failure.

Arrhythmias

Both binge drinking and long-term drinking can affect how quickly a heart beats. The heart depends on an internal pacemaker system to keep it pumping consistently and at the right speed. Alcohol disturbs this pacemaker system and causes the heart to beat too rapidly, or irregularly. These heart rate abnormalities are called arrhythmias. Two types of alcohol induced arrhythmias are:

- **Atrial fibrillation**: In this form of arrhythmia, the heart's upper, or atrial, chambers shudder weakly but do not contract. Blood can collect and even clot in these upper chambers. If a blood clot travels from the heart to the brain, a stroke can occur; if it travels to other organs such as the lungs, an embolism, or blood vessel blockage, occurs.
- **Ventricular tachycardia**: This form of arrhythmia occurs in the heart's lower, or ventricular, chambers. Electrical signals travel throughout the heart's muscles, triggering contractions that keep blood flowing at the right pace. Alcohol Induced damage to heart muscle cells can cause these electrical impulses to circle through the ventricle too many times, causing too many contractions. The heart beats too quickly, and so does not fill up with enough blood between each beat. As a result, the rest of the body does not get enough blood. Ventricular tachycardia causes dizziness, lightheadedness, unconsciousness, cardiac arrest, and even sudden death.

Strokes

A stroke occurs when blood cannot reach the brain. In about 80 percent of strokes, a blood clot prevents blood flow to the brain. These are called ischemic strokes. Sometimes, blood accumulates in the brain, or in the spaces surrounding it. This causes hemorrhagic strokes.

Both binge drinking and long-term heavy drinking can lead to strokes even in people without coronary heart disease. Recent studies show that people who binge drink are about 56 percent more likely than people who never binge drink to suffer an ischemic stroke over 10 years. Binge drinkers also are about 39 percent more likely to suffer any type of stroke than people who never binge drink. In addition, alcohol exacerbates the problems that often lead to strokes, including hypertension, arrhythmias, and cardiomyopathy.

Hypertension

Chronic alcohol use, as well as binge drinking, can cause high blood pressure, or hypertension. Your blood pressure is a measurement of the pressure your heart creates as it beats, and the pressure inside your veins and arteries. Healthy blood vessels stretch like elastic as the heart pumps blood through them. Hypertension develops when the blood vessels stiffen, making them less flexible. Heavy alcohol consumption triggers the release of certain stress hormones that in turn constrict blood vessels. This elevates blood pressure. In addition, alcohol may affect the function of the muscles within the blood vessels, causing them to constrict and elevate blood pressure.

Know the Benefits

Research shows that healthy people who drink moderate amounts of alcohol may have a lower risk of developing coronary heart disease than nondrinkers. Moderate drinking is usually defined as no more than two drinks in a given day for men and one drink per day for women who are not pregnant or trying to conceive.

A variety of factors, including diet, genetics, high blood pressure, and age, can cause fat to build up in your arteries, resulting in coronary heart disease. An excess of fat narrows the coronary arteries, which are the blood vessels that supply blood directly to the heart. Clogged arteries reduce blood supply to the heart muscle, and make it easier for blood clots to form. Blood clots can lead to both heart attacks and strokes. According to recent studies, drinking moderately can protect your heart from these conditions. Moderate drinking helps inhibit and reduce the buildup of fat in the arteries. It can raise the levels of high-density lipoproteins (HDL)—or "good" cholesterol—in the blood, which wards off heart disease. It can help guard against heart attack and stroke by preventing blood clots from forming and by dissolving blood clots that do develop. Drinking moderately also may help keep blood pressure levels in check.

These benefits may not apply to people with existing medical conditions, or who regularly take certain medications. In addition, researchers discourage people from beginning to drink just for the health benefits. Rather, you can use this research to help you spark a conversation with your medical professional about the best path for you.

Effects on the Liver

Know the Facts

Liver disease is one of the leading causes of illness and death in the United States. More than 2 million Americans suffer from liver disease caused by alcohol.

In general, liver disease strikes people who drink heavily over many years. While many of us recognize that excessive alcohol consumption can lead to liver disease, we might not know why. Understanding the connections between alcohol and the liver can help you make smarter decisions about drinking and take better control of your health.

Know the Function

Your liver works hard to keep your body productive and healthy. It stores energy and nutrients. It generates proteins and enzymes your body uses to function and ward off disease. It also rids your body of substances that can be dangerous—including alcohol.

The liver breaks down most of the alcohol a person consumes. But the process of breaking alcohol down generates toxins even more harmful than alcohol itself. These byproducts damage liver cells, promote inflammation, and weaken the body's natural defenses. Eventually, these problems can disrupt the body's metabolism and impair the function of other organs. Because the liver plays such a vital role in alcohol detoxification, it is especially vulnerable to damage from excessive alcohol.

Know the Consequences

Heavy drinking—even for just a few days at a time—can cause fat to build up in the liver. This condition, called steatosis, or fatty liver, is the earliest stage of alcoholic liver disease and the most common alcohol induced liver disorder. The excessive fat makes it more difficult for the liver to operate and leaves it open to developing dangerous inflammations, like alcoholic hepatitis.

For some, alcoholic hepatitis does not present obvious symptoms. For others, though, alcoholic hepatitis can cause fever, nausea, appetite loss, abdominal pain, and even mental confusion. As it increases in severity, alcoholic hepatitis dangerously enlarges the liver, and causes jaundice, excessive bleeding, and clotting difficulties.

Another liver condition associated with heavy drinking is fibrosis, which causes scar tissue to build up in the liver. Alcohol alters the chemicals in the liver needed to break down and remove this scar tissue. As a result, liver function suffers.

If you continue to drink, this excessive scar tissue builds up and creates a condition called cirrhosis, which is a slow deterioration of the liver. Cirrhosis prevents the liver from performing critical functions, including managing infections, removing harmful substances from the blood, and absorbing nutrients.

A variety of complications, including jaundice, insulin resistance and type 2 diabetes, and even liver cancer, can result as cirrhosis weakens liver function.

Risk factors ranging from genetics and gender, to alcohol accessibility, social customs around drinking, and even diet can affect a person's individual susceptibility to alcoholic liver disease. Statistics show that about one in five heavy drinkers will develop alcoholic hepatitis, while one in four will develop cirrhosis.

Know There Is a Bright Side

The good news is that a variety of lifestyle changes can help treat alcoholic liver disease. The most critical lifestyle change is abstinence from alcohol. Quitting drinking will help prevent further injury to your liver. Cigarette smoking, obesity, and poor nutrition all contribute to alcoholic liver disease. It is important to stop smoking and improve your eating habits to keep liver disease in check. But when conditions like cirrhosis become severe, a liver transplant may be the primary treatment option.

Effects on the Pancreas

Know the Facts

Each year, acute pancreatitis sends more than 200,000 Americans to the hospital. Many of those who suffer from pancreatic problems are also heavy drinkers. Habitual and excessive drinking damages the pancreas, and commonly causes pancreatitis. Learning more about the links between alcohol and pancreatic problems can help you make better decisions to protect your health.

Know the Function

The pancreas plays an important role in food digestion and its conversion into fuel to power your body. It sends enzymes into the small intestine to digest carbohydrates, proteins, and fat. It also secretes insulin and glucagon, hormones that regulate the process of utilizing glucose, the body's main source of energy. Insulin and glucagon control glucose levels, which helps all cells use the energy glucose provides. Insulin also ensures that extra glucose gets stored away as either glycogen or fat. When you drink, alcohol damages pancreatic cells and influences metabolic processes involving insulin. This process leaves the pancreas open to dangerous inflammations.

Know the Risks

A pancreas unaffected by alcohol sends enzymes out to the small intestine to metabolize food. Alcohol jumbles this process. It causes the pancreas to secrete its digestive juices internally, rather than sending the enzymes to the small intestine. These enzymes, as well as acetaldehyde—a substance produced from metabolizing, or breaking down the alcohol—are harmful to the pancreas. If you consume alcohol excessively over a long time, this continued process can cause inflammation, as well as swelling of tissues and blood vessels. This inflammation is called pancreatitis, and it prevents the pancreas from working properly. Pancreatitis occurs as a sudden attack, called acute pancreatitis. As excessive drinking continues, the inflammation can become constant. This condition is known as chronic pancreatitis.

Pancreatitis is also a risk factor for the development of pancreatic cancer. A heavy drinker may not be able to detect the buildup of pancreatic damage until the problems set off an attack. An acute pancreatic attack causes symptoms including:

- Abdominal pain, which may radiate up the back
- Nausea and vomiting
- Fever
- Rapid heart rate
- Diarrhea
- Sweating

Chronic pancreatitis causes these symptoms as well as severe abdominal pain, significant reduction in pancreatic function and digestion, and blood sugar problems. Chronic pancreatitis can slowly destroy the pancreas and lead to diabetes or even death. While a single drinking binge will not automatically lead to pancreatitis, the risk of developing the disease increases as excessive drinking continues over time. These risks apply to all heavy drinkers, but only about 5 percent of people with alcohol dependence develop pancreatitis. Some people are more susceptible to the disease than others, but researchers have not yet identified exactly what environmental and genetic factors play the biggest role.

Treatment Helps—But Does Not Cure

Abstinence from alcohol can slow the progression of pancreatitis and reduce its painful symptoms. A low fat diet also may help. It is also critical to guard against infections and to get supportive treatment. Treatment options, including enzyme replacement therapy or insulin, can improve pancreatic function. In some cases, surgery is necessary to relieve pain, clear blockages, and reduce attacks. The effects of alcoholic pancreatitis can be managed, but not easily reversed.

Effects on the Immune System

Germs and bacteria surround us everywhere. Luckily, our immune system is designed to protect our bodies from the scores of foreign substances that can make us sick. Drinking too much alcohol weakens the immune system, making your body a much easier target for disease. Understanding the effect alcohol can have on your immune system can inform the decisions you make about drinking alcohol.

Know the Facts

Your immune system is often compared to an army. This army defends your body from infection and disease. Your skin and the mucous that lines your respiratory and gastrointestinal tracts help block bacteria from entering or staying in your body. If foreign substances somehow make it through these barriers, your immune system kicks into gear with two defensive systems: innate and adaptive.

The innate system exists in your body before you are exposed to foreign substances like bacteria, viruses, fungi, or parasites. These substances, which are called antigens, can invade your body and make you sick. The components of the innate system include:

- **White blood cells (WBCs):** White blood cells form your first line of defense against infection. They surround and swallow foreign bodies quickly.
- **Natural killer (NK) cells:** Natural killers are special WBCs that detect and destroy cells infected with cancer or viruses.

- **Cytokines**: White blood cells send out these chemical messengers directly to an infected site. Cytokines trigger inflammatory responses, like dilating blood vessels and increasing blood flow to the affected area. They also call on more WBCs to swarm an infected area.

The adaptive system kicks in after you are exposed to an infection for the first time. The next time you encounter the same infection, your adaptive system fights it off even faster and more efficiently than the first time. The components of the adaptive system include:

- **T-lymphocyte cells**: T-cells reinforce the work of white blood cells by targeting individual foreign substances. T-cells can identify and destroy a vast array of bacteria and viruses. They can also kill infected cells and secrete cytokines.
- **B-lymphocyte cells**: B-cells produce antibodies that fight off harmful substances by sticking to them and making them stand out to other immune cells.
- **Antibodies**: After B-cells encounter antigens, they produce antibodies. These are proteins that target specific antigens and then remember how to combat the antigen.

Know the Risks

Alcohol suppresses both the innate and the adaptive immune systems. Chronic alcohol use reduces the ability of white blood cells to effectively engulf and swallow harmful bacteria. Excessive drinking also disrupts the production of cytokines, causing your body to either produce too much or not enough of these chemical messengers. An abundance of cytokines can damage your tissues, whereas a lack of cytokines leaves you open to infection.

Chronic alcohol use also suppresses the development of T-cells and may impair the ability of NK cells to attack tumor cells. This reduced function makes you more vulnerable to bacteria and viruses, and less capable of destroying cancerous cells.

With a compromised immune system, chronic drinkers are more liable to contract diseases like pneumonia and tuberculosis than people who do not drink too much. There is also data linking alcohol's damage to the immune system with an increased susceptibility to contracting HIV infection. HIV develops faster in chronic drinkers who already have the virus.

Drinking a lot on a single occasion also can compromise your immune system. Drinking to intoxication can slow your body's ability to produce cytokines that ward off infections by causing inflammations. Without these inflammatory responses, your body's ability to defend itself against bacteria is significantly reduced. A study shows that slower inflammatory cytokine production can reduce your ability to fight off infections for up to 24 hours after getting drunk.

Still Looking for the Bright Side

At this point, scientists do not know whether abstinence, reduced drinking, or other measures will help reverse the effects of alcohol on the immune system.

Nevertheless, it is important to keep in mind that avoiding drinking helps minimize the burden on your immune system, particularly if you are fighting a viral or bacterial infection.

Chapter 8

Alcohol-Related Problems: Across Gender and Lifespan

Chapter Contents

Section 8.1

Alcohol Use in Adolescence

This section includes text excerpted from "Alcohol Use in Adolescence," U.S. Department of Health and Human Services (HHS), January 19, 2018.

Alcohol use is a common and risky behavior among adolescents in the United States, with more than three in five high school students reporting having had at least one drink. Fortunately, parents and practitioners who work with youth can play a vital role in influencing their use of alcohol. The following section explores how common alcohol use is among adolescents, the risks associated with its use, and strategies adults can use to help youth make healthy decisions.

How Common Is Adolescent Alcohol Use?

- Adolescents use alcohol more than any other drug, including tobacco and marijuana. In 2016, nearly one in five 12- to 20-year-olds reported drinking alcohol in the past month.
- Adolescents are more likely to drink as they get older. In 2017, one in three students in 12th grade reported drinking in the past month, compared with one in five students in 10th grade and one in 14 students in 8th grade.
- Binge drinking is the most commonly reported—and most dangerous—way that adolescents consume alcohol. Binge drinking is defined, for males, as drinking five or more drinks on one occasion, and, for females, four or more drinks on one occasion. The threshold for binge drinking is lower for females because of physical differences that make them more vulnerable than males to the effects of alcohol. Three out of five youth who drink alcohol also report binge drinking. In 2017, 17 percent of students in 12th grade reported binge drinking in the past month compared to 10 percent of students in 10th grade and 4 percent of students in 8th grade.

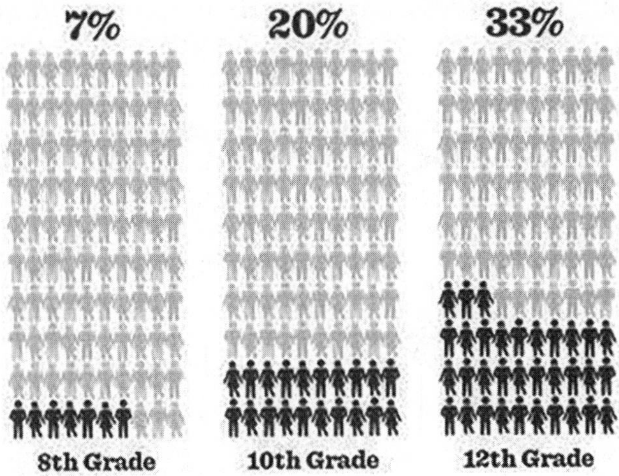

Figure 8.1. *Drinking Prevalence by Grade*

- Rates of underage alcohol use and binge drinking decreased from 2002–2015, and have remained relatively stable since then.

Risks of Adolescent Alcohol Use

Adolescents who drink alcohol are more likely to:

- **Experience injury or death.** Adolescents who drink put themselves at risk of injury or death from alcohol poisoning or alcohol related accidents. Drinking and driving is especially deadly for adolescents: one in seven drivers ages 16–20 involved in fatal crashes in 2016 had alcohol in their systems. Unfortunately, it is relatively common for adolescent to drive or ride with someone under the influence of alcohol. In 2015, one in thirteen high school students reported drinking and driving, and one in five high school students rode with a driver who had been drinking.
- **Have impaired judgment.** Consuming alcohol lowers inhibitions and impairs judgment, exposing adolescents to serious dangers, including risky sexual behavior as well as physical and sexual assault.
- **Have difficulty at school.** Adolescent drinking is associated with having trouble at school, including missing class and having low grades.

- **Have alcohol interfere with brain development.** Research shows that adolescents' brains continue developing into their 20s. Alcohol use can negatively influence this development, potentially affecting both brain structure and function.
- **Have alcohol addiction and related problems.** Adolescents who start drinking early are at risk of suffering from alcohol addiction. Adolescents who start drinking before the age of 15 are four times more likely at some point in their lives meet the criteria for alcohol dependence. Additionally, there are long-term alcohol related consequences including chronic diseases such as high blood pressure, psychological disorders, and various cancers.
- **Have legal problems.** It is illegal for anyone under age 21 to purchase or publicly consume alcohol in all 50 states. Youth who violate the law risk serious legal consequences.

Section 8.2

Alcohol and Women's Health Issues

This section includes text excerpted from "Fact Sheets—Excessive Alcohol Use and Risks to Women's Health," Centers for Disease Control and Prevention (CDC), March 7, 2016.

Although men are more likely to drink alcohol and drink in larger amounts, gender differences in body structure and chemistry cause women to absorb more alcohol, and take longer to break it down and remove it from their bodies (i.e., to metabolize it). In other words, upon drinking equal amounts, women have higher alcohol levels in their blood than men, and the immediate effects of alcohol occur more quickly and last longer in women than men. These differences also make it more likely that drinking will cause long-term health problems in women than men.

Drinking Levels among Women

- Approximately 46 percent of adult women report drinking alcohol in the last 30 days.

- Approximately 12 percent of adult women report binge drinking 3 times a month, averaging 5 drinks per binge.
- Most (90%) people who binge drink are not alcoholics or alcohol dependent.
- About 2.5 percent of women and 4.5 percent of men met the diagnostic criteria for alcohol dependence in the past year.

Reproductive Health Outcomes

- National surveys show that about 1 in 2 women of child-bearing age (i.e., aged 18–44 years) drink alcohol, and 18 percent of women who drink alcohol in this age group binge drink
- Excessive drinking may disrupt the menstrual cycle and increase the risk of infertility
- Women who binge drink are more likely to have unprotected sex and multiple sex partners. These activities increase the risks of unintended pregnancy and sexually transmitted diseases (STDs).

Pregnancy Outcomes

- About 10 percent of pregnant women drink alcohol.
- Women who drink alcohol while pregnant increase their risk of having a baby with fetal alcohol spectrum disorders (FASDs). The most severe form is fetal alcohol syndrome (FAS), which causes mental retardation and birth defects.
- FASD are completely preventable if a woman does not drink while pregnant or while she may become pregnant. It is not safe to drink at any time during pregnancy.
- Excessive drinking increases a woman's risk of miscarriage, stillbirth, and premature delivery.
- Women who drink alcohol while pregnant are also more likely to have a baby die from sudden infant death syndrome (SIDS). This risk substantially increases if a woman binge drinks during her first trimester of pregnancy.

Other Health Concerns

- **Liver disease:** The risk of cirrhosis and other alcohol-related liver diseases is higher for women than for men.

- **Impact on the brain:** Excessive drinking may result in memory loss and shrinkage of the brain. Research suggests that women are more vulnerable than men to the brain damaging effects of excessive alcohol use, and the damage tends to appear with shorter periods of excessive drinking for women than for men.
- **Impact on the heart:** Studies have shown that women who drink excessively are at increased risk for damage to the heart muscle than men even for women drinking at lower levels.
- **Cancer:** Alcohol consumption increases the risk of cancer of the mouth, throat, esophagus, liver, colon, and breast among women. The risk of breast cancer increases as alcohol use increases.
- **Sexual assault:** Binge drinking is a risk factor for sexual assault, especially among young women in college settings. Each year, about 1 in 20 college women are sexually assaulted. Research suggests that there is an increase in the risk of rape or sexual assault when both the attacker and victim have used alcohol prior to the attack.

Section 8.3

Men's Health Risks from Excessive Alcohol Use

This section includes text excerpted from "Fact Sheets—Excessive Alcohol Use and Risks to Men's Health," Centers for Disease Control and Prevention (CDC), March 7, 2016.

Men are more likely than women to drink excessively. Excessive drinking is associated with significant increases in short-term risks to health and safety, and the risk increases as the amount of drinking increases. Men are also more likely than women to take other risks (e.g., drive fast or without a safety belt), when combined with excessive drinking, further increasing their risk of injury or death.

Drinking Levels among Men

- Approximately, 58 percent of adult men report drinking alcohol in the last 30 days.
- Approximately, 23 percent of adult men report binge drinking 5 times a month, averaging 8 drinks per binge.
- Men are almost two times more likely to binge drink than women.
- Most (90%) people who binge drink are not alcoholics or alcohol dependent.
- About 4.5 percent of men and 2.5 percent of women met the diagnostic criteria for alcohol dependence in the past year.

Injuries and Deaths as a Result of Excessive Alcohol Use

- Men consistently have higher rates of alcohol-related deaths and hospitalizations than women.
- Among drivers in fatal motor-vehicle traffic crashes, men are almost twice as likely as women to have been intoxicated (i.e., a blood alcohol concentration of 0.08% or greater).
- Excessive alcohol consumption increases aggression and, as a result, can increase the risk of physically assaulting another person.
- Men are more likely than women to commit suicide, and more likely to have been drinking prior to committing suicide.

Reproductive Health and Sexual Function

Excessive alcohol use can interfere with testicular function and male hormone production resulting in impotence, infertility, and reduction of male secondary sex characteristics such as facial and chest hair. Excessive alcohol use is commonly involved in sexual assault. Also, alcohol use by men increases the chances of engaging in risky sexual activity including unprotected sex, sex with multiple partners, or sex with a partner at risk for sexually transmitted diseases.

Section 8.4

Alcohol Use in Older People

This section includes text excerpted from "Facts about Aging and Alcohol," National Institute on Aging (NIA), National Institutes of Health (NIH), May 16, 2017.

Sometimes trouble with alcohol in older people is mistaken for other conditions related to aging—for example, a problem with balance. But, how the body handles alcohol can change with age. You may have the same drinking habits, but your body has changed.

Alcohol may act differently in older people than in younger people. Some older people can feel "high" without increasing the amount of alcohol they drink. This "high" can make them more likely to have accidents, including falls and fractures and car crashes. Also, older women are more sensitive than men to the effects of alcohol.

Drinking too much alcohol over a long time can:

- Lead to some kinds of cancer, liver damage, immune system disorders, and brain damage
- Worsen some health conditions such as osteoporosis, diabetes, high blood pressure, stroke, ulcers, memory loss, and mood disorders
- Make some medical problems hard for doctors to find and treat—for example, alcohol causes changes in the heart and blood vessels. These changes can dull pain that might be a warning sign of a heart attack
- Cause some older people to be forgetful and confused—these symptoms could be mistaken for signs of Alzheimer disease (AD)

How Alcohol Affects Safety

Drinking even a small amount of alcohol can lead to dangerous or even deadly situations. Drinking can impair a person's judgment, coordination, and reaction time. This increases the risk of falls, household accidents, and car crashes. Alcohol is a factor in 30 percent of suicides, 40 percent of crashes and burns, 50 percent of drownings and homicides, and 60 percent of falls. People who plan to drive, use machinery, or perform other activities that require attention, skill, or coordination should not drink.

In older adults, too much alcohol can lead to balance problems and falls, which can result in hip or arm fractures and other injuries. Older people have thinner bones than younger people, so their bones break more easily. Studies show that the rate of hip fractures in older adults increases with alcohol use.

Adults of all ages who drink and drive are at higher risk of traffic accidents and related problems than those who do not drink. Drinking slows reaction times and coordination and interferes with eye movement and information processing. People who drink even a moderate amount can have traffic accidents, possibly resulting in injury or death to themselves and others. Even without alcohol, the risk of crashes goes up starting at age 55. Also, older drivers tend to be more seriously hurt in crashes than younger drivers. Alcohol adds to these age related risks.

In addition, alcohol misuse and abuse can strain relationships with family members, friends, and others. At the extreme, heavy drinking can contribute to domestic violence and child abuse or neglect. Alcohol use is often involved when people become violent, as well as when they are violently attacked. If you feel that alcohol is endangering you or someone else, call 911 or get other help right away.

Chapter 9

Understanding the Development of an Addiction

Warning Signs of Addiction

Warning signs of substance abuse or addiction may include:

- sleep difficulties
- anxiety or depression
- memory problems
- mood swings (temper flare-ups, irritability, defensiveness)
- rapid increases in the amount of medication needed
- frequent requests for refills of certain medicines
- a person not seeming like themselves (showing a general lack of interest or being overly energetic)
- "doctor shopping" (moving from provider to provider in an effort to get several prescriptions for the same medication)
- use of more than one pharmacy
- false or forged prescriptions

This chapter includes text excerpted from "Biology of Addiction," *NIH News in Health*, National Institutes of Health (NIH), October 2015.

Drugs and Alcohol Can Hijack Your Brain

People with addiction lose control over their actions. They crave and seek out drugs, alcohol, or other substances no matter what the cost—even at the risk of damaging friendships, hurting family, or losing jobs. What is it about addiction that makes people behave in such destructive ways? And why is it so hard to quit?

The National Institutes of Health (NIH) funded scientists are working to learn more about the biology of addiction. They've shown that addiction is a long-lasting and complex brain disease, and that current treatments can help people control their addictions. But even for those who've successfully quit, there's always a risk of the addiction returning, which is called relapse.

The biological basis of addiction helps to explain why people need much more than good intentions or willpower to break their addictions.

"A common misperception is that addiction is a choice or moral problem, and all you have to do is stop. But nothing could be further from the truth," says Dr. George Koob, director of NIH's National Institute on Alcohol Abuse and Alcoholism (NIAAA). "The brain actually changes with addiction, and it takes a good deal of work to get it back to its normal state. The more drugs or alcohol you've taken, the more disruptive it is to the brain."

Researchers have found that much of addiction's power lies in its ability to hijack and even destroy key brain regions that are meant to help us survive.

A healthy brain rewards healthy behaviors—like exercising, eating, or bonding with loved ones. It does this by switching on brain circuits that make you feel wonderful, which then motivates you to repeat those behaviors. In contrast, when you're in danger, a healthy brain pushes your body to react quickly with fear or alarm, so you'll get out of harm's way. If you're tempted by something questionable—like eating ice cream before dinner or buying things you can't afford—the front regions of your brain can help you decide if the consequences are worth the actions.

But when you're becoming addicted to a substance, that normal hardwiring of helpful brain processes can begin to work against you. Drugs or alcohol can hijack the pleasure/reward circuits in your brain and hook you into wanting more and more. Addiction can also send your emotional danger sensing circuits into overdrive, making you feel anxious and stressed when you're not using the drugs or alcohol. At this stage, people often use drugs or alcohol to keep from feeling bad rather than for their pleasurable effects.

To add to that, repeated use of drugs can damage the essential decision-making center at the front of the brain. This area, known as the prefrontal cortex, is the very region that should help you recognize the harms of using addictive substances.

"Brain imaging studies of people addicted to drugs or alcohol show decreased activity in this frontal cortex," says Dr. Nora Volkow, director of NIH's National Institute on Drug Abuse (NIDA). "When the frontal cortex isn't working properly, people can't make the decision to stop taking the drug—even if they realize the price of taking that drug may be extremely high, and they might lose custody of their children or end up in jail. Nonetheless, they take it."

Scientists don't yet understand why some people become addicted while others don't. Addiction tends to run in families, and certain types of genes have been linked to different forms of addiction. But not all members of an affected family are necessarily prone to addiction. "As with heart disease or diabetes, there's no one gene that makes you vulnerable," Koob says.

Other factors can also raise your chances of addiction. "Growing up with an alcoholic; being abused as a child; being exposed to extraordinary stress—all of these social factors can contribute to the risk for alcohol addiction or drug abuse," Koob says. "And with drugs or underage drinking, the earlier you start, the greater the likelihood of having alcohol use disorder or addiction later in life."

Teens are especially vulnerable to possible addiction because their brains are not yet fully developed—particularly the frontal regions that help with impulse control and assessing risk. Pleasure circuits in adolescent brains also operate in overdrive, making drug and alcohol use even more rewarding and enticing.

NIH is launching a new nationwide study to learn more about how teen brains are altered by alcohol, tobacco, marijuana, and other drugs. Researchers will use brain scans and other tools to assess more than 10,000 youth over a 10-year span. The study will track the links between substance use and brain changes, academic achievement, intelligence quotient (IQ), thinking skills, and mental health over time.

Although there's much still to learn, we do know that prevention is critical to reducing the harms of addiction. "Childhood and adolescence are times when parents can get involved and teach their kids about a healthy lifestyle and activities that can protect against the use of drugs," Volkow says. "Physical activity is important, as well as getting engaged in work, science projects, art, or social networks that do not promote use of drugs."

To treat addiction, scientists have identified several medications and behavioral therapies—especially when used in combination—that can help people stop using specific substances and prevent relapse. Unfortunately, no medications are yet available to treat addiction to stimulants such as cocaine or methamphetamine, but behavioral therapies can help.

"Treatment depends to a large extent on the severity of addiction and the individual person," Koob adds. "Some people can stop cigarette smoking and alcohol use disorders on their own. More severe cases might require months or even years of treatment and follow-up, with real efforts by the individual and usually complete abstinence from the substance afterward."

NIH-funded researchers are also evaluating experimental therapies that might enhance the effectiveness of established treatments. Mindfulness meditation and magnetic stimulation of the brain are being assessed for their ability to strengthen brain circuits that have been harmed by addiction. Scientists are also examining the potential of vaccines against nicotine, cocaine, and other drugs, which might prevent the drug from entering the brain.

"Addiction is a devastating disease, with a relatively high death rate and serious social consequences," Volkow says. "We're exploring multiple strategies so individuals will eventually have more treatment options, which will increase their chances of success to help them stop taking the drug."

Chapter 10

The Genetics of Alcoholism

Genes Influence Alcohol Use Disorder (AUD)

Alcohol use disorder (AUD) often seems to run in families, and we may hear about scientific studies of an "alcoholism gene." Genetics certainly influence our likelihood of developing AUD, but the story isn't so simple. Research shows that genes are responsible for about half of the risk for AUD. Therefore, genes alone do not determine whether someone will develop AUD. Environmental factors, as well as gene and environment interactions account for the remainder of the risk.

Multiple genes play a role in a person's risk for developing AUD. There are genes that increase a person's risk, as well as those that may decrease that risk, directly or indirectly. For instance, some people of Asian descent carry a gene variant that alters their rate of alcohol metabolism, causing them to have symptoms like flushing, nausea, and rapid heartbeat when they drink. Many people who experience these effects avoid alcohol, which helps protect them from developing AUD. As we have learned more about the role genes play in our

---

This chapter contains text excerpted from the following sources: Text beginning with the heading "Genes Influence Alcohol Use Disorder (AUD)" is excerpted from "Genetics of Alcohol Use Disorder," National Institute on Alcohol Abuse and Alcoholism (NIAAA), May 17, 2012. Reviewed April 2018; Text beginning with the heading "Genetics and Epigenetics of Addiction" is excerpted from "Genetics and Epigenetics of Addiction," National Institute on Drug Abuse (NIDA), February 2016.

health, researchers have discovered that different factors can alter the expression of our genes. This field is called epigenetics. Scientists are learning more and more about how epigenetics can affect our risk for developing AUD.

Genes Affect Alcohol Treatment

Scientists are also exploring how genes may influence the effectiveness of treatments for AUD. For instance, the drug naltrexone has been shown to help some, but not all, patients with AUD to reduce their drinking. Research has shown that patients with AUD who also have variations in a specific gene respond positively to treatment with the drug, while those without the specific gene do not. A fuller understanding of how genes influence treatment outcomes will help doctors prescribe the treatment that is most likely to help each patient.

Genetics and Epigenetics of Addiction

Why do some people become addicted while others don't? Family studies that include identical twins, fraternal twins, adoptees, and siblings suggest that as much as half of a person's risk of becoming addicted to nicotine, alcohol, or other drugs depends on his or her genetic makeup. Pinning down the biological basis for this risk is an important avenue of research for scientists trying to solve the problem of drug addiction.

Genes—functional units of deoxyribonucleic acid (DNA) that make up the human genome—provide the information that directs a body's basic cellular activities. Research on the human genome has shown that, on average, the DNA sequences of any two people are 99.9 percent the same. However, that 0.1 percent variation is profoundly important—it's still 3 million differences in the nearly 3 billion base pairs of DNA sequence. These differences contribute to visible variations, like height and hair color, and invisible traits, such as increased risk for or protection from certain diseases such as heart attack, stroke, diabetes, and addiction.

Some diseases, such as sickle cell anemia or cystic fibrosis, are caused by an error, known as a mutation, in a single gene. Some mutations, like the *BRCA 1* and *BRCA 2* mutations that are linked to a much higher risk of breast and ovarian cancer, have become critical medical tools in evaluating a patient's risk for serious diseases. Medical researchers have had striking success at unraveling the genetics of these single-gene disorders, though finding treatments or cures has not been as simple. Most diseases, including addiction, are complex, and variations in many different genes contribute to a person's overall level of risk or protection. The good news is that scientists are actively pursuing many more paths to treatment and prevention of these more complex illnesses.

Linking Genes to Health: Genome-Wide Association Studies

Recent advances in DNA analysis are helping researchers untangle complex genetic interactions by examining a person's entire genome all at once. Technologies such as genome-wide association studies (GWAS), whole genome sequencing, and exome sequencing (looking at just the protein-coding genes) identify subtle variations in DNA sequence called single-nucleotide polymorphisms (SNPs). SNPs are differences in just a single letter of the genetic code from one person to another. If a SNP appears more often in people with a disease than those without, it is thought to either directly affect susceptibility to that disease or be a marker for another variation that does.

GWAS and sequencing are extremely powerful tools because they can find a connection between a known gene or genes and a disorder, and can identify genes that may have been overlooked or were previously unknown. Through these methods, scientists can gather more evidence from affected families or use animal models and biochemical experiments to verify and understand the link between a gene and the risk of addiction. These findings would then be the basis for developing new treatment and intervention approaches.

The Role of the Environment in Diseases Like Addiction

That old saying "nature or nurture" might be better phrased "nature and nurture" because research shows that a person's health is the result of dynamic interactions between genes and the environment. For example, both genetics and lifestyle factors—such as diet, physical activity, and stress—affect high blood pressure risk. National Institute on Drug Abuse (NIDA) research has led to discoveries about how a person's surroundings affect drug use in particular.

For example, a community that provides healthy after-school activities has been shown to reduce vulnerability to drug addiction, and recent data show that access to exercise can discourage drug-seeking behavior, an effect that is more pronounced in males than in females.

In addition, studies suggest that an animal's drug use can be affected by that of its cage mate, showing that some social influences can enhance risk or protection. In addition, exposure to drugs or stress in a person's social or cultural environment can alter both gene expression and gene function, which, in some cases, may persist throughout a person's life. Research also suggests that genes can play a part in how a person responds to his or her environment, placing some people at higher risk for disease than others.

Epigenetics: Where Genes Meet the Environment

Epigenetics is the study of functional, and sometimes inherited, changes in the regulation of gene activity and expression that are not dependent on gene sequence. "Epi-" itself means "above" or "in addition to." Environmental exposures or choices people make can actually "mark"—or remodel—the structure of DNA at the cell level or even at the level of the whole organism. So, although each cell type in the human body effectively contains the same genetic information, epigenetic regulatory systems enable the development of different cell types (e.g., skin, liver, or nerve cells) in response to the environment. These epigenetic marks can affect health and even the expression of the traits passed to children. For example, when a person uses cocaine, it can mark the DNA, increasing the production of proteins common in addiction. Increased levels of these altered proteins correspond with drug-seeking behaviors in animals.

Histones, as another example, are like protein spools that provide an organizational structure for genes. Genes coil around histones, tightening or loosening to control gene expression. Drug exposure can affect specific histones, modifying gene expression in localized brain regions. Science has shown that manipulation of histone-modifying enzymes and binding proteins may have promise in treating substance use disorders.

The development of multidimensional data sets that include and integrate genetic and epigenetic information provides unique insights into the molecular genetic processes underlying the causes and consequences of drug addiction. Studying and using these data types to identify biological factors involved in substance abuse is increasingly important because technologic advances have improved the ability of researchers to single out individual genes or brain processes that may inform new prevention and treatment interventions.

Genetics and Precision Medicine

Clinicians often find substantial variability in how individual patients respond to treatment. Part of that variability is due to genetics. Genes influence the numbers and types of receptors in people's brains, how quickly their bodies metabolize drugs, and how well they respond to different medications. Learning more about the genetic, epigenetic, and neurobiological bases of addiction will eventually advance the science of addiction.

Scientists will be able to translate this knowledge into new treatments directed at specific targets in the brain or to treatment approaches that can be customized for each patient—called pharmacogenomics. This emerging science, often called precision medicine, promises to harness the power of genomic information to improve treatments for addiction by tailoring the treatment to the person's specific genetic makeup. By knowing a person's genomic information, healthcare providers will be better equipped to match patients with the most suitable treatments and medication dosages and to avoid or minimize adverse reactions.

Chapter 11

Alcohol Use Disorder: A Comparison between DSM–IV and DSM–5

The *Diagnostic and Statistical Manual of Mental Disorders* (DSM) initially developed out of a need to collect statistical information about mental disorders in the United States. The first attempt to collect information on mental health began in the 1840 census. By the 1880 census, the Bureau of the Census had developed seven categories of mental illness. In 1917, the Bureau of the Census began collecting uniform statistics from mental hospitals across the country.

Not long afterward, the American Psychiatric Association (APA) and the New York Academy of Medicine (NYAM) collaborated to produce a "nationally acceptable psychiatric nomenclature" for diagnosing patients with severe psychiatric and neurological disorders. After World War I, the Army and Veterans Administration broadened the nomenclature to include disorders affecting veterans.

In 1952, the APA Committee on Nomenclature and Statistics published the first edition of the *Diagnostic and Statistical Manual: Mental Disorders (DSM–I)*. The DSM–I included a glossary describing diagnostic categories and included an emphasis on how to use the

This chapter includes text excerpted from "Alcohol Use Disorder: A Comparison between DSM–IV and DSM–5," National Institute on Alcohol Abuse and Alcoholism (NIAAA), July 2016.

manual for making clinical diagnoses. The DSM–II, which was very similar to the DSM–I, was published in 1968. The DSM–III, published in 1980, introduced several innovations, including explicit diagnostic criteria for the various disorders, that are now a recognizable feature of the DSM. A 1987 revision to the DSM–III, called the DSM–III–R, clarified some of these criteria and also addressed inconsistencies in the diagnostic system. A comprehensive review of the scientific literature strengthened the empirical basis of the next edition, the DSM–IV, which was published in 1994. The DSM–IV–TR, a revision published in 2000, provided additional information on diagnosis. Since 1952, each subsequent edition of the DSM aimed to improve clinicians' ability to understand and diagnose a wide range of conditions.

Differences in DSM–IV and DSM–5

In May 2013, the APA issued the 5th edition of the *Diagnostic and Statistical Manual of Mental Disorders (DSM–5)*. Although there is considerable overlap between DSM–5 and DSM–IV, the prior edition, there are several important differences:

Changes Disorder Terminology

- DSM–IV described two distinct disorders, alcohol abuse, and alcohol dependence, with specific criteria for each.
- DSM–5 integrates the two DSM–IV disorders, alcohol abuse, and alcohol dependence, into a single disorder called alcohol use disorder (AUD) with mild, moderate, and severe subclassifications.

Changes Diagnostic Thresholds

- Under DSM–IV, the diagnostic criteria for abuse and dependence were distinct: anyone meeting one or more of the "abuse" criteria (see table 11.1—1 through 4) within a 12-month period would receive the "abuse" diagnosis. Anyone with three or more of the "dependence" criteria (see table 11.1—5 through 11) during the same 12-month period would receive a "dependence" diagnosis.
- Under DSM–5, anyone meeting any two of the 11 criteria during the same 12-month period would receive a diagnosis of AUD. The severity of an AUD—mild, moderate, or severe—is based on the number of criteria met.

Alcohol Use Disorder: A Comparison between DSM–IV and DSM–5

Removes Criterion

- DSM–5 eliminates legal problems as a criterion.

Adds Criterion

- DSM–5 adds craving as a criterion for an AUD diagnosis. It was not included in DSM–IV.

Revises Some Descriptions

- DSM–5 modifies some of the criteria descriptions with updated language.

Table 11.1. A Comparison between DSM–IV and DSM–5

DSM–IV **In the past year, have you:**			**DSM–5** **In the past year, have you:**	
Any 1 = ALCOHOL ABUSE	Found that drinking—or being sick from drinking—often interfered with taking care of your home or family? Or caused job troubles? Or school problems?	1	Had times when you ended up drinking more, or longer, than you intended?	The presence of at least 2 of these symptoms indicates an **Alcohol Use Disorder (AUD).** The severity of the AUD is defined as: **Mild:** The presence of 2–3 symptoms **Moderate:** The presence of 4–5 symptoms **Severe:** The presence of 6 or more symptoms
	More than once gotten into situations while or after drinking that increased your chances of getting hurt (such as driving, swimming, using machinery, walking in a dangerous area, or having unsafe sex)?	2	More than once wanted to cut down or stop drinking, or tried to, but couldn't?	

Table 11.1. Continued

DSM–IV **In the past year, have you:**			**DSM–5** **In the past year, have you:**	
	More than once gotten arrested, been held at a police station, or had other legal problems because of your drinking? ****This is not included in DSM–5****	3	Spent a lot of time drinking? Or being sick or getting over other aftereffects?	
	Continued to drink even though it was causing trouble with your family or friends?	4	Wanted a drink so badly you couldn't think of anything else? ****This is new to DSM–5****	
Any 3 = ALCOHOL DEPENDENCE	Had to drink much more than you once did to get the effect you want? Or found that your usual number of drinks had much less effect than before?	5	Found that drinking—or being sick from drinking—often interfered with taking care of your home or family? Or caused job troubles? Or school problems?	

Table 11.1. Continued

DSM–IV In the past year, have you:			**DSM–5 In the past year, have you:**	
	Found that when the effects of alcohol were wearing off, you had withdrawal symptoms, such as trouble sleeping, shakiness, restlessness, nausea, sweating, a racing heart, or a seizure? Or sensed things that were not there?	6	Continued to drink even though it was causing trouble with your family or friends?	
	Had times when you ended up drinking more, or longer, than you intended?	7	Given up or cut back on activities that were important or interesting to you, or gave you pleasure, in order to drink?	
	More than once wanted to cut down or stop drinking, or tried to, but couldn't?	8	More than once gotten into situations while or after drinking that increased your chances of getting hurt (such as driving, swimming, using machinery, walking in a dangerous area, or having unsafe sex)?	

Table 11.1. Continued

DSM–IV **In the past year, have you:**			**DSM–5** **In the past year, have you:**	
	Spent a lot of time drinking? Or being sick or getting over other aftereffects?	9	Continued to drink even though it was making you feel depressed or anxious or adding to another health problem? Or after having had a memory blackout?	
	Given up or cut back on activities that were important or interesting to you, or gave you pleasure, in order to drink?	10	Had to drink much more than you once did to get the effect you want? Or found that your usual number of drinks had much less effect than before?	
	Continued to drink even though it was making you feel depressed or anxious or adding to another health problem? Or after having had a memory blackout?	11	Found that when the effects of alcohol were wearing off, you had withdrawal symptoms, such as trouble sleeping, shakiness, restlessness, nausea, sweating, a racing heart, or a seizure? Or sensed things that were not there?	

Chapter 12

Alcohol Myths and Facts

The following are the myths and facts about alcohol.

Myth: I can drink and still be in control.

Fact: Drinking impairs your judgment, which increases the likelihood that you will do something you'll later regret such as having unprotected sex, being involved in date rape, damaging property, or being victimized by others.

Myth: Drinking isn't all that dangerous.

Fact: Among college students, alcohol contributes to deaths from alcohol-related unintentional injuries, as well as assaults, sexual assaults, or date rapes, and poor academic performance.

Myth: I can sober up quickly if I have to.

Fact: It takes about 2 hours for the adult body to eliminate the alcohol content of a single drink, depending on your weight. Nothing can speed up this process—not even coffee or cold showers.

Myth: It's okay for me to drink to keep up with my boyfriend.

Fact: Women process alcohol differently. No matter how much he drinks, if you drink the same amount as your boyfriend, you will be more intoxicated and more impaired.

This chapter includes text excerpted from "Alcohol Myths," College Drinking, National Institute on Alcohol Abuse and Alcoholism (NIAAA), August 8, 2016.

Myth: Beer doesn't have as much alcohol as hard liquor.

Fact: A 12-ounce bottle of beer has the same amount of alcohol as a standard shot of 80-proof liquor (either straight or in a mixed drink) or 5-oz. of wine.

Myth: I'd be better off if I learn to "hold my liquor."

Fact: If you have to drink increasingly larger amounts of alcohol to get a "buzz" or get "high," you are developing tolerance. Tolerance is actually a warning sign that you're developing more serious problems with alcohol.

Myth: I can manage to drive well enough after a few drinks.

Fact: The effects of alcohol start sooner than people realize, with mild impairment (up to 0.05 BAC (blood alcohol content)) starting to affect speech, memory, attention, coordination, and balance. And if you are under 21, driving after drinking any amount of alcohol is illegal and you could lose your license. The risks of a fatal crash for drivers with positive BAC compared with other drivers (i.e., the relative risk) increase with increasing BAC, and the risks increase more steeply for drivers younger than age 21 than for older drivers.

Part Two

The Problem of Underage Drinking

Chapter 13

Overview of Underage Drinking Policy in the United States

Underage drinking presents an enormous public health issue. Alcohol is the drug of choice among children and adolescents. Annually, about 5,000 youth under age 21 die from motor vehicle crashes, other unintentional injuries, and homicides and suicides that involve underage drinking. As the lead federal agency for supporting and conducting basic and applied research on alcohol problems, the National Institute on Alcohol Abuse and Alcoholism (NIAAA) is spearheading an Initiative on Underage Drinking to intensify research, evaluation, and outreach efforts in this important area. The Alcohol Policy Information System (APIS) website presents information on ten policy topics that are particularly relevant to underage drinking.

This chapter contains text excerpted from the following sources: Text in this chapter begins with excerpts from "Highlight on Underage Drinking," National Institute on Alcohol Abuse and Alcoholism (NIAAA), January 2, 2006. Reviewed April 2018; Text under the heading "Alcohol Policy Information System" is excerpted from "Underage Drinking: Possession/Consumption/Internal Possession of Alcohol," National Institute on Alcohol Abuse and Alcoholism (NIAAA), February 1, 2001. Reviewed April 2018.

Underage Drinking Policy in the United States

State laws restricting access to alcoholic beverages by young people were first enacted early in the 20th century. These laws prohibited sales of alcohol to young people but did not directly prohibit consumption of alcoholic beverages by young people or prohibit the sharing of alcohol to youth by adults. Underage drinking policies in the United States have become more restrictive over time. The 18th Amendment to the U.S. Constitution, ratified in 1919, prohibited the sale of all intoxicating liquors in the United States, superseding state laws on the sale of alcoholic beverages to young people. Following the repeal of the 18th Amendment in 1933, restrictions on possession and consumption of alcoholic beverages by youth and noncommercial provision of alcohol to youth by adults became the norm. Most states applied these restrictions to those under the age of 21, making the minimum legal drinking age the same as the minimum age then required for voting in federal elections.

Between 1970 and 1975, 29 states lowered their minimum drinking ages from 21 to 18, 19, or 20, following the enactment of the 26th Amendment to the U.S. Constitution, which granted 18- to 20-year-olds the right to vote. In the 1980s, states began to return the minimum drinking age to 21. This reversal reflected both increased public concern about underage drinking and research findings linking lower minimum drinking ages with increases in alcohol-related motor vehicle crashes.

In 1984, Congress enacted the National Minimum Drinking Age Act, which remains in effect. This law requires that a portion of federal highway funds be withheld from any states that do not prohibit persons under 21 years of age from purchasing or publicly possessing alcoholic beverages. The U.S. Supreme Court held in 1987 that Congress was within constitutional bounds in attaching such conditions to the receipt of federal funds to encourage uniformity in states' drinking ages. By 1988, every State had passed legislation to meet the federal funding requirements. The result is that all states currently prohibit minors (a term widely used in this context to refer to persons under the age of 21) from possessing alcoholic beverages; most states also prohibit minors from purchasing and consuming alcoholic beverages. In addition, most states prohibit adults from furnishing alcoholic beverages to minors and some states prohibit "internal possession" of alcoholic beverages by minors. These prohibitions are subject to a number of exceptions that vary from state to state. These exceptions can be seen in the information presented for the ten APIS policy topics relevant to underage drinking.

In addition to minimum drinking age laws, states have adopted a variety of other policies to address underage drinking. Some of these policies apply to youth directly, e.g., using false identification to purchase alcohol, loss of driving privileges for alcohol violations by minors ("use/lose" laws), and lower blood alcohol concentration levels for drivers under 21 ("zero-tolerance laws"). Other policies include minimum ages for both alcohol sellers and for servers and bartenders, keg registration requirements, and criminal penalties for hosting underage parties.

In 2006, Congress enacted The Sober Truth on Preventing Underage Drinking (STOP) Act, which authorized $18 million in federal funds to combat underage drinking. Provisions of the act include: enhancement of an interagency committee to coordinate efforts by federal agencies to address the issue; annual reporting to Congress about state-level efforts to combat underage drinking, including annual state report cards; a national media campaign aimed at adults; assessments of youth exposure to media messages; increased resources for community coalitions to enhance prevention efforts; and funding for new research on underage drinking, including short-and long-term effects on adolescent brain development.

In 2007, the then Acting U.S. Surgeon General Kenneth P. Moritsugu unveiled a *Call to Action on Underage Drinking*. Developed in collaboration with the National Institute on Alcohol Abuse and Alcoholism (NIAAA) and the Substance Abuse and Mental Health Services Administration (SAMHSA), the *Call to Action* identifies six goals to be achieved by government, school officials, parents, other adults, and young people. These goals include:

1. facilitating healthy adolescent development and preventing and reducing underage drinking
2. engaging parents, schools, communities, government, social systems, and youth in a national effort to prevent and reduce underage drinking and its consequences
3. promoting understanding of underage drinking across individual adolescent characteristics as well as across environmental, ethnic, cultural, and gender differences
4. conducting research on adolescent alcohol use and its consequences
5. improving public health monitoring of underage drinking and underage drinking policies
6. promoting policy consistency across levels of government

In November of 2016, U.S. Surgeon General Dr. Vivek Murthy issued a report finding alcohol and drug misuse and severe substance use disorders, commonly called addiction, to be one of America's most pressing public health concerns. The report (Facing Addiction in America: The Surgeon General's Report on Alcohol, Drugs, and Health) marks the first time a U.S. Surgeon General has dedicated a report to substance misuse and related disorders. Among the report's key findings is that "well-supported scientific evidence shows that adolescence is a critical 'at-risk period' for substance use and addiction; all addictive drugs, including alcohol and marijuana, have especially harmful effects on the adolescent brain, which is still undergoing significant development."

The Institute of Medicine (IOM) notes that underage drinking strategies such as those outlined here demonstrate a broad societal commitment to reduce underage drinking. The IOM further notes that "the effectiveness of laws to restrict access to alcohol by youths can be increased by closing gaps in coverage, promoting compliance, and strengthening enforcement.

Alcohol Policy Information System

The alcohol policy information system (APIS) provides detailed information on a wide variety of alcohol-related policies in the United States at both state and federal levels, as well as policy information regarding the recreational use of cannabis.

All states prohibit possession of alcoholic beverages (with certain exceptions) by those under age 21. In addition, most but not all states have statutes that specifically prohibit consumption of alcoholic beverages by those under the age of 21. Many states that prohibit possession and/or consumption apply various statutory exceptions to these provisions.

States that prohibit underage consumption may allow different exceptions for consumption than those that apply to underage possession.

In recent years, a number of states have passed laws prohibiting the "internal possession" of alcohol by persons under 21 years of age. These provisions typically require evidence of alcohol in the minor's body, but do not require any specific evidence of possession or consumption. Internal possession laws are especially useful to law enforcement in making arrests or issuing citations when breaking up underage drinking parties. Internal possession laws allow officers to bring charges against underage persons who are neither holding nor drinking alcoholic beverages in the presence of law enforcement officers. As with laws prohibiting underage possession and consumption, states that prohibit internal possession may apply various statutory exceptions to these provisions.

APIS codes a state as having an internal possession law if its statutes or regulations prohibit a person under the age of 21 from having alcohol in her or his system as determined by a blood, breath or urine test. Laws that punish persons under the age of 21 for displaying "indicators of consumption," or for "exhibiting the effects" of having consumed alcohol, are not considered to be internal possession laws for the purpose of APIS coding.

Although all states prohibit possession of alcohol by minors, some states do not specifically prohibit underage alcohol consumption. In addition, states that prohibit underage possession and/or consumption may or may not address the issue of internal possession.

The APIS tables for underage possession/consumption/internal possession of alcohol report data on prohibitions of three closely related behaviors:

1. Possession of alcoholic beverages
2. Consumption of alcoholic beverages
3. Internal possession of alcoholic beverages

Exceptions

Some states allow an exception to possession, consumption, or internal possession prohibitions when a family member consents and/or is present. States vary widely in terms of which relatives may consent or must be present for this exception to apply and in what circumstances the exception applies. Sometimes a reference is made simply to "family" or "family member" without further elaboration.

APIS codes two types of family member exceptions. The first is an exception for either the consent or presence of a parent or guardian. The second is an exception for either the consent or presence of the spouse of a married minor.

When a statute or regulation is unclear as to which family members must be present and/or consent, APIS assumes that parents, guardians, and spouses are all included. Further detail and explanations for such statutes and regulations are provided in row and/or jurisdiction notes in the comparison tables. Some jurisdictions limit family member exceptions to specific locations. For example, minors might be allowed to possess or consume alcohol with parental consent in their parents' residence, but not elsewhere.

Some states allow exceptions to possession, consumption, or internal possession prohibitions on private property. States vary in the extent of the private property exception, which may extend to all private locations, private residences only, or in the home of a parent or guardian only. In some jurisdictions, a location exception is conditional on the presence and/or consent of a parent, legal guardian, or spouse.

With respect specifically to consumption laws, some states prohibit underage consumption only on licensed premises. Because the number of underage persons who drink on licensed premises is small, APIS codes such states as having no law prohibiting consumption.

Chapter 14

Current Drinking Patterns among Underage Drinkers

Underage Drinking

Underage drinking is a serious public health problem in the United States. Alcohol is the most widely used substance of abuse among America's youth, and drinking by young people poses enormous health and safety risks. The consequences of underage drinking can affect everyone—regardless of age or drinking status. We all feel the effects of the aggressive behavior, property damage, injuries, violence, and deaths that can result from underage drinking. This is not simply a problem for some families—it is a nationwide concern.

Underage Drinking Statistics

Many young people drink alcohol

- By age 15, about 33 percent of teens have had at least 1 drink
- By age 18, about 60 percent of teens have had at least 1 drink
- In 2015, 7.7 million young people ages 12–20 reported that they drank alcohol beyond "just a few sips" in the past month

---

This chapter includes text excerpted from "Underage Drinking," National Institute of Alcohol Abuse and Alcoholism (NIAAA), February 2017.

Youth ages 12–20 often binge drink

People ages 12 through 20 drink 11 percent of all alcohol consumed in the United States. Although youth drink less often than adults do, when they do drink, they drink more. That is because young people consume more than 90 percent of their alcohol by binge drinking. Binge drinking is consuming many drinks on an occasion. Drinking alcohol and binge drinking become more prevalent as young people get older.

- 5.1 million young people reported binge drinking (for males 5 or more drinks and for females 4 or more drinks on the same occasion within a few hours) at least once in the past month
- 1.3 million young people reported binge drinking on 5 or more days over the past month

Drinking Patterns Vary by Age and Gender

As adolescents get older, they tend to drink more. The prevalence of drinking by boys and girls is similar, although among older adolescents, boys binge more than girls.

Underage Drinking Is Dangerous

Underage drinking poses a range of risks and negative consequences. It is dangerous because it:

Causes Many Deaths

Based on data from 2006–2010, the Centers for Disease Control and Prevention (CDC) estimates that, on average, alcohol is a factor in the deaths of 4,358 young people under age 21 each year. This includes:

- 1,580 deaths from motor vehicle crashes
- 1,269 from homicides
- 245 from alcohol poisoning, falls, burns, and drowning
- 492 from suicides

Causes Many Injuries

Drinking alcohol can cause kids to have accidents and get hurt. In 2011 alone, about 188,000 people under age 21 visited an emergency room for alcohol-related injuries.

Impairs Judgment

Drinking can lead to poor decisions about engaging in risky behavior, including drinking and driving, sexual activity (such as unprotected sex), and aggressive or violent behavior.

Increases the Risk of Physical and Sexual Assault

Underage youth who drink are more likely to carry out or be the victim of a physical or sexual assault after drinking than others their age who do not drink.

Can Lead to Other Problems

Drinking may cause youth to have trouble in school or with the law. Drinking alcohol also is associated with the use of other drugs.

Increases the Risk of Alcohol Problems Later in Life

Research shows that people who start drinking before the age of 15 are 4 times more likely to meet the criteria for alcohol dependence at some point in their lives.

Interferes with Brain Development

Research shows that young people's brains keep developing well into their 20s. Alcohol can alter this development, potentially affecting both brain structure and function. This may cause cognitive or learning problems and/or make the brain more prone to alcohol dependence. This is especially a risk when people start drinking young and drink heavily.

Reasons Young People Drink

As children mature, it is natural for them to assert their independence, seek new challenges, and try taking risks. Underage drinking is a risk that attracts many developing adolescents and teens. Many want to try alcohol, but often do not fully recognize its effects on their health and behavior. Other reasons young people drink alcohol include:

- Peer pressure
- Increased independence, or desire for it
- Stress

In addition, many youth may have easy access to alcohol. In 2015, among 12- to 14-year-olds who reported that they drank alcohol in the past month, 95.1 percent reported that they got it for free the last time they drank. In many cases, adolescents have access to alcohol through family members, or find it at home.

Preventing Underage Drinking

Preventing underage drinking is a complex challenge. Any successful approach must consider many factors, including:

- Genetics
- Personality
- Rate of maturation and development
- Level of risk
- Social factors
- Environmental factors

Several key approaches have been found to be successful. They are:

Environmental Interventions

This approach makes alcohol harder to get—for example, by raising the price of alcohol and keeping the minimum drinking age at 21. Enacting zero-tolerance laws that outlaw driving after any amount of drinking for people under 21 also can help prevent problems.

Individual-Level Interventions

This approach seeks to change the way young people think about alcohol, so they are better able to resist pressures to drink.

School-Based Interventions

These are programs that provide students with the knowledge, skills, motivation, and opportunities they need to remain alcohol free.

Family-Based Interventions

These are efforts to empower parents to set and enforce clear rules against drinking, as well as improve communication between children and parents about alcohol.

The Role Parents Play

Parents and teachers can play a big role in shaping young people's attitudes toward drinking. Parents, in particular, can have either a positive or negative influence.

Parents can help their children avoid alcohol problems by:

- Talking about the dangers of drinking
- Drinking responsibly, if they choose to drink
- Serving as positive role models in general
- Not making alcohol available
- Getting to know their children's friends
- Having regular conversations about life in general
- Connecting with other parents about sending clear messages about the importance of not drinking alcohol
- Supervising all parties to make sure there is no alcohol
- Encouraging kids to participate in healthy and fun activities that do not involve alcohol

Research shows that children whose parents are actively involved in their lives are less likely to drink alcohol. On the other hand, research shows that a child with a parent who binge drinks is much more likely to binge drink than a child whose parents do not binge drink.

Warning Signs of Underage Drinking

Adolescence is a time of change and growth, including behavior changes. These changes usually are a normal part of growing up but sometimes can point to an alcohol problem. Parents and teachers should pay close attention to the following warning signs that may indicate underage drinking:

- Changes in mood, including anger and irritability
- Academic and/or behavioral problems in school
- Rebelliousness
- Changing groups of friends
- Low energy level
- Less interest in activities and/or care in appearance

- Finding alcohol among a young person's things
- Smelling alcohol on a young person's breath
- Problems concentrating and/or remembering
- Slurred speech
- Coordination problems

Treating Underage Drinking Problems

Screening young people for alcohol use and alcohol use disorder is very important and may avoid problems down the road. Screening by a health practitioner (e.g., pediatrician) provides an opportunity to identify problems early and address them before they escalate. It also allows young people to ask questions of a knowledgeable adult. National Institute on Alcohol Abuse and Alcoholism (NIAAA) and the American Academy of Pediatrics (AAP) both recommend that all youth be regularly screened for alcohol use.

Some young people can experience serious problems as a result of drinking, including alcohol use disorder, which require intervention by trained professionals. Professional treatment options include:

- Seeing a counselor, psychologist, psychiatrist, or other trained professional
- Participating in outpatient or inpatient treatment at a substance abuse treatment facility or other licensed program

Chapter 15

Does Advertising Play a Role in Underage Drinking?

Chapter Contents

Section 15.1

Alcohol Advertising

This section includes text excerpted from "Alcohol Advertising," Federal Trade Commission (FTC), September 2013. Reviewed April 2018.

These days, advertising is almost everywhere we go—on television, in the bus, on the street, and on the Internet. Alcohol advertising is no exception. And, as is the case with most advertising, alcohol advertising makes the product look great!

Alcohol ads typically associate a brand with cool, sexy people and a fun activity. The various elements in alcohol ads are specifically chosen to communicate ideas like this product is for people like me; this alcohol product makes occasions better; this product is popular, or stylish, or creative, and people want to be seen drinking this product. Ultimately, these concepts come together to suggest: if I use this product, I can be cool, sexy, and successful like the people in the ad, having fun like they seem to be.

So What Can a Parent Do?

Use "media literacy" techniques to help your teen view ads critically. From time to time, when your family sits down to watch television, use the occasion as a teachable moment. Tailor the moment given your teen's age and attention level. Pick an ad, and draw out their thoughts by asking questions like:

- Who created or paid for the ad, and why?
- What do they want you to do?
- What techniques are being used to make the scene and the product look attractive? For example,
    - Who are the people in the ad and how do they look?
    - What are they doing, and where?
    - Does the ad try to associate the brand with fun, or sports, or humor? How?

- Does the ad suggest that alcohol somehow makes the situation better?
- How does this ad make you feel? Is this an accident, or did the advertiser intend it?
- What message is the ad trying to get you to believe?
- What values and lifestyles are represented by this ad?
- What isn't the ad saying? Does it show anything bad about alcohol?

Exercises like this can help your teen better understand that alcohol ads communicate the advertiser's point of view and learn how to challenge what an ad is saying, internally. With time, the exercises will help your teen realize that they don't have to buy into an advertiser's message. Educators call it learning to read between the lines, and it is relevant to all media messages, both commercial and noncommercial advertisement.

Alcohol Advertising Regulation

The First Amendment provides substantial protections to speech, and thus substantially limits the government's ability to regulate truthful, nondeceptive alcohol advertising based on concerns about underage appeal. For this reason, the Federal Trade Commission (FTC) has long encouraged the alcohol industry to adopt and comply with self-regulatory standards to reduce the extent to which alcohol advertising targets teens, whether by placement or content.

Most alcohol advertisers have pledged to comply with one of three voluntary self-regulatory codes designed to limit targeting of teens. Among other provisions, these codes direct that no more than 28.4 percent of the audience for an ad may consist of people under 21, based on reliable audience data; and that ad content should not appeal primarily to people under 21.

The FTC monitors compliance with these codes formally and informally. It has published the results of three major studies on alcohol advertising and industry self-regulation. If you believe that an ad doesn't comply with codes, consider filing a complaint. You can submit a complaint with:

- the Distilled Spirits Council, for complaints regarding distilled spirits ads, or ads for wine or beer by distilled spirits companies;

- the Beer Institute, for beer ads, or;
- the Wine Institute, for wine ads.

In addition, the FTC collects complaints about potentially deceptive business practices, identity theft, and privacy violations to identify patterns of wrongdoing and determine how best to allocate FTC resources. The FTC does not, however, resolve individual consumer complaints.

Section 15.2

Advertising Regulations for Alcoholic Beverages

This section includes text excerpted from "Alcohol Beverage Advertising," Alcohol and Tobacco Tax and Trade Bureau (TTB), U.S. Department of the Treasury (USDT), January 14, 2015.

What Is an Advertisement?

The Alcohol and Tobacco Tax and Trade Bureau (TTB) regulations define the term "advertisement" as any written or verbal statement, illustration, or depiction, which is in, or calculated to induce sales in, interstate or foreign commerce, or is disseminated by mail. Examples include ads in newspapers or magazines, trade booklets, menus, wine cards, leaflets, circulars, mailers, book inserts, catalogs, promotional materials, or sales pamphlets. The definition includes any written, printed, graphic, or other matter accompanying the container; markings on cases, billboards signs, or other outdoor display; and broadcasts made via radio, television, or in any other media. Though not specifically listed, this definition includes websites and other Internet-based advertising such as social media.

Does TTB Approve Alcohol Beverage Advertisements?

The Federal Alcohol Administration (FAA) Act does not require alcohol beverage advertisements to be approved prior to appearing in print or broadcast. TTB does, however, offer industry members, free of charge, a voluntary advertising preclearance service. To submit an advertisement for preclearance review, you may e-mails it to market.compliance@ttb.gov.

What Information Is Required on an Alcohol Beverage Advertisement?

With few exceptions, the following information is required on advertisements of alcohol beverages:

Wine (27 CFR 4.62)

- Name and address (city and state) of the permittee responsible for the advertisement; and
- Class, type or distinctive designation to which the product belongs, corresponding with the information shown on the approved label. For example:
    - Red wine, white wine, sparkling wine; or
    - Cabernet Sauvignon, chardonnay; or
    - Champagne, bordeaux; or
    - Red wine with natural flavors.

Distilled Spirits (27 CFR 5.63)

- Name and address (city and state) of the permittee responsible for the advertisement;
- Class and type to which the product belongs, corresponding with the information shown on the approved label. For example:
    - Whiskey, gin, brandy; or
    - Vodka, bourbon, cognac; or
    - Neutral spirits with natural flavor and caramel color;
    - Alcohol content shown as percent alcohol by volume (proof may be shown as additional information); and
    - Percentage of neutral spirits and name of commodity, as required for certain distilled spirits.

Malt Beverages (27 CFR 7.52)

- Name and address (city and state) of the permittee responsible for the advertisement; and
- Class to which the product belongs, corresponding with the information shown on the approved label. For example:
    - Lager, ale, stout;
    - Raspberry ale, stout brewed with pumpkin and cinnamon.

Learn more about the advertising regulations listed in the Code of Federal Regulations (CFR) for: wine (27 CFR part 4, subpart G), distilled spirits (27 CFR part 5, subpart H), and malt beverages (27 CFR part 7, subpart F).

What Is Prohibited from Appearing in an Alcohol Beverage Advertisement?

For a complete listing of prohibited practices, please see:

- Wine: 27 CFR 4.64
- Distilled spirits: 27 CFR 5.65
- Malt beverages: 27 CFR 7.54

Monitoring Advertisements in the Marketplace

TTB monitors the advertising of alcohol beverages through a combination of:

- Preclearance of advertising material: At the industry member's request, TTB reviews the member's advertisement for compliance with the appropriate advertising regulations. This service is offered at no charge.
- Referrals and/or complaints: Review of advertisements for compliance when the general public, other government agencies, an employee within TTB, or another industry member refers to TTB an advertisement that they believe is in violation of our laws and regulations.
- Internal selections for review: TTB market compliance specialists independently select advertisements from a variety of media and review those advertisements for compliance with the advertising regulations.

Advertisement Complaints

If you have a complaint about an advertisement that you feel is in violation of TTB regulations, you may send an e-mails to Market.Compliance@ttb.gov.

Chapter 16

How Alcohol Affects Development

Chapter Contents

Section 16.1

Developmental Perspective on Underage Alcohol Use

This section includes text excerpted from "Effects and Consequences of Underage Drinking," U.S. Department of Justice (DOJ), September 2012. Reviewed April 2018.

Effects and Consequences of Underage Drinking

By raising the drinking age to 21 across the United States, Congress has provided a highly effective strategy to increase youth health and safety. Tens of thousands of lives have been saved in traffic crashes alone. Nonetheless, youth and young adults under age 21 often drink alcoholic beverages. Alcohol consumption is often accepted as normal adolescent and young adult behavior. According to a report from the National Institute on Drug Abuse (NIDA), by the time teenagers reached grade 12, almost 71 percent had used alcohol at least once in their lives and 41.2 percent had drunk alcohol during the past month. Older adolescents and young adults drink at even higher levels, especially those who attend college. Despite the significant progress that has been made in reducing adolescent drinking and related problems, when a behavior is as pervasive as alcohol use among youth and young adults under age 21, the general public may be tempted to question the emphasis being placed on it. Alcohol use is often considered a rite of passage, and adults who furnish alcohol to minors often abet this use. This casual attitude ignores the serious consequences of alcohol abuse by minors. This section discusses adolescents' neurological, social, and emotional development and examines why youth begin drinking alcohol.

Adolescent Social and Emotional Development

Adolescents have unique social and emotional characteristics and undergo physical and cognitive changes that can affect their social and emotional development. Some of these characteristics and changes can increase the likelihood that youth will find themselves in dangerous and risky situations when using alcohol at a time when they are particularly vulnerable to negative outcomes from drinking. Understanding adolescents' social and emotional development can provide greater insight into underage drinking, its dangers, and ways to prevent it.

As adolescents struggle for independence and create a personal identity, relationships with their family and peers change. Peer groups may become more important to youth than their families, and peers often provide some of the same functions that family did earlier. Peers become the bridge between the family and the adult social roles the young person must assume. Youth look to their peers for support, approval, and belonging. They tend to choose peers who are similar to themselves. To gain acceptance from their peers, youth tend to dress alike, use similar speech patterns, be enamored of the same heroes, and listen to the same music. They want to steer clear of humiliation, so they try to look and act like their peers to avoid disapproval and negative judgments. Peer pressure often convinces youth to engage in activities to gain one another's approval. This tendency may lead to alcohol use. On the other hand, some youth face social rejection or neglect and have few peer relationships. These youth are at higher risk for a variety of problems, such as social isolation or withdrawal, lack of appropriate social skills development, and low self-esteem. Furthermore, rejection or neglect may contribute to these youth joining together in antisocial groups. Whether their peers accept or reject them, youth develop new behavior patterns during adolescence. A variety of adolescent behavioral characteristics that guide social development are described below:

- **Experimentation.** Youth try different social roles and identities to discover who they are. This may include harmless experiments such as new hairstyles, makeup, dress, and music, or more harmful experimentation such as alcohol and drug use.
- **Rebellion.** Youth rebel against adult authority as a means of learning to make decisions. They often do exactly the opposite of what adults want them to do. Sources of conflict may include curfews, smoking, drinking alcohol, the use of other psychoactive substances, or academic performance.
- **Talking and socializing.** Youth may talk on the telephone, send text messages, interact on social media sites (e.g., Instagram, Facebook, Twitter), or hang out with friends at the mall to socialize. The peer group provides a social form of self-evaluation, and youth need feedback from their peers.

- **Preoccupation with themselves.** Youth tend to focus on their needs. They feel they are the topic of others' conversations and others are watching them constantly. They may spend long periods of time self-grooming, monopolizing the telephone or computer, or engaging in other self-centered activities.
- **Risk taking.** Youth often do not realize the consequences that their behavior will have and may take risks because they believe nothing bad will happen to them. Adolescents undergo many physical and mental changes before they become adults. In addition to their predisposition to peer pressure and social experimentation, adolescents' brains continue to develop through their mid-twenties and may be highly vulnerable to the effects of alcohol and other substances.

Section 16.2

Alcohol Use and Adolescent Development

This section includes text excerpted from "Alcohol and Puberty: Mechanisms of Delayed Development," National Institute on Alcohol Abuse and Alcoholism (NIAAA), February 16, 2017.

Alcohol and Puberty: Mechanisms of Delayed Development

Adolescence represents a vulnerable period for developing youth. Alcohol use and misuse are especially problematic behaviors during this time. Adolescents are more sensitive to alcohol and less tolerant of its detrimental effects than are adults. Research in humans and animals has revealed that early alcohol consumption can result in delayed pubertal development. Animal studies have shown that alcohol detrimentally affects neuroendocrine systems within the hypothalamic region of the brain that are associated with the normal, timely onset of the pubertal process. To effectively restore development and shorten recovery time associated with the adverse effects of alcohol on puberty, researchers must first understand the molecular and physiological mechanisms by which alcohol interferes with critical hypothalamic functions.

Despite efforts to prevent underage alcohol use, drinking does occur as early as the 6th grade. According to a recent national survey, 9.7 percent of 8th graders and 21.5 percent of 10th graders reported using alcohol at least once in the previous 30 days. This is important because people who begin drinking between ages 11 and 14 are at increased risk for developing alcohol use disorder, compared with those who begin drinking at later ages. These high-risk age groups also are exactly within the pubertal time frame. Some of the younger adolescents may not have begun the pubertal process. Others, however, are subject to the process being slowed or halted by alcohol, thus impeding further development. Following a brief summary of alcohol's effects on puberty in humans, this review describes the neuroendocrine processes that control puberty and research using animal models to assess the effects of prepubertal alcohol exposure.

Early research demonstrated that alcohol use by adolescent boys causes suppressed serum levels of growth hormone (GH), luteinizing hormone (LH), and testosterone, as well as lower bone density. In adolescent girls, alcohol use caused suppressed serum GH and estradiol (E2) levels. Other studies found evidence for disruptions in stature, weight distribution, and a risk for nutritional deficiencies. More recently, studies in girls have shown that prepubertal alcohol use was associated with delayed breast development and onset of menarche. This research suggested that prepubertal girls who use alcohol have four times the chance of delayed onset of puberty than those who do not. This finding is confirmed in animal models, which show that alcohol acts within the hypothalamic region of the brain to suppress key puberty-related genes and hormones responsible for the normal timing of development.

Basic Neuroendocrine Control of Puberty

The onset of puberty results from a complex series of interactions between nerve cells (i.e., neurons) and glial cells (i.e., nonneuronal brain cells) within the hypothalamus that are governed by metabolic signals, as well as genetic and environmental influences. Although age at puberty varies widely between and among mammalian species, the main event that signals puberty onset is basically similar, in that it relies on the increased pulsatile secretory activity of a hypothalamic neuropeptide, luteinizing hormone-releasing hormone (LHRH). This event occurs through the enhanced developmental responsiveness of the LHRH-producing neurons and their nerve terminals to excitatory inputs, such as insulin-like growth factor-1 (IGF-1) and the kisspeptins (Kp), a family of neuropeptide products of the *KiSS-1* gene, as well as leptin, transforming growth factor, and excitatory amino acids.

In addition to the development of excitatory inputs, the timing of puberty is influenced by a concomitant and gradual removal of prepubertal inhibitory inputs, such as γ aminobutyric acid (GABA) and the opioid peptides β endorphin and dynorphin. This alteration, often referred to as a "brake" on the pubertal process, is responsible for keeping prepubertal LHRH secretion low. As LHRH secretion increases, it drives the timing of puberty in both sexes by stimulating pituitary gonadotropin secretions, which in turn stimulate gonadal steroid synthesis and secretions for further maturation of the hypothalamus and reproductive organs. Although all of the excitatory and inhibitory influences noted above have been shown to be involved in the pubertal process, the mechanism-of-action portion of this review will concentrate on the most current findings about some of these modulators in relation to their upstream and downstream influences on the pubertal process.

Overall Effects of Alcohol on Puberty-Related Hormones and Indices of Pubertal Development

Initial studies using both female and male rodents revealed that chronic alcohol administration caused delayed puberty. Over the years, researchers have attempted to correlate the timing of puberty with specific puberty-related hormones following chronic prepubertal alcohol exposure. In female rats, alcohol caused delayed vaginal opening and the age at first estrus, as well as suppressed serum levels of GH and LH but not follicle-stimulating hormone (FSH). In this regard, the differential effects of alcohol on LH and FSH were not surprising, because this previously had been shown in adult rats. Significantly, several studies have shown that prepubertal alcohol exposure in females caused suppressed circulating levels of E2, a clear indication of impaired ovarian development and activity. Although less is known about the prepubertal effects of alcohol in males, it has been shown to cause an early suppression in serum LH and to reduce the serum levels of GH and testosterone. Prepubertal alcohol use also can lead to lower testicular weight and smaller secondary sex organs.

Additional research conducted in an animal model that more closely resembled humans, female rhesus monkeys, found that chronically administered alcohol resulted in suppressed GH, LH, and E2, exactly as described above in immature female rats. Furthermore, these actions were associated with the altered development of a regular monthly pattern of menstruation.

In addition to the effects of alcohol on GH and LH, research has shown that prepubertal alcohol administration caused suppressed serum IGF-1 in immature female rats and rhesus monkeys, thereby reducing the amount of peptide available to the prepubertal hypothalamus. This is relevant because IGF-1 normally can act centrally to influence both the hypothalamic–pituitary–gonadal axis and the hypothalamic-pituitary GH axis at puberty. Specifically, IGF-1 has been shown to act at the hypothalamic level to stimulate LHRH/LH secretion and advance the time of puberty in female rodents. The ability of IGF-1 to regulate GH through its actions on hypothalamic growth hormone–releasing hormone and somatostatin (i.e., somatotropin release–inhibiting factor), the latter being a GH-release inhibitor, have been well documented.

It is important to note that the central control of these two hypothalamic systems is complex and interrelated, especially regarding the important integrative and bidirectional influences of IGF-1 on their respective neuro-secretions. Although a detailed discussion of these basic interrelationships is beyond the scope of this review, it also is worth noting that alcohol can affect both of these systems at multiple levels. For example, in addition to the aforementioned alcohol-related suppression of LHRH/LH resulting in suppressed serum E2, alcohol also causes altered hypothalamic growth hormone–releasing hormone synthesis and secretion. This then results in decreased pulsatile GH release, which in turn downregulates IGF-1 synthesis by liver hepatocytes. The resulting alcohol-induced suppression in circulating IGF-1 causes suppressed body growth and interferes with the maturation and function of several organ systems. Furthermore, the accompanying reduction in circulating IGF-1 to feedback on the hypothalamus further reduces the secretion of LH and GH.

All of the above hormones are critical for puberty. However, alcohol's suppression of the pituitary secretion of LH has become a primary focus of research on pubertal onset, because this gonadotropin is regulated by LHRH, the hypothalamic peptide responsible for beginning the pubertal process. Researchers now are examining whether the alcohol-induced effect to suppress LH is a result of a hypothalamic or pituitary site of action.

The Hypothalamic Site of Alcohol's Actions

Studies in female rats, which showed increased hypothalamic LHRH content after chronic prepubertal alcohol administration, offered the first indirect evidence that alcohol affects this part of the brain. Subsequently, alcohol was shown to block the stimulatory effects of norepinephrine, IGF-1, leptin, and N-methyl-dl-aspartic acid (NMA) on the in vitro release of prepubertal LHRH. Although important, these collective observations did not rule out the possibility that alcohol also may act at the level of the pituitary.

To definitively assess the site of alcohol action, prepubertal rhesus monkeys that had been chronically exposed to alcohol were subjected to hypothalamic and pituitary response tests. The hypothalamic stimulation test showed that the NMA-induced LH secretion observed in the nonalcohol treated monkeys was blocked in the alcohol-treated monkeys. This is significant, because NMA causes LH release by first stimulating hypothalamic LHRH secretion and does not act at the pituitary level. Three weeks later, these same animals were given LHRH to test pituitary responsiveness. Results indicated that the LH response to the peptide was the same in both nonalcohol treated and alcohol-treated monkeys, conclusively demonstrating the hypothalamic site of action.

Mechanisms of Action

Upstream Effects of Alcohol on LHRH Synthesis

The majority of LHRH-synthesizing neurons are localized within the brain preoptic area and the region just posterior to it referred to as the anterior hypothalamic area. This latter area also contains the anteroventral periventricular (AVPV) nucleus. Neurons in the AVPV nucleus produce kisspeptins, which regulate prepubertal LHRH synthesis and are critical for the onset of puberty. Thus, research focused on discerning which factors affect prepubertal *KiSS-1* expression. Chronic prepubertal alcohol exposure was shown to cause suppressed *KiSS-1* gene expression in the AVPV nucleus of female rats, an action associated with a decrease in the usual level of phosphorylated Akt. Akt is a transduction signal that mediates the actions of IGF-1, a peptide known to activate puberty in rats and rhesus monkeys. Understanding IGF-1's ability to regulate *KiSS-1* was essential to further research. In studies with rats, an injection of IGF-1 directly into the brain's third ventricle caused the upregulation of prepubertal *KiSS-1* gene expression in the AVPV nucleus 6 hours later. Subsequently, alcohol was shown to block the IGF-1 induction of *KiSS-1* in the AVPV nucleus by inhibiting IGF-1 receptor (IGF-1R)-induced phosphorylation of Akt. Further investigation will determine whether the suppressed Akt activity occurred directly at the level of Kp-containing neurons or through an interneuron or glial cell that also expresses the IGF-1R. However, the fact that alcohol can interfere with this pathway to LHRH synthesis is important, because once the onset of puberty begins, the synthesis of this peptide must keep pace with its release to drive the pubertal process.

Downstream Effects of Alcohol on LHRH Release

Alcohol is known to alter several downstream signals in the hypothalamus that collectively reduce LHRH release at puberty. Although the numerous excitatory substances mentioned above influence LHRH at puberty, the role of *KiSS-1* and Kp also are noteworthy. *KiSS-1* expression increases in the hypothalamus as puberty approaches, and Kp is a potent stimulator of prepubertal LHRH secretion. By suppressing prepubertal *KiSS-1*/Kp, alcohol contributes to decreased LHRH secretion at a time when increases are needed as puberty approaches. In addition, alcohol has been shown to stimulate the release of GABA and the opioid peptides, which, as stated above, are known inhibitors of LHRH release. Alcohol also can activate the hypothalamic–pituitary–adrenal axis, and the hormones involved in the stimulation of this stress axis can suppress LH secretion. Furthermore, the newly described gene *Lin28b* also is associated with the brake on puberty, and its expression has been shown to gradually decrease as puberty approaches.

Recent research assessed whether alcohol would alter the normal pubertal rise in Kp and decrease in Lin28b protein. Chronic alcohol exposure reversed these actions within the brain region known as the medial basal hypothalamus (MBH) in prepubertal female rats by suppressing Akt, *KiSS-1*, and Kp, while stimulating the synthesis of Lin28b. In addition, research showed that Lin28b induced dynorphin (DYN) synthesis and that alcohol stimulated DYN release. DYN inhibits Kp and LHRH secretion. Because the MBH contains neurons that coexpress Kp and DYN, these observations are relevant to the control of prepubertal LHRH secretion. Although LHRH neurons are not localized within the MBH of the rat, they are in primates, including humans. Therefore, both the release and synthesis of LHRH in the MBH of primates may be affected by alcohol.

In addition to alcohol's actions on neuronal inputs controlling prepubertal LHRH secretion discussed above, alcohol may affect neuronal-to-glial and glial-to-glial inputs facilitating LHRH release within the MBH. LHRH secretory activity can be modulated by a specific neuronal-glial gene family that synthesizes signaling proteins involved in bidirectional communications at puberty. Chronic prepubertal alcohol exposure decreases the synthesis of glial protein tyrosine phosphatase-β, which is required for binding to the neuronal components contactin and contactin-associated protein-1. This finding demonstrates that alcohol can alter these interactions and interfere with glial–neuronal communications.

Glial-to-glial interactions also are affected by alcohol. Once released, glial-derived epidermal growth factor and transforming growth factor α (TGFα) both bind to the erbB1 receptor on adjacent glial cells and stimulate the release of prostaglandin E2, a well-known stimulator of LHRH secretion. Alcohol exposure initially was shown to inhibit PGE2 release induced by epidermal growth factor/TGFα. In addition, glial-derived IGF-1 binds to IGF-1R on adjacent glial cells, which produce TGFα, and alcohol exposure altered the synthesis and release of TGFα and PGE2, thereby resulting in decreased prepubertal LHRH secretion. Furthermore, specialized glial cells within the MBH known as tanycytes release glial-derived TGFβ1, causing retraction of their processes and allowing for better entry of LHRH into the system of blood vessels that connect the hypothalamus with the pituitary (i.e., hypophyseal portal system). Alcohol blocks IGF-1 from stimulating the synthesis and release of TGFβ1 by altering the IGF-1R synthesis and Akt phosphorylation, therefore further contributing to diminished LHRH secretion.

Alcohol use and misuse by adolescents increases the risk for altered neuroendocrine function, potentially modifying the timing of pubertal development. This review highlights results of research with animal models showing the site and mechanisms by which alcohol causes puberty-related problems. These studies demonstrate that alcohol acts within the hypothalamus to alter the expression and function of excitatory and inhibitory puberty-related genes and neuro-hormones, which are critical for the timely increase in LHRH secretion and the onset of puberty. More research in this field is needed and would no doubt promote a better understanding of normal mechanisms controlling events leading to increased LHRH release at puberty, as well as the cause-and-effect relationships by which alcohol can differentially affect them.

Advancing knowledge in this area will allow researchers to begin to identify potential treatment substances that may lessen the impact and shorten the recovery time of adolescents who show signs of delayed development associated with alcohol use and misuse. It also is significant that delayed puberty is known to be associated with altered gonadal steroid production, which is needed for the development and function of several body systems. Furthermore, delayed pubertal development correlates with other health concerns such as altered bone density or height and weight issues, as well as psychological problems. Thus, the neuroendocrine consequences of alcohol use can result in far-reaching adolescent health concerns.

Chapter 17

Alcohol, Energy Drinks, and Youth: A Dangerous Mix

Dangers of Mixing Alcohol and Energy Drinks[1]

Energy drinks typically contain caffeine, plant-based stimulants, simple sugars, and other additives. Mixing alcohol with energy drinks is a popular practice, especially among young people in the United States.

- In 2015, 13 percent of students in grades 8, 10, and 12 and 33.5 percent of young adults aged 19–28 reported consuming alcohol mixed with energy drinks at least once in the past year.
- In a study among Michigan high school students, those who binge drank were more than twice as likely to mix alcohol with energy drinks as nonbinge drinkers (49.0% versus 18.2%). Liquor was the usual type of alcohol consumed by students who reported mixing alcohol and energy drinks (52.7%).

This chapter includes text excerpted from documents published by three public domain sources. Text under headings marked 1 are excerpted from "Alcohol and Public Health—Fact Sheets—Alcohol and Caffeine," Centers for Disease Control and Prevention (CDC), June 9, 2017; Text under heading marked 2 is excerpted from "Dangers of Teen Drinking," Federal Trade Commission (FTC), September 2013. Reviewed April 2018; Text under heading marked 3 is excerpted from "Alcohol," National Institute on Drug Abuse (NIDA) for Teens, January 2016.

- Drinkers aged 15–23 who mix alcohol with energy drinks are 4 times more likely to binge drink at high intensity (i.e., consume 6 or more drinks per binge episode) than drinkers who do not mix alcohol with energy drinks.
- Drinkers who mix alcohol with energy drinks are more likely than drinkers who do not mix alcohol with energy drinks to report unwanted or unprotected sex, driving drunk or riding with a driver who was intoxicated, or sustaining alcohol-related injuries.

Dangers of Mixing Alcohol and Caffeine[1]

- The *Dietary Guidelines for Americans* (DGA) cautions against mixing alcohol with caffeine.
- When alcohol is mixed with caffeine, the caffeine can mask the depressant effects of alcohol, making drinkers feel more alert than they would otherwise. As a result, they may drink more alcohol and become more impaired than they realize, increasing the risk of alcohol-attributable harms.
- Caffeine has no effect on the metabolism of alcohol by the liver and thus does not reduce breath or blood alcohol concentrations (it does not "sober you up") or reduce impairment due to alcohol consumption.

Caffeinated Alcoholic Beverages[1]

- Caffeinated alcoholic beverages (CABs) were premixed beverages popular in the 2000s that combined alcohol, caffeine, and other stimulants. They were malt or distilled spirits-based beverages and they usually had a higher alcohol content than beer (e.g., 12% alcohol by volume compared to 4–5% for beer).
- CABs were heavily marketed in youth-friendly media (e.g., social media) and with youth-oriented graphics and messaging that connected the consumption of these beverages with extreme sports or other risk-taking behaviors.
- In November 2010, the U.S. Food and Drug Administration (FDA) told the manufacturers of seven CABs that their drinks could no longer stay on the market in their current form, stating that "FDA does not find support for the claim that the addition of caffeine to these alcoholic beverages is 'generally recognized as safe,' which is the legal standard."

- Producers of CABs responded by removing caffeine and other stimulants from their products. However some producers continued to sell these products without caffeine.

Dangers of Underage Drinking[2]

Fatalities

Underage drivers are more susceptible than adults to the alcohol-induced impairment of driving skills. The National Highway Traffic Safety Administration (NHTSA) estimates that 21-year-old minimum drinking age laws have reduced alcohol traffic fatalities by 13 percent and have saved an estimated 28,765 lives since 1975. Still, about 1155 persons under 21 die every year in car crashes involving underage drinking.

Further, the majority of underage drinking related deaths are not traffic related. Instead, they are due to other fatal accidents, including homicides, suicides, poisoning, burns, falls, and drownings.

Emergency Room Visits and Hospitalization

In 2011, 189,000 persons under 21 visited emergency departments due to alcohol use. This represents 43 percent of all underage emergency departments visits due to drug abuse.

In 2008, almost 40,000 youth ages 15–20 were admitted to hospitals due to alcohol problems. In most cases, the primary or secondary diagnosis was acute intoxication. One quarter of the patients also had experienced a physical injury due to a traffic accident, being assaulted, or getting into a fight. The mean length of stay was 4.9 days and the mean cost was $19,200 per stay.

Altered Brain Development

The human brain continues to develop into a person's early 20's. There is concerning evidence from small-scale human brain imaging studies that underage drinking can harm the developing brain. In the long term, heavy alcohol use by teens can alter the trajectory of brain development and cause lingering cognitive defects; whether these defects are permanent is not now known.

Reduced Academic Performance

There is a relationship between binge drinking and grades. A government study published in 2007 showed that approximately two-thirds of students with "mostly A's" are nondrinkers, while nearly half of the students with "mostly D's and F's" report binge drinking.

Risky Sex

Current teen drinkers are twice as likely to have sex as nondrinkers. Adolescents who drink are also more likely to engage in risky sex, like having sex with someone they don't know or failing to use birth control.

Other Dangerous Behaviors

As compared to nondrinkers, teens who drink are more likely to get into a car with a driver who has been drinking, smoke pot, use inhalants, or carry a weapon. Binge drinking substantially increases the likelihood of these activities.

Public Health Impact of Excessive Alcohol Use[1]

- Excessive alcohol use is responsible for about 88,000 deaths in the United States each year and $249 billion in economic costs in 2010.
- Binge drinking (consuming 4 or more drinks per occasion for women or 5 or more drinks per occasion for men) is responsible for more than half of these deaths and three-quarters of economic costs.
- Binge drinking is also associated with many health and social problems, including alcohol-impaired driving, interpersonal violence, risky sexual activity, and unintended pregnancy.
- Most people younger than age 21 who drink report binge drinking, usually on multiple occasions.

Consequences of Underage Drinking[3]

There are increased risks and a range of negative consequences related to underage drinking. It is dangerous because it:

- **Causes many deaths.** On average, alcohol plays a role in the deaths of 4,358 young people under age 21 every year. These deaths include:
    - 1,580 deaths from car crashes

- 1,269 from murders
- 245 from alcohol poisoning, falls, burns, and drowning
- 492 from suicides

- **Causes many injuries.** Drinking alcohol can cause young people to have accidents and get hurt. In 2011 alone, about 188,000 people under age 21 visited an emergency room for injuries related to drinking alcohol.
- **Increases the risk of physical and sexual assault.** Young people under age 21 who drink are more likely to carry out or be the victim of a physical or sexual assault after drinking than others their age who do not drink.
- **Can lead to other problems.** Drinking can cause teens to have trouble in school or with the law. Teens who drink are more likely to use other drugs than teens who don't.
- **Can lead to developing an alcohol use disorder (AUD).** AUDs are medical conditions that doctors diagnose when someone's drinking causes them distress or harm. In 2014 about 679,000 young people ages 12–17 had an AUD. Even more important, the younger the use of alcohol the more likely one is to develop an AUD later in life.
- **Increases the risk of cancer.** Drinking alcohol increases your risk of developing various cancers, including cancers of the mouth, esophagus, pharynx, larynx, liver, and breast.

Prevention Strategies[1]

- The Community Preventive Services Task Force (CPSTF) recommends effective population-based strategies for preventing excessive alcohol consumption and related harms, including increasing alcohol excise taxes, limiting alcohol outlet density, and commercial host (dram shop) liability for service to underage or intoxicated customers.
- States and communities have also developed educational strategies to alert consumers to the risks of mixing alcohol with energy drinks. At least one community enacted an ordinance requiring retailers to post warning signs informing consumers of the risks of mixing alcohol and energy drinks.

- Monitoring and reducing youth exposure to alcohol advertising through "no-buy" lists could also help reduce underage drinking. No-buy lists identify television programming that advertisers can avoid to improve compliance with the alcohol industry's self-regulated alcohol marketing guidelines.

Chapter 18

Alcohol Use on College Campuses

Chapter Contents

Section 18.1

Drinking on Campus: Scope of the Problem

This section includes text excerpted from "College Drinking," National Institute on Alcohol Abuse and Alcoholism (NIAAA), December 2015.

Harmful and underage college drinking are significant public health problems, and they exact an enormous toll on the intellectual and social lives of students on campuses across the United States. Drinking at college has become a ritual that students often see as an integral part of their higher education experience. Many students come to college with established drinking habits, and the college environment can exacerbate the problem. According to a national survey, almost 60 percent of college students ages 18–22 drank alcohol in the past month, and almost two out of three of them engaged in binge drinking during that same timeframe.

Consequences of Harmful and Underage College Drinking

Drinking affects college students, their families, and college communities at large. Researchers estimate that each year:

Death

About 1,825 college students between the ages of 18 and 24 die from alcohol-related unintentional injuries, including motor-vehicle crashes.

Assault

About 696,000 students between the ages of 18 and 24 are assaulted by another student who has been drinking.

Sexual assault

About 97,000 students between the ages of 18 and 24 report experiencing alcohol-related sexual assault or date rape.

Academic problems

About 1 in 4 college students report academic consequences from drinking, including missing class, falling behind in class, doing poorly on exams or papers, and receiving lower grades overall. In a national survey of college students, binge drinkers who consumed alcohol at least 3 times per week were roughly 6 times more likely than those who drank but never binged to perform poorly on a test or project as a result of drinking (40% versus 7%) and 5 times more likely to have missed a class (64% versus 12%).

Alcohol use disorder (AUD)

About 20 percent of college students meet the criteria for an AUD.

Other consequences

These include suicide attempts, health problems, injuries, unsafe sex, and driving under the influence of alcohol, as well as vandalism, property damage, and involvement with the police.

Factors Affecting Student Drinking

Although the majority of students come to college already having some experience with alcohol, certain aspects of college life, such as unstructured time, the widespread availability of alcohol, inconsistent enforcement of underage drinking laws, and limited interactions with parents and other adults, can intensify the problem. In fact, college students have higher binge-drinking rates and a higher incidence of driving under the influence of alcohol than their noncollege peers. The first 6 weeks of freshman year are a vulnerable time for heavy drinking and alcohol-related consequences because of student expectations and social pressures at the start of the academic year.

Factors related to specific college environments also are significant. Students attending schools with strong Greek systems and with prominent athletic programs tend to drink more than students at other types of schools. In terms of living arrangements, alcohol consumption is highest among students living in fraternities and sororities and lowest among commuting students who live with their families. An often-overlooked preventive factor involves the continuing influence of parents. Research shows that students who choose not to drink often do so because their parents discussed alcohol use and its adverse consequences with them.

Section 18.2

CollegeAIM

This section includes text excerpted from "CollegeAIM—Introduction," National Institute on Alcohol Abuse and Alcoholism (NIAAA), September 22, 2015.

The National Institute on Alcohol Abuse and Alcoholism (NIAAA) developed the CollegeAIM guide and website to help college personnel choose wisely among the many potential interventions to address harmful and underage college student drinking.

The centerpiece of the guide is a user-friendly, matrix-based tool developed with input from leading college alcohol researchers, along with college student life and alcohol and other drug (AOD) program staff. With this "college alcohol intervention matrix"—or CollegeAIM tool—school officials can easily use research-based information to inform decisions about alcohol intervention strategies.

Why Intervene? College Drinking Is a Big Deal

While some see college drinking, even to excess, as a harmless rite of passage, it often results in adverse consequences for students and their schools.

Consequences for Students

- Academic fallout: Missed classes, poor school performance, withdrawal from courses, and dropping out
- Health problems: Alcohol use disorder and other alcohol-related problems, such as sleep issues and depression
- Acute risks: Impaired driving, unsafe sex, fights, sexual assaults, suicide attempts, unintentional injuries, overdoses, and death.

Even students who don't drink may experience secondhand effects, such as disrupted study and sleep, or being the victim of an alcohol-related assault.

Consequences for Schools

- Higher costs for healthcare and security
- Costs related to campus vandalism
- Costs related to attrition and the need for additional recruitment
- Damage to a school's reputation

College drinking is a big deal. The problem is complex and challenging, but you can reduce the likelihood of alcohol-related harm to your students. Commit to a plan using evidence-based interventions.

Where Does CollegeAIM Fit into an Overall Prevention Planning Process?

CollegeAIM, with its matrix-based tool, guide, website, and related resources, is meant to be used in conjunction with your school's own processes for anticipating and responding to the needs of your student body, campus environment, and surrounding community. You probably already apply a variation of these steps for college prevention programs:

- Assess the problems on your campus and set priorities,
- Select strategies by exploring evidence-based interventions,
- Plan how you'll carry out the chosen strategies and how you'll measure results, and
- Take action—implement the chosen strategies, evaluate them, and refine your program.

Section 18.3

Sexual Violence and Alcohol Use on Campus

This section includes text excerpted from "Sexual Assault and Alcohol," National Institute on Drug Abuse (NIDA), September 14, 2016.

Sexual Assault and Alcohol: What the Research Evidence Tells Us

Recognize the Complexity of the Association

Alcohol use does not cause sexual assault, but it can be a major contributing factor.

- Research studies have found that about half of sexual assaults on college campuses involve a situation in which the perpetrator, the victim, or both were consuming alcohol. Sexual assaults were more likely to occur in settings where alcohol was consumed (e.g., parties, bars). Potential perpetrators seek out such settings as a way of finding vulnerable individuals. Alcohol should be seen as a risk factor for—not a cause of—unwanted sexual advances and other forms of sexual assault.

Sexual assaults involving alcohol more often occur among individuals who know each other casually as acquaintances, rather than among individuals in romantic relationships.

Alcohol consumption is associated with aggression and loss of inhibition.

- Several decades of research have demonstrated that alcohol can increase the likelihood of intimate partner violence. When a relationship situation is potentially dangerous, alcohol can be seen as "adding fuel to the fire." Alcohol might increase sexual arousal, disinhibition, and aggression among perpetrators; heavier drinkers also have personality characteristics that are associated with perpetration (e.g., antisocial behavior, orientation toward impersonal sex). Perpetrators might also use alcohol as a means to justify their behavior or diminish their level of responsibility.

Reducing Alcohol Use Is One Piece of a Multifaceted Approach to Reducing Sexual Assault

Reducing underage and excessive drinking among college students is good practice to promote the safety and health of students.

- Excessive alcohol consumption among college students is a contributory factor for unintentional injury risk, fatalities, and sexual assault. 18–21 Alcohol use is related to the risk for sexual assault in the way that icy sidewalks can contribute to falls: People can fall on a dry sidewalk, but the presence of ice increases a person's susceptibility for experiencing a dangerous fall. Similarly, sexual assault can and does occur without alcohol consumption by the perpetrator or victim, but the presence of alcohol increases a person's susceptibility for experiencing a sexual assault.

Eliminating stigma around alcohol-involved sexual victimization is essential to support victims.

- Victims who were drinking at the time of a sexual assault report high levels of distress, self-blame, and negative reactions from others. They often fear they will not be believed or will be blamed. Support services must be comprehensive and help victims overcome the traumatic aftermath of victimization, regardless of whether the victim was drinking.

Reducing alcohol use through individual—and environmental—level interventions is an important component of a comprehensive campus strategy to reduce sexual assault.

- An experimental study compared the risk for completed rapes among female participants who were randomly assigned to a resistance training program (which included targeting excessive drinking) or to a control group. After one year, 5.2 percent of the women who received the training experienced a rape versus 9.8 percent of the control group. Attempted rape was also significantly different at one year between the groups (3.4% versus 9.3%).

- Helping potential victims to be less susceptible to assailants is only one part of the solution. To address sexual assault comprehensively, approaches must recognize the complex causes of violence against women and men, encourage bystanders to intervene, provide guidance regarding healthy relationships early in life, and reduce alcohol availability.

Section 18.4

Academic Performance and Alcohol Use

This section includes text excerpted from "Adolescent and School Health—Health and Academics," Centers for Disease Control and Prevention (CDC), September 7, 2017.

The academic success of America's youth is strongly linked with their health, and is one way to predict adult health outcomes.

Healthy Students Are Better Learners

Health-risk behaviors such as early sexual initiation, violence, and substance use are consistently linked to poor grades and test scores and lower educational attainment. In turn, academic success is an excellent indicator for the overall well-being of youth and a primary predictor and determinant of adult health outcomes. Leading national education organizations recognize the close relationship between health and education, as well as the need to foster health and well-being within the educational environment for all students.

Schools Are the Right Place for a Healthy Start

Schools play a critical role in promoting the health and safety of young people and helping them establish lifelong healthy behaviors. Research shows that school health programs reduce the prevalence of health risk behaviors among young people and have a positive effect on academic performance. Centers for Disease Control and Prevention (CDC) analyzes research findings to develop guidelines and strategies for schools to address health risk behaviors among students and creates tools to help schools implement these guidelines.

Making the Connection: Alcohol and Academic Grades

Data from the National Youth Risk Behavior Survey (YRBS) show that students with higher academic grades are less likely to drink alcohol, begin drinking at a young age, or engage in binge drinking. It is important to remember that these associations do not prove causation. School health professionals, school officials, and other decision-makers can use this information to better understand the associations between alcohol use and grades, as well as to develop and reinforce policies, practices, and programs that promote healthy behaviors.

Key Findings

Compared to students with lower grades, students with higher grades are less likely to:

- Drink alcohol before the age of 13 years
- Currently drink alcohol
- Drink 5 or more drinks of alcohol in a row within a couple of hours

Drinking Alcohol Behaviors

- 12 percent of U.S. high school students with mostly A's drank alcohol (other than a few sips) for the first time before the age of 13 years, compared to 34 percent of students with mostly D/F's
- 24 percent of U.S. high school students with mostly A's currently drank alcohol (at least 1 drink of alcohol on at least 1 day during the 30 days before the survey), compared to 52 percent of students with mostly D/F's
- 11 percent of U.S. high school students with mostly A's drank 5 or more drinks of alcohol in a row within a couple of hours on at least 1 day during the 30 days before the survey, compared to 34 percent of students with mostly D/F's

These results from the YRBS provide evidence of a significant association between academic grades and drinking alcohol. Further research is warranted to determine whether higher grades in school lead to lower alcohol consumption and delayed alcohol initiation, if lower alcohol consumption and delayed alcohol initiation lead to higher grades, or some other factors lead to these alcohol-related behaviors. There is a close relationship between health and education. By working together, education and health agencies, parents and communities can ensure that students are healthy and ready to learn in school.

About the Data

The National YRBS monitors priority health-risk behaviors that contribute to the leading causes of death, disability, and social problems among youth and adults in the United States. It is conducted every 2 years during the spring and provides data representative of 9th through 12th grade students in public and private schools throughout the nation. In 2015, students completing the YRBS were asked, "During the past 12 months, how would you describe your grades in school?" and given seven response options (Mostly A's, Mostly B's, Mostly C's, Mostly D's, Mostly F's, None of these grades, Not sure). In 2015, 32 percent of students received mostly A's, 38 percent received mostly B's, 20 percent received mostly C's, 6 percent received mostly D's or F's, and 4 percent reported receiving none of these grades or not sure.

Section 18.5

What Policy-Makers Need to Know about College Drinking

This section includes text excerpted from "College Drinking," National Institute on Alcohol Abuse and Alcoholism (NIAAA), December 2015.

Addressing College Drinking

Ongoing research continues to improve our understanding of how to address the persistent and costly problem of harmful and underage student drinking. Successful efforts typically involve a mix of strategies that target individual students, the student body as a whole, and the broader college community.

Strategies Targeting Individual Students

Individual-level interventions target students, including those in higher-risk groups such as first year students, student athletes, members of Greek organizations, and mandated students. They are designed to change students' knowledge, attitudes, and behaviors related to alcohol so that they drink less, take fewer risks, and experience fewer harmful consequences. Categories of individual-level interventions include the following:

- Education and awareness programs
- Cognitive-behavioral skills-based approaches
- Motivation and feedback-related approaches
- Behavioral interventions by health professionals

Strategies Targeting the Campus and Surrounding Community

Environmental-level strategies target the campus community and student body as a whole, and are designed to change the campus and community environments in which student drinking occurs. Often, a major goal is to reduce the availability of alcohol, because research shows that reducing alcohol availability cuts consumption and harmful consequences on campuses as well as in the general population.

A Mix of Strategies Is Best

For more information on individual- and environmental-level strategies, the National Institute on Alcohol Abuse and Alcoholism (NIAAA) CollegeAIM guide (and interactive website) rates nearly 60 alcohol interventions in terms of effectiveness, costs, and other factors—and presents the information in a user-friendly and accessible way.

In general, the most effective interventions in CollegeAIM (which stands for College Alcohol Intervention Matrix) represent a range of counseling options and policies related to sales and access. Yet, while school officials should be aware of the strategies that came out on top in the ratings—and those that rated poorly—they should use CollegeAIM as a resource to find the best mix of individual and environmental strategies for their unique circumstances. After analyzing alcohol problems at their own schools, officials can use the CollegeAIM ratings to find the best combination of interventions for their students and budgets.

The greatest chance for creating a safer campus will likely come from a combination of individual—and environmental—level interventions that work together to maximize positive effects. Strong leadership from a concerned college president, in combination with an involved campus community and a comprehensive program of evidence-based strategies, can help address harmful student drinking.

Chapter 19

Family Guide to Underage Drinking Prevention

Chapter Contents

Section 19.1

Parental Involvement in Alcohol Use Prevention

This section includes text excerpted from "Parenting to Prevent Childhood Alcohol Use," National Institute on Alcohol Abuse and Alcoholism (NIAAA), February 2017.

Drinking alcohol undoubtedly is a part of American culture, as are conversations between parents and children about its risks and potential benefits. However, information about alcohol can seem contradictory. Alcohol affects people differently at different stages of life—small amounts may have health benefits for certain adults, but for children and adolescents, alcohol can interfere with normal brain development. Alcohol's differing effects and parents' changing role in their children's lives as they mature and seek greater independence can make talking about alcohol a challenge. Parents may have trouble setting concrete family policies for alcohol use. And they may find it difficult to communicate with children and adolescents about alcohol-related issues.

Research shows, however, that teens and young adults do believe their parents should have a say in whether they drink alcohol. Parenting styles are important—teens raised with a combination of encouragement, warmth, and appropriate discipline are more likely to respect their parents' boundaries. Understanding parental influence on children through conscious and unconscious efforts, as well as when and how to talk with children about alcohol, can help parents have more influence than they might think on a child's alcohol use. Parents can play an important role in helping their children develop healthy attitudes toward drinking while minimizing its risk.

Alcohol Use by Young People

Adolescent alcohol use remains a pervasive problem. The percentage of teenagers who drink alcohol is slowly declining; however, numbers are still quite high. About 22.8 percent of adolescents report drinking by 8th grade, and about 46.3 percent report being drunk at least once by 12th grade.

Parenting Style

Accumulating evidence suggests that alcohol use—and in particular binge drinking—may have negative effects on adolescent development and increase the risk for alcohol dependence later in life. This underscores the need for parents to help delay or prevent the onset of drinking as long as possible. Parenting styles may influence whether their children follow their advice regarding alcohol use. Every parent is unique, but the ways in which each parent interacts with his or her children can be broadly categorized into four styles:

- Authoritarian parents typically exert high control and discipline with low warmth and responsiveness. For example, they respond to bad grades with punishment but let good grades go unnoticed.
- Permissive parents typically exert low control and discipline with high warmth and responsiveness. For example, they deem any grades at all acceptable and fail to correct behavior that may lead to bad grades.
- Neglectful parents exert low control and discipline as well as low warmth and responsiveness. For example, they show no interest at all in a child's school performance.
- Authoritative parents exert high control and discipline along with high warmth and responsiveness. For example, they offer praise for good grades and use thoughtful discipline and guidance to help improve low grades.

Regardless of the developmental outcome examined—body image, academic success, or substance abuse—children raised by authoritative parents tend to fare better than their peers. This is certainly true when it comes to the issue of underage drinking, in part because children raised by such parents learn approaches to problem-solving and emotional expression that help protect against the psychological dysfunction that often precedes alcohol misuse. The combination of discipline and support by authoritative parents promotes healthy decision making about alcohol and other potential threats to healthy development.

Modeling

Some parents wonder whether allowing their children to drink in the home will help them develop an appropriate relationship with alcohol. According to most studies this does not appear to be the case.

In a study of 6th, 7th, and 8th graders, researchers observed that students whose parents allowed them to drink at home and/or provided them with alcohol experienced the steepest escalation in drinking. Other studies suggest that adolescents who are allowed to drink at home drink more heavily outside of the home. In contrast, adolescents are less likely to drink heavily if they live in homes where parents have specific rules against drinking at a young age and also drink responsibly themselves. However, not all studies suggest that parental provision of alcohol to teens leads to trouble. For instance, one study showed that drinking with a parent in the proper context (such as a sip of alcohol at an important family function) can be a protective factor against excessive drinking. In other contexts, parental provision of alcohol serves as a direct risk factor for excessive drinking, as is the case when parents provide alcohol for parties attended or hosted by their adolescents. Collectively, the literature suggests that permissive attitudes toward adolescent drinking, particularly when combined with poor communication and unhealthy modeling, can lead teens into unhealthy relationships with alcohol.

Genetics

Regardless of what parents may teach their children about alcohol, some genetic factors are present from birth and cannot be changed. Genes appear to influence the development of drinking behaviors in several ways. Some people, particularly those of Asian ancestry, have a natural and unpleasant response to alcohol that helps prevent them from drinking too much. Other people have a naturally high tolerance to alcohol, meaning that to feel alcohol's effects, they must drink more than others. Some personality traits are genetic, and those, like impulsivity, can put a person at risk for problem drinking. Psychiatric problems may be caused by genetic traits, and such problems can increase risk for alcohol abuse and dependence. Finally, having a parent with a drinking problem increases a child's risk for developing an alcohol problem of his or her own.

Do Teens Listen?

Adolescents do listen to their parents when it comes to issues such as drinking and smoking, particularly if the messages are conveyed consistently and with authority. Research suggests that only 19 percent of teens feel that parents should have a say in the music they listen to, and 26 percent believe their parents should influence what clothing they wear. However, the majority—around 80 percent—feel that parents should have a say in whether they drink alcohol. Those who do not think that parents have authority over these issues are four times more likely than other teens to drink alcohol and three times more likely to have plans to drink if they have not already started.

Whether teens defer to parents on the issue of drinking is statistically linked to how parents parent. Specifically, authoritative parents—those who provide a healthy and consistent balance of discipline and support—are the most likely to have teenagers who respect the boundaries they have established around drinking and other behaviors; whereas adolescents exposed to permissive, authoritarian, or neglectful parenting are less influenced by what their parents say about drinking.

Research suggests that, regardless of parenting styles, adolescents who are aware that their parents would be upset with them if they drank are less likely to do so, highlighting the importance of communication between parents and teens as a protective measure against underage alcohol use.

What Can Parents Do?

Parents influence whether and when adolescents begin drinking as well as how their children drink. Family policies about adolescent drinking in the home and the way parents themselves drink are important. For instance, if you choose to drink, always model responsible alcohol consumption. But what else can parents do to help minimize the likelihood that their adolescent will choose to drink and that such drinking, if it does occur, will become problematic? Studies have shown that it is important to:

- Talk early and often, in developmentally appropriate ways, with children and teens about your concerns—and theirs—regarding alcohol. Adolescents who know their parents' opinions about youth drinking are more likely to fall in line with their expectations.
- Establish policies early on, and be consistent in setting expectations and enforcing rules. Adolescents do feel that parents should have a say in decisions about drinking, and they maintain this deference to parental authority as long as they perceive the message to be legitimate. Consistency is central to legitimacy.

- Work with other parents to monitor where kids are gathering and what they are doing. Being involved in the lives of adolescents is key to keeping them safe.
- Work in and with the community to promote dialogue about underage drinking and the creation and implementation of action steps to address it
- Be aware of your state's laws about providing alcohol to your own children
- Never provide alcohol to someone else's child

Children and adolescents often feel competing urges to comply with and resist parental influences. During childhood, the balance usually tilts toward compliance, but during adolescence, the balance often shifts toward resistance as teens prepare for the autonomy of adulthood. With open, respectful communication and explanations of boundaries and expectations, parents can continue to influence their children's decisions well into adolescence and beyond. This is especially important in young people's decisions regarding whether and how to drink—decisions that can have lifelong consequences.

Section 19.2

Talk to Your Child about Alcohol

This section contains text excerpted from the following sources: Text under the heading "Talking with Teens about Alcohol" is excerpted from "Talking with Teens about Alcohol," U.S. Department of Health and Human Services (HHS), October 17, 2016; Text beginning with the heading "Why You Should Talk with Your Child about Alcohol" is excerpted from "Answering Your Child's Tough Questions about Alcohol," Substance Abuse and Mental Health Services Administration (SAMHSA), September 20, 2017.

Talking with Teens about Alcohol

Alcohol use by teens is sometimes considered a "gateway" to a wide range of other high-risk activities, including premature sexual activity and use of illegal drugs. Alcohol is harmful to young people and early use has lasting, sometimes tragic, consequences for them. Although many factors influence whether teens use alcohol, one thing is clear: parents play a central role in teens' decisions.

How You Make a Difference

- **Be realistic about the risks and costs.** Despite glorified or humorous portrayals in the media, underage alcohol use contributes to a wide range of risks for teens, including:
    - Alcohol-related injury or death (particularly associated with drinking and driving or riding with an intoxicated driver)
    - Earlier sexual intercourse and unprotected sex
    - Having multiple sexual partners and having casual, unprotected sex when alcohol is being consumed
    - Decreased school attendance and achievement
    - Potentially altered brain functioning
- **Understand what predicts a young person's alcohol use.** A variety of studies have found a wide range of factors that affect whether a young person drinks—and whether this drinking will become a significant problem.
- **Do not allow teens to drink in the home.** Though some people advocate letting adolescents drink at home so they can learn to consume alcohol responsibly, available research indicates that doing so increases the risks of underage drinking. Those whose parents provide alcohol have the greatest increases in drinking behavior, and they are more likely to drink more heavily away from home.
- **If you choose to drink, model responsible alcohol attitudes and consumption.** How you respond to situations that include alcohol—especially when your teens are around—sends a strong message.
    - Limit how much, how often, and where you drink. Do not drink in high-risk situations such as when driving, operating a boat, or operating machinery.
    - Avoid making alcohol seem essential for relaxing or having a good time. Don't laugh at or glorify the people who have had

too much to drink, whether it is in your community, in the news, or on television.

- If your teen asks why you can drink and he or she can't, say something like, "Alcohol isn't good for growing bodies and minds," or "Consuming alcohol well requires first developing adult skills and showing responsibility in many different areas of life."
- Always offer nonalcoholic drink options when you entertain in your home or workplace so that teens know that some adults do not drink. (About one-third of U.S. adults do not drink alcohol.)
- If you or your partner struggles with alcohol abuse, seek professional help from a physician or addiction counselor. You can find treatment options through the Substance Abuse Treatment Facility Locator, a service of the Substance Abuse and Mental Health Services Administration (SAMHSA).

- **Start early.** Setting and enforcing clear expectations about not using alcohol as a teenager are key to delaying first use. That's important, since the younger adolescents are when they first use alcohol the more likely they are to deal with its negative consequences.
- **Keep communication open.** Be interested in your teen's life, and be open to information he or she may share. Not only will this make it easier to talk about difficult issues regarding alcohol and other topics, but it also will give you information about where your teen may be facing pressure or temptation to use alcohol.
- **Set clear, specific rules about alcohol use.** Teens who have well-defined, alcohol-specific rules are less likely to start drinking. Those who start later are likely to drink less.
- **Address drinking and driving.** Be clear that teens should never drive with any alcohol in their system or ride with someone who has been drinking. Have a clear plan for what to do if your teen is in a situation that could involve alcohol and driving. This could include an agreement to call you for help at any time, with no questions asked at the time (though consequences would be in place after the immediate danger has passed).
- **Adjust as your teen grows up and faces new situations.** As teens get older, they will face new challenges and situations. In

addition, they will pull away from some of the protective structures of adolescence and become more independent. Major personal or family changes (such as parental divorce or a move to a new town) require rebuilding the positive supports that keep your teen on track.

- **Band together with other parents.** Other parents are likely to share some of your same concerns. Create a pact to work together to keep parties and get-togethers alcohol-free (for example, by ensuring that an adult is around when parties happen).
- **Support broader school and community efforts.** Underage drinking is not a teen problem or a family problem. It is a community problem that requires many people and systems working together, including efforts in the schools to support and reinforce appropriate rules and consequences. As you're able, link to and support these broader efforts, recognizing the value that broader efforts can provide for parents.
- **Intervene if you suspect that teens are using alcohol.** Talk to teens right away and work with them (and other parents) to prevent further underage alcohol use.
    - Ask teens directly, describing the reasons for your concern. Ask for their side of the story. Avoid being judgmental, but share your perspective and expectations.
    - If your teen has used alcohol, set appropriate consequences. Use it as an opportunity to help him or her learn from mistakes. What should happen the next time, or what will you do to ensure there are not other similar opportunities to get alcohol?
    - If you suspect your teen has a serious drinking problem, get professional help. Many physicians and addiction counselors can offer information on treatment options. You can also find treatment options in your area through the Substance Abuse Treatment Facility Locator.

Talk with Your Teen

- **Clarify your expectations.** Set clear ground rules for not drinking and set specific consequences if your teen does drink. Discuss your expectations that they do not drink alcohol as teenagers and the reasons for it, including the laws, risks, and consequences.

- **Talk early and often.** Share your concerns about alcohol. Listen to their concerns, questions, and perspectives. Use advertisements, news stories, or personal incidents to raise the issue. Ask teens what they think about alcohol use on television, on the Internet, in movies, or among friends.
- **Counter the "everybody's doing it" message.** Remind teens that not everyone drinks, particularly teenagers (for whom drinking is also illegal). One in three adults chooses to not consume alcohol. Let them know that abstaining from alcohol is, for many, a responsible and acceptable choice.
- **Find out what's happening with friends, at school, and places they spend time.** Directly ask if friends talk about alcohol use and where alcohol is readily available. Find out whether or how your teen feels pressure from others to use alcohol. Check in regularly, since the situation may change as your teen gets older.

Why You Should Talk with Your Child about Alcohol

The chance that children will use alcohol increases as they get older. About 10 percent of 12-year-olds say they have tried alcohol, but by age 15, that number jumps to 50 percent. The sooner you talk to your children about alcohol, the greater chance you have of influencing their decisions about drinking.

Parents play a critical role in children's decisions to experiment with alcohol. Studies have shown that parents have a significant influence on young people's decisions about alcohol consumption, especially when parents create supportive and nurturing environments in which their children can make their own decisions. In fact, around 80 percent of children feel that parents should have a say in whether they drink alcohol.

The conversation is often more effective before children start drinking. If you talk to your kids directly and honestly, they are more likely to respect your rules and advice about alcohol use. When parents know about underage alcohol use, they can protect their children from many of the high-risk behaviors associated with it.

Some children may try alcohol as early as 9 years old. Most 6-year-olds know that alcohol is only for adults. Between the ages of 9 and 13, children start to view alcohol more positively. Many children begin to think underage drinking is OK. Some even start to experiment. It is never too early to talk to your children about alcohol.

If you do not talk about it, you are still saying something. What you say to your children about alcohol is up to you. But remember, parents who do not discourage underage drinking may have an indirect influence on their children's alcohol use.

Question Children May Ask about Alcohol

Some questions about alcohol can be hard to answer, so it's important to be prepared. The following are common questions and answers about underage drinking.

"I got invited to a party. Can I go?"

Ask your child if an adult will be present at the party or if he or she thinks children will be drinking. Remind your child that even being at a party where there is underage drinking can get him or her into trouble. Use this time to establish or reinforce your rules about alcohol and outline the behavior you expect.

"Did you drink when you were a kid?"

Don't let your past stop you from talking to your child about underage drinking. If you drank as a teenager, be honest. Acknowledge that it was risky. Make sure to emphasize that we now know even more about the risks to children who drink underage. You could even give your child an example of a painful moment that occurred because of your underage drinking.

"Why do you drink?"

Make a distinction between alcohol use among children and among adults. Explain to your child your reasons for drinking: whether it is to enhance a meal, share good times with friends, or celebrate a special occasion. Point out that if you choose to drink, it is always in moderation. Tell your child that some people should not drink at all, including underage children.

"What if my friends ask me to drink?"

Helping your child say "no" to peer pressure is one of the most important things you can do to keep him or her alcohol-free. Work with your child to think of a way to handle this situation, whether it is simply saying, "No, I don't drink," or saying, "I promised my mom (or dad) that I wouldn't drink."

"You drink alcohol, so why can't I?"

Remind your child that underage drinking is against the law, and for good reason. Point out that adults are fully developed mentally and physically so they can handle drinking. Children's minds and bodies, however, are still growing, so alcohol can have a greater effect on their judgment and health.

"Why is alcohol bad for me?"

Don't try to scare your child about drinking or tell him or her, "You can't handle it." Instead, tell your child that alcohol can be bad for his or her growing brain, interferes with judgment, and can make him or her sick. Once children hear the facts and your opinions about them, it is easier for you to make rules and enforce them.

Section 19.3

Talk with Your High School Grads about Celebrating Safely

This section includes text excerpted from "Parents—Talk with Your High School Grads about Celebrating Safely," National Institute on Alcohol Abuse and Alcoholism (NIAAA), October 2016.

Graduation

Graduation is a time to celebrate. But before your high school seniors begin their parties, take the time to talk with them about keeping events alcohol-free—it just may save a life.

It's about Your Teen

A teenager's brain is still developing, and it is very sensitive to alcohol's effects on judgment and decision-making. Tragedies can—and do—happen, so underage drinking should not be a part of any end-of-year celebration.

The Effects of Alcohol Can Be Deceptive

If you are asked to explain the reasons behind your rules, you can describe the effects of alcohol on the human body:

When people drink alcohol, they may temporarily feel elated and happy, but they should not be fooled. As blood alcohol content rises, the effects on the body—and the potential risks—multiply.

- Inhibitions and memory become affected, so people may say and do things that they will regret later and possibly not remember doing at all
- Decision-making skills are affected. When they drink, some people may become restless and aggressive. They may be at greater risk for having an alcohol-related traffic crash, getting into fights, or making unwise decisions about sex.
- Coordination and physical control are also impacted. When drinking leads to loss of balance, slurred speech, and blurred vision, even normal activities can become more dangerous.
- Consuming too much alcohol can also lead to death. If people drink too much, they will eventually get sleepy and pass out. Reflexes like gagging and breathing can be suppressed. That means they could vomit and choke, or just stop breathing completely.

Think about It

Drinking to celebrate graduation can result in vandalism, arrests, sexual assaults, trips to the emergency room, alcohol-related traffic crashes, and worse. Drinking by teens can put them—and their friends—in real danger. Ask them to consider this question: Is that any way to celebrate?

Talking with Your Graduate

It is critical to talk with your graduate because research shows that parents do make a difference. By serving as positive role models, talking to other parents and your teens, supervising parties to make sure no alcohol is served, and supporting alcohol-free school celebrations, you can help prevent a life-changing mistake.

Remember

Tell your graduate to play it safe and party right—and alcohol-free—at graduation. Because a well-deserved celebration shouldn't end in tragedy.

Chapter 20

Efforts to Prevent and Reduce Alcohol Problems in Adolescents

Chapter Contents

Section 20.1

How to Tell If Your Child Is Drinking Alcohol

This section includes text excerpted from "How to Tell If Your Child Is Drinking Alcohol," Substance Abuse and Mental Health Services Administration (SAMHSA), September 20, 2017.

Learn how to tell if your child is drinking alcohol.

Warning Signs

Although the following signs may indicate a problem with alcohol or other drugs, some also reflect normal growing pains. Experts believe that a drinking problem is more likely if you notice several of these signs at the same time, if they occur suddenly, or if some of them are extreme in nature.

- Mood changes: flare-ups of temper, irritability, and defensiveness
- School problems: poor attendance, low grades, and/or recent disciplinary action
- Rebellion against family rules
- Friend changes: switching friends and a reluctance to let you get to know the new friends
- A "nothing matters" attitude: sloppy appearance, a lack of involvement in former interests, and general low energy
- Alcohol presence: finding it in your child's room or backpack or smelling alcohol on his or her breath
- Physical or mental problems: memory lapses, poor concentration, bloodshot eyes, lack of coordination, or slurred speech

Finding Help

Do Not Play the Blame Game

It is hard for most parents to believe that their child might be caught up in underage alcohol use and in need of professional help.

Do not feel bad if you did not see the warning signs until your child was in trouble or until someone told you about the problem. When most parents find out about their child's underage drinking, they feel shocked and stunned and wonder where they went wrong. In getting help for a child who drinks, the first thing to do is to try not to blame yourself or your child. The important thing is to act now to find the best available services to help your child stop using alcohol and begin building an alcohol-free future.

Talk with People You Know

If you are seeking treatment for a child's mental health or substance abuse problem, you can start by talking with people you know such as family members, friends, school teachers, counselors, clergy, and your doctor. Your health insurance company can give you a list of mental health and substance abuse providers. If your employer has an employee assistance program, you can get a referral there. Your child's school may suggest a good substance abuse treatment program. If not, the school district is likely to have a substance abuse prevention and counseling program. Contact them for help.

Contact a Professional

Your county's health department probably has substance abuse services and is another good source for information. The county agency may be called "alcohol and drug programs" or "behavioral health" or it may be in a mental health services division. A call to the county health agency's general information number should point you in the right direction.

Section 20.2

What You Can Do to Prevent Your Child from Drinking

This section contains text excerpted from the following sources: Text beginning with the heading "Be Aware of Factors That May Increase the Risk of a Child's Alcohol Use" is excerpted from "What You Can Do to Prevent Your Child from Drinking," Substance Abuse and Mental Health Services Administration (SAMHSA), September 20, 2017; Text under the heading "Stopping Teens' Easy Access to Alcohol" is excerpted from "Stopping Teens' Easy Access to Alcohol," Federal Trade Commission (FTC), September 2013. Reviewed April 2018.

Be Aware of Factors That May Increase the Risk of a Child's Alcohol Use

- Significant social transitions such as graduating to middle or high school or getting a driver's license
- A history of social and emotional problems
- Depression and other serious emotional problems
- A family history of alcoholism
- Contact with peers involved in troubling activities

Be a Positive Adult Role Model

- Stay away from alcohol in high-risk situations. For example, do not operate a vehicle after drinking alcohol.
- Get help if you think you have an alcohol-related problem
- Do not give alcohol to your children. Tell them that any alcohol in your home is off limits to them and to their friends.

Work with Schools, Communities, and the Government to Protect Children from Underage Alcohol Use by Ensuring

- Schools and the community support and reward young people's decisions not to drink
- Schools and the community identify and intervene with children engaged in underage drinking early
- Rules about underage drinking are in place at home, at school, and in your community
- Agreements of acceptable behavior are established, well-known, and applied consistently
- Parties and social events at home and elsewhere do not permit underage drinking

Support Your Children and Give Them Space to Grow

- Be involved in your children's lives
- Encourage your children's growing independence, but set appropriate limits
- Make it easy for your children to share information about their lives
- Know where your children are, what they are doing, whom they are with, and whom they are friends with
- Make an effort to get to know the parents of your children's friends. Share your rules about not allowing alcohol use
- Find ways for your children to be involved in family life such as doing chores or caring for a younger sibling
- Set clear rules, including rules about alcohol use. Enforce the rules you set
- Help your children find ways to have fun without alcohol
- Do not let your children attend parties at which alcohol is served. Do not allow alcohol at parties in your own home.
- Help your children avoid dangerous situations such as riding in a car driven by someone who has been drinking

- Help your children get professional help if you are worried about their involvement with alcohol
- Create a pledge between yourself and your children that promises they will not drink alcohol

Stopping Teens' Easy Access to Alcohol

Teen drinking is not inevitable. More than 58 percent of high school seniors do not drink alcohol, reducing their current risk of injury. One way to prevent teens from drinking is to cut off easy access to alcohol. Unfortunately, right now most teens report that it is easy to get alcohol. Almost 72 percent of teens who drink get alcohol without having to pay for it. They get it from friends or family members, at parties, or by taking it without permission. Underage drinkers who pay for alcohol usually give money to someone else to buy it.

Here's what you can do to reduce easy access to alcohol:

At Home

- Make sure teens can't access alcohol without your knowledge. Unmonitored alcohol, including alcohol stored in a cabinet, basement or garage, can be a temptation. When in doubt, lock it up.
- Exercise your influence. Data shows that teens continue to care what their parents think, even while they are in high school and college. Let your teen know that you don't want them to drink and that most teens in fact don't drink.
- Talk to your kids about how to say no to a drink. The National Institute on Alcohol Abuse and Alcoholism (NIAAA) suggests these responses:
    - No, thanks.
    - I don't feel like it. Do you have any soda?
    - Alcohol's not my thing.
    - Are you talking to me? Forget it.
    - You're pressuring me. I said no.
    - Please back off.

In Your Community

It may have happened already. A neighbor announces she is hosting a teen party, but you shouldn't worry—she's taking the car keys from every kid who comes in. Or a colleague says he's serving alcohol to his high school son's friends so they can "learn to drink responsibly."

- Speak out, because silence can be misinterpreted. If you hear about a situation, say that you don't want other people serving alcohol to your teen or condoning teen drinking. Let your friends, neighbors, and family members know that the minimum drinking age is a policy that protects teens, and that you don't want your teen to drink.
- Take action before a situation arises. Start talking to the parents of your teen's friends early—for example, when your kid is in 6th grade. Tell them about the risks of teen drinking and let them know that you don't want anyone to allow your teen to drink alcohol.
- Talk to adults who host teen parties. Let them know that the overwhelming majority of parents support the legal drinking age and agree that it is not okay to serve alcohol to someone else's teen—and not okay to turn a blind eye to teens' alcohol consumption.
- Talk to your school board, school principals, teachers, and coaches. Let them know that it is unsafe, illegal, and irresponsible to condone teen drinking. Ask them to discourage this activity.
- Talk to management at restaurants, town halls, and other venues where teen parties are held. Let them know that parents in your community do not want teens to have access to alcohol.
- Let local law enforcement know that you encourage active policing of noisy teen parties that may signal alcohol use.
- Tell local alcohol retailers that you want them to check ID before selling alcohol. Limiting alcohol sales to legal purchasers is an important goal and worth the time it takes.

Section 20.3

School Interventions to Prevent Alcohol Abuse

This section includes text excerpted from "School-Based Programs to Prevent and Reduce Alcohol Use among Youth," National Institute on Alcohol Abuse and Alcoholism (NIAAA), December 7, 2011. Reviewed April 2018.

Schools are an important setting for interventions aimed at preventing alcohol use and abuse among adolescents. A range of school-based interventions have been developed to prevent or delay the onset of alcohol use, most of which are targeted to middle-school students. Most of these interventions seek to reduce risk factors for alcohol use at the individual level, whereas other interventions also address social and/or environmental risk factors. Not all interventions that have been developed and implemented have been found to be effective. In-depth analyses have indicated that to be most effective, interventions should be theory-driven, address social norms around alcohol use, build personal and social skills helping students resist pressure to use alcohol, involve interactive teaching approaches, use peer leaders, integrate other segments of the population into the program, be delivered over several sessions and years, provide training and support to facilitators, and be culturally and developmentally appropriate. Additional research is needed to develop interventions for elementary-school and high-school students and for special populations.

Because alcohol use typically begins during adolescence and because no other community institution has as much continuous and intensive contact with underage youth, schools can be an important setting for intervention. This section describes school-based approaches to alcohol prevention, highlighting evidence-based examples of this method of intervention, and suggests directions for future research. This section primarily is based on several recent reviews focusing on alcohol prevention among underage youth conducted by Foxcroft and colleagues, Komro and Toomey, and—the most comprehensive and critical review of this field to date—Spoth and colleagues. Although these previous reviews addressed interventions in a variety of contexts (e.g., families, schools, and communities), the present section highlights key findings specific to school-based interventions.

Characteristics of School-Based Alcohol Prevention Programs

Rates of initiation of drinking rise rapidly starting at age 10 (i.e., grades 4 and 5) and peak between ages 13 and 14 (i.e., grades 8 and 9). At that point, more than 50 percent of adolescents report ever having consumed alcohol in their lifetime. Given this natural history of alcohol use in adolescence, most school-based programs have been developed for and delivered in middle schools; programs aimed at elementary schools (especially grades 3–5) and high schools are less common. Of particular concern to contemporary research with underage youth is heavy drinking, including harmful behaviors, such as binge drinking and drunkenness.

The primary goal of school-based alcohol prevention programs is to prevent or delay the onset of alcohol use, although some programs also seek to reduce the overall prevalence of alcohol use. Interventions earlier in life (i.e., during elementary school) target risk factors for later alcohol use (e.g., early aggression) because alcohol use itself is not yet relevant to this age group. Any reduction in alcohol-related behavior is assumed to lead to subsequent reductions in alcohol-related problems (e.g., injuries or alcohol dependence), although the latter often are not measured in primary prevention studies.

School-based alcohol interventions are designed to reduce risk factors for early alcohol use primarily at the individual level (e.g., by enhancing student's knowledge and skills), although the most successful school-based programs address social and environmental risk factors (e.g., alcohol-related norms) as well. Some school-based programs focus on the general population of adolescents (i.e., are universal programs), whereas others target adolescents who are particularly at risk (i.e., are selective or indicated programs). The research literature on the efficacy of school-based alcohol prevention programs is large, encompassing several decades of study. The review by Spoth and colleagues provides several examples of effective school-based programs, which will be discussed in detail below. Not all school-based alcohol prevention programs for youth are effective, however. The review by Foxcroft and colleagues, especially, emphasizes this point with regard to long-term (3 years or more) outcomes of primary prevention efforts such as school-based programs.

Examples of Evidence-Based, School-Based Alcohol Prevention Programs

The review by Spoth and colleagues provides support for the efficacy of school-based programs, at least in the short-term (defined as at least 6 months after the intervention was implemented). This review considered alcohol prevention interventions across three developmental periods (i.e., younger than age 10 years, age 10–15 years, and age 16 years or older), aligned with reviews of other etiologic work during the same developmental stages. Of more than 400 studies that the investigators screened, only 127 interventions could be evaluated for their efficacy according to the inclusion criteria specified by the researchers. Of these 127 studies, 41 showed evidence of a positive effect—that is, they could be classified as "most promising" (n = 12) or having "mixed or emerging" evidence (n = 29).

Two-thirds of the most-promising interventions that were identified by Spoth and colleagues either were exclusively school-based (n = 2) or included a large school-based component within a multiple-component or multiple-domain intervention (n = 6). Most-promising interventions were identified for all three age-groups studied. At the elementary-school level, interventions classified as most promising included the following:

- Seattle Social Development Project
- Linking the Interests of Families and Teachers
- Raising Healthy Children
- Preventive Treatment Program

At the middle-school level, the most promising interventions included the following:

- Project Northland
- Project STAR, or Midwestern Prevention Project
- Keepin' it REAL

At the high-school level, only the Project Toward No Drug Abuse (TND) was classified as most promising, although Project Northland also has been implemented and shown to be successful with high-school students. Other school-based programs that may be familiar to readers who conduct research in this area, such as Promoting Alternative THinking Strategies (PATHS), Life Skills Training were identified as either having mixed (e.g., Life Skills Training, Project Alert) or emerging (e.g., Promoting Alternative Thinking Strategies) evidence, along with 26 other interventions. Seventeen of 29 "mixed or emerging evidence" interventions either were exclusively school-based (n = 11) or included a school-based component (n = 6).

Although the review by Spoth and colleagues offers concrete examples of evidence-based interventions, it does not address why some school-based interventions were effective and others were not. Other recent literature reviews and meta-analyses have examined this issue. The findings suggest that the following elements are essential to developing and implementing effective school-based alcohol prevention interventions:

The interventions are theory-driven, with a particular focus on the social-influences model, which emphasizes helping students identify and resist social influences (e.g., by peers and media) to use alcohol.

- The interventions address social norms around alcohol use, reinforcing that alcohol use is not common or acceptable among youth.
- The interventions build personal and social skills that help students resist pressure to use alcohol.
- The interventions use interactive teaching techniques (e.g., small-group activities and role plays) to engage students.
- The interventions use same-aged students (i.e., peer leaders) to facilitate delivery of the program.
- The interventions integrate additional components to connect other segments of the community (e.g., parents) to the program.
- The interventions are conducted across multiple sessions and multiple years to ensure that an adequate "dose" of prevention is received by students and schools.
- The interventions provide adequate training and support for program facilitators (i.e., teachers, students).
- The interventions are both culturally and developmentally appropriate for the students they serve.

Two projects that are examples of programs meeting the criteria noted above are Project Northland and Communities that Care. These community-wide programs used evidence-based school curricula, supplemented with parental involvement, peer leadership, and community action to achieve reductions in the onset of alcohol use in early adolescence. Communities that Care is described in more detail in the article by Fagan and colleagues that focuses on community-based preventive interventions.

Table 20.1. School-Based Alcohol Prevention Interventions

The Most Promising School-Based Alcohol Prevention Interventions Identified by Spoth and Colleagues
Children younger than 10 years of age Linking the Interests of Families and Teachers Raising Healthy Children Seattle Social Development Project
Adolescents ages 10–15 years keepin' it REAL Midwestern Prevention Project/Project STAR Project Northland
Older participants ages 16 to more than 20 years Project Toward No Drug Abuse

Future Directions for School-Based Alcohol Prevention Interventions

Although the understanding of effective interventions to prevent underage alcohol use has grown substantially over the last few decades, especially for school-based approaches, additional research is warranted to fill remaining gaps in the knowledge base. For example, the existing literature does not include sufficient evidence to support or refute the short- or long-term efficacy of school-based interventions in elementary- or high-school settings and does not fully address interventions for special populations, including culturally specific programming. These points are considered in more detail below as suggestions for future directions for school-based research. Readers are directed to the reviews by Spoth and colleagues for additional discussion of needed improvements in conducting and reporting this research.

School-Based Interventions for Elementary-School and High-School Settings

As noted above, the majority of school-based alcohol prevention interventions have been conducted in middle schools. By comparison, far fewer interventions have been developed for elementary schools and high schools. In the review by Spoth and colleagues, only one school-based intervention for high-school students could be classified as most promising, and only one could be classified as having mixed or emerging evidence. However, alcohol use is particularly problematic during the high-school years. Nationwide, almost half of high-school seniors report consuming alcohol in the previous month, and one-third were drunk in the last month. Accordingly, sustained intervention throughout high school likely is necessary to maintain any changes in developmental trajectories of alcohol use achieved through interventions delivered in middle school, as was demonstrated by the high-school component of Project Northland. Further efforts to curb more problematic patterns of alcohol use, such as binge drinking, also are warranted during this period.

Additional efforts to design, develop, and test school-based interventions for younger age-groups (e.g., "tweens") are needed as well, given that school-based interventions seem to be most efficacious when delivered as a primary prevention program, with the strongest effects found in youth who have not yet begun to experiment with alcohol. Early onset of alcohol use during the teen or preteen years is of great concern because it can have substantial physical, social, and emotional health consequences for children and adolescents, including impairment of key brain functions and development. Of note, a large proportion of young adolescents use or begin to use alcohol before middle school. For example, in Project Northland Chicago, 17 percent of these urban sixth graders had started drinking alcohol before they entered middle school, and the proportion was even higher (i.e., 37%) in rural Minnesota, in the original Project Northland; moreover, these students were much less responsive to the intervention than students who had not begun drinking. These high rates of early alcohol use make it worthwhile to introduce earlier, universal approaches to alcohol prevention. For example, Spoth and colleagues suggested intervening in grades 3, 4, and 5; however, none of the existing school-based programs aimed at the later elementary-school years met the criteria for inclusion in their review.

School-Based Interventions for Special Populations

To date, the large majority of school-based interventions have been implemented with primarily White urban and suburban youth. The problem of alcohol use, however, is not limited to these populations. Alcohol use rates among school-going youth often are higher in rural settings, especially rates of binge drinking (i.e., five or more drinks in one sitting in the last 2 weeks) and drunkenness. With respect to ethnic groups, rates of alcohol use among Hispanic eighth graders exceed those of White eighth graders, followed by African Americans. Accordingly, the need for alcohol use prevention interventions tailored for these special populations is great. Although the body of research on this topic is growing, it requires even more attention. As Schinke and colleagues noted in a Cochrane review, culturally focused interventions may be an especially valuable approach to intervention over the long term. However, additional development and rigorous evaluation of this approach is required.

In their review, Spoth and colleagues identified a few school-based alcohol prevention interventions specifically designed for special populations (e.g., minority youth, rural youth) with promising or emerging evidence. For example, keepin' it REAL is a culturally grounded alcohol prevention program developed for and tested in Mexican and Mexican-American middle-school students. Instead of "translating" an existing school-based program originally designed for majority youth for use in this population, Hecht and colleagues crafted a successful program grounded from the beginning in ethnic norms and values. Their multicultural version, based on Latino, European-American, and African American norms and values, was especially effective at reducing alcohol use over time. Approaches like these that influence the deeper structure of an intervention might be necessary to effectively meet the needs of special populations as additional efforts are considered and subsequently undertaken to adapt existing evidence-based interventions for use in nonmajority, understudied groups.

Efforts to date to translate or adapt existing evidence-based interventions for special populations and settings have produced mixed results. For example, the adaptation of Project Northland for use with a multiethnic population in Chicago was unsuccessful at changing alcohol use behaviors among those urban middle-school youth, even though the adaptation included not only surface-structure changes (e.g., changes in text and graphics) but also the deep-structure changes (e.g., incorporating culturally specific values and norms) alluded to above. The original Project Northland in Minnesota had pursued a more proximal approach to intervention, with staff who were housed at the schools and with special emphasis given to school- and after-school-based activities, supplemented with parental involvement. The Chicago adaptation, in contrast, placed more emphasis on more distal intervention strategies, using staff who were housed in the community and emphasizing community organization to reduce access to alcohol. The results achieved with the two variants of the intervention suggest that in middle-school school students may require a more focused, hands-on approach to alcohol prevention. On the other hand, the Chicago implementation may have been less successful because alcohol use was less of a concern or priority in this population. Thus, in the Minnesota sample, alcohol use was the most serious problem found in the region of the State where the intervention was implemented, whereas in the Chicago sample other concerns (e.g., regarding other drugs or violence) were more prominent. Therefore, community needs, priorities, and readiness—as well as the question of how these can be shaped successfully—need to be considered carefully as translation research unfolds.

A final program worthy of note is Drug Abuse Resistance Education (D.A.R.E.). Although reviews of this program consistently show that it has little if any impact on alcohol and drug use, it continues to be widely used across the United States. To capitalize on the powerful dissemination mechanism of the D.A.R.E. program, Perry and colleagues developed and evaluated D.A.R.E. Plus, which was successful in reducing tobacco and alcohol use among boys. These positive outcomes were attributed to the "Plus" components, such as peer leadership, parental education, and neighborhood involvement, because the D.A.R.E. program alone did not demonstrate these outcomes.

Section 20.4

Adolescent Exposure to Substance Use Prevention Messages

This section includes text excerpted from "Exposure to Substance Use Prevention Messages among Adolescents," Substance Abuse and Mental Health Services Administration (SAMHSA), October 3, 2017.

Underage substance use is preventable, and adolescents are subjected to influences that may increase their risk for substance use or protect them from it. Substance use prevention programs are designed to reduce the influence of risk factors and increase the influence of protective factors. Parents can also affect substance use through conversations with their children. Research indicates that parents play a major role in their children's decisions, particularly with regard to health risk behaviors. Substance use prevention messages and programs are also provided through the media, schools, and other sources and have been shown to have an association with reduction in alcohol and illicit drug use. Providing adolescents with credible, accurate, and age-appropriate information about the harm associated with substance use is a key component in prevention programming. Prevention programming can be made more effective by gaining a better understanding of the ways in which adolescents are given prevention messages. Similarly, prevention programming can be better targeted to address underserved populations if the characteristics of adolescents not exposed to prevention messages or programs are known.

The National Survey on Drug Use and Health (NSDUH) is an annual survey of the civilian, noninstitutionalized population of the United States aged 12 years old or older and is the primary source for statistical information on illicit drug use, alcohol use, substance use disorders, and mental health issues. One of NSDUH's strengths is the large, nationally representative sample, which allows for the examination of specific subgroups in the United States, such as adolescents. NSDUH is a face-to-face household interview survey that is fielded continuously throughout the year.

NSDUH asks adolescents aged 12–17 whether they have been exposed to prevention messages in the past 12 months through parental sources (i.e., talked with at least one of their parents during the past year about the dangers of tobacco, alcohol, or drug use) and media sources outside of school (i.e., seen or heard any alcohol or drug prevention messages from sources such as posters, pamphlets, radio, or television). In addition, adolescents are asked whether they have been exposed to prevention messages in the past 12 months through school sources (i.e., special classes about drugs or alcohol in school; films, lectures, discussions, or printed information about drugs or alcohol in regular school classes such as health or physical education; or films, lectures, discussions, or distribution of printed information about drugs or alcohol outside of regular classes such as in a special assembly).

Adolescents are also asked about whether they have participated in the past 12 months in an alcohol, tobacco, or drug prevention program outside of school. Adolescents are also asked about whether they have participated in the past 12 months in an alcohol, tobacco, or drug prevention program outside of school.

This section examines adolescents' exposure to substance use prevention messages using data from the 2002–2015 NSDUHs. It also uses 2015 NSDUH data to examine exposure to prevention messages by key demographic characteristics. The 2015 estimates are based on a total sample size of 17,000 adolescents aged 12–17. All differences discussed in this report are statistically significant at the 0.05 level.

Trends in Exposure to Prevention Messages

From 2002–2015, about 3 out of 4 adolescents aged 12–17 were exposed to substance use prevention messages in the media or at school and about 1 out of 2 adolescents talked to their parents about substance use (Figure 20.1). In 2015, 73.3 percent of adolescents aged 12–17 had seen or heard drug or alcohol use prevention messages in the past year from media sources outside of school, such as posters, pamphlets, the radio, or television (Figure 20.1). The percentage of adolescents who had seen substance use prevention messages from a

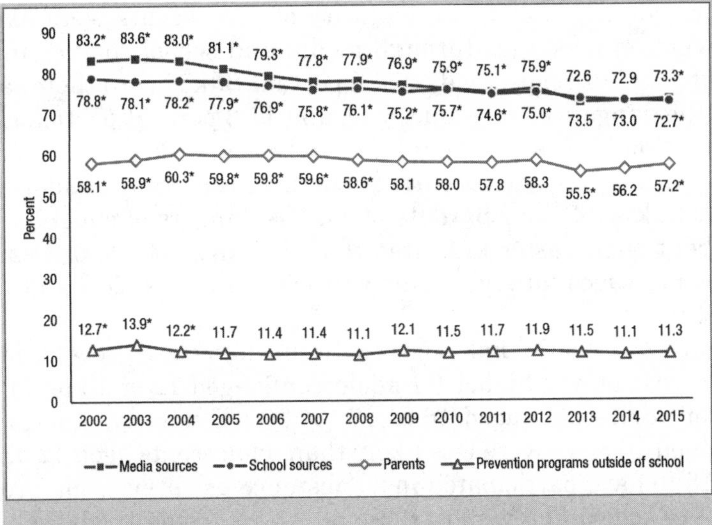

* Difference between this estimate and the 2015 estimate is statistically significant at the .05 level.

Note: Only adolescents who were enrolled in school at the time of the interview were included in the estimates of exposure to prevention messages from school-based sources.

Figure 20.1. *Trends in Exposure to Substance Use Prevention Messages in the past Year among Adolescents Aged 12–17: 2002–2015*

media source was lower in 2015 than the percentages in 2002–2012, but it was similar to the percentages in 2013 and 2014.

In 2015, 72.7 percent of adolescents who were enrolled in school in the past year had seen or heard drug or alcohol use prevention messages at school. The percentage of adolescents in school who saw or heard substance use prevention messages at school was lower in 2015 than the percentages in 2002–2012, but it was similar to the percentages in 2013 and 2014. In 2002, for example, 78.8 percent of adolescents who were enrolled in school were exposed to substance use prevention messages at school. In 2015, about 1 in 9 adolescents (11.3 %) had participated in alcohol, tobacco, or drug use prevention programs outside of school in the past year. This estimate was similar to the percentages from 2005–2014, but it was lower than the percentages in 2002–2004. Nevertheless, in any given year since 2002, the majority of adolescents did not participate in prevention programs outside of school in the past year.

Exposure to Prevention Messages

As previously noted, the majority of adolescents were exposed to prevention messages through media and school sources in 2015 (73.3 and 72.7%, respectively), 57.2 percent talked with their parents about the dangers of substance use, and 11.3 percent participated in a prevention program outside of school (Figure 20.1). Nonexposure to prevention messages occurred where 42.8 percent of adolescents did not talk with their parents about the dangers of substance use, and about one-quarter indicated that they did not see or hear prevention messages through media and school sources (26.7 and 27.3%, respectively).

Figure 20.2 shows that exposure to substance use prevention messages in school was higher for adolescents aged 12 or 13 or 14 or 15 than for adolescents aged 16 or 17 (67.9%). Similarly, older adolescents aged 16 or 17 were less likely than adolescents aged 12 or 13 or 14 or 15 to have participated in a substance use prevention program outside of school (9.5 versus 12.9 and 11.5%, respectively). Younger adolescents were less likely than older adolescents to have seen prevention messages via media sources. Older adolescents aged 16 or 17 were less likely than adolescents aged 14 or 15 to have talked with their parents about substance use (55.6 versus 59.0%); however, there were no differences in the percentage of adolescents aged 12 or 13 who talked with parents compared with the percentage of adolescents aged 14 or 15 or 16 or 17.

The trends in exposure to prevention messages were also examined by age group. Exposure to prevention messages in school and via media sources were generally lower in 2015 than in prior years for adolescent each age group. There are have been fewer changes in the trends in adolescent exposure to prevention messaging by talking to their parents or from sources outside of school by age group.

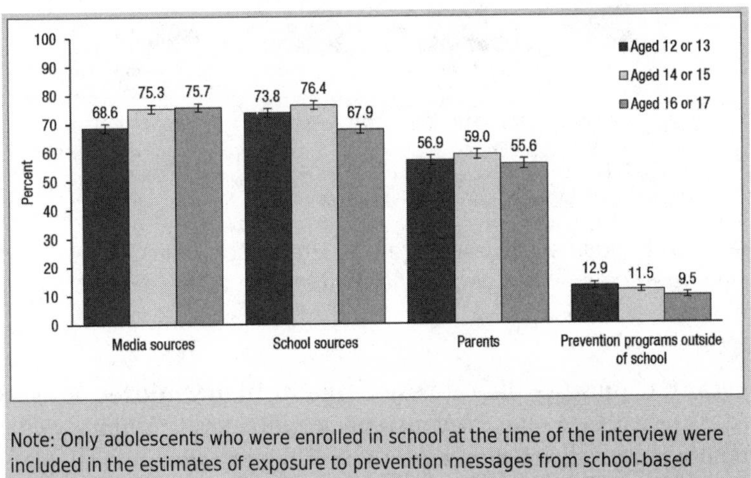

Note: Only adolescents who were enrolled in school at the time of the interview were included in the estimates of exposure to prevention messages from school-based sources.

Figure 20.2. *Exposure to Substance Use Prevention Messages in the past Year among Adolescents Aged 12–17, by Age Group: 2015*

In 2015, female adolescents were more likely than males to have been exposed to prevention messages through media sources, to have been exposed to prevention messages through school sources, and to have talked with a parent about the dangers of substance use in the past year (Figure 20.3). For example, 75.0 percent of females were exposed to prevention messages through media sources compared with 71.8 percent of males. Males were more likely than females to have participated in a substance use prevention program outside of school (11.9 versus 10.6%).

Between the early 2000s and 2011, the percentages of adolescents who were exposed to drug or alcohol use prevention messages in the past year through media and school sources generally declined; however, in each year, the majority of adolescents were exposed to substance use prevention messages through these sources. The percentage of adolescents who talked with their parents about the dangers of substance use has declined slightly since 2002, and in 2015, about 42.8 percent of adolescents did not have such conversations. Research

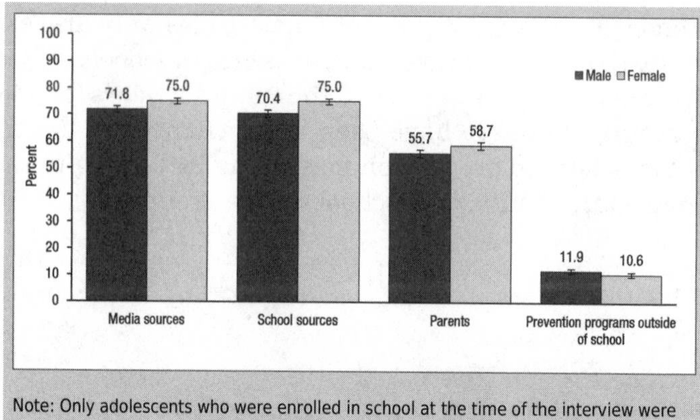

Note: Only adolescents who were enrolled in school at the time of the interview were included in the estimates of exposure to prevention messages from school-based sources.

Figure 20.3. *Exposure to Substance Use Prevention Messages in the past Year among Adolescents Aged 12–17, by Gender: 2015*

suggests that parents play a major role in their children's decisions regarding substance use. Prevention specialists may want to continue to promote parent discussion with their children regarding the dangers of substance use. The Substance Abuse and Mental Health Services Administration's (SAMHSA) "Talk. They Hear You." campaign aims to reduce underage drinking by providing parents with information and resources they need to address the issue of alcohol with their children.

Although the majority of adolescents are receiving prevention messages, practitioners, policymakers, educators, and parents may also want to consider the percentage of adolescents who were not exposed to prevention messages through these sources. For example, 27.3 percent of in-school adolescents did not see or hear prevention messages through school sources. These findings suggest the need for continued monitoring of exposure to prevention messaging to assess whether the nation's adolescents are seeing or hearing substance use prevention messages. However, the cross-sectional nature of the NSDUH data precludes making any causal connections between perceptions of risk and actual substance use. For example, it is not possible to determine based on these data whether respondents' perceptions of low risk of harm from substance use preceded and influenced their decision to engage in substance use or if their substance use preceded and influenced their perceptions of low risk of harm. It would be useful to conduct longitudinal research that explores whether increases in the percentages of people perceiving great risk of harm from substance use coincide with decreases in use.

Chapter 21

Community-Based Alcohol Abuse Prevention

Chapter Contents

Section 21.1

Strategies for Local Alcohol-Related Policies and Practices

This section includes text excerpted from "Preventing Excessive Alcohol Consumption," Centers for Disease Control and Prevention (CDC), May 2015.

Excessive alcohol consumption is a risk factor for many health and social problems, contributing to 88,000 deaths each year in the United States. The estimated economic cost of excessive drinking in the United States was $223.5 billion. Drinking too much can cause immediate harm such as injuries from motor vehicle crashes, violence, and alcohol poisoning, and drinking too much overtime can cause chronic diseases, such as cancer and heart disease.

The following content is designed to help public health program planners, community advocates, educators, and policymakers find proven intervention strategies—including programs, services, and policies—for preventing excessive alcohol consumption and related harms. It can help decision-makers in both public and private sectors make choices about what intervention strategies are best for their communities. This section summarizes to help select intervention strategies you can adapt for your community to:

- Reduce excessive alcohol use, including binge drinking and underage drinking
- Reduce the risk of chronic conditions such as liver disease, high blood pressure, heart disease, and cancer
- Reduce violent crime, motor vehicle injuries, and alcohol-exposed pregnancies
- Reduce youth access to alcohol

The Public Health Challenge

Excessive Drinking Has a Substantial Public Health Impact

Table 21.1. Average Annual Alcohol-Attributable Deaths in the United States (2006–2010)

Cause	Number of Annual Fatalities
Chronic Causes (e.g., Liver Disease)	38,253
Acute Causes (e.g., Homicide)	49,544
Total for all causes	87,798

- Drinking too much alcohol is responsible for 88,000 deaths annually, including 1 in 10 deaths among working-age adults in the United States.
- Excessive alcohol use costs the United States $223.5 billion—or $1.90 per drink—in 2006 due to lost workplace productivity, healthcare expenses, and crime. Federal, state, and local governments paid 42 percent of these costs—or 80 cents per drink.
- About 9 in 10 excessive drinkers are not alcohol dependent, or addicted to alcohol

Binge Drinking Is the Main Problem

- Binge drinking is defined as having 4 or more drinks on an occasion (2–3 hours) for women, or 5 or more drinks on an occasion for men.
- Binge drinking is the most common and most dangerous pattern of excessive drinking. It is responsible for more than half of the deaths and three-quarters of the economic costs associated with excessive alcohol use.
- 1 in 6 adults binge drinks about four times a month, consuming about eight drinks per binge.
- About 1 in 4 high school students report binge drinking.

Evaluating the Evidence

- The Task Force findings and recommendations for interventions strategies to prevent excessive alcohol consumption are based on systematic reviews of the available evidence.
- The systematic reviews look at the results of research and evaluation studies published in peer-reviewed journals and other sources.

- Each systematic review looks at the intervention strategy's effectiveness and how it works in different populations and settings. If found effective, cost and return on investment are also reviewed when available.

Summarizing the Findings on Excessive Alcohol Consumption

Six of the ten Task Force recommendations related to reducing excessive alcohol consumption are below:

- **Increasing alcohol taxes.** Increasing the price of alcohol by raising taxes has proven effective in reducing consumption, leading to fewer deaths and injuries due to motor vehicle crashes, liver disease, violence, and other alcohol-related problems. For every 10 percent increase in price, alcohol consumption is expected to decrease by more than 7 percent. Public health effects are expected to be proportional to the size of the tax increase. Higher alcohol prices may also reduce underage drinking.
- **Dram shop liability.** Dram shop (or commercial host) liability refers to laws that hold alcohol retailers liable for injuries or deaths caused by a patron who was illegally served or sold alcohol because they were either intoxicated or under the age of 21 at the time of service. Commercial host liability is effective in preventing and reducing alcohol-related harms. For example, there was a median 6.4 percent reduction in deaths resulting from motor vehicle crashes in states with commercial host liability.
- **Regulation of alcohol outlet density.** Alcohol outlet density refers to the number and concentration of alcohol retailers (e.g., bars, restaurants, and liquor stores) in an area. Higher alcohol outlet density is associated with excessive alcohol use and related harms, including injuries and violence. Alcohol outlet density is often regulated by licensing or zoning regulations. States vary in the extent to which they allow local governments to regulate the licensing and placement of retail alcohol outlets.
- **Electronic screening and brief interventions (e-SBI).** The delivery of screening and brief interventions for excessive alcohol use using electronic devices, such as computers, is effective for reducing self-reported excessive alcohol consumption

and alcohol-related problems among intervention participants. Some e-SBI programs are fully automated while others combine screening by a health professional with the automated delivery of counseling services. The use of e-SBI can reduce the amount of time required to deliver screening and counseling services.

- **Enhanced enforcement of laws prohibiting sales to minors.** Enforcing minimum drinking age laws through retailer compliance checks and sanctions is effective in reducing sales of alcohol to minors in commercial settings by a median of 42 percent. Enhanced enforcement programs are often part of multi-component, community-based efforts to curb underage drinking.

The Task Force recommends against the further privatization of retail alcohol sales in settings with current government control of retail sales. Privatization, which allows nongovernmental retailers to sell a type of alcoholic beverage (e.g., distilled spirits), was found to increase the per capita sales of the privatized beverage type by a median of 44.4 percent, and decrease the sale of other types of alcohol by 2.2 percent. Privatization often results in increases in alcohol outlet density, days and hours of sales, and alcohol advertising, which are associated with increased consumption and alcohol-related harms.

Task Force Findings on Excessive Alcohol Consumption

The Community Preventive Services Task Force (CPSTF) has released the following findings on what works in public health to prevent excessive alcohol consumption and related harms. Use the findings to identify intervention strategies you could use for your community.

Understanding the Findings

The Task Force bases its findings and recommendations on systematic reviews of the scientific literature. With oversight from the Task Force, scientists and subject matter experts from the Centers for Disease Control and Prevention (CDC) conduct these reviews in collaboration with a wide range of government, academic, policy, and practice-based partners. Based on the strength of the evidence, the Task Force assigns each intervention to one of the categories below.

Intervention	Task Force Finding
Interventions Directed to the General Population	
Increasing alcohol taxes	●
Regulation of alcohol outlet density	●
Dram shop liability	●
Maintaining limits on days of sale	●
Maintaining limits on hours of sale	●
Electronic screening and brief interventions (e-SBI)	●
Overservice law enforcement initiatives	◆
Responsible beverage service training	◆
Privatization of retail alcohol sales	▲
Interventions Directed to Underage Drinkers	
Enhanced enforcement of laws prohibiting sales to minors	●

Figure 21.1. *Types of Interventions That Prevent Excessive Alcohol Consumption*

CATEGORY	DESCRIPTION	ICON
Recommended	There is strong or sufficient evidence that the intervention is **effective**. This finding is based on the number of studies, how well the studies were designed and carried out, and the consistency and strength of the results.	●
Insufficient Evidence	There is **not enough evidence** to determine whether the intervention is effective. This does not mean the intervention does not work. There is not enough research available or the results are too inconsistent to make a firm conclusion about the intervention's effectiveness. The Task Force encourages those who use interventions with insufficient evidence to evaluate their efforts.	◆
Recommended Against	There is strong or sufficient evidence that the strategy is **harmful or not effective**.	▲

Figure 21.2. *Effectiveness of Interventions*

Section 21.2

Town Hall Meetings Mobilize Communities to Prevent and Reduce Underage Alcohol Use

This section includes text excerpted from "Town Hall Meetings Mobilize Communities to Prevent and Reduce Underage Alcohol Use: Moving Communities beyond Awareness to Action," Substance Abuse and Mental Health Services Administration (SAMHSA), 2014. Reviewed April 2018.

Town Hall Meetings as a Strategic Response to the Problem

U.S. Surgeon General Kenneth P. Moritsugu, M.D., M.P.H., called upon all communities to confront underage drinking as "a widespread and persistent public health and safety problem that creates serious personal, social, and economic consequences for adolescents, their families, communities, and the nation as a whole."

Among the actions recommended by the Surgeon General are that communities should:

- Promote the idea that underage alcohol use is a local problem that local citizens can solve through concerted and dedicated action;
- Establish organizations and coalitions committed to forming a local culture that disapproves of underage alcohol use, that works diligently to prevent and reduce it, and that is dedicated to informing the public about the extent and consequences of underage drinking; and
- Work to ensure that members of the community are aware of the latest research on adolescent alcohol use and, in particular, the adverse consequences of alcohol use on underage drinkers and other members of the community who suffer from its second-hand effects.

Town Hall Meetings, which bring diverse community stakeholders together to confront the issue of underage drinking, are a strategic response to the Surgeon General's recommendations and provide an effective tool for meeting requirements of SAMHSA's Strategic Prevention Framework and other federal grants.

Some states use Town Hall Meetings as an essential part of their overall strategic approach to underage drinking prevention:

- California provides statewide support for CBOs that sign up to conduct Town Hall Meetings with a package of state-produced printed materials (e.g., posters, brochures, California-specific fact sheets) containing underage drinking prevention messages and information. Host CBOs include many chapters of Friday Night Live, the state's youth prevention program, which trains high school students to organize and participate in local Town Hall Meetings and be spokespersons for effective alcohol control policies. A state analysis of 2010 Town Hall Meetings found that more than 20 percent of event organizers planned to introduce a local social host ordinance. In 2012, 92 SAMHSA-sponsored Town Hall Meetings were held in California.
- In Iowa, a final Town Hall Meeting serves as a summary of issues and recommendations stemming from statewide and coordinated events. This input is compiled as a report to the state to help it assess its progress in reducing and preventing alcohol use and its consequences. In 2012, 34 SAMHSA-sponsored Town Hall Meetings were held across Iowa.
- Massachusetts' Town Hall Meetings provide strong support for the primary focus of the state's SAMHSA Block Grant to prevent underage drinking among youth between the ages of 12 and 18, and the Massachusetts Bureau of Substance Abuse Services' efforts to foster environmental prevention statewide. For example, communities used Town Hall Meetings during 2012 to inform their members about the potential legal consequences related to the state's social host law. In 2012, 60 SAMHSA-sponsored Town Hall Meetings were held across Massachusetts. Massachusetts Lieutenant Governor Tim Murray provided top-level support and participated in a kickoff event for statewide Town Hall Meetings.
- In Texas, Texans Standing Tall takes the lead in promoting evidence-based alcohol prevention policies. The group uses Town Hall Meetings, fashioned in Texas as "regional policy forums,"

to organize communities to make strategic use of evidence-based strategies. Texans Standing Tall also conducts its own rigorous evaluation of these community gatherings and reports impressive survey responses from its Town Hall Meeting participants. More than half (54.7%) said they spoke with decision-makers about their policy and enforcement concerns; 70.8 percent said that their community participation and involvement in underage drinking prevention increased because of the Town Hall Meetings they attended.

- Washington has been a strong and consistent partner in the Town Hall Meeting initiative. In 2012, 74 CBOs across Washington planned 77 Town Hall Meetings to support the state's Coalition to Reduce Underage Drinking's (RUaD) objective to promote social host responsibility ordinances and enforcement. Several Town Hall Meetings adopted the RUaD campaign theme of "Let's Draw the Line Between Youth and Alcohol." Promotion of SAMHSA-supported Town Hall Meetings on the RUaD website ensured that the majority of local groups who signed on for the SAMHSA initiative were already a part of the state's network of organizations targeting underage drinking in their communities and actively supporting the state's prevention agenda.

Section 21.3

Communities That Care (CTC): An Evidence-Based Substance-Use Prevention System

This section includes text excerpted from "Communities That Care System Helps Prevent Problem Behaviors in Youth Through 12th Grade," National Institute on Drug Abuse (NIDA), December 31, 2014. Reviewed April 2018.

The latest evaluation of a 24-town trial of Communities That Care (CTC) found that CTC-associated reductions in current substance use and delinquency, which had been observed when the children were in grades 8 and 10, were no longer evident in 12th grade. A benefit of

CTC persisted, however: Although similar percentages of youths who had lived in CTC-using and comparison towns while in middle school reported that they had avoided those behaviors in 12th grade, higher percentages of those in CTC-using towns had done so in all previous grades as well.

Communities adopting CTC select from a roster of evidence-based prevention interventions those that target what school surveys of young people indicate are the most pertinent risk factors for the most pressing behavioral problems. CTC developer Dr. J. David Hawkins and colleagues at the University of Seattle in Washington initiated the trial in 2004, randomly assigning 12 towns to implement the program and 12 others to serve as control communities.

Altogether, more than 4,400 5th graders entered the trial, 55 percent of whom received CTC-sponsored interventions in their families, schools, and communities. In follow-up surveys when they were in 8th and 10th grade, students in the CTC communities reported lower rates of initiation of tobacco use, alcohol use, and delinquent activity than those in the comparison towns, as well as less current tobacco and alcohol use and binge drinking (see Prevention Program Averts Initiation of Alcohol and Tobacco Use and Prevention System Has Lasting Effects, Benefit Exceeds Costs). The researchers estimated that the program-associated reductions in problem behaviors would save the CTC towns more than $5 for every dollar invested in the program.

More than 90 percent of the original student participants responded to the survey that forms the basis of the new evaluation, including 75 percent who were attending 12th grade and 25 percent who had left school. Those from the CTC communities were about 30 percent more likely than those in the control communities to have never used any substance—including alcohol, cigarettes, and marijuana—over the 8 years since the study began. They also were almost 20 percent more likely to have never engaged in delinquent behavior. The survey results also disclosed, however, that the portions of participants who had used drugs, alcohol, or tobacco within the last year were similar in the CTC and control towns.

Dr. Hawkins comments that CTC continued to benefit youths through 12th grade, even though the CTC communities in this study focused on preventive interventions for youths in grades 6 through 9. He suggests that extending the interventions to target risk factors through the high school years could strengthen effects on substance use and delinquent behaviors on the cusp of adulthood.

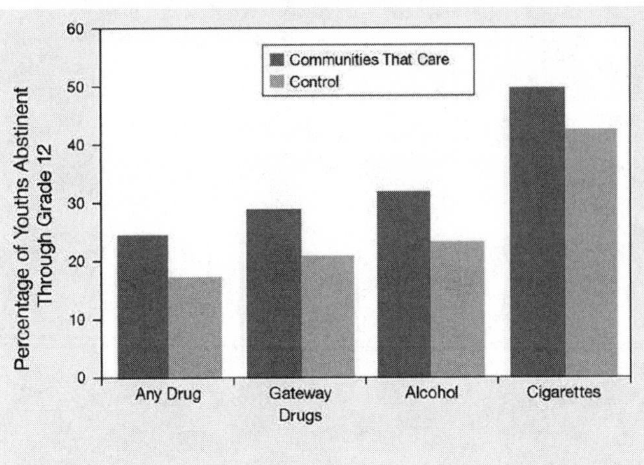

Figure 21.3. *Percentages of Youths Reporting That They Had Never Used Drugs, Alcohol, or Cigarettes*

Chapter 22

The Minimum Legal Drinking Age (MLDA) Law

A Minimum Legal Drinking Age (MLDA) of 21 Saves Lives and Protects Health

Minimum Legal Drinking Age (MLDA) laws specify the legal age when an individual can purchase or publicly consume alcoholic beverages. The MLDA in the United States is 21 years. However, prior to the enactment of the National Minimum Drinking Age Act of 1984, the legal age when alcohol could be purchased varied from state to state.

An age 21 MLDA is recommended by the:

- American Academy of Pediatrics (AAP)
- Community Preventive Services Task Force (CPSTF)
- Mothers Against Drunk Driving (MADD)
- National Highway Traffic Safety Administration (NHTSA)
- National Prevention Council
- National Academy of Sciences (National Research Council and Institute of Medicine)

This chapter includes text excerpted from "Alcohol and Public Health—Fact Sheets—Age 21 Minimum Legal Drinking Age," Centers for Disease Control and Prevention (CDC), October 20, 2016.

The Age 21 MLDA Saves Lives and Improves Health

- **Fewer motor vehicle crashes**: States that increased the legal drinking age to 21 saw a 16 percent median decline in motor vehicle crashes.
- **Decreased drinking**:
  - After all states adopted an age 21 MLDA, drinking during the previous month among persons aged 18–20 years declined from 59 percent in 1985 to 40 percent in 1991.
  - Drinking among people aged 21–25 also declined significantly when states adopted the age 21 MLDA, from 70 percent in 1985 to 56 percent in 1991.
- **Other outcomes**: There is also evidence that the age 21 MLDA protects drinkers from alcohol and other drug dependence, adverse birth outcomes, and suicide and homicide.

Drinking by Those under the Age of 21 Is a Public Health Problem

- Excessive drinking contributes to more than 4,300 deaths among people below the age of 21 in the United States each year.
- Underage drinking cost the U.S. economy $24 billion in 2010.
- There were about 189,000 emergency department visits by people under age 21 for injuries and other conditions linked to alcohol in 2010.
- More than 90 percent of the alcohol consumed by those under age 21 is consumed by binge drinkers (defined as 5 or more drinks per occasion for boys; 4 or more drinks per occasion for girls).

Drinking by those below the age of 21 is also strongly linked with:

- Death from alcohol poisoning
- Unintentional injuries, such as car crashes, falls, burns, and drowning
- Suicide and violence, such as fighting and sexual assault
- Changes in brain development
- School performance problems, such as higher absenteeism and poor or failing grades

- Alcohol dependence later in life
- Other risk behaviors such as smoking, abuse of other drugs, and risky sexual behaviors

Alcohol-Impaired Driving

Drinking by those below the age of 21 is strongly associated with alcohol-impaired driving.

The 2015 Youth Risk Behavior Survey found that among high school students, during the past 30 days.

- 8 percent drove after drinking alcohol
- 20 percent rode with a driver who had been drinking alcohol

Rates of Drinking and Binge Drinking among Those under 21

The 2015 Youth Risk Behavior Surveillance System found that among high school students, 33 percent drank alcohol and 18 percent binge drank during the past 30 days. In 2015, the Monitoring the Future Survey reported that 10 percent of 8th graders and 35 percent of 12th graders drank alcohol during the past 30 days, and 5 percent of 8th graders and 17 percent of 12th graders binge drank during the past 2 weeks.

Enforcing the Age 21 MLDA

Communities can enhance the effectiveness of age 21 MLDA laws by actively enforcing them.

- A Community Guide review found that enhanced enforcement of laws prohibiting alcohol sales to minors reduced the ability of youthful-looking decoys to purchase alcoholic beverages by a median of 42 percent.
- Alcohol sales to minors are still a common problem in communities
    - For example, in 2014, the New York City Department of Health and Mental Hygiene and the New York State Liquor Authority found that more than half (58%) of the licensed alcohol retailers in the City sold alcohol to underage decoys.

Part Three

The Physical Effects and Consequences of Alcohol Abuse

Chapter 23

Blood Alcohol Concentration (BAC)

Chapter Contents

Section 23.1

BAC and Alcohol Impairment

This section contains text excerpted from the following sources: Text beginning with the heading "What Is Blood Alcohol Concentration (BAC)?" is excerpted from the "The ABCs of BAC," National Highway Traffic Safety Administration (NHTSA), July 2016; Text under the heading "Estimating Blood Alcohol Levels in Children" is excerpted from "Estimating Blood Alcohol Levels in Children," National Institute on Alcohol Abuse and Alcoholism (NIAAA), September 2009. Reviewed April 2018.

What Is Blood Alcohol Concentration (BAC)?

The amount of alcohol in a person's body is measured by the weight of the alcohol in a certain volume of blood (measured in grams per deciliter). This is called the blood alcohol concentration. Alcohol is absorbed directly through the walls of the stomach and the small intestine, goes into the bloodstream, and travels throughout the body and to the brain. Alcohol is quickly absorbed and can be measured within 30–70 minutes after a person has had a drink.

Does the Type of Alcohol I Drink Affect My BAC?

No. A drink is a drink, is a drink. A typical drink equals about half an ounce of alcohol (.54 ounces, to be exact). This is the approximate amount of alcohol found in one shot of distilled spirits, one 5-ounce glass of wine, and one 12-ounce beer.

What Affects My BAC?

How fast a person's BAC rises varies based on a number of factors:

- **The number of drinks.** The more you drink, the higher your BAC.
- **How fast you drink.** When alcohol is consumed quickly, you will reach a higher BAC than when it is consumed over a longer period of time.
- **Your gender.** Women generally have less water and more body fat per pound of body weight than men. Alcohol does not go into

fat cells as easily as other cells, so more alcohol remains in the blood of women.

- **Your weight.** The more you weigh, the more water is present in your body. This water dilutes the alcohol and lowers the BAC.
- **Food in your stomach.** Absorption will be slowed if you've had something to eat.

What about Other Medications or Drugs?

Medications or drugs will not change your BAC. However, if you drink alcohol while taking certain medications or drugs, you may feel—and be—more impaired, which can affect your ability to perform driving-related tasks.

When Am I Impaired?

Because of the number of factors that affect BAC, it is very difficult to assess your own BAC or impairment. Even small amounts of alcohol affect one's brain and the ability to drive. People often swear they are "fine" after several drinks—but in fact, the failure to recognize alcohol impairment is often a symptom of impairment.

While the lower stages of alcohol impairment are undetectable to others, the drinker knows vaguely when the "buzz" begins. A person will likely be too impaired to drive before looking or maybe even feeling "drunk."

How Will I Know I'm Impaired, and Why Should I Care?

Alcohol steadily decreases a person's ability to drive a motor vehicle safely. The more you drink, the greater the effect. As with BAC, the signs of impairment differ with the individual.

Drivers with a BAC of .08 are approximately 4 times more likely to crash than drivers with a BAC of zero. At a BAC of .15, drivers are at least 12 times more likely to crash than drivers with a BAC of zero. The risk of crashing is even greater for young males. Further, many studies have shown that even small amounts of alcohol can impair a person's ability to drive.

Every state has passed a law making it illegal to drive with a BAC of .08 or higher. A driver also can be arrested with a BAC below .08 when a law enforcement officer has probable cause, based on the driver's behavior.

The following table contains some of the more common symptoms people exhibit at various BAC levels, and the probable effects on driving ability.

Table 23.1. Blood Alcohol Concentration and Alcohol Impairment

Blood Alcohol Concentration (BAC)	Typical Effects	Predictable Effects on Driving
0.02	• Some loss of judgment • Relaxation • Slight body warmth • Altered mood	• Decline in visual functions (rapid tracking of a moving target) • Decline in ability to perform two tasks at the same time (divided attention)
0.05	• Exaggerated behavior • May have loss of small-muscle control (e.g., focusing your eyes) • Impaired judgment • Usually good feeling • Lowered alertness • Release of inhibition	• Reduced coordination • Reduced ability to track moving objects • Difficulty steering • Reduced response to emergency driving situation
0.08	• Muscle coordination becomes poor (e.g., balance, speech, vision, reaction time, and hearing) • Harder to detect danger • Impaired judgment, self-control, reasoning, and memory	• Concentration • Short-term memory loss • Speed control • Reduced information processing capability (e.g., signal detection, visual search) • Impaired perception
0.10	• Clear deterioration of reaction time and control • Slurred speech, poor coordination, and slowed thinking	• Reduced ability to maintain lane position and brake appropriately
0.15	• Far less muscle control than normal • Vomiting may occur (unless this level is reached slowly or a person has developed a high tolerance for alcohol) • Significant loss of balance	• Substantial impairment in vehicle control, attention to driving task, and unnecessary visual and auditory information processing

What Can I Do to Stay Safe When I Plan on Drinking?

If you plan on drinking, plan not to drive. You should:

- Plan a safe way home in advance and never drive after drinking
- Designate a sober driver
- Use a taxi, call a sober friend or family member, or use public transportation
- Download National Highway Traffic Safety Administration's (NHTSA) SaferRide mobile app, to easily call a taxi or a friend for a ride home. The app can also help you identify your location, if needed.
- Always wear your seatbelt. It's your best defense against impaired drivers.

Estimating Blood Alcohol Levels in Children

Drink for drink, the average blood alcohol concentrations (BACs) attained by children and adolescents are much higher than those seen among college students or adults, according to a study supported by National Institute of Arthritis Abuse and Alcoholism (NIAAA).

Using previously published health surveys and scientific reports, researchers derived total body water data and alcohol elimination rates—key variables in the BAC equation—for individuals ranging in age from 9–17. With that information, researchers were able to modify the equation used for estimating BACs in adults to estimate the BACs that theoretically would result after children and adolescents consume various numbers of drinks. No alcohol was provided to children or adolescents as part of this research.

With the modified equation, researchers can better determine how to assess child or adolescent binge drinking. NIAAA defines binge drinking as a pattern of alcohol consumption that brings BAC to .08 grams percent or above, the legal limit for driving in all 50 States. For the typical adult male, this pattern corresponds to consuming 5 or more drinks in about 2 hours (4 or more drinks for adult females). A drink is defined as an alcohol beverage that contains 0.6 fluid ounces or 14 grams of "pure" alcohol, the approximate content in a 12-ounce regular beer, 5-ounce glass of wine, or a 1½ -ounce shot of 80-proof distilled spirits.

The study determined that girls aged 9–17 can be "legally intoxicated" after having as few as 3 drinks in a 2-hour period. Similarly, the study's authors estimate that a BAC of .08 or higher would also result among boys aged 9–13 who consume 3 drinks within 2 hours.

According to the study's author, John E. Donovan, Ph.D., the findings suggest that children may experience physical and psychological effects after drinking less than a full drink. Research has shown that the expectation of experiencing such effects increases the likelihood of starting to drink and of involvement in problem drinking in adolescence.

Section 23.2

Alcohol Use Disorders

This section contains text excerpted from the following sources: Text beginning with the heading "What Are Alcohol Use Disorders (AUDs)?" is excerpted from "Alcohol," National Institute on Drug Abuse (NIDA) for Teens, January 2016; Text under the heading "How Many People Die of Alcohol Poisoning?" is excerpted from "Vital Signs—Alcohol Poisoning Deaths," Centers for Disease Control and Prevention (CDC), January 6, 2015.

What Are Alcohol Use Disorders (AUDs)?

Alcohol use disorders (AUDs) are medical conditions that doctors diagnose when someone's drinking causes them distress or harm.

What Is a Standard Drink?

Many people are surprised to learn what counts as a drink. The amount of liquid in your glass, can, or bottle is not necessarily equal to how much alcohol is in your drink. A standard drink is:

- 12 ounces of beer (about 5% alcohol)
- 8 ounces of malt liquor—beer with a high alcohol content (about 7% alcohol)
- 5 ounces of table wine (about 12% alcohol)
- 1.5 ounces (a "shot") of liquor, like gin, rum, vodka, tequila, or whiskey (about 40% alcohol)

No level of drinking is safe or legal for anyone under age 21, but unfortunately, many teens drink—and they often drink multiple drinks, which is very dangerous.

How Does Alcohol Affect the Teenage Brain?

When teens drink, alcohol affects their brains in the short-term—but repeated drinking can also impact it down the road, especially as their brains grow and develop.

Short-Term Consequences of Intoxication (Being "Drunk")

- An intoxicated person has a harder time making good decisions.
- A person is less aware that his/her behavior may be inappropriate or risky.
- A person may be more likely to engage in risky behavior, including drinking and driving, sexual activity (like unprotected sex) and aggressive or violent behavior.
- A person is less likely to recognize potential danger.

Long-Term Consequences as the Teen Brain Develops

- Research shows that drinking during the teen years could interfere with normal brain development and change the brain in ways that:
    - Have negative effects on information processing and learning
    - Increase the risk of developing an alcohol use disorder later in life

How Does Alcohol Affect Your Body?

People who drink are affected even before they show signs of being drunk, especially when it comes to decision-making abilities. At first, alcohol causes people to feel upbeat and excited. But this is temporary and they shouldn't be fooled.

If drinking continues, the effects on the body—and the potential risks—multiply. Here's what can happen:

- **Inhibitions and memory:** People may say and do things that they will regret later, or possibly not remember at all. Inhibitions are lost leading to poor decision making.

- **Decision-making skills:** When they drink, individuals are more likely to be impulsive. They may be at greater risk for having an alcohol-related traffic crash, getting into fights, or making unwise decisions about sex.
- **Coordination and physical control:** When drinking leads to loss of balance, slurred speech, and blurred vision, even normal activities can become more dangerous.
- **Death:** Drinking too much alcohol can also lead to death. If people drink too much, they will eventually get sleepy and pass out. Reflexes like gagging and breathing can be suppressed. That means they could vomit and choke, or stop breathing completely.

And finally, it's easy to misjudge how long alcohol's effects last. Alcohol continues to affect the brain and body long after the last drink has been finished. Even after someone stops drinking, alcohol in the stomach and intestine continues to enter the bloodstream, impairing judgment and coordination for hours.

What Is Alcohol Poisoning and How Can I Help Someone Who May Be Suffering from It?

Alcohol poisoning occurs when there is so much alcohol in a person's bloodstream that areas of the brain controlling basic life-support systems—such as breathing, heart rate, and temperature control—begin to shut down.

Symptoms of alcohol poisoning include:

- Confusion
- Difficulty remaining conscious
- Vomiting
- Seizures
- Trouble with breathing
- Slow heart rate
- Clammy skin
- Dulled responses, such as no gag reflex (which prevents choking)
- Extremely low body temperature
- Death

If you suspect someone has alcohol poisoning, call 911 and get medical help immediately. Cold showers, hot coffee, or walking will NOT reverse the effects of alcohol overdose and could actually make things worse.

How Many People Die of Alcohol Poisoning?

On average, 6 people died every day from alcohol poisoning in the United States from 2010–2012. Alcohol poisoning is caused by drinking large quantities of alcohol in a short period of time. Very high levels of alcohol in the body can shut down critical areas of the brain that control breathing, heart rate, and body temperature, resulting in death. Alcohol poisoning deaths affect people of all ages but are most common among middle-aged adults and men.

There are 2,200 alcohol poisoning deaths in the United States each year.

Alcohol poisoning deaths:

- Most people who die are 35–64 years old
- Most people who die are men
- Most alcohol poisoning deaths are among non-Hispanic whites. Although a smaller share of the U.S. population, American Indians/Alaska Natives have the most alcohol poisoning deaths per million people of any of the races.
- Alaska has the most alcohol poisoning deaths per million people, while Alabama has the least.
- Alcohol dependence (alcoholism) was identified as a factor in 30 percent of alcohol poisoning deaths.

Binge drinking can lead to death from alcohol poisoning:

- Binge drinking (4 or more drinks for women or 5 or more drinks for men in a short period of time) typically leads to a blood alcohol concentration (BAC) that exceeds 0.08 g/dL, the legal limit for driving in all states.
- U.S. adults who binge drink consume an average of about 8 drinks per binge, which can result in even higher levels of alcohol in the body.
- The more you drink the greater your risk of death.

States and communities can take steps to reduce alcohol poisoning deaths by preventing binge drinking, including:

- Partnering with police, community groups, health departments, and doctors, nurses, and other healthcare providers to reduce binge drinking and related harms
- Tracking the role of alcohol in injuries and deaths
- Supporting proven programs and policies that decrease binge drinking. States with stronger alcohol policies have less binge drinking

Chapter 24

Alcohol Hangover

An alcohol hangover, which goes by its less-known name Veisalgia in scientific parlance, is one of the most commonly experienced consequences of alcohol consumption, and is characterized by a cluster of unpleasant symptoms that occur between 8 and 16 hours after a bout of heavy intake of alcohol. These symptoms, which include both physical and mental consequences, typically differ in severity and may depend on the amount of alcohol consumed. Although several studies have analyzed an alcohol hangover, it still remains a poorly understood phenomenon, both in terms of etiology and management, and has long been associated with negative socioeconomic consequences, mainly from poor performance and absenteeism in academic and work settings.

Pathology of an Alcohol Hangover

Studies of the blood and urine samples of people who have imbibed too much alcohol show a marked relationship between hangover severity and concentration of blood acetaldehyde, a toxic intermediate byproduct of alcohol metabolism in the body. The most significant correlation, however, was the one between hangover severity and immune factors. The fact that the body considers alcohol a toxin strongly implicates the immune system in the pathology of an alcohol hangover, and may explain the inflammatory response provoked by alcohol and its metabolites in the development of a hangover. Several extraneous factors can also increase the severity of a hangover without actually causing it. These include genetic susceptibility, sleep deprivation, smoking, and congeners (byproducts of alcohol fermentation such as methanol, acetaldehyde, tannins, and others), which all appear to play a role in aggravating hangover symptoms. Interestingly, there exists a small subset of drinkers who have hangover immunity and are either totally free of symptoms or experience very mild symptoms. Studies on the exact differences in how alcohol is metabolized in the hangover and hangover-immune group are still underway and may help unravel the pathology of an alcohol hangover and provide important leads to its etiology, prevention, and treatment.

Symptoms of an Alcohol Hangover

Hangover symptoms occur as the blood alcohol concentration (BAC) drops. These symptoms are typically characterized by a general feeling of misery that can last up to 24 hours. An alcohol hangover involves multiple body systems, including the endocrine, gastrointestinal, and neurological systems. Alcohol can interfere with blood sugar metabolism and lead to hypoglycemia (low blood sugar). Alcohol also inhibits the production of vasopressin, the hormone responsible for reabsorption of water and minerals by the kidneys. This diuretic effect leads to a water and electrolyte imbalance that can cause dehydration, fatigue, and loss of coordination the morning after heavy drinking. Hangovers may also cause cognitive impairment that can affect concentration and negatively impact everyday activities such as learning, driving, or job performance. Other symptoms frequently associated with a hangover include headaches, nausea, dizziness, anxiety, irritability, loss of appetite, and hypersensitivity to light and sound.

Hangover Treatment

Alcohol hangovers are as old as alcohol itself and have led to the formulation of numerous cures and prophylactic measures to manage their symptoms. Although scientific evidence for the efficacy of treating or preventing the pathological mechanism behind a hangover is generally lacking, many types of medication can successfully alleviate common hangover symptoms such as headache, nausea, and vomiting. Analgesics such as aspirin and ibuprofen are the most commonly used over-the-counter hangover medications. These drugs are generally harmless, but some have the potential for hepatotoxicity, particularly if the BAC is high. Many people also use natural hangover remedies such as ginseng, prickly pear cactus, ginger, milk thistle, and angostura to resolve hangover symptoms; however, the effectiveness of these remedies has not been proven through scientific studies. Claims of numerous miracle cures for a hangover notwithstanding, a hangover usually runs its course and resolves on its own after 24 hours even without medication.

Hangover Myth

The popular adage "hair of the dog that bit you" goes back to an ancient belief that drinking more alcohol helps cure a hangover. This is a myth. While it may be possible to delay the onset of symptoms only until the BAC drops again, drinking more can only add to the existing toxicity. Moreover, drinking again after a heavy drinking episode may do more harm than good, as the body needs at least 48 hours to recover from the deleterious effects of alcohol intake, whether or not one is experiencing the symptoms of a hangover.

Hangover Prevention

Abstinence and responsible drinking are the only guarantees to preventing an alcohol hangover.

Some tips for moderating alcohol intake and lowering the risk of hangover follow:

- **Choose beverages with fewer congeners** since consuming them is less likely to result in a hangover.
- **Avoid drinking on an empty stomach** since alcohol is more rapidly absorbed into the bloodstream in this instance. Eating while drinking is also a good way to slow down alcohol absorption.
- **Sip water between drinks** to cut down alcohol intake and maintain adequate levels of hydration.
- **Take it slow**; know your limits and stick to them without feeling pressured to drink more.

References

1. "Hangover Treatment," MedlinePlus, March 5, 2018.

2. "Alcohol Hangover," National Institute on Alcohol Abuse and Alcoholism (NIAAA), 1998.
3. "The Alcohol Hangover Research Group Consensus Statement on Best Practice in Alcohol Hangover Research," National Center for Biotechnology Information (NCBI), June 2010.
4. "Hangover," Mayo Clinic, December 16, 2017.

Chapter 25

Alcohol Changes the Brain

Chapter Contents

Section 25.1

Alcohol Tolerance and Withdrawal

This section includes text excerpted from "Alcohol Alert—Neuroscience Pathways to Alcohol Dependence," National Institute on Alcohol Abuse and Alcoholism (NIAAA), April 2009. Reviewed April 2018.

Why does drinking alcohol have such profound effects on thought, mood, and behavior? And why does alcohol dependence develop and persist in some people and not in others? Scientists are addressing these questions and others through neuroscience—the study of the brain, where both alcohol intoxication and dependence begin. Through neuroscience research, scientists are gaining a better understanding of how alcohol changes the brain and how those changes in turn influence certain behaviors.

To function normally, the brain must maintain a careful balance of chemicals called neurotransmitters—small molecules involved in the brain's communication system that ultimately help regulate the body's function and behavior. Just as a heavyweight can tip a scale, alcohol intoxication can alter the delicate balance among different types of neurotransmitter chemicals and can lead to drowsiness, loss of coordination, and euphoria—hallmarks of alcohol intoxication.

Remarkably, with ongoing exposure to alcohol, the brain starts to adapt to these chemical changes. When alcohol is present in the brain for long periods—as with long-term heavy drinking—the brain seeks to compensate for its effects. To restore a balanced state, the function of certain neurotransmitters begins to change so that the brain can perform more normally in the presence of alcohol. These long-term chemical changes are believed to be responsible for the harmful effects of alcohol, such as alcohol dependence.

Thanks to rapidly advancing technology, researchers know more than ever about how alcohol affects the brain and how the brain responds and adapts to these effects. This section summarizes some of what we know about alcohol's short and long-term effects on the brain and how breakthroughs in neuroscience are leading to better treatments for alcohol-related problems.

How Alcohol Changes the Brain: Tolerance and Withdrawal

As the brain adapts to alcohol's presence over time, a heavy drinker may begin to respond to alcohol differently than someone who drinks only moderately. Some of these changes may be behind alcohol's effects, including alcohol tolerance (i.e., having to drink more in order to become intoxicated) and alcohol withdrawal symptoms. These effects are associated with alcohol dependence.

When the brain is exposed to alcohol, it may become tolerant—or insensitive—to alcohol's effects. Thus, as a person continues to drink heavily, he or she may need more alcohol than before to become intoxicated. As tolerance increases, drinking may escalate, putting a heavy drinker at risk for a number of health problems—including alcohol dependence. Even as the brain becomes tolerant to alcohol, other changes in the brain may increase some people's sensitivity to alcohol. Desire for alcohol may transition into a pathological craving for these effects. This craving is strongly associated with alcohol dependence.

Other changes in the brain increase a heavy drinker's risk for experiencing alcohol withdrawal—a collection of symptoms that can appear when a person with alcohol dependence suddenly stops drinking. Withdrawal symptoms can be severe, especially during the 48 hours immediately following a bout of drinking. Typical symptoms include profuse sweating, racing heart rate, and feelings of restlessness and anxiety. Research shows that alcohol-dependent people may continue drinking to avoid experiencing withdrawal. Feelings of anxiety associated with alcohol withdrawal can persist long after the initial withdrawal symptoms have ceased, and some researchers believe that—over the long-term—this anxiety is a driving force behind alcohol use relapse.

The Brain's Unique Communication System

Tolerance and withdrawal are tangible evidence of alcohol's influence on the brain. Scientists now understand some of the mechanisms that lead to these changes—changes that begin with the brain's unique communication system. The brain communicates through a complex system of electrical and chemical signals. These signals are vital to brain function, sending messages throughout the brain, which, in turn, regulate every aspect of the body's function. Neurotransmitter chemicals play a key role in this signal transmission.

Under normal circumstances, the brain's balance of neurotransmitters allows the body and brain to function unimpaired.

Alcohol can cause changes that upset this balance, impairing brain function. For example, the brain balances the activity of inhibitory neurotransmitters, which work to delay or stop nerve signals, with that of excitatory neurotransmitters, which work to speed up these signals. Alcohol can slow signal transmission in the brain, contributing to some of the effects associated with alcohol intoxication, including sleepiness and sedation. As the brain grows used to alcohol, it compensates for alcohol's slowing effects by increasing the activity of excitatory neurotransmitters, speeding up signal transmission.

In this way, the brain attempts to restore itself to a normal state in the presence of alcohol. If the influence of alcohol is suddenly removed (that is, if a long-term heavy drinker stops drinking suddenly), the brain may have to readjust once again, this may lead to the unpleasant feelings associated with alcohol withdrawal, such as experiencing "the shakes" or increased anxiety.

Section 25.2

Drinking and Memory Lapses

This section contains text excerpted from the following sources: Text under the heading "Alcohol Blackout" is excerpted from "Alcohol," National Institute on Drug Abuse (NIDA) for Teens, January 2016; Text beginning with the heading " Blackouts and Memory Lapses" is excerpted from "Alcohol Alert—Alcohol's Damaging Effects on the Brain," National Institute on Alcohol Abuse and Alcoholism (NIAAA), October 20, 2004. Reviewed April 2018.

Alcohol Blackout

An alcohol blackout is a gap in a person's memory for events that took place while he or she was drinking. When a blackout happens, a person's brain does not create memories for these events as they are happening. For people who have had a blackout, it can be frightening to wake up the next day and not remember what they did the night before.

Blackouts and Memory Lapses

Alcohol can produce detectable impairments in memory after only a few drinks and, as the amount of alcohol increases, so does the degree of impairment. Large quantities of alcohol, especially when consumed quickly and on an empty stomach, can produce a blackout, or an interval of time for which the intoxicated person cannot recall key details of events, or even entire events.

Blackouts are much more common among social drinkers than previously assumed and should be viewed as a potential consequence of acute intoxication regardless of age or whether the drinker is clinically dependent on alcohol. White and colleagues surveyed 772 college undergraduates about their experiences with blackouts and asked, "Have you ever awoken after a night of drinking not able to remember things that you did or places that you went?" Of the students who had ever consumed alcohol, 51 percent reported blacking out at some point in their lives, and 40 percent reported experiencing a blackout in the year before the survey. Of those who reported drinking in the 2 weeks before the survey, 9.4 percent said they blacked out during that time. The students reported learning later that they had participated in a wide range of potentially dangerous events they could not remember, including vandalism, unprotected sex, and driving.

Equal numbers of men and women reported experiencing blackouts, despite the fact that the men drank significantly more often and more heavily than the women. This outcome suggests that regardless of the amount of alcohol consumption, females—a group infrequently studied in the literature on blackouts—are at greater risk than males for experiencing blackouts. A woman's tendency to black out more easily probably results from differences in how men and women metabolize alcohol. Females also may be more susceptible than males to milder forms of alcohol-induced memory impairments, even when men and women consume comparable amounts of alcohol.

Binge Drinking and Blackouts

Drinkers who experience blackouts typically drink too much and too quickly, which causes their blood alcohol levels to rise very rapidly. College students may be at particular risk for experiencing a blackout, as an alarming number of college students engage in binge drinking. Binge drinking, for a typical adult, is defined as consuming five or more drinks in about 2 hours for men, or four or more drinks for women.

Section 25.3

Adolescent Brain Is Vulnerable to Alcohol Exposure

This section includes text excerpted from "Effects and Consequences of Underage Drinking," Office of Juvenile Justice and Delinquency Prevention (OJJDP), U.S. Department of Justice (DOJ), September 10, 2012. Reviewed April 2018.

Effects and Consequences of Underage Drinking

Many people begin to drink alcohol during adolescence and young adulthood. Alcohol consumption during this developmental period may have profound effects on brain structure and function. Heavy drinking has been shown to affect the neuropsychological performance (e.g., memory functions) of young people and may impair the growth and integrity of certain brain structures. Furthermore, alcohol consumption during adolescence may alter measures of brain functioning, such as blood flow in certain brain regions and electrical brain activities. Not all adolescents and young adults are equally sensitive to the effects of alcohol consumption, however. Moderating factors—such as family history of alcohol and other drug use disorders, gender, age at onset of drinking, drinking patterns, use of other drugs, and co-occurring psychiatric disorders—may influence the extent to which alcohol consumption interferes with an adolescent's normal brain development and functioning.

Several decades of research have shown that chronic heavy drinking is associated with adverse effects on the central nervous system and have revealed some of the processes that give rise to these effects. Yet it remains unclear when in the course of a person's "drinking career" these central nervous system changes may emerge. Research suggests that heavy drinking may already affect brain functioning in early adolescence, even in physically healthy youths. This issue is important and interesting for at least two reasons. First, the brain continues to develop throughout adolescence and into young adulthood, and insults to the brain during this period therefore could have an impact on long-term brain function. Consistent with this assumption, animal studies have demonstrated that alcohol exposure during adolescence and young adulthood can significantly interfere with an animal's normal brain development and function. Second, young adulthood is a period when most people make critical educational, occupational, and social decisions, and impaired cognitive functioning at this time could substantially affect their futures.

Questions regarding alcohol's influence on brain development and function during adolescence are especially pertinent because heavy drinking is quite common among young people. For example, in one survey, 36 percent of 19- to 28-year-olds reported having consumed five or more drinks in a row in the preceding 2 weeks. Another survey determined that 7 percent of 18- to 25-year-olds meet the diagnostic criteria for alcohol dependence. Thus, a substantial number of adolescents and young adults could be at risk for alcohol-related impairment of brain development and brain function.

Neurological Consequences of Underage Drinking

If youth experiment with alcohol, this use may have negative effects on the brain, which continues to develop until the mid-twenties. Psychoactive substances such as alcohol produce pleasurable feelings and may diminish stress and emotional pain. These chemicals can turn on the brain's reward system, which makes people want to repeat the use of substances to obtain the same feelings. Eventually, substance use can alter the structure and chemical makeup of the brain, leading to brain disorders. In addition, adolescents have a diminished sensitivity to intoxication, making it possible for them to drink more alcohol without feeling very intoxicated. This may be because they have higher metabolic rates.

Alcohol use by adolescents is associated with abnormalities in the volume of the prefrontal cortex, the part of the brain that controls reasoning and impulse. In particular, females are vulnerable to the effects of alcohol on this part of the brain. Severe or chronic alcohol use among female adolescents may limit the development of their prefrontal cortex more than it does for males. Low prefrontal cortex development may lead to deficiencies in reasoning and impulsive behavior.

Alcohol can activate the pleasure-producing chemistry of the brain and release a pleasure-enhancing chemical called dopamine. Dopamine is released in the brain when an action satisfies a basic need or desire. With repeated alcohol use, the brain's natural capacity to produce dopamine is reduced. This leads to feelings of depression, anger, boredom, anxiety, and frustration.

With the use of alcohol and other drugs over time, youth may fail to advance to more complex stages of thinking and social interaction. Youth with alcohol-use disorders often perform worse on memory tests and have diminished abilities to plan. Effects may also include hallucinations, psychotic episodes, changes in sleep patterns, and changes in the ability to concentrate.

Section 25.4

Wernicke-Korsakoff Syndrome (Alcoholic Encephalopathy)

This section includes text excerpted from "Wernicke-Korsakoff Syndrome," Genetic and Rare Diseases Information Center (GARD), National Center for Advancing Translational Sciences (NCATS), April 1, 2018.

Wernicke-Korsakoff syndrome (WKS) is a brain disorder, due to thiamine deficiency that has been associated with both Wernicke encephalopathy (WE) and Korsakoff syndrome (KS). The term refers to two different syndromes, each representing a different stage of the disease. WE represents the "acute" phase and KS represents the "chronic" phase. However, they are used interchangeably in many sites. WE is characterized by confusion, abnormal stance and gait (ataxia), and abnormal eye movements (nystagmus). KS is observed in a small number of patients. It is a type of dementia, characterized by memory loss and confabulation (filling in of memory gaps with data the patient can readily recall) and involvement of the heart, vascular, and nervous system. WKS mainly results from chronic alcohol use, but also from dietary deficiencies, prolonged vomiting, eating disorders, systemic diseases (cancer, acquired immune deficiency syndrome (AIDS), infections), bariatric surgery, transplants, or the effects of chemotherapy. Studies indicate that there may be some genetic predisposition for the disease. Treatment involves supplementing the diet with thiamine. WE is an acute syndrome and requires emergency treatment to prevent death and neurologic complications. In cases where the diagnosis is not confirmed, patients should still be treated while additional evaluations are completed.

Symptoms

Although these conditions may appear to be two different disorders, they are generally considered to be different stages of WKS. Wernicke encephalopathy (WE) represents the "acute" phase and Korsakoff amnesic syndrome represents the "chronic" phase. The symptoms of WE commonly include:

- Encephalopathy (profound disorientation or mental confusion, inability to think clearly and indifference)
- Vision problems (including double vision, abnormal eye movements (nystagmus) and eyelid drooping)
- Loss of muscle coordination (ataxia)

Other symptoms may include:

- Delirium tremor
- Coma
- Hypothermia
- Hypotension

Korsakoff syndrome (KS) is seen most frequently in people who abuse alcohol after they experience an episode of WE. Most patients with KS show typical WE lesions in the brain. The main features of KS are impairments in acquiring new information or establishing new memories, and in retrieving previous memories.

The symptoms include:

- Loss of memory and inability to form new memories
- Making of stories (confabulation)
- Seeing or hearing things that are not really there (hallucinations)
- Disorientation
- Vision impairment

Attention and social behavior are relatively preserved. Affected subjects are able to carry on a socially appropriate conversation that may seem normal to an unsuspecting spectator. Patients with KS are as a rule unaware of their illness. Some patients may have severe cognitive function and global dementia.

In people with memory impairment, lesions in an area of the brain known as the anterior thalamus are commonly found. The shrinking of the mamillary bodies is also specific for WE, so when damaged or very small mamillary bodies are found in a demented patient, it is thought that the dementia may be due to alcohol abuse and malnutrition.

Cause

Wernicke-Korsakoff is caused by thiamine deficiency. Thiamine is a cofactor for several key enzymes important in energy metabolism. Thiamine requirements depend on metabolic rate, with the greatest need during periods of high metabolic demand and high glucose intake.

Because of the role of thiamine in cerebral energy utilization, it has been proposed that its deficiency initiates neuronal injury by inhibiting metabolism in brain regions with high metabolic requirements and high thiamine turnover.

Thiamine deficiency in alcohol abusers results from a combination of inadequate dietary intake, reduced gastrointestinal absorption, decreased hepatic storage, and impaired utilization.

Some studies indicate that there may be a genetic predisposition for the disease. Variants in the high-affinity thiamine transporter gene have also been implicated. The *SLC19A2* gene provides instructions for making a protein called thiamine transporter 1. This protein is located on the surface of cells, where it works to bring vitamin B1 (thiamine) into cells.

Treatment

The goals of treatment are to control symptoms as much as possible and to prevent progression of the disorder. Some people may need to be hospitalized initially to control the symptoms. Wernicke encephalopathy is an acute syndrome and requires emergency treatment to prevent death and neurologic problems. For this reason, even if the diagnosis is not confirmed, patients should be treated while additional evaluations are completed.

Treatment involves replacement of thiamine and providing proper nutrition and hydration. Intravenous thiamine is the treatment of choice. After the initial dose, daily doses of thiamine are usually recommended. Supplementation of electrolytes, particularly magnesium and potassium (often low in people with alcoholism), may be required in addition to thiamine. In those who are chronically malnourished, the remainder of the B vitamins should also be supplemented. Supplementation can be tapered as the patient resumes normal intake and shows improvement.

Because long-term alcohol use is the most common cause for WKS, avoiding alcohol provides the best chance for recovery. Referral to an alcohol recovery program should be part of the treatment regimen.

Due to difficulties with movement, patients should be provided with assistance when walking during the initial phase of treatment. Patients may require physical therapy to assist with movement. Walking difficulties may be permanent, depending on the severity at initial presentation and the timeliness of therapy.

Patients with KS rarely recover. Many patients require at least some form of supervision and social support, either at home or in a chronic care facility.

Prognosis

Most symptoms (such as uncoordinated movement and vision difficulties) can be reversed if detected and treated promptly. Without treatment, these disorders can be disabling and life-threatening. Patients with KS rarely recover. Many patients require at least some form of supervision and social support, either at home or in a chronic care facility.

Chapter 26

Alcohol-Induced Liver Disease

Chapter Contents

Section 26.1

Overview and Progression of Liver Disease

This section includes text excerpted from "Overview of the Liver," U.S. Department of Veterans Affairs (VA), February 13, 2018.

Your liver is one of the largest and most important organs in your body. You have only one liver. It is the size of a football and weighs about 3 pounds in the average-size person. It is reddish-brown. Your liver is located on the right side of your abdomen behind your lower ribs, and your ribs help to protect your liver.

The Liver Is a Filter

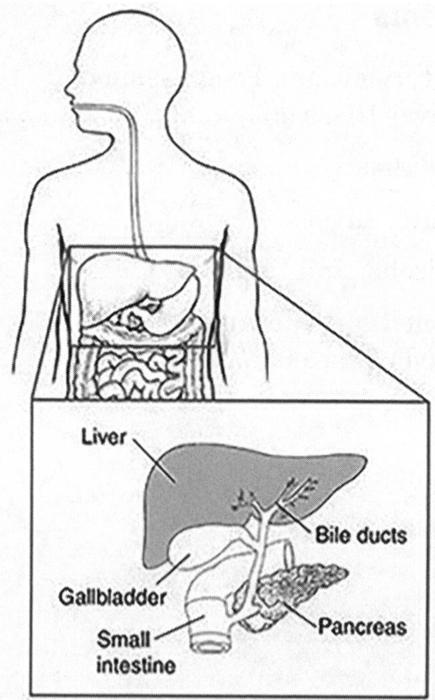

Figure 26.1. *Liver* (Source: "Cirrhosis," National Institute of Diabetes and Digestive and Kidney Diseases (NIDDK).)

Your liver has many important jobs. One of the jobs that the liver does is to act as a "filter" for your body. The liver filters or detoxifies the blood. Almost all the blood in your body passes through the liver. As blood passes through the liver, it breaks down substances, such as prescription or over-the-counter (OTC) drugs, street drugs, alcohol, and caffeine. Our bodies naturally produce some harmful (toxic) chemicals or poisons, and those are also broken down by the liver. In this way the liver acts as a filter to clean your blood.

The Liver Is a Factory

The liver is also a "chemical factory"—performing over 500 chemical functions in your body. The liver takes certain materials in your body and turns them into something else. For example, your liver turns proteins and sugars into things that your body needs.

The liver produces blood-clotting factors that are needed to help you heal after an injury. It also stores vitamins, hormones, cholesterol, and minerals. Your liver lets go of these chemicals and nutrients when your body needs them, and they flow into your bloodstream. The liver also produces a greenish fluid called bile. Tubes, called "bile ducts," connect the liver and another organ, the gallbladder, to the small intestine. The bile that is made by the liver helps to digest fats in the small intestine.

Liver Functions

- Filters your blood
- Makes proteins, including blood-clotting factors (needed to help you heal)
- Stores vitamins, sugars, fats, and other nutrients
- Helps regulate hormones
- Releases chemicals and nutrients into the body when needed
- Makes bile needed for digesting fats
- And much more

Liver Disease and Other Complications

Liver disease is caused by damage to the liver. Liver damage can be caused by many things, including:

- Drinking alcohol heavily

- Viruses (such as the hepatitis viruses)
- Being very overweight
- Certain medications—for example, acetaminophen (Tylenol), can cause severe liver damage in people who also have heavy alcohol use
- Exposure to industrial chemicals, including cleaning solvents, aerosolized paints, and paint thinners

Liver damage can lead to livers that are swollen, shrunken, hard, or scarred. Such livers do not work well, and you can get very sick, or even die, if your liver stops working altogether.

Symptoms of Liver Disease

Acute

If something happens to the liver suddenly, it is "acute." Some acute liver problems will cause symptoms suddenly as well. Symptoms of acute liver disease can include:

- Tiredness or weakness
- Jaundice (yellowing of the eyes and skin)
- Fever
- Nausea and vomiting
- Dark urine or very pale colored stools
- Pain under the ribs on the right side

Up to half of all people with acute liver disease have no symptoms at all. Some types of acute liver disease get better without treatment, and the liver heals itself entirely. On rare occasions an acute liver injury can require hospitalization and even liver transplant right away.

Chronic

If something is continuing to affect the liver over time, after 6 months it is "chronic." Many people with chronic liver problems will have no symptoms at all and may not even know they have a liver problem. Sometimes they develop symptoms only when the liver has been damaged for many years.

Section 26.2

Cirrhosis

This section includes text excerpted from "Cirrhosis: A Patient's Guide," U.S. Department of Veterans Affairs (VA), February 14, 2018.

What Is Cirrhosis?

The liver is the largest organ inside our body. It helps our body digest food, store energy, and remove poisons. When something attacks and damages the liver, liver cells are killed and scar tissue is formed. This scarring process is called fibrosis, and it happens little by little over many years. When the whole liver is scarred, it shrinks and gets hard. This is called cirrhosis, and usually this damage cannot be undone. Any illness that affects the liver over a long period of time may lead to fibrosis and, eventually, cirrhosis. Heavy drinking and viruses (like hepatitis C or hepatitis B) are common causes of cirrhosis. However, there are other causes as well. Cirrhosis may be caused by a buildup of fat in the liver of people who are overweight or have diabetes. Some people inherit genes for certain conditions that cause liver disease, such as genes that will cause iron buildup in the liver. In other diseases, bile collects in the liver and causes damage that can lead to cirrhosis. Other causes include certain prescribed and over-the-counter (OTC) medicines, environmental poisons, and autoimmune hepatitis, a condition in which a person's own immune system attacks the liver as if it were a foreign body.

What Happens When You Have Cirrhosis?

Because the liver becomes lumpy and stiff in cirrhosis, blood cannot flow through it easily, so pressure builds up in the vein that brings blood to the liver. This vein is called the portal vein. When pressure is high in the portal vein, the condition is called portal hypertension. In order to relieve this pressure, the blood passes through other veins. Some of these veins, called varices, can be found in the pipe that carries food from your mouth to your stomach (the esophagus) or in your stomach itself.

When you have cirrhosis, the high pressure in the portal vein backs up into another organ called the spleen, which gets big and destroys more platelets than usual. Platelets are blood particles that help with blood clotting.

When you have cirrhosis, entrance of blood to the liver is blocked and substances such as ammonia that would normally be cleaned by the liver, escape into the general circulation. Aside from the problems with liver blood flow, when cirrhosis is advanced there aren't enough healthy worker cells to get all the work done, so these cells cannot make the good substances such as albumin and clotting factors that the liver normally makes. Liver cancer, called hepatocellular carcinoma (HCC) can also occur in cirrhosis when some of the sick liver cells start to multiply out of control.

What Are the Symptoms of Cirrhosis?

At first, you may have no symptoms at all (this is called compensated cirrhosis). In fact, a person may live many years with cirrhosis without being aware that his or her liver is scarred. This is because the pressure in the portal vein is not yet too high and there are still enough healthy liver cells to keep up with the body's needs.

But if nothing is done about the cause of cirrhosis (if you continue to drink, for example) or if your hepatitis is not treated, the pressure in the portal vein gets higher and the few remaining worker cells get overwhelmed.

Then you may notice symptoms like low energy, poor appetite, weight loss, or loss of muscle mass. You can also develop the following serious problems:

1. Internal bleeding from large blood vessels in the esophagus, called bleeding varices;
2. A buildup of fluid in the belly, called ascites;
3. Confusion from the buildup of toxins in the blood, called encephalopathy; or
4. Yellowing of the eyes and skin, called jaundice.

As mentioned before, another serious complication of cirrhosis is liver cancer, which may occur in the compensated or decompensated stage. There may be no signs of liver cancer until the cancer has grown very large and causes pain.

What Is Decompensated Cirrhosis?

If you experience any of the serious problems described below, your disease has progressed from compensated cirrhosis to decompensated cirrhosis. You are then at risk of dying from life-threatening complications of liver disease, unless your sick liver can be replaced with a healthy liver (liver transplant).

Bleeding Varices (Internal Bleeding)

Large blood vessels (varices) in the food tube get bigger and bigger over time and can burst open. When this happens, you may vomit blood or notice your stool is black and tarry. If either of these things happens, you should go to the emergency room immediately to get help and stop the bleeding.

The risk of bleeding from varices can be reduced by taking special blood pressure medicines (called beta blockers) or by a special procedure in which tiny rubber bands are tied around the varices.

If you vomit blood or your stool turns black and tarry, you should go to the emergency room immediately. These are signs that varices may have begun to bleed, and this can be life-threatening.

Ascites (Fluid in the Belly)

Another problem caused by high pressure in the veins of the liver is ascites. Fluid leaks out into the belly and it begins to fill it up. This can make the abdomen enlarge like a balloon filled with water. The legs can get swollen too. This can be very uncomfortable. Eating can be a problem because there is less room for food. Even breathing can be a problem, especially when you are lying down. But the most dangerous problem associated with ascites is infection, which can be life-threatening. Ascites may go away with a low-salt diet, and with diuretics (water pills) ordered by your provider. But sometimes a provider must actually drain the fluid from the belly using a special kind of needle.

If you have ascites and you suddenly get a fever or belly pain, you should go to the emergency room immediately. These could be signs of a serious infection that can be life-threatening.

Encephalopathy (Confusion)

A liver that is working poorly may not be able to get rid of toxic substances like ammonia (which comes from the intestines), and it may allow these substances to go into the brain and cause confusion.

Besides confusion, toxins in the brain cause changes in your sleep, your mood, your concentration, and your memory. If it gets really bad, these toxins can even cause a coma. These changes are all symptoms of hepatic encephalopathy. If you have encephalopathy, you may have problems driving, writing, calculating, and performing other activities of daily living. Signs of encephalopathy are trembling and hand "flapping."

Encephalopathy may occur when you have an infection or when you have internal bleeding, and it may also occur if you are constipated or take too many water pills or take tranquilizers or sleeping pills. Your doctor might recommend lactulose. Lactulose is a syrup that makes your bowels move more often (up to two or three times a day) and helps get rid of ammonia.

If you are not acting like yourself, if you are confused, or if you are very sleepy, you should be taken to the emergency room immediately. These symptoms could be a sign of a serious medical problem. You should not drive when you have these symptoms.

Jaundice (Yellowing of the Eyes and Skin)

A liver that is working poorly cannot get rid of bilirubin, a substance that produces a yellowing of the eyes and skin called jaundice. Too much alcohol and some medicines can also lead to jaundice. If you suddenly develop jaundice, you should go to the emergency room immediately.

How Do You Know If You Have Cirrhosis?

Often, you cannot know whether you have cirrhosis until the disease is advanced. Only your healthcare provider can tell you if you have cirrhosis.

There are many signs of cirrhosis that your provider may find. You may have red palms or small spider-like veins on your face or your body. You may have developed fluid in your abdomen.

Your provider may do some blood tests that point to cirrhosis. Other tests can also give your provider a good idea of whether you have cirrhosis, such as an ultrasound, a computerized axial tomography (CAT) scan, a magnetic resonance imaging (MRI), or a liver-spleen scan.

Sometimes, you may need a liver biopsy. A liver biopsy shows how much scarring your liver has and will help your healthcare provider figure out what is causing the damage and how best to treat it.

What Will Your Healthcare Provider Do about Cirrhosis?

People with cirrhosis need to see a healthcare provider from time to time. If you have compensated cirrhosis, these visits may be scheduled every year or even as often as every 3–6 months. These visits will let your provider watch for the development of complications. The provider can order the screening tests that can catch these complications early. Then they can be treated or even delayed.

If you have decompensated cirrhosis, you may need to see your provider more often so that the complications that have developed already can be managed well.

People with cirrhosis have to have an upper endoscopy from time to time. This is a test in which you swallow a thin tube with a camera so that your provider can look for varices in the esophagus (food tube) and the stomach. If you have no varices, the endoscopy will be repeated every few years to see whether they show up. If you have large varices, you will get treatment to reduce the chance of bleeding.

You also will have a blood test and an ultrasound (or sometimes a CAT scan or an MRI) to look for signs of liver cancer and to check for ascites. It is important for your healthcare provider to look for cancer on a regular basis. If the cancer is caught early, there are often ways to treat it. If fluid (ascites) is found in your belly, medications (for example, water pills) and changes in your diet (like a low-salt diet) may help control this fluid. If these methods stop working, you can have a procedure called paracentesis. This procedure is used when your belly gets large and hard, which may happen every so often. You will go to a special procedures department where a trained provider will empty your belly of fluid using a special needle.

If you have developed decompensated cirrhosis, your provider may discuss the need for you to be considered for a liver transplant. You will want a healthcare provider who really knows you and can help you to decide if a transplant is right for you. Your provider will help you find out if your body can tolerate this operation, and, if it can, help you and your loved ones get ready for the transplant procedure.

When to Go to the Emergency Room

Use the following guidelines to determine if you need to go to the emergency room.

Go to the Emergency Room (or call 911, say you have cirrhosis, and tell them what's happening)

Bleeding

- My stools are black and tarry
- I'm vomiting blood

Confusion

- My head is cloudy
- I'm so confused and sleepy I can't do anything

Fever

- I have a fever and I can't stop shaking

Jaundice

- My eyes are suddenly turning yellow

What You and Your Provider Should Do to Take Good Care of Your Liver

You and your provider can do the following things to keep your liver as healthy as possible for as long as possible (Take this list with you to discuss with your provider.)

- Schedule liver clinic visits every 6 months, or more often if you have decompensated cirrhosis
- Have blood tests (to see how well the liver is working and to check for liver cancer) and an ultrasound (or CT or MRI) every 6–12 months
- Have an endoscopy to screen for varices (repeated every few years if you have no varices or only small ones)
- Take medicines called beta blockers when varices are large, to reduce the chance of bleeding
- Take medicines called diuretics (spironolactone alone or with furosemide) to decrease ascites, and have regular blood tests to check for kidney health
- Talk about how much alcohol you are drinking at every clinic visit
- Go over your medicine list at every clinic visit
- Talk about whether and when a liver transplant workup should be started for you

- Discuss and update your Child-Pugh-Turcotte (CPT) score and your Model for End-Stage Liver Disease (MELD) score at each visit. These scores are ratings that tell how sick your liver is and how urgently you need a transplant.

Section 26.3

Fatty Liver

This section includes text excerpted from "Fatty Liver Disease," MedlinePlus, National Institutes of Health (NIH), April 26, 2017.

What Is Fatty Liver Disease?

Your liver is the largest organ inside your body. It helps your body digest food, store energy, and remove poisons. Fatty liver disease is a condition in which fat builds up in your liver. There are two main types:

Nonalcoholic Fatty Liver Disease (NAFLD)

Nonalcoholic fatty liver disease (NAFLD) is a type of fatty liver disease that is not related to heavy alcohol use. There are two kinds:

- Simple fatty liver, in which you have fat in your liver but little or no inflammation or liver cell damage. Simple fatty liver typically does not get bad enough to cause liver damage or complications.
- Nonalcoholic steatohepatitis (NASH), in which you have inflammation and liver cell damage, as well as fat in your liver. Inflammation and liver cell damage can cause fibrosis, or scarring, of the liver. NASH may lead to cirrhosis or liver cancer.

Alcoholic Fatty Liver Disease

Alcoholic fatty liver disease is due to heavy alcohol use. Your liver breaks down most of the alcohol you drink, so it can be removed from your body. But the process of breaking it down can generate harmful substances. These substances can damage liver cells, promote inflammation, and weaken your body's natural defenses. The more alcohol that you drink, the more you damage your liver. Alcoholic fatty liver disease is the earliest stage of alcohol-related liver disease. The next stages are alcoholic hepatitis and cirrhosis.

Who Gets Fatty Liver Disease?

Researchers do not know the cause of nonalcoholic fatty liver (NAFLD). They do know that it is more common in people who:

- Have type 2 diabetes and prediabetes
- Have obesity
- Are middle aged or older (although children can also get it)
- Are Hispanic, followed by non-Hispanic whites. It is less common in African Americans.
- Have high levels of fats in the blood, such as cholesterol and triglycerides
- Have high blood pressure
- Take certain drugs, such as corticosteroids and some cancer drugs
- Have certain metabolic disorders, including metabolic syndrome
- Have rapid weight loss
- Have certain infections, such as hepatitis C
- Have been exposed to some toxins

NAFLD affects about 25 percent of people in the world. As the rates of obesity, type 2 diabetes, and high cholesterol are rising in the United States, so is the rate of NAFLD. NAFLD is the most common chronic liver disorder in the United States.

Alcoholic fatty liver disease only happens in people who are heavy drinkers, especially those who have been drinking for a long period of time. The risk is higher for heavy drinkers who are women, have obesity, or have certain genetic mutations.

What Are the Symptoms of Fatty Liver Disease?

Both NAFLD and alcoholic fatty liver disease are usually silent diseases with few or no symptoms. If you do have symptoms, you may feel tired or have discomfort in the upper right side of your abdomen.

How Do I Know If I Have Fatty Liver Disease?

Because there are often no symptoms, it is not easy to find fatty liver disease. Your doctor may suspect that you have it if you get abnormal results on liver tests that you had for other reasons. To make a diagnosis, your doctor will use:

- Your medical history
- A physical exam
- Various tests, including blood and imaging tests, and sometimes a biopsy

As part of the medical history, your doctor will ask about your alcohol use, to find out whether fat in your liver is a sign of alcoholic fatty liver disease or nonalcoholic fatty liver (NAFLD). He or she will also ask which medicines you take, to try to determine whether a medicine is causing your NAFLD.

During the physical exam, your doctor will examine your body and check your weight and height. Your doctor will look for signs of fatty liver disease, such as:

- An enlarged liver
- Signs of cirrhosis, such as jaundice, a condition that causes your skin and whites of your eyes to turn yellow

You will likely have blood tests, including liver function tests and blood count tests. In some cases you may also have imaging tests, like those that check for fat in the liver and the stiffness of your liver. Liver stiffness can mean fibrosis, which is scarring of the liver. In some cases you may also need a liver biopsy to confirm the diagnosis, and to check how bad the liver damage is.

What Are the Treatments for Fatty Liver Disease?

Doctors recommend weight loss for nonalcoholic fatty liver. Weight loss can reduce fat in the liver, inflammation, and fibrosis. If your doctor thinks that a certain medicine is the cause of your NAFLD, you should stop taking that medicine. But check with your doctor before stopping the medicine. You may need to get off the medicine gradually, and you might need to switch to another medicine instead.

There are no medicines that have been approved to treat NAFLD. Studies are investigating whether a certain diabetes medicine or vitamin E can help, but more studies are needed.

The most important part of treating alcohol-related fatty liver disease is to stop drinking alcohol. If you need help doing that, you may want to see a therapist or participate in an alcohol recovery program. There are also medicines that can help, either by reducing your cravings or making you feel sick if you drink alcohol.

Both alcoholic fatty liver disease and one type of nonalcoholic fatty liver disease (nonalcoholic steatohepatitis) can lead to cirrhosis. Doctors can treat the health problems caused by cirrhosis with medicines, operations, and other medical procedures. If the cirrhosis leads to liver failure, you may need a liver transplant.

What Are Some Lifestyle Changes That Can Help with Fatty Liver Disease?

If you have any of the types of fatty liver disease, there are some lifestyle changes that can help:

- Eat a healthy diet, limiting salt and sugar, plus eating lots of fruits, vegetables, and whole grains
- Get vaccinations for hepatitis A and B, the flu and pneumococcal disease. If you get hepatitis A or B along with fatty liver, it is more likely to lead to liver failure. People with chronic liver disease are more likely to get infections, so the other two vaccinations are also important.
- Get regular exercise, which can help you lose weight and reduce fat in the liver
- Talk with your doctor before using dietary supplements, such as vitamins, or any complementary or alternative medicines or medical practices. Some herbal remedies can damage your liver.

Section 26.4

Alcohol and Hepatitis C

This section includes text excerpted from "Hepatitis C and Alcohol," U.S. Department of Veterans Affairs (VA), February 14, 2018.

Alcohol and hepatitis C are certainly the two primary causes of cirrhosis and liver transplantation in the United States and Europe. Many patients with hepatitis C from these regions also have a history of problematic alcohol use, and thus have liver injury from both agents. An unequivocal first step in the management of patients with hepatitis C virus (HCV) who have an "alcohol problem" is ensuring that alcohol cessation is put in place. This section describes what has been shown about the interaction between alcohol intake and chronic hepatitis C infection.

Several factors have made this area of study difficult:

- The fact that alcohol intake varies over time in nearly everyone, and is thus very difficult to quantify
- Alcohol likely affects individuals differently (for example, it seems that only 20% of heavy drinkers develop cirrhosis)
- These limitations should be considered in the interpretation of the studies discussed

Alcohol and Liver Disease in Patients with Hepatitis C Virus (HCV)

Since the discovery of the hepatitis C virus in 1989, heavy alcohol consumption and hepatitis C have been known to interact with each other in causing liver disease. Poynard et al were among the first to demonstrate that heavy alcohol intake (50 grams/day or more in their study) contributes to fibrosis on liver biopsy in patients with HCV independent from other predictors. This intake is equivalent to 5 or more drinks per day (an average "drink"—one 12-oz. beer, 5 ounces of wine, or one 1.25 ounce shot of hard liquor—contains approximately 10 grams of alcohol).

Numerous other studies have confirmed that heavy alcohol intake contributes to HCV-associated liver disease. Notable among them is the study by Roudot-Thoraval et al, which evaluated more than 6,600 patients. Heavy alcohol intake in this study was associated with significantly more cirrhosis than was smaller amounts of alcohol intake. Another important study was that of Ostapowicz et al, in which patients with HCV who had undergone a liver biopsy had a detailed lifetime alcohol history obtained. Daily alcohol intake was not associated with fibrosis in multivariate analysis, but patients with cirrhosis had greater total lifetime alcohol consumption than did patients who did not have cirrhosis.

Limitations of studies published to date have included grouping subjects by fixed categories of alcohol intake, and using case-control methodology, with cases often having cirrhosis and controls having little liver disease. Studies including light drinkers have had conflicting results. Ostapowicz et al found no significant relationship between light or moderate alcohol intake and fibrosis on liver biopsy. A second prospective study, this one of inner-city injection drug users, found a statistically significant increase in the adjusted incidence of cirrhosis when 90-260 g/week were consumed, and a further increase when >260 g/week were consumed.

Two studies suggest a similar role for light or moderate alcohol use on liver disease in patients with HCV. A group of 800 American patients who had lifetime alcohol use estimated at the time of liver biopsy were found to have more liver scarring if they had drunk >50 g/day of alcohol, and lower amounts of alcohol were associated with fibrosis, but to a lesser extent. A French study of similar design found that quantity of alcohol drunk within 6 months prior to liver biopsy also was associated with fibrosis, and in a similar pattern: <31 g/day exerted some effect, 31–50 g/day a greater effect.

Overall, data that light alcohol use leads to some increase in liver scarring in patients with hepatitis C are emerging, but this effect is less than that seen in heavy drinkers.

Alcohol and Hepatitis C Virus Therapy

Active alcohol intake is considered a relative contraindication to interferon-based therapy. This recommendation is based on the documented noncompliance of heavy drinkers with different medical therapies, and the fact that the side effects of interferon therapy make it extremely difficult to comply with, even in patients without ongoing substance abuse. Because abstinence prior to therapy is considered standard management, major trials of anti-hepatitis C therapy excluded active drinkers, and did not evaluate alcohol history as a predictor variable in treatment response. As such, the effects of alcohol on HCV treatment response come only from much smaller studies.

Nearly all studies of the effect of alcohol on treatment responses have been with interferon monotherapy, and none has been blinded or randomized. Examples include two Japanese studies, one in which 16 of 53 patients were defined as heavy drinkers, and only 6 percent of all drinkers normalized their alanine aminotransferase (ALT) during treatment, compared with 30 percent of nondrinkers. A second study found that ALT normalization segregated directly with alcohol intake, 53 percent in nondrinkers, 43 percent in those consuming <70 g/day of alcohol, and 0 percent in those consuming >70 g/day.

An Italian study required abstinence from alcohol for 6 months prior to and during interferon monotherapy. Sustained virological response was significantly reduced in those with >75 g/day alcohol consumption prior to abstinence, compared with nondrinkers (33%). In the only published study examining the role of alcohol on response in patients treated with interferon and ribavirin, a German group treated 81 patients whose alcohol use histories were characterized prior to, during, and after interferon and ribavirin therapy. Twenty-one patients (26%) reported alcohol use while on therapy, 6 requiring inpatient treatment for detoxification. No significant differences were found, however, in therapeutic outcome and ALT levels after treatment based on alcohol consumption before or during combination therapy.

Published studies mostly suggest a negative effect of alcohol on the response to hepatitis C therapy. However, these were all small, nonrandomized, unblinded studies, so basing firm conclusions on them is difficult. Moreover, none of the studies reported patient compliance with therapy. As such, it remains unknown whether observed response differences seen in drinkers actually reflect biological differences, or whether the heavy drinkers were merely less compliant with therapy.

Alcohol and Hepatocellular Cancer in Patients with Hepatitis C Virus

Heavy alcohol intake is clearly associated with cirrhosis, alone and particularly in combination with HCV. Cirrhosis has been shown to be the primary risk factor for hepatocellular carcinoma (HCC). Thus, alcohol is clearly associated with HCC through causing cirrhosis. It remains unclear, however, whether alcohol leads to liver cancer independent from its effect on cirrhosis.

A number of studies have suggested that alcohol is associated with HCC independent of its association with cirrhosis. Aizawa et al included histological stage in their multivariate model, and found alcohol to be associated with HCC independent of histological stage. However, stage had often been ascertained 5–15 years prior to HCC diagnosis. A large, case-control study of patients with HCV found that alcohol consumption >60 g/day was associated with twice the risk of HCC as was abstinence or light alcohol consumption. A cross-sectional study from France, however, found that alcohol use was not independently associated with HCC, only cirrhosis was. A population-based study from Taiwan confirmed the importance of HCV as a risk factor for HCC, with having an antibody to HCV multiplying the risk of liver cancer 3.6-fold. Alcohol intake added to this risk, with a further threefold increased incidence of HCC in patients with HCV who drank alcohol.

Alcohol has also been connected to outcomes in patients diagnosed with HCC. In a Japanese cohort of 53 patients who underwent resection of HCC, patients who continued to consume >80 g/day of alcohol had a significantly diminished median disease-free survival (12.6 months) compared with those drinking <80 g/day (25.4 mos).

To summarize, drinking alcohol has been related to HCC development in patients with chronic hepatitis C. The demonstration of this association at a population level, as well as the association between alcohol and HCC recurrence, suggests a direct connection between alcohol and HCC independent of the effect of alcohol on fibrosis, but this has not been proven.

Patients with chronic hepatitis C infection likely should not drink alcohol. Heavy alcohol use has been found in multiple studies to be associated with fibrosis progression and cirrhosis. Light and moderate alcohol consumption also seem to contribute to liver disease.

Both past and current heavy alcohol use also have been associated with a decrease in patients' responses to interferon-based therapy, but studies largely have been retrospective and small, and have not addressed the question of whether patient compliance with therapy is also affected by alcohol. Alcohol intake in patients with HCV also has been related to HCC. This may be principally through the association between alcohol and cirrhosis; studies have not demonstrated a connection between alcohol and HCC independent from the association between alcohol and cirrhosis. Future studies with careful quantification and documentation of the timing of alcohol intake will shed additional light on all these questions.

Section 26.5

Nutrition Therapy in Alcoholic Liver Disease

This section includes text excerpted from "The Role of Nutritional Therapy in Alcoholic Liver Disease," National Institute on Alcohol Abuse and Alcoholism (NIAAA), June 26, 2007. Reviewed April 2018.

The study of malnutrition in patients with alcoholic liver disease (ALD) is based on several general concepts and observations. Researchers and clinicians previously believed that malnutrition was the primary cause of liver injury in ALD rather than the consequence of excessive alcohol consumption. This view was based on the prevalence of malnutrition in alcoholics and those with clinical evidence of liver (i.e., hepatic) dysfunction resulting from alcohol consumption. It now is widely accepted that the quantity and duration of alcohol consumption are the principal agents in the development of alcoholic liver injury. This is based on animal and human data showing that ALD can develop in well-nourished individuals who consume large amounts of alcohol. However, a great deal of variability exists regarding the individual development of progressive alcoholic liver injury. Although more than 90 percent of people with excessive alcohol consumption will develop fatty liver (defined as greater than 5 percent fat in the liver), only up to 35 percent will develop inflammation of the liver caused by alcohol (i.e., alcoholic hepatitis) and only 20 percent will progress to scarring of the liver (i.e., cirrhosis). Clearly, other risk factors, including genetic predisposition, obesity, concomitant viral hepatitis infection, and poor nutrition, may contribute variably to the development of ALD.

Indeed, in a large study of hospitalized patients with varying severity of ALD, malnutrition (especially the type caused by deficient protein and calories) was closely associated (although not necessarily causal) with the severity of liver injury. All patients with clinical evidence of ALD (regardless of severity) exhibited some features of malnutrition. With regard to the possible value of nutritional therapy, it would seem logical that patients with more severe deficits would benefit more, although convincing proof of this, to our knowledge, is not available.

Diversity of Liver Injury

Alcoholic liver injury is known to evolve through various stages. Patients exhibit a variety of clinical symptoms and signs in liver histology. As previously mentioned, almost everyone with heavy alcohol consumption develops fatty liver. This often is a rather benign disorder and considered reversible upon cessation of alcohol intake. In some cases, continued drinking may result in the development of alcoholic hepatitis, which may—and often does—end in severe clinical disease. The severity of disease and liver dysfunction correlates with an increasing short-term mortality. It is in this acutely diseased group that optimal nutritional therapy might have the most impact. Continued drinking in this group of patients may lead to the development of excess scar tissue in the liver (i.e., fibrosis) and the subsequent anatomical changes of cirrhosis. Cirrhosis is considered a late stage of the disease, clinically manifested by progressive liver dysfunction with associated yellowing of skin and whites of the eyes (i.e., jaundice)—caused by decreased liver clearance of bilirubin, fluid accumulation in the abdomen (i.e., ascites), and impaired brain function caused by the accumulation of ammonia in the brain tissues (i.e., encephalopathy).

These three disorders may occur separately or often in association with each other. In many instances, these stages of liver injury may be difficult to distinguish either clinically or by laboratory measures of liver dysfunction. Prior studies regarding nutritional therapy in ALD often did not differentiate between these various types of liver disease, complicating researchers' abilities to assess the true benefit of nutritional therapy. This has been a problem in the assessment of such data in the past as well as for the present authors.

Basis for Malnutrition in ALD

The signs and symptoms of nutritional deficits in ALD patients have been well characterized and include muscle wasting, decreased lean body mass, various vitamin deficiencies, and decreased measurable serum proteins. A complete description of specific nutritional deficits is beyond the scope of this review; however, it is important to consider the factors that contribute to malnutrition in individuals with ALD, as they may have an influence on the administration of nutritional therapy. There are many reasons for the deficits and abnormalities that occur as a result of malnutrition. These are outlined below and include decreased dietary intake and poor absorption and digestion of nutrients.

Decreased Food Intake

People with ALD will substitute calories from food with calories from alcohol. It has been shown in patients with ALD that calories from alcohol may contribute more than 50 percent of their total calories, with calories from protein comprising only 6–10 percent. In addition, the proportion of calories from alcohol appears to increase, whereas those from food decrease with escalating liver dysfunction. This increase in alcohol calories and decrease in food calories may be partially explained by the diversion of funds from the purchase of food to that of alcohol; however, hospitalized patients with ALD given adequate access to nutrition still demonstrate decreased ingestion of nonalcohol calories. This decreased desire for food (i.e., anorexia) also correlates with the severity of liver injury. Anorexia is pervasive in ALD and is a key reason for decreased dietary intake of nonalcohol calories.

Poor Absorption and Digestion of Nutrients

Another factor contributing to poor nutrition in patients with ALD is the malabsorption and maldigestion of various nutrients from the gut. This may relate to the impaired output of bile from the liver, resulting in decreased absorption of fat and fat-soluble vitamins. The possibility of concomitant pancreatitis causing decreased output of enzymes necessary for absorption of fats and proteins also can occur with alcohol abuse. Moreover, there may be a direct effect of alcohol on the gut itself. Alcohol has been demonstrated to decrease the intestinal absorption of amino acids and various vitamins, particularly thiamine, folate, and B12. Malabsorption also may occur through mechanical alterations in the gut. This may be attributed to increased intestinal swelling (i.e., edema) from a lack of structural proteins in the gut wall, decreased intestinal enzyme activity (i.e., lactase) required for carbohydrate digestion and absorption, and/or decreased absorption from increased swelling of the gut. The latter is attributed to increased pressure in the draining vein (i.e., portal vein) and lymphatic vessels connecting the intestines with the liver. The changes in intestinal digestion and absorption appear to reverse once the patient ceases drinking and starts to follow a normal diet, suggesting that nutritional replacement may be of special benefit.

Finally, the preferential metabolism of alcohol by the liver alters the metabolism of sugars (i.e., carbohydrates), fats (i.e., lipids), and proteins (i.e., amino acids/nitrogen). Abnormal breakdown of fat results in the formation of triglycerides that are deposited in the liver, manifesting as fatty liver. Altered fat metabolism also may propagate fibrosis by increasing collagen formation. The altered functional mass of the liver from these increased deposits of fat and collagen may result in decreased stores of vitamins and carbohydrates. Glycogen, the storage form of carbohydrates in the liver, serves as an energy reserve for periods of increased energy need. Inadequate glycogen reserves cause the body to make use of other metabolic pathways for energy, such as the breakdown of muscle. This may explain the increased muscle wasting, increased nitrogen excretion in the stool, and negative nitrogen balance seen in patients with ALD. It is important to note that in healthy individuals these alternate pathways of energy usually are found only after periods of prolonged fasting or starvation. Patients with ALD, however, may begin to use alternative pathways after only an overnight fast, suggesting that the frequency of feeding is as important as the type of feeding.

Role of Malnutrition in ALD

It is not precisely known how alcohol causes liver damage. The net effect of nutrition on the development of ALD may involve multiple factors, including free-radical damage and increased risk of infection.

Free-Radical Damage

It has been observed that one of the toxic byproducts of alcohol metabolism (i.e., free radicals) may cause damage to the liver. Free-radical damage also occurs as a result of oxidation of lipids in cellular membranes and in the internal constituents (i.e., mitochondria) of the cell. This improper oxidation of fat can, in turn, lead to the increased fat deposition and fibrosis, described previously. Cell damage from this improper oxidation also results in an inflammatory response and the generation of various signaling chemicals (i.e., cytokines), which may further contribute to tissue injury.

The liver has a built-in defense against harmful oxidation in glutathione, a compound that assists in the removal of the toxic byproducts of alcohol metabolism. Glutathione availability depends on the presence of certain amino acids that may be deficient in patients with ALD. One of these amino acids, S-adenosylmethionine (SAM), serves as a precursor for glutathione. Evidence exists that SAM is deficient in patients with ALD. Furthermore, membrane integrity depends on the availability of SAM, in addition to an ample supply of phospholipids.

SAM is involved in the processing of phospholipids needed for cell membrane repair. It also has been observed that patients with ALD are deficient in vitamins (e.g., vitamin E) that may offer a protective effect as antioxidants.

Increased Risk of Infection

Patients with ALD are at increased risk of infection partly because alcohol directly suppresses the immune system but also because the altered protein metabolism observed in ALD results in decreased circulating antibodies needed to fight infection. The intestinal system also works as a barrier to prevent bacteria from inside the gut from crossing the intestinal wall and causing infection. In addition, the cells of the gut secrete an antibody that is unique to the gut and assists with fighting infection. There is evidence that the gut's role as a barrier to infection decreases with poor nutrition, as well as with excess alcohol intake. Research in animals has shown that improved nutrition results in decreased translocation of bacterial organisms across the gut and a subsequent decrease in bacterial infections. Generally, it is accepted that patients with advanced ALD have an increased risk of morbidity and mortality with surgical procedures. This increased risk may be related to higher infection risk and poor wound healing. Considering that chronic ALD, after cessation of drinking, is one of the more common indications for liver transplant, it is reasonable to suggest that improved nutrition in patients with ALD can improve the outcomes of surgical procedures by decreasing infection and improving wound healing.

In brief summary, the decreased ability to process hepatic fat, as well as the lack of key proteins and amino acids that may decrease the liver's ability to neutralize the effects of free radicals generated by alcohol metabolism, may, in turn, result in damage to cell membranes and promote inflammation and cell death (i.e., necrosis). Such events also may lead to fibrosis and even cirrhosis. Thus, theoretically, improved nutrition could ameliorate these adverse events, enhance hepatic regeneration, and decrease the risk of infection, which is a common complication of advanced ALD and a leading cause of patient mortality.

Chapter 27

Alcohol and Cardiovascular Disease

Chapter Contents

Section 27.1

Alcohol's Effects on the Cardiovascular System

This section includes text excerpted from "Alcohol's Effects on the Cardiovascular System," National Institute on Alcohol Abuse and Alcoholism (NIAAA), February 16, 2017.

Alcohol use has complex effects on cardiovascular (CV) health. The associations between drinking and CV diseases such as hypertension, coronary heart disease, stroke, peripheral arterial disease, and cardiomyopathy have been studied extensively. Although many behavioral, genetic, and biologic variants influence the interconnection between alcohol use and CV disease, dose and pattern of alcohol consumption seem to modulate this most. Low-to-moderate alcohol use may mitigate certain mechanisms such as risk and hemostatic factors affecting atherosclerosis and inflammation, pathophysiologic processes integral to most CV disease. But any positive aspects of drinking must be weighed against serious physiological effects, including mitochondrial dysfunction and changes in circulation, inflammatory response, oxidative stress, and programmed cell death, as well as anatomical damage to the CV system, especially the heart itself. Several promising avenues exist for future research-related to alcohol use and CV disease. These include using direct biomarkers of alcohol to confirm self-report of alcohol consumption levels; studying potential mediation of various genetic, socioeconomic, and racial and ethnic factors that may affect alcohol use and CV disease; reviewing alcohol–medication interactions in cardiac patients; and examining CV effects of alcohol use in young adults and in older adults.

Data from numerous epidemiologic studies over the last two decades have revealed complex associations between alcohol use and cardiovascular (CV) conditions such as hypertension (HTN), coronary heart disease (CHD), stroke, peripheral arterial disease (PAD), and cardiomyopathy. In particular, these associations are strongly modulated by the dose and pattern of alcohol consumption. Low-to-moderate daily alcohol consumption (i.e., <15 to 20 g/day, 1–2 standard drinks) is associated with a reduced risk of CV disease and mortality, whereas greater amounts of alcohol consumption and a binge pattern of drinking have been linked to an increased risk. Consequently, the effects of alcohol consumption can be a double-edged sword.

Mechanisms Related to Alcohol's Positive and Adverse Effects on CV Conditions

Many of the CV conditions associated with alcohol share the pathophysiologic process of atherosclerosis and inflammation. Therefore, alcohol may exert its protective or enhancing effects on these conditions by modifying three broad categories of mechanisms: risk factors (e.g., lipid profiles, carotid intima-medial thickness (cIMT), and insulin sensitivity), hemostatic factors (e.g., fibrinogen levels and platelet reactivity), and inflammation. In addition, and specific to CHD, alcohol consumption may modulate ischemia–reperfusion mechanisms as blood flow is restored to tissues after oxygen deprivation. Some of these potential mechanisms are briefly reviewed below.

Risk Factors

One common risk factor for CV disease is the composition of the lipids found in the blood, and the effects of alcohol consumption on lipid profiles have been extensively studied. Many researchers have found that alcohol intake increases HDL cholesterol (HDL-c) levels, HDL ("good cholesterol") particle concentration, apolipoprotein A-I, and HDL-c subfractions. Findings have been equivocal for other lipids, such as low-density lipoprotein cholesterol (LDL-c) (the estimated amount of cholesterol within LDL particles, or "bad cholesterol") and triglyceride levels. High triglyceride levels in the bloodstream have been linked to atherosclerosis and, by extension, increased risk of CHD and stroke. However, a recently conducted Mendelian randomization study reported that low-to-moderate alcohol consumption reduced triglyceride and LDL-c and increased HDL-c, in particular the HDL2-c subfraction. Interestingly, the researchers found a nonlinear effect of alcohol consumption on HDL2-c levels. This supports the findings from other studies that the alcohol-induced changes in HDL-c do not fully account for the lower risk of CHD in moderate alcohol drinkers.

Other risk factors that are surrogate markers of atherosclerosis and future CHD events, such as cIMT, also have been examined. The relationship between alcohol consumption and cIMT was inconsistent. It was also reported that older adults (age >70) consuming 1–6 drinks/week had lower cIMT compared with abstainers and those having

≥14 drinks/week. This is in contrast to results from other large population-based studies of older (age >70) or middle-aged (ages 45–64) adults, which did not find a relationship between level of alcohol intake and cIMT.

Some reports suggest that low-to-moderate alcohol consumption is associated with favorable effects in insulin sensitivity and glucose metabolism, key risk factors in the development of diabetes. Randomized placebo-controlled trials conducted with nondiabetic postmenopausal women showed that 2 drinks per day significantly lowered insulin levels during fasting and after meals and increased insulin sensitivity. Increased insulin sensitivity, which is the opposite of insulin resistance, is associated with a reduced risk for the development of type 2 diabetes and CHD.

Hemostatic Factors

Alcohol consumption can be associated with both a favorable hemostatic/coagulation profile as well as an adverse one. Several epidemiologic and randomized controlled studies have found alcohol consumption decreases coagulation factors such as fibrinogen, which is a CV risk marker at elevated levels. In addition to being essential to the coagulation cascade, fibrinogen also may play a proinflammatory role in the development of certain CV diseases, including vascular wall disease and atherosclerosis. Findings from a meta-analysis of 42 studies suggested that 30 g of alcohol/day (2 standard drinks) was associated with a 7.5 mg/dl (-17.7 to 32.7) decrease in fibrinogen concentration. Similarly, the results from a small randomized crossover trial (2015) found that women consuming alcohol (146–218 g/week, ~2–3 standard drinks/day) for 4 weeks showed a 14 percent reduction in fibrinogen levels.

Platelets and their role in clotting also affect CV disease. Altered platelet responses (e.g., increased platelet activation/aggregation) leads to blood-clot formation (or thrombosis) in certain CV conditions. Anticlotting therapies are therefore the cornerstone of managing acute coronary syndromes. Not surprisingly, alcohol consumption has complex and varying effects on platelet function. Studies using different methodologies have shown that low-to-moderate alcohol consumption decreases platelet activation and aggregation in certain cases. On the other hand, significant daily alcohol consumption increases platelet aggregation and reactivity. Infection or other stressful events also can lead to immune-triggered platelet production, a condition called rebound thrombocytosis, which may occur immediately after withdrawal from both heavy and one-time heavy (binge) drinking. Although highly individualized and dose dependent, alcohol use also can increase bleeding time (i.e., taking longer to develop a clot).

Inflammation

The effects of alcohol consumption on inflammation are twofold. Lower doses are associated with reduced inflammation, as indicated by markers such as C-reactive protein and certain interleukins. Conversely, higher levels induce oxidative stress and a wide variety of inflammatory markers. Oxidative stress in particular is likely a key event in the development of alcoholic cardiomyopathy. Data from numerous types of research studies show that alcohol may alter levels of antioxidant enzymes and stimulate oxidative damage, and it may therefore be involved in the pathogenesis of many types of alcohol-induced diseases.

Ischemic Preconditioning

Another mechanism underlying the cardioprotective effects of low-to-moderate alcohol consumption and CHD in particular may be related to a phenomenon known as ischemic preconditioning, which produces resistance to the loss of blood supply (and oxygen) to organs or tissues. If the blood supply is impaired briefly (usually for <5 minutes) and then restored so that blood flow resumes, and the process is repeated two or more times, the cells downstream of the tissue or organ are protected from a final ischemic insult, when the blood supply is cut off. In the heart, this would protect the heart muscle (myocardium) from subsequent, more prolonged episodes of restricted blood flow (ischemia) followed by injury when that blood flow returns to the heart (called reperfusion injury or ischemia–reperfusion injury. Ischemic preconditioning results in smaller infarct sizes, fewer and less severe arrhythmias, and prevention of endothelial cell dysfunction. During the ischemic phase, the flow of oxygen and nutrients to the tissues is reduced, most significantly to the heart, brain, and kidneys. In contrast, during the reperfusion phase, despite restoration of blood flow, a series of dysfunctional biochemical and metabolic changes are initiated that lead to extensive accumulation of reactive oxygen species (ROS). ROS induce a number of changes. One is the opening of the mitochondrial permeability transition pore, which is formed in the mitochondria during ischemic incidents, contributing to reperfusion injury and cell death. Others include recruitment of neutrophils (white blood cells

(WBC) that are among the first inflammatory cells to respond during inflammation) and dysfunction of the sarcoplasmic reticulum, which can affect calcium ion storage and release into muscle fibers.

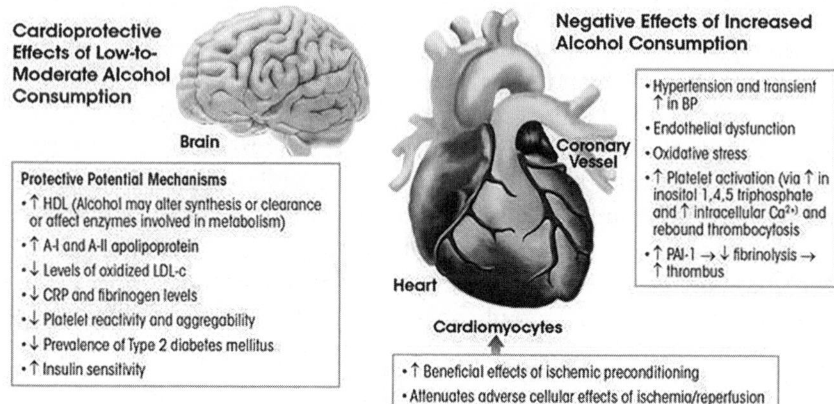

Figure 27.1. *Mechanisms Related to the Positive and Adverse Effects of Alcohol on Cardiovascular Conditions*

BP = blood pressure, Ca2+ = calcium, CRP = C-reactive protein, DM = diabetes mellitus, HDL = high-density lipoprotein, LDL = low-density lipoprotein, PAI-1 = plasminogen activator inhibitor-1

Impact of Drinking Patterns and Types of Alcoholic Beverages on Risk

Drinking patterns, and in particular a binge pattern of drinking and higher frequency of binge drinking, are associated with a heightened risk of CV conditions such as Hypertension (HTN), stroke, and myocardial infarction (MI), as well as sudden death or increased mortality after MI. A systematic review found that excessive ethanol intake (>150 g ethanol/week) was associated with a doubled risk of subarachnoid hemorrhage. The latter findings may relate to the overall large quantity of alcohol consumed (~12 standard drinks/week) rather than a binge pattern.

Binge drinking in younger individuals also may increase the risk of stroke. Acute intake on weekends and holidays of >40 g ethanol was significantly associated with cerebral infarction within 24 hours in young (ages 16–40) and middle-aged (ages 41–60) subjects. One possible mechanism for the binge-associated increased stroke risk is

HTN. However, at least in younger people, HTN prevalence is low, suggesting that other mechanisms may be involved.

It has been debated whether beverage type has differential effects. Some investigators have suggested that drinking wine may offer more protection against CV disease because it contains polyphenols, such as resveratrol and flavonoids, which are micronutrients with antioxidant activity. However, among studies designed to examine the influence of beverage type, no differences have been found in CV disease outcomes or biologic markers, such as HDL-c. Differential associations of CV risk with certain beverage types such as wine instead have been attributable to other lifestyle factors (e.g., increased physical activity) or drinking with meals. The findings from INTERHEART, in which "any alcohol use" had no cardioprotective effects in certain populations, such as in people of South Asian ethnicity who live in South Asia (e.g., India, Bangladesh, Nepal), led to speculation about beverage type, beverage quality, and drinking pattern as important mediators.

Finally, in studies of people from certain Eastern European countries, investigators have failed to find a cardioprotective effect with any level of ethanol consumption. This suggests that alcoholic beverage type may be an important mediator, because in countries such as Russia, spirits are the alcoholic beverage of choice. However, the negative associations between alcohol consumption and CV outcomes in these countries also may relate to pervasive patterns of binge drinking.

Section 27.2

Alcohol-Induced Heart Disease

This section contains text excerpted from the following sources: Text in this section begins with excerpts from " Alcohol and You: An Interactive Body," College Drinking, National Institute on Alcohol Abuse and Alcoholism (NIAAA), September 17, 2010. Reviewed April 2018; Text beginning with the heading "Alcohol Consumption and CHD" is excerpted from "Alcohol's Effects on the Cardiovascular System," National Institute on Alcohol Abuse and Alcoholism (NIAAA), February 16, 2017.

Long-term heavy drinking weakens the heart muscle, causing a condition called alcoholic cardiomyopathy. A weakened heart droops and stretches and cannot contract effectively. As a result, it cannot pump enough blood to sufficiently nourish the organs. In some cases, this blood flow shortage causes severe damage to organs and tissues. Symptoms of cardiomyopathy include shortness of breath and other breathing difficulties, fatigue, swollen legs and feet, and irregular heartbeat. It can even lead to heart failure.

Both binge drinking and long-term drinking can affect how quickly a heart beats. The heart depends on an internal pacemaker system to keep it pumping consistently and at the right speed. Alcohol disturbs this pacemaker system and causes the heart to beat too rapidly, or irregularly. These heart rate abnormalities are called arrhythmias. Drinking to excess on a particular occasion, especially when you generally don't drink, can trigger either of these irregularities. Over the long-term, chronic drinking changes the course of electrical impulses that drive the heart's beating, which creates arrhythmia.

Both binge drinking and long-term heavy drinking can lead to strokes, even in people without coronary heart disease. Recent studies show that people who binge drink are about 56 percent more likely than people who never binge drink to suffer an ischemic stroke over 10 years. Binge drinkers also are about 39 percent more likely to suffer any type of stroke than people who never binge drink. In addition, alcohol exacerbates the problems that often lead to strokes, including hypertension, arrhythmias, and cardiomyopathy.

Alcohol Consumption and CHD

Studies, which included both men and women, showed that various alcohol consumption levels (g/day) among active drinkers compared with nondrinkers were associated with a reduced relative risk for CV mortality, incident CHD, and CHD mortality. Alcohol consumption levels between 2.5 g/day and 30–60 g/day (<1 standard drink/day to ~5 drinks/day) were cardioprotective for both CV mortality and CHD mortality. However, the association between alcohol consumption and CV mortality was insignificant when alcohol consumption was >60 g/day, but remained significantly reduced for CHD mortality.

Alcohol and Heart Failure

Several studies and meta-analyses have been conducted to determine the relationship between alcohol consumption and the risk of developing heart failure in healthy subjects, as well as in those with a history of MI or CHD. Heart failure is a syndrome that often results from an MI or CHD. Studies also have examined the "safety" of alcoholic beverage consumption in subjects with heart failure.

A meta-analysis of prospective studies of healthy people ages 21–81, Larsson and colleagues reported that, compared with nondrinkers, the risk for heart failure across different levels of alcohol consumption was greatest for those consuming 12 drinks per week, intermediate for those consuming 3 drinks/week as well as for those consuming 14 drinks/week, and least for those consuming 7 drinks/week. Based on dose-response analysis, consumption of 7 drinks/week was associated with a 17 percent lower risk of developing heart failure.

In contrast, Wannamethee and colleagues examined different levels of alcohol consumption and risk for heart failure in an older population (mean age ~68) and found no evidence that light-to-moderate drinking had a protective effect on incident heart failure in this age group. On the other hand, drinking ≥5 drinks/day (or ≥35 drinks/week) was associated with a significant risk of heart failure. Thus, low levels of alcohol consumption (1–2 drinks, but not everyday) in patients with heart failure may not exacerbate the condition, especially in those with heart failure attributable to ischemic CHD. Because heart failure patients usually are older (over age 65) and often are prescribed numerous medications, both the effects of age and of medication use should be carefully considered by patients, clinicians, and researchers.

Acute and Long-Term Effects of Alcohol on the Myocardium

Acute Effects

The acute effects of alcohol on the myocardium include a weakening of the heart's ability to contract (negative inotropic effect). Data from isolated papillary and heart muscle cell (myocyte) experiments demonstrate that acute physiologic intoxicating doses of alcohol (80–250 mg%) can have a negative inotropic effect. These effects also may involve an irregular and often very fast heart rate (arrhythmia) during which the heart's upper chambers (atria) contract chaotically out of coordination with its lower chambers (ventricles), known as atrial fibrillation, or (rarely) sudden cardiac death.

Investigators have used a variety of noninvasive tests to evaluate the acute effects of alcohol consumption on myocardial function and hemodynamics in healthy humans. As with isolated animal heart experiments, some investigators have found that acute alcohol exposure (blood alcohol levels 40–110 mg%) depresses myocardial systolic function in humans. However, these changes were transient, with small changes from baseline.

Other researchers have reported that acute alcohol consumption resulting in blood alcohol levels of 100–120 mg percent exerted no effect on cardiac performance. It is important to note that most studies were performed >30 years ago with young subjects (mean age 23–35) and with small sample sizes (n = 4–12). As a result, whether or how these findings generalize to older healthy people and those with CV disease is unknown. However, in an elderly community-based population (i.e., the Atherosclerosis Risk in Communities Study, mean age at time of study 74–76 years), Gonçalves and colleagues examined the effects of different levels of weekly alcohol consumption on alterations in cardiac structure and function. These investigators found increasing amounts of alcohol were associated with mild alterations in cardiac structure and function, which were greater in women. In the United States, it is estimated that by 2060 there will be 98 million adults age >65, more than twice the number in 2014. In addition, recent research indicates that this generation will potentially consume alcohol at higher rates than previous generations. Consequently, more research may be necessary to better understand the effects of alcohol consumption on the CV systems of older adults.

Certain arrhythmias, such as atrial fibrillation, may be the most serious consequence of consuming large amounts of alcohol, and in particular binge drinking. Larsson and colleagues have reported that binge drinking (defined by these researchers as having more than 5 drinks on a single occasion) was associated with an increased risk of new-onset atrial fibrillation. Atrial fibrillation is one of the most common arrhythmias and is strongly associated with adverse CV events, such as stroke. Results from retrospective studies enrolling adults ages 40–60 also have linked binge drinking to a heightened risk of sudden death.

Long-Term Effects

Alcoholic cardiomyopathy (ACM) is a heart-muscle disease found in individuals with a history of long-term heavy alcohol consumption. It is characterized by a dilated left ventricle (LV), normal or reduced LV wall thickness, increased LV mass, and (in advanced stages) a reduced LV ejection fraction (<40%). There are no specific immunohistochemical or immunological biomarkers or other criteria for an ACM diagnosis. Therefore, a key factor in diagnosing ACM is a long-term history of heavy alcohol abuse without CHD or other cardiac conditions such as inflammation of and damage to the myocardium, known as myocarditis.

ACM's exact prevalence remains elusive. The proportion of cardiomyopathy cases attributable to alcohol abuse has ranged from 23–40 percent. Recently, Guzzo-Merello and colleagues reported that, among 282 patients with a dilated cardiomyopathy phenotype, 33 percent had ACM. Both men and women can develop ACM. However, some reports indicate that alcohol-dependent women develop ACM after consuming less alcohol over a shorter period than do age-matched alcohol-dependent men.

In humans, the exact amount and duration of alcohol consumption associated with development of ACM remains unknown. The point at which alcohol-induced abnormalities appear over the course of a person's lifetime drinking also is not well established and is highly individualized. This suggests either protective or adverse interaction effects of genetic or lifestyle factors.

Long-term heavy alcohol consumption induces adverse histological, cellular, and structural changes within the myocardium. As with other alcohol-induced pathologies, mechanisms contributing to ACM include oxidative stress, apoptotic (programmed) cell death, impaired mitochondrial bioenergetics and stress, derangements in fatty acid metabolism and transport, and accelerated protein breakdown. These mechanisms contribute to the myocyte cellular changes that lead to intrinsic cell dysfunction, such as sarcoplasmic reticular dysfunction and changes in intracellular calcium handling and myocyte loss. However, modulatory influences related to drinking patterns, genetic susceptibility, nutritional factors, ethnicity, and gender also many play a role.

Section 27.3

Binge Drinking and Blood Pressure

This section contains text excerpted from the following sources: Text in this section begins with excerpts from "Alcohol and You: An Interactive Body," College Drinking, National Institute on Alcohol Abuse and Alcoholism (NIAAA), September 17, 2010. Reviewed April 2018; Text beginning with the heading "Potential Biologic Mechanisms Underlying Alcohol-Induced BP Effects" is excerpted from "Alcohol's Effects on the Cardiovascular System," National Institute on Alcohol Abuse and Alcoholism (NIAAA), February 16, 2017.

Chronic alcohol use, as well as binge drinking, can cause high blood pressure, or hypertension. Your blood pressure is a measurement of the pressure your heart creates as it beats, and the pressure inside your veins and arteries. Heavy alcohol consumption triggers the release of certain stress hormones that in turn constrict blood vessels. This elevates blood pressure. In addition, alcohol may affect the function of the muscles within the blood vessels, causing them to constrict and elevate blood pressure.

Potential Biologic Mechanisms Underlying Alcohol-Induced BP Effects

Several mechanisms may underlie alcohol's effects on blood pressure. These include impairments in cells that lead to buildup of plaque in arteries (i.e., through alterations in endothelial cell function and nitric oxide availability), and disruptions in arterial-vascular function (i.e., through myogenic mechanisms and changes in baroreceptor function), and hormonal imbalances that control the body's fluid and

BP regulation (through the renin–angiotensin–aldosterone system (RAAS)). Some adverse BP-related mechanisms that may be triggered by alcohol include changes in intracellular calcium levels, baroreflex control, and heart rate and activation of other neurohormonal systems besides the RAAS, such as the sympathetic nervous system.

Several reports indicate that alcohol first exerts a seemingly positive effect, followed by a more negative impact (i.e., it is biphasic) on the endothelial–nitric oxide–generating system. The endothelium is a key regulator of vascular function. Endothelial dysfunction is an early indicator of blood vessel damage and atherosclerosis, as well as a strong prognostic factor for future CV events. Low-to-moderate levels of alcohol consumption may initially improve endothelial function, whereas high daily levels and binge drinking may impair it.

Other studies have shown that low-to-moderate concentrations of ethanol (20 mM) increase endogenous nitric oxide synthase (eNOS) expression in certain cells (i.e., human umbilical-vein endothelial cells). Low-to-moderate ethanol consumption in rats (36% of caloric intake) for 6 weeks increased nitric oxide production and eNOS expression in the aortic vascular wall. Nitric oxide helps regulate vascular tone. eNOS has a protective function in the cardiovascular system, which is attributed to nitric oxide production. However, higher daily ethanol (blood alcohol levels >29 mM) for 6 weeks in another animal model was associated with decreased eNOS expression, increased release of endothelial-derived vasoconstrictor prostanoids, and greater responsiveness of mesenteric arterioles to phenylephrine. Taken together, these findings show lower amounts of alcohol may have a positive effect on nitric oxide signaling, but higher amounts alter this system and change arteriolar reactivity, which may led to an increased risk for HTN.

In humans, endothelial function is assessed by measuring the widening (i.e., dilation) of the brachial artery under different conditions. Some research noted that endothelial function is impaired in abstinent individuals with a long-term history of alcohol abuse or alcoholism. Other studies have examined the effect of a single binge-drinking episode and found impairment in brachial artery endothelial-dependent and -independent vasodilation. Therefore, as in animal studies, the effects of ethanol on endothelial function in humans likely depend on the dose and duration of ethanol consumption.

Vascular wall oxidative stress also is a key mechanism in ethanol-induced HTN. Oxidative stress is an imbalance between production of free radicals and the body's ability to detoxify or fight off their harmful effects through neutralization by antioxidants. Various studies with animals and humans indicate that ethanol can increase the development of reactive oxygen species (ROS), leading to increases in redox-signaling pathways and decreases in protective antioxidant levels. Alcohol also can increase levels of co-enzymes or reducing equivalents (e.g., reduced nicotinamide adenine dinucleotide phosphate (NADPH)), which lead to increases in ROS formation and decreases in eNOS activity.

Studies on Alcohol Intake and Blood Pressure

In healthy adults, consuming low-to-moderate amounts of alcohol each day typically has no short-term (i.e., acute) or substantial impact on hemodynamics or blood pressure (BP). However, data suggest that binge drinking (more than 5 standard drinks in a single sitting) is associated with transient increases in BP that range from 4–7 mmHg for systolic BP.

In a systematic review and meta-analysis that included 16 prospective studies on the effects of alcohol consumption on the risk of hypertension (systolic BP >140 mmHg/diastolic BP >90 mmHg), Briasoulis and colleagues found that consuming more than 20 g ethanol/day (~1–2 drinks/day) significantly increased risk of hypertension (HTN) in women, and higher amounts (31–40 g/day) increased risk of HTN in men. In women, there was a J-shaped relationship between alcohol consumption and HTN, where consumption of <10 g/day was associated with a reduced risk of HTN, whereas in men the alcohol-risk relationship was more linear (figure 27.2).

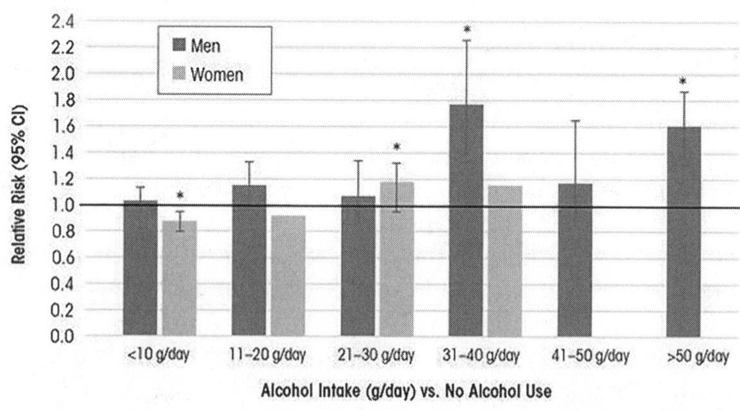

Figure 27.2. *Incidence of Hypertension in Men and Women*

*Note: *Indicates data significantly different from nondrinkers. For females, data at higher alcohol consumption levels (>40 g/day) were not analyzed.*

Results from another meta-analysis of 12 cohort studies found a similar dose–response relationship between alcohol consumption and HTN for males. A J-shaped relationship for females showed protective effects at or below consumption levels of 15 g/day. These data highlight how gender may be an important modifier of the alcohol threshold level and can shape the alcohol benefit–risk relationship.

The discrepancy in findings across studies suggests that other characteristics differ among the study subjects. However (and importantly), the meta-analysis by Briasoulis and colleagues included all of the former studies and found that in the pooled analysis, for both men and women, consuming >20 g ethanol/day (~1–2 drinks/day) was associated with a higher risk of developing HTN.

Mori and colleagues examined the dose-dependent effects of drinking on BP measured at regular intervals in healthy premenopausal women ages 20–45. These repeated measurements allowed comparison of BP among 24 participants at 3 drinking levels, each for a 4-week consumption interval. The study included periods of low-volume and higher-volume alcohol consumption as well as of drinking alcohol-free red wine for each participant, whether or not she initially had been a lower-level or higher-level drinker as defined by the study. Awake systolic BP and diastolic BP were 2.3 mmHg/1.3 mmHg higher in women who consumed greater amounts of alcohol (146–218 g/week, ~2–3 standard drinks/day) than in those who drank less (42–73 g/week, ~0.5–1 standard drink/day) or none at all. There was no BP-lowering effect with lower alcohol amounts. In women, these findings support the data from meta-analyses and prospective studies, suggesting that greater amounts of alcohol consumption may increase BP and contribute to the development of HTN. However, findings from this study do not support a BP-lowering effect at the lower level of alcohol consumption (42–73 g alcohol/week, or ~3–5 standard drinks). Interestingly, in the Mori study, higher alcohol consumption was associated with a 10 percent increase in high-density lipoproteins (HDLs, which remove cholesterol from the blood and are associated with reduced risk of atherosclerosis and heart disease) and a 14 percent reduction in levels of fibrinogen (a glycoprotein that helps form blood clots).

To summarize, in both men and women, alcohol consumption at levels above about 1–2 drinks per day is associated with HTN. The alcohol–risk relationship tends to be J shaped in women and linear in men. More research is needed to determine if certain ethnic or socioeconomic groups are more vulnerable to alcohol-induced HTN. The American Society of Hypertension (ASH) and the International Society of Hypertension (ISH) recommended that men limit their alcohol consumption to no more than 2 drinks a day, and women to no more than 1 drink a day. To put the importance of BP control into perspective, at a population level, a 2-mmHg increase in BP increases mortality from stroke by 10 percent and from coronary artery disease by 7 percent.

Chapter 28

Alcoholic Neuropathy

Chronic alcohol abuse is often associated with damage to the peripheral nervous system, the network of nerves that communicates between the central nervous system (CNS)—the brain and spinal cord—and all other parts of the body. Alcoholic neuropathy, also known as alcoholic polyneuropathy, is primarily caused by degeneration of the axon (the long neuronal process that transmits electrical impulses from one neuron to the next). Axonal degeneration, in turn, leads to demyelination (damage to the myelin sheath enveloping the neurons), which can disrupt messages between the CNS and the rest of the body. A potentially incapacitating condition, alcoholic neuropathy usually has a gradual onset, but may have a rapidly progressive onset in some cases.

Symptoms of alcoholic neuropathy depend largely on the type of neuron involved and include impairment of sensory, motor, and autonomic functions. Neuropathic pain associated with sensory nerve damage is one of the most prominent clinical presentations of alcoholic neuropathy. This pain can adversely affect quality of life and emotional well being. Damage to motor neurons is usually characterized by muscle weakness, muscle atrophy, cramps, and fasciculations (muscle twitches), while severe cases of neuropathy may present autonomic symptoms caused by malfunction of internal organs.

Pathophysiology: Pathways Involved

Studies of alcoholic neuropathy largely attribute alcohol-induced neuropathy to a nutritional deficiency, particularly of thiamine (vitamin B1) and, to a lesser extent, other B vitamins (folic acid and cobalamin). Thiamine, the vitamin associated with glucose metabolism, is closely linked with the biosynthesis of neurotransmitters and provides a defense against oxidative stress in cells of the nervous system. Ethanol impairs gastrointestinal absorption of thiamine and also its cellular utilization. These impairments have been established as the cause of alcohol-linked neurological sequelae (such as Wernicke-Korsakoff syndrome), alcohol-induced cognitive impairment, and alcoholic dementia. While nutritional deficiencies may be one of the factors contributing to alcohol-induced brain injury, studies also indicate that other mechanisms may also be responsible for the neurotoxic effects caused by ethanol. The exact pathogenesis of alcoholic neuropathy remains elusive, but several studies point toward certain possible metabolic pathways involved in the development of alcoholic neuropathy. One such mechanism relates to the formation of free radicals by oxidative stress and consequent damage to neurons.

Symptoms

A classic symptom of alcoholic neuropathy is pain—often accompanied by burning sensations and particularly in the extremities. Initial symptoms may vary from mild numbness or paresthesia (tingling or prickling sensations) to allodynia (pain caused by innocuous stimuli such as light touch). Chronic neuropathy may lead to severe symptoms that include muscle wastage, impaired gait, paralysis, and malfunction of organs or glands. These may manifest as a loss of bladder control, sexual dysfunction, orthostatic hypotension, and arrhythmia (irregular heartbeat). Symptoms may extend over days, months, or years. Their onset, in some cases, may also be sudden, progressing rapidly and resolving slowly as the damaged neurons heal. In severe cases, symptoms may progress gradually with intermittent periods of relief and relapse.

Diagnosis

The healthcare provider makes a diagnosis of alcoholic neuropathy based on the patient's medical history and physical and neurological examinations. A known history of alcoholism and family history of diabetes or neurological disease may provide important insight into the possible causes of neuropathy. Blood tests are carried out to determine nutritional deficiencies linked to alcohol use and nerve health. A liver function test may also be performed to determine neuropathy related to alcoholic liver disease. A battery of tests is usually carried out to eliminate other potential causes of neuropathy (such as diabetes, autoimmune disease, neuromas, cancer, infections, endocrine disorders, or repetitive stress).

Once a diagnosis of neuropathy has been confirmed, additional tests may be ordered to establish the nature and extent of the neuropathy:

- **Nerve conduction velocity (NCV)** measures the degree of damage in nerve fibers and determines whether symptoms are caused by axonal degeneration or by damage to the myelin sheath. A nerve fiber, electrically stimulated with a probe, responds by generating its own electrical signal, which is then measured by an electrode placed in its path.
- **Electromyography (EMG) tests** can help make a differential diagnosis of muscle and nerve disorders as both conditions can present with a similar constellation of symptoms. A fine needle is inserted into the muscle to record the electrical activity of the muscle during rest and forceful contraction. Any abnormal electrical activity can help establish motor neuropathy and differentiate between nerve and muscle disorders.
- **Magnetic resonance imaging (MRI)** can help diagnose other aetiological factors of neuropathy, such as tumors, herniated discs, or other abnormalities.
- **Nerve/skin biopsy tests** that involve removing and examining a sample of nerve/skin tissue may be used to determine the degree of nerve damage associated with neuropathy. Nerve biopsy is an invasive procedure that may cause adverse neuropathic side effects and is not usually recommended. Skin biopsy, in contrast, is less invasive and devoid of harmful effects.

Clinical Management

The treatment protocol for alcoholic neuropathy focuses on arresting further damage to the peripheral nerves through lifestyle modifications (alcohol abstinence and exercise), and nutritional modifications, including a balanced diet and supplementation of B vitamins. While the prognosis is usually good for mild neuropathy, long-term alcohol use can cause irreversible neurological damage and treatment outcomes may not be very encouraging. Dysesthesias (abnormal, painful sensations) associated with alcoholic neuropathy is typically managed with anticonvulsants, such as gabapentin or amitriptyline, in conjunction with other over-the-counter pain medications, such as aspirin or acetaminophen. Anticonvulsants are anticholinergic agents that can block neurotransmitters in the central and peripheral nervous system and have both analgesic, as well as sedative effects. Other classes of drugs—including antidepressants, antiarrhythmic medications, and narcotic agents—can also modulate pain through their action on the CNS and peripheral nerves. These medications may be prescribed for chronic painful neuropathies.

While pain medication may provide symptomatic relief, their addiction potential and undesirable side effects render them unsuitable for long-term use. Currently, treatment modalities address pain alleviation but, for the most part, are ineffective in targeting the basic pathological phenomena underlying alcoholic neuropathy. Studies involving alternative therapies that are typically without side effects and aim to address multiple pathological pathways—such as oxidative stress and nutrient deficiencies, associated with the development of alcoholic neuropathy—are underway, however.

References

1. "Peripheral Neuropathy Information Page," National Institute of Neurological Disorders and Stroke (NINDS), May 24, 2017.
2. Res, Pain. J. "An Integrated Perspective on Diabetic, Alcoholic, and Drug-Induced Neuropathy, Etiology, and Treatment in the US," U.S. National Library of Medicine (NLM), 2017.
3. "Peripheral Neuropathy," Mayo Clinic, August 9, 2017.

Chapter 29

Alcohol and the Lung

One of a pair of organs in the chest that supplies the body with oxygen, and removes carbon dioxide from the body. During breathing,

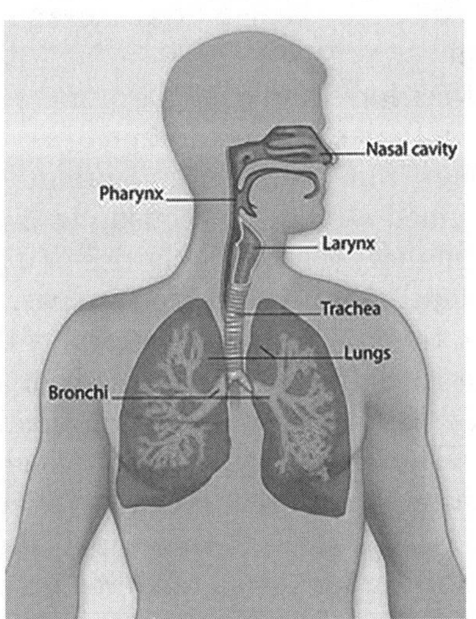

Figure 29.1. *Lung* (Source: "What Is Lung Cancer?" Centers for Disease Control and Prevention (CDC).)

This chapter contains text excerpted from the following sources: Text in this chapter begins with excerpts from "NCI Dictionary of Cancer Terms—Definition of Lung," National Cancer Institute (NCI), September 14, 2016; Text beginning with the heading "Lung and Its Function" is excerpted from "Alcohol and the Lung," National Institute on Alcohol Abuse and Alcoholism (NIAAA), February 16, 2017.

oxygen is taken into the lungs, where it passes into the blood and travels to the body's tissues. Carbon dioxide, a waste product made by the body's tissues, is carried to the lungs, where it is breathed out. There are different tests to measure lung function. Also called pulmonary function.

Lung and Its Functions

Among the many organ systems affected by harmful alcohol use, the lungs are particularly susceptible to infections and injury. The mechanisms responsible for rendering people with alcohol use disorder (AUD) vulnerable to lung damage include alterations in host defenses of the upper and lower airways, disruption of alveolar epithelial barrier integrity, and alveolar macrophage immune dysfunction. Collectively, these derangements encompass what has been termed the "alcoholic lung" phenotype. Alcohol-related reductions in antioxidant levels also may contribute to lung disease in people with underlying AUD. In addition, researchers have identified several regulatory molecules that may play crucial roles in the alcohol-induced disease processes. Although there currently are no approved therapies to combat the detrimental effects of chronic alcohol consumption on the respiratory system, these molecules may be potential therapeutic targets to guide future investigation.

Few social practices have had a longer or more complicated history in human civilization than the consumption of alcohol. As documented in academic writings, but even more commonly in art and music, humans have consumed alcohol for thousands of years, and drinking is either a celebrated facet of social activities or a proscribed practice, depending on the local moral or religious views. In the latter years of the 18th century, the first Surgeon General of the United States of America, Benjamin Rush (for whom the medical school in Chicago is named), noted that excessive alcohol consumption was associated with pneumonia. After about a century, William Osler wrote that alcohol abuse was the most important risk factor for pneumonia. As modern medicine evolved throughout the 20th century, it became abundantly clear that alcohol use disorder (AUD) rendered people more susceptible to a wide variety of lung infections, including bacterial pneumonias and tuberculosis, and increased morbidity and mortality. In a now-classic modern citation, Perlino and Rimland coined the term "alcoholic leukopenic pneumococcal sepsis syndrome" when they published a case series of patients with underlying AUD who suffered from pneumococcal pneumonia and sepsis associated with leukopenia that was associated with a mortality of more than 80 percent. Excessive alcohol consumption seems to increase susceptibility to pneumonia through multiple mechanisms. The major factors include an increased risk of aspiration, abnormalities in the way particles are eliminated from the conducting airways through the mucus (i.e., in mucociliary clearance), and impaired activity of one branch of the immune system (i.e., innate immunity) within the lower airways.

Researchers have identified an association between underlying AUD and acute respiratory distress syndrome (ARDS). ARDS is a severe form of acute lung injury that occurs as a complication of diverse insults, including sepsis, massive aspiration, and trauma; it has a mortality rate of 30–50 percent, even with state-of-the-art modern medical care in an intensive care unit. A seminal study demonstrated for the first time that AUD independently conferred an approximately two-fold increase in risk of developing ARDS. A subsequent prospective study focusing only on patients with severe sepsis revealed that the relative risk of developing ARDS was closer to fourfold higher in those with an underlying AUD; this effect was independent of factors such as age, smoking, severity of illness, and nutritional status. Other investigators have confirmed these associations. Taken together, all of these findings indicate that drinking patterns that define AUD are associated with a significantly increased risk of serious lung infections and acute lung injury and thereby contribute to the deaths of tens of thousands of Americans every year, and many more worldwide.

Alcohol and the Airways

The potential influence of alcohol consumption on airway health and disease has been documented for a long time. Chronic alcohol ingestion constantly subjects the drinker's airways to high concentrations of alcohol vapor, as best evidenced by the use of alcohol breath tests (i.e., Breathalyzer). The volatile nature of alcohol is exploited in this common field sobriety test, which is reliably used as a surrogate to quantify blood alcohol concentrations. Interestingly, the alcohol vapor found in the airways is not caused by inhalation but is a result of the ready diffusion of alcohol from the airway blood supply across the airway epithelium and into the airways themselves. This process explains why alcohol vapor in the breath may be used to determine blood alcohol concentration. The alcohol then is deposited and metabolized in the airways. This process leads to the formation of reactive aldehydes (e.g., acetaldehyde), which in turn can interact and form harmful adducts with proteins and deoxyribonucleic acid (DNA). The formation of these adducts may disrupt normal cellular functions, induce inflammation, and impair healing. Taken together, these findings demonstrate that the airways—including the oral cavity and extending all the way to the alveolar space—are subjected to high concentrations of alcohol and its deleterious metabolites during intoxication.

Within the upper airways, chronic alcohol consumption leads to several alterations. First, chronic heavy drinking often is associated with poor tooth development and arrangement (i.e., dentition) as well as poor oral hygiene, and although these usually are attributed to poor nutritional and lifestyle choices, clinical studies have established that they also result, to some extent, from the direct effects of alcohol exposure on the upper airway. Specifically, alcohol decreases saliva production in the salivary glands located in front of the ears (i.e., the parotid glands), thereby eliminating an important mucosal defense within the oral cavity. As a result, heavy drinkers are susceptible to dental caries and gingivitis, conditions that may be exacerbated by concurrent tobacco use, which is common in people with AUD. This alters the microenvironment of the mouth, making it more susceptible to colonization with certain bacteria, including gram-negative bacilli. Moreover, acute alcohol intoxication and the resulting decrease in the level of consciousness promotes aspiration of oral secretions into the lower airways because of diminished gag and upper-airway reflexes that would normally protect against this phenomenon. These modifications in the upper airways seem to contribute to the increased risk of lung infections, including those caused by more virulent gram-negative organisms, in chronic heavy drinkers.

This risk further is exacerbated by the negative effects of chronic alcohol ingestion on the lower airways. In particular, animal models have established that chronic excessive alcohol ingestion causes dysfunction of the mucociliary apparatus, an important host defense mechanism responsible for clearing harmful pathogens and mucus from the lower airways. An early experimental study in sheep investigating the effects of alcohol on ciliary beat frequency (CBF) demonstrated a dose-dependent effect, such that low alcohol concentrations actually stimulated CBF, whereas high concentrations impaired it. Mechanistic studies found that whereas short-term alcohol exposure causes a transient increase in CBF, chronic exposure desensitizes the cilia so that they cannot respond to stimulation. Alcohol-induced failure of the mucociliary system could interfere with the clearance of pathogens from the airways and thereby may contribute to the increased risk of pulmonary infections in people with chronic heavy alcohol use.

Although alcohol's influences on upper and lower airway host defenses collectively are harmful, its role in causing specific diseases, such as asthma, within the conducting airways is less clear, despite some interesting historical references. For example, some documentation in Egyptian papyri dating back to about 2000 B.C.E. suggests the use of alcohol in the treatment of asthma, although one cannot be certain of the accuracy of the asthma diagnosis in these ancient writings. After about 1,000 years, Hippocrates—who is regarded as the father of Western medicine—noted that wine has a variety of medicinal uses and is specifically beneficial for reducing sputum production; again, however, it is not clear if he was referring to asthma as we currently define the syndrome. Salter (1863) described the successful use of alcohol to treat three patients with intractable asthma who had failed all other treatments. In contrast, more modern epidemiological data suggest that chronic heavy drinking is associated with increased odds of all-cause mortality and hospitalization among patients with asthma, although a direct link between asthma control and alcohol use was not investigated.

To supplement the various anecdotal reports of using alcohol in the treatment of airway diseases, early mechanistic investigations demonstrated that alcohol itself seems to have bronchodilating properties in asthmatics. However, the effects differed depending on the alcohol concentration used as well as on the route of administration (i.e., intravenous versus oral). Moreover, these observations directly conflict with findings that many asthmatics actually report exacerbations of their disease after alcohol ingestion. In an attempt to explain some of these discrepancies, Breslin and colleagues (1973) compared the effects of exposure to different types of alcohol in a clinical study. These analyses found that whereas pure alcohol did not appear to induce bronchial reactivity, some alcoholic beverages worsened asthma symptoms. These findings were the first to suggest that the nonalcohol components and additives of alcoholic beverages may be responsible for inducing asthma, rather than alcohol itself. Similar findings were seen in studies that examined the effects of red wine in asthma. However, researchers have not yet been able to determine conclusively if alcohol ingestion has any clinically significant effects on asthma. For example, Bouchard and colleagues (2012) showed that alcohol exposure triggered asthma-like pulmonary inflammation in an allergen-sensitized mouse model. The alcohol-exposed mice exhibited increased numbers of certain inflammatory cells (i.e., eosinophils) in fluid obtained from the lungs (i.e., bronchoalveolar lavage fluid), increased production of the main component of mucus (i.e., mucin), and constriction of the small airways (i.e., decreased bronchiole patency). These effects were not seen in mice that were exposed to alcohol but were not allergen sensitized, suggesting that alcohol can be an important trigger for airway reactivity in the context of an underlying allergic component. In contrast, Oldenburg and colleagues demonstrated that alcohol actually reduced airway hyperresponsiveness and airway inflammation in a mouse model of allergic asthma.

One potential explanation for the disparate findings in the literature regarding alcohol's role in airway disease is that some forms (i.e., phenotypes) of asthma may be more sensitive to the effects of alcohol than others. One subtype of asthma called aspirin-sensitive asthma or aspirin-exacerbated respiratory disease represents less than 10 percent of all asthma cases but accounts for a disproportionately high number of severe asthma cases and can be extremely difficult to diagnose and treat. Interestingly, alcohol-induced respiratory symptoms are more common in patients with aspirin-exacerbated respiratory disease than in aspirin-tolerant asthmatics. These findings suggest that the potential irritant versus bronchodilator effects of alcohol may vary by disease subtype; however, further investigation is necessary to validate these observations.

Alcohol and Acute Lung Injury

ARDS is a severe form of lung injury characterized by fluid accumulation in the lung that is not related to heart problems (i.e., noncardiogenic pulmonary edema) as well as by flooding of the alveolar airspaces with protein-like (i.e., proteinaceous) fluid. ARDS develops in response to inflammatory stresses, including sepsis, trauma, gastric aspiration, pneumonia, and massive blood transfusions. Originally described by Ashbaugh and colleagues, ARDS is characterized by alveolar epithelial and endothelial barrier disruption, dysfunction of the lipoprotein complex (i.e., surfactant) coating the lung surfaces, and intense inflammation. Together, these alterations profoundly disrupt gas exchange and cause severe respiratory failure. Although much has been learned about the underlying pathophysiology of this syndrome over the past four decades, treatment of ARDS remains essentially supportive, and despite aggressive treatment in intensive care units and mechanical ventilation, the mortality rate for ARDS remains unacceptably high at 30–50 percent.

The association between alcohol abuse and acute lung injury only has been identified within the past 20 years, when Moss and colleagues analyzed a patient database at the University of Colorado and reported that patients who were admitted to the hospital with a critical illness and who had underlying alcohol abuse were at about twofold-increased risk for developing ARDS. This original study was limited by the uncertain accuracy regarding the diagnosis of an underlying AUD in the database. However, a subsequent prospective study of 220 patients with septic shock, in whom a more precise diagnosis of an AUD was established using the Short Michigan Alcoholism Screening Test (SMAST), determined that the incidence of ARDS in patients with AUD was 70 percent (46 of 66), compared with 31 percent (47 of 154) in patients without AUD ($P< 0.001$). After controlling for potentially confounding variables, the relative risk of ARDS in alcoholic versus nonalcoholic patients was 3.7:1. Overall, 49 percent (46 of 93) of those patients that developed ARDS had an underlying AUD, consistent with the findings of the previous study, in which 51 percent of the patients who developed ARDS were classified as alcoholics. If these findings are extrapolated to the population at large, then alcohol abuse contributes to the development of acute lung injury in tens of thousands of patients in the United States each year.

Alcohol-Related Mechanisms of Lung Injury

The recognition that excessive chronic alcohol ingestion has such a dramatic and independent effect on the risk of acute lung injury prompted a search for the underlying mechanisms. Because one of the cardinal features of ARDS is disruption of the alveolar epithelial barrier that regulates the fluid content of the airspace, this was a logical target for investigation. Maintaining the fluid balance of the alveolar space is critical for normal gas exchange. Acute lung injury involves the rapid development of noncardiogenic pulmonary edema, and patients with impaired alveolar epithelial fluid clearance are three times more likely to die from ARDS than patients with a maximal ability to clear lung fluid. Although the fluid balance in the lungs is regulated by the concerted actions of both epithelial and endothelial barriers, it is the alveolar epithelium which primarily prevents protein and fluid flow into airspaces. A pathological hallmark of ARDS is heterogeneous damage of the alveolar epithelium, with complete loss of the epithelial surface in some areas, whereas other alveoli remain relatively intact. Therefore, at a cellular level the extent of the alveolar epithelial damage may not be as widespread or as uniform as chest X-rays may suggest, and preservation and repair of the alveolar epithelium are key to survival.

In experimental animal models, chronic alcohol ingestion for as little as 6 weeks renders the lung susceptible to acute edematous injury. In these same models, chronic alcohol ingestion produces a lasting defect in the ability of the alveolar epithelium to form and/or maintain a tight physical barrier; specifically, primary alveolar epithelial cells isolated from alcohol-fed animals form relatively leakier monolayers in culture, even if there is no alcohol in the culture medium. In addition, the permeability of the alveolar epithelium to large proteins in vivo is increased approximately fivefold in the alcohol-fed rats. The mechanisms by which alcohol impairs the alveolar epithelial barrier are still being investigated. Animal models suggest that chronic alcohol ingestion interferes with the expression and formation of tight junction complexes within the alveolar epithelium. Tight junctions are closely associated areas of two cells where the membranes of the cells join together; they are critically necessary to form an impermeable barrier that can limit the passage of even very small molecules across cell layers. Only a few studies of alcohol's effects on the alveolar epithelium have been conducted in humans. The findings indicate that people with AUD have impaired alveolar-capillary permeability at baseline and develop more pulmonary edema in the setting of ARDS compared with people without AUD.

The experimental evidence that alcohol can cause a profound defect in the physical barrier of the alveolar epithelium led to the question of why alcohol abuse alone, in the absence of an acute stress such as sepsis, does not cause pulmonary edema. Additional studies revealed that alcohol causes a concurrent, and perhaps compensatory, increase in salt and water transport across the epithelium. This transport is mediated by specific epithelial sodium channels located in the apical membrane and by protein pumps (i.e., Na/K-ATPase complexes) in the basolateral membrane of the epithelial cells. The expression and function of both the Na/K-ATPase complexes and epithelial sodium channels are increased in the alveolar epithelium of alcohol-fed animals. Thus, as long as there are no additional stresses, the alcoholic lung seems to be able to limit edema formation by upregulating salt and water transport across the epithelium, thereby compensating for the marked increase in the leakage of fluid between cells (i.e., paracellular leakage) into the airways. In the presence of an acute inflammatory stress, such as sepsis or aspiration, however, the paracellular leak increases dramatically, and the alveoli flood with proteinaceous edema fluid that overwhelms the already upregulated transepithelial pumping mechanisms. This scenario is supported by findings in laboratory animals that even at baseline, the lungs of alcohol-exposed animals are unable to clear a salt and water challenge as efficiently, despite the compensatory increase in epithelial sodium channel and Na/K-ATPase function, reflecting the severe permeability defect in the paracellular barrier mechanisms.

Alcohol, Alveolar Macrophages, and Pneumonia

Lung infections are major causes of morbidity and mortality worldwide. Data from the Centers for Disease Control and Prevention (CDC) consistently show that pneumonia is one of the top 10 causes of death in the United States and remains the leading cause of death from an infection. Alcoholism has been linked to pulmonary infections for over 200 years. Additionally, studies have demonstrated that people who abuse alcohol are not only more likely to develop pneumonia, but also are susceptible to more severe forms of the disease, are more likely to experience complications, and require greater use of resources. A prospective study by Adamuz and colleagues examined features associated with increased use of healthcare services and risk for readmission in patients discharged with pneumonia. Interestingly, the only independent risk factor associated with increased healthcare utilization after discharge was alcohol abuse. Similarly, Chalmers and colleagues demonstrated in a multivariate regression model that alcohol abuse was among independent risk factors that were significantly associated with the development of certain complications (i.e., complicated para-pneumonic effusion or empyema) in patients with community-acquired pneumonia.

Another experimental study using a pulmonary infection model of respiratory syncytial virus in mice found that chronic alcohol ingestion caused not only more severe infections, but also influenced the levels of various signaling molecules (i.e., cytokines), inducing a more robust proinflammatory cytokine profile. In this particular study, pulmonary inflammation in alcohol-exposed mice persisted for 7 days after infection, compared with 3–5 days in the control animals. Moreover, some alcohol-exposed mice showed severe inflammation with hemorrhage and edema. These results corroborate findings that infection in the setting of alcohol exposure increases the risk of complications such as ARDS. Similarly, other studies showed that people with AUD not only are more prone to develop community-acquired pneumonia, but are likely to suffer from infections that portend a worse prognosis and are more likely to be caused by virulent microorganisms that are more challenging to treat.

The mechanisms by which chronic and excessive alcohol consumption increases susceptibility to pneumonia are multifactorial. In addition to the already-discussed alterations in bacterial colonization and impaired host defenses in the upper and lower airways, increasing evidence suggests that chronic alcohol ingestion negatively impacts the immune functions of alveolar macrophages in a manner that is similar to its effects on epithelial barrier function. The alveolar macrophage is the primary immune cell in the alveolar space and is responsible for maintaining homeostasis of the lower airways through phagocytosis of pathogens and removal of debris. Animal studies have shown that chronic alcohol exposure causes significant alveolar macrophage dysfunction, leaving these normally active immune cells poorly equipped to phagocytose or kill invading organisms. Alveolar macrophages in alcohol-exposed animals also exhibit decreased production of important chemokines and mediators, which impairs their ability to recruit other cell types, namely neutrophils, during times of stress and infection. Although the majority of data focuses on the effects of chronic alcohol ingestion, experimental evidence further suggests that even acute exposure has similar detrimental effects on alveolar macrophage immune function, although these defects readily resolve. Taken together, these alcohol-mediated defects in alveolar macrophage function contribute to increased vulnerability to pulmonary infections.

Potential Therapeutic Strategies for the Alcoholic Lung

Currently, there are no specific therapies that can modify the alcoholic lung in the clinical setting. Clearly, as with all alcohol-related health issues, the ideal treatment would be abstinence in people with underlying AUD and/or a safe level of consumption in people who choose to drink for social reasons. However, this ideal will be impossible to achieve in any meaningful timeframe and it therefore is critical to identify, test, and validate therapeutic strategies that can limit the morbidity and mortality of alcohol-related diseases, including acute lung injury and pneumonia.

For identifying candidate approaches, it is important to recognize that a large percentage of people with AUD are otherwise healthy and can be identified by relatively simple health-screening questionnaires well before they develop serious organ dysfunction. Also, many people with AUD seek treatment, and structured alcohol treatment programs offer an opportunity to initiate adjunctive therapies designed to enhance lung health. For example, as discussed previously, clinical studies have shown that even otherwise-healthy people with AUD have glutathione and zinc deficiency within the alveolar space. Moreover, animal studies found that dietary supplementation with zinc and/or a glutathione precursor such as SAMe can enhance lung health even in the context of chronic alcohol ingestion. This trial currently is in progress with the goal of determining whether these supplements, alone or in combination, can enhance glutathione and zinc bioavailability in the alveolar space and improve alveolar macrophage immune function.

Another potential therapeutic target is Nrf2, which can be activated by plant-derived compounds (i.e., phytochemicals), such as sulforaphane. One clinical study evaluating the effects of 7-day treatment with the Nrf2 activator Protandim® in patients with AUD did not identify any significant improvement in glutathione levels or epithelial function. However, it is possible that combination therapy with an Nrf2 activator plus zinc and/or SAMe may be more effective than zinc and/or SAMe alone, and clinical trials in the near future hopefully will be able to answer that question.

The goal of these treatments clearly would not be to make it safe(r) to consume excessive amounts of alcohol. However, just as clinicians try to mitigate the health effects of metabolic syndrome in obese patients using medications that target diabetes, hypertension, or dyslipidemia while the patients struggle with weight loss, it is imperative to decrease the risk of pneumonia, acute lung injury, and other life-threatening complications while people with AUD work to achieve abstinence. There also may be some concerns about alcoholic patients' compliance with chronic oral treatments, such as zinc and SAMe supplements. However, many patients with AUD seek care for their addiction precisely because they are motivated to become or remain healthy and, consequently, are likely to adhere to their treatment regimen. Moreover, inadequate adherence to medical regimens is not a concern unique to this patient population but occurs in patients with many chronic medical conditions; examples include the low use of continuous positive airway pressure therapy for obstructive sleep apnea and poor adherence with anti-diabetic medications in adults with type 2 diabetes. Even if patients seeking treatment for AUD have equally low adherence rates, tens of thousands of individuals could benefit from these relatively simple and inexpensive treatments every year in the United States alone. Researchers and clinicians are just beginning to scratch the surface of this challenging problem, but the rapid pace of experimental and clinical research in the past two decades offers hope that in the relatively near future the devastating effects of AUD on lung health can be ameliorated.

Chapter 30

Alcohol Abuse Affects Bone Health

Chapter Contents

Section 30.1

The Link between Alcohol and Osteoporosis

This section includes text excerpted from "What People Recovering from Alcoholism Need to Know about Osteoporosis," National Institutes of Health (NIH), April 1, 2016.

According to the National Institute on Alcohol Abuse and Alcoholism (NIAAA), approximately 17 million adults ages 18 and older have an alcohol use disorder (AUD). Alcoholism is a disease characterized by a dependency on alcohol. Because alcohol affects almost every organ in the body, chronic heavy drinking is associated with many serious health problems, including pancreatitis, liver disease, heart disease, cancer, and osteoporosis. Maintaining sobriety is undoubtedly the most important health goal for individuals recovering from alcoholism. However, attention to other aspects of health, including bone health, can help increase the likelihood of a healthy future, free from the devastating consequences of osteoporosis and fracture.

What Is Osteoporosis?

Osteoporosis is a condition in which bones become less dense and more likely to fracture. Fractures from osteoporosis can result in significant pain and disability. In the United States, more than 53 million people either already have osteoporosis or are at high risk due to low bone mass.

Risk factors for developing osteoporosis include:

- thinness or small frame
- being postmenopausal and particularly having had early menopause
- abnormal absence of menstrual periods (amenorrhea)
- prolonged use of certain medications, such as those used to treat lupus, asthma, thyroid deficiencies, and seizures
- low calcium intake
- lack of physical activity

- smoking
- excessive alcohol intake

Osteoporosis often can be prevented. It is known as a silent disease because, if undetected, bone loss can progress for many years without symptoms until a fracture occurs. Osteoporosis has been called a childhood disease with old age consequences because building healthy bones in one's youth helps prevent osteoporosis and fractures later in life. However, it is never too late to adopt new habits for healthy bones.

Alcohol and Osteoporosis

Alcohol negatively affects bone health for several reasons. To begin with, excessive alcohol interferes with the balance of calcium, an essential nutrient for healthy bones. Calcium balance may be further disrupted by alcohol's ability to interfere with the production of vitamin D, a vitamin essential for calcium absorption.

In addition, chronic heavy drinking can cause hormone deficiencies in men and women. Men with alcoholism may produce less testosterone, a hormone linked to the production of osteoblasts (the cells that stimulate bone formation). In women, chronic alcohol exposure can trigger irregular menstrual cycles, a factor that reduces estrogen levels, increasing the risk for osteoporosis. Also, cortisol levels may be elevated in people with alcoholism. Cortisol is known to decrease bone formation and increase bone breakdown.

Because of the effects of alcohol on balance and gait, people with alcoholism tend to fall more frequently than those without the disorder. Heavy alcohol consumption has been linked to an increase in the risk of fracture, including the most serious kind—hip fracture. Vertebral fractures are also more common in those who abuse alcohol.

Osteoporosis Management Strategies

The most effective strategy for alcohol-induced bone loss is abstinence. People with alcoholism who abstain from drinking tend to have a rapid recovery of osteoblastic (bone-building) activity. Some studies have even found that lost bone can be partially restored when alcohol abuse ends.

Nutrition. Because of the negative nutritional effects of chronic alcohol use, people recovering from alcoholism should make healthy nutritional habits a top priority. As far as bone health is concerned, a well-balanced diet rich in calcium and vitamin D is critical. Good sources of calcium include low-fat dairy products; dark green, leafy vegetables; and calcium-fortified foods and beverages. Supplements can help ensure that you get adequate amounts of calcium each day, especially in people with a proven milk allergy. The Institute of Medicine recommends a daily calcium intake of 1,000 mg (milligrams) for men and women up to age 50. Women over age 50 and men over age 70 should increase their intake to 1,200 mg daily.

Vitamin D plays an important role in calcium absorption and bone health. Food sources of vitamin D include egg yolks, saltwater fish, and liver. Many people, especially those who are older or housebound, may need vitamin D supplements to achieve the recommended intake of 600–800 IU (International Units) each day.

Exercise. Like muscle, bone is living tissue that responds to exercise by becoming stronger. The best exercise for your bones is weight-bearing exercise that forces you to work against gravity. Some examples include walking, climbing stairs, weight training, and dancing. Regular exercise, such as walking, may help prevent bone loss and will provide many other health benefits.

Healthy lifestyle. Smoking is bad for bones as well as the heart and lungs. Women who smoke tend to go through menopause earlier, resulting in earlier reduction in levels of the bone-preserving hormone estrogen and triggering earlier bone loss. In addition, smokers may absorb less calcium from their diets.

Bone Density Test. A bone mineral density (BMD) test measures bone density in various parts of the body. This safe and painless test can detect osteoporosis before a fracture occurs and can predict one's chances of fracturing in the future. The BMD test can help determine whether medication should be considered. Individuals in recovery are encouraged to talk to their healthcare providers about whether they might be candidates for a BMD test.

Medication. Several medications are available for the prevention and/or treatment of osteoporosis, including: bisphosphonates; estrogen agonists/antagonists (also called selective estrogen receptor modulators or SERMS); calcitonin; parathyroid hormone; estrogen therapy; hormone therapy; and a RANK ligand (RANKL) inhibitor.

Section 30.2

Excessive Alcohol Intake Is a Risk Factor for Osteonecrosis

This section includes text excerpted from "Osteonecrosis," National Institute of Arthritis and Musculoskeletal and Skin Diseases (NIAMS), October 30, 2015.

Excessive alcohol use causes fatty substances to build up in the blood vessels. This can cause a decreased blood supply to the bone, which can lead to osteonecrosis.

What Is Osteonecrosis?

Osteonecrosis is a bone disease. It results from the loss of blood supply to the bone. Without blood, the bone tissue dies. This causes the bone to collapse. It may also cause the joints that surround the bone to collapse. If you have osteonecrosis, you may have pain or be limited in your physical activity. Osteonecrosis can develop in any bone, most often in the:

- Thighbone (femur)
- Upper arm bone (humerus)
- Knees
- Shoulders
- Ankles

It is also called:

- Avascular necrosis
- Aseptic necrosis
- Ischemic necrosis

Who Gets It?

Anyone can get osteonecrosis, but it is most common in men and people in their 30s, 40s, and 50s.

Symptoms

Osteonecrosis does not always cause symptoms, especially when it first develops. As the disease gets worse, you may feel pain when you put your weight on a joint that is affected by osteonecrosis. Over time, you may feel pain in the joint even when you are resting. Pain caused by osteonecrosis may be mild or severe. If it causes your bone and joint to collapse, you may have severe pain and not be able to use the joint. For instance, if you have osteonecrosis in the hip, you may not be able to walk.

Is There a Test?

There is no single test for osteonecrosis. If your doctor suspects you have osteonecrosis, he or she will take your medical history and do a physical exam.

Your doctor may also order one or more tests to see which bones are affected. These tests include:

- X-ray
- Magnetic resonance imaging (MRI)
- Computed tomography (CT) scan
- Bone scan
- Bone biopsy
- Measure of the pressure inside the bone

How Is It Treated?

Most people with osteonecrosis need treatment.

The goals of treatments are to:

- Improve use of the joint
- Stop further damage
- Protect bones and joints

Your treatment options may include surgery or nonsurgical treatments, such as medicines. Your doctor will determine the best treatment for you based on several factors, including:

- Your age
- The stage of the disease

- Where and how much bone has osteonecrosis
- The cause, if known. If the cause is steroid or alcohol use, treatment may not work unless you stop using those substances.

Nonsurgical Treatments

Nonsurgical treatments do not cure osteonecrosis, but they may help manage the disease. Your doctor may recommend one or more nonsurgical treatments, especially if the disease is in its early stages.

Medications

- Nonsteroidal anti-inflammatory drugs (NSAIDs) are used to reduce pain and swelling
- If you have blood-clotting problems, blood thinners may be used to prevent clots that block the blood supply to the bone
- If you take steroid medicines, cholesterol-lowering drugs may be used to reduce fat in the blood

Taking Weight off the Joint

Your doctor may suggest you limit your activity or use crutches to take weight off joints with osteonecrosis. This may slow bone damage and allow some healing. If combined with NSAIDs, it may help you avoid or delay surgery.

Range-of-Motion Exercises

Your doctor may recommend you exercise the joints with osteonecrosis to help improve their range of motion.

Electrical Stimulation

Your doctor may recommend electrical stimulation therapy to help bone growth.

Surgery

Most people with osteonecrosis eventually need surgery as the disease worsens. Some people with early-stage disease may need surgery if nonsurgical treatments do not help.

There are four types of surgery. Your doctor will decide if you need surgery and what type is best for you.

- **Core decompression surgery**, which lowers the pressure inside the bone. This increases blood flow to the bone.
- **Osteotomy**, which reshapes the bone. This reduces stress on the damaged joint.
- **Bone graft,** which takes healthy bone from one part of the body and uses it to replace diseased bone
- **Total joint replacement,** which replaces the joint with a manufactured one

Chapter 31

Other Organs at Risk from Alcohol Abuse

Chapter Contents

Section 31.1

Alcohol and Gut-Derived Inflammation

This section includes text excerpted from "Alcohol and Gut-Derived Inflammation," National Institute on Alcohol Abuse and Alcoholism (NIAAA), February 16, 2017.

In large amounts, alcohol and its metabolites can overwhelm the gastrointestinal tract (GI) and liver and lead to damage both within the GI and in other organs. Specifically, alcohol and its metabolites promote intestinal inflammation through multiple pathways. That inflammatory response, in turn, exacerbates alcohol-induced organ damage, creating a vicious cycle and leading to additional deleterious effects of alcohol both locally and systemically.

The gastrointestinal (GI) tract, as the first line of contact with anything ingested into the body, is at particular risk for damage by toxins. And mounting research suggests that poor gastrointestinal health plays a significant role in the body's overall health. Connecting the dots, anything that may cause GI damage, may have consequences far beyond the intestines. In fact, researchers have begun to discover that alcohol, particularly if consumed chronically and in larger amounts, induces a process initiated in the gut that promotes inflammation throughout the body. This alcohol-induced intestinal inflammation may be at the root of multiple organ dysfunctions and chronic disorders associated with alcohol consumption, including chronic liver disease, neurological disease, GI cancers, and inflammatory bowel syndrome. This section summarizes the mechanisms by which chronic alcohol intake leads to intestinal inflammation. These mechanisms include alcohol's influences on intestinal microbiota, on the integrity of the barrier between the intestine and the rest of the body, and on immune function within and outside the GI tract. The factors that can modify alcohol-induced gut inflammation and organ damage and the resulting pathologies that are a consequence of gut-derived inflammation are described. Although there may be large gender, racial, and interindividual variations in alcohol's effect on the GI tract, depending on differences in alcohol absorption, distribution, and elimination, they are not the focus of the current review.

Alcohol Metabolism and the Gut

Once consumed, alcohol is absorbed mainly in the upper intestinal tract by diffusion and then enters the liver via the portal vein. Therefore, the effect of alcohol on the distal small intestine and colon should largely come from its circulatory levels. That said, the luminal concentration of alcohol in the latter parts of the small intestine, close to the colon, reaches up to 200 mg/100 ml within an hour of drinking 2–2½ standard alcoholic drinks (0.8 g/kg).

The majority of alcohol metabolism in humans occurs in the liver, in cells called hepatocytes. During social drinking, defined here as an average of two standard drinks, the body typically processes the ingested alcohol with no deleterious effects through a process called oxidative conversion, during which the enzyme alcohol dehydrogenase (ADH) converts alcohol into the toxin acetaldehyde. Acetaldehyde dehydrogenase (ALDH) then converts acetaldehyde into acetate. Another alcohol metabolism pathway, the microsomal ethanol—oxidizing system (MEOS), handles a small portion of alcohol metabolism in social drinkers but a significant portion of alcohol metabolism when the body needs to process larger amounts of alcohol. MEOS leads to the production of oxygen free radicals, which can cause cellular damage. Although the majority of alcohol metabolism occurs in hepatocytes, the enzymes involved in the oxidative metabolism of alcohol also are present in the intestinal mucosa and intestinal bacteria also produce acetaldehyde in the GI tract. In addition, less commonly, nonoxidative alcohol metabolism occurs in the intestines via reactions with membrane phospholipids and/or free fatty acids. This alternative pathway may become particularly relevant when intestinal injuries occur after chronic alcohol consumption.

Therefore, both the small and large intestine can be affected by alcohol and its metabolites as the result of its oxidative and nonoxidative metabolism. Metabolism of alcohol in the GI tract can then lead to disruption of tissue homeostasis toward a chronic state of intestinal inflammation. As will be discussed in this review, mounting evidence shows that alcohol induces intestinal inflammation through various pathways, including changes in intestinal microbiota composition and function, increased permeability of the intestinal mucosa, and disruptions of the immune system of the intestinal mucosa.

Underlying Mechanisms for Alcohol and Gut-Derived Inflammation

Alcohol and Intestinal Microbiota

The intestine houses more than 500 bacterial species and achieves bacterial homeostasis when the ratio between "good" bacteria and pathogenic bacteria is appropriately balanced. "Dysbiosis" occurs when disease or environmental factors disrupt the bacterial balance. Disruption to the normal gut flora also occurs when there is an overall overgrowth of bacteria. Studies show that alcohol promotes both dysbiosis and bacterial overgrowth, which in turn leads to an increase in the release of endotoxins, produced by gram-negative bacteria. Endotoxins activate proteins and immune cells that promote inflammation. This section discusses evidence supporting alcohol's role in altering intestinal microbiota.

Bacterial Overgrowth

Studies in animals and humans confirm that alcohol increases intestinal bacteria. This overgrowth may be stimulated directly by alcohol, but some studies suggest that it also could be an indirect byproduct of poor digestive and intestinal function caused by alcohol consumption. For example, studies of patients with liver cirrhosis (both caused by alcohol and not) found an association between patients with abnormal intestinal motility—the intestine's ability to move food along—and bacterial overgrowth. Other studies found a connection between alcohol, bile acid, and bacterial overgrowth. Specifically, alcohol can alter bile-acid metabolism and, in turn, bile acids can affect intestinal bacteria. Studies in rats show that alcohol decreases certain bile acids and treating rats with bile acids reversed bacterial overgrowth.

Bacterial Dysbiosis

More studies use deoxyribonucleic acid (DNA) sequencing technology to assess intestinal microbiota populations and indicate a correlation between alcohol and changes in the ratio between beneficial or "good" bacteria, such as strains of Lactobacillus and Bifidobacterium, and pathogenic bacteria, such as proteobacteria and bacilli. For example, mice chronically fed alcohol display a decrease in good bacteria and an increase in bacteria that boost endotoxin production. In another study, researchers found a significant shift in intestinal microbiota composition in rats chronically fed alcohol, but they could prevent the shift by giving the rats Lactobacillus GG bacteria and a diet that included probiotic oats. Connecting dysbiosis to alcohol-induced health problems, several studies find that probiotic and synbiotic interventions, which stimulate the growth of beneficial bacteria, attenuate liver injury in rats and liver dysfunction in cirrhotic patients. Alcohol-induced bacterial overgrowth also may increase the risk of inflammation because intestinal bacteria can independently metabolize alcohol, producing excess acetaldehyde in the colon, which increases production of proinflammatory alcohol metabolites.

Alcohol-Induced Intestinal Hyperpermeability

The intestinal barrier regulates the passage of materials between the GI tract and the bloodstream, allowing for the absorption by the blood of key nutrients and preventing the absorption of noxious substances. It is made up of a layer of water, mucous gel, and epithelial and connective tissue. The epithelial layer can become leaky or "permeable," allowing pathogens and other deleterious substances into the bloodstream.

Studies in humans demonstrate that a subset of people with alcohol use disorder (AUD) in fact have increased intestinal permeability, measured using a method called Cr-EDTA, which examines excretion of orally administered chromium. In addition, those people with AUD and with increased permeability are more likely to have liver disease, indicating that intestinal permeability may be a mediator of organ damage in some people with AUD. Another study showed that not only is gut permeability increased in people with AUD, it is increased enough to allow large macromolecules through the intestinal barrier. Endotoxins—also known as lipopolysaccharides (LPS)—are large macromolecules and, as expected, the same study found that plasma endotoxin levels increased in parallel with increases in gut permeability.

But exactly how does alcohol induce intestinal permeability? The short answer is by disrupting the epithelial cells themselves (transepithelial permeability) and by disrupting the spaces between the epithelial cells (paracellular permeability), which consist of tight junctions, the cytoskeleton, and several associated proteins. Trans-epithelial permeability is caused by direct cellular damage. For example:

- Alcohol causes cell death, which leads to changes in the intestine that include mucosal ulcerations, erosions, and loss of epithelium mainly at the villi tips

- Acetaldehyde forms DNA adducts that cause direct cellular damage
- Reactive oxygen species (ROS) released during alcohol metabolism cause direct cellular damage via oxidative stress

Alcohol and its metabolites cause paracellular permeability by acting on the tight-junction complex, which melds two adjoining cells together. For example, acetaldehyde destabilizes tight junctions by redistributing proteins; alcohol and its metabolites alter the expression of tight-junction proteins; and alcohol nonoxidative metabolites cause tight-junction redistribution, disrupting its barrier function. In addition, studies show that alcohol destabilizes cells' cytoskeletons, the cell borders that give them their structure. There also is growing evidence that alcohol causes the overexpression of microRNAs (miRNAs), which are small stretches of noncoding ribonucleic acid (RNA) that silence gene expression. Specifically, alcohol can lead to overexpression of miRNAs that influence genes associated with gut-barrier integrity.

Alcohol Modulation of Mucosal Immunity

Gut inflammation results from an inflammatory response mounted by the immune system against alcohol and its metabolites. Alcohol affects intestinal mucosal immunity via several mechanisms. In particular, it may first decrease the innate immune response in the mucosa, resulting in increased susceptibility to intestinal pathogens. Subsequently, as found in studies in cell cultures, alcohol may trigger an immune system response and upregulation of molecules that promote the inflammatory response, including a release of inflammatory immune cells, such as leukocytes and mast cells.

Alcohol's Effect on Immunity and Inflammation

Alcohol can induce intestinal inflammation through a cascade of mechanisms that subsequently lead to inflammation and organ dysfunction throughout the body, in particular in the liver and brain. One mechanism is by increasing bacterial loads and the permeability of the intestinal wall allowing bacteria to leak through, leading to local and systemic effects by affecting mucosal immunity and via endotoxin release, respectively. Alcohol also affects mucosal immunity by suppressing one of the intestine's main lines of defense against bacteria, Paneth cells that secrete antibacterial compounds. Suppressed Paneth cells secrete fewer antibacterial compounds, which can allow additional intestinal bacterial overgrowth and allow their byproducts (i.e., endotoxins) entrance through the intestinal barrier. The bacteria, via endotoxins, trigger an inflammatory response by the intestine's immune system, causing a release of proinflammatory cytokines. The endotoxins and cytokines can then enter the liver, directly interacting with hepatocytes and with liver immune cells, causing local cytokine release that leads to fibrosis and causes additional inflammation. The gut inflammation can also spread endotoxins and cytokines into the bloodstream where they can enter the central nervous system (CNS), causing neuroinflammation.

As mentioned earlier, alcohol-related bacterial overgrowth and dysbiosis may lead to increased endotoxin production in the gut, which can bind to cells on the intestinal mucosa, causing local inflammation, and translocate to extraintestinal sites, causing systemic inflammation. Studies also show that alcohol can directly modulate both innate and adaptive immunity, further contributing to gut and gut-derived inflammation. For example, a study in mice found that alcohol inhibits the intestine's immune response for clearing hazardous bacteria, and other studies find that alcohol suppresses intestinal mucosal immune cell activity. Additional studies find myriad ways that alcohol affects mucosal immunity, including the following:

- By reducing the amount of antimicrobial molecules intestinal cells secrete, which leads to bacterial overgrowth
- By suppressing the signaling molecule, interleukin-22, which negatively affects antimicrobial peptides (e.g., Reg3β and Reg3γ) and intestinal mucosal integrity; and
- By suppressing signal molecules and immune T cells and thereby suppressing the intestinal mucosal immune response and bacterial clearance

Modifying Factors for Alcohol-Induced Gut-Derived Inflammation

As described above, alcohol causes gut-derived inflammation, which is related to other alcohol-associated pathologies. However, not all people with AUD develop disease, and those who do have varying degrees of disease severity. Although the extent of disease depends in large part on the extent of alcohol use and likely involves inherent individual characteristics, including genetics, race, and age, there are some adjustable factors that affect alcohol-induced intestinal inflammation and, therefore, may prevent or slow the progression of alcohol-related disease. Here, we discuss the roles of two adjustable environmental factors: circadian rhythm and diet.

Circadian Disruption

Circadian rhythm, also known as the biological clock, refers to an internal cycling of various biological processes. Chronic alcohol use can lead to a disrupted biological clock, which in turn can have a wide range of health-related consequences.

In terms of gut-related inflammation, studies in cell cultures, mice, and humans suggest that a disrupted circadian rhythm exacerbates alcohol-related gut leakiness. For example, one study found that alcohol-fed CLOCK mutant mice—who have a disrupted circadian cycle—showed more evidence of gut leakiness than alcohol-fed wild-type mice. A study in humans, including a group of shift workers who often have disrupted circadian rhythm, came to a similar conclusion. The researchers assessed circadian rhythm by measuring participants' blood melatonin levels, using low melatonin as a marker for disrupted circadian rhythm. They found that low melatonin correlated with gut leakiness in people with AUD.

Although it is unclear how circadian disruption amplifies alcohol-induced gut permeability, there are some hints from most studies done on this. For example, gut microbes have circadian oscillations, and circadian disruption can lead to dysbiosis in mice fed a high-fat diet, which in turn can induce intestinal inflammation and hyperpermeability. In addition, timing of lipid metabolism and bile-acid synthesis are regulated by the local hepatic circadian rhythm. Together, the evidence on circadian rhythm suggests a looping cycle where circadian disruption promotes alcohol-induced intestinal inflammation and alcohol disturbs circadian rhythm, which may further propagate intestinal hyperpermeability and inflammation.

Diet

Various studies show that nutrition can modify alcohol-induced gut inflammation and, subsequently, extraintestinal organ damage. Because people with AUD typically have altered diet composition, a focus on changing dietary habits might attenuate alcohol-related diseases. The following section reviews a sampling of studies on different diets and alcohol use.

Fat

Studies examining high-fat diets find conflicting results. Some find fats propagate alcohol's effects on the intestine, and some find they attenuate alcohol's harmful effects. The contrast likely reflects the variety of fats found in high-fat foods. Generally, studies seem to support the idea that unsaturated fats increase gut permeability and some kinds of saturated fats are protective.

Studies have examined the effects of several types of saturated fats given as supplements to alcohol-exposed mice. One found that tributyrin, a triglyceride fat found in butter and margarine, prevented alcohol-induced tight-junction disruption, which in turn protects against intestinal hyperpermeability. Another examined saturated long-chain fatty acids (SLCFAs), which are found in coconut oil, peanut oil, and dairy products. The researchers observed that the intestinal bacteria in mice chronically fed ethanol produced far less SLCFAs than mice not fed ethanol, and they also had lower levels of tight-junction proteins. That changed after the researchers gave the ethanol-fed mice SLCFA supplementation. Indeed, the mice given supplementation had higher levels of tight-junction proteins than ethanol-fed mice without supplementation. SLCFA supplements also prevented dysbiosis.

Unsaturated fats had less favorable effects. In one study, mice fed alcohol and unsaturated fats had increased fatty liver changes and suppressed mRNA expression of tight-junction proteins compared with mice fed alcohol and saturated fat. These findings suggest that an unsaturated-fat diet in conjunction with chronic alcohol use increases intestinal permeability.

Oats

Oats, which are rich in fat, fiber, protein, vitamins, and minerals, have long been associated with cardiovascular health and, examined for a possible role in gastrointestinal health. Several preclinical studies suggest that oats may attenuate alcohol's deleterious effects on the digestive system. In one study, two groups of rats received increasing doses of alcohol and either oats or regular rat chow for a period of 10 weeks. The oats-fed rats had significantly lower endotoxin levels than the chow-fed animals. Another study found that alcohol-fed rats given oat supplementation showed fewer signs of gut inflammation and alcohol-induced hyperpermeability than rats fed alcohol and regular rat chow. Researchers examined supplementation with glutamine, an amino acid found in oats. The study in mice found that glutamine supplements ameliorated alcohol-induced intestinal leakiness and improved alcohol-induced liver injury.

Vitamins and Minerals

People with AUD often are deficient in certain vitamins and minerals, including zinc and vitamin D, either from direct effects of alcohol consumption or poor diet. Those deficiencies, in turn, may have deleterious effects on the digestive system. A study in mice found a relationship between zinc deficiency and gut leakiness. The study compared mice fed alcohol and a zinc-deficient diet with mice fed alcohol and a zinc-adequate diet. The zinc-deficient mice showed increased intestinal permeability and higher plasma endotoxin levels.

Another study, conducted in intestinal cell culture and mice, examined whether vitamin D might protect gut health from alcohol exposure. In the cells, treating with vitamin D protected the cells from ethanol damage. In the mice, higher vitamin D levels measured in blood correlated with increased resistance to changes that lead to intestinal injury. These findings suggest that vitamin D deficiency may promote the deleterious effects of alcohol on the gut barrier and, perhaps, that vitamin D supplementation may attenuate those effects.

The Clinical Relevance of the Alcohol-Induced, Gut-Derived Inflammation

Alcohol-induced gut inflammation is believed to promote several disease states both within the GI tract, in the form of gastrointestinal cancers and inflammatory bowel disease, and outside the GI tract, in the form of, for example, liver disease and neuroinflammation. The following section briefly reviews a sample of the conditions associated with alcohol-related gut inflammation.

Alcohol and GI Cancers

Chronic alcohol consumption is associated with increased risk of major gastrointestinal cancers including cancer of the esophagus, stomach, and colon (colorectal cancer). The risk generally increases as alcohol consumption increases and in combination with other lifestyle-related factors, such as smoking tobacco or metabolic syndrome. And although alcohol was initially thought to act as a direct carcinogen, research instead suggests that alcohol-induced gut inflammation may be at fault.

Systemic inflammation seen in metabolic syndrome and obesity increases risk of several types of epithelial cancers, including those in the gastrointestinal tract, suggesting that the systemic inflammatory state created by alcohol-induced gut inflammation also may contribute to alcohol-induced carcinogenesis in the GI tract and other organs. This process can snowball because, as cells transition to a cancerous state, ADH activity increases while ALDH activity may decrease. This leads to an increased oxidation rate and a decreased ability to clear alcohol metabolites, which in turn can further promote carcinogenesis through direct effects on DNA, oxidative stress, and gut inflammation.

Alcohol and Inflammatory Bowel Disease (IBD)

Several lifestyle factors such as smoking and diet affect the incidence and severity of IBD, most likely by modulating gut inflammation. Alcohol consumption also may influence the course of IBD through associated gut inflammation; however, its effect in patients with IBD only has been studied in a few small studies. One study, for example, examined the impact of 1 week of moderate (24–36 g ethanol daily) red wine consumption on clinical disease activity and other noninvasive markers associated with increased risk of future disease flare. The study found no significant changes in indices of clinical disease but did find subclinical increases in markers for disease activity, including intestinal permeability. Such findings suggest that chronic alcohol consumption could increase the long-term risk for disease flare in IBD and supports the need for additional study.

Gut–Liver Axis (GLA)

Approximately 20–30 percent of heavy drinkers (people who drink more than 30 grams/day for at least 10 years) develop clinically significant alcoholic liver disease, including alcoholic steatohepatitis and cirrhosis. Several factors, such as the amount and duration of alcohol consumption, obesity, and gender, seem to moderate a person's risk and progression of alcoholic liver disease. In addition, studies find that alcohol-induced gut inflammation can contribute to liver injury by increasing intestinal permeability and the likelihood that gut-derived endotoxins enter the liver. One study found that people with AUD who also have liver disease are much more likely to have intestinal permeability: more than 40 times more likely than people without AUD and more than 20 times more likely than people with AUD who do not have liver disease. In alcohol-fed rats, gut leakiness is evident

2 weeks after alcohol initiation; after another 2 weeks, endotoxemia develops and then liver injury, suggesting an intermediary role for endotoxemia on liver injury.

Once gut leakiness begins, endotoxins can enter the liver via the portal vein that drains from the gut. In the liver, gut-derived substances interact with the liver's hepatocytes, parenchymal cells, and immune cells. Alcohol exposure increases LPS levels in portal and systemic circulation, and that can have a host of deleterious effects:

- Initiating endotoxin-mediated hepatocellular damage by activating the innate immune system and leading to an increase in ROS and inflammatory cytokines, leukotrienes, and chemokines
- Activating signaling pathways that lead to proinflammatory cytokine release associated with liver fibrosis
- Activating immune cells that can lead to liver inflammation and eventual fibrosis

Gut-Brain Axis (GBA)

It is well established that the brain helps control the gut, but research suggests the opposite also is true: the gut can influence brain function. In fact, some evidence suggests that alcohol-induced intestinal permeability and LPS can influence psychological and cognitive function. For example, among a group of alcohol-dependent, noncirrhotic patients hospitalized for detoxification, the subset that showed signs of intestinal permeability and LPS also had higher scores on measures of depression, anxiety, and alcohol cravings and scored worse on measures of selective attention. These findings suggest that some of the biological and behavioral changes seen in people with AUD may extend from the systemic inflammatory response triggered by changes in the gut.

Although the mechanisms by which the gut-brain axis conveys the effect(s) of alcohol on the central nervous system (CNS) are not well established, several studies suggest that systemic inflammation, like that caused by alcohol-provoked leaky gut, can influence the nervous system in several ways. For example, alcohol-induced gut inflammation can result in a systemic inflammation that subsequently affects neuronal function and may drive some symptoms of alcohol withdrawal, including autonomic disturbances and anxiety. In addition, elevated cytokines caused by the inflammatory response may be able to enter the brain and disrupt the blood–brain barrier, starting a vicious cycle that perpetuates alcohol's effects on the CNS. Alcohol-induced dysbiosis may have its own effect on the CNS via vagal afferent nerve fibers, which influence areas of the brain implicated in AUD, including the thalamus, hippocampus, amygdala, and prefrontal cortex. Specifically, accumulating evidence suggests that alcohol-induced dysbiosis and gut microbiome may contribute to modifications in the vagal response and neuroinflammation in the CNS linked with alcohol-associated behaviors. Other studies link microbiota alterations and endotoxins with neuroinflammation and anxiety-like behavior. Studies in mice and humans suggest that antimicrobials and probiotics can positively influence brain function in healthy people, holding out promise that targeting gut microbiota in people with AUD might help defray alcohol's influence on brain function.

Conclusions

Through multiple pathways, alcohol induces gut inflammation, which in turn promotes broad-spectrum pathologies both inside and outside the GI tract. In fact, many alcohol-related disorders, including cancers, liver disease, and neurological pathologies, may be exacerbated or directly affected by this alcohol-induced gut inflammation. The inflammation itself results from oxidative and nonoxidative pathways of alcohol metabolism that lead to a leaky gut, bacterial overgrowth, dysbiosis, and alterations in the mucosal immune system. As research uncovers the mechanisms by which alcohol affects gut inflammation and how that inflammation influences disease, researchers may be able to develop better strategies to prevent, or treat, conditions associated with chronic alcoholism. Already, studies are suggesting ways to modify diet and intestinal flora that may help alleviate some of the risks associated with chronic heavy drinking. Controlled trials are needed to assess the use of dietary supplementation with micronutrients in preventing or reversing alcohol effects.

Section 31.2

Alcoholism: A Common Cause of Pancreatitis

This section includes text excerpted from "Pancreatitis," National Institute of Diabetes and Digestive and Kidney Diseases (NIDDK), November 2017.

What Is Pancreatitis?

Pancreatitis is a potentially fatal inflammation of the pancreas often associated with long-term alcohol consumption. The pancreas is a large gland behind the stomach, close to the first part of the small intestine, called the duodenum. The pancreas has two main functions—to make insulin and to make digestive juices, or enzymes, to help you digest food. These enzymes digest food in the intestine. Pancreatitis occurs when the enzymes damage the pancreas, which causes inflammation. Pancreatitis can be acute or chronic. Either form is serious and can lead to complications.

Acute Pancreatitis

Acute pancreatitis occurs suddenly and is a short-term condition. Most people with acute pancreatitis get better, and it goes away in several days with treatment. Some people can have a more severe form of acute pancreatitis, which requires a lengthy hospital stay.

Chronic Pancreatitis

Chronic pancreatitis is a long-lasting condition. The pancreas does not heal or improve. Instead, it gets worse over time, which can lead to lasting damage to your pancreas.

How Common Is Pancreatitis?

Acute pancreatitis has become more common, for reasons that are not clear. Each year, about 275,000 hospital stays for acute pancreatitis occur in the United States. Although pancreatitis is rare in children, the number of children with acute pancreatitis has grown. Chronic pancreatitis is less common, with about 86,000 hospital stays per year.

Symptoms of Pancreatitis

The main symptom of acute and chronic pancreatitis is pain in your upper abdomen that may spread to your back. People with acute or chronic pancreatitis may feel the pain in different ways.

Acute Pancreatitis

Acute pancreatitis usually starts with pain that:

- begins slowly or suddenly in your upper abdomen
- sometimes spreads to your back
- can be mild or severe
- may last for several days

Other symptoms may include:

- fever
- nausea and vomiting
- fast heartbeat
- swollen or tender abdomen

People with acute pancreatitis usually look and feel seriously ill and need to see a doctor right away.

Chronic Pancreatitis

Most people with chronic pancreatitis feel pain in the upper abdomen, although some people have no pain at all. The pain may:

- spread to your back
- become constant and severe
- become worse after eating
- go away as your condition gets worse

People with chronic pancreatitis may not have symptoms until they have complications.

Other symptoms may include:

- diarrhea
- nausea
- greasy, foul-smelling stools
- vomiting
- weight loss

What Causes Pancreatitis?

The most common causes of both acute and chronic pancreatitis are:

- heavy alcohol use
- gallstones
- genetic disorders of your pancreas
- some medicines

Other causes include:

- infections, such as viruses or parasites
- injury to your abdomen
- pancreatic cancer
- having a procedure called endoscopic retrograde cholangiopancreatography (ERCP) to treat another condition
- pancreas divisum

Diagnosis of Pancreatitis

To diagnose pancreatitis and find its causes, doctors use:

- your medical history
- a physical exam
- lab and imaging tests

A healthcare professional will ask:

- about your symptoms

- if you have a history of health conditions or concerns that make you more likely to get pancreatitis—including medicines you are taking
- if you have a personal or family medical history of pancreatitis or gallstones

During a physical exam, the healthcare professional will:

- examine your body
- check your abdomen for pain, swelling, or tenderness

What Tests Do Healthcare Professionals Use to Diagnose Pancreatitis?

Healthcare professionals may use lab or imaging tests to diagnose pancreatitis and find its causes. Diagnosing chronic pancreatitis can be hard in the early stages. Your doctor will also test for other conditions that have similar symptoms, such as peptic ulcers or pancreatic cancer.

Treatment for Pancreatitis

Treatment for acute or chronic pancreatitis may include:

- a hospital stay to treat dehydration with intravenous (IV) fluids and, if you can swallow them, fluids by mouth
- pain medicine, and antibiotics by mouth or through an IV if you have an infection in your pancreas
- a low-fat diet, or nutrition by feeding tube or IV if you can't eat

Your doctor may send you to a gastroenterologist or surgeon for one of the following treatments, depending on the type of pancreatitis that you have.

Acute Pancreatitis

Mild acute pancreatitis usually goes away in a few days with rest and treatment. If your pancreatitis is more severe, your treatment may also include:

Surgery. Your doctor may recommend surgery to remove the gallbladder, called cholecystectomy, if gallstones cause your pancreatitis. Having surgery within a few days after you are admitted to the hospital lowers the chance of complications. If you have severe pancreatitis, your doctor may advise delaying surgery to first treat complications.

Procedures. Your doctor or specialist will drain fluid in your abdomen if you have an abscess or infected pseudocyst, or a large pseudocyst causing pain or bleeding. Your doctor may remove damaged tissue from your pancreas.

Endoscopic Cholangiopancreatography (ERCP). Doctors use ERCP to treat both acute and chronic pancreatitis. ERCP combines upper gastrointestinal endoscopy and X-rays to treat narrowing or blockage of a bile or pancreatic duct. Your gastroenterologist may use ERCP to remove gallstones blocking the bile or pancreatic ducts.

Chronic Pancreatitis

Treatment for chronic pancreatitis may help relieve pain, improve how well the pancreas works, and manage complications. Your doctor may prescribe or provide the following:

Medicines and vitamins. Your doctor may give you enzyme pills to help with digestion, or vitamins A, D, E, and K if you have malabsorption. He or she may also give you vitamin B-12 shots if you need them.

Treatment for diabetes. Chronic pancreatitis may cause diabetes. If you get diabetes, your doctor and healthcare team will work with you to create an eating plan and a routine of medicine, blood glucose monitoring, and regular checkups.

Surgery. Your doctor may recommend surgery to relieve pressure or blockage in your pancreatic duct, or to remove a damaged or infected part of your pancreas. Surgery is done in a hospital, where you may have to stay a few days. In patients who do not get better with other treatments, surgeons may perform pancreatic islet transplantation following surgery to remove your whole pancreas.

Procedures. Your doctor may suggest a nerve block, which is a shot of numbing medicine through your skin and directly into nerves that carry the pain message from your pancreas. If you have stones blocking your pancreatic duct, your doctor may use a procedure to break up and remove the stones.

How Can I Help Manage My Pancreatitis?

Stop Drinking Alcohol

Healthcare professionals strongly advise people with pancreatitis to stop drinking alcohol, even if your pancreatitis is mild or in the early stages. Continuing to drink alcohol when you have acute pancreatitis can lead to:

- more episodes of acute pancreatitis
- chronic pancreatitis

When people with chronic pancreatitis caused by alcohol use continue to drink alcohol, the condition is more likely to lead to severe complications and even death. Talk with your healthcare professional if you need help to stop drinking alcohol.

Stop Smoking

Healthcare professionals strongly advise people with pancreatitis to stop smoking, even if your pancreatitis is mild or in the early stages. Smoking with acute pancreatitis, especially if it's caused by alcohol use, greatly raises the chances that your pancreatitis will become chronic. Smoking with pancreatitis also may raise your risk of pancreatic cancer. Talk with your healthcare professional if you need help to stop smoking.

How Can I Help Prevent Pancreatitis?

You can't prevent pancreatitis, but you can take steps to help you stay healthy.

Avoid Alcohol Use

Alcohol use can cause acute and chronic pancreatitis. Talk with your healthcare professional if you need help to stop drinking alcohol.

Maintain a Healthy Weight or Lose Weight Safely

Maintaining a healthy lifestyle and a healthy weight—or losing weight if needed—can help to:

- make your pancreas work better

- lower your chance of getting gallstones, a leading cause of pancreatitis
- prevent obesity—a risk factor for pancreatitis
- prevent diabetes—a risk factor for pancreatitis

Avoid Smoking

Smoking is a common risk factor for pancreatitis—and the chances of getting pancreatitis are even higher in people who smoke and drink alcohol. Talk with your healthcare professional if you need help to stop smoking.

Eating, Diet, and Nutrition for Pancreatitis

During pancreatitis treatment, your doctor may tell you not to eat or drink for a while. Instead, your doctor may use a feeding tube to give you nutrition. Once you may start eating again, he or she will prescribe a healthy, low-fat eating plan that includes small, frequent meals. If you have pancreatitis, drink plenty of fluids and limit caffeine. Healthcare professionals strongly advise people with pancreatitis not to drink any alcohol, even if your pancreatitis is mild. Having an eating plan high in fat and calories can lead to high levels of fat in your blood, which raises your risk of pancreatitis. You can lower your chances of getting pancreatitis by sticking with a low-fat, healthy eating plan.

Section 31.3

Alcohol Misuse and Kidney Injury

This section includes text excerpted from "Alcohol Misuse and Kidney Injury: Epidemiological Evidence and Potential Mechanisms," National Institute of Alcohol Abuse and Alcoholism (NIAAA), February 16, 2017.

Chronic alcohol consumption is a well-known risk factor for tissue injury. The link between alcohol use disorder (AUD) and kidney injury is intriguing but controversial, and the molecular mechanisms by which alcohol may damage the kidneys are poorly understood. Epidemiological studies attempting to link AUD and kidney disease are, to date, inconclusive, and there is little experimental evidence directly linking alcohol consumption to kidney injury. However, studies conducted primarily in other organs and tissues suggest several possible mechanisms by which alcohol may promote kidney dysfunction. One possible mechanism is oxidative stress resulting from increased production of reactive oxygen species, which leads to an excessive amount of free radicals, which in turn trigger tissue injury and increase inflammation. In addition, AUD's effect on other major organs (liver, heart, intestines, and skeletal muscle) appears to promote unfavorable pathological processes that are harmful to the kidneys. Notably, these mechanisms have not yet been validated experimentally in the kidney. Additional research is needed to clarify if alcohol does indeed promote kidney injury and the mechanisms by which alcohol-induced kidney injury may occur.

Alcohol use disorder (AUD) is a substantial public health problem, affecting 15.7 million people age 12 and older in the United States. In 2012, 5.9 percent of all global deaths were attributable to alcohol—7.6 percent for men and 4.0 percent for women. Moreover, alcohol-attributable deaths have increased worldwide, making alcohol the fifth leading risk factor for premature death and disability in 2010 and the first among people ages 15–49.

Among the major consequences of chronic AUD that contribute to alcohol-related morbidity and mortality are liver cirrhosis, liver cancer, pancreatitis, and cardiovascular complications. To date, the epidemiological evidence connecting AUD and an increased incidence of chronic kidney disease is controversial. However, several preclinical studies suggest that alcohol consumption has a profound effect on the kidney and imply that there may be an independent pathologic entity, which we refer to here as "alcoholic kidney injury."

Studies conducted primarily in other organs and tissues suggest several possible mechanisms by which alcohol may promote kidney dysfunction. In particular, alcoholic kidney injury may be associated with a complex interaction of ethanol-induced oxidative stress and pro-inflammatory alterations. This may be complicated by the interplay between the kidneys and other organs, including the liver, intestines, skeletal muscle, and cardiovascular system. This brief synopsis reviews the evidence in support of these hypotheses.

Kidney Diseases and AUD: Lessons from Epidemiology

It is well established that cardiovascular diseases (including hypertension and ischemic heart disease) and diabetic microvascular complications are major risk factors for the development of chronic kidney diseases. In turn, heavy alcohol consumption is implicated in the development of these cardiac diseases, with chronic, heavy drinkers at higher risk than those who consume small to moderate amounts of alcohol.

That said, epidemiological data have yet to confirm a relationship between alcohol consumption and chronic kidney disease. A meta-analysis found little support for such a relationship. The researchers performed an extensive literature search using online databases (MEDLINE, EMBASE, and Cochrane Databases) to identify studies investigating the association between high alcohol consumption and chronic kidney disease, end-stage renal disease, or proteinuria (i.e., excess protein in the urine that indicates kidney damage). Their analysis included 20 studies representing a total of 292, 431 patients. The researchers reported that the pooled risk ratios of chronic kidney disease, proteinuria, and end-stage renal disease in patients with high alcohol consumption were 0.83, 0.85, and 1.00, respectively, indicating decreased risk or no risk of kidney disease in heavy alcohol consumers.

Other studies report similar findings, showing that the incidence of kidney disease is comparable or even lower in heavier drinkers (more than 210 g/week alcohol consumption) than in those who drink moderately (70–210 g/week alcohol consumption). In contrast, some studies find that heavy alcohol consumption may predict poorer outcome in patients with chronic kidney diseases. For example, White and colleagues reported that heavier drinkers (those consuming more than 30 g of alcohol/week) were at higher risk of incident albuminuria, which is typically a symptom of kidney disease. Japanese and Italian cohort studies revealed a U-shaped association between alcohol consumption and incidence of proteinuria. It is possible that the contradictory findings are the result of varying effects of different types of alcoholic beverages on the kidney, or the result of different alcohol consumption patterns in different countries. In addition, the self-reporting nature of drinking behaviors and the amount of alcohol consumed may bias some of the conclusions as shown, for example, by Parekh and Klag, who found that people who drink heavily underreport their alcohol consumption.

Although research suggests several potential mechanisms by which alcohol may directly or indirectly affect the kidneys, they have not yet been validated experimentally. Future research will hopefully explore these hypotheses to provide a better understanding of alcoholic kidney injury. Highlighting the effects of other organs on kidney and renal function; however, it should be noted that alcoholic kidney injury itself may have negative metabolic consequences. One such complication is impaired vitamin D metabolism, which may influence the function of several other organs, creating a vicious cycle.

The treatment of alcoholic kidney injury is still largely symptomatic, despite accumulating knowledge about underlying mechanisms. Both preclinical and human studies highlight the central role of oxidative stress and inflammation in triggering and driving the pathological processes associated with alcoholic kidney injury. Early diagnosis of this condition and rigorous abstinence from alcohol are very important for slowing down the progression of the disease and allowing the kidneys to regenerate.

Chapter 32

How Alcohol Interacts with Other Diseases and Disorders

Chapter Contents

Section 32.1

Influence of Alcohol on Immune System

This section includes text excerpted from "Alcohol Alert," National Institute on Alcohol Abuse and Alcoholism (NIAAA), January 25, 2017.

Many people are aware that excessive drinking can be harmful to the liver and other vital organs; however, there is another, less obvious, body system that is vulnerable to the negative effects of alcohol: the immune system. Because of alcohol's effects on the immune system, people who drink to excess are at increased risk of contracting infectious diseases, may have more complications after surgery, and often take longer to recover from illness, compared with those who drink at lower levels. Disruptions in immune system function also contribute to organ damage associated with alcohol consumption.

What Is the Immune System?

Our bodies are constantly exposed to a barrage of microbes, including viruses, bacteria, and fungi. Some of these are necessary for our well-being, such as the bacteria that live in the intestine and help with digestion; others can cause illness or have other toxic effects. The immune system is the body's defense against infectious disease, helping to distinguish, for example, between "good" and "bad" bacteria and eliminating harmful organisms (so-called pathogens) from the body. Equally important, however, is the immune system's ability to detect tissue damage and orchestrate the body's response, including removing damaged tissue and assisting in subsequent tissue repair and regeneration. To perform all of these functions, the immune system relies on an elaborate network of highly specialized cells that interact in a tightly orchestrated way. Some of these defense and damage-response networks are in place at birth; this is called our innate immunity. Other parts of the immune system develop throughout life, allowing the body to "learn" and adapt whenever it encounters a new pathogen; this is called our adaptive immunity.

The innate immune system includes physical barriers, such as the skin, that prevent organisms from entering the body directly;

physiological barriers, such as enzymes in the stomach and intestines, that destroy many pathogens and toxins that enter the body with food; and specialized immune cells that work throughout the body to combat infection and disease. The innate immune system mounts the first swift response to pathogens or tissue damage, seeking to attack and destroy invaders or eliminate damaged cells. An example of innate immune system activation is the initial inflammation, often characterized by redness and pain, that occurs in response to an infection or infection-free tissue injury. The adaptive immune system, on the other hand, mounts a longer-lasting response, involving numerous types of immune cells and molecules. It not only protects the body from pathogens that bypass the defenses of the innate immune system, but it "remembers" each particular pathogen it encounters. Therefore, if the pathogen should invade a second time, the body can launch an even speedier and more targeted counterattack.

Highly specialized immune cells, including white blood cells, are key players in innate and adaptive immunity, particularly cells called monocytes and macrophages, neutrophils, natural killer (NK) cells, dendritic cells, T cells, and B cells. These cells circulate in the bloodstream and also reside in primary and secondary lymphoid organs, including the thymus, bone marrow, and lymph nodes and spleen, as well as in organs like the liver and brain. This widespread distribution allows the body to respond to not only general infections but also localized infections and tissue injury. To optimally exert their effects, the immune cells communicate with each other and with various other cells in the body through signaling molecules called cytokines, which trigger specific immune responses. In addition, B cells produce proteins called antibodies or immunoglobulins, which recognize foreign molecules and bind to them, thus marking them for destruction.

Considering the important roles of the immune system, and the many players and interactions that contribute to its proper functioning, it is not surprising that disruptions to the system—for example, those related to alcohol consumption—can adversely affect health.

Alcohol's Effects on the Immune System

Alcohol consumption can alter the number, survival, and function of most immune cells. Although these alterations alone may not be sufficient to adversely affect one's health, if a person is exposed to a second "hit," such as a virus, his or her immune system may be unable to respond properly, increasing the risk of infection. The specific effects of alcohol on the immune system depend largely on how often and how much a person drinks. Even a single episode of binge drinking can have measurable effects on the immune system, from within the first 20 minutes to several hours after alcohol ingestion. Over the long term, alcohol misuse weakens the immune system and increases the risk and severity of viral and bacterial infections, including human immunodeficiency virus (HIV), hepatitis B and C, and lung infections. It can reduce the effectiveness of vaccines and contribute to a host of diseases, including alcoholic liver disease, alcoholic pancreatitis, inflammation in the gastrointestinal tract and brain, and cancer. Alcohol also adversely affects the immune system through its effect on the liver. An important component of the innate immune system, the liver produces a wide variety of antibacterial proteins.

If the liver is severely damaged by alcohol, it is less capable of producing these proteins, thereby increasing our susceptibility to bacterial infection. Indeed, bacterial infection is one of the most common complications of severe alcoholic hepatitis and alcoholic cirrhosis. Consuming alcohol during pregnancy can disrupt development of the fetal immune system. It can increase risk of infection and disease in infants after birth and possibly throughout their lives. One study found that the effect of prenatal alcohol exposure on neonatal infection is most significant if alcohol exposure occurred in the second trimester of pregnancy, a time when the immune system is developing. The risk is even more significant for babies who are born prematurely. Additional research is needed to determine how maternal drinking affects the fetal immune system and whether these effects can be reversed or reduced.

Alcohol's Impact on Immunity in the Gastrointestinal (GI) Tract

In addition to its direct effects on the immune system, alcohol can have an indirect impact on immunity through its actions in the stomach and intestines (GI tract). The GI tract is one of the first parts of the body to come into contact with alcohol and, as a result, bears the brunt of alcohol's harmful effects. The intestine is home to a wide variety of bacteria necessary for proper digestion; however, these bacteria can become problematic if they are not well-controlled and held in careful balance with each other.

Chronic alcohol consumption alters the composition of bacteria in our gastrointestinal (GI) tract, collectively known as microbiota. It reduces the numbers of beneficial bacteria and allows an increase in unhealthy bacteria. This imbalance limits the ability of immune cells in the GI tract to distinguish between normal and disease-causing organisms, and it is associated with diseases such as irritable bowel syndrome, food allergies, diabetes, cancer, obesity, and cardiovascular disease.

Chronic alcohol exposure, and indeed even a single episode of binge drinking, can also damage the wall of the intestine, allowing bacterial toxins and other harmful byproducts to leak from the intestine into the bloodstream. Once in the bloodstream, these compounds are transported to vital organs such as the liver, where they can activate inflammation and increase the risk, and even severity, of diseases such as alcoholic liver disease. The migration of bacteria from the gut into the bloodstream also can lead to systemic infections, sepsis, and multiple organ failure.

Alcohol's Impact on Immunity in the Liver

The central function of the liver is metabolizing, or breaking down, nutrients from digested food and detoxifying toxic substances after they pass through the gut. The liver is the chief organ for metabolizing and eliminating alcohol from the body and, as such, it is especially susceptible to damage caused by alcohol and its toxic byproducts. Alcohol-induced liver damage can lead to activation of immune cells within the liver as part of the inflammatory response to tissue injury. In addition, alcohol can harm the liver by promoting the leakage of bacterial toxins from the gut into the bloodstream, as noted above, which also activates the liver's inflammatory response.

With chronic, excessive alcohol use, this acute inflammatory response persists to become chronic inflammation, and results in further damage, impaired tissue repair, and the development of increasingly severe forms of liver disease, including hepatitis, fibrosis (i.e., scar tissue formation), and, ultimately, cirrhosis of the liver.

Other Health Consequences due to Alcohol's Impact on Immunity

In addition to those described above, a variety of other illnesses have been linked to the effects of alcohol on the immune system. Several of these adverse health consequences are discussed below.

Respiratory Diseases

Alcohol damages numerous components of the lung's defense system, increasing susceptibility to pneumonia, tuberculosis, and other respiratory infections. For example, heavy drinking hampers the ability of innate immune cells to identify and destroy bacteria that enter the airways and can produce lung infection. Heavy drinking also impairs the function of immune cells that recognize and destroy the pathogen that causes tuberculosis. In individuals with dormant tuberculosis infections, alcohol misuse can weaken the immune system, causing the pathogen to become active.

Finally, long-term drinking damages the body's first line of defense against respiratory infections—namely, the cells lining the airways that are covered with tiny hairs (i.e., cilia), which trap pathogens and other inhaled particles before they can reach the lungs and cause disease.

The potential consequences of lung infections—or any kind of lung damage—also are more severe in people who drink heavily. As one example, they are at increased risk of a life-threatening condition called acute respiratory distress syndrome (ARDS), which causes widespread inflammation of the lungs and leads to decreased oxygen levels in the blood. ARDS can result from lung infections and, particularly, bacterial pneumonia. It is two to four times more common in people with a history of chronic alcohol misuse.

Cancer

Alcohol has been linked to an increased risk of cancer, including cancers of the liver, mouth and throat (i.e., upper aerodigestive tract), large intestine, and breast. The risk of harm differs depending on the type of cancer, the amount of alcohol consumed, and even genetic factors.

For example, heavy drinkers with a genetic mutation leading to a deficiency in aldehyde dehydrogenase 2, an enzyme that metabolizes acetaldehyde, a toxic byproduct of alcohol, are at considerably elevated risk for cancer of the esophagus. Alcohol's effects on the immune system also may make cancer cells more aggressive. Normally, immune cells from both the innate and the adaptive immune system, and the molecules they produce, help to eliminate cancer cells and control cancer growth and progression. However, alcohol-induced disruption of immune cells may allow the cancer to grow and progress. As a result, cancer patients who drink heavily are more likely to die from cancer-related complications (and to die sooner) than those who drink less.

Human Immunodeficiency Virus (HIV) Infection

The complex interaction between alcohol, immunity, and disease is particularly relevant to HIV infection. HIV attacks the immune system by destroying a type of T cell vital to fighting infections. The destruction of these cells leaves people with HIV vulnerable to other infections, diseases, and complications. Many studies examining the connection between alcohol, HIV, and the immune system have focused on the mucosa—the cell layer that lines various parts of the body, including the lungs, airways, GI tract, and genitalia. These mucosas are the body's initial defense against invading pathogens. Converging evidence indicates that alcohol misuse disrupts mucosa function and, in doing so, increases risk of HIV, accelerates HIV progression, and contributes to other infections and inflammation.

Recovery from Traumatic Injury

About one-third of all patients with wounds such as burns, broken bones, and brain and other tissue injuries have blood alcohol levels above the legal limit at the time of injury. Alcohol intoxication not only increases the risk of such injuries, but it can adversely affect outcomes for these patients. These effects appear to be particularly attributed to altered immune function, which makes patients more vulnerable to subsequent challenges to the immune system, such as surgery or infection. As a result, these patients are more likely to die during the recovery period. Alcohol intoxication is especially harmful for people with burn injuries. Approximately 50 percent of burn patients have detectable blood alcohol levels when they are admitted to the hospital. These patients have more complications, require longer hospital stays, and have greater mortality rates compared with patients who are not intoxicated at the time of injury. Patients with burn injuries are especially susceptible to infection of the lung. Alcohol intoxication at the time of injury further increases the risk of such infections by suppressing the immune system. Similarly, both burn injuries and alcohol disrupt the barrier function of the intestine, allowing bacteria to enter the bloodstream and increasing the risk of infection throughout the body.

Immune Activity in the Brain

Data collected indicate that alcohol-induced immune activation contributes to neuropathology and perhaps even alcohol use disorder. Animal studies find that alcohol consumption increases neuronal damage via the activation of immune factors. Studies also have found that mice bred for high alcohol consumption exhibit an increase in the expression of certain genes involved in immune signaling, suggesting a role for immune cells in drinking behavior.

Though human research in this area is limited, studies using postmortem human brains have found that immune factors are increased in the brains of people who had alcohol use disorder. These studies have also found that the expression in the brain of certain immune factors is correlated with lifetime alcohol consumption. In addition, immune molecules, such as inflammatory cytokines, produced when bacteria leak from the gut into the bloodstream, can be transported to the brain where they produce a long-lasting inflammatory response.

Much more research is needed to determine how neuroinflammation occurs; how it affects brain function at the molecular, cellular, and circuit levels; and how the brain and peripheral immune systems communicate. Nonetheless, this is a promising avenue of research with the potential to enhance our understanding of alcohol use disorder and other alcohol-related conditions.

Practical Implications for Patients Who Drink

Alcohol's effects on the immune system have important implications for treating critically ill patients with a history of alcohol use disorder. Such patients are more likely to require hospitalization, have longer hospital stays, or need treatment in an intensive care unit. They also are more likely to die from their illnesses. In addition, these patients are at increased risk of numerous complications, such as persistent fever, pneumonia, blood infections, ARDS, or confusion and disorientation. Finally, they may need higher doses of certain medications to achieve effective treatment. Treating patients who drink excessively for serious medical problems is, therefore, particularly challenging. Physicians need to be aware of a patient's alcohol use to be able to offer the best treatment and to prevent more serious or even fatal complications.

Conclusion

Considerable progress has been made in bringing to light the relationship between alcohol and the immune system. However, the immune system is exceedingly complex, and there still are many gaps in our understanding of just how alcohol affects immunity and, ultimately, health. Scientists are working to better define the ways in which alcohol interacts with and hampers the immune system. The knowledge gained from this research is expected to lead to new ways of preventing and treating alcohol-related illnesses, enabling physicians to bolster weakened immune responses and tailor treatment to the unique needs of patients with alcohol use disorder.

Section 32.2

Alcohol Use Increases Likelihood of Acquiring Sexually Transmitted Diseases (STDs)

This section includes text excerpted from "Sexually Transmitted Diseases," HIV.gov, U.S. Department of Health and Human Services (HHS), May 15, 2017.

What Do I Need to Know about STDs?

Living healthy with human immunodeficiency virus (HIV) includes preventing other sexually transmitted diseases (STDs). An STD is an infection that's passed from person to person through sexual contact. HIV is an example of an STD.

Other types of STDs include:

- Chlamydia
- Genital herpes
- Gonorrhea
- Hepatitis B and C
- Human papillomavirus (HPV), and
- Syphilis

The only way to avoid getting other STDs is to not have vaginal, anal, or oral sex. If you are sexually active, you can do the following things to lower your chances of getting other STDs:

- Choose less risky sexual behaviors
- Use condoms consistently and correctly
- Reduce the number of people with whom you have sex

- Limit or eliminate drug and alcohol use before and during sex
- Have an honest and open talk with your healthcare provider and ask how frequently you should be tested for STDs.

For people living with HIV, it can be harder to treat STDs. STDs increase your viral load in your genital fluids, and some types of STDs can lower your CD4 count. Because HIV weakens the CD4 cells in the immune system, your body has a harder time fighting off STDs. This also means that if you are living with HIV and also have an STD, you may be able to transmit HIV to your partner(s) even if your viral load is undetectable. In fact, people living HIV who are also infected with another STD are 3–5 times as likely as others living with HIV to spread HIV through sexual contact.

It's important for people with HIV to get tested and treated for other STDs. Being tested and treated for STDs helps you maintain good health and avoid transmitting an STD unknowingly. If you have HIV and are sexually active, get tested at least once a year.

Encourage your partner(s) to do the same. You or your partner(s) can have an STD without having symptoms. You and your partner should determine what sexual behaviors and prevention practices are going to be used in your relationship—and outside of it if you are not exclusive. The goal of this communication is to keep you both healthy and free from new infections. Your healthcare provider can offer you the best care if you discuss your sexual history openly. Locate a provider near you.

Alcohol Use

Alcohol use can be harmful to your health and get out of hand for some people. Modest use of alcohol can help your heart health in some circumstances, but it can also lead to long-term effects that are harmful and reduce your ability to fight off STDs.

How Can Alcohol and STDs Affect My Health?

Alcohol use, abuse, and dependence may damage your body and brain. This damage to your body and brain can negatively affect your health and well-being in many ways. These are just some examples.

- Physical effects

    - Drinking too much can damage your brain, liver, and immune system. Chronic drinkers with STDs may be at greater risk for disease progression than those who drink very little or not at all.
    - Making it easier for your body to get an infection
    - Alcohol may interfere with medicines that are part of an overall treatment plan
- Other effects
    - The after-effects of alcohol "high" can create feelings of depression, exhaustion, pain, and/or irritability
    - Getting high may cause you to forget to take your HIV medicines or forget to make and keep doctor and clinic appointments

Alcohol dependency can make it hard for you to maintain your house, job, relationships, and social supports—all of which are important for your well-being

How Can I Find Treatment or Support Programs?

Choosing to stop consuming alcohol is not easy, but it can be done. Quitting will improve your health, well-being, and relationships with others.

- Based on your level of dependence, you may need medical treatment and/or psychological therapy to help you quit. Talk with your healthcare provider to explore treatment options that are specific to your type of substance use.
- Peer support and faith-based recovery groups may also help you manage alcohol use and dependence

Section 32.3

Human Immunodeficiency Virus (HIV) and Alcohol Use

This section includes text excerpted from "Drugs, Alcohol and HIV: Entire Lesson," U.S. Department of Veterans Affairs (VA), February 8, 2018.

If you've just found out that you are HIV positive, you might be wondering what alcohol will do to your body. (Recreational drugs are drugs that aren't being used for medical purposes, such as beer, cocaine, amphetamines, and pot; this also includes prescription medicines that are being used for pleasure.) You may be wondering whether these drugs are bad for your immune system. And what about your HIV medications—can recreational drugs affect those? Is using alcohol bad for you? Each person is different, and a lot depends on how much you use, and how often you use them. However, most experts would agree that, in large amounts alcohol is bad for your immune system and your overall health. Remember, if you have HIV, your immune system is already weakened.

Alcohol Effects on Your Immune System

Drinking too much alcohol can weaken your immune system. A weaker immune system will have a harder time fighting off common infections (such as a cold), as well as human immunodeficiency virus (HIV)-related infections. A weaker immune system also increases the chance that you will experience more side effects from your HIV medications. All of these things can make it easier for you to get infections. The organ in your body that alcohol affects most is your liver. The liver rounds up waste from chemicals that you put in your body. A weaker liver means less efficient "housekeeping" and, probably, a weaker you. If you also have hepatitis C (or any other kind of hepatitis), your liver is already working very hard to fight the disease itself and deal with the strong drugs that you may be taking for your hepatitis treatment.

Alcohol Interactions with Your HIV Meds

HIV medications can be hard on your body, so when you are taking these medications, it is important that your liver works as well as possible. The liver is responsible for getting rid of waste products from the medications. Once you are HIV positive, your body may react differently to alcohol. Many people find that it takes longer to recover from consuming alcohol than it did before they had HIV. Remember that having HIV means a major change has taken place in your body. You may choose to use alcohol in moderation, but be sure to respect your body. Pay attention to what and how much you eat, drink, smoke, and take into your body.

Alcohol and Safer Sex

Alcohol may affect your ability to make decisions. Even though you use condoms regularly and practice safer sex when you're not high, you may be willing to take more risks and not use a condom when you're under the influence of alcohol. Alcohol can also affect the decisions you make about safer sex. For example, if you have too much to drink, you may not be able to remember where you put the condoms, and decide simply not to use them. These are decisions you probably would not make if you were sober. These actions put your partner at risk for HIV and put you at risk for other sexually transmitted diseases. Remember to keep condoms handy in places where you might have sex. Also, try to limit the amount of alcohol you drink if you know you are going to have sex.

Section 32.4

Alcohol Increases Cancer Risks

This section includes text excerpted from "Alcohol and Cancer Risk," National Cancer Institute (NCI), June 24, 2013. Reviewed April 2018.

The Link between Alcoholism and Cancer

Based on extensive reviews of research studies, there is a strong scientific consensus of an association between alcohol drinking and several types of cancer. In the *Report on Carcinogens*, the National Toxicology Program of the U.S. Department of Health and Human Services (HHS) lists consumption of alcoholic beverages as a known human carcinogen. The research evidence indicates that the more alcohol a person drinks—particularly the more alcohol a person drinks regularly over time—the higher his or her risk of developing an alcohol-associated cancer.

Clear patterns have emerged between alcohol consumption and the development of the following types of cancer:

Head and Neck Cancer

Alcohol consumption is a major risk factor for certain head and neck cancers, particularly cancers of the oral cavity (excluding the lips), pharynx (throat), and larynx (voice box). People who consume 50 or more grams of alcohol per day (approximately 3.5 or more drinks per day) have at least a two to three times greater risk of developing these cancers than nondrinkers. Moreover, the risks of these cancers are substantially higher among persons who consume this amount of alcohol and also use tobacco.

Esophageal Cancer

Alcohol consumption is a major risk factor for a particular type of esophageal cancer called esophageal squamous cell carcinoma. In addition, people who inherit a deficiency in an enzyme that metabolizes alcohol have been found to have substantially increased risks of alcohol-related esophageal squamous cell carcinoma.

Liver Cancer

Alcohol consumption is an independent risk factor for, and a primary cause of, liver cancer (hepatocellular carcinoma). (Chronic infection with hepatitis B virus and hepatitis C virus are the other major causes of liver cancer.)

Breast Cancer

More than 100 epidemiologic studies have looked at the association between alcohol consumption and the risk of breast cancer in women. These studies have consistently found an increased risk of breast cancer associated with increasing alcohol intake. A meta-analysis of 53 of these studies (which included a total of 58,000 women with breast cancer) showed that women who drank more than 45 grams of alcohol per day (approximately three drinks) had 1.5 times the risk of developing breast cancer as nondrinkers (a modestly increased risk). The risk of breast cancer was higher across all levels of alcohol intake: for every 10 grams of alcohol consumed per day (slightly less than one drink), researchers observed a small (7%) increase in the risk of breast cancer.

Colorectal Cancer

Alcohol consumption is associated with a modestly increased risk of cancers of the colon and rectum. A meta-analysis of 57 cohort and case-control studies that examined the association between alcohol consumption and colorectal cancer risk showed that people who regularly drank 50 or more grams of alcohol per day (approximately 3.5 drinks) had 1.5 times the risk of developing colorectal cancer as nondrinkers or occasional drinkers. For every 10 grams of alcohol consumed per day, there was a small (7%) increase in the risk of colorectal cancer.

Research on Alcohol Consumption and Other Cancers

Numerous studies have examined the association between alcohol consumption and the risk of other cancers, including cancers of the pancreas, ovary, prostate, stomach, uterus, and bladder. For these cancers, either no association with alcohol use has been found or the evidence for an association is inconsistent.

However, for two cancers—renal cell (kidney) cancer and non-Hodgkin lymphoma (NHL)—multiple studies have shown that increased alcohol consumption is associated with a decreased risk of cancer. A meta-analysis of the NHL studies (which included 18,759 people with NHL) found a 15 percent lower risk of NHL among alcohol drinkers compared with nondrinkers. The mechanisms by which alcohol consumption would decrease the risks of either renal cell cancer or NHL are not understood.

How Does Alcohol Increase the Risk of Cancer?

Researchers have identified multiple ways that alcohol may increase the risk of cancer, including:

- metabolizing (breaking down) ethanol in alcoholic drinks to acetaldehyde, which is a toxic chemical and a probable human carcinogen; acetaldehyde can damage both deoxyribonucleic acid (DNA) (the genetic material that makes up genes) and proteins

- generating reactive oxygen species (chemically reactive molecules that contain oxygen), which can damage DNA, proteins, and lipids (fats) through a process called oxidation
- impairing the body's ability to break down and absorb a variety of nutrients that may be associated with cancer risk, including vitamin A; nutrients in the vitamin B complex, such as folate; vitamin C; vitamin D; vitamin E; and carotenoids
- increasing blood levels of estrogen, a sex hormone linked to the risk of breast cancer

Alcoholic beverages may also contain a variety of carcinogenic contaminants that are introduced during fermentation and production, such as nitrosamines, asbestos fibers, phenols, and hydrocarbons.

How Does the Combination of Alcohol and Tobacco Affect Cancer Risk?

Epidemiologic research shows that people who use both alcohol and tobacco have much greater risks of developing cancers of the oral cavity, pharynx (throat), larynx, and esophagus than people who use either alcohol or tobacco alone. In fact, for oral and pharyngeal cancers, the risks associated with using both alcohol and tobacco are multiplicative; that is, they are greater than would be expected from adding the individual risks associated with alcohol and tobacco together.

Can a Person's Genes Affect Their Risk of Alcohol-Related Cancers?

A person's risk of alcohol-related cancers is influenced by their genes, specifically the genes that encode enzymes involved in metabolizing (breaking down) alcohol.

For example, one way the body metabolizes alcohol is through the activity of an enzyme called alcohol dehydrogenase, or ADH. Many individuals of Chinese, Korean, and especially Japanese descent carry a version of the gene for ADH that codes for a "superactive" form of the enzyme. This superactive ADH enzyme speeds the conversion of alcohol (ethanol) to toxic acetaldehyde. As a result, when people who have the superactive enzyme drink alcohol, acetaldehyde builds up. Among people of Japanese descent, those who have this superactive

ADH have a higher risk of pancreatic cancer than those with the more common form of ADH.

Another enzyme, called aldehyde dehydrogenase 2 (ALDH2), metabolizes toxic acetaldehyde to nontoxic substances. Some people, particularly those of East Asian descent, carry a variant of the gene for ALDH2 that codes for a defective form of the enzyme. In people who have the defective enzyme, acetaldehyde builds up when they drink alcohol. The accumulation of acetaldehyde has such unpleasant effects (including facial flushing and heart palpitations) that most people who have inherited the ALDH2 variant are unable to consume large amounts of alcohol. Therefore, most people with the defective form of ALDH2 have a low risk of developing alcohol-related cancers.

However, some individuals with the defective form of ALDH2 can become tolerant to the unpleasant effects of acetaldehyde and consume large amounts of alcohol. Epidemiologic studies have shown that such individuals have a higher risk of alcohol-related esophageal cancer, as well as of head and neck cancers, than individuals with the fully active enzyme who drink comparable amounts of alcohol. These increased risks are seen only among people who carry the ALDH2 variant and drink alcohol—they are not observed in people who carry the variant but do not drink alcohol.

Can Drinking Red Wine Help Prevent Cancer?

Researchers conducting studies using purified proteins, human cells, and laboratory animals have found that certain substances in red wine, such as resveratrol, have anticancer properties. Grapes, raspberries, peanuts, and some other plants also contain resveratrol. However, clinical trials in humans have not provided evidence that resveratrol is effective in preventing or treating cancer. Few epidemiologic studies have looked specifically at the association between red wine consumption and cancer risk in humans.

What Happens to Cancer Risk after a Person Stops Drinking Alcohol?

Most of the studies that have examined whether cancer risk declines after a person stops drinking alcohol have focused on head and neck cancers and on esophageal cancer. In general, these studies have found that stopping alcohol consumption is not associated with immediate reductions in cancer risk; instead, it may take years for the risks of cancer to return to those of never drinkers.

For example, a pooled analysis of 13 case-control studies of cancer of the oral cavity and pharynx combined found that alcohol-associated cancer risk did not begin to decrease until at least 10 years after stopping alcohol drinking. Even 16 years after they stopped drinking alcohol, the risk of cancer was still higher for ex-drinkers than for never drinkers. In several studies, the risk of esophageal cancer was also found to decrease slowly with increasing time since stopping alcohol drinking. A pooled analysis of five case–control studies found that the risk of esophageal cancer did not approach that of never drinkers for at least 15 years after stopping alcohol drinking.

Is It Safe for Someone to Drink Alcohol While Undergoing Cancer Chemotherapy?

As with most questions related to a specific individual's cancer treatment, it is best for a patient to check with their healthcare team about whether or not it is safe to drink alcohol during or immediately following chemotherapy treatment. The doctors and nurses administering the treatment will be able to give specific advice about whether drinking alcohol is safe with particular chemotherapy drugs and/or other medications prescribed along with chemotherapy.

Section 32.5

Alcohol and Hypoglycemia in Diabetics

This section includes text excerpted from "Low Blood Glucose (Hypoglycemia)," National Institute of Diabetes and Digestive and Kidney Diseases (NIDDK), August 30, 2016.

Alcohol makes it harder for your body to keep your blood glucose level steady, especially if you haven't eaten in a while. The effects of alcohol can also keep you from feeling the symptoms of hypoglycemia, which may lead to severe hypoglycemia.

Hypoglycemia, also called low blood glucose or low blood sugar, occurs when the level of glucose in your blood drops below normal. For many people with diabetes, that means a level of 70 milligrams per deciliter (mg/dL) or less. Your numbers might be different, so check with your healthcare provider to find out what level is too low for you.

What Are the Symptoms of Hypoglycemia?

Symptoms of hypoglycemia tend to come on quickly and can vary from person to person. You may have one or more mild-to-moderate symptoms listed below. Sometimes people don't feel any symptoms. Severe hypoglycemia is when your blood glucose level becomes so low that you're unable to treat yourself and need help from another person. Severe hypoglycemia is dangerous and needs to be treated right away. This condition is more common in people with type 1 diabetes.

Some symptoms of hypoglycemia during sleep are:

- crying out or having nightmares
- sweating enough to make your pajamas or sheets damp
- feeling tired, irritable, or confused after waking up

How Can I Prevent Hypoglycemia If I Have Diabetes?

If you are taking insulin, a sulfonylurea, or a meglitinide, using your diabetes management plan and working with your healthcare team to adjust your plan as needed can help you prevent hypoglycemia. The following actions can also help prevent hypoglycemia:

Eat Regular Meals and Snacks

Your meal plan is key to preventing hypoglycemia. Eat regular meals and snacks with the correct amount of carbohydrates to help keep your blood glucose level from going too low. Also, if you drink alcoholic beverages, it's best to eat some food at the same time.

Check Blood Glucose Levels

Knowing your blood glucose level can help you decide how much medicine to take, what food to eat, and how physically active to be. To find out your blood glucose level, check yourself with a blood glucose meter as often as your doctor advises.

Hypoglycemia Unawareness

Sometimes people with diabetes don't feel or recognize the symptoms of hypoglycemia, a problem called hypoglycemia unawareness. If you have had hypoglycemia without feeling any symptoms, you may need to check your blood glucose more often so you know when you need to treat your hypoglycemia or take steps to prevent it. Be sure to check your blood glucose before you drive. If you have hypoglycemia unawareness or have hypoglycemia often, ask your healthcare provider about a continuous glucose monitor (CGM). A CGM checks your blood glucose level at regular times throughout the day and night. CGMs can tell you if your blood glucose is falling quickly and sound an alarm if your blood glucose falls too low. CGM alarms can wake you up if you have hypoglycemia during sleep.

Be Physically Active Safely

Physical activity can lower your blood glucose during the activity and for hours afterward. To help prevent hypoglycemia, you may need to check your blood glucose before, during, and after physical activity and adjust your medicine or carbohydrate intake. For example, you might eat a snack before being physically active or decrease your insulin dose as directed by your healthcare provider to keep your blood glucose from dropping too low.

Work with Your Healthcare Team

Tell your healthcare team if you have had hypoglycemia. Your healthcare team may adjust your diabetes medicines or other aspects of your management plan. Learn about balancing your medicines, eating plan, and physical activity to prevent hypoglycemia. Ask if you should have a glucagon emergency kit to carry with you at all times.

How Do I Treat Hypoglycemia?

If you begin to feel one or more hypoglycemia symptoms, check your blood glucose. If your blood glucose level is below your target or less than 70, eat or drink 15 grams of carbohydrates right away. Examples include:

- four glucose tablets or one tube of glucose gel
- 1/2 cup (4 ounces) of fruit juice—not low-calorie or reduced sugar*
- 1/2 can (4–6 ounces) of soda—not low-calorie or reduced sugar
- 1 tablespoon of sugar, honey, or corn syrup
- 2 tablespoons of raisins

Wait 15 minutes and check your blood glucose again. If your glucose level is still low, eat or drink another 15 grams of glucose or carbohydrates. Check your blood glucose again after another 15 minutes. Repeat these steps until your glucose level is back to normal.

If your next meal is more than 1 hour away, have a snack to keep your blood glucose level in your target range. Try crackers or a piece of fruit.

Note: (*) People who have kidney disease shouldn't drink orange juice for their 15 grams of carbohydrates because it contains a lot of potassium. Apple, grape, or cranberry juice are good options.

Treating Hypoglycemia If You Take Acarbose or Miglitol

If you take acarbose or miglitol along with diabetes medicines that can cause hypoglycemia, you will need to take glucose tablets or glucose gel if your blood glucose level is too low. Eating or drinking other sources of carbohydrates won't raise your blood glucose level quickly enough.

What If I Have Severe Hypoglycemia and Can't Treat Myself?

Someone will need to give you a glucagon injection if you have severe hypoglycemia. An injection of glucagon will quickly raise your blood glucose level. Talk with your healthcare provider about when and how to use a glucagon emergency kit. If you have an emergency kit, check the date on the package to make sure it hasn't expired.

If you are likely to have severe hypoglycemia, teach your family, friends, and coworkers when and how to give you a glucagon injection. Also, tell your family, friends, and coworkers to call 911 right away after giving you a glucagon injection or if you don't have a glucagon emergency kit with you. If you have hypoglycemia often or have had severe hypoglycemia, you should wear a medical alert bracelet or pendant. A medical alert ID tells other people that you have diabetes and need care right away. Getting prompt care can help prevent the serious problems that hypoglycemia can cause.

Section 32.6

Alcohol and Sleep Difficulties

This section includes text excerpted from "Your Guide to Healthy Sleep," National Heart, Lung, and Blood Institute (NHLBI), August 2011. Reviewed April 2018.

Jet Lag and Alcohol

To relieve the stress of travel and make it easier to fall asleep, you're more likely to sleep lighter and wake up in the middle of the night when the effects of the alcohol wear off. Caffeine can help keep you awake longer, but caffeine also can make it harder for you to fall asleep if its effects haven't worn off by the time you are ready to go to bed.

Driving and Sleep Deprivation

Don't drink alcohol. Just one beer when you are sleep deprived will affect you as much as two or three beers when you are well rested. Although alcohol is a sedative that makes it easier to fall asleep, it prevents deep sleep and rapid eye movement (REM) sleep, allowing only the lighter stages of sleep. People who drink alcohol also tend to wake-up in the middle of the night when the effects of an alcoholic "nightcap" wear off.

Snoring

Long the material for jokes, snoring is generally accepted as common and annoying in adults but as nothing to worry about. However, snoring is no laughing matter. Frequent, loud snoring is often a sign of sleep apnea and may increase your risk of developing cardiovascular disease (CVD) and diabetes. Snoring also may lead to daytime sleepiness and impaired performance.

Snoring is caused by a narrowing or partial blockage of the airways at the back of your mouth, throat, or nose. This obstruction results in increased air turbulence when breathing in, causing the soft tissues in your upper airways to vibrate. The end result is a noisy snore that can disrupt the sleep of your bed partner. This narrowing of the airways is typically caused by the soft palate, tongue, and throat relaxing while you sleep, but allergies or sinus problems also can contribute to a narrowing of the airways, as can being overweight and having extra soft tissue around your upper airways.

Snoring in older children and adults may be relieved by less invasive measures, however. These measures include losing weight, refraining from use of tobacco, sleeping on the side rather than on the back, or elevating the head while sleeping. Treating chronic congestion and refraining from alcohol or sedatives before sleeping also may decrease snoring. In some adults, snoring can be relieved by dental appliances that reposition the soft tissues in the mouth. Although numerous over-the-counter (OTC) nasal strips and sprays claim to relieve snoring, no scientific evidence supports those claims.

Chronic Insomnia

Chronic insomnia is often caused by sleep-disrupting behavior such as drinking alcohol, exercising shortly before bedtime, ingesting caffeine late in the day, watching TV or reading while in bed, or irregular sleep schedules due to shift work or other causes.

The benefits of these treatments are limited, and they have risks. Some may help you fall asleep but leave you feeling unrefreshed in the morning. Others have longer lasting effects and leave you feeling still tired and groggy in the morning. Some also may lose their effectiveness over time. Doctors may prescribe sedating antidepressants for insomnia, but the effectiveness of these medicines in people who do not have depression is not known, and there are significant side effects.

Avoid Alcohol and Caffeine

Although it may be tempting to drink alcohol to relieve the stress of travel and make it easier to fall asleep, you're more likely to sleep lighter and wake up in the middle of the night when the effects of the alcohol wear off. Caffeine can help keep you awake longer, but caffeine also can make it harder for you to fall asleep if its effects haven't worn off by the time you are ready to go to bed. Therefore, it's best to use caffeine only during the morning and not during the afternoon.

Chapter 33

Facts about Aging and Alcohol

You can become more sensitive to alcohol as you get older.

"I'll be 68 in March. I've had a beer or two every night since I was in my mid-30s. Never had a problem until a few months ago. Lately, when I drink my beer, I feel a little tipsy. My son says I'm slurring my words. What's going on?"

As people age, they may become more sensitive to alcohol's effects. The same amount of alcohol can have a greater effect on an older person than on someone who is younger. Over time, someone whose drinking habits haven't changed may find she or he has a problem.

Heavy Drinking Can Make Some Health Problems Worse

"I take medicine to keep my diabetes under control. Every night I have a couple of shots of whiskey. Now my doctor says I need to stop drinking. It isn't going to be easy, but I guess it's something I need to do to stay healthy."

Heavy drinking can make some health problems worse. It is important to talk to your doctor if you have problems like high blood sugar (diabetes). Heavy drinking can also cause health problems such as weak bones (osteoporosis).

This chapter includes text excerpted from "Older Adults and Alcohol," National Institute on Aging (NIA), National Institutes of Health (NIH), December 2015.

Older adults are more likely to have health problems that can be made worse by alcohol. Some of these health problems are:

- stroke
- high blood pressure
- memory loss
- mood disorders

Talk with your doctor or other healthcare worker about how alcohol can affect your health.

Medicines and Alcohol Don't Mix

"I was taking strong medicine for a bad cold. When I had my usual glass of wine at dinner, I felt dizzy. That's never happened before."

Many prescriptions, over-the-counter medicines, and herbal remedies can be dangerous or even deadly when mixed with alcohol. Always ask your doctor or pharmacist if you can safely drink alcohol. Read the labels on all of your medicines. Some labels say, "Do not use with alcohol."

Some problems mixing medicine and alcohol:

- Taking aspirin and drinking alcohol can raise the chance of bleeding in your stomach.
- You can get very sleepy if you drink alcohol and take cold or allergy medicines.
- Some cough syrups have a high amount of alcohol in them.
- Drinking alcohol while taking some sleeping pills, pain pills, or anxiety or depression medicine can be very dangerous.
- You can hurt your liver if you drink and take a lot of painkillers that have the word "acetaminophen" on the label. Always check the warning labels.

Reasons to Stop Drinking

I would like to quit drinking because:

- I want to be healthy by keeping my high blood sugar (diabetes) under control.
- I want to lower my blood pressure.

- I want to keep my liver working right.
- I don't want to hurt anyone by driving after I've been drinking.
- I don't want to fall and hurt myself.
- I'm tired of feeling sleepy or sick the morning after I drink.
- I want to enjoy the things I used to do.
- I want to stop feeling embarrassed about how I act when drinking.

Some people can cut back on their drinking. Some people need to stop drinking altogether. Making a change in your drinking habits can be hard. Don't give up! If you do not reach your goal the first time, try again. Ask your family and friends for help. Talk to your doctor if you are having trouble quitting. Get the help you need.

There Is Help

If you think you have a drinking problem, here are some things you can do:

- Find a support group for older adults with alcohol problems.
- Talk to a healthcare professional like your doctor.
- Ask about medicines that might help.
- Visit a trained counselor who knows about alcohol problems and how they affect older adults.
- Choose individual, group, or family therapy, depending on what works for you.
- Join a 12-step program such as AA, which is short for Alcoholics Anonymous. AA groups offer support and have programs for people who want to quit drinking.

Tips to Stop Drinking

- Remove alcohol from your home.
- Eat food when you are drinking—don't drink on an empty stomach. When you drink, sip slowly.
- Say "no thanks" or "I'll have something else instead" when offered a drink.

- Avoid drinking when you are angry or upset or if you've had a bad day.
- Stay away from people who drink a lot and the places where you used to drink. Plan what you will do if you are tempted to drink.
- Call your doctor or other healthcare worker, the senior center near you, or your local Area Agency on Aging to find the names of places where you can get help.
- Reward yourself for not drinking! Use the time and money spent on drinking to do something you enjoy.

Have you been a heavy drinker for years or do you drink often? It is important to talk to your doctor before making a change in your drinking. There may be some side effects from a sudden change. Medicine can help.

Tips for Helping a Family Member or Friend

Step One: Talk

- Talk about your worries when the person is sober. Try to say what you think or feel, like "I am concerned about your drinking."
- Give facts. Some people find it helpful just to get information. You could say, "I want to share some things I've learned about older adults and alcohol."
- Try to stay away from labels like "alcoholic."
- Ask if you can go to the doctor with your family member or friend.

Step Two: Offer Your Help

- Suggest things to do that don't include drinking.
- Encourage counseling or attending a group meeting. Offer to drive to and from these support meetings.
- Give your support during treatment.

Step Three: Take Care of Yourself

- You need support, too. Think about what you need to stay safe and healthy.

- Involve other family members or friends so you are not in this alone. Talk honestly about how you are feeling. Try to say what support or help you need.
- Try going to counseling or special meetings that offer support to families and friends of people with drinking problems. There may be programs at your local hospital or clinic. For example, Al-Anon is a support group for friends and family of people with a drinking problem. Find a meeting near you by calling 888-425-2666.

Frequently Asked Questions (FAQs)

Q: I have been drinking for most of my adult life. Is it too late to quit?

A: No. Many older adults decide to quit drinking later in life. Treatment can work! Changing an old habit is not easy, but it can be done.

Q: My neighbor was never much of a drinker, but since he retired I see him sitting in the backyard every day, drinking. Is it really possible for someone to start to have a drinking problem later in life?

A: Some adults do develop a drinking problem when they get older. Health worries, boredom after retirement, or the death of friends and loved ones are some of the reasons why older people start drinking. Feeling tense or depressed can also sometimes be a trigger for drinking.

Q: What counts as one drink?

A:

- One 12-ounce can or bottle of regular beer, ale, or wine cooler
- One 8- or 9-ounce can or bottle of malt liquor
- One 5-ounce glass of red or white wine
- One 1.5-ounce shot glass of distilled spirits (gin, rum, tequila, vodka, whiskey, etc.). The label on the bottle will say 80 proof or less.
- Drinks may be stronger than you think. Some mixed drinks may have more than one 1.5-ounce shot of liquor in them.

It is helpful to understand the "standard" drink sizes in order to follow health guidelines. However, it also is important to keep in mind that drinks may be stronger than you think they are if the actual serving sizes are larger than the standard sizes. In addition, drinks within the same beverage category, such as beer, can contain different percentages of alcohol.

Q: What's too much for a person over age 65 to drink each week? Each day?

A: Everyone is different. If you are healthy and 65 years or older, you should not have more than 7 drinks in a week. Don't have more than 3 drinks on any given day. Do you have a health problem? Are you taking certain medicines? You may need to drink less or not drink at all. Talk to your doctor.

Q: Is it true that drinking a glass of red wine every day is good for my health?

A: This may be true for some people, but if you have a problem with alcohol, it's better for you to avoid drinking at all. You can get many of the same health benefits from a glass of grape juice. Ask your doctor or another healthcare worker for advice.

Q: I am worried that my cousin Ruby has a drinking problem. We play cards every week and she drinks through most of the game. The other women in our group have noticed this as well. When I told Ruby we were worried, she just laughed. Is there anything we can do?

A: It isn't always easy to get people to say that they have a drinking problem. Some older adults may be ashamed about their drinking. Others may feel their drinking doesn't hurt anyone.

Chapter 34

Use with Caution: Alcohol and Medications

Chapter Contents

Section 34.1

Harmful Interactions: Mixing Alcohol with Medicines

This section includes text excerpted from "Harmful Interactions: Mixing Alcohol with Medicines," National Institute on Alcohol Abuse and Alcoholism (NIAAA), March 7, 2014. Reviewed April 2018.

The danger is real. Mixing alcohol with certain medications can cause nausea and vomiting, headaches, drowsiness, fainting, or loss of coordination. It also can put you at risk for internal bleeding, heart problems, and difficulties in breathing. In addition to these dangers, alcohol can make a medication less effective or even useless, or it may make the medication harmful or toxic to your body. You might never have suspected can react with alcohol, including many medications which can be purchased "over-the-counter"—that is, without a prescription. Even some herbal remedies can have harmful effects when combined with alcohol.

Medications are typically safe and effective when used appropriately. Your pharmacist or other healthcare provider can help you determine which medications interact harmfully with alcohol. Mixing alcohol and medicines can be harmful. Alcohol, like some medicines, can make you sleepy, drowsy, or lightheaded. Drinking alcohol while taking medicines can intensify these effects. You may have trouble concentrating or performing mechanical skills. Small amounts of alcohol can make it dangerous to drive, and when you mix alcohol with certain medicines you put yourself at even greater risk. Combining alcohol with some medicines can lead to falls and serious injuries, especially among older people.

Medicines May Have Many Ingredients

Some medications including many popular painkillers and cough, cold, and allergy remedies—contain more than one ingredient that can react with alcohol. Read the label on the medication bottle to find out exactly what ingredients a medicine contains. Ask your pharmacist if you have any questions about how alcohol might interact with a drug you are taking.

Some Medicines Contain Alcohol

Certain medicines contain up to 10 percent alcohol. Cough syrup and laxatives may have some of the highest alcohol concentrations.

Alcohol Affects Women Differently

Women in general have a higher risk for problems than men. When a woman drinks, the alcohol in her bloodstream typically reaches a higher level than a man's even if both are drinking the same amount. This is because women's bodies generally have less water than men's bodies. Because alcohol mixes with body water, a given amount of alcohol is more concentrated in a woman's body than in a man's. As a result, women are more susceptible to alcohol-related damage to organs such as the liver.

Older People Face Greater Risk

Older people are at particularly high risk for harmful alcohol–medication interactions. Aging slows the body's ability to break down alcohol, so alcohol remains in a person's system longer. Older people also are more likely to take a medication that interacts with alcohol—in fact, they often need to take more than one of these medications.

Timing Is Important

Alcohol and medicines can interact harmfully even if they are not taken at the same time.

Words of Caution

Mixing alcohol and medicines puts you at risk for dangerous reactions. Protect yourself by avoiding alcohol if you are taking a medication and don't know its effect. To learn more about a medicine and whether it will interact with alcohol, talk to your pharmacist or other healthcare provider.

Section 34.2

Medications for the Treatment of Alcohol Use Disorder

This section includes text excerpted from "Medications for the Treatment of Alcohol Use Disorder," U.S. Department of Veterans Affairs (VA), September 28, 2016.

Medication-assisted treatment is used for people with an alcohol use disorder. It uses medication, in combination with counseling and behavior therapies, to treat alcohol use disorder and sustain recovery. Medication can help to:

- Regain a stable state of mind, free from alcohol-induced highs and lows
- Provide freedom from thinking about alcohol all the time
- Reduce problems of craving
- Focus on lifestyle changes that lead back to healthy living

Taking medication for alcohol use disorder is like taking medication to treat any other medical condition. It is not substituting one drug for another. Used properly, medication does not create a new addiction. Currently, there are four medications that are recommended by U.S. Department of Veterans Affairs (VA) and Department of Defense (DoD) for treating alcohol use disorder:

- Acamprosate
- Disulfiram
- Naltrexone
- Topiramate

Each medication acts differently and has different side effects. None of these medications will get rid of symptoms of withdrawal.

Some medication may be safely taken for years

Plans to stop taking medication should be discussed with a healthcare provider because abruptly stopping medication can cause serious health problems.

Medication is matched to you

Meeting with a healthcare provider is the first step in starting a medication program to reduce or stop drinking alcohol. You and your healthcare provider can work together to select a medication that is right for you.

Talk to your healthcare provider about:

- Your treatment goals
- Safe withdrawal management, to include the need for medication or a hospital admission
- Medications to help with your long-term recovery
- All medications that you are taking, such as over-the counter medications, herbal supplements, and even those prescribed by another provider, as they may cause problems or interfere with your recovery
- Future office visits and treatment schedule
- How to avoid situations which might tempt you to drink alcohol
- A counseling plan and available support groups

Counseling can be offered as part of medication-assisted treatment or by itself. It consists of talking with a mental health provider either one-on-one or in a group with others in treatment. Counseling can provide encouragement, motivation to stick with treatment, and coping skills to avoid relapse.

In group counseling and mutual support groups, people connect with others in treatment and can begin to build a network of people to support recovery.

Support from family and friends can be very helpful during treatment and recovery. Some treatment programs offer counseling for loved ones because being close to someone with an addiction can be hard. Counseling is useful for family and friends to learn about:

- Addiction
- How to help
- How to handle other problems

How Can You Reduce the Risks Associated with Drinking Too Much Alcohol?

A person with an alcohol use disorder can recover and regain a healthy life. For some, alcohol use disorder can be a chronic disease, like heart disease or diabetes, but it can be managed. Most people with a serious drinking problem need help to return to normal, healthy living. They can get this help with treatment from healthcare providers, to include physicians.

Treatment helps people to:

- Stop drinking
- Get through withdrawal and cope with cravings
- Address issues tied to the addiction, such as low self-worth, a bad work or home situation, or spending time with people who encourage alcohol or drug use
- Begin making healthier choices—a way of living referred to as recovery

Chapter 35

Alcohol-Induced Organ Injury: The Role of Nutrition

Alcohol and nutrition have the potential to interact at multiple levels. For example, heavy alcohol consumption can interfere with normal nutrition, resulting in overall malnutrition or in deficiencies of important micronutrients, such as zinc, by reducing their absorption or increasing their loss. Interactions between alcohol consumption and nutrition also can affect epigenetic regulation of gene expression by influencing multiple regulatory mechanisms, including methylation and acetylation of histone proteins and deoxyribonucleic acid (DNA). These effects may contribute to alcohol-related organ or tissue injury. The impact of alcohol—nutrition interactions has been assessed for several organs and tissues, including the intestine, where heavy alcohol use can increase intestinal permeability, and the liver, where the degree of malnutrition can be associated with the severity of liver injury and liver disease. Alcohol—nutrition interactions also play a role in alcohol-related lung injury, brain injury, and immune dysfunction. Therefore, treatment involving nutrient supplementation (e.g., with zinc or S-adenosylmethionine) may help prevent or attenuate some types of alcohol-induced organ damage.

The effect of alcohol on organ health and injury is complex and influenced by a host of different factors, such as dose of alcohol consumed;

This chapter includes text excerpted from "Development, Prevention, and Treatment of Alcohol-Induced Organ Injury: The Role of Nutrition," National Institute on Alcohol Abuse and Alcoholism (NIAAA), December 15, 2015.

duration and pattern of drinking (e.g., binge drinking); and, as reviewed in this chapter, potential interactions with nutrition. The 2015–2020 *Dietary Guidelines for Americans* (U.S. Department of Health and Human Services (HHS) and U.S. Department of Agriculture (USDA)) highlight the concept of the standard drink and the fact that if alcohol is consumed, it should be in moderation (i.e., up to 1 drink per day for women and 2 drinks per day for men in adults of legal drinking age). It is becoming increasingly accepted that this moderate form of drinking may have health benefits that seem to lessen many types of organ injury. This concept was popularized in 1991, when Morley Safer presented information on the television show 60 Minutes related to the "French paradox"—that is, the observation that the French seemed to have lower rates of heart attacks despite higher fat consumption. This outcome was postulated as possibly resulting from the beneficial effects of wine consumption by the French. Subsequent studies have shown that all forms of alcohol, when consumed in moderation, seem to lower the risk of coronary artery disease. The beneficial effect can be represented by a J-shaped curve, in which low alcohol consumption has protective effects compared with abstention, whereas excessive alcohol consumption is harmful. Moderate drinking also may have beneficial effects on several other organs and organ systems, including the following:

- Decreased risk of ischemic stroke
- Protection against type 2 diabetes
- Decrease in rheumatoid arthritis
- Improved cognition
- Decreased progression of liver disease to fibrosis in obese individuals
- Improved renal function

Indeed, moderate alcohol consumption may be associated with an overall modest survival benefit. Moderate alcohol consumption also has been shown to decrease biomarkers of inflammation, such as C-reactive protein, and reduced inflammation could be one unifying mechanism underlying alcohol's protective effects. On the other hand, long-term heavy alcohol abuse can cause organ injury, which may, at least in part, result from alcohol–nutrient interactions and alcohol-related nutrient deficiencies. As described in this chapter, people who abuse alcohol frequently consume large amounts of alcohol, which may contribute to the displacement of needed nutrients. Indeed, recent analyses of nutritional status and alcohol consumption in people with alcohol use disorder (AUD) who were admitted to a rehabilitation program demonstrated that the participants generally had a normal body mass index, were not overtly malnourished, and did not have clinical evidence of alcohol-induced organ injury. However, these people were consuming, on average, 14 drinks per day, which would amount to about 2,000 calories per day or more consumed as alcohol. Considering that the participants had a normal body mass index, this suggests that they replaced normal nutrients with alcoholic beverages, resulting in potential nutrient deficiencies. Nutritional supplementation may either help ameliorate such deficiencies or have pharmacologic effects.

Alcohol and nutrition can interact at multiple levels. For example, alcohol metabolism can result in the generation of reactive oxygen species, which can deplete endogenous nutritional antioxidant stores and contribute to oxidative stress. Heavy alcohol consumption also can cause poor intestinal absorption of certain nutrients (e.g., zinc) or increase nutrient losses (e.g., by increasing zinc and magnesium excretion in the urine). Moreover, nutrition can have a far-reaching impact through altering epigenetic mechanisms, such as methylation and acetylation of DNA and associated proteins. Finally, the degree of alcohol-related malnutrition can be associated with the severity of organ injury (e.g., alcoholic hepatitis). This chapter reviews how nutritional alterations may predispose to alcohol-induced organ injury and how nutritional supplementation may prevent and/or treat alcohol-induced organ injury. The chapter specifically highlights the effects of certain alcohol–nutrient interactions, with a focus on zinc and linoleic acid, and their impact on epigenetics and selected organ injury.

Nutrition and Nutritional Alterations Following Alcohol Use/Abuse

From a nutrition perspective, alcohol is a significant source of calories, but these can be considered "empty" calories—that is, they contain few micronutrients, such as vitamins and minerals, normally found in most food sources. The main site of beverage alcohol (i.e., ethanol) metabolism is the liver, where ethanol is converted to carbon dioxide and water, with an energy yield of 7 kcal/g of alcohol. Regular alcohol intake can be a major source of calories, because beer has approximately 150 kcal per 12-ounce can and bourbon or scotch with a mixer has approximately 125 kcal per drink. Thus, a person can easily consume 200–500 calories or more per day by consuming 2–3 drinks. For people attempting weight reduction, alcohol consumption therefore can be considered a source of unwanted and empty calories. Moreover, when alcohol intake is combined with fructose-containing sugared drinks, the intake of empty calories increases even further, enhancing the opportunity for alcohol-induced organ injury. Finally, alcohol can be an expensive source of calories compared with traditional foods, and this may become a major problem for people with limited incomes.

The issue of alcohol as a nutrient becomes more prominent when dealing with people with AUD and those with alcohol-induced organ injury. Analyses of the nutritional status of people with AUD admitted to treatment programs found that these individuals often consumed 35–50 percent of their total calories as alcohol, and some exhibited inadequate micronutrient intake and micronutrient serum levels. However, most had little or no evidence of protein-calorie malnutrition and loss of muscle mass. In contrast, patients admitted to hospitals for severe alcoholic hepatitis who also consumed 50 percent of their total calories as alcohol not only regularly showed depletion of certain micronutrients but also loss of muscle mass. The below paragraphs focus on the micronutrient zinc, which may be deficient or have altered metabolism with heavy alcohol consumption, and a macronutrient (i.e., dietary fat) that may play a role in alcohol-induced organ injury.

Zinc

Zinc is an essential trace element required for normal cell growth, development, and differentiation, including such processes as deoxyribonucleic acid (DNA) synthesis, ribonucleic acid (RNA) transcription, and cell division and activation. It is a critical component of many proteins/enzymes, including zinc-dependent transcription factors. Zinc deficiency or altered zinc metabolism is frequently observed in heavy alcohol drinkers and may result from decreased dietary intake, increased urinary excretion, abnormal activation of certain zinc transporters, and induction of hepatic metallothionein. Zinc deficiency may manifest itself in many ways in alcoholics, ranging from raised, crusting skin lesions around the eyes, nose, and mouth to impaired wound healing or liver regeneration, altered mental status, or altered immune function. Importantly, oxidative stress (e.g., resulting from ethanol metabolism) may cause release of zinc from critical zinc-finger proteins and cause loss of DNA-binding activity. Specifically, oxidative stress causes modification of certain amino acids (i.e., cysteine residues) that hold the zinc in place in zinc-finger proteins such as hepatocyte nuclear factor 4 (HNF4), a transcription factor that is essential for liver development.

Zinc supplementation has been documented to block or attenuate experimental organ injury and dysfunction in the gut, liver, lung, and brain through multiple pathways. Thus, zinc may strengthen the integrity of the intestinal wall by stabilizing tight junctions, reduce transfer of toxic bacterial molecules (e.g., endotoxin) into the blood, lower the levels of metabolic toxins such as ammonia in the blood, decrease production of inflammation-promoting (i.e., proinflammatory) cytokines, reduce oxidative stress, and attenuate apoptotic cell death. The dose of zinc used for treatment of alcohol-induced organ injury such as liver disease usually is 50 mg of elemental zinc taken with a meal to decrease the potential side effect of nausea. Intake of greater than 50 mg of elemental zinc per day can cause dose-related side effects, such as copper deficiency resulting from reduced copper absorption.

Dietary Fats

The critical role for specific types of dietary fat (i.e., saturated versus unsaturated fats) in intestinal and liver injury has been demonstrated and extensively studied in preclinical animal models of alcohol feeding using various sources of dietary lipids. Experimental evidence has shown that dietary saturated fats (SFs) attenuated, and unsaturated fats (USFs) enhanced, alcohol-induced liver damage. Thus, in contrast to the general assumption that SFs are less healthy than USFs, in this situation SFs had a protective effect and USFs had a harmful effect.

Nutrition–Alcohol Interactions and Epigenetics

In virtually every cell type, epigenetic mechanisms—that is, modifications to the genetic material that do not alter the DNA sequence—play a critical role in both the physiologic and pathologic regulation of gene expression. These mechanisms, which involve chromatin remodeling initiated by posttranslational modifications of histones and changes in DNA methylation status, can activate or deactivate gene transcription. The proteins that are involved in posttranslational histone modifications and DNA methylation changes require a variety of cofactors, including acetyl coenzyme A, S-adenosylmethionine (SAM), nicotinamide adenine dinucleotide, and zinc. A person's nutritional status can significantly influence the availability of these cofactors and, consequently, epigenetic mechanisms, gene expression, and disease pathogenesis. Chronic alcohol consumption is known to affect nutritional status at many levels, including nutrient intake, absorption, utilization, and excretion, causing nutritional disturbances and deficiencies in these cofactors. Research has determined that alcohol-induced nutrient fluctuations can impact transcriptional activity and expression of genes by modulating epigenetic parameters, including histone modifications and DNA methylation. Hence, in people with AUD, the combined effects of alcohol metabolism and compromised nutrition are likely to influence epigenetic mechanisms, gene expression, and disease pathogenesis involving intestinal barrier dysfunction, immune suppression, and organ injury.

Examples of Nutrition–Alcohol Interactions in Alcohol-Induced Organ/Tissue Injury Intestine

The intestinal mucosa plays a critical role in preventing passage of toxins from the intestine into the bloodstream, as well as in immune function, detoxification, and metabolism. The importance of the gut in alcohol-mediated multiorgan pathology is becoming increasingly recognized. Clinical and experimental data have demonstrated that the gut-derived bacterial product, lipopolysaccharide, also referred to as endotoxin, plays a crucial role in the development and progression of alcohol-induced organ injuries, including alcoholic liver disease (ALD). Significantly increased endotoxin levels in the blood (i.e., endotoxemia) have been found in patients with different stages of ALD, including fatty liver, hepatitis, and cirrhosis.

Multiple mechanisms contribute to alcohol-associated endotoxemia, including alcohol-mediated alterations in the composition of the bacterial population of the gut (i.e., gut microbiome) and increased lipopolysaccharide translocation as a result of disruption of intestinal barrier integrity.

Liver Injury

Patients with severe alcoholic hepatitis almost invariably demonstrate some form of malnutrition. Probably the most detailed information concerning malnutrition in ALD comes from two large studies from the Veterans Health Administration (VA) Cooperative Studies Program in patients with alcoholic hepatitis. In these studies, almost 50 percent of the patients' energy intake was derived from alcohol. Although they frequently showed no inadequate calorie intake, the patients often exhibited insufficient intake of protein and critical micronutrients. The severity of liver disease generally correlated with the severity of malnutrition. During treatment, the patients received a balanced 2,500-kcal hospital diet (monitored by a dietitian) that they were encouraged to consume. Investigators found that voluntary oral food intake correlated in a stepwise fashion with 6-month mortality data. Thus, patients who voluntarily consumed more than 3,000 kcal per day had virtually no mortality, whereas those who consumed less than 1,000 kcal per day had a 6-month mortality of more than 80 percent. Moreover, the degree of malnutrition correlated with the development of serious complications, such as encephalopathy, ascites, and hepatorenal syndrome.

Initial interest in nutrition therapy for ALD was stimulated by Patek and colleagues (1948) who demonstrated that a "nutritious diet" improved the 5-year outcome of patients with alcoholic cirrhosis compared with historic control subjects. Subsequently, nutritional supplementation through a feeding tube was shown to significantly improve liver function in in-patients with ALD compared with inpatients who ate a hospital diet. Probably the most important data supporting nutrition therapy came from a multicenter study by Cabré and colleagues (2000), who randomly assigned patients with severe alcoholic hepatitis to receive either the glucocorticoid prednisone (40 mg daily) or a liver-specific formula containing 2,000 calories per day through a feeding tube. The 1-month mortality was the same in both groups, but the 1-year mortality was significantly lower in the enteral-nutrition group than in the glucocorticoid group, mainly because they experienced fewer infectious complications. This study clearly documented the importance of enteral nutrition in severe alcoholic hepatitis. Oral/enteral nutrition is preferable over parenteral nutrition because of lower costs, risk of sepsis from the parenteral nutrition line, preservation of the integrity of the gut mucosa, and prevention of bacterial translocation and multiple-organ failure.

Enteral nutrition supplements also have been shown to improve nutritional status and immune function in outpatients with alcoholic cirrhosis as well as to reduce hospitalization. The concept of an outpatient late-evening snack (prior to bedtime) was established after studies demonstrated altered energy metabolism in people with liver cirrhosis. These patients exhibit depleted hepatic glycogen stores, which force the body to depend on fat and protein stores, leading to catabolism during an overnight fast. A randomized controlled trial demonstrated that provision of a late-evening nutritional supplement (compared with daytime supplements) over a 12-month period could improve body protein stores in patients with cirrhosis. The nighttime snack resulted in body protein accrual equivalent to about 2 kg of lean tissue sustained over 12 months, whereas this benefit was not observed with daytime snacks. Thus, late-evening snacks are valuable nutritional interventions in outpatients with alcoholic cirrhosis.

Many types of nutritional supplements have yielded positive effects in animal models of ALD, especially antioxidants. However, human studies using specific nutrients or combination therapy are limited and generally have shown equivocal or negative results. Larger, well-designed studies are required.

Lung Injury

Chronic alcohol abuse alters the phenotype of the lung and makes it more susceptible to subsequent challenges, such as bacterial infection and acute lung injury. One of the mechanisms that contribute to increased susceptibility to infection and injury is alcohol-induced oxidative stress. Oxidative stress is defined as an imbalance between oxidants and antioxidants, and the way cells sense and respond to such an imbalance is a key determinant of disease initiation/progression or resolution. Oxidant-sensing and -signaling pathways rely primarily on proteins with reactive thiol-containing cysteine residues. The reactivity of a given protein thiol can be fine tuned by its local redox environment—that is, by the ratio of reduced versus oxidized molecules in the cell. This redox environment largely is controlled by two low-molecular-weight thiol-disulfide redox couples: one composed of the amino acid cysteine (Cys), which is the reduced partner of the pair, and its disulfide cystine (CySS), which serves as the oxidized partner. The other redox pair comprises glutathione (GSH) as the reduced partner and its disulfide GSSG as the oxidized partner. The two pairs are related but have different roles. Cys is one of the three component amino acids making up GSH, so it is not surprising that they share similar chemical properties. However, these redox control systems are compartmentalized; GSH/GSSG provides control mechanisms within cells and in the lung-lining fluid, whereas Cys/CySS predominates in the extracellular fluids of plasma and interstitium. The extracellular Cys/CySS redox state has been shown to have a direct effect on the production of two important proinflammatory cytokines, namely production of transforming growth factor β by lung fibroblasts and interleukin-1 β by monocytes.

Accumulating evidence suggests that the Cys/CySS and GSH/GSSG redox couples can be controlled by the diet. Dietary supplementation with the cysteine precursors N-acetylcysteine or procysteine has been used extensively to counteract the effects of oxidative stress. Although the effects of these cysteine precursors usually are attributed to enhanced GSH synthesis, they also are effective even when given in combination with a GSH-synthesis inhibitor (e.g., buthionine sulfoximine). Recent studies showed that supplementing the diet with a combination of cysteine and methionine could prevent oxidation of the plasma Cys/CySS redox couple and decrease circulating levels of proinflammatory interleukin-1 β in endotoxin-challenged mice. Similar diets also can alter the plasma Cys/CySS redox state in humans. It will be interesting to determine whether this type of dietary intervention can protect against lung injury in chronic alcoholics.

Zinc deficiency, particularly within immune cells in the lungs (i.e., alveolar macrophages), also contributes to increased susceptibility to bacterial infection in chronic alcoholics. Studies in rats showed that chronic alcohol feeding decreased bacterial clearance from lung and oxidized Cys/CySS in the alveolar space. Dietary zinc supplementation blocked both of these effects.

Brain Injury

Prenatal alcohol exposure can result in a range of detrimental effects, including damage to the developing brain, that are collectively known as fetal alcohol spectrum disorders (FASD). Early autopsy studies, as well as more recent magnetic resonance imaging studies in both animal models and humans have revealed a variety of brain abnormalities, including reduced brain size (i.e., microcephaly) and anomalies of specific brain structures (e.g., the cerebrum, cerebellum, hippocampus, basal ganglia, and corpus callosum) after prenatal alcohol exposure. These ethanol-induced brain insults contribute to the learning deficits, impairment in memory, difficulties with motor planning, and problems in regulating emotions and behavior observed in children with FASD.

Alcohol can damage the developing embryo through multiple mechanisms. Oxidative stress seems to play an important role in ethanol-induced programmed cell death (i.e., apoptosis) and morphological abnormalities. In addition, accumulating evidence suggests that changes in epigenetic regulation are involved in the pathogenesis of FASD. For example, in animal studies, prenatal alcohol exposure increased the proportion of offspring with an unusual coat color by inducing hypermethylation of a specific gene, Avy locus. Moreover, recent studies demonstrated that microRNA 125b can prevent ethanol-induced apoptosis of certain embryonal cells (i.e., neural crest cells) by targeting two specific genes called *Bak1* and *PUMA*.

It also is well known that nutritional deficiencies contribute to the pathogenesis of FASD and to ethanol-induced damage to the developing brain. Heavy maternal alcohol consumption results in deficiency in nutrients that are critical for fetal development and maternal health, including vitamins A and D, thiamin, folate, and zinc. Moreover, as in adult brains, DHA deficiency occurred in the developing brain of animals prenatally exposed to ethanol. Finally, studies have shown that diets low in nutrients exacerbate alcohol-induced brain damage in the offspring.

Immune Dysfunction

Excessive alcohol consumption has deleterious effects on the immune system. Several clinical and experimental studies have suggested that long-term alcohol use can lead to the dysregulation of both cell-mediated and humoral immunity. Epidemiologic studies have documented that alcohol-induced impairment of the immune system leads to increased susceptibility to opportunistic infections and development of certain tumors. Although many types of immune cells are affected by alcohol, including neutrophils, natural killer cells, and monocytes/macrophages, several observations suggest that the major effect of ethanol involves the impairment of thymus-derived lymphocytes (T lymphocytes or T cells). Because a subgroup of T-lymphocytes (i.e., CD4+ T cells) are the central regulators of the immune system, including cell-mediated and humoral immunity, loss of their survival and function constitutes a critical part of alcohol-induced immune dysfunction.

Alterations in nutrition and nutrient metabolism are common in chronic alcoholics and may contribute to alcohol-induced organ injury. Conversely, nutritional supplementation may prevent the development or attenuate the progression of alcohol-induced organ injury. Nutritional supplements may alleviate a nutrient deficiency or act as pharmacologic agents. Such nutrients also may have epigenetic effects. Nutritional supplementation as a therapy is especially attractive because there are currently no U.S. Food and Drug Administration (FDA)–approved therapies for most forms of alcohol-induced organ injury and nutrient supplements are readily available.

Part Four

The Effects of Alcohol on Reproductive and Fetal Health

Chapter 36

Infertility and Alcohol

Understanding Infertility

Have you known someone who had trouble getting pregnant? Have you had trouble yourself? Infertility is a common disease of the reproductive system that affects both women and men.

For most women, infertility is defined as not being able to get pregnant after one year of trying. For women over 35, infertility may be diagnosed after six months. Problems with the ovaries, fallopian tubes, and uterus can all cause infertility, but one of the most important risk factors is age. A woman's chance of becoming pregnant decreases rapidly every year after 30, because she has fewer healthy eggs left, is more likely to have a miscarriage, and may develop other health conditions that can cause fertility problems. Smoking, alcohol use, stress, and extreme weight gain or loss can also affect a woman's ability to

---

This chapter contains text excerpted from the following sources: Text under the heading "Understanding Infertility" is excerpted from "Understanding Infertility," Office on Women's Health (OWH), U.S. Department of Health and Human Services (HHS), April 22, 2014. Reviewed April 2018; Text beginning with the heading "What Increases a Woman's Risk of Infertility?" is excerpted from "Reproductive Health—Infertility FAQs," Centers for Disease Control and Prevention (CDC), March 30, 2017; Text under the heading "Alcohol and the Female Reproductive System" is excerpted from "Alcohol's Effects on Female Reproductive Function," National Institute on Alcohol Abuse and Alcoholism (NIAAA), June 2003. Reviewed April 2018; Text under the heading "Alcohol and the Male Reproductive System" is excerpted from "Alcohol and the Male Reproductive System," National Institute on Alcohol Abuse and Alcoholism (NIAAA), April 1, 2002. Reviewed April 2018.

get and stay pregnant. Women who are having difficulty conceiving should talk to their doctor.

Infertility isn't just a woman's condition. Of the nearly 4 million men who seek help, 18 percent have physical problems that contribute to infertility. Medical conditions like diabetes and cystic fibrosis, trauma, infection, and treatment with chemotherapy or radiation can all affect a man's fertility, as can smoking, heavy alcohol use, testosterone supplementation, anabolic steroid use, illicit drug use, and exposure to environmental toxins.

Infertility can have devastating physical, emotional, and financial effects. But there is hope. Surgery, medications, intrauterine insemination, and assisted reproductive technology have all helped people with infertility have healthy pregnancies. But they can be expensive and time-consuming, and they don't work for everyone. Also, health insurers don't always cover the costs.

Infertility is a common problem, but it can be hard to talk about. People affected by infertility may experience anger, loss, stress, and guilt. Nonprofit and support groups offer resources and support for people dealing with infertility.

If a friend or loved one is struggling with infertility, it can be hard to know how you can support them. Learning about infertility and sharing the message that it is a common and important health concern for many people is a great first step. Some nonprofit groups have tips on what to say, what not to say, and how to support your loved ones.

What Increases a Woman's Risk of Infertility?

Female fertility is known to decline with:

- Aging decreases a woman's chances of having a baby in the following ways:
- She has a smaller number of eggs left
- Her eggs are not as healthy
- She is more likely to have health conditions that can cause fertility problems
- She is more likely to have a miscarriage
- Excessive alcohol use
- Smoking
- Extreme weight gain or loss

- Excessive physical or emotional stress that results in amenorrhea (absent periods)

Is Infertility Just a Woman's Problem?

No, infertility is not always a woman's problem. Both men and women can contribute to infertility.

Many couples struggle with infertility and seek help to become pregnant, but it is often thought of as only a woman's condition. However, in about 35 percent of couples with infertility, a male factor is identified along with a female factor. In about 8 percent of couples with infertility, a male factor is the only identifiable cause.

Almost 9 percent of men aged 25–44 years in the United States reported that they or their partner saw a doctor for advice, testing, or treatment for infertility during their lifetime.

What Increases a Man's Risk of Infertility?

Male fertility is known to decline with:

- Age. Although advanced age plays a much more important role in predicting female infertility, couples in which the male partner is 40 years old or older are more likely to report difficulty conceiving
- Excessive alcohol use
- Smoking
- Use of marijuana
- Being overweight or obese
- Exposure to testosterone
- Exposure to radiation
- Frequent exposure of the testes to high temperatures, such as that which may occur in men confined to a wheelchair, or through frequent sauna or hot tub use
- Exposure to certain medications such as flutamide, cyproterone, bicalutamide, spironolactone, ketoconazole, or cimetidine
- Exposure to environmental toxins including exposure to pesticides, lead, cadmium, or mercury

Alcohol and the Female Reproductive System

Rapid hormonal changes occurring during puberty make females especially vulnerable to the deleterious effects of alcohol exposure during this time. Thus, the high incidence of alcohol consumption among middle school and high school students in the United States is a matter of great concern. A national survey of students revealed that 22.4 percent of 8th graders and 50 percent of 12th graders reported consuming alcohol in the 30 days before the survey.

Alcohol markedly disrupts normal menstrual cycling in female humans and rats. Alcoholic women are known to have a variety of menstrual and reproductive disorders, from irregular menstrual cycles to complete cessation of menses, absence of ovulation (i.e., anovulation), and infertility. Alcohol abuse has also been associated with early menopause. However, alcoholics often have other health problems such as liver disease and malnutrition, so reproductive deficits may not be directly related to alcohol use.

In human females, alcohol ingestion, even in amounts insufficient to cause major damage to the liver or other organs, may lead to menstrual irregularities. It is important to stress that alcohol ingestion at the wrong time, even in amounts insufficient to cause permanent tissue damage, can disrupt the delicate balance critical to maintaining human female reproductive hormonal cycles and result in infertility. A study of healthy nonalcoholic women found that a substantial portion who drank small amounts of alcohol (i.e., social drinkers) stopped cycling normally and became at least temporarily infertile. This anovulation was associated with a reduced or absent pituitary luteinizing hormone (LH) secretion. All the affected women had reported normal menstrual cycles before the study. This finding is consistent with epidemiologic data from a representative national sample of 917 women, which showed increased rates of menstrual disturbances and infertility associated with increasing self-reported alcohol consumption. Thus, alcohol-induced disruption of female fertility is a clinical problem that merits further study.

Alcohol consumption temporarily increases testosterone levels. Because testosterone is a well-known suppressor of the hypothalamic-pituitary unit, an increase in testosterone could therefore disturb normal female cycling.

Alcohol and the Male Reproductive System

Alcohol use affects all three parts of the hypothalamic-pituitary-gonadal (HPG) axis, a system of endocrine glands and hormones involved in male reproduction. Alcohol use is associated with low testosterone and altered levels of additional reproductive hormones. Researchers are investigating several potential mechanisms for alcohol's damage. These mechanisms are related to alcohol metabolism, alcohol-related cell damage, and other hormonal reactions associated with alcohol consumption. Chronic alcohol use in male rats also has been shown to affect their reproductive ability and the health of their offspring.

The endocrine system, which is made up of several hormone-producing organs throughout the body, is integral to all normal body functions, including growth, development, metabolism, and reproduction. This system of endocrine glands and hormones includes a brain region called the hypothalamus; the pituitary gland, located at the base of the brain; and the male gonads (testes).

Research with animals has consistently demonstrated an association between both acute (i.e., one time, one occasion) and chronic (i.e., long-term) alcohol consumption and low testosterone. As testosterone levels decrease, levels of luteinizing hormone (LH) and follicle-stimulating hormone (FSH) would be expected to increase to stimulate the production of more testosterone. However, studies with young (i.e., pubertal) male rats indicate that both acute and chronic alcohol exposure result in profound testosterone suppression accompanied by lower or normal LH and FSH levels, when elevated levels are expected. This suggests that the hypothalamic cells which produce LHRH do not function correctly when the feedback normally provided by testosterone is removed (i.e., when testosterone levels decrease). Thus it appears that alcohol's damaging effects on reproduction are mediated at all three levels of the male reproductive unit: the hypothalamus, pituitary, and testes.

Heavy alcohol consumption over long periods of time results in severe cell damage that leads to cell death. Cell death occurs via two distinct mechanisms: necrosis and apoptosis. Necrosis occurs when exposure to a noxious stimulus, such as alcohol, causes the loss of the cell's metabolic functions and damage to the cell membrane. In apoptosis, the cell actively participates in the cell death processes by activating a cascade of biochemical reactions that ultimately lead to cell shrinkage and fragmentation of the nucleus. When a cell undergoes apoptosis, the entire cell, including the nucleus, separates into numerous fragments (i.e., apoptotic bodies).

Few studies have addressed the effects of the male parent's alcohol use on his reproductive ability and his offspring's health. As a model of teenage drinking, researchers have studied the effects of alcohol exposure on peripubertal male rats. This research demonstrated the deleterious effects of paternal alcohol consumption on the offspring. Two months of alcohol feeding to male animals as they progressed through puberty resulted in their having lower body weights and reduced testosterone levels, compared with animals that did not receive alcohol. Despite this, after a 1-week abstinence from alcohol, those animals were able to successfully mate, although successful mating resulting in conception was significantly reduced and the number of successful pregnancies was diminished.

Research over the past 25 years has greatly expanded knowledge of alcohol's effects on male reproduction. Areas fertile for investigation include mechanisms of alcohol-induced oxidative damage and apoptosis in the testes, the consequences of paternal alcohol exposure for their offspring, and the effects of alcohol use on leptin and male reproduction.

Chapter 37

Alcohol Use among Pregnant Women and Recent Mothers

Alcohol Use in Pregnancy

There is no known safe amount of alcohol use during pregnancy or while trying to get pregnant. There is also no safe time during pregnancy to drink. All types of alcohol are equally harmful, including all wines and beer. When a pregnant woman drinks alcohol, so does her baby. Women also should not drink alcohol if they are sexually active and do not use effective contraception (birth control). This is because a woman might get pregnant and expose her baby to alcohol before she knows she is pregnant. Nearly half of all pregnancies in the United States are unplanned. Most women will not know they are pregnant for up to 4–6 weeks. Fetal alcohol spectrum disorders (FASDs) are completely preventable if a woman does not drink alcohol during pregnancy.

This chapter includes text excerpted from "Fetal Alcohol Spectrum Disorders (FASDs)— Alcohol Use in Pregnancy," Centers for Disease Control and Prevention (CDC), July 21, 2016.

Why Alcohol Is Dangerous

Alcohol in the mother's blood passes to the baby through the umbilical cord. Drinking alcohol during pregnancy can cause miscarriage, stillbirth, and a range of lifelong physical, behavioral, and intellectual disabilities. These disabilities are known as FASDs. Children with FASDs might have the following characteristics and behaviors:

- Abnormal facial features, such as a smooth ridge between the nose and upper lip (this ridge is called the philtrum)
- Small head size
- Shorter-than-average height
- Low body weight
- Poor coordination
- Hyperactive behavior
- Difficulty with attention
- Poor memory
- Difficulty in school (especially with math)
- Learning disabilities
- Speech and language delays
- Intellectual disability or low intelligence quotient (IQ)
- Poor reasoning and judgment skills
- Sleep and sucking problems as a baby
- Vision or hearing problems
- Problems with the heart, kidney, or bones

How Much Alcohol Is Dangerous

There is no known safe amount of alcohol to drink while pregnant.

When Alcohol Is Dangerous

There is no safe time to drink alcohol during pregnancy. Alcohol can cause problems for the developing baby throughout pregnancy, including before a woman knows she is pregnant. Drinking alcohol in the first three months of pregnancy can cause the baby to have abnormal facial features. Growth and central nervous system problems (e.g., low birth weight, behavioral problems) can occur from drinking alcohol anytime during pregnancy. The baby's brain is developing throughout pregnancy and can be affected by exposure to alcohol at any time. If a woman is drinking alcohol during pregnancy, it is never too late to stop. The sooner a woman stops drinking, the better it will be for both her baby and herself.

Chapter 38

Fetal Alcohol Spectrum Disorders (FASD)

Fetal alcohol spectrum disorders (FASDs) are a group of conditions that can occur in a person whose mother drank alcohol during pregnancy. These effects can include physical problems and problems with behavior and learning. Often, a person with an FASD has a mix of these problems.

Causes

FASDs are caused by a woman drinking alcohol during pregnancy. Alcohol in the mother's blood passes to the baby through the umbilical cord. When a woman drinks alcohol, so does her baby. There is no known safe amount of alcohol during pregnancy or when trying to get pregnant. There is also no safe time to drink during pregnancy. Alcohol can cause problems for a developing baby throughout pregnancy, including before a woman knows she's pregnant. All types of alcohol are equally harmful, including all wines and beer.

Signs and Symptoms

FASDs refer to the whole range of effects that can happen to a person whose mother drank alcohol during pregnancy. These conditions

---

This chapter includes text excerpted from "Fetal Alcohol Spectrum Disorders (FASDs)—Facts about FASDs," Centers for Disease Control and Prevention (CDC), June 6, 2017.

can affect each person in different ways, and can range from mild to severe. A person with an FASD might have:

- Abnormal facial features, such as a smooth ridge between the nose and upper lip (this ridge is called the philtrum)
- Small head size
- Shorter-than-average height
- Low body weight
- Poor coordination
- Hyperactive behavior
- Difficulty with attention
- Poor memory
- Difficulty in school (especially with math)
- Learning disabilities
- Speech and language delays
- Intellectual disability or low intelligence quotient (IQ)
- Poor reasoning and judgment skills
- Sleep and sucking problems as a baby
- Vision or hearing problems
- Problems with the heart, kidneys, or bones

Types of FASDs

Different terms are used to describe FASDs, depending on the type of symptoms.

- **Fetal alcohol syndrome (FAS):** FAS represents the most involved end of the FASD spectrum. Fetal death is the most extreme outcome from drinking alcohol during pregnancy. People with FAS might have abnormal facial features, growth problems, and central nervous system (CNS) problems. People with FAS can have problems with learning, memory, attention span, communication, vision, or hearing. They might have a mix of these problems. People with FAS often have a hard time in school and trouble getting along with others.

- **Alcohol-related neurodevelopmental disorder (ARND):** People with ARND might have intellectual disabilities and problems with behavior and learning. They might do poorly in school and have difficulties with math, memory, attention, judgment, and poor impulse control.
- **Alcohol-related birth defects (ARBD):** People with ARBD might have problems with the heart, kidneys, or bones or with hearing. They might have a mix of these.
- **Neurobehavioral disorder associated with prenatal alcohol exposure (ND-PAE):** ND-PAE was first included as a recognized condition in the Diagnostic and Statistical Manual 5 (DSM 5) of the American Psychiatric Association (APA) in 2013. A child or youth with ND-PAE will have problems in three areas:
    1. Thinking and memory, where the child may have trouble planning or may forget material he or she has already learned
    2. Behavior problems, such as severe tantrums, mood issues (for example, irritability), and difficulty shifting attention from one task to another
    3. Trouble with day-to-day living, which can include problems with bathing, dressing for the weather, and playing with other children

In addition, to be diagnosed with ND-PAE, the mother of the child must have consumed more than minimal levels of alcohol before the child's birth, which APA defines as more than 13 alcoholic drinks per month of pregnancy (that is, any 30-day period of pregnancy) or more than 2 alcoholic drinks in one sitting.

Diagnosis

The term FASDs is not meant for use as a clinical diagnosis. The Centers for Disease Control and Prevention (CDC) worked with a group of experts and organizations to review the research and develop guidelines for diagnosing FAS. The guidelines were developed for FAS only. CDC and its partners are working to put together diagnostic criteria for other FASDs, such as ARND. Diagnosing FAS can be hard because there is no medical test, like a blood test, for it. And other disorders, such as attention deficit hyperactivity disorder (ADHD) and Williams syndrome (WS), have some symptoms like FAS.

To diagnose FAS, doctors look for:

- Abnormal facial features (e.g., smooth ridge between nose and upper lip)
- Lower-than-average height, weight, or both
- CNS problems (e.g., small head size, problems with attention and hyperactivity, poor coordination)
- Prenatal alcohol exposure (PAE); although confirmation is not required to make a diagnosis

Prevention

To prevent FASDs, a woman should not drink alcohol while she is pregnant, or when she might get pregnant. This is because a woman could get pregnant and not know for up to 4–6 weeks. In the United States, nearly half of pregnancies are unplanned.

If a woman is drinking alcohol during pregnancy, it is never too late to stop drinking. Because brain growth takes place throughout pregnancy, the sooner a woman stops drinking the safer it will be for her and her baby. FASDs are completely preventable if a woman does not drink alcohol during pregnancy—so why take the risk?

Treatment

FASDs last a lifetime. There is no cure for FASDs, but research shows that early intervention treatment services can improve a child's development. There are many types of treatment options, including medication to help with some symptoms, behavior and education therapy, parent training, and other alternative approaches. No one treatment is right for every child. Good treatment plans will include close monitoring, follow-ups, and changes as needed along the way. Also, "protective factors" can help reduce the effects of FASDs and help people with these conditions reach their full potential.

Protective factors include:

- Diagnosis before 6 years of age
- Loving, nurturing, and stable home environment during the school years
- Absence of violence
- Involvement in special education and social services

Chapter 39

Adopting and Fostering Children with FASD

Parenting has been called the toughest but most fulfilling job in the world. Parenting children with special needs, such as fetal alcohol spectrum disorders (FASD), brings its own set of challenges. Many parents of children with an FASD are adoptive or foster parents. Some knew about FASD when they welcomed their children into their family, while others did not. In any case, information is the key to success in raising children with an FASD. Learning about FASD can help parents understand how their children are affected, which parenting strategies work best, and how to get services and support. For people who want to adopt or foster a child with an FASD, knowing the facts can help them make an informed decision.

What Is Fetal Alcohol Spectrum Disorders (FASD)?

"FASD" is an umbrella term describing the range of effects that can occur in an individual whose mother drank alcohol during pregnancy. These effects may include physical, mental, behavioral, and/or learning disabilities (LD) with possible lifelong implications. The term FASD is not intended for use as a clinical diagnosis. It refers to conditions such

---

This chapter includes text excerpted from "Adopting and Fostering Children with Fetal Alcohol Spectrum Disorders," Substance Abuse and Mental Health Services Administration (SAMHSA), May 12, 2007. Reviewed April 2018.

as fetal alcohol syndrome (FAS), alcohol-related neurodevelopmental disorder (ARND), and alcohol-related birth defects (ARBD). In the United States, FASD occurs in about 10 per 1,000 live births, or about 40,000 babies per year.

There is little information available about FASD and adoption or foster care. One study of children in foster care in Washington state revealed a rate of FAS 10–15 times higher than in the general population, suggesting that children in foster care are more likely to have an FASD. Estimates for international adoptions vary by country. In Russian orphanages, the rate of FAS alone has been estimated at 1–10 per 100.

Meeting the Challenges Associated with FASD

Brain damage and physical defects are the primary disabilities associated with FASD. Lifelong behavioral or cognitive problems may include:

- Mental retardation (MR)
- Learning disabilities (LD)
- Hyperactivity
- Attention deficits
- Problems with impulse control, social skills, language, and memory

These challenges can lead to other problems called secondary disabilities, which may include:

- Disrupted school experience
- Alcohol and substance abuse
- Mental illness
- Dependent living
- Problems with employment
- Inappropriate sexual behavior
- Involvement in the criminal or juvenile justice system
- Confinement (prison or inpatient treatment for mental health or substance abuse problems)

A child with an FASD is likely to need services throughout his or her life and may never be able to live independently. The lifetime cost for one child with FAS can be $2 million. Despite their challenges, children with an FASD have a number of strengths. For example, they tend to be caring, creative, determined, and eager to please. They also respond well to structure, consistency, concrete communication, and close supervision. With a supportive home, an early diagnosis, and appropriate services, many children with an FASD can avoid secondary disabilities and reach their full potential.

Gathering Information

Many children who have an FASD lack an accurate diagnosis and their problems may not be clear. Prospective parents may request a copy of a child's complete medical and family history. However, because records may not tell the whole story, they may also ask specific questions about:

- Possible prenatal exposure to alcohol or drugs
- The physical and mental health of the mother and any siblings
- The developmental history of the child, including possible delays
- Independent evaluations from a physician

Most states require adoption and foster care agencies to share information with prospective parents about the health and social history of the child and birth parents. Some states require more information sharing than others, but few specifically address alcohol. Full investigation and disclosure is best for everyone so that placements are successful, parents are prepared, and children get the help they need.

Chapter 40

FASD May Co-Occur with Mental Illness

Everyone is born with a certain amount of potential. Reaching it can often be a challenge, especially for people with fetal alcohol spectrum disorders (FASD) who may also have co-occurring mental illness. A co-occurring disorder exists simultaneously with another disorder. This co-occurring disorder often complicates treatment and interferes with the person's ability to function.

What Are Fetal Alcohol Spectrum Disorders (FASD)?

"Fetal alcohol spectrum disorders" (FASD) is an umbrella term describing the range of effects that can occur in an individual who was prenatally exposed to alcohol. These effects may include physical, mental, behavioral, and/or learning disabilities (LD) with possible lifelong implications. FASD is not a diagnostic term used by clinicians.

What Are Co-Occurring Disorders?

Co-occurring disorders is the term used when an individual has both a mental illness as well as a drug or alcohol abuse-related disorder.

This chapter includes text excerpted from "How Fetal Alcohol Spectrum Disorders Co-Occur with Mental Illness," Substance Abuse and Mental Health Services Administration (SAMHSA), 2007. Reviewed April 2018.

A person with an FASD who is also diagnosed with a mental illness is said to have a co-occurring disorder.

FASD and Co-Occurring Disorders: What Are the Risks?

Often, a person with a co-occurring FASD and mental illness not diagnosed with an FASD. This can cause anger and frustration. Failure to recognize co-occurring disorders can increase the risk of:

- Misdiagnosis or inappropriate treatment
- Unemployment or underemployment
- Psychiatric hospitalization
- Family, school, and relationship problems
- Homelessness
- Alcohol and drug abuse
- Legal problems
- Premature death (suicide, accident, murder)

Recognizing an FASD as a co-occurring disorder can help decrease anger and frustration among individuals, families, and providers. Individuals may be relieved to have an explanation for their difficulties. Families can understand the nature of the problems and provide support. Service providers can focus on ways to make treatment programs more effective.

Which Disorders Co-Occur with FASD?

Prenatal alcohol exposure can cause behavioral, cognitive, and psychological problems. Signs and symptoms of an FASD are similar to some mental illnesses. In many cases, the signs and symptoms of an FASD go unrecognized or are misdiagnosed as a mental illness or brain injury. Individuals with an FASD may also receive multiple diagnoses, such as attention deficit hyperactivity disorder (ADHD), oppositional defiant disorder (ODD), and anxiety disorder. Therefore, it is important to determine whether the symptoms are a result of prenatal alcohol exposure or have another root cause.

If an FASD is unrecognized, treatments may be ineffective. When the best possible diagnostic and treatment methods do not work, consider the possibility of an FASD. An FASD assessment may be in order, including neuropsychological tests, by a clinician familiar with FASD. FASD can co-occur with many disorders, such as:

- Major depressive or bipolar disorder
- Psychotic disorders
- Autism or Asperger syndrome (AS)
- Schizophrenia
- Personality or conduct disorders (CD)
- Reactive attachment disorder (RAD)
- Traumatic brain injury (TBI)

Some conditions, such as RAD, may result from frequent changes in home placement and other environmental factors. In addition, an FASD can lead to many of the psychosocial stressors, such as:

- Educational problems
- Occupational problems
- Financial problems
- Legal problems
- Relationship problems

The *Diagnostic and Statistical Manual of Mental Disorders, Fourth Edition (DSM-IV)* has no codes for FASDs. For insurance purposes, providers may list a co-occurring mental illness as the primary diagnosis. Regardless of which diagnostic code is used, an FASD must be seriously considered when developing an individual's treatment plan.

How Can We Recognize Co-Occurring Conditions?

Co-occurring disorders among persons with an FASD may occur more often in individuals with a family history of mental illness than those in families without such history. Some conditions, such as schizophrenia, mood disorders, and ADHD, have genetic vulnerability. Because persons with an FASD are likely to have co-occurring conditions, getting an accurate diagnosis is critical. A thorough diagnostic workup should be completed, including:

- Maternal alcohol history

- Medical history, including information such as head circumference and length of eye openings, seizures, and poor coordination
- Individual and family mental health history
- Evaluation of any developmental disabilities
- Medical and psychiatric evaluation
- Neuropsychological tests
- Adaptive functioning tests

The cognitive impairments in FASD can hinder the ability to succeed in treatment. Such impairments include:

- Difficulty following multiple directions at home, school, work, and treatment settings
- Difficulty participating in treatment that requires receptive language skills, such as group therapy or 12-step programs
- Difficulty processing information outside sessions and applying what they have learned (e.g., can recite rules but repeatedly break them because they forget them)
- Tendency to process information literally (e.g., told to "take a cab home," one young man stole a cab)
- Difficulty grasping the concept of historic time and future time. Reward systems that involve earning points one week for rewards the next may be ineffective

What Can Treatment Personnel Do?

To produce the best outcomes, it is necessary to diagnose and treat all conditions simultaneously. Treatment personnel should avoid over or underdiagnosing. Communicating with families to get as much information as possible is key to an accurate diagnosis and effective treatment. Most importantly, treatment personnel should focus on positive outcomes for their clients. Instead of viewing individuals as failing if they do not do well in a program, staff need to view the program as not providing what the individual needs to succeed. Treatment personnel need to investigate the cause of any behavior, such as failure to understand instructions. Understanding the individual's disorders, needs, and strengths will help in developing an effective approach that enables the person to succeed. Correctly identifying all co-occurring disorders and treating them appropriately can lead to improved outcomes for the individual, family, and service providers.

Part Five

Mental Health Problems Associated with Alcohol Abuse

Chapter 41

Alcoholism, Substance Abuse, and Addictive Behavior

Alcoholism

Alcohol abuse is a pattern of drinking that is harmful to the drinker or others. The following situations, occurring repeatedly in a 12-month period, would be indicators of alcohol abuse:

- Missing work or skipping child care responsibilities because of drinking
- Drinking in situations that are dangerous, such as before or while driving
- Being arrested for driving under the influence of alcohol or for hurting someone while drunk
- Continuing to drink even though there are ongoing alcohol-related tensions with friends and family

---

This chapter includes text excerpted from "Alcoholism, Substance Abuse, and Addictive Behavior," Office on Women's Health (OWH), U.S. Department of Health and Human Services (HHS), August 13, 2015.

Alcoholism is a disease. It is chronic, or lifelong, and it can get worse over time and be life-threatening. Alcoholism is based in the brain. These are some of the typical characteristics of alcoholism:

- Craving: A strong need to drink
- Loss of control: The inability to stop drinking
- Physical dependence: Withdrawal symptoms, such as nausea, sweating, shakiness, and anxiety, when alcohol use is stopped after a period of heavy drinking
- Tolerance: The need for increasing amounts of alcohol to get "high"

Know the Risks

Research suggests that a woman is more likely to drink too much if she has any of the following:

- Parents and siblings (or other blood relatives) with alcohol problems
- A partner who drinks too much
- The ability to "hold her liquor" more than others
- A history of depression
- A history of childhood physical or sexual abuse

The presence of any of these factors is a good reason to be especially careful with drinking.

How Do You Know If You Have a Problem?

Answering the following four questions can help you find out if you or someone close to you has a drinking problem.

- Have you ever felt you should cut down on your drinking?
- Have people annoyed you by criticizing your drinking?
- Have you ever felt bad or guilty about your drinking?
- Have you ever had a drink first thing in the morning to steady your nerves or to get rid of a hangover?

One "yes" answer suggests a possible alcohol problem. If you responded "yes" to more than one question, it is very likely that you have a problem with alcohol. In either case, it is important that you see your healthcare provider right away to discuss your responses to these questions.

Even if you answered "no" to all of the above questions, if you are having drinking-related problems with your job, relationships, health, or with the law, you should still seek help.

Treatment for Alcohol Problems

Treatment for an alcohol problem depends on its severity. Routine doctor visits are an ideal time to discuss alcohol use and its potential problems. Healthcare professionals can help a woman take a good hard look at what effect alcohol is having on her life and can give advice on ways to stop drinking or to cut down.

Alcoholism treatment works for many people. But like other chronic illnesses, such as diabetes, high blood pressure, and asthma, there are varying levels of success when it comes to treatment. Some people stop drinking and remain sober. Others have long periods of sobriety with bouts of relapse. And still others cannot stop drinking for any length of time. With treatment, one thing is clear, however: the longer a person stops drinking alcohol, the more likely he or she will be able to stay sober.

Substance Abuse

Many people do not understand why people become addicted to drugs. The truth is: drugs change the brain and cause repeated drug abuse. Drug addiction is a brain disease. Drug use leads to changes in the structure and function of the brain. Although it is true that for most people the initial decision to take drugs is voluntary, over time, the changes in the brain caused by repeated drug abuse can affect a person's self-control and ability to make sound decisions. At the same time, drugs cause the brain to send intense impulses to take more drugs.

Treatment

Drug abuse is a treatable disease. There are many effective treatments for drug abuse. Some important points about substance abuse treatment include:

- Medical and behavioral therapy, alone or used together, are used to treat drug abuse.

- Sometimes treatment can be done on an outpatient basis.
- Severe drug abuse usually requires residential treatment, where the patient sleeps at the treatment center.
- Treatment can take place within the criminal justice systems, which can stop a convicted person from returning to criminal behavior.
- Studies show that treatment does not need to be voluntary to work.

Addictive Behavior

Why Do Some People Become Addicted, While Others Do Not?

Nothing can predict whether or not a person will become addicted to drugs. But there are some risk factors for drug addiction, including:

- **Biology.** Genes, gender, ethnicity, and the presence of other mental disorders may increase risk for drug abuse and addiction.
- **Environment.** Peer pressure, physical and sexual abuse, stress, and family relationships can influence the course of drug abuse and addiction in a person's life.
- **Development.** Although taking drugs at any age can lead to addiction, the earlier that drug use begins, the more likely it is to progress to more serious abuse.

Chapter 42

Alcohol and Mental Health

Alcohol Addiction as Mental Illness

Did you know that addiction alcohol is a mental illness? Alcoholic use disorder changes normal desires and priorities. It changes normal behaviors and interferes with the ability to work, go to school, and to have good relationships with friends and family. Having two illnesses at the same time is known as "comorbidity" and it can make treating each disorder more difficult.

Alcohol Use Disorders

Alcohol use disorders can refer to alcohol use or alcohol dependence. Symptoms of these disorders may include:

- Behavioral changes, such as:
    - Drop in attendance and performance at work or school

This chapter contains text excerpted from the following sources: Text under the heading "Alcohol Addiction as Mental Illness" is excerpted from "Substance Use and Mental Health," National Institute of Mental Health (NIMH), May 2016; Text beginning with heading "Alcohol Use Disorders" is excerpted from "Mental Health and Substance Use Disorders," MentalHealth.gov, U.S. Department of Health and Human Services (HHS), September 26, 2017; Text beginning with heading "Prevention of Alcohol Abuse and Mental Illness" is excerpted from "Prevention of Substance Abuse and Mental Illness," Substance Abuse and Mental Health Services Administration (SAMHSA), September 20, 2017.

    - Frequently getting into trouble (fights, accidents, illegal activities)
    - Using alcohol/substances in physically hazardous situations such as while driving or operating a machine
    - Engaging in secretive or suspicious behaviors
    - Changes in appetite or sleep patterns
    - Unexplained change in personality or attitude
    - Sudden mood swings, irritability, or angry outbursts
    - Periods of unusual hyperactivity, agitation, or giddiness
    - Lacking of motivation
    - Appearing fearful, anxious, or paranoid, with no reason
- Physical changes, such as:
    - Bloodshot eyes and abnormally sized pupils
    - Sudden weight loss or weight gain
    - Deterioration of physical appearance
    - Unusual smells on breath, body, or clothing
    - Tremors, slurred speech, or impaired coordination
- Social changes, such as:
    - Sudden change in friends, favorite hangouts, and hobbies
    - Legal problems related to substance/alcohol use
    - Unexplained need for money or financial problems
    - Using alcohol/substances even though it causes problems in relationships

Alcohol Use Disorders and Mental Health

Mental health problems and alcohol use disorders sometimes occur together. This is because:

- Certain illegal drugs or alcohol can cause people with an addiction to experience one or more symptoms of a mental health problem
- Mental health problems can sometimes lead to alcohol or drug use, as some people with a mental health problem may misuse these substances as a form of self-medication

- Mental and alcohol use disorders share some underlying causes, including changes in brain composition, genetic vulnerabilities, and early exposure to stress or trauma

More than one in four adults living with serious mental health problems also has a substance/alcohol use problem. Substance/alcohol use problems occur more frequently with certain mental health problems, including:

- Depression
- Anxiety disorders
- Schizophrenia
- Personality disorders

Recovering from Mental Health Problems and Alcohol Use

Someone with a mental health problem and alcohol use disorder must treat both issues. Treatment for both mental health problems and alcohol use disorders may include rehabilitation, medications, support groups, and talk therapy.

Prevention of Alcohol Abuse and Mental Illness

Promoting mental health and preventing mental and/or alcohol use disorders are fundamental to the Substance Abuse and Mental Health Services Administration's (SAMHSA) mission to reduce the impact of behavioral health conditions in America's communities.

Mental and alcohol use disorders can have a powerful effect on the health of individuals, their families, and their communities. In 2014, an estimated 9.8 million adults aged 18 and older in the United States had a serious mental illness, and 1.7 million of which were aged 18–25. Also 15.7 million adults (aged 18 or older) and 2.8 million youth (aged 12–17) had a major depressive episode during the past year. In 2014, an estimated 22.5 million Americans aged 12 and older self-reported needing treatment for alcohol or illicit drug use, and 11.8 million adults self-reported needing mental health treatment or counseling in the past year. These disorders are among the top conditions that cause disability and carry a high burden of disease in the United States, resulting in significant costs to families, employers, and publicly funded health systems. By 2020, mental and alcohol use disorders will surpass all physical diseases as a major cause of disability worldwide.

In addition, alcohol and drug use can lead to other chronic diseases such as diabetes and heart disease. Addressing the impact of alcohol use alone is estimated to cost Americans more than $600 billion each year.

Preventing mental and/or alcohol use disorders and related problems in children, adolescents, and young adults is critical to Americans' behavioral and physical health. Behaviors and symptoms that signal the development of a behavioral disorder often manifest two to four years before a disorder is present. In addition, people with a mental health issue are more likely to use alcohol or drugs than those not affected by a mental illness. Results from the National Survey on Drug Use and Health (NSDUH) report showed that of those adults with any mental illness, 18.2 percent had a alcohol use disorder, while those adults with no mental illness only had a 6.3 percent rate of alcohol use disorder in the past year. If communities and families can intervene early, behavioral health disorders might be prevented, or symptoms can be mitigated.

Continuum of Care

A comprehensive approach to behavioral health also means seeing prevention as part of an overall continuum of care. The Behavioral Health Continuum of Care Model recognizes multiple opportunities for addressing behavioral health problems and disorders. Based on the Mental Health Intervention Spectrum, first introduced in a 1994 Institute of Medicine (IOM) report, the model includes the following components:

- **Promotion:** These strategies are designed to create environments and conditions that support behavioral health and the ability of individuals to withstand challenges. Promotion strategies also reinforce the entire continuum of behavioral health services.
- **Prevention:** Delivered prior to the onset of a disorder, these interventions are intended to prevent or reduce the risk of developing a behavioral health problem, such as underage alcohol use, prescription drug misuse and abuse, and illicit drug use
- **Treatment:** These services are for people diagnosed with a alcohol use or other behavioral health disorder.
- **Recovery:** These services support individuals' abilities to live productive lives in the community and can often help with abstinence.

Chapter 43

Anxiety and Alcohol Use Disorders

The co-occurrence of anxiety disorders and alcohol use disorders (AUDs) is relatively common and is associated with a complex clinical presentation. Sound diagnosis and treatment planning requires that clinicians have an integrated understanding of the developmental pathways and course of this comorbidity. Moreover, standard interventions for anxiety disorders or AUDs may need to be modified and combined in targeted ways to accommodate the unique needs of people who have both disorders. Optimal combination of evidence-based treatments should be based on a comparative balance that considers the advantages and disadvantages of sequential, parallel, and integrated approaches.

Co-occurring anxiety disorders and alcohol use disorders (AUDs) are of great interest to researchers and clinicians. Cumulative evidence from epidemiological and clinical studies over the past few decades has highlighted both the frequency and clinical impact of this comorbidity. Investigations into the unique connections between specific anxiety disorders and AUDs have shown that this association is multifaceted and complex, underscoring the importance of careful diagnostic scrutiny. Of clinical relevance, treatment for people with comorbid anxiety

---

This chapter includes text excerpted from "Anxiety and Alcohol Use Disorders: Comorbidity and Treatment Considerations," National Institute on Alcohol Abuse and Alcoholism (NIAAA), November 21, 2012. Reviewed April 2018.

and AUDs can be complicated, and both the methods used and the timing of the interventions are relevant factors in treatment planning and delivery.

Prevalence of Comorbid Anxiety and AUDs

The respective prevalences of comorbid anxiety disorders and AUDs from each of these epidemiological studies are summarized in table 43.1. These data show that, across different large-scale studies, at different times, and both in the United States and abroad, anxiety and AUDs co-occur at rates greater than would be expected by chance alone. The odds ratios (ORs) characterizing the comorbidity between an AUD and any anxiety disorder in these studies ranged between 2.1 and 3.3—in other words, the two conditions co-occurred about two to three times as often as would be expected by chance alone.

Table 43.1. Adjusted Odds Ratios of the 12-Month Comorbidity between Certain Anxiety Disorders and Alcohol Use Disorders across Epidemiological Samples

Types of Disorders	ECA	NCS	NSMH & WB	NESARC
Agoraphobia	2.7	2.6	2.3	3.6
Generalized anxiety disorder	—	4.6	3.3	3
Obsessive–compulsive disorder	—	—	2.7	—
Panic disorder	4.1	1.7	3.9	3.5
Simple phobia	2	2.2	—	2.3
Social phobia	1.8	2.8	3.2	2.3
Any	2.1	2.6	3.3	2.7

Development of Comorbid Anxiety and AUDs

The question of how anxiety and AUDs coalesce has intrigued investigators and clinicians for decades and still is a subject of debate. Three primary pathways have been proposed:

- The common-factor model that uses a third variable to explain the co-occurrence of anxiety and AUDs
- The self-medication pathway, which posits that people consume alcohol to cope with anxiety disorders, leading to co-occurring AUDs

- The substance-induced pathway, wherein AUDs lead to increased anxiety and vulnerability for co-occurring anxiety disorders

Gender Differences in Comorbid Anxiety and Alcohol Use Disorders

Numerous studies have attempted to evaluate possible gender differences in the frequency of comorbid anxiety disorders and alcohol use disorders (AUDs). Population surveys consistently show that anxiety disorders are more common among women, whereas AUDs are more common among men. To account for these base-rate differences when estimating gender-specific comorbidity rates for anxiety disorders and AUDs in the National Comorbidity Survey, Kessler and colleagues used adjusted odds ratios (ORs). These analyses found that among alcohol-dependent men in the sample, 35.8 percent (OR = 2.22) had a co-occurring anxiety disorder, compared with 60.7 percent (OR = 3.08) among alcohol-dependent women. Moreover, not only did women in the study have an increased likelihood of independent anxiety disorders compared with men, but prior anxiety disorders also were more strongly predictive of alcohol dependence among the women. Furthermore, a multisite trial in Germany demonstrated that anxiety disorders had a substantial influence on the course and severity of alcoholism in women. Thus, in this treatment-seeking sample women who had an anxiety disorder reported an accelerated temporal sequence of alcoholism, including the onset of first drink, regular drinking, and incidence of alcohol withdrawal than women with no anxiety disorder.

One potential explanation for these findings is that the reasons for using alcohol may differ by gender. For example, women may be more prone than men to self-medicate for mood problems with substances such as alcohol. Furthermore, empirical inspection of gender differences in stress-related drinking has shown that women report higher levels of stress and have a stronger connection between stress and drinking. Together, these results suggest that women may be more likely to rely on alcohol to manage anxiety.

The findings suggest that women are more likely than men to have both disorders, and the presence of anxiety disorders may exacerbate the course and severity of alcohol problems in women. Furthermore, treatment for women with this comorbidity may be especially complex, both because they are likely to use alcohol to self-medicate for stress and because women with social phobia may be reluctant to participate in treatment (e.g., Alcoholics Anonymous) that could otherwise be effective. These factors spotlight the importance of probing for anxiety disorders in women entering alcohol treatment and reinforce the need to remain sensitive to the different ways that gender can influence the process and outcomes of therapy.

Mutual Maintenance of Anxiety and AUDs

Once comorbidity between anxiety disorders and AUDs has been established, the two disorders may influence and maintain each other in ways that are independent of the developmental pathway. In other words, the processes involved in the initiation and the maintenance of comorbidity may differ in meaningful ways. One hypothesis emerging from the comorbidity literature is that anxiety and AUDs become intertwined in a reciprocal, perpetuating cycle. This positive feedback loop often is characterized as a feed-forward or mutual-maintenance pattern. For example, a person who copes with anxiety by self-medicating with increasing amounts of alcohol likely will experience greater alcohol-related consequences (e.g., poor job performance, interpersonal problems, and anxiety induction from alcohol withdrawal), thus exacerbating the initial anxiety and leading to further drinking, which in turn sustains and/or amplifies the cycle.

Evidence that comorbid anxiety disorders can worsen and perpetuate AUDs and impair alcohol treatment response includes the following findings:

- People with social anxiety disorder endorsed greater alcohol dependence severity and had more dependence symptoms than alcoholics without social phobia
- The presence of social anxiety disorder and generalized anxiety disorder predicted increased long-term mental distress among treatment-seeking, substance-dependent patients
- Alcoholic inpatients with anxiety disorders had increased severity of alcohol withdrawal
- Comorbid panic disorder with agoraphobia and generalized anxiety disorder were related to increased risk of persistent alcohol dependence
- Symptoms of generalized anxiety disorder and social anxiety disorder can interfere with substance use treatment
- Anxiety disorders are associated with elevated risk for relapse following alcohol treatment.

Treatment Considerations for Comorbid Anxiety and AUDs

When a diagnosis has been established, the treatment provider also needs to take into consideration the unique factors associated with this comorbidity when selecting the appropriate treatment protocol. A variety of pharmacotherapy and psychotherapy approaches are available to address anxiety and AUDs. Each modality has proven to be efficacious for these problems in isolation, and several evidence-based treatment alternatives for each disorder are available. However, it sometimes may be necessary to modify these treatment approaches for comorbid individuals because even strategies considered the gold standard for one disorder potentially can have a negative impact on individuals with the other disorder.

Pharmacotherapy for Anxiety Disorders

Medication-based treatments for anxiety include an assortment of agents from several classes of medication, including benzodiazepines, tricyclic antidepressant drugs (TCAs), monoamine oxidase inhibitors (MAO-Is), and serotonergic-based medications (e.g., selective serotonin reuptake inhibitors (SSRIs), serotonin-norepinephrine reuptake inhibitors (SNRIs), and the 5-HT1a partial agonist buspirone).

Benzodiazepines. Benzodiazepines can be very safe and effective agents for the short-term management of anxiety disorders. These medications are well-tolerated and have few medical scenarios in which they must not be used (i.e., few contraindications), although patients with pulmonary disorders may be sensitive to the depressant effects of these agents on the central nervous system.

MAO-Is and TCAs. Caution also is suggested with the use of MAO-Is and TCAs for comorbid individuals. Although MAO-Is are quite effective in reducing anxiety, patients taking these agents may suffer a sudden severe increase in blood pressure (i.e., hypertensive crisis) after consuming certain foods and beverages that contain the amino acid tyramine, resulting in dietary restrictions for MAO-I users. These beverages include certain beers (e.g., imported beers, beer on tap, and nonalcoholic or reduced-alcohol beers), red wines, sherry, liqueurs, and vermouth, which is critical to know when treating people who also have alcohol problems. TCAs also should be used with caution among people with co-occurring AUDs and be prescribed only after other treatments have been ruled out because these medications

Table 43.2. FDA Approved and Evidence-Based Treatments for Anxiety and Alcohol Use Disorders

FDA Approved Therapies	Generalized Anxiety Disorder	Obsessive–Compulsive Disorder	Panic Disorder	Social Anxiety Disorder	Alcohol Use Disorders
Pharmacotherapy	Buspirone Duloxetine Escitalopram Paroxetine Venlafaxine	Clomipramine Fluoxetine Fluvoxamine Paroxetine Sertraline	Alprazolam Clonazepam Fluoxetine Paroxetine Sertraline Venlafaxine	Fluvoxamine Paroxetine Sertraline Venlafaxine	Acamprosate Disulfiram Naltrexone Topiramate
Psychotherapy	Cognitive and behavioral therapies	Cognitive therapy; exposure and response prevention	Applied relaxation; cognitive and behavioral therapies; psychoanalytic therapy	Cognitive and behavioral therapies	Behavioral couples therapy; brief intervention; cognitive and behavioral therapies; community reinforcement approach; motivational interviewing; relapse prevention therapy; social skills training; 12-step facilitation

can have an enhanced adverse-effect profile in this population. Moreover, the impaired judgment and impulsivity among persons with co-occurring alcohol use problems may increase the risks of taking an overdose of the medications that can result in toxicity and, potentially, suicidality. Finally, TCAs may react with alcohol in the brain to cause respiratory depression.

Serotonergic-based Medications. Medications that target a brain signaling system which uses the neurotransmitter serotonin and its receptors perhaps are the safest and most widely used agents to treat anxiety disorders. These agents include the SSRIs, SNRIs, and the serotonin partial agonist buspirone. At present, SSRIs (e.g., fluoxetine, paroxetine, and sertraline) and SNRIs (e.g., venlafaxine and duloxetine) generally are used as first-line treatment in this area because they consistently demonstrate anxiolytic efficacy, including in patients with comorbid AUDs. Moreover, serotonergic agents have favorable properties, such as being well-tolerated and having virtually no abuse potential. Another welcome characteristic of SSRIs in patients with comorbid AUDs is that, in contrast to TCAs, they do not interact with alcohol to increase the risk of respiratory depression. With both SSRIs and SNRIs it is advisable to inform patients that it may take about 1–2 weeks before these medications show full effectiveness. In addition, there is a risk of an electrolyte imbalance involving decreased sodium concentrations in the blood (i.e., hyponatremia), which can reduce the seizure threshold. This may be especially relevant during alcohol withdrawal, and clinicians therefore should monitor fluid intake and sodium levels during these periods.

Buspirone specifically is approved by the U.S. Food and Drug Administration (FDA) for the management of generalized anxiety disorder. Similar to other serotonergic-based medications, buspirone has a desirable safety profile but a relatively delayed onset of anxiolytic effects.

Psychotherapy for Anxiety Disorders

The psychosocial treatment of choice for anxiety disorders is established more clearly, with a family of strategies known collectively as cognitive behavioral therapies (CBTs) considered the practice standard for people with anxiety problems. Meta-analyses of CBTs for anxiety disorders have shown strong evidence for their efficacy. The CBT approaches to anxiety consist of two overarching strategies:

1. Exposure to feared stimuli

2. Anxiety management techniques, such as cognitive restructuring, applied relaxation, and coping skills training

Pharmacotherapy for AUDs

There currently are three medications that have received FDA approval for the maintenance treatment of alcoholism:

1. Disulfiram, an agent that interferes with ethanol metabolism and induces an adverse reaction (e.g., flushing, nausea, and rapid heartbeat) when a person consumes alcohol
2. Naltrexone, an antagonist acting at receptors for signaling molecules, endogenous opioids, that can interfere with the rewarding properties of alcohol and reduce craving; it is available in both short- and long-acting formulations
3. Acamprosate, an agent that acts on the gamma-aminobutyric acid (GABA) system, counteracting alcohol's effects on this system

Administration of medications for AUDs may require some adjustment for individuals who also have anxiety disorders compared with the regimen for alcoholics without this comorbidity.

Psychotherapy for AUDs

Psychosocial approaches to treating AUDs have evolved markedly over the past few decades. The historical roots of this treatment modality largely can be traced back to the development of Alcoholics Anonymous (AA) in Akron, Ohio, in the 1930s and 1940s. It has been estimated that nearly 1 in every 10 Americans has attended at least one AA meeting, and it is "the most frequently consulted source of help for drinking problems." Anecdotal and research evidence suggests that AA participation can promote positive alcohol-related outcomes, lending some credence to the oft-quoted adage, "It works if you work it." Several alternative treatments have been developed since and have received favorable empirical support. In a systematic analysis of 10 published reviews of evidence-based psychosocial therapies for AUDs, a majority of the reviews found support for CBTs, the community reinforcement approach (CRA), motivational interviewing (MI), relapse prevention therapy (RPT), social skills training (SST), behavioral marital (couples) therapy (BCT), and brief intervention (BI).

The administration of these psychosocial treatment strategies for alcohol problems can be less straightforward with individuals who have comorbid anxiety and AUDs.

Conclusion

Regardless of the method of onset, however, once anxiety and AUDs co-occur, the mutual maintenance model suggests that these comorbid disorders can become engaged in a feed-forward cycle that could be progressive if left untreated. It is important to be mindful of the unique developmental and maintenance characteristics associated with this comorbidity, because these elements have a considerable influence on both diagnosis and treatment planning.

Fortunately, several evidence-based strategies are available for treating anxiety and AUDs, including both pharmacotherapy and psychotherapy approaches. As these and other lines of research in comorbid anxiety and AUDs continue to mature, future studies should provide further insights into the special considerations, treatment needs, and ideal therapeutic strategies for individuals with these dual problems.

Chapter 44

Psychiatric Disorders Associated with Alcoholism

The thinking, memory, and feeling parts of the human brain change, and alcohol can interfere with these important changes and actually shrink the thinking and memory parts.

Research shows that drinking an excessive amount of alcohol can make an area of the brain called the frontal lobes smaller. The frontal lobes help us make decisions, think about things, and pay attention. People who drink an excessive amount of alcohol have problems in these areas. Alcohol also can shrink the hippocampus, the brain area that helps with learning and memory. For weeks and months after a person stops drinking heavily, these parts of the brain still struggle to work correctly.

Drinking at a young age also makes alcoholism more likely later in life. So the decision to drink when you're still a teen could have negative effects on brain development over time. So be kind to your brain and think before you drink.

This chapter contains text excerpted from the following sources: Text in this chapter begins with excerpts from "Real Teens Ask: Got Alcohol on the Brain?" National Institute on Drug Abuse (NIDA) for Teens, May 24, 2011. Reviewed April 2018; Text beginning with the heading "Independent Major Depression" is excerpted from "Alcoholism and Psychiatric Disorders," National Institute on Alcohol Abuse and Alcoholism (NIAAA), November 2002. Reviewed April 2018.

Independent Major Depression

Mood disturbances (which frequently are not severe enough to qualify as "disorders") are arguably the most common psychiatric complaint among treatment-seeking alcoholic patients, affecting upwards of 80 percent of alcoholics at some point in their drinking careers. These mood problems may be characterized as one of the following:

- An expected, time-limited consequence of alcohol's depressant effects on the brain
- A more organized constellation of symptoms and signs (i.e., a syndrome) reflecting an alcohol-induced mood disorder with depressive features
- An independent major depressive disorder coexisting with or even predating alcoholism

When one applies these more precise definitional criteria and classifies only those patients as depressive who meet the criteria for a syndrome of a major depressive episode, approximately 30–40 percent of alcoholics experience a comorbid depressive disorder.

Some controversy exists as to the precise cause-and-effect relationship between depression and alcoholism, with some authors pointing out that depressive episodes frequently predate the onset of alcoholism, especially in women. Several studies found that approximately 60 percent of alcoholics who experience a major depressive episode, especially men, meet the criteria for an alcohol-induced mood disorder with depressive features. The remaining approximately 40 percent of alcoholic women and men who suffer a depressive episode likely have an independent major depressive disorder—that is, they experienced a major depressive episode before the onset of alcoholism or continue to exhibit depressive symptoms and signs even during lengthy periods of alcohol abstinence.

In a study of 2,954 alcoholics, Schuckit and colleagues found that patients with alcohol–induced depression appear to have different characteristics from patients with independent depressive disorders. For example, compared with patients with alcohol–induced depression, patients with independent depression were more likely to be Caucasian, married, and female; less experienced with other illicit drugs; less often treated for alcoholism; more likely to have a history of a prior suicide attempt; and more likely to have a family history of a major mood disorder.

Bipolar Disorder

According to two major epidemiological surveys conducted in the past 20 years, bipolar disorder (i.e., mania or manic–depressive illness) is the second-most common axis I disorder associated with alcohol dependence. (The axis I disorders most commonly associated with alcoholism are other drug use disorders.) Among manic patients, 50–60 percent abuse or become dependent on alcohol or other drugs (AODs) at some point in their illness. Diagnosing bipolar disorder in alcoholic patients can be particularly challenging. Several factors, such as the underreporting of symptoms (particularly symptoms of mania), the complex effects of alcohol on mood states, and common features shared by both illnesses (e.g., excessive involvement in pleasurable activities with high potential for painful consequences) reduce diagnostic accuracy. Bipolar patients are also likely to abuse drugs other than alcohol (e.g., stimulant drugs such as cocaine or methamphetamine), further complicating the diagnosis. As will be described in greater detail later, it can be helpful for an accurate diagnosis to obtain a careful history of the chronological order of both illnesses because approximately 60 percent of patients with both alcoholism and bipolar disorder started using AODs before the onset of affective episodes.

ASPD and Other Externalizing Disorders

Among the axis II personality disorders, ASPD (and the related conduct disorder, which often occurs during childhood in people who subsequently will develop ASPD) has long been recognized to be closely associated with alcoholism. Epidemiologic analyses found that compared with nonalcoholics, alcohol-dependent men are 4–8 times more likely, and alcoholic women are 12–17 times more likely, to have comorbid ASPD. Thus, approximately 15–20 percent of alcoholic men and 10 percent of alcoholic women have comorbid ASPD, compared with 4 percent of men and approximately 0.8 percent of women in the general population. Patients with ASPD are likely to develop alcohol dependence at an earlier age than their nonantisocial counterparts and are also more prone to having other drug use disorders.

In addition to ASPD, other conditions marked by an externalization of impulsive aggressive behaviors, such as attention deficit hyperactivity disorder (ADHD), are also associated with increased risk of alcohol-related problems.

Chapter 45

Alcohol's Association with Suicide

A number of national surveys have helped shed light on the relationship between alcohol and other drug use and suicidal behavior. A review of minimum-age drinking laws and suicides among youth ages 18–20 found that lower minimum-age drinking laws were associated with higher youth suicide rates. In a large study following adults who drink alcohol, suicide ideation was reported among persons with depression. In another survey, persons who reported that they had made a suicide attempt during their lifetime were more likely to have had a depressive disorder, and many also had an alcohol and/or substance abuse disorder. In a study of all nontraffic injury deaths associated with alcohol intoxication, over 20 percent were suicides.

In studies that examine risk factors among people who have completed suicide, substance use and abuse occurs more frequently among youth and adults, compared to older persons. For particular groups at risk, such as American Indians and Alaskan Natives, depression and alcohol use and abuse are the most common risk factors for completed

---

This chapter contains text excerpted from the following sources: Text in this chapter begins with excerpts from "Does Alcohol and Other Drug Abuse Increase the Risk for Suicide?" U.S. Department of Health and Human Services (HHS), May 7, 2008. Reviewed April 2018; Text beginning with the heading "Background" is excerpted from "Suicides Due to Alcohol and/or Drug Overdose—A Data Brief from the National Violent Death Reporting System," Centers for Disease Control and Prevention (CDC), February 3, 2011. Reviewed April 2018.

suicide. Alcohol and substance abuse problems contribute to suicidal behavior in several ways. Persons who are dependent on substances often have a number of other risk factors for suicide. In addition to being depressed, they are also likely to have social and financial problems. Substance use and abuse can be common among persons prone to being impulsive, and among persons who engage in many types of high-risk behaviors that result in self-harm. Fortunately, there are a number of effective prevention efforts that reduce risk for substance abuse in youth, and there are effective treatments for alcohol and substance use problems. Researchers are currently testing treatments specifically for persons with substance abuse problems who are also suicidal, or have attempted suicide in the past.

Background

Suicide occurs when a person ends his or her own life. It is the 11th leading cause of death among Americans, and every year more than 33,000 people end their own lives. Suicide is found in every age, racial, and ethnic group to differing degrees. There are a number of factors that increase the likelihood a person will take his or her own life; one of these is abusing substances such as alcohol and drugs. Alcohol and drug abuse are second only to depression and other mood disorders as the most frequent risk factors for suicidal behavior. Alcohol and some drugs can result in a loss of inhibition, may increase impulsive behavior, can lead to changes in the brain that result in depression over time, and can be disruptive to relationships—resulting in alienation and a loss of social connection. Furthermore, excessive acute drug and/or alcohol ingestion could result in death.

Results

Poisoning was the third-leading method of suicide, following firearm and hanging/strangulation. Seventy-five percent of suicides by poisoning were due to alcohol and/or drug overdose versus other types of poison such as carbon monoxide. Less than half (47%) of those who died by alcohol and/or drug overdose were known to have an alcohol or substance abuse problem.

Substances Used in Suicides

- Sixty-nine percent of individuals who died by suicide due to substance overdose had ingested one type of drug; 25 percent ingested two or more types of drugs.

- Poisoning is a leading method in suicide deaths, and drugs and/or alcohol make up 75 percent of suicide deaths due to poisoning.
- In suicides resulting from more than one substance, about one-third occur due to a combination of alcohol and prescription drugs. Almost another third are due to a combination of over-the-counter (OTC) drugs and prescription drugs.

Of Those Who Consumed a Single Drug Type

- Prescription drugs such as those in the opioid, benzodiazepine, and antidepressant class (e.g., oxycodone, diazepam, and fluoxetine) were the leading type used in suicide deaths. From 2005–2007, 79 percent of suicides due to substance overdose were due to prescription drugs only.
- OTC drugs such as acetaminophen were the second leading substance type used in suicides. They represented 10 percent of suicides due to substance overdose.
- Street/recreational drugs and alcohol made up the smallest proportion of these suicides (2% and less than 1% respectively).

Of Those Who Consumed More than One Type of Drug

- Alcohol and prescription drugs were ingested in 31 percent of suicides due to multiple substance overdose.
- Prescription drugs and OTC drugs were ingested in 30 percent of cases.
- Other (unspecified) combinations of substances were ingested in 24 percent of cases.
- Street/recreational drugs and prescription drugs were ingested in 12 percent of cases.
- Alcohol, street/recreational drugs, and prescription drugs were ingested in 2 percent of cases.
- Alcohol and street recreational drugs were ingested in <1 percent of cases.

Distribution by Demographic Group

- Females die in disproportionate numbers from suicide due to alcohol and/or drug overdose. From 2005–2007, 34 percent of female suicides were due to alcohol and/or drug overdose, versus 8 percent of males.

- 15 percent of suicides among white non-Hispanics were due to alcohol and/or drug overdose; this equals almost two times the percentage of black non-Hispanics in the same category (8%).
- 18 percent of suicide decedents between ages 40 and 64 died from alcohol and/or drug overdose; this equals more than four times the percentage of those aged 17 years and younger in the same category.
- The percent of total suicides due to alcohol and/or drugs in NVDRS-funded states range from 5.8–19.8 percent.

Table 45.1. Number and Percent of Suicides due to Drug and/or Alcohol Ingestion, by Decedent Sex, Race/Ethnicity, and Age Group, 16 NVDRS States, 2005–2007

Characteristic	Number	Percentage of Total Suicides due to Poisoning by Drugs/Alcohol
Sex		
Male	1698	8
Female	2008	34
Race/Ethnicity		
Hispanic	131	10
White, non-Hispanic	3322	15
Black, non-Hispanic	138	8
American Indian/Alaska Native, non-Hispanic	50	10
Asian/Pacific Islander, non-Hispanic	45	11
Unknown/Other	20	10
Age Group (years)		
<17	31	4
18-39	1079	11
40-64	2313	18
>65	282	7
Unknown	1	10

Table 45.2. Number and Percent of Suicides due to Drug and/or Alcohol Ingestion, by State, 2005–2007

State	No.	Percentage of Total Suicides due to Poisoning by Drugs/Alcohol
Alaska	25	6
Colorado	368	17
Georgia	205	7
Kentucky	125	7
Maryland	179	13
Massachusetts	280	20
New Jersey	304	17
New Mexico	118	11
North Carolina	490	15
Oklahoma	231	15
Oregon	275	16
Rhode Island	42	17
South Carolina	173	11
Utah	170	16
Virginia	407	16
Wisconsin	314	16
Total	3706	14

Implications and Recommendations

Alcohol and drug overdose account for a substantial number of suicides, and many of these deaths can be prevented by limiting access to substances. If lethal substances are not available when people are under psychological or emotional stress and despair, the ability to commit suicide is limited. Many of the substances used in suicides are either easily available—as in the case of over-the-counter drugs such as acetaminophen—or, like opioids, antidepressants, and benzodiazepines, are commonly prescribed to treat various physical and mental health conditions. Effective mental health treatment, which often includes pharmacologic therapy, is important to prevent suicide; however to adequately promote the safety and well-being of individuals at risk of suicide, consumers, family members, and others should be aware of the associated risk these substances pose. There are actions that state and local communities, policy-makers, and family members can take to reduce the number of suicides due to substance overdose.

Develop guidelines for safer prescribing and dispensing of medications. The National Strategy for Suicide Prevention (NSSP) calls for the development of guidelines for safer dispensing of medications for individuals at heightened risk of suicide. Policy makers should initiate strategies shown to be effective in preventing suicide. These include requiring bubble/blister packaging of analgesic pills instead of bottle packaging; limiting the number of pills pharmaceutical and nonpharmaceutical outlets can sell at one time, and providing printed warnings about the dangers of overdose with each sale of analgesics. Physicians and other clinicians should be educated about safe prescribing practices for suicidal individuals. Related efforts to address unintentional poisoning may also address suicide. For example, many states are developing statewide electronic databases to collect information on substances dispensed. This effort can provide valuable information on substance use and abuse trends that can affect drug policy and overdose prevention.

Teach families of suicidal individuals the importance of limiting access to substances in the home. Educational and skill-building interventions shown to be effective in reducing access to lethal substances should be implemented broadly in high-risk populations. Examples include educating parents and other family members in emergency departments, hospitals, and other clinical settings. Families should be educated on strategies to limit access at home to prescription drugs, over-the-counter analgesics, and alcohol. They should be educated about the potential dangers of alcohol in suicidal individuals and its ability to amplify the harmful effects of medications and other substances that can result in severe respiratory depression and death.

Promote connectedness between health, mental health, and substance abuse providers and other community-based support organizations to build a safety net for suicidal individuals. Increasing linkages between primary care, mental health, and substance abuse service providers and other community-based support organizations may allow for better identification, assessment, management, and treatment of at-risk individuals. A "team approach" can help ensure that those likely to work with suicidal individuals know appropriate actions to take to see that needed services are actually delivered and appropriate standards of care, monitoring, and follow-up are provided.

Build social support networks for persons who are suicidal. Individuals who have regular interactions with social support networks that may include family, friends, teachers, and school administrators, and a faith community can be protected from many of the factors that increase suicide risk such as alcohol and drug abuse. Families, friends, spiritual leaders, and other advisors of suicidal individuals can be instrumental in preventing suicide by maintaining open channels of communication about feelings of despair. They can encourage suicidal individuals to seek professional help and support them in other actions to save their life.

If you or someone you know is struggling with feelings of hopelessness and/or thinking about suicide, call the National Suicide Prevention Lifeline, 800-273-TALK (800-273-8255), to speak with a trained counselor and be connected with helpful resources in your area.

Part Six

Alcohol's Impact on Family, Work, and the Community

Chapter 46

Children Living with Alcohol-Abusing Parents

Chapter Contents

Section 46.1

Children of Alcoholics

This section includes text excerpted from "Children of Alcoholics—A Guide to Community Action," Substance Abuse and Mental Health Services Administration (SAMHSA), April 13, 2004. Reviewed April 2018.

Often, the people hurt most by alcohol abuse and alcoholism don't even drink; they are the children of alcoholic parents. These children are more likely to experience mental and physical problems and are at a greater risk of being neglected and/or abused. Children of alcoholics (COAs) are two to four times more likely than other children to become addicted to alcohol themselves. Every community experiences the devastating effects of alcoholism on children. Together, we can break the cycle of alcohol problems in families.

How Many Children of Alcoholics Are There?

More than 6 million children live with at least one parent who abuses or is dependent on alcohol or an illicit drug.

Why Should We Be Concerned about Children of Alcoholics?

- Alcoholism tends to run in families. Children of alcoholics (COAs) are four times more likely than non-COAs to develop alcoholism or drug problems.
- COAs are at higher risk than others for depression, anxiety disorders, problems with cognitive and verbal skills, and parental abuse or neglect. They are significantly more likely than other children to be abused or neglected by their parents or guardians and are more likely to enter foster care.
- If not prevented, the difficulties faced by COAs can place increased burdens on State and local Governments. These include increased costs for healthcare, mental health services,

child welfare, education, police and juvenile justice, and lost economic opportunity.

How Are Families with Alcoholism Different from Other Families?

- Families with alcoholism have higher levels of conflict than other families. Lack of adequate parenting and poor home management and family communication skills often leave children without effective training and role modeling.
- Families with alcoholism often lack structure and discipline for their children; as a result, the children often are expected to take on responsibilities normally assigned to older youth or adults.

How Can We Help Prevent Children of Alcoholics from Repeating Their Families' Alcohol-Related Problems?

- Although they are at increased risk, many COAs do not develop alcohol or drug use disorders or other serious problems in their lives. Often, they appear to be resilient, bolstered by protective factors and the support of caring adults in their lives.
- COAs can be helped, whether or not the alcohol-abusing family members are receiving help. Prevention programs often help COAs reduce stress; deal with emotional issues; and develop self-esteem, coping skills, and social support.
- Children who cope effectively with alcoholism in their families often rely on support from a nonalcoholic parent, grandparent, teacher, or other caring adult. Support groups, faith communities, and trained professionals also are available to help.

What Can Others Do to Help Children of Alcoholics Avoid Alcohol Abuse and Other Serious Problems?

- Simple acts of kindness and compassion can make a difference for COAs. By making yourself available to listen, discuss feelings, share interests, and support their efforts to make friends, you can help COAs cope with their present situations and develop the resilience and skills necessary for their futures.

- Tell them they are not alone, that responsible adults are available to help them, and that millions of others have had similar experiences and have grown up to lead healthy, satisfying lives.
- Remind them that their families' problems are not their fault and not their responsibility to solve. Their jobs are to be children and help take good care of themselves; learn the facts about alcohol, tobacco, and drugs; recognize their risks; and learn how to avoid repeating their families' alcohol abuse patterns.
- Encourage them to ask for help. Assure them that getting help is a sign of strength. Offer your own examples and be prepared to help them connect with caring, trustworthy adults and with student assistance programs and other services designed to provide them with further skill-building and support.
- Reach out to your community by participating in the annual Children of Alcoholics Week during the week of February 14. Help break through the barriers of shame, silence, and isolation to help these children live healthy, happy lives—despite their family problems.

Section 46.2

The Number of Children Living with Substance-Abusing Parents

This section includes text excerpted from "Children Living with Parents Who Have a Substance Use Disorders," Substance Abuse and Mental Health Services Administration (SAMHSA), August 24, 2017.

Substance use disorders (SUDs) are characterized by recurrent use of alcohol or drugs (or both) that results in problems such as being unable to control use of the substance; failing to meet obligations at work, home, or school; having poor health; and spending an increased amount of time getting, using, or recovering from the effects of using the substance. Parent substance use and parent experience of an SUD can have negative effects on children. Children with a parent who has an SUD are more likely than children who do not have a parent with an SUD to have lower socioeconomic status and increased difficulties in academic and social settings and family functioning. Children having a parent with an SUD are at risk of experiencing direct effects, such as parental abuse or neglect, or indirect effects, such as fewer household resources. Previous research indicates that the negative effects of parent SUDs may differ depending on the type of SUD the parent has (i.e., alcohol or illicit drugs). Policymakers can use information on the number of children living with parents with an SUD for developing targeted prevention and outreach programs.

The Center for Behavioral Health Statistics and Quality (CBHSQ) Report presents estimates of the number of children aged 17 or younger who lived with a parent with an SUD, alcohol use disorder, or illicit drug use disorder based on combined data from the 2009–2014 National Surveys on Drug Use and Health (NSDUHs). NSDUH is an annual survey of the U.S. civilian, noninstitutionalized population aged 12 or older. One of NSDUH's strengths is the stability of the survey design, which allows for multiple years of data to be combined to examine substance use and mental health issues in the United States.

NSDUH asks respondents who report using alcohol or illicit drugs in the year before the interview a series of questions designed to measure symptoms of SUD based on criteria specified in the fourth edition of the *Diagnostic and Statistical Manual of Mental Disorders (DSM-IV)*, including withdrawal; tolerance; use in dangerous situations; trouble with the law; and interference in major obligations at work, school, or home during the past year. NSDUH also allows for estimating of alcohol use disorder and illicit drug use disorder separately. In NSDUH, illicit drugs include marijuana, cocaine, heroin, hallucinogens, and inhalants, as well as the nonmedical use of prescription-type psychotherapeutic drugs. Adults with an SUD may have an alcohol use disorder, an illicit drug use disorder, or both an alcohol and an illicit drug use disorder. All estimates in this chapter are annual averages from the combined 2009–2014 NSDUH data.

The estimate of children with at least one parent who had an SUD is a composite measure. This measure is calculated using information gathered from adult respondents aged 18 or older including the respondent's SUD status; the number of biological, step, adoptive, or foster children aged 17 or younger living in the respondent's household; and whether another parent is also living in the respondent's household at the time of the interview.

The total number of children residing with at least one parent with an SUD was estimated by determining:

1. The number of children who live in a single-parent household with a father who has an SUD
2. The number of children who live in a single-parent household with a mother who has an SUD
3. The number of children who live in a two-parent household with a mother who has an SUD
4. The number of children who live in a two-parent household with a mother who does not have an SUD but where the other parent has an SUD

The first three groups are estimated by using the parent's analytic weight multiplied by the number of children aged 17 or younger in the household. The fourth group is estimated by applying a conditional probability (that in a two-parent household in which the mother does not have an SUD but the other parent does) to the mother respondent's analytic weight multiplied by the number of children aged 17 or younger in the household. The total number of children from these four groups constitutes the number of children residing with at least one parent where at least one parent has an SUD. The analysis is based on a sample size of 22,200 adults aged 18 or older with at least 1 related child aged 17 or younger residing in the household.

Children Living with a Parent Who Had a Substance Use Disorder

This section presents information on the number of children who are living with at least one parent with an SUD related to their use of alcohol or illicit drugs. Previous research has shown that children of parents with an SUD were found to be of lower socioeconomic status and had more difficulties in academic, social, and family functioning when compared with children of parents who do not have an SUD. These children are also more likely to have higher rates of mental and behavioral disorders. Children who are exposed to a parent with SUDs are more likely to develop SUD symptoms themselves.

Based on combined 2009–2014 NSDUH data, an annual average of 8.7 million children aged 17 or younger live in households in the United States with at least one parent who had an SUD. This represents about 12.3 percent of children aged 17 or younger who resided with at least one parent with an SUD. An annual average of 1.5 million children aged 0–2 (12.8% of this age group), 1.4 million children aged 3–5 (12.1% of this age group), 2.8 million children aged 6–11 (11.8% of this age group), and 3.0 million children aged 12–17 (12.5% of this age group) lived with at least one parent who had an SUD.

Data can also be examined by household composition (i.e., two-parent or single-parent households). It should be noted that, for two-parent households, it is not possible to determine whether both parents in the household had SUD. About 7.0 million children aged 17 or younger resided in a two-parent household with at least one parent who had a past year SUD, and 1.7 million resided in a single-parent household with a parent who had a past year SUD. In other words, 13.9 percent of children residing in two-parent households lived with at least one parent who had a past year SUD, and 8.4 percent of children residing in single-parent households lived with a parent who had an SUD. Among the 1.7 million children residing in single-parent households with a parent who had a past year SUD, about 344,000 lived with their fathers and 1.4 million lived with their mothers. Thus, about 11.8 percent of children residing in father-only households lived with a father who had a past year SUD, and 7.8 percent of children residing in mother-only households lived with a mother who had a past year SUD.

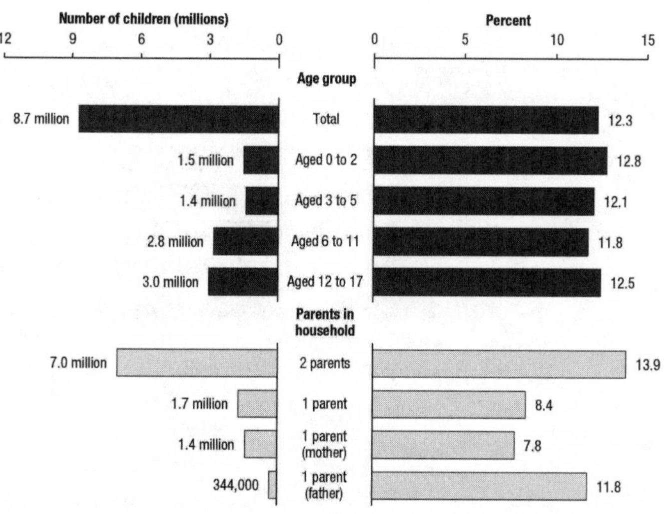

Figure 46.1. *Children Living with a Parent Who Had a Substance Use Disorder*

Children Living with a Parent Who Had an Alcohol Use Disorder

NSDUH data can be used to estimate the number of children who are living with at least one parent with an alcohol use disorder. Alcohol use disorder includes drinking-related behavior that may cause people to physically endanger themselves or others; get into trouble with the law; experience difficulties in relationships or jobs; and fail to fulfill major obligations at work, school, or home. Previous research has found that children of parents with an alcohol use disorder are at greater risk for depression, anxiety disorders, problems with cognitive and verbal skills, and parental abuse or neglect. Furthermore, they are four times more likely than other children to develop symptoms of an alcohol use disorder themselves.

Overall, about 7.5 million (10.5%) children aged 17 or younger lived in households with at least one parent who had an alcohol use disorder. An annual average of 1.2 million children aged 0–2 (10.1% of this age group), 1.2 million children aged 3–5 (9.9% of this age group), 2.4 million children aged 6–11 (10.2% of this age group), and 2.7 million children aged 12–17 (11.3% of this age group) lived with at least one parent who had an alcohol use disorder.

About 6.1 million children aged 17 or younger resided in a two-parent household with at least one parent who had an alcohol use disorder, and 1.4 million children resided in a single-parent household with at

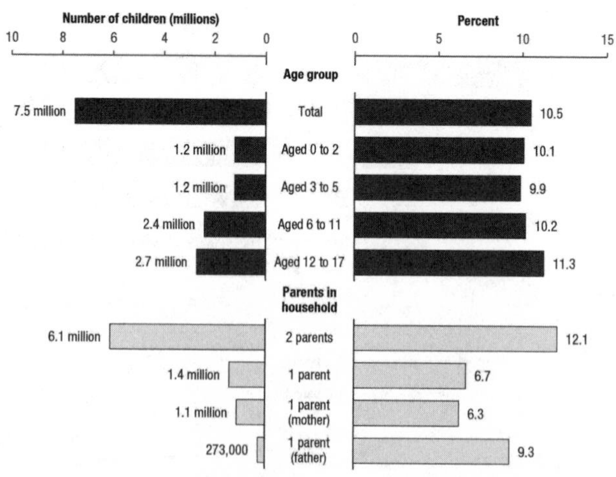

Figure 46.2. *Children Living with a Parent Who Had an Alcohol Use Disorder*

least one parent who had an alcohol use disorder. In other words, about 12.1 percent of children residing in two-parent households lived with at least one parent who had a past year alcohol use disorder, and 6.7 percent of children residing in single-parent households lived with a parent who had an alcohol use disorder. Among the 1.4 million children residing in single-parent households with a parent who had an alcohol use disorder, 273,000 lived with their fathers and 1.1 million lived with their mothers. About 9.3 percent of children residing in father-only households lived with a father who had an alcohol use disorder, and 6.3 percent of children residing in mother-only households lived with a mother who had an alcohol use disorder.

Discussion

SUDs can have a profound influence on the lives of people and their families, particularly children. The data in this chapter indicate that about 1 in 8 children in the United States aged 17 or younger were residing in homes with at least one parent who had an SUD. The rate of 1 in 8 children having at least one parent with an SUD was consistent across four age groups ranging from younger than 3 years to adolescents aged 12–17. Although many children living in households with a substance-using parent will not experience abuse or neglect, they are at increased risk for child maltreatment and child welfare involvement compared with other children. In addition, these children are at an increased risk for engaging in substance use themselves. The consistency of the prevalence across age groups in the percentage of children living with at least one parent with an SUD suggest that prevention and intervention efforts targeting older and younger children may be beneficial for reducing the impact of parent SUDs.

The annual average of 8.7 million children aged 17 or younger living in U.S. households with at least one parent who had an SUD highlights the potential breadth of substance use prevention and treatment needs for the whole family—from substance use treatment for the affected adults to prevention and supportive services for the children. As substance use and SUDs among parents often occur in households that face other challenges (e.g., mental illness, poverty, domestic violence), the recovery process may need to extend beyond substance use treatment to produce the changes in a family that are necessary to ensure a healthy family environment for a child.

According to NSDUH data, approximately 20.2 million adults aged 18 or older had a past year SUD, including 16.3 million with an alcohol use disorder and 6.2 million with an illicit drug use disorder; however, only 7.6 percent of adults with past year SUD received substance use treatment in the past year (data not shown). The expense of substance use treatment can be a financial barrier for people who need it; however, the long-term potential impact of parent substance use on their children suggests that substance use treatment intervention for parents may be essential to the well-being of their children. When a parent has an SUD, the whole family may be part of the recovery process, and each household member may need support. Many resources are available to help children when a parent uses substances or has an SUD.

Section 46.3

What to Do If a Family Member Abuses Alcohol

This section contains text excerpted from the following sources: Text in this section begins with excerpts from "Families in Recovery: Share Experiences to Support Recovery," Substance Abuse and Mental Health Services Administration (SAMHSA), March 1, 2016; Text beginning with the heading "Facts on Substance Use Disorder" is excerpted from "Substance Use Disorders Affects Families," U.S. Department of Veterans Affairs (VA), March 23, 2012. Reviewed April 2018; Text under the heading "SAMHSA's National Helpline" is excerpted from "SAMHSA's National Helpline," Substance Abuse and Mental Health Services Administration (SAMHSA), September 15, 2017.

When a family member has a mental and/or substance use disorder, the effects are felt by their immediate and extended family members. Family members may experience feelings of abandonment, anxiety, fear, anger, concern, embarrassment, or guilt. They may also wish to ignore or cut ties with a person misusing substances. This is true for traditional families as well as nontraditional families, which may include stepchildren, same-sex couples, and individuals who consider or include their friends as their family unit. However, individuals and family members can find encouragement and hope through the recovery process and support each other on the path to healing.

Millions of family members are affected by mental and/or substance use disorders:

- An estimated 43.6 million individuals aged 18 or older had any mental illness in the past year.
- An estimated 21.5 million individuals aged 12 or older were classified with a substance use disorder in the past year.
- Approximately 7.9 million adults had co-occurring substance use disorder and any mental illness in the past year.

When considering family recovery, it is also important to acknowledge the impact of growing up in a home where there may be dysfunction due to a family member's mental and/or substance use disorder. With robust evidence indicating that genes influence both alcohol dependence and dependence on illicit drugs, generations within a family often have to navigate the learned behaviors of substance misuse, as well as the knowledge that their genetic makeup may put them at an increased risk for developing a mental and/or substance use disorder.

Finding Support

Family members benefit from knowing they are not alone in helping loved ones through the recovery journey. They also need support, and self-care is critical. Individuals can focus on their well-being while caring for a loved one by:

- Joining a family support group to meet others experiencing similar challenges.
- Participating in family programs in which education and treatment sessions include loved ones.
- Attending individual therapy to learn appropriate coping skills.
- Eating healthy meals and getting adequate sleep.
- Managing stress by engaging in hobbies and getting exercise.
- Sharing their stories with the virtual recovery community and reading about others who have similar experiences.

Research shows that families play a major role in helping to prevent mental and/or substance use disorders, identifying when someone has a problem, and connecting those in need with the treatment resources and services they need to begin and stay on their recovery journey.

Families are in a unique position to recognize the signs and symptoms of a mental and/or substance use disorder in a loved one.

Having actively involved family members can also promote positive behavioral health since family members monitor each other's behavior, take responsibility for each other's well-being, and can offer or recommend assistance and support.

The idea of talking to a loved one about a mental illness or substance use disorder can seem overwhelming. However, understanding that the recovery journey is not a one-size-fits-all process and coming from a place of love and support can help a loved one accept help.

Promoting Recovery

Families experiencing the recovery process can find strength and resiliency from other families and learn how to better support a loved one's recovery journey. As family members adjust to the emotions and stresses of caring for someone with a mental and/or substance use disorder, some of the best support often comes from others who are, or have been, in similar circumstances.

Resources for family members who need support include:

- **Al-Anon Family Groups** (www.al-anon.alateen.org): Offers the opportunity to learn from the experiences of others who have a loved one with an alcohol use/misuse disorder.
- **Mental Health America (MHA)—Mental Illness and the Family: Recognizing Warning Signs and How to Cope** (www.mentalhealthamerica.net/recognizing-warning-signs): Provides information on how to recognize mental illness, along with other resources for people living with a mental illness or who know people living with mental illness.
- **National Alliance on Mental Illness (NAMI) Family Support Group** (www.nami.org/find-support/nami-programs/nami-family-support-group): Provides a peer-led support group for family members, caregivers, and loved ones of individuals living with mental illness.
- **The 20 Minute Guide** (the20minuteguide.com/parents/#.VFqXTTF9fe): Offers a set of interactive tools and strategies for any family member or friend who wants to help a loved one get help for a substance use disorder.

- **The Campaign to Change Direction** (www.changedirection.org): Provides resources to individuals and communities who wish to "change the story" in America about mental health, mental illness, and wellness.
- **Faces & Voices of Recovery Guide to Mutual Aid Resources** (www.facesandvoicesofrecovery.org/resources/mutual-aid-resources/mutual-aid-resources.html): Publishes the Guide to Mutual Aid Resources, including a list of resources for families and friends looking for mutual aid support groups.
- **Learn to Cope** (www.learn2cope.org): Offers education, resources, peer support, and hope for parents and family members coping with a loved one addicted to opiates or other drugs.
- **National Association for Children of Alcoholics (NACoA)** (www.nacoa.net): Provides resources to help support children and families affected by alcoholism and other drug dependencies.
- **Adult Children of Alcoholics World Service Organization (ACA WSO)** (www.adultchildren.org): Offers the opportunity for men and women who grew up in alcoholic or otherwise dysfunctional homes to learn from the experiences of others and to practice their own recovery.
- **Substance Abuse and Mental Health Services Administration's (SAMHSA) National Helpline, 800-662-HELP (800-662-4357)—or 800-487-4889 (TDD)** (www.samhsa.gov/find-help/national-helpline): Provides 24-hour, free, and confidential treatment referral and information about mental and/or substance use disorders, prevention, treatment, and recovery in English and Spanish.
- **The National Clearinghouse on Families and Youth (NCFY)** (ncfy.acf.hhs.gov/about/free-resources): Provides free information for communities, organizations, and individuals interested in developing new and effective strategies for supporting young people and their families.
- **The National Responsible Fatherhood Clearinghouse (NRFC)** (fatherhood.gov): Offers resources for fathers, practitioners, programs/federal grantees, states, and the public at-large who are serving or supporting strong fathers and families.

Family recovery involves providing essential support and becoming the champion of a loved one's recovery; this is a reality for millions of Americans. The hope, help, and healing of family recovery is a powerful way to break the intergenerational cycle of mental and/or substance use disorders.

Facts on Substance Use Disorder

- One of the most important signs of a substance use disorder is using drugs or alcohol even when using them causes severe physical, psychological and emotional pain.
- Substance misuse can get worse over time, hurting the person using drugs or alcohol and the entire family.
- Substance abuse/dependence is a serious problem:
    - It affects people of every race, ethnicity, gender and location.
    - In 2014, about 8 percent of people in the United States were affected by a substance use disorder.
    - Excessive alcohol and illicit drug use cost the United States approximately $416 billion per year in crime, lost work productivity, foster care, medical care and other social problems.
- Substance abuse/dependence is an illness that can be treated; millions of Americans and their families are in healthy recovery from substance use disorder.

Does Your Family Member Have a Substance Abuse/ Dependence Problem?

When your family member has been drinking or using drugs does he or she do any of the following:

- Embarrass you?
- Blame you for things?
- Break promises?
- Drive under the influence?
- Make bad decisions?
- Behave badly?

What Are the Possible Effects of Substance Abuse/Dependence on My Family?

Substance abuse/dependence causes stress on the family, which can lead to many family problems.

- **Health effects:** Substance abuse/dependence can increase the risk for human immunodeficiency virus (HIV), fetal alcohol syndrome (FAS), premature death, injury, and increased risk taking
- **Effects on children:** Children whose parents have a substance use disorder have an increased risk of the following problems:
  - **Alcohol misuse:** They are about four times more likely than the general population to develop alcohol problems
  - **Conduct problems:** They may feel frustrated and have an increased risk of aggressive behavior and crime
  - **Academic problems:** Learning difficulties, lower concentration and disruptiveness
  - **Emotional problems:** Anger, poor self-esteem, withdrawal and sadness
- **Marital problems:** When a family member has alcohol use disorder, there is an increased chance of divorce
- **Legal problems:** Problems such as unpaid bills, driving under the influence, and crime
- **Financial problems:** Loss of a job and money; a family member may forget to pay or ignore bills because of substance abuse/dependence

Reminders for Families

- Substance use disorder affects the entire family and close friends, even if only one person has it
- It's not your fault!
  - It is a disorder
  - You need and deserve help for yourself and your family members
  - Your family member with the disorder is responsible for making it stop
- People with a history of substance use disorder in their families are more likely to have a substance use disorder

- You are not alone!
    - More than 10 percent of U.S. children live with a parent who misuses or is addicted to alcohol
    - Thousands live with parental drug abuse
    - A lot of people come from families with a substance use disorder

Action Steps

1. Ask for help: If someone close to you misuses alcohol or drugs, the first step is to be open about the problem and ask for help.
    - Children who have alcohol or drug abuse/dependence in the family can get help by talking with adults and peers such as teachers, doctors, school counselors, and support groups.
2. Support your loved one's efforts to seek help: Finding services for your family also supports your loved one's next steps toward recovery.
    - Family support and motivation are important for successful treatment
    - Treatment works
3. Find out about treatment options: There are many treatments that work for addiction; the final step to recovery is when alcohol or substance abuse/dependence stops.
4. Talk with children: It is important to talk with children about what is happening in the family and to help them talk about their fears and feelings; children need to trust the adults in their lives and to believe that they will support them.

SAMHSA's National Helpline

SAMHSA's National Helpline, 800-662-HELP (800-662-4357) (also known as the Treatment Referral Routing Service) is a confidential, free, 24-hour-a-day, 365-day-a-year, information service, in English and Spanish, for individuals and family members facing mental and/or substance use disorders. This service provides referrals to local treatment facilities, support groups, and community-based organizations. Callers can also order free publications and other information.

Do I Need Health Insurance to Receive This Service?

The referral service is free of charge. If you have no insurance or are underinsured, SAMHSA will refer you to your state office, which is responsible for state-funded treatment programs. In addition, it can often refer you to facilities that charge on a sliding fee scale or accept Medicare or Medicaid. If you have health insurance, you are encouraged to contact your insurer for a list of participating healthcare providers and facilities.

Will My Information Be Kept Confidential?

The service is confidential. SAMHSA will not ask you for any personal information. SAMHSA may ask for your zip code or other pertinent geographic information in order to track calls being routed to other offices or to accurately identify the local resources appropriate to your needs.

Section 46.4

Impact of Alcoholism on Family and Children

This section includes text excerpted from "Parental Substance Use and the Child Welfare System," Child Welfare Information Gateway, U.S. Department of Health and Human Services (HHS), October 31, 2014. Reviewed April 2018.

Many families receiving child welfare services are affected by parental substance use. Identifying substance abuse and meeting the complex needs of parents with substance use disorders and those of their children can be challenging. Over the past two decades, innovative approaches coupled with new research and program evaluation have helped point to new directions for more effective, collaborative, and holistic service delivery to support both parents and children. This bulletin provides child welfare workers and related professionals with information on the intersection of substance use disorders and child maltreatment and describes strategies for prevention, intervention, and treatment, including examples of effective programs and practices.

The Relationship between Substance Use Disorders and Child Maltreatment

It is difficult to provide precise, current statistics on the number of families in child welfare affected by parental substance use or dependency since there is no ongoing, standardized, national data collection on the topic. In a report to Congress, the U.S. Department of Health and Human Services (HHS) reported that studies showed that between one-third and two-thirds of child maltreatment cases were affected by substance use to some degree. More recent research reviews suggest that the range may be even wider. The variation in estimates may be attributable, in part, to differences in the populations studied and the type of child welfare involvement (e.g., reports, substantiation, out-of-home placement); differences in how substance use (or substance abuse or substance use disorder) is defined and measured; and variations in state and local child welfare policies and practices for case documentation of substance abuse.

Children of Parents with Substance Use Disorders

An estimated 12 percent of children in this country live with a parent who is dependent on or abuses alcohol or other drugs. Based on data from the period 2002–2007, the National Survey on Drug Use and Health (NSDUH) reported that 8.3 million children under 18 years of age lived with at least one substance-dependent or substance-abusing parent. Of these children, approximately 7.3 million lived with a parent who was dependent on or abused alcohol, and about 2.2 million lived with a parent who was dependent on or abused illicit drugs. While many of these children will not experience abuse or neglect, they are at increased risk for maltreatment and entering the child welfare system.

For more than 400,000 infants each year (about 10% of all births), substance exposure begins prenatally. State and local surveys have documented prenatal substance use as high as 30 percent in some populations. Based on NSDUH data from 2011 and 2012, approximately 5.9 percent of pregnant women aged 15–44 were current illicit drug users. Younger pregnant women generally reported the greatest substance use, with rates approaching 18.3 percent among 15- to 17-year-olds. Among pregnant women aged 15–44 years old, about 8.5 percent reported current alcohol use, 2.7 percent reported binge drinking, and 0.3 percent reported heavy drinking.

Parental Substance Abuse as a Risk Factor for Maltreatment and Child Welfare Involvement

Parental substance abuse is recognized as a risk factor for child maltreatment and child welfare involvement. Research shows that children with parents who abuse alcohol or drugs are more likely to experience abuse or neglect than children in other households. One longitudinal study identified parental substance abuse (specifically, maternal drug use) as one of five key factors that predicted a report to child protective services (CPS) for abuse or neglect. Once a report is substantiated, children of parents with substance use issues are more likely to be placed in out-of-home care and more likely to stay in care longer than other children. The National Survey of Child and Adolescent Well-Being (NSCAW) estimates that 61 percent of infants and 41 percent of older children in out-of-home care are from families with active alcohol or drug abuse.

According to data in the Adoption and Foster Care Analysis and Reporting System (AFCARS), parental substance abuse is frequently reported as a reason for removal, particularly in combination with neglect. For almost 31 percent of all children placed in foster care in 2012, parental alcohol or drug use was the documented reason for removal, and in several states that percentage surpassed 60 percent. Nevertheless, many caregivers whose children remain at home after an investigation also have substance abuse issues. NSCAW found that the need for substance abuse services among in-home caregivers receiving child welfare services was substantially higher than that of adults nationwide (29% as compared with 20%, respectively, for parents ages 18–25, and 29% versus 7% for parents over age 26).

Role of Co-Occurring Issues

While the link between substance abuse and child maltreatment is well documented, it is not clear how much is a direct causal connection and how much can be attributed to other co-occurring issues. National data reveal that slightly more than one-third of adults with substance use disorders have a co-occurring mental illness. Research on women with substance abuse problems shows high rates of post-traumatic stress disorder (PTSD), most commonly stemming from a history of childhood physical and/or sexual assault. Many parents with substance abuse problems also experience social isolation, poverty, unstable housing, and domestic violence. These co-occurring issues may contribute to both the substance use and the child maltreatment. Evidence increasingly points to a critical role of stress and reactions within the brain to stress, which can lead to both drug-seeking activity and inadequate caregiving.

Impact of Parental Substance Use on Children

The ways parents with substance use disorders behave and interact with their children can have a multifaceted impact on the children. The effects can be both indirect (e.g., through a chaotic living environment) and direct (e.g., physical or sexual abuse). Parental substance use can affect parenting, prenatal development, and early childhood and adolescent development. It is important to recognize, however, that not all children of parents with substance use issues will suffer abuse, neglect, or other negative outcomes.

Parenting

A parent's substance use disorder may affect his or her ability to function effectively in a parental role. Ineffective or inconsistent parenting can be due to the following:

- Physical or mental impairments caused by alcohol or other drugs
- Reduced capacity to respond to a child's cues and needs
- Difficulties regulating emotions and controlling anger and impulsivity
- Disruptions in healthy parent–child attachment
- Spending limited funds on alcohol and drugs rather than food or other household needs
- Spending time seeking out, manufacturing, or using alcohol or other drugs
- Incarceration, which can result in inadequate or inappropriate supervision for children
- Estrangement from family and other social supports

Family life for children with one or both parents that abuse drugs or alcohol often can be chaotic and unpredictable. Children's basic needs—including nutrition, supervision, and nurturing—may go unmet, which can result in neglect. These families often experience a number of other problems—such as mental illness, domestic violence, unemployment, and housing instability—that also affect parenting and contribute to high levels of stress. A parent with a substance abuse disorder may be unable to regulate stress and other emotions, which can lead to impulsive and reactive behavior that may escalate to physical abuse.

Different substances may have different effects on parenting and safety. For example, the threats to a child of a parent who becomes sedated and inattentive after drinking excessively differ from the threats posed by a parent who exhibits aggressive side effects from methamphetamine use. Dangers may be posed not only from use of illegal drugs, but also, and increasingly, from abuse of prescription drugs (pain relievers, anti-anxiety medicines, and sleeping pills). Polysubstance use (multiple drugs) may make it difficult to determine the specific and compounded effects on any individual. Further, risks for the child's safety may differ depending upon the level and severity of parental substance use and associated adverse effects.

Prenatal and Infant Development

The effects of parental substance use disorders on a child can begin before the child is born. Maternal drug and alcohol use during pregnancy have been associated with premature birth, low birth weight, slowed growth, and a variety of physical, emotional, behavioral, and cognitive problems. Research suggests powerful effects of legal drugs, such as tobacco, as well as illegal drugs on prenatal and early childhood development.

Fetal alcohol spectrum disorders (FASDs) are a set of conditions that affect an estimated 40,000 infants born each year to mothers who drank alcohol during pregnancy. Children with FASD may experience mild to severe physical, mental, behavioral, and/or learning disabilities, some of which may have lifelong implications (e.g., brain damage, physical defects, attention deficits). In addition, increasing numbers of newborns—approximately 3 per 1,000 hospital births each year—are affected by neonatal abstinence syndrome (NAS), a group of problems that occur in a newborn who was exposed prenatally to addictive illegal or prescription drugs.

The full impact of prenatal substance exposure depends on a number of factors. These include the frequency, timing, and type of substances used by pregnant women; co-occurring environmental deficiencies; and the extent of prenatal care. Research suggests that some of the negative outcomes of prenatal exposure can be improved by supportive home environments and positive parenting practices.

Child and Adolescent Development

Children and youth of parents who use or abuse substances and have parenting difficulties have an increased chance of experiencing a variety of negative outcomes:

- Poor cognitive, social, and emotional development
- Depression, anxiety, and other trauma and mental health symptoms
- Physical and health issues
- Substance use problems

Parental substance use can affect the well-being of children and youth in complex ways. For example, an infant who receives inconsistent care and nurturing from a parent engaged in addiction-related behaviors may suffer from attachment difficulties that can then interfere with the growing child's emotional development. Adolescent children of parents with substance use disorders, particularly those who have experienced child maltreatment and foster care, may turn to substances themselves as a coping mechanism. In addition, children of parents with substance use issues are more likely to experience trauma and its effects, which include difficulties with concentration and learning, controlling physical and emotional responses to stress, and forming trusting relationships.

Child Welfare Laws Related to Parental Substance Use

In response to concerns over the potential negative impact on children of parental substance abuse and illegal drug-related activities, approximately 47 states and the District of Columbia (DC) have child protection laws that address some aspect of parental substance use. Some states have expanded their civil definitions of child abuse and neglect to include a caregiver's use of a controlled substance that impairs the ability to adequately care for a child and/or exposure of a child to illegal drug activity (e.g., sale or distribution of drugs, home-based meth labs). Exposure of children to illegal drug activity is also addressed in 33 states' criminal statutes.

Federal and state laws also address prenatal drug exposure. The Child Abuse Prevention and Treatment Act (CAPTA) requires states receiving CAPTA funds to have policies and procedures for healthcare personnel to notify CPS of substance-exposed newborns and to develop procedures for safe care of affected infants. As yet, there are no national data on CAPTA-related reports for substance-exposed newborns. In some state statutes, substance abuse during pregnancy is considered child abuse and/or grounds for termination of parental rights. State statutes and state and local policies vary widely in their requirements for reporting suspected prenatal drug abuse, testing for drug exposure, CPS response, forced admission to treatment of pregnant women who use drugs, and priority access for pregnant women to state funded treatment programs.

Service Delivery Challenges

Despite the fact that a large percentage of parents who are investigated in child protection cases require treatment for alcohol or drug dependence, the percentage of parents who actually receive services is limited, compared to the need. Also, many parents who begin treatment do not complete it. Historically, insufficient collaboration has hindered the ability of child welfare, substance abuse treatment, and family/dependency court systems to support these families.

Child welfare agencies face a number of difficulties in serving children and families affected by parental substance use disorders, including:

- Insufficient service availability or scope of services to meet existing needs
- Inadequate funds for services and/or dependence on client insurance coverage
- Difficulties in engaging and retaining parents in treatment
- Knowledge gaps among child welfare workers to meet the comprehensive needs of families with substance use issues
- Lack of coordination between the child welfare system and other services and systems, including hospitals that may screen for drug exposure, treatment agencies, mental health services, criminal justice system, and family/dependency courts
- Differences in perspectives and timeframes, reflecting different guiding policies, philosophies, and goals in child welfare and substance abuse treatment systems (for example, a focus on the safety and wellbeing of the child without sufficient focus on parents' recovery)

A critical challenge for child welfare professionals is meeting legislative requirements regarding child permanency while allowing for sufficient progress in substance abuse recovery and development of parenting capacity. The Adoption and Safe Families Act (ASFA) requires that a child welfare agency file a petition for termination of parental rights if a child has been in foster care for 15 of the past 22 months, unless it is not in the best interest of the child. Many agencies struggle with adhering to this timeframe due to problems with accessing substance abuse services in a timely manner. In addition, treatment may take many months (often longer than the ASFA timeline allows), and achieving sufficient stability to care for children may take even longer. Addressing addiction can require extended recovery periods, and relapses can occur.

Innovative Prevention and Treatment Approaches

While parental substance abuse continues to be a major challenge in child welfare, the past two decades have witnessed some new and more effective approaches and innovative programs to address child protection for families where substance abuse is an issue. Some examples of promising and innovative prevention and treatment approaches include the following:

- **Promotion of protective factors,** such as social connections, concrete supports, and parenting knowledge, to support families and buffer risks.
- **Early identification of at-risk families** in substance abuse treatment programs and through expanded prenatal screening initiatives so that prevention services can be provided to promote child safety and well-being in the home.
- **Priority and timely access** to substance abuse treatment slots for mothers involved in the child welfare system.
- **Gender-sensitive treatment** and support services that respond to the specific needs, characteristics, and co-occurring issues of women who have substance use disorders.
- **Family-centered treatment services,** including inpatient treatment for mothers in facilities where they can have their children with them and programs that provide services to each family member.
- **Recovery coaches or mentoring** of parents to support treatment, recovery, and parenting.

- **Shared family care** in which a family experiencing parental substance use and child maltreatment is placed with a host family for support and mentoring.

Find more information on specific programs and service models:

- National Center on Substance Abuse and Child Welfare (NCSACW), Regional Partnership Grant (RPG) Program: Overview of Grantees' Services and Interventions
- NRC for In-Home Services, In-Home Programs for Drug Affected Families
- Substance Abuse and Mental Health Services Administration's (SAMHSA) National Registry of Evidence-Based Programs and Practices (NREPP)

Promising Child Welfare Casework Practices

In working with families affected by substance abuse, child welfare workers can use a variety of strategies to help meet parents' needs while also promoting safety, permanency, and well-being of their children. To begin, workers need to build their understanding of parental substance use issues, its signs, the effects on parenting and child safety, and what to expect during a parent's treatment and recovery. Specific casework practice strategies reflect:

Family engagement. Engagement strategies that help motivate parents to enter and remain in substance abuse services are critical to enhancing treatment outcomes. An essential part of this process is partnering with parents to develop plans that address individual needs, such as a woman's own trauma history, as well as needs for support services like child care and transportation. Child welfare workers can help create supportive environments, build nonjudgmental relationships, and implement evidence-based motivational approaches, such as motivational interviewing.

Routine screening and assessment. Screening family members for possible substance use disorders with the use of brief, validated, and culturally appropriate tools should be a routine part of child welfare investigation and case monitoring. Once a substance use issue has been identified through screening, alcohol and drug treatment providers can conduct more in-depth assessments of its nature and extent, the impact on the child, and recommended treatment. Find more information on screening tools and collaborative strategies:

- Screening and Assessment for Family Engagement, Retention and Recovery (SAFERR)
- Protecting Children in Families Affected by Substance Use Disorders (SUDs)

Individualized treatment and case plans. Caseworkers can help match parents with evidence-based treatment programs and support services that meet their specific needs. Working collaboratively with families, alcohol and drug treatment professionals, and the courts, caseworkers can help develop and coordinate case and treatment plans.

Support of parents in treatment and recovery. Child welfare workers can support parents in their efforts to build coping and parenting skills, help them pay attention to triggers for substance-using behaviors, and work collaboratively on safety plans to protect children during a potential relapse. Workers also can help coordinate services, make formal and informal connections, and encourage parents in looking forward to their role as caregivers.

Providing services for children of parents with substance use issues. Given the developmental and emotional effects of parental substance abuse on children and youth in child welfare, it is important that child welfare workers collaborate with behavioral/mental health professionals to conduct screenings and assessments and link children and youth to appropriate, evidence-based services that promote wellness. Individualized services should address the child or youth's strengths and needs, trauma symptoms, effects associated with prenatal or postnatal exposure to parental substance use, and risk for developing substance use disorders themselves.

Permanency planning. ASFA and treatment timeframes become significant considerations in permanency plans and reunification goals in families affected by substance abuse. Concurrent planning, in which an alternative permanency plan is pursued at the same time as the reunification plan, can play an important part in ensuring that children achieve permanency in a timely manner. For instance, guardianship by a relative or adoption by foster parents might be the concurrent goal if family reunification is not viable.

For child welfare training and other resources related to improving the safety, permanency, well-being, and recovery outcomes for children and families, visit the NCSACW website.

Chapter 47

Intimate Partner Violence

Intimate partner violence (IPV) is a serious, preventable public health problem that affects millions of Americans. The term "intimate partner violence" describes physical violence, sexual violence, stalking, and psychological aggression (including coercive acts) by a current or former intimate partner.

An intimate partner is a person with whom one has a close personal relationship that can be characterized by the following:

- Emotional connectedness
- Regular contact
- Ongoing physical contact and/or sexual behavior
- Identity as a couple
- Familiarity and knowledge about each other's lives

The relationship need not involve all of these dimensions. Examples of intimate partners include current or former spouses, boyfriends or girlfriends, dating partners, or sexual partners. IPV can occur between heterosexual or same-sex couples and does not require sexual intimacy.

This chapter includes text excerpted from "Intimate Partner Violence—Definitions," Centers for Disease Control and Prevention (CDC), August 22, 2017.

IPV can vary in frequency and severity. It occurs on a continuum, ranging from one episode that might or might not have lasting impact to chronic and severe episodes over a period of years.

There are four main types of IPV.

- Physical violence is the intentional use of physical force with the potential for causing death, disability, injury, or harm. Physical violence includes, but is not limited to, scratching; pushing; shoving; throwing; grabbing; biting; choking; shaking; aggressive hair pulling; slapping; punching; hitting; burning; use of a weapon; and use of restraints or one's body, size, or strength against another person. Physical violence also includes coercing other people to commit any of the above acts.
- Sexual violence is divided into five categories. Any of these acts constitute sexual violence, whether attempted or completed. Additionally all of these acts occur without the victim's freely given consent, including cases in which the victim is unable to consent due to being too intoxicated (e.g., incapacitation, lack of consciousness, or lack of awareness) through their voluntary or involuntary use of alcohol or drugs.
    1. **Rape or penetration of victim:** This includes completed or attempted, forced or alcohol/drug-facilitated unwanted vaginal, oral, or anal insertion. Forced penetration occurs through the perpetrator's use of physical force against the victim or threats to physically harm the victim.
    2. **Victim was made to penetrate someone else**: This includes completed or attempted, forced or alcohol/drug-facilitated incidents when the victim was made to sexually penetrate a perpetrator or someone else without the victim's consent.
    3. **Nonphysically pressured unwanted penetration:** This includes incidents in which the victim was pressured verbally or through intimidation or misuse of authority to consent or acquiesce to being penetrated.
    4. **Unwanted sexual contact**: This includes intentional touching of the victim or making the victim touch the perpetrator, either directly or through the clothing, on the genitalia, anus, groin, breast, inner thigh, or buttocks without the victim's consent

5. **Noncontact unwanted sexual experiences**: This includes unwanted sexual events that are not of a physical nature that occur without the victim's consent. Examples include unwanted exposure to sexual situations (e.g., pornography); verbal or behavioral sexual harassment; threats of sexual violence to accomplish some other end; and /or unwanted filming, taking or disseminating photographs of a sexual nature of another person.

- Stalking is a pattern of repeated, unwanted, attention, and contact that causes fear or concern for one's own safety or the safety of someone else (e.g., family member or friend). Some examples include repeated, unwanted phone calls, e-mails, or text messages; leaving cards, letters, flowers, or other items when the victim does not want them; watching or following from a distance; spying; approaching or showing up in places when the victim does not want to see them; sneaking into the victim's home or car; damaging the victim's personal property; harming or threatening the victim's pet; and making threats to physically harm the victim.
- Psychological aggression is the use of verbal and nonverbal communication with the intent to harm another person mentally or emotionally, and/or to exert control over another person. Psychological aggression can include expressive aggression (e.g., name-calling, humiliating); coercive control (e.g., limiting access to transportation, money, friends, and family; excessive monitoring of whereabouts); threats of physical or sexual violence; control of reproductive or sexual health (e.g., refusal to use birth control; coerced pregnancy termination); exploitation of victim's vulnerability (e.g., immigration status, disability); exploitation of perpetrator's vulnerability; and presenting false information to the victim with the intent of making them doubt their own memory or perception (e.g., mind games).

Risk and Protective Factors

Persons with certain risk factors are more likely to become perpetrators or victims of intimate partner violence (IPV). Those risk factors contribute to IPV but might not be direct causes. Not everyone who is identified as "at risk" becomes involved in violence.

Some risk factors for IPV victimization and perpetration are the same, while others are associated with one another. For example, childhood physical or sexual victimization is a risk factor for future IPV perpetration and victimization.

A combination of individual, relational, community, and societal factors contribute to the risk of becoming an IPV perpetrator or victim. Understanding these multilevel factors can help identify various opportunities for prevention.

Individual Risk Factors

- Heavy alcohol and drug use
- Low self-esteem
- Low income
- Low academic achievement
- Young age
- Aggressive or delinquent behavior as a youth
- Depression
- Anger and hostility
- Antisocial personality traits
- Borderline personality traits
- Prior history of being physically abusive
- Having few friends and being isolated from other people
- Unemployment
- Emotional dependence and insecurity
- Belief in strict gender roles (e.g., male dominance and aggression in relationships)
- Desire for power and control in relationships
- Perpetrating psychological aggression
- Being a victim of physical or psychological abuse (consistently one of the strongest predictors of perpetration)
- History of experiencing poor parenting as a child
- History of experiencing physical discipline as a child

Relationship Factors

- Marital conflict—fights, tension, and other struggles
- Marital instability—divorces or separations
- Dominance and control of the relationship by one partner over the other
- Economic stress
- Unhealthy family relationships and interactions

Community Factors

- Poverty and associated factors (e.g., overcrowding, food instability, etc.)
- Low social capital—lack of institutions, relationships, and norms that shape a community's social interactions
- Weak community sanctions against IPV (e.g., unwillingness of neighbors to intervene in situations where they witness violence)

Societal Factors

Traditional gender norms (e.g., belief that women should stay at home, not enter the workforce, and be submissive; men should support the family and make the decisions)

Cost to Society

- Costs of intimate partner violence (IPV) against women alone in 1995 exceeded an estimated $5.8 billion. These costs included nearly $4.1 billion in the direct costs of medical and mental healthcare and nearly $1.8 billion in the indirect costs of lost productivity. This is generally considered an underestimate because the costs associated with the criminal justice system were not included.
- When updated to 2003 dollars, IPV costs exceeded $8.3 billion, which included $460 million for rape, $6.2 billion for physical assault, $461 million for stalking, and $1.2 billion in the value of lost lives.
- The increased annual healthcare costs for victims of IPV can persist as much as 15 years after the cessation of abuse.

- Victims of severe IPV lose nearly 8 million days of paid work—the equivalent of more than 32,000 full-time jobs—and almost 5.6 million days of household productivity each year.
- Women who experience severe aggression by men (e.g., not being allowed to go to work or school, or having their lives or their children's lives threatened) are more likely to have been unemployed in the past, have health problems, and be receiving public assistance.

Consequences

Approximately 27 percent of women and 11 percent of men in the United States have experienced contact sexual violence, physical violence, or stalking by an intimate partner and reported at least one measured impact related to these or other forms of violence in that relationship. In general, victims of repeated violence over time experience more serious consequences than victims of one-time incidents. The following list describes some, but not all, of the consequences of IPV.

Physical

Nearly in 4 women (23%) and 1 in 7 men (14%) aged 18 and older in the United States have been the victim of severe physical violence by an intimate partner in their lifetime. Nearly, 14 percent of women and 4 percent of men have been injured as a result of IPV that included contact sexual violence, physical violence, or stalking by an intimate partner in their lifetime. In 2010, 241 males and 1095 females were murdered by an intimate partner.

Apart from deaths and injuries, physical violence by an intimate partner is associated with a number of adverse health outcomes. Several health conditions associated with intimate partner violence may be a direct result of the physical violence (for example, bruises, knife wounds, broken bones, traumatic brain injury, back or pelvic pain, headaches). Other conditions are the result of the impact of intimate partner violence on the cardiovascular, gastrointestinal, endocrine and immune systems through chronic stress or other mechanisms.

Examples of health conditions associated with IPV include:

- Asthma
- Bladder and kidney infections
- Circulatory conditions

- Cardiovascular disease
- Fibromyalgia
- Irritable bowel syndrome
- Chronic pain syndromes
- Central nervous system disorders
- Gastrointestinal disorders
- Joint disease
- Migraines and headaches

Children might become injured during IPV incidents between their parents. A large overlap exists between IPV and child maltreatment.

Reproductive

- Gynecological disorders
- Pelvic inflammatory disease
- Sexual dysfunction
- Sexually transmitted infections (STIs), including human immunodeficiency virus (HIV)/acquired immunodeficiency syndrome (AIDS)
- Delayed prenatal care
- Preterm delivery
- Pregnancy difficulties like low birth weight babies and perinatal deaths
- Unintended pregnancy

Psychological

Physical violence is typically accompanied by emotional or psychological abuse. IPV—whether sexual, physical, or psychological—can lead to various psychological consequences for victims.

- Anxiety
- Depression
- Symptoms of posttraumatic stress disorder (PTSD)
- Antisocial behavior

- Suicidal behavior in females
- Low self-esteem
- Inability to trust others, especially in intimate relationships
- Fear of intimacy
- Emotional detachment
- Sleep disturbances
- Flashbacks
- Replaying assault in the mind

Social

Victims of IPV sometimes face the following social consequences:

- Restricted access to services
- Strained relationships with health providers and employers
- Isolation from social networks
- Homelessness

Health Behaviors

Women with a history of IPV are more likely to display behaviors that present further health risks (e.g., substance abuse, alcoholism, suicide attempts) than women without a history of IPV.

IPV is associated with a variety of negative health behaviors. Studies show that the more severe the violence, the stronger its relationship to negative health behaviors by victims.

- Engaging in high-risk sexual behavior
    - Unprotected sex
    - Decreased condom use
    - Early sexual initiation
    - Choosing unhealthy sexual partners
    - Multiple sex partners
    - Trading sex for food, money, or other items

- Using harmful substances
    - Smoking cigarettes
    - Drinking alcohol
    - Drinking alcohol and driving
    - Illicit drug use
- Unhealthy diet-related behaviors
    - Fasting
    - Vomiting
    - Abusing diet pills
    - Overeating
- Overuse of health services

Chapter 48

Alcohol-Impaired Vehicle Operation

Chapter Contents

Section 48.1

Driving under the Influence of Alcohol

This section contains text excerpted from the following sources: Text in this section begins with excerpts from "Motor Vehicle Safety—Impaired Driving: Get the Facts," Centers for Disease Control and Prevention (CDC), June 16, 2017; Text beginning with the heading "How Alcohol Affects Driving Ability" is excerpted from "Drunk Driving," National Highway Traffic Safety Administration (NHTSA), April 1, 2018.

Every day, 28 people in the United States die in motor vehicle crashes that involve an alcohol-impaired driver. This is one death every 51 minutes. The annual cost of alcohol-related crashes totals more than $44 billion. There are effective measures that can help prevent injuries and deaths from alcohol-impaired driving.

The Problem

- In 2015, 10,265 people died in alcohol-impaired driving crashes, accounting for nearly one-third (29%) of all traffic-related deaths in the United States.
- Of the 1,132 traffic deaths among children ages 0–14 years in 2015, 209 (16%) involved an alcohol-impaired driver
- In 2015, nearly 1.1 million drivers were arrested for driving under the influence of alcohol or narcotics. That's one percent of the 111 million self-reported episodes of alcohol-impaired driving among U.S. adults each year.
- Drugs other than alcohol (legal and illegal) are involved in about 16 percent of motor vehicle crashes
- Marijuana use is increasing and 13 percent of nighttime, weekend drivers have marijuana in their system.
- Marijuana users were about 25 percent more likely to be involved in a crash than drivers with no evidence of marijuana use, however other factors—such as age and gender—may account for the increased crash risk among marijuana users.

Prevention

Effective measures include:

- Actively enforcing existing 0.08 percent BAC laws, minimum legal drinking age laws, and zero tolerance laws for drivers younger than 21 years old in all states
- Requiring ignition interlocks for all offenders, including first-time offenders
- Using sobriety checkpoints
- Putting health promotion efforts into practice that influence economic, organizational, policy, and school/community action
- Using community-based approaches to alcohol control and DWI prevention
- Requiring mandatory substance abuse assessment and treatment, if needed, for DWI offenders
- Raising the unit price of alcohol by increasing taxes

Areas for continued research:

- Reducing the illegal BAC threshold to 0.05 percent
- Mandatory blood alcohol testing when traffic crashes result in injury
- Does marijuana impair driving? How and at what level?
- Does marijuana use increase the risk of motor vehicle crashes?

How Alcohol Affects Driving Ability

Every day, almost 29 people in the United States die in alcohol-impaired vehicle crashes—that's one person every 50 minutes in 2016. Drunk-driving fatalities have fallen by a third in the last three decades; however, drunk-driving crashes claim more than 10,000 lives per year. In 2010, the most recent year for which cost data is available, these deaths and damages contributed to a cost of $44B per year.

Alcohol is a substance that reduces the function of the brain, impairing thinking, reasoning, and muscle coordination. All these abilities are essential to operating a vehicle safely. As alcohol levels rise in a person's system, the negative effects on the central nervous system increase, too. Alcohol is absorbed directly through the walls of the stomach and small intestine. Then it passes into the bloodstream where it accumulates until it is metabolized by the liver.

Alcohol level is measured by the weight of the alcohol in a certain volume of blood. This is called blood alcohol concentration, or BAC. At a BAC of .08 grams of alcohol per deciliter of blood (g/dL), crash risk increases exponentially. Because of this risk, it's illegal in all 50 States, the District of Columbia and Puerto Rico to drive with a BAC of .08 or higher. However, even a small amount of alcohol can affect driving ability. In 2016, there were 2,017 people killed in alcohol-related crashes where drivers had lower alcohol levels (BACs of .01 to .07 g/dL). BAC is measured with a breathalyzer, a device that measures the amount of alcohol in a driver's breath, or by a blood test.

The Effects of Blood Alcohol Concentration

Table 48.1. Effects of Blood Alcohol Concentration (BAC)

Blood Alcohol Concentration (BAC)*	Typical Effects	Predictable Effects on Driving
0.02	Some loss of judgment; relaxation, slight body warmth, altered mood	Decline in visual functions (rapid tracking of a moving target), decline in ability to perform two tasks at the same time (divided attention)
0.05	Exaggerated behavior, may have loss of small-muscle control (e.g., focusing your eyes), impaired judgment, usually good feeling, lowered alertness, release of inhibition	Reduced coordination, reduced ability to track moving objects, difficulty steering, reduced response to emergency driving situations
0.08	Muscle coordination becomes poor (e.g., balance, speech, vision, reaction time, and hearing), harder to detect danger; judgment, self-control, reasoning, and memory are impaired	Concentration, short-term memory loss, speed control, reduced information processing capability (e.g., signal detection, visual search), impaired perception
0.1	Clear deterioration of reaction time and control, slurred speech, poor coordination, and slowed thinking	Reduced ability to maintain lane position and brake appropriately

Table 48.1. Continued

Blood Alcohol Concentration (BAC)*	Typical Effects	Predictable Effects on Driving
0.15	Far less muscle control than normal, vomiting may occur (unless this level is reached slowly or a person has developed a tolerance for alcohol), major loss of balance	Substantial impairment in vehicle control, attention to driving task, and in necessary visual and auditory information processing

Risk Factors of Drunk Driving

Driving after drinking is deadly. Yet it still continues to happen across the United States. If you drive while impaired, you could get arrested, or worse—be involved in a traffic crash that causes serious injury or death.

Approximately one-third of all traffic crash fatalities in the United States involve drunk drivers (with blood alcohol concentrations (BACs) of .08 or higher). In 2016, there were 10,497 people killed in these preventable crashes. In fact, on average over the 10-year period from 2006–2016, more than 10,000 people died every year in drunk-driving crashes.

In every State, it's illegal to drive with a BAC of .08 or higher, yet one person was killed in a drunk-driving crash every 50 minutes in the United States in 2016.

Men are more likely than women to be driving drunk in fatal crashes. In 2016, 21 percent of males were drunk in these crashes, compared to 14 percent for females.

Take steps to prevent drunk driving:

- If you will be drinking, plan on not driving. Plan your safe ride home before you start the party. Designate a sober driver ahead of time.
- If you drink, do not drive for any reason. Call a taxi, phone a sober friend or family member, use public transportation, etc. Download National Highway Traffic Safety Administration's (NHTSA) SaferRide mobile app (play.google.com/store/apps/details?id=com.nhtsa.SaferRide&hl=en), which helps you identify your location and call a taxi or friend to pick you up.
- If someone you know has been drinking, do not let that person get behind the wheel. Take their keys and help them arrange a sober ride home.

- If you see an impaired driver on the road, contact local law enforcement. Your actions could help save someone's life.

Consequences

Driving a vehicle while impaired is a dangerous crime. Tough enforcement of drunk-driving laws has been a major factor in reducing alcohol-impaired-driving deaths since the 1980s. Charges range from misdemeanors to felony offenses, and penalties for impaired driving can include driver's license revocation, fines, and jail time. It's also extremely expensive. A first-time offense can cost the driver upwards of $10,000 in fines and legal fees.

Some States require offenders to install ignition interlock devices at the driver's own expense. An ignition interlock device is a breath test device connected to a vehicle's ignition. The vehicle will not start unless the driver blows into the interlock and has a BAC below a preset low limit, usually .02 g/dL. National Highway Traffic Safety Administration (NHTSA) strongly supports the expansion of ignition interlocks as a proven technology that keeps drunk drivers from getting behind the wheel.

Responsible Behavior

Being a responsible driver is simple—if you are drinking, do not drive.

1. Before drinking, choose a nondrinking friend as a designated driver.
2. Don't let your friends drive impaired.
3. If you have been drinking, call a taxi or ride service. Get NHTSA's SaferRide app to help you call a friend or family member, pinpoint your location, and arrange to be picked up.
4. If you're hosting a party where alcohol will be served, make sure all guests leave with a sober driver.
5. Always wear your seatbelt—it's your best defense against impaired drivers.

Section 48.2

Crashes and Fatalities Involving Alcohol-Impaired Drivers

This section includes text excerpted from "Traffic Safety Facts: 2016 Data," National Highway Traffic Safety Administration (NHTSA), October 2017.

Drivers are considered to be alcohol-impaired when their blood alcohol concentrations (BACs) are 0.08 grams per deciliter (g/dL) or higher. Thus, any fatal crash involving a driver with a BAC of 0.08 g/dL or higher is considered to be an alcohol-impaired-driving crash, and fatalities occurring in those crashes are considered to be alcohol-impaired-driving fatalities. The term "drunk driving" is used instead of alcohol-impaired driving in some other National Highway Traffic Safety Administration (NHTSA) communication and material. The term "driver" refers to the operator of any motor vehicle, including a motorcycle.

Estimates of alcohol-impaired driving are generated using BAC values reported to the Fatality Analysis Reporting System (FARS) and BAC values imputed when they are not reported. In this section, National Highway Traffic Safety Administration (NHTSA) uses the term "alcohol-impaired" in evaluating the FARS statistics. In all cases throughout this section, use of the term does not indicate that a crash or a fatality was caused by alcohol impairment, only that an alcohol-impaired driver was involved in the crash.

This section contains information on fatal motor vehicle crashes and fatalities based on data from FARS. FARS is a census of fatal crashes in the 50 states, the District of Columbia, and Puerto Rico (Puerto Rico is not included in U.S. totals).

All 50 States, the District of Columbia, and Puerto Rico have by law set a threshold making it illegal to drive with a BAC of 0.08 g/dL or higher. In 2016, there were 10,497 people killed in alcohol-impaired driving crashes, an average of 1 alcohol-impaired-driving fatality every 50 minutes. These alcohol impaired-driving fatalities accounted for 28 percent of all motor vehicle traffic fatalities in the United States in 2016. Of the 10,497 people who died in alcohol-impaired-driving crashes in 2016, there were 6,479 drivers (62%) who had BACs of 0.08 g/dL or higher. The remaining fatalities consisted of 3,070 motor vehicle occupants (29%) and 948 nonoccupants (9%).

Fatalities in alcohol-impaired-driving crashes increased by 1.7 percent (10,320–10,497 fatalities) from 2015–2016. Alcohol-impaired-driving fatalities in the past 10 years have declined by 20 percent from 13,041 in 2007 to 10,497 in 2016. The national rate of alcohol-impaired-driving fatalities in motor vehicle crashes in 2016 was 0.33 per 100 million vehicle miles traveled (VMT), which has been the same since 2014. The alcohol-impaired-driving fatality rate in the past 10 years has declined by 23 percent, from 0.43 in 2007 to 0.33 in 2016.

Economic Cost for All Traffic Crashes

The estimated economic cost of all motor vehicle traffic crashes in the United States in 2010 (the most recent year for which cost data is available) was $242 billion, of which $44 billion resulted from alcohol-impaired crashes (involving alcohol-impaired drivers or alcohol-impaired nonoccupants). Included in the economic costs are:

- Lost productivity
- Workplace losses
- Legal and court expenses
- Medical costs
- Emergency medical services
- Insurance administration
- Congestion
- Property damage

These costs represent the tangible losses that result from motor vehicle traffic crashes. However, in cases of serious injury or death, such costs fail to capture the relatively intangible value of lost quality-of-life that results from these injuries. When quality-of-life valuations are considered, the total value of societal harm from motor vehicle traffic crashes in the United States in 2010 was an estimated $836 billion, of which $201.1 billion resulted from alcohol-impaired crashes.

Children

A total of 1,233 children 14 and younger were killed in motor vehicle traffic crashes in 2016. Of these 1,233 fatalities, 214 children (17%) died in alcohol-impaired-driving crashes. Of these 214 child deaths:

- 115 (54%) were occupants of vehicles with drivers who had BACs of .08 g/dL or higher
- 61 (29%) were occupants of other vehicles

- 36 (17%) were nonoccupants (pedestrians, pedalcyclists, or other nonoccupants)
- 2 (<1%) were drivers

Environmental Characteristics

This section has the information about the setting surrounding alcohol-impaired drivers involved in fatal crashes in 2016 including month, land use, weather, light condition, and roadway function class. In 2016 based on known values of alcohol-impaired drivers involved in fatal crashes:

- More occurred in July (9.5%), May (9.1%), and October (9.1%) than the other months
- 50 percent occurred in both urban and rural areas
- 92 percent occurred in clear/cloudy conditions compared to 6 percent in rainy conditions and 2 percent in other conditions
- 70 percent occurred in the dark compared to 26 percent in daylight, 3 percent in dusk, and 1 percent in dawn
- 86 percent occurred on noninterstate roads compared to 14 percent on interstate roads

Section 48.3

Driving after Drinking

This section includes text excerpted from "Drinking and Driving," Centers for Disease Control and Prevention (CDC), October 3, 2011. Reviewed April 2018.

U.S. adults drank too much and got behind the wheel about 112 million times in 2010. Though episodes of driving after drinking too much ("drinking and driving") have gone down by 30 percent during the past 5 years, it remains a serious problem in the United States. Alcohol-impaired drivers are involved in about 1 in 3 crash deaths, resulting in nearly 11,000 deaths in 2009.

Driving drunk is never OK. Choose not to drink and drive and help others do the same.

Problem

People who drink and drive put everyone on the road in danger.

Certain groups are more likely to drink and drive than others.

- Men were responsible for 4 in 5 episodes (81%) of drinking and driving in 2010.
- Young men ages 21–34 made up only 11 percent of the U.S. adult population in 2010, yet were responsible for 32 percent of all instances of drinking and driving.
- 85 percent of drinking and driving episodes were reported by people who also reported binge drinking. Binge drinking means 5 or more drinks for men or 4 or more drinks for women during a short period of time.

There are proven ways to prevent people from drinking and driving.

- At sobriety checkpoints, police stop drivers to judge if they are driving under the influence of alcohol. More widespread, frequent use of these checkpoints could save about 1,500–3,000 lives on the road each year.
- Minimum legal drinking age laws prohibit selling alcohol to people under age 21 in all 50 states and the District of Columbia. Keeping and enforcing 21 as the minimum legal drinking age helps keep young, inexperienced drivers from drinking and driving.
- Ignition interlocks prevent drivers who were convicted of alcohol-impaired driving from operating their vehicles if they have been drinking. Interlocks are effective in reducing re-arrest rates from drinking and driving by about two-thirds while the device is on the vehicle.

Your best defense against a drunk driver is to buckle up every time.

Every person in every seat should be buckled up on every trip. Seat belts reduce serious injuries and deaths from crashes by about 50 percent. Primary enforcement seat belt laws allow police to stop vehicles just because someone is not wearing a seatbelt. These state laws are effective in increasing seat belt use.

What Can Be Done

States can:

- Enforce 0.08 percent blood alcohol concentration and minimum legal drinking age laws
- Expand the use of sobriety checkpoints
- Require ignition interlocks for everyone convicted of drinking and driving, starting with their first offense
- Consider including strategies to reduce binge drinking—such as increasing alcohol taxes—to reduce drinking and driving, since the two behaviors are linked
- Pass primary enforcement seat belt laws that cover everyone in the car

Employers can:

- Set policies that immediately take away all work-related driving privileges for any employee cited for drinking and driving while using a company or personal vehicle for work purposes
- Use workplace health promotion programs to communicate the dangers of drinking and driving, including information directed to family members

Health professionals can:

- Help patients realize that car crashes are the leading cause of death for everyone ages 5–34 and that 1 in 3 crash deaths involves a drunk driver
- Routinely screen patients for risky drinking patterns, including binge drinking, and provide a brief intervention—a 10–15 minute counseling session—for patients who screen positive

Everyone can:

- Choose not to drink and drive and help others do the same.
    - Before drinking, designate a nondrinking driver when with a group
    - If out drinking, get a ride home or call a taxi

    - Don't let friends drink and drive
- Choose not to binge drink themselves and help others not to do it.
- Talk with a doctor or nurse about drinking and driving and request counseling if drinking is causing health, work, or social problems.
- Buckle up every time, no matter how short the trip. Encourage passengers in the car to buckle up, including those in the back seat.

Section 48.4

Boating Under the Influence of Alcohol

This section includes text excerpted from "BUI Initiatives—USCG Boating Safety," U.S. Coast Guard Boating Safety Division, October 1, 2002. Reviewed April 2018.

Every boater needs to understand the risks of boating under the influence of alcohol or drugs (BUI). It is illegal to operate a boat while under the influence of alcohol or drugs in every state. The U.S. Coast Guard also enforces a federal law that prohibits BUI. This law pertains to ALL boats (from canoes and rowboats to the largest ships) and includes foreign vessels that operate in U.S. waters, as well as U.S. vessels on the high seas.

Dangers of BUI

Alcohol affects judgment, vision, balance, and coordination. These impairments increase the likelihood of accidents afloat for both passengers and boat operators. U.S. Coast Guard data shows that in boating deaths involving alcohol use, over half the victims capsized their boats and/or fell overboard.

Alcohol is even more hazardous on the water than on land. The marine environment motion, vibration, engine noise, sun, wind, and spray accelerates a drinker's impairment. These stressors cause fatigue that makes a boat operator's coordination, judgment and reaction time decline even faster when using alcohol.

Alcohol can also be more dangerous to boaters because boat operators are often less experienced and less confident on the water than on the highway. Recreational boaters don't have the benefit of experiencing daily boat operation. In fact, boaters average only 110 hours on the water per year.

Alcohol Effects

Alcohol has many physical effects that directly threaten safety and well-being on the water.

When a boater or passenger drinks, the following occur:

- Cognitive abilities and judgment deteriorate, making it harder to process information, assess situations, and make good choices.
- Physical performance is impaired—evidenced by balance problems, lack of coordination, and increased reaction time.
- Vision is affected, including decreased peripheral vision, reduced depth perception, decreased night vision, poor focus, and difficulty in distinguishing colors (particularly red and green).
- Inner ear disturbances can make it impossible for a person who falls into the water to distinguish up from down.
- Alcohol creates a physical sensation of warmth—which may prevent a person in cold water from getting out before hypothermia sets in.

As a result of these factors, a boat operator with a blood alcohol concentration above 0.10 percent is estimated to be more than 10 times as likely to die in a boating accident than an operator with zero blood alcohol concentration. Passengers are also at greatly increased risk for injury and death—especially if they are also using alcohol.

Estimating Impairment

This table gives a guide to average impacts of alcohol consumption. However, many factors, including prescription medications and fatigue, can affect an individual's response to alcohol, and impairment can occur much more quickly as a result. There is NO safe threshold for drinking and operating a boat, so do not assume you are safe just because you fall into the "rarely" or "possibly" influenced categories.

Table 48.2. Approximate Blood Alcohol Percentage

Drinks	**Body Weight in Pounds**								**Influenced**
	100	**120**	**140**	**160**	**180**	**200**	**220**	**240**	
1	0.04	0.04	0.03	0.03	0.02	0.02	0.02	0.02	**RARELY**
2	0.09*	0.07*	0.06*	0.06*	0.05*	0.04	0.04	0.04	
3	0.13	0.11	0.09*	0.08*	0.07*	0.07*	0.06*	0.06*	
4	0.18	0.15	0.13	0.11	0.1	0.09*	0.08*	0.07*	**POSSIBLY***
5	0.22	0.18	0.16	0.14	0.12	0.11	0.1	0.09*	
6	0.26	0.22	0.19	0.17	0.15	0.13	0.12	0.11	
7	0.31	0.26	0.22	0.19	0.17	0.15	0.14	0.13	**DEFINITELY**
8	0.35	0.29	0.25	0.22	0.2	0.18	0.16	0.15	
9	0.4	0.33	0.28	0.25	0.22	0.2	0.18	0.17	
10	0.44	0.37	0.31	0.28	0.24	0.22	0.2	0.18	

The asterisk (*) indicates estimated levels of impairment that could mean the individual is possibly influenced.

Enforcement and Penalties

The U.S. Coast Guard and every state have stringent penalties for violating BUI laws. Penalties can include large fines, suspension or revocation of boat operator privileges, and jail terms. The Coast Guard and the states cooperate fully in enforcement in order to remove impaired boat operators from the waters.

In waters that are overseen solely by the states, the states have the authority to enforce their own BUI statutes. In state waters that are also subject to U.S. jurisdiction, there is concurrent jurisdiction. That means if a boater is apprehended under Federal law in these waters, the Coast Guard will (unless precluded by state law) request that state law enforcement officers take the intoxicated boater into custody.

When the Coast Guard determines that an operator is impaired, the voyage may be terminated. The vessel will be brought to mooring by the Coast Guard or a competent and un-intoxicated person on board the recreational vessel. Depending on the circumstances, the Coast Guard may arrest the operator, detain the operator until sober, or turn the operator over to state or local authorities.

Tips for Avoiding BUI

Boating, fishing and other water sports are fun in their own right. Alcohol can turn a great day on the water into the tragedy of a lifetime.

Consider these alternatives to using alcohol while afloat:

- Take along a variety of cool drinks, such as sodas, water, iced tea, lemonade or nonalcoholic beer.
- Bring plenty of food and snacks.
- Wear clothes that will help keep you and your passengers cool.
- Plan to limit your trip to a reasonable time to avoid fatigue. Remember that it's common to become tired more quickly on the water.
- If you want to make alcohol part of your day's entertainment, plan to have a party ashore at the dock, in a picnic area, at a boating club, or in your backyard. Choose a location where you'll have time between the fun and getting back into your car or boat.
- If you dock somewhere for lunch or dinner and drink alcohol with your meal, wait a reasonable time (estimated at a minimum of an hour per drink) before operating your boat.

- Having no alcohol while aboard is the safest way to enjoy the water intoxicated passengers are also at risk of injury and falls overboard.
- Spread the word on the dangers of BUI. Many recreational boaters forget that a boat is a vehicle and that safe operation is a legal and personal responsibility.

Chapter 49

Preventing Alcohol-Impaired Driving

Chapter Contents

Section 49.1

Mass Media Campaigns to Prevent Alcohol-Impaired Driving

This section includes text excerpted from "Recommendation for Use of Mass Media Campaigns to Reduce Alcohol-Impaired Driving," Centers for Disease Control and Prevention (CDC), December 31, 2008. Reviewed April 2018.

Role of Mass Media Campaigns in Alcohol-Impaired Driving

Motor vehicle-related injuries kill more children and young adults than any other single cause in the United States, and are the leading overall cause of injury deaths for all ages. In 2002, alcohol-related motor vehicle crashes resulted in 17,419 deaths and more than 300,000 injuries. Each year, these crashes result in more than $50 billion in economic costs.

The accompanying systematic review found strong evidence that mass media campaigns are effective in reducing alcohol-impaired driving and alcohol-related crashes (i.e., those in which the driver had a blood alcohol concentration (BAC) of at least 0.01 g/dL) if they are carefully planned, well-executed, and attain adequate audience exposure, and if they are implemented in conjunction with other ongoing prevention activities, such as enforcement of laws against alcohol-impaired driving. Based on this evidence, the Task Force on Community Preventive Services (the Task Force) recommends that mass media campaigns that meet these criteria be implemented to reduce alcohol-impaired driving and its consequences. Such campaigns can be effective whether they focus on publicizing existing laws and enforcement activities or on the health and social consequences of alcohol-impaired driving.

In addition to recommending mass media campaigns, the Task Force has previously recommended five other approaches to preventing alcohol-impaired driving: sobriety checkpoints, 0.08 blood alcohol concentration laws, minimum legal drinking age laws, lower blood alcohol concentration laws for young or inexperienced drivers, and intervention training programs for servers of alcoholic beverages.

Although these recommendations are based on evaluations of each intervention as a distinct activity, it is important to remember that optimal prevention of alcohol-impaired driving requires a comprehensive and systematic approach to changing drinking and driving behavior. Because of the strong potential for a synergistic effect between well-planned mass media campaigns and other interventions with demonstrated effectiveness, communities should consider including such mass media campaigns in their multifaceted programs to reduce alcohol-impaired driving.

Section 49.2

Sobriety Checkpoints

This section includes text excerpted from "Sobriety Checkpoints," Centers for Disease Control and Prevention (CDC), December 2, 2015.

A sobriety checkpoint is a predetermined location at which law enforcement officers stop vehicles at a predetermined location to check whether the driver is impaired. They either stop every vehicle or stop vehicles at some regular interval, such as every third or tenth vehicle. The purpose of checkpoints is to deter driving after drinking by increasing the perceived risk of arrest. To do this, checkpoints should be highly visible, publicized extensively, and conducted regularly. Fell, Lacey, and Voas provide an overview of checkpoint operations, use, effectiveness, and issues.

History of Sobriety Checkpoints

Sobriety checkpoints were first introduced in Scandinavia in the 1930s and became common in the United States in the early 1980s. In 1990, the U.S. Supreme Court ruled in favor of the constitutionality of sobriety checkpoints; however, the debate over checkpoints has continued, and some individual state courts have deemed them illegal for violating state constitutions.

Use of Sobriety Checkpoint

Sobriety checkpoints are authorized in 38 states and the District of Columbia, but few states conduct them often. According to Global Health Security Agenda (GHSA), only 13 states conduct checkpoints on a weekly basis. The main reasons checkpoints are not used more frequently are lack of law enforcement personnel and lack of funding.

Effectiveness of Sobriety Checkpoints

Centers for Disease Control and Prevention (CDC) systematic review of 11 high-quality studies found that checkpoints reduced alcohol-related fatal, injury, and property damage crashes each by about 20 percent. Similarly, a meta-analysis found that checkpoints reduce alcohol-related crashes by 17 percent, and all crashes by 10–15 percent. Till date the National Highway Traffic Safety Administration (NHTSA) has supported a number of efforts to reduce alcohol-impaired driving using sobriety checkpoints. Evaluations of statewide campaigns in Connecticut and West Virginia involving sobriety checkpoints and extensive paid media found decreases in alcohol-related fatalities following the program, as well as fewer drivers with positive BACs at roadside surveys. In addition, a study examining demonstration programs in 7 states found reductions in alcohol-related fatalities between 11 and 20 percent in states that employed numerous checkpoints or other highly visible impaired driving enforcement operations and intensive publicity of the enforcement activities, including paid advertising. States with lower levels of enforcement and publicity did not demonstrate a decrease in fatalities relative to neighboring states.

Research on Effectiveness

Nunn and Newby examined the effectiveness of 22 sobriety checkpoints implemented over one year at nine checkpoint locations in Indianapolis, Indiana, using various methodologies (pre/post, difference in differences, and interrupted time series). Impairment rates (impaired-driver collisions per 100 collisions) decreased insignificantly in non-downtown locations and increased significantly in downtown areas. Sobriety checkpoints also resulted in a small significant reduction in the number of alcohol-related crashes when compared with similar control locations, with differences more pronounced in downtown areas. Finally, the time-series analysis found that the number of impaired collisions in postcheckpoint periods was approximately 19 percent less than in the precheckpoint periods.

Measuring Effectiveness

Because sobriety checkpoints are intended to deter impaired driving, an appropriate measure would be the number of impaired drivers deterred, but this is not easily identified. Instead, traffic enforcement agencies track changes in alcohol-related crashes, injuries, and fatalities. Measures can also include the number of stops and the number of driving while intoxicated (DWI) arrests per checkpoint or awareness or perceptions of the checkpoints obtained through surveys.

Costs

The main costs are for law enforcement time and for publicity. A typical checkpoint requires several hours from each law enforcement officer involved. Law enforcement costs can be reduced by operating checkpoints with 3–5 officers, perhaps supplemented by volunteers, instead of the 10–12 or more officers used in some jurisdictions. Law enforcement agencies in two rural West Virginia counties were able to sustain a year-long program of weekly low-staff checkpoints. The proportion of nighttime drivers with BACs of 0.05 and higher was 70 percent lower in these counties compared to drivers in comparison counties that did not operate additional checkpoints. NHTSA has a guidebook available to assist law enforcement agencies in planning, operating and evaluating low-staff sobriety checkpoints. "Checkpoint publicity can be costly if paid media are used, although publicity can also include earned media."

Time to Implement

Checkpoints can be implemented very quickly if officers are trained in detecting impaired drivers, SFST (Standardized Field Sobriety Test), and checkpoint operational procedures.

Other Issues

Legality

Checkpoints currently are permitted in 38 states and the District of Columbia. Checkpoints are permitted under the United States Constitution but some state courts have held that checkpoints violate their state's constitution. Some state legislatures have not authorized checkpoints. States where checkpoints are not permitted may use saturation patrols.

Visibility

According to NHTSA, checkpoints must be highly visible and publicized extensively to be effective. Communication and enforcement plans should be coordinated. Messages should clearly and unambiguously support enforcement. Paid media may be necessary to complement news stories and other earned media, especially in a continuing checkpoint program.

Arrests

The primary purpose of checkpoints is to deter impaired driving, not to increase arrests. Police generally arrest impaired drivers detected at checkpoints and publicize those arrests, but arrests at checkpoints should not be used as a measure of checkpoint effectiveness. The number of drivers evaluated at checkpoints would be a more appropriate measure.

Other Offenses

Checkpoints may also be used to check for valid driver's licenses, seat belt use, outstanding warrants, stolen vehicles, and other traffic and criminal infractions.

Combining Checkpoints with Other Activities

To enhance the visibility of their law enforcement operations, some jurisdictions combine checkpoints with other activities, such as saturation patrols. For example, some law enforcement agencies conduct both checkpoints and saturation patrols during the same weekend. Others alternate checkpoints and saturation patrols on different weekends as part of a larger impaired-driving enforcement effort.

Chapter 50

Alcohol and Stress in the Military

Members of the armed forces are not immune to the substance use problems that affect the rest of society. Although illicit drug use is lower among U.S. military personnel than among civilians, heavy alcohol and tobacco use, and especially prescription drug abuse, are much more prevalent and are on the rise. The stresses of deployment during wartime and the unique culture of the military account for some of these differences. Zero-tolerance policies and stigma pose difficulties in identifying and treating substance use problems in military personnel, as does lack of confidentiality that deters many who need treatment from seeking it.

Those with multiple deployments and combat exposure are at greatest risk of developing substance use problems. They are more apt to engage in new-onset heavy weekly drinking and binge drinking, to suffer alcohol and other drug-related problems, and to have greater prescribed use of behavioral health medications. They are also more likely to start smoking or relapse to smoking.

Drinking and Smoking

Alcohol use is also higher among men and women in military service than among civilians. Almost half of active duty service members (47%)

This chapter includes text excerpted from "Substance Abuse in the Military," National Institute on Drug Abuse (NIDA), March 2013. Reviewed April 2018

reported binge drinking in 2008—up from 35 percent in 1998. In 2008, 20 percent of military personnel reported binge drinking every week in the past month; the rate was considerably higher—27 percent—among those with high combat exposure. In 2008, 30 percent of all service members were current cigarette smokers—comparable to the rate for civilians (29%). However, as with alcohol use, smoking rates are significantly higher among personnel who have been exposed to combat.

Addressing the Problem

A report prepared for the U.S. Department of Defense (DoD) by the Institute of Medicine (IOM Report) recommended ways of addressing the problem of substance use in the military, including increasing the use of evidence-based prevention and treatment interventions and expanding access to care. The report recommends broadening insurance coverage to include effective outpatient treatments and better equipping healthcare providers to recognize and screen for substance use problems so they can refer patients to appropriate, evidence-based treatment when needed. It also recommends measures like limiting access to alcohol on bases.

The IOM Report also notes that addressing substance use in the military will require increasing confidentiality and shifting a cultural climate in which drug problems are stigmatized and evoke fear in people suffering from them.

Branches of the military have already taken steps to curb prescription drug abuse. The Army, for example, has implemented changes that include limiting the duration of prescriptions for opioid pain relievers to 6 months and having a pharmacist monitor a soldier's medications when multiple prescriptions are being used.

National Institute on Drug Abuse (NIDA) and other government agencies are currently funding research to better understand the causes of drug abuse and other mental health problems among military personnel, veterans, and their families and how best to prevent and treat them.

Chapter 51

Alcohol-Related Fire Fatalities

Establishing a Relationship between Alcohol and Casualties of Fire

- Alcohol abuse is a leading risk factor for unintentional injuries, the fifth leading cause of death in the United States. The overall costs resulting from unintentional injuries and deaths totaled $517 billion. Nearly 7 percent of the adult population meet the diagnostic criteria for alcohol abuse.
- Nearly half of adult emergency room patients treated for trauma are alcohol-impaired.
- Fires are the fourth leading cause of unintentional injuries; studies indicate that up to 40 percent of residential fire death victims are alcohol-impaired.
- Burn victims with high alcohol blood levels are more likely to die than burn victims with no alcohol impairment.

This chapter contains text excerpted from the following sources: Text beginning with the heading "Establishing a Relationship between Alcohol and Casualties of Fire" is excerpted from "Establishing a Relationship between Alcohol and Casualties of Fire," U.S. Fire Administration (USFA), July 2003, Reviewed April 2018; Text under the heading "Alcohol and Fire Safety Tips" is excerpted from "Alcohol and Fire Are a Lethal Mixture," U.S. Fire Administration (USFA), September 16, 2015.

- Children are not exempt from the effects of alcohol and fire, primarily through no fault of their own. Fire fatalities in these instances can be attributed to the caregivers' impaired judgment.
- Smoking combined with alcohol abuse exacerbates the risk of fires, fire injuries, and fire deaths.

This report links alcohol abuse with the risk of unintentional injuries, with specific focus on fire injuries where alcohol may be a contributing factor. Alcohol abuse and resulting unintentional injuries impose a burden on individuals, those around them, and society as a whole. Alcohol abuse is a leading risk factor for unintentional injury and is associated with increased risk of injury in automobile crashes, falls, fires, drowning, homicides, and suicides.

Use and Effects of Alcohol

Alcohol is a major contributing factor to unintended injuries in the United States. Studies have estimated that nearly half of alcohol-related deaths are the result of injuries sustained from motor vehicle crashes, falls, fires, drownings, homicides, and suicides. Alcohol depresses the central nervous system, potentially to the point of stupor, coma, and death; and individuals who consume large quantities of alcohol experience disordered thought patterns, impaired judgment, impaired perception, and a decrease in generalized motor control.

Alcohol is widely used in U.S. society. It is heavily advertised and is embedded in everyday life, including religious traditions. Although the 20-year trend in the rate of alcohol consumption is down 12 percent, this downward trend does not minimize the potential devastating effect that alcohol may have on abusers.

The role of alcohol as a risk factor for unintentional injury stems primarily from reduced cognitive function, impaired physical coordination and performance, and increased risk-taking behavior. Injuries tend to be more serious among the alcohol-impaired, because alcohol affects the physiology of the victim. Alcohol consumption has consequences not only for the health and well being of those who drink but, by extension, the lives of those around them. A classic example of this is the intoxicated driver who fails to fasten his seat belt. This individual not only risks greater injury to himself, but as a result of his impaired senses is a high risk to other drivers and pedestrians. The following statistics give a glimpse of the magnitude of alcohol use in the United States:

- Approximately 14 million people (7% of the adult population) meet the diagnostic criteria for alcohol abuse or alcoholism.
- More than half of all adults have a close family member who is or had been an alcoholic.
- Approximately one–fourth of children younger than 18 is exposed to alcohol abuse or alcohol dependence in the family.
- Between 20 percent and 30 percent of patients seen in hospital emergency departments have alcohol problems.

Unintentional Injuries

Unintentional injuries are the fifth leading cause of death in the United States, behind heart, cancer, cerebrovascular, and chronic lower respiratory diseases. Over 97,000 people died from unintentional injuries in 1999. Of those, 3,348 resulted from fire and burns.

The national trend of unintentional injuries has declined 43 percent over the past 40 years. This downward trend may be attributed to local, state, and national prevention and educational campaigns; to better technology (e.g., airbags in automobiles, smoke alarms and built-in fire protection systems); and to improvements in product safety and stricter building codes. Nevertheless, wage losses, medical expenses, property damage, employer costs, fire losses, and other expenses related to unintentional injury and fatalities ran to an estimated $516.9 billion.

Alcohol's Involvement in Unintentional Injuries

Alcohol abuse is a leading risk factor for unintentional injuries. The short-term physiological effects of alcohol diminish motor coordination and balance and impair perception and judgment. Alcohol is also thought to perpetuate accident-prone behavior. Studies have estimated that nearly half of adult trauma patients receiving treatment in emergency rooms have been injured while under the influence of alcohol. For example, traffic crashes involving alcohol killed more than 16,000 people, alcohol was involved in 39 percent of all fatal traffic crashes, up to 77 percent of deaths from falls involved alcohol, and the victim had been drinking in up to 47 percent of drowning deaths. The end result of acute alcohol intoxication is carelessness.

Alcohol and Fire Casualties

Fires are the fourth leading cause of unintentional injuries in the United States, after motor vehicle crashes, poisonings, and drownings.

More than 3,500 people died of unintended exposure to smoke, fire, and flames. Scientists have estimated that alcohol is involved in 40 percent of all residential fire deaths. One study on published medical examiner results revealed that 42 percent of unintentional fire and burn fatalities were intoxicated (with a blood alcohol level greater than or equal 0.1). Another study found that alcoholics in Toronto have a fire death risk 9.7 times that of the city's population. Further, a study of decedents in North Carolina found that 53 percent (69 of 130) adult victims were intoxicated, and in Alabama, more than half of the victims older than 17 tested positive for alcohol. Of the 374 fire fatalities in Minnesota, 133 (36%) were found to have positive blood alcohol concentrations.

Chronic alcohol use has been shown to disrupt the immune system response to a significant burn.

Because alcohol and burns each the suppress immune response, the synergistic effect is an extremely suppressed immune response.

Burn victims who had been drinking are three times more likely to die than burn victims with no

alcohol present in their blood streams. Public perception of alcohol's contribution to fatal fire injuries may be underestimated. This suggests that because public awareness of alcohol's contribution to fire fatalities and injuries is underestimated, the public pays too little attention to the potential fire risk posed by alcohol abuse.

Children. Children are not exempt from the harmful effects of alcohol, primarily through no fault of their own (e.g., involvement in traffic accidents). Children up to age 14 were involved in 5 percent of unintentional fire injuries, but this same group accounted for 20 percent of all fire deaths and 14 percent of all fire injuries. One study found that, of juvenile fatalities examined, 15 percent died in fires where the surviving adult was impaired by alcohol or drugs.

Case after case revealed that fire deaths of children were attributed to the parents' failure to perceive and respond to a fire emergency because of impairment of their sensory, judgment, or physical functions by alcohol consumption. Although anecdotal, the inference that caregivers who are alcohol impaired contribute to children casualties is compelling.

Smoking. Smoking is the fifth most frequent cause of residential fire, the leading cause of fire deaths, and the second most common cause of fire-related injuries. Smoking combined with alcohol is often identified as factors in fire deaths in residences, where the majority of fire fatalities occurs. Smokers consume more alcohol than do nonsmokers. Alcohol abusers and smokers are an especially dangerous combination since smoking materials represent a ready-made fire threat while at the same time alcohol consumption decreases the chances of detecting, mitigating, and escaping a fire. Data from Minnesota is particularly revealing. Smoking, the leading cause of fatal fires in Minnesota, accounted for 26 percent of fire fatalities (94 deaths). Of these fatalities from smoking-related fires, 62 percent (58 of 94) had a blood alcohol level meeting or exceeding the state standard of 0.1.

Awareness Campaigns

Fire casualties are emerging as an unintentional injury subset highly influenced by problematic drinking behaviors. Because the public's perception of this problem may be low, it may be possible to minimize fire risk by increasing the awareness of those who drink and those who are surrounded by regular drinkers. Educational campaigns warning the public of the dangers of drunk driving have been successful, and the same can be done to shed light on the subtle dangers of alcohol and fire.

Alcohol and Fire Safety Tips

- After a party or get-together where alcohol was consumed, check for smoking materials, especially under cushions. Chairs and sofas catch on fire easily and burn fast.
- Don't consume alcohol and cook—you could fall asleep and cause a devastating fire.
- Make sure a working smoke alarm is installed; it significantly increases your chances of escaping and surviving a deadly fire.

Part Seven

Treatment and Recovery

Chapter 52

Helping Someone Who Has a Problem with Alcohol

Remember—you can't make a person deal with a drinking problem. You can offer support and get help for yourself.

Step One: Talk

- Talk about your worries when the person is sober. Try to say what you think or feel, like "I am concerned about your drinking."
- Give facts. Some people find it helpful just to get information. You could say, "I want to share some things I've learned about adults and alcohol."
- Try to stay away from labels like "alcoholic."
- Ask if you can go to the doctor with your family member or friend

---

This chapter contains text excerpted from the following sources: Text in this chapter begins with excerpts from "How to Help Someone You Know with a Drinking Problem," National Institute on Aging (NIA), National Institutes of Health (NIH), May 16, 2017; Text beginning with the heading "If My Friend or Loved One Asks for My Help, Where Do I Start?" is excerpted from "What to Do If Your Adult Friend or Loved One Has a Problem with Drugs," National Institute on Drug Abuse (NIDA), January 2016.

Step Two: Offer Your Help

- Suggest things to do that don't include drinking
- Encourage counseling or attending a group meeting. Offer to drive to and from these support meetings.
- Give your support during treatment

Step Three: Take Care of Yourself

- You need support, too. Think about what you need to stay safe and healthy.
- Involve other family members or friends so you are not in this alone. Talk honestly about how you are feeling. Try to say what support or help you need.
- Try going to counseling or special meetings that offer support to families and friends of people with drinking problems. There may be programs at your local hospital or clinic.

If My Friend or Loved One Asks for My Help, Where Do I Start?

If someone you care about has asked for help, he or she has taken an important first step. If that person is resistant to help, see if you can at least convince him or her to get an evaluation from a doctor.

You can always take steps to locate an appropriate physician or health professional, and leave the information with your friend. You can call health professionals in advance to see if they are comfortable speaking with their patients about addiction. If not, ask for a referral to another doctor with more expertise in the area of addiction. There are 3,500 board-certified physicians who specialize in addiction in the United States.

Emphasize to your friend or loved one that it takes a lot of courage to seek help for a alcohol problem because there is a lot of hard work ahead. There is a great deal of scientific evidence that treatment works, and people recover every day. Like other chronic diseases, addiction can be managed successfully. Treatment enables people to counteract the powerfully disruptive effects of drugs on the brain and behavior and to regain control of their lives. Like many diseases, it can take several attempts at treatment to find the right approach. But assure your friend or loved one that you will be supportive in his or her courageous effort.

My Friend Has Considered Treatment but Is Afraid of What Others Will Think. What Can I Tell My Friend?

Many employers, friends, and family members will be compassionate if they see a person is making a sincere effort to recover from a substance abuse problem. But you can also reassure your friend that laws protect the privacy of a person seeking drug treatment—or in fact, any medical treatment. Healthcare providers may not share information with anyone else without a patient's permission. Some jobs may require a doctor's note saying an employee is being treated for a medical condition, but the nature of the condition need not be specified.

If My Friend or Loved One Refuses to Cooperate, Should We Conduct an Intervention?

Many people are compelled to enter treatment by the pressure of their family, friends, or a court system. However, there is no evidence that confrontational "interventions" like those familiar from TV programs are effective at convincing people they have a problem or motivating them to change. It is even possible for such confrontational encounters to escalate into violence or backfire in other ways. Instead, you should focus on creating incentives to at least get the person to a doctor. Often people will listen to professionals rather than have conversations with friends and family members, as the latter encounters can sometimes be driven by fear, accusations, and emotions.

Can I Explore Treatment Centers Even If My Friend Is Not Willing to Go into Treatment?

Yes. If you find centers that might appeal to your friend, either by their location or medical approach, it might encourage him or her to enter treatment. You can call this helpline and get some advice on how to proceed: 800-662-HELP (800-662-4357) (This service is supported by the U.S. Department of Health and Human Services (HHS).) You can also look for a treatment center online, which will allow you to search for a treatment center in your area and also give you information about the kind of addiction or patients it treats.

You can also search the following directories to find board-certified addiction specialists near you. We recommend that you search both directories. The American Board of Addiction Medicine (ABAM) directory lists physicians who are board-certified in addiction medicine. Many of these physicians are primary care doctors. The American

Board of Psychiatry and Neurology (ABPN) directory lists psychiatrists who are board-certified in addiction psychiatry. These physicians specialize in mental health.

What Should I Look for in a Treatment Center?

Treatment approaches must be tailored to address each patient's substance abuse patterns and also other medical, psychiatric, and social problems. Some treatment centers offer outpatient treatment programs, which allow patients to continue to perform some daily responsibilities. However, many people do better in inpatient (residential) treatment. An addiction specialist can advise your friend or loved one about the most promising options.

Who Will Be Providing Treatment?

There are different kinds of specialists who are involved in addiction care, including doctors, nurses, therapists, social workers, and others. In some treatment programs, different specialists work as a team to help patients recover from addiction.

What Is Treatment Like?

Everyone entering treatment for a substance use disorder is unique. That is why the patient and the treatment staff work together to develop an individualized treatment plan. It may include some type of behavioral treatment ("talk therapy") designed to engage the patient in the treatment process, alter destructive attitudes and behaviors related to drug use, and increase healthy life skills. Behavioral treatment can also enhance the effectiveness of medications that might be available and help patients stay in treatment longer. Treatment for substance use disorders can be delivered in many different settings using a variety of different approaches.

Do Most Treatment Centers Offer Medication?

Some do, and that is a good question to ask them. Medications are currently available to treat addictions to alcohol, nicotine, and opioids (heroin and prescription pain relievers), and your loved one's treatment team may recommend one of those medications. There are also medicines to treat mental health conditions (such as depression) that might be contributing to the addiction. In addition, medication is sometimes prescribed to help with the symptoms associated with drug withdrawal. When medication is available, it can be combined with behavioral therapy to ensure success for most patients. Some treatment centers follow the philosophy that they should not treat a drug addiction with other drugs, but research shows that medication can help in many cases.

My Friend Was in Rehab before but Relapsed Afterward. How Do We Know Treatment Will Work This Time?

This means your friend has already learned many of the skills needed to recover from addiction and should try it again. The fear of relapse should not get in the way of trying treatment again. People being treated or recovering from addiction relapse about as often as do people with other chronic diseases, such as hypertension, diabetes, and asthma. Treatment of any chronic disease involves changing deeply imbedded behaviors, and relapse sometimes goes with the territory—it doesn't mean treatment failed. A return to drug abuse indicates that treatment needs to be started again or adjusted, and your friend might benefit from a different treatment approach.

How Can People Find a Treatment Center They Can Afford?

If they have health insurance, it may cover substance abuse treatment services. Many insurance plans cover inpatient stays. When setting up appointments with treatment centers, you can ask about payment options and what insurance plans they take. They can also advise you on potential low-cost options.

To find treatment—and to learn about payment options—try the Behavioral Health Treatment Services Locator provided by the Substance Abuse and Mental Health Services Administration (SAMHSA). This free tool offers payment information for each of the treatment services listed, including information on sliding fee scales and payment assistance. Its "Frequently Asked Questions" section addresses cost of treatment.

You can also call the treatment helpline at 800-662-HELP (800-662-4357) or 800-487-4889 (TTY) to ask about treatment centers that offer low- or no-cost treatment. You can also contact your state substance abuse agency—many states will help pay for substance abuse treatment.

Note that the new Mental Health Parity and Addiction Equity Act ensures that co-pays, deductibles, and visit limits are generally not more restrictive for mental health and substance abuse disorder benefits than they are for medical and surgical benefits. The Affordable Care Act builds on this law and requires coverage of mental health and substance use disorder services as one of ten essential health benefits categories. Under the essential health benefits rule, individual and small group health plans are required to comply with these parity regulations. When you research payment options, be sure you are speaking to people familiar with the new rules (old websites and pamphlets will not necessarily be accurate).

If My Friend Does Go into Treatment, How Can I Offer Support?

This is a great conversation to have with your friend's treatment provider. Different patients need different levels of support. If there are difficult dynamics in a family group or set of friends, the counselor may recommend little contact for a while. It is important to tell friends struggling with addiction that you admire their courage for tackling this medical problem directly through treatment and that as long as they stick with the treatment plan, you will offer encouragement and support. When residential treatment is over, your friend will have to re-enter the community and it will be a difficult time. There will be triggers everywhere that could promote a relapse—such as driving by places where the person once took drugs, or seeing friends who provided those drugs. You can encourage your friend to avoid these triggers, and you can make an effort to ask him or her what those triggers are. However, people addicted to drugs have to fight much of this struggle on their own, without the help and advice of friends, using the knowledge and skills learned in treatment. Offer as much love and support you can as long as your friend continues to follow the treatment plan. If your he or she relapses, you should encourage additional treatment.

Chapter 53

Strategies for Reducing Alcohol Consumption or Quitting

Tips to Avoid Alcohol

Small changes can make a big difference in reducing your chances of having alcohol-related problems. Whatever strategies you choose, give them a fair trial. If one approach doesn't work, try something else. But if you haven't made progress in cutting down after 2–3 months, consider quitting drinking altogether, seeking professional help, or both.

Here are some strategies to try, and you can add your own at the end. Check off perhaps two or three to try in the next week or two:

- **Keep track.** Keep track of how much you drink. Find a way that works for you: Carry a drinking tracker card in your wallet, make check marks on a kitchen calendar, or enter notes in a mobile phone notepad or personal digital assistant. Making note of each drink before you drink it may help you slow down when needed.
- **Count and measure.** Know the standard drink sizes so you can count your drinks accurately. Measure drinks at home. Away from home, it can be hard to keep track, especially with mixed

---

This chapter includes text excerpted from "Tips to Try," National Institute on Alcohol Abuse and Alcoholism (NIAAA), March 6, 2009. Reviewed April 2018.

drinks, and at times, you may be getting more alcohol than you think. With wine, you may need to ask the host or server not to "top off" a partially filled glass.

- **Set goals.** Decide how many days a week you want to drink and how many drinks you'll have on those days. It's a good idea to have some days when you don't drink. People who always stay within the low-risk limits when they drink have the lowest rates of alcohol-related problems.
- **Pace and space.** When you do drink, pace yourself. Sip slowly. Have no more than one standard drink with alcohol per hour. Have "drink spacers"—make every other drink a nonalcoholic one, such as water, soda, or juice.
- **Include food.** Don't drink on an empty stomach. Eat some food so the alcohol will be absorbed into your system more slowly.
- **Find alternatives.** If drinking has occupied a lot of your time, then fill free time by developing new, healthy activities, hobbies, and relationships, or renewing ones you've missed. If you have counted on alcohol to be more comfortable in social situations, manage moods, or cope with problems, then seek other, healthy ways to deal with those areas of your life.
- **Avoid "triggers."** What triggers your urge to drink? If certain people or places make you drink even when you don't want to, try to avoid them. If certain activities, times of day, or feelings trigger the urge, plan something else to do instead of drinking. If drinking at home is a problem, keep little or no alcohol there.
- **Plan to handle urges.** When you cannot avoid a trigger and an urge hits, consider these options: Remind yourself of your reasons for changing (it can help to carry them in writing or store them in an electronic message you can access easily). Or talk things through with someone you trust. Or get involved with a healthy, distracting activity, such as physical exercise or a hobby that doesn't involve drinking. Or, instead of fighting the feeling, accept it and ride it out without giving in, knowing that it will soon crest like a wave and pass.
- **Know your "no."** You're likely to be offered a drink at times when you don't want one. Have a polite, convincing "no, thanks" ready. The faster you can say no to these offers, the less likely you are to give in. If you hesitate, it allows you time to think of excuses to go along.

Reminder Strategies

Change can be hard, so it helps to have concrete reminders of why and how you've decided to do it. Some standard options include carrying a change plan in your wallet or posting sticky notes at home. Also, consider these high-tech ideas:

- Fill out a change plan, e-mails it to your personal (nonwork) account, store it in a private online folder, and review it weekly
- Store your goals, reasons, or strategies in your mobile phone as short text messages or notepad entries that you can retrieve when an urge hits.
- Set up an automated mobile phone or e-mails calendar alerts that deliver reminders when you choose, such as a few hours before you usually go out. (E-mails providers such as Gmail and Yahoo mail have online calendars with alert options.)
- Create passwords that are motivating phrases in code, which you'll reinforce each time you log in, such as 1Day@aTime, 1stThings1st! or 0Pain=0Gain.

Choose Your Approach

This chapter will be most useful for people who have become dependent on alcohol and thus may find it difficult to quit without some support. Several proven treatment approaches are available. One size doesn't fit all, however. It's a good idea to do some research to find options that appeal to you, as you are more likely to stick with them. Chances are excellent that you'll pull together an approach that works for you.

Suggestions for getting started:

- Social support to stop drinking
- Professional help

Social Support to Stop Drinking

One potential challenge when people stop drinking is rebuilding a life without alcohol. It may be important to:

- Educate family and friends
- Develop new interests and social groups
- Find rewarding ways to spend your time that don't involve alcohol
- Ask for help from others

When asking for support from friends or significant others, be specific. This could include:

- Not offering you alcohol
- Not using alcohol around you
- Giving words of support and withholding criticism
- Not asking you to take on new demands right now
- Going to a group like Al-Anon

Consider joining Alcoholics Anonymous or another mutual support group. Recovering people who attend groups regularly do better than those who do not. Groups can vary widely, so shop around for one that's comfortable. You'll get more out of it if you become actively involved by having a sponsor and reaching out to other members for assistance.

Professional Help

Advances in alcoholism treatments have provided more choices for patients and health professionals.

- **Medications to treat alcoholism.** The U.S. Food and Drug Administration (FDA) has approved three medications for treating alcohol dependence: naltrexone, acamprosate, and disulfiram. Some medications already approved for other conditions have also shown promise for treating alcohol dependence and problem drinking, including varenicline, gabapentin, and topiramate. Of the FDA approved medications, the two newer ones (naltrexone and acamprosate) can make it easier to quit drinking by offsetting changes in the brain caused by alcoholism. They don't make you sick if you do drink, unlike the older approved medication (disulfiram). None of these medications is addictive. They can be combined with mutual-support groups or behavioral treatments. As an alternative to specialty treatment, your regular doctor can treat alcohol problems using the new medications and several brief office visits for support.
- **Behavioral treatments.** Often known as alcohol counseling or "talk therapy," behavioral treatments also work well. Several counseling approaches are about equally effective—cognitive-behavioral, motivational enhancement, marital and family counseling, or a combination. Getting help in itself appears to be more important than the particular approach used, as long as it offers empathy, avoids heavy-handed confrontation, strengthens

motivation, and provides concrete ways to change drinking behavior.

- **Specialized, intensive treatment programs.** Some people will need more intensive programs. See Help Links (www.rethinkingdrinking.niaaa.nih.gov/Help-links/Default.aspx#Treatment) for a treatment locator. If you need a referral to a program, ask your doctor.

Chapter 54

The Differences between Brief Intervention and Treatment for Alcoholism

Chapter Contents

Section 54.1

Brief Interventions to Moderate Alcohol Consumption

This section includes text excerpted from "Alcohol Screening and Brief Intervention—a Guide for Public Health Practitioners," Substance Abuse and Mental Health Services Administration (SAMHSA), April 15, 2009. Reviewed April 2018.

Screening and brief intervention (SBI) is a structured set of questions designed to identify individuals at risk for alcohol use problems, followed by a brief discussion between an individual and a service provider, with referral to specialized treatment as needed. Screening asks several questions to determine whether individuals are misusing alcohol—that is, are they drinking too much, too often, or experiencing harm from their drinking. The provider evaluates the answers and then shares the results and their significance with the individual. Brief interventions are counseling sessions that last 5–15 minutes. Their purpose is to increase the person's awareness of his or her alcohol use and its consequences and then motivate the person to either reduce risky drinking or seek treatment, if needed. The provider works with the person on willingness and readiness to change his or her drinking behavior.

Screening and Brief Intervention

Healthcare providers use screening and brief intervention to reduce the impact of substance abuse. Screening and brief intervention:

- is designed for use by service providers who do not specialize in addiction treatment
- uses motivational approaches based on how ready the person is to change behavior
- gives feedback and suggestions respectfully in the form of useful information, without judgment or accusations
- has been shown by research to be effective in reducing alcohol use and alcohol-related adverse consequences, including injury

Background on SBI

The first research studies of SBI were conducted more than 40 years ago. However, it was not until effective assessments of alcohol use were developed in the 1980s that SBI became a useful public health strategy for addressing alcohol misuse.

Early screening tools, such as the Michigan Alcohol Screening Test (MAST) and the Cut-Down, Annoyed, Guilty Eye-Opener (CAGE), were developed to detect alcohol dependence and refer to treatment. Swedish research showed that more systematic screening along with brief interventions in primary care settings could reach large numbers of at-risk drinkers and help them reduce their alcohol use. These findings led the World Health Organization (WHO) to start a program in 1981 to develop an internationally valid screening tool and study the effectiveness of brief interventions for at-risk drinkers. The result was the Alcohol Use Disorders Identification Test (AUDIT) and the first study of effectiveness of brief intervention across different countries. The WHO program then expanded to study ways to implement SBI in primary care settings and to develop national plans to integrate SBI into the healthcare systems of developed and developing nations.

At present, there are large-scale SBI programs in Brazil, South Africa, Europe, and the United States. The Substance Abuse and Mental Health Services Administration (SAMHSA), through its Screening, Brief Intervention, and Referral to Treatment (SBIRT) program, conducts science-based demonstration projects across the country that assess and disseminate information on new SBI methods.

Effectiveness of SBI

Several systematic reviews have shown that SBI is effective:

- in helping at-risk drinkers. Drinkers who are alcohol dependent typically need more intensive treatment
- in helping both men and women, including pregnant women
- with a wide age range, including adolescents, adults, and older adults
- in both primary care and emergency department settings

Since at-risk drinkers make up a large percentage of all drinkers, SBI can have a very significant impact on improving the health of the population as a whole. Large numbers of people can be helped to reduce risky drinking or to maintain their drinking at safe levels by just one or a few brief meetings with a provider.

A key review showed small decreases in hazardous drinking 6–12 months after SBI among people who had not sought alcohol treatment. Among people who did seek treatment, SBI was as successful as the more intensive types of treatment.

Another review of SBI demonstrated the effectiveness of brief interventions in adult primary care. The U.S. Preventive Services Task Force (USPSTF) found that 6–12 months after brief counseling (up to 15 minutes and at least one follow-up contact), the participants had decreased their average number of drinks per week by anywhere from 13–34 percent. The percentage of participants drinking at safe or moderate levels was 10–19 percent greater than among those who did not receive the brief intervention. The brief interventions were effective with people from 17–70 years old. Based on this review, the U.S. Preventive Services Task Force wrote a recommendation statement supporting the use of brief interventions in adult primary care.

A recent report on findings from SAMHSA's SBIRT program also shows that large numbers of people who are at risk of developing serious alcohol problems can be identified through screening. The combination of screening, brief intervention, and referral to treatment can decrease the frequency and severity of alcohol use and increase the percentage of people who obtain the specialized treatment they need.

Cost-Effectiveness of SBI

The cost-effectiveness of SBI has been shown in several countries. SBI does not require investments in extensive training, expensive instruments or lengthy amounts of time to conduct. One study in physician offices showed that SBI not only led to significant decreases in alcohol use but also to a decrease in hospital days and emergency department visits. The cost of the intervention was $205 per person; it saved $712 in healthcare costs. This means that for every dollar spent, $4.30 was saved in future healthcare costs. The cost benefit increased dramatically (from 4.3–39) when factoring in reductions in motor vehicle crashes and legal costs.

Cost-effectiveness varies depending on how SBI is used. Emergency departments and trauma centers, which have a higher proportion of patients with alcohol use problems than the general healthcare system, have found SBI to be very cost-effective. One study of trauma patients in emergency departments and hospitals found a net savings of $89 in healthcare costs alone per patient screened and $330 for each patient offered an intervention. The number and length of sessions per client also significantly affect the cost.

SBI in the Context of a Public Health Approach

The effectiveness of SBI in helping individuals reduce their drinking can be increased when SBI is carried out in communities that are using public health strategies to address alcohol problems in a comprehensive way. This comprehensive approach includes community education for the general public and for merchants who sell alcohol; development and enforcement of laws and policies that affect the price, availability, and advertising of alcohol; collaboration among organizations and coalition building to address issues related to alcohol use; health insurance coverage for SBI; and ready access to alternative activities, such as alcohol-free recreation programs, dances, and drop-in centers.

Screening and Brief Intervention: What You Need to Know

Screening is used to identify anyone who is at risk of having a specific health condition. However, it does not provide a diagnosis. Screening for alcohol misuse assesses whether an individual may have an alcohol use disorder or is at risk of experiencing problems from alcohol use. Screening is followed by brief intervention targeted toward at-risk drinkers rather than those who are dependent on alcohol. Many at-risk drinkers still have enough control over their drinking that they can cut down or quit with just the help from a brief intervention. However, if further help is needed, you should be prepared to make appropriate referrals.

Screening can be conducted by a variety of different public health professionals in many community-based settings, including your office, during home visits, or at public events such as health fairs. It can be offered through face-to-face interview or as a self-administered paper or computer-based questionnaire. If a self-administered instrument is used, it is more efficient for the client to complete it before meeting with you, perhaps in a waiting room. However, if the issue of alcohol use comes up during your meeting, it can be useful to conduct the screening right then. It is important to start by asking if the person would be willing to answer some questions to help discuss his or her alcohol use.

There are many different alcohol screening tools available. Some are designed for specific populations, such as adolescents or pregnant women. Some are available in other languages in addition to English. The tools also vary in whether they ask about alcohol use patterns such as amount and frequency, alcohol-related problems, or both. Another way these tools differ is in the number of questions they ask and the amount of time they take to administer and score.

Some people should not drink alcohol at all. They include:

- Children and adolescents (people under age 21)
- People who cannot keep their drinking to a moderate level
- Women who are pregnant, planning to become pregnant, or breastfeeding
- People who take prescription or over-the-counter medications that can interact with alcohol
- People who have a health condition that can be made worse by alcohol
- People who are or will be driving, operating machinery, or doing other activities that require alertness, coordination, or skill

A brief intervention consists of one or more time-limited conversations between an at-risk drinker and a practitioner. The goals are to

1. help the drinker increase awareness of his or her alcohol use and its consequences and
2. encourage the person to create a plan to change his or her drinking behavior to stay within safe limits.

The conversations are typically 5–15 minutes, although they can last up to 30–60 minutes for as many as four sessions.

Section 54.2

Integration of Healthcare Systems and Substance Use Disorders

This section contains text excerpted from the following sources: Text in this section begins with excerpts from "Health Care Systems and Substance Use Disorders," Surgeongeneral.gov, U.S. Department of Health and Human Services (HHS), November 2016; Text under the heading "Effectiveness of Alcohol Screening and Brief Interventions in Medical Settings" is excerpted from "Putting the Screen in Screening: Technology-Based Alcohol Screening and Brief Interventions in Medical Settings," National Institute on Alcohol Abuse and Alcoholism (NIAAA), 2014. Reviewed April 2018; Text under the heading "SBI in Trauma/Emergency Rooms" is excerpted from "SBIRT Screening, Brief Intervention and Referral to Treatment," Substance Abuse and Mental Health Services Administration (SAMHSA), April 25, 2011. Reviewed April 2018.

Healthcare systems are made up of diverse healthcare organizations ranging from primary care, specialty substance use disorder treatment (including residential and outpatient settings), mental healthcare, infectious disease clinics, school clinics, community health centers, hospitals, emergency departments, and others.

It is known that most people with substance use disorders do not seek treatment on their own, many because they do not believe they need it or they are not ready for it, and others because they are not aware that treatment exists or how to access it. But individuals with substance use disorders often do access the healthcare system for other reasons, including acute health problems like illness, injury, or overdose, as well as chronic health conditions such as Human immunodeficiency virus infection and acquired immune deficiency syndrome (HIV/AIDS), heart disease, or depression. Thus, screening for substance misuse and substance use disorders in diverse healthcare settings is the first step to identifying substance use problems and engaging patients in the appropriate level of care.

Mild substance use disorders may respond to brief counseling sessions in primary care, while severe substance use disorders are often chronic conditions requiring substance use disorder treatment like specialty residential or intensive outpatient treatment as well as long-term management through primary care. A wide range of healthcare settings is needed to effectively meet the diverse needs of patients.

Primary care has a central role in this process, because it is the site for most preventive and ongoing clinical care for patients—the patient's anchor in the healthcare system. For example, primary care settings can serve as a conduit to help patients engage in and maintain recovery. Also, approaches such as screening, brief intervention, and referral to treatment (SBIRT) provide primary care providers with tools for addressing patients' substance misuse. Based upon the strength of the evidence for their effectiveness, the U.S. Preventive Services Task Force (USPSTF) has recommended alcohol screening and brief behavioral counseling interventions for adults in primary care and given the supporting evidence for these services a "B" grade. This is significant because under the Affordable Care Act (ACA), preventive services given a grade of A or B by the USPSTF must be covered by most health plans without cost-sharing. The USPSTF recommendation supports the expectation that primary care providers will soon routinely screen adults of all ages for unhealthy alcohol use as they now do for blood pressure and weight. Relatedly, the National Commission on Prevention Priorities (NCPP) of the Partnership for Prevention ranks primary care-based interventions to reduce alcohol misuse among the most valuable clinical preventive services.

Reasons Why Integrating Substance Use Disorder Services and Mainstream Healthcare Is Necessary

A number of strong arguments underpin the growing momentum to integrate substance use disorder services and mainstream healthcare. The main argument is that substance use disorders are medical conditions like any other, and recognition of that fact means it no longer makes sense to keep substance use disorders segregated from other health issues. A number of other realities support the need for integration.

- Substance use, mental disorders, and other general medical conditions are often interconnected
- Integration has the potential to reduce health disparities
- Delivering substance use disorder services in mainstream healthcare can be cost-effective and may reduce intake/treatment wait times at substance use disorder treatment facilities

- Integration can lead to improved health outcomes through better care coordination.

Substance Use Disorders, Mental Disorders, and Other Medical Conditions Are Interconnected

Many individuals who come to mainstream healthcare settings, such as primary care, obstetrics and gynecology, emergency departments, and hospitals, also have a substance use disorder. In a study within one health plan, one third of the most common and costly medical conditions were markedly more prevalent among patients with substance use disorders than they were among similar health system members who did not have a substance use disorder. Similarly, many individuals who present at specialty substance use disorder treatment programs have other medical conditions, including hypertension, HIV/AIDS, coronary artery disease, hepatitis, chronic liver disease, and psychiatric disorders.

Because substance use complicates many other medical conditions, early identification and management of substance misuse or use disorders presents an important opportunity to improve health outcomes and reduce healthcare costs. Research shows that primary care patients with mild or moderate substance use have higher rates of other medical problems, including injury, hypertension, and psychiatric disorders, as well as higher costs. Alcohol misuse is associated with liver and pancreatic diseases; hypertension; reproductive system disorders; trauma; stroke; and cancers of the oral cavity, esophagus, larynx, pharynx, liver, colon, and rectum. Even one drink per day may increase the risk of breast cancer.

In addition to the health problems faced by individuals engaged in substance use mentioned above, substance use can adversely affect a developing fetus. In the United States, fetal alcohol spectrum disorders (FASD) remain highly prevalent and problematic, even though they are preventable. A study of children in public and private schools in a Midwestern community calculated rates of FASD to be as high as 6–9 per 1,000.

Adolescents with substance use disorders experience higher rates of other physical and mental illnesses, as well as diminished overall health and well-being. Sexually transmitted infections (STIs) and HIV/AIDS, appetite changes and weight loss, dermatological problems, gastrointestinal problems, headaches, insomnia and chronic fatigue, and heart, lung, and abdominal abnormalities are only some of the problems that affect the health of young people who misuse alcohol and drugs. A study of adolescents entering specialty substance use disorder treatment—as compared with age-matched adolescent patients without a substance use disorder—found higher rates of clinically diagnosed sinusitis, asthma, abdominal pain, sleep disorders, injuries and overdoses.

In addition to the physical health problems described above, mental health problems are also over-represented among adolescents with substance use disorders, particularly attention-deficit hyperactivity disorder, conduct disorders, anxiety disorders, and mood disorders. In addition, alcohol and drug use are associated with serious personal and social problems for users and for those around them including elevated rates of morbidity and mortality related to traffic crashes, intimate partner violence, risky sex, and unintentional injuries, including death from overdose.

Integration Can Lead to Improved Health Outcomes through Better Care Coordination

Treatment of substance use disorders has historically been provided episodically, when a person experiences a crisis or a relapse occurs. This is neither good quality nor efficient care, because severe substance use disorders are chronic health problems, similar to other health conditions and with similar outcomes. Studies conducted over extended periods of time have found that annual primary care visits were associated with better outcomes and reduced healthcare costs following substance use disorder treatment, but research on models of chronic care management is only beginning and thus far no consensus has emerged on the best approach. These types of long-term studies will be more informative as the substance use disorder treatment, healthcare, and mental health systems become more integrated and as researchers buildon disease management models that are effective for other medical conditions.

In addition to chronic care management for severely affected individuals, coordinating services for those with mild or moderate problems is also important. Studies of various methods for integrating substance use services and general medical care have typically shown beneficial outcomes. The effectiveness of providing alcohol screening and brief counseling in primary care is supported by a robust evidence base, and a growing literature is showing its benefits as a first tool in managing chronic health conditions that may arise from, or be exacerbated by, alcohol use. Primary care-based alcohol use disorder case management involving pharmacotherapy and psychosocial support has been found to increase engagement in specialty substance use disorder treatment and to decrease heavy drinking.

A fundamental concept in care coordination between the healthcare, substance use disorder treatment, and mental health systems is that there should be "no wrong door." This means that no matter wherein the healthcare system the need for substance use disorder treatment is identified the patient will be effectively linked with appropriate services.

Effectiveness of Alcohol Screening And Brief Interventions In Medical Settings

Alcohol is strongly linked to the leading causes of adolescent and adult mortality and health problems, making medical settings such as primary care and emergency departments important venues for addressing alcohol use. Extensive research evidence supports the effectiveness of alcohol screening and brief interventions (SBIs) in medical settings, but this valuable strategy remains underused, with medical staff citing lack of time and training as major implementation barriers. Technology-based tools may offer a way to improve efficiency and quality of SBI delivery in such settings. The small but growing evidence base generally shows strong feasibility and acceptability of technology-based SBI in medical settings. However, evidence for effectiveness in changing alcohol use is limited in this young field.

Alcohol-related screening and brief interventions (SBIs) in medical settings have the potential to transform the treatment of alcohol misuse and prevent considerable alcohol-related harm. Rapid screening and assessment tools allow healthcare providers to quickly assess the extent of patients' alcohol use, identify those with problematic use, provide them with an immediate brief intervention, and refer patients with more severe alcohol use disorders to a substance abuse specialist when available. SBIs have proven effective for detecting potential alcohol problems and reducing the severity of problems in a wide range of populations and settings—so much so that agencies focused on preventing and treating alcohol use, including the U.S. Preventive Services Task Force (USPSTF), the National Institute on Alcohol Abuse and Alcoholism (NIAAA), and the Substance Abuse and Mental Health Services Administration (SAMHSA), recommend that primary care and other medical settings expand their SBI use for patients ages 18 years and older. Although the USPSTF cited insufficient evidence to recommend SBIs for adolescents, recognition of and evidence for the potential utility of SBIs for adolescents have been building in recent years, leading the American Academy of Pediatrics to recommend that all pediatricians use SBIs in their practices as part of routine care.

Despite the push for using SBIs in medical settings, they remain underused. In a recent national survey of U.S. adults, only one in six (15.7%) respondents reported discussing alcohol use with a health professional in the past year, with state-specific estimates ranging from 8.7–25.5 percent. The percentage was higher (34.9%), but still inadequate, among those with 10 or more binge-drinking episodes in the past month. An often-cited barrier to SBI implementation is lack of time. Computer-facilitated SBI delivery may offer a solution for busy medical settings, allowing more widespread implementation.

Technology-Based SBIs

Technology-based SBIs could help increase the frequency and quality of SBI use in medical settings by enhancing efficiency and standardizing implementation. In terms of screening, touchscreen devices or standalone computers with Internet connections can allow patients to enter information in the waiting room prior to an appointment. Programs automatically score the screening results that staff can print or electronically transmit to practitioners. This reduces clinician time needed for administering and scoring a questionnaire during the visit. In addition, programs can be loaded with validated measures that improve the quality of screening and can automatically select appropriate questions according to the patient's age and previous responses. Patients also may be more willing to disclose sensitive information to a computer than to a person, and integration of computerized screening results with electronic health records may boost screening and documentation rates.

Similarly, computer-facilitated brief intervention delivery has the potential advantages of greater standardization, lower cost, and greater ease of implementation compared with face-to-face delivery. As with screening, programs can automatically tailor intervention content to individual patients. Interventions vary based on the program, but, as with face-to-face SBIs, computer-based SBI tools often follow screening with personalized feedback that includes a summary of patients' consumption patterns and risk status, a comparison of their consumption with recommended limits, estimated blood alcohol concentrations for their heaviest drinking occasion in the reported time frame, and a comparison between their consumption and consumption reported by others in their peer group. More extensive programs may incorporate intervention strategies based on principles of evidence-based face-to-face treatments, such as motivational interviewing and cognitive-behavioral therapy (CBT).

Using technology for SBIs in medical settings may be especially valuable for reaching young people who are highly engaged with technology and nearly universal access to computers, cell phones, and the Internet. Indeed, using technology-facilitated alcohol SBIs in medical settings to reach adolescents may be a powerful mechanism to reduce medical costs and gain productive years of life, since alcohol use disorders are strongly linked to the leading causes of adolescent and adult mortality, including motor-vehicle crashes and suicide.

This high level of online engagement has fueled a surge of interest in the potential of standalone web-based SBI programs to address problematic alcohol use, particularly among college students. These programs provide a means to inexpensively reach people less likely to access traditional health services. The lack of interpersonal contact with these programs may contribute to lower participation rates and adherence over time. In addition, alcohol use is strongly linked to many physical and mental health problems, such as cancer, cirrhosis, and depression. Therefore, standalone programs are unlikely to obviate the need for SBIs in medical settings.

SBIs for Pregnant Women

Previous studies have shown the benefits of SBIs for addressing alcohol and drug use in pregnant women. However, only one published randomized-controlled trial has examined a computerized SBI for alcohol use during pregnancy. This early-stage randomized controlled trial in an urban prenatal care clinic included a convenience sample of 50 pregnant women that either screened positive on the T-ACE alcohol screening tool or had drinking patterns before pregnancy that exceeded National Institute on Alcohol Abuse and Alcoholism (NIAAA) drinking limits for women. Participants randomly completed either the computerized SBI or an unrelated questionnaire. Those receiving the intervention gave it high marks for ease of use, likability, and respectfulness. Both intervention and control groups showed significant and equivalent reductions in drinking at the 1-month follow-up, although babies born to women in the intervention group had higher newborn birth weights.

More recently, Pollick and colleagues found high acceptability of, and user satisfaction with, a computerized brief intervention for alcohol use in pregnancy (C-BIAP) in a qualitative pilot study among 18 pregnant African American women. Given the paucity of studies in this population, and that alcohol use in pregnant and parenting women additionally can cause secondary lifelong harm to the fetus or infant, more studies are critically needed to elucidate the utility of computerized strategies to enhance the efficient and effective implementation of alcohol SBIs in prenatal and antenatal clinics.

SBI in Trauma/Emergency Rooms

Over 20,000 (7.6 million per year) people enter emergency departments everyday for alcohol-related injuries and illnesses. Alcohol dependence is not the only problem facing many Americans. For every one person that is dependent on alcohol, six or more are at-risk or have already experienced problems as a result of their use. Approximately 40 percent of the patients admitted to trauma centers have a positive BAC. If drug use is included, approximately 60 percent of patients seen in trauma centers are under the influence of alcohol or drugs when admitted. Also, 26 percent of patients that have a negative toxicology screen have screened positive for alcohol or other drug misuse, abuse or dependence. McGlynn and her colleagues found that only 15.5 percent of traumatically injured inpatients had any medical record indication that substance use had been assessed. They found that 7 percent are intoxicated and another 20 percent screen positive for alcohol misuse or abuse. Because of the role alcohol plays in contributing to illness, injury and even death, it is important to have protocols in place to take advantage of a "teachable moment" by implementing screening and brief intervention as part of routine care.

The American College of Surgeons' Committee on Trauma (ACS-COT) requires that Level I and Level II trauma centers have a mechanism to identify problem drinkers and that Level I centers have the capability to provide brief interventions for screen-positive patients. New CPT codes created by the American Medical Association (AMA) allow Medicare and commercial insurers to reimburse physicians for alcohol and drug screening and intervention. Thus, the initiative to have SBIRT a common practice in trauma centers is not only mandated, but also can now be reimbursed.

Chapter 55

Treatment Options for Alcohol Use Disorders

When Is It Time for Treatment?

Alcohol-related problems—which result from drinking too much, too fast, or too often—are among the most significant public health issues in the United States. Many people struggle with controlling their drinking at some time in their lives. Approximately 17 million adults ages 18 and older have an alcohol use disorder (AUD) and 1 in 10 children live in a home with a parent who has a drinking problem.

Does Treatment Work?

The good news is that no matter how severe the problem may seem, most people with an alcohol use disorder can benefit from some form of treatment. Research shows that about one-third of people who are treated for alcohol problems have no further symptoms 1-year later. Many others substantially reduce their drinking and report fewer alcohol-related problems.

This chapter includes text excerpted from "Treatment for Alcohol Problems: Finding and Getting Help," National Institute on Alcohol Abuse and Alcoholism (NIAAA), 2014. Reviewed April 2018.

Signs of an Alcohol Problem

Alcohol use disorder (AUD) is a medical condition that doctors diagnose when a patient's drinking causes distress or harm. The condition can range from mild to severe and is diagnosed when a patient answers "yes" to two or more of the following questions.

In the past year, have you:

- Had times when you ended up drinking more, or longer than you intended?
- More than once wanted to cut down or stop drinking, or tried to, but couldn't?
- Spent a lot of time drinking? Or being sick or getting over the aftereffects?
- Experienced craving—a strong need, or urge, to drink?
- Found that drinking—or being sick from drinking—often interfered with taking care of your home or family? Or caused job troubles? Or school problems?
- Continued to drink even though it was causing trouble with your family or friends?
- Given up or cut back on activities that were important or interesting to you, or gave you pleasure, in order to drink?
- More than once gotten into situations while or after drinking that increased your chances of getting hurt (such as driving, swimming, using machinery, walking in a dangerous area, or having unsafe sex)?
- Continued to drink even though it was making you feel depressed or anxious or adding to another health problem? Or after having had a memory blackout?
- Had to drink much more than you once did to get the effect you want? Or found that your usual number of drinks had much less effect than before?
- Found that when the effects of alcohol were wearing off, you had withdrawal symptoms, such as trouble sleeping, shakiness, irritability, anxiety, depression, restlessness, nausea, or sweating? Or sensed things that were not there?

If you have any of these symptoms, your drinking may already be a cause for concern. The more symptoms you have, the more urgent the need for change. A health professional can conduct a formal assessment of your symptoms to see if an alcohol use disorder is present. For an online assessment of your drinking pattern, go to RethinkingDrinking.niaaa.nih.gov.

Options for Treatment

When asked how alcohol problems are treated, people commonly think of 12-step programs or 28-day inpatient rehab but may have difficulty naming other options. In fact, there are a variety of treatment methods currently available, thanks to significant advances in the field over the past 60 years. Ultimately, there is no one-size-fits-all solution, and what may work for one person may not be a good fit for someone else. Simply understanding the different options can be an important first step.

Types of Treatment

Behavioral Treatments

Behavioral treatments are aimed at changing drinking behavior through counseling. They are led by health professionals and supported by studies showing they can be beneficial.

Medications

Three medications are currently approved in the United States to help people stop or reduce their drinking and prevent relapse. They are prescribed by a primary care physician or other health professional and may be used alone or in combination with counseling.

Mutual-Support Groups

Alcoholics Anonymous (AA) and other 12-step programs provide peer support for people quitting or cutting back on their drinking. Combined with treatment led by health professionals, mutual-support groups can offer a valuably added layer of support. Due to the anonymous nature of mutual-support groups, it is difficult for researchers to determine their success rates compared with those led by health professionals.

Starting with a Primary Care Doctor

For anyone thinking about treatment, talking to a primary care physician is an important first step—he or she can be a good source for treatment referrals and medications. A primary care physician can also:

- Evaluate whether a patient's drinking pattern is risky
- Help craft a treatment plan
- Evaluate overall health
- Assess if medications for alcohol may be appropriate

Treatments Led by Health Professionals

Medications

Some are surprised to learn that there are medications on the market approved to treat alcohol dependence. The newer types of these medications work by offsetting changes in the brain caused by alcoholism. All approved medications are nonaddictive and can be used alone or in combination with other forms of treatment.

Behavioral Treatments

Also known as alcohol counseling, behavioral treatments involve working with a health professional to identify and help change the behaviors that lead to heavy drinking. Behavioral treatments share certain features, which can include:

- Developing the skills needed to stop or reduce drinking
- Helping to build a strong social support system
- Working to set reachable goals
- Coping with or avoiding the triggers that might cause the relapse

Types of Behavioral Treatments

- Cognitive-behavioral therapy (CBT) can take place one-on-one with a therapist or in small groups. This form of therapy is focused on identifying the feelings and situations (called "cues") that lead to heavy drinking and managing stress that can lead to relapse. The goal is to change the thought processes that lead to excessive drinking and to develop the skills necessary to cope with everyday situations that might trigger problem drinking.

- Motivational enhancement therapy (MET) is conducted over a short period of time to build and strengthen motivation to change drinking behavior. The therapy focuses on identifying the pros and cons of seeking treatment, forming a plan for making changes in one's drinking, building confidence, and developing the skills needed to stick to the plan.
- Marital and family counseling incorporates spouses and other family members in the treatment process and can play an important role in repairing and improving family relationships. Studies show that strong family support through family therapy increases the chances of maintaining abstinence (stopping drinking), compared with patients undergoing individual counseling.
- Brief interventions are short, one-on-one or small-group counseling sessions that are time limited. The counselor provides information about the individual's drinking pattern and potential risks. After receiving personalized feedback, the counselor will work with the client to set goals and provide ideas for helping to make a change.

Ultimately, choosing to get treatment may be more important than the approach used, as long as the approach avoids heavy confrontation and incorporates empathy, motivational support, and a focus on changing drinking behavior.

What FDA-Approved Medications Are Available?

Certain medications have been shown to effectively help people stop or reduce their drinking and avoid relapse.

Medications

The U.S. Food and Drug Administration (FDA) has approved three medications for treating alcohol dependence, and others are being tested to determine if they are effective.

- Naltrexone can help people reduce heavy drinking
- Acamprosate makes it easier to maintain abstinence
- Disulfiram blocks the breakdown (metabolism) of alcohol by the body, causing unpleasant symptoms such as nausea and flushing of the skin. Those unpleasant effects can help some people avoid drinking while taking disulfiram.

It is important to remember that not all people will respond to medications, but for a subset of individuals, they can be an important tool in overcoming alcohol dependence. Scientists are working to develop a larger menu of pharmaceutical treatments that could be tailored to individual needs. As more medications become available, people may be able to try multiple medications to find which they respond to best.

"Isn't Taking Medications Just Trading One Addiction for Another?"

This is not an uncommon concern, but the short answer is "no." All medications approved for treating alcohol dependence are nonaddictive. These medicines are designed to help manage a chronic disease, just as someone might take drugs to keep their asthma or diabetes in check.

Looking Ahead: The Future of Treatment

Progress continues to be made as researchers seek out new and better treatments for alcohol problems. By studying the underlying causes of alcoholism in the brain and body, National Institute on Alcohol Abuse and Alcoholism (NIAAA) is working to identify key cellular or molecular structures—called "targets"—that could lead to the development of new medications.

Personalized Medicine

Ideally, health professionals would be able to identify which alcoholism treatment is most effective for each person. NIAAA and other organizations are conducting research to identify genes and other factors that can predict how well someone will respond to a particular treatment. These advances could optimize how treatment decisions are made in the future.

NIAAA Research—Leading to Future Breakthroughs

Certain medications already approved for other uses have shown promise for treating alcohol dependence and problem drinking:

- The anti-smoking drug varenicline (marketed under the name Chantix) significantly reduced alcohol consumption and craving among people with alcoholism.
- Gabapentin, a medication used to treat pain conditions and epilepsy, was shown to increase abstinence and reduce heavy

drinking. Those taking the medication also reported fewer alcohol cravings and improved mood and sleep.

- The anti-epileptic medication topiramate was shown to help people curb problem drinking, particularly among those with a certain genetic makeup that appears to be linked to the treatment's effectiveness.

Tips for Selecting Treatment

Professionals in the alcohol treatment field offer advice on what to consider when choosing a treatment program. Overall, gather as much information as you can about the program or provider before making a decision on treatment. If you know someone who has first-hand knowledge of the program, it may help to ask about his or her personal experience. Here are some questions you can ask that may help guide your choice:

- **What kind of treatment does the program or provider offer?**

  It is important to gauge if the facility provides all the currently available methods or relies on one approach. You may want to learn if the program or provider offers medication and if mental health issues are addressed together with addiction treatment.

- **Is treatment tailored to the individual?**

  Matching the right therapy to the individual is important to its success. No single treatment will benefit everyone. It may also be helpful to determine whether treatment will be adapted to meet changing needs as they arise.

- **What is expected of the patient?**

  You will want to understand what will be asked of you in order to decide what treatment best suits your needs.

- **Is treatment success measured?**

  By assessing whether and how the program or provider measures success, you may be able to better compare your options.

- **How does the program or provider handle relapse?**

  Relapse is common and you will want to know how it is addressed. For more information on relapse, see Relapse Is Part of the Process.

When seeking professional help, it is important you feel respected and understood and that you have a feeling of trust that this person, group, or organization can help you. Remember, though, that relationships with doctors, therapists, and other health professionals can take time to develop.

Additional Considerations

Treatment Setting—Inpatient or Outpatient?

In addition to choosing the type of treatment that's best for you, you'll also have to decide if that treatment is inpatient (you would stay at a facility) or outpatient (you stay in your home during treatment). Inpatient facilities tend to be more intensive and costly. Your healthcare provider can help you evaluate the pros and cons of each.

Cost May Be a Factor When Selecting a Treatment Approach

Evaluate the coverage in your health insurance plan to determine how much of the costs your insurance will cover and how much you will have to pay. Ask different programs if they offer sliding scale fees—some programs may offer lower prices or payment plans for individuals without health insurance.

An Ongoing Process

Overcoming an alcohol use disorder is an ongoing process, one which can include setbacks.

The Importance of Persistence

Because an alcohol use disorder can be a chronic relapsing disease, persistence is key. It is rare that someone would go to treatment once and then never drink again. More often, people must repeatedly try to quit or cut back, experience recurrences, learn from them, and then keep trying. For many, continued follow-up with a treatment provider is critical to overcoming problem drinking.

Relapse Is Part of the Process

Relapse is common among people who overcome alcohol problems. People with drinking problems are most likely to relapse during periods of stress or when exposed to people or places associated with past drinking. Just as some people with diabetes or asthma may have flare-ups of their disease, a relapse to drinking can be seen as a temporary set-back to full recovery and not a complete failure. Seeking professional help can prevent relapse—behavioral therapies can help people develop skills to avoid and overcome triggers, such as stress, that might lead to drinking. Most people benefit from regular checkups with a treatment provider. Medications also can deter drinking during times when individuals may be at greater risk of relapse (e.g., divorce, a death of a family member).

Mental Health Issues and Alcohol Use Disorder

Depression and anxiety often go hand in hand with heavy drinking. Studies show that people who are alcohol dependent are 2–3 times as likely to suffer from major depression or anxiety over their lifetime. When addressing drinking problems, it's important to also seek treatment for any accompanying medical and mental health issues.

Advice for Friends and Family Members

Caring for a person who has problems with alcohol can be very stressful. It is important that as you try to help your loved one, you find a way to take care of yourself as well. It may help to seek support from others, including friends, family, community, and support groups. If you are developing your own symptoms of depression or anxiety, think about seeking professional help for yourself. Remember that your loved one is ultimately responsible for managing his or her illness.

However, your participation can make a big difference. Based on clinical experience, many health providers believe that support from friends and family members is important in overcoming alcohol problems. But friends and family may feel unsure about how best to provide the support needed.

Remember that changing deep habits is hard, takes time, and requires repeated efforts. We usually experience failures along the way, learn from them, and then keep going. Alcohol use disorders are no different. Try to be patient with your loved one. Overcoming this disorder is not easy or quick.

Pay attention to your loved one when he or she is doing better or simply making an effort. Too often we are so angry or discouraged that we take it for granted when things are going better. A word of appreciation or acknowledgment of a success can go a long way.

Chapter 56

Alcohol Treatment: Need, Utilization, and Barriers

Treatment techniques and tools to address alcohol use disorders (AUDs) have multiplied over the last 30 years, moving beyond models based on Alcoholics Anonymous (AA) and its offshoot, the Minnesota Model. Care providers now can prescribe medications to aid people as they work to reduce their drinking. If a traditional mutual-help group model of care does not appeal to a patient, he or she has other behavioral therapy options. And web-based approaches provide access to therapy 24 hours a day, 7 days a week.

Despite these developments, however, the majority of people with alcohol use disorders (AUDs) in the United States go untreated. According to data from National Institute on Alcohol Abuse and Alcoholism (NIAAA) 2001–2002 National Epidemiologic Survey on Alcohol and Related Conditions (NESARC), only 14.6 percent of people with alcohol abuse or dependence receive treatment. Another survey of people who experienced the onset of alcohol dependence a year before the study found that only 25 percent ever received treatment. Though some people with AUDs do actually recover on their own without formal treatment, some achieve partial remission, and some cycle in and out of alcohol problems throughout their lives, novel approaches and

---

This chapter includes text excerpted from "Exploring Treatment Options for Alcohol Use Disorders," National Institute on Alcohol Abuse and Alcoholism (NIAAA), September 12, 2011. Reviewed April 2018.

further access to treatment could play an important role in helping people to reduce their drinking.

This picture of a largely untreated population of patients has prompted researchers to explore better ways of engaging people who might not have considered treatment as an option for addressing their problems with alcohol. Improving diagnosis is one area under exploration, including screening for alcohol abuse and alcoholism and providing brief interventions in a variety of settings, such as primary care clinics and emergency departments. Scientists are examining the effectiveness of medications for treating patients and preventing relapse to drinking. Research also suggests that a large proportion of people with co-occurring psychological or medical conditions remain underserved by existing treatment systems; greater coordination of care might improve responses to AUD treatment for this group.

Broadening the Reach of Treatment

Although medications and behavioral therapies traditionally have been developed and studied within specialty alcoholism treatment settings, that is beginning to change. Studies show that effective treatment can be administered in a variety of settings and should be considered a routine component of healthcare. As physicians gain experience and comfort with alcohol treatment options, they will be more likely to identify and help people with AUDs and to help them better manage their drinking throughout their lives.

Medications

Primary care providers are accustomed to prescribing medications for a number of illnesses, but generally are unfamiliar with medicines to treat alcohol problems. Medicines approved by the U.S. Food and Drug Administration (FDA) to treat alcohol dependence include disulfiram (Antabuse®), oral naltrexone, extended-release naltrexone (Vivitrol®), and acamprosate (Campral®). Medications marketed for other illnesses also have shown efficacy in treating AUDs, such as topiramate, which is approved to treat epilepsy and migraines.

New compounds under study also are showing promise. For example, some compounds targeting certain brain systems are being used for alcohol withdrawal and for relapse prevention. Also, researchers are studying medicines approved for smoking cessation for their impact on heavy drinking.

Positive results are found when medications are combined with behavioral treatment. Now scientists are assessing the appropriate level of counseling to use in conjunction with medication and the best methods to enhance patients' medication adherence. Such approaches include establishing a plan for adhering to the medication, solving any problems that appear, and teaching strategies for self-change. Maintaining contact with patients and emphasizing adherence appear to be key to successful treatment with medications, and these aspects are especially well suited to primary care settings where doctors maintain ongoing relationships with their patients.

Behavioral Therapies

Medications are one tool to stop or reduce drinking, but successful long-term recovery centers on changing a person's behaviors and expectations about alcohol. Many treatment approaches, including mutual-help groups like Alcoholics Anonymous (AA), focus on behavioral principles such as reinforcement and behavior modeling (for instance, these groups provide sponsors who guide participants through the program) to help patients make those changes. Since the mid-1980s, therapies have become available that combine behavioral principles of reinforcement and punishment with various therapeutic techniques designed to encourage healthy behavior change. Many of these therapies can be adapted for use outside specialty alcoholism treatment settings, such as primary care, emergency departments, community centers, and schools.

Behavioral therapies are especially effective in encouraging self-change—or the ability of some people to quit drinking on their own. These approaches use goal setting, self-monitoring of drinking, analysis of drinking situations, and learning alternate coping skills. Couples and family therapies analyze drinking behaviors and aim to improve relationship factors, such as improving communication, avoiding conflicts, and learning to solve problems that might lead to drinking.

Care providers can offer these treatments not only in different settings but in varying doses. For example, brief interventions enable doctors to help patients in identifying high-risk situations when they might use alcohol and discuss skills for coping with those situations without drinking. Such therapies can be delivered in a physician's office in an hour or less. One study determined that brief physician advice delivered across two doctor visits and two follow-up phone calls resulted in reduced alcohol use and binge drinking for up to 4 years after the intervention.

With such a variety of approaches available now, scientists are examining whether certain patient characteristics predict better responses to different approaches. Although no such patterns have yet emerged from research, core components of effective therapies have been identified that may prove useful in helping a care provider decide which treatment is best for a particular person. These components include enhancing social support, working with the patient to develop goals and to provide ideas for obtaining those goals, modeling and rewarding good behavior, and reviewing ways to cope with the triggers that lead to drinking. Matching a patient to therapies that address an area where he or she shows the greatest need may prove most effective.

Screening

A potentially powerful way to improve problem drinkers' access to treatment is to make routine screening part of primary care. Asking the single question of how often the patient exceeded the daily maximum drinking limits in the prior year (i.e., 4 drinks for men, 3 drinks for women) can screen effectively for unhealthy alcohol use. A simple question can then become the opportune moment for a brief intervention.

Mutual-Help Groups (MHGs)

Despite developments in medications and behavioral therapies, MHGs remain the most commonly sought source of help for AUDs in the United States. MHGs are groups of two or more people who share a problem and come together to provide problem-specific help and support to one another. Although AA has the largest following, groups catering to populations with different demographics and preferences (e.g., women and younger people) also can be found.

One reason for the popularity of MHGs may be their inherent flexibility and responsiveness. People can attend MHGs as frequently and for as long as they want without insurance and without divulging personal information. Often, people can attend MHGs at convenient times, like evenings and weekends, when they are at higher risk of a relapse to drinking. MHGs also are more cost-effective than formal treatment. For example, patients can attend AA at no cost, which translates into about 45 percent lower overall treatment costs than costs for patients in outpatient care while achieving similar outcomes.

Although high-quality clinical trials assessing MHGs are difficult because of their voluntary and anonymous nature, studies that follow drinkers during and after treatment have shown that MHGs compare well with more formal treatment. AA participants in a 16-year study did as well in achieving abstinence at the 8-year mark as those in formal treatment (approaching 50%), and a group that participated in both AA and formal treatment performed better than formal treatment alone at years 1 and 3. Other studies show that people involved in MHGs had more friend support resources than those in outpatient programs. Indeed, some scientists believe the improvement in participants' social network and the support they receive for abstinence may explain the success of MHGs. Also, people can have access to this support for as long as they need it.

Thus, MHGs remain a staple treatment tool and provide a good alternative for physicians to consider when counseling patients. One method doctors use to encourage patients to try MHGs, called twelve-step facilitation (TSF) therapy, dispels myths and encourages patients to attend meetings. Studies of TSF, show that if physicians actively refer their patients to MHGs by making arrangements for them to attend meetings or setting up introductions to group members, patients do become more involved. Patients who receive TSF also have shown higher rates of continuous abstinence than those receiving some other behavioral therapies.

Emerging Technologies

From social networking sites and news outlets to online learning, the Internet is changing the way people communicate and obtain information. Internet and computer-based technologies are infiltrating many levels of AUD care, from screening to recovery. Early evidence suggests that they improve access to services and promote treatment effectiveness.

The Internet gives patients the option of receiving treatment 24 hours a day, 7 days a week. It enables a patient in a rural setting to access much of the same care as those in urban settings, provided he or she has Internet access. Using web-based therapy, patients can compare their drinking patterns with those of people like them or take a test that indicates the severity of their drinking concerns. These tools are cost-effective ways of engaging people in treatment. For those who want to reduce their drinking, Internet tools can provide drinking diaries, goal-setting exercises, and relapse-prevention techniques. These may prove useful for patients most interested in self-help. While the tools have most often been studied under circumstances of face-to-face contact with a care provider, some studies of online versions of the tools suggest that people who use them do reduce their drinking.

In addition to improving the accessibility of screening and other tools, emerging technologies also are being used to help clinicians maintain better contact with their patients through the use of mobile phone-based counseling and online counseling. Here, monitoring tools such as interactive voice response programs can collect information from patients and help caregivers keep track of patients' progress and signal the potential need for intervention.

One new program for helping patients with long-term management of their own AUDs takes advantage of the capabilities of smartphones. Known as the Alcohol–Comprehensive Health Enhancement Support System (A-CHESS), the program uses smartphones to provide patients with information, adherence strategies, decision-making tools, reminders, and social support services in easy-to-use formats. The phone application is customizable to focus on particular patients' needs and enhances their autonomy by providing a tool that provides resources patients can select when needed.

Reaching out to Potential Patients

Because such a high proportion of people with unhealthy alcohol use—from risk drinking and abuse to dependence—go untreated, it may be advantageous to expand treatment to include other settings, such as primary care offices, emergency departments, and even community centers. Involving healthcare providers such as psychiatrists, psychologists, and social workers also may help. Even still, these measures may not be enough. Studies suggest that the majority of those with alcohol problems recognize the problem as much as a decade before they seek treatment, which implies there may be an opportunity for reaching patients earlier. Understanding the factors that influence people's decisions to seek care and learning how to engage them will direct this effort.

Characteristics of Treatment Seeking

Only 15–25 percent of people with drinking problems seek help from doctors, treatment programs, or MHGs. Many do not use treatment services until they are forced to do so by a court, a family member, or an employer. People in alcohol treatment, then, often have the most serious problems, such as comorbid health, mental health, and psychosocial problems. However, studies also show that 66–75 percent of risky drinkers do make positive changes, including reaching abstinence or stable moderation, on their own. People who resolve drinking problems on their own more commonly become moderate drinkers than those who receive treatment.

Research suggests that a person's denial that he or she has a drinking problem is not a primary reason people do not seek treatment. One possible reason people do not seek treatment earlier is that both alcohol problems and treatment remain stigmatized in society. Other barriers to treatment include a belief that the problem is not serious enough to warrant treatment. People also report that a lack of insurance, worries about privacy, and problems making or keeping appointments keep them from treatment.

The consequences of heavy drinking—particularly social consequences—do drive people to seek help. Positive change and treatment-seeking are more likely among people whose social networks encourage them to get help and discourage heavy drinking, while help-seeking is likely among those whose networks accept heavy drinking.

Strategies for Promoting Treatment Seeking

To remove barriers to treatment, programs are starting to view people with AUDs and their social networks as consumers of services who can choose among many available alternatives. Programs are making services more user-friendly and attractive by providing convenient appointments, parking, and child care. They also can offer treatment goals that do not necessarily require abstinence in the near term but allow for more gradual approaches to change.

Some programs have gone a step further, offering "treatment on demand." Rather than working to change a person's motivations directly, these programs simply promote rapid treatment entry as soon as an individual's motivation shifts in favor of change. Another approach, the Community Reinforcement and Family Training (CRAFT) model, works to change the patient's environment to make a nonsubstance-using lifestyle more rewarding than one focused on drinking. In the CRAFT model, concerned significant others (CSOs) are the focus of the therapy instead of the substance abusers. CSOs receive training to change their interactions with the substance-using person, reducing their enabling behaviors and improving their communication strategies.

Keeping Patients in Recovery

Unfortunately, even after entering treatment, many patients drop out—either during the initial phases or later during follow-up care. Some of the same concerns that prevent people from entering treatment make them especially reluctant to continue with care. Generally, patients in AUD treatment begin with intensive outpatient treatment of two to three sessions per week lasting between 30 and 60 days, followed by a continuing care phase when patients are encouraged to attend self-help meetings. Yet, alcohol problems typically are chronic, involving cycles of abstinence, relapse, and treatment. This has led researchers to design approaches that provide a continuum of care, blurring the traditional distinction between intensive initial phases and followup with MHGs or individual therapy. That research shows that interventions with a longer duration (i.e., at least 12 months) or in which patients are actively engaged through telephone calls, home visits, or by involving a patient's support network—such as family, friends, and employers—have the most success. Researchers also are investigating ways to make remaining active in treatment more appealing, including the use of incentives—such as providing monetary rewards or support with housing, employment, or alcohol-free social activities—to keep patients from dropping out of treatment. Also, programs can take into account patients' preferences for the type and intensity of their treatment and, importantly, be able to detect and adapt to each patient's changing likelihood of relapse. As noted above, smartphones and the Internet can play a role in identifying fluctuations in a patient's needs.

Treating Patients with Co-Occurring Disorders

Although engaging and keeping people with AUDs in treatment are essential areas for improvement in service delivery, another dimension that can add significantly to the success of treatment is improving care for those with co-occurring psychological or medical disorders (CODs). More than half (51.4%) of those with a lifetime alcohol or other drug disorder also have a co-occurring mental health disorder. In addition, research suggests that people with alcohol or other drug problems have a higher prevalence of general health problems, and in particular diseases such as human immunodeficiency virus (HIV), hepatitis B and C, viruses, asthma, hypertension, and others. All this complicates treatment and frequently contributes to poorer outcomes. Better integration of care is key. Researchers have proposed several ways to approach COD treatment. For example, is it better for separate providers to treat one disorder at a time? Or is it more advantageous for a single clinician to treat both disorders simultaneously? Unfortunately, to date, few studies have yet been able to make recommendations about the effectiveness of one strategy versus another.

What is clear is that primary care settings offer a promising environment for incorporating both AUD and mental health services, as this is where the services would be less stigmatized and potentially reach more patients. Considering the reviews and recommendations from groups such as the Institute of Medicine, which reported on the state of integrated care, trends in care will continue to shift for those with CODs.

Considering Financing

Methods of reimbursement, such as fee-for-service versus fixed-budget, create incentives that influence the accessibility, quantity, and quality of care—sometimes negatively. Patients cite lack of insurance coverage as a reason they do not enter AUD treatment. Additionally, insurance reimbursement often does not pay for extended follow-up care. The setting for treatment services and the amount of services a patient can receive largely depend on what insurance companies and public payers such as States are willing to finance. One thing, however, that influences payers is new legislation; several recent policy changes are likely to affect AUD treatment services.

Conclusion

People with AUDs differ in their degree of severity, in their co-occurring conditions, and in the social systems that support either their recovery or their continued abusive drinking. In recognizing this, the field is seeking ways to better tailor care and to make that care responsive to a patient's changing needs. Emerging technologies likely will make these goals easier and perhaps more cost-effective. Simultaneously, changes in policies and insurance coverage can help create new, more flexible systems that reflect the latest research findings. Also, it will be important to embrace the existing treatment framework—such as medications, behavioral therapies, and mutual help groups—that have been shown to have a significant impact on many people's efforts to change their drinking.

Chapter 57

Detoxification: One Part of Alcohol Abuse Treatment

History of Detoxification Services

Prior to the 1970s, public intoxication was treated as a criminal offense. People arrested for it were held in the "drunk tanks" of local jails where they underwent withdrawal with little or no medical intervention. Shifts in the medical field, in perceptions of addiction, and in social policy changed the way that people with dependency on drugs, including alcohol, were viewed and treated. Two notable events were particularly instrumental in changing attitudes. In 1958, the American Medical Association (AMA) took the official position that alcoholism is a disease. This declaration suggested that alcoholism was a medical problem requiring medical intervention. In 1971, the National Conference of Commissioners on Uniform State Laws adopted the Uniform Alcoholism and Intoxication Treatment Act, which recommended that "alcoholics not be subjected to criminal prosecution because of their consumption of alcoholic beverages but rather should be afforded a continuum of treatment in order that they may lead normal lives as productive members of society." While this recommendation did not carry the weight of law, it made a major change in the legal implications of

---

This chapter includes text excerpted from "Detoxification and Substance Abuse Treatment," Substance Abuse and Mental Health Services Administration (SAMHSA), May 26, 2006. Reviewed April 2018.

addiction. With these changes came more humane treatment of people with addictions.

Several methods of detoxification have evolved that reflect a more humanitarian view of people with substance use disorders. In the "medical model," detoxification is characterized by the use of physician and nursing staff and the administration of medication to assist people through withdrawal safely. The "social model" rejects the use of medication and the need for routine medical care, relying instead on a supportive nonhospital environment to ease the passage through withdrawal. At present, it is rare to find a "pure" detoxification model. For example, some social model programs use medication to ease withdrawal but generally employ nonmedical staff to monitor withdrawal and conduct triage (i.e., sorting patients according to the severity of their disorders). Likewise, medical programs generally have some components to address social/personal aspects of addiction.

Just as the treatment and the conceptualization of addiction have changed, so too have the patterns of substance use and the accompanying detoxification needs. The popularity of cocaine, heroin, and other substances has led to the need for different kinds of detoxification services. At the same time, public health officials have increased investments in detoxification services and substance abuse treatment, especially after 1985, as a means to inhibit the spread of human immunodeficiency virus (HIV) infection and acquired immunodeficiency syndrome (AIDS) among people who inject drugs. More recently, people with substance use disorders are more likely to abuse more than one drug simultaneously (i.e., polydrug abuse). The AMA continues to maintain its position that substance dependence is a disease, and it encourages physicians and other clinicians, health organizations, and policymakers to base all their activities on this premise. As treatment regimens have become more sophisticated and polydrug abuse more common, detoxification has evolved into a compassionate science.

Definition of Detoxification

Detoxification is a set of interventions aimed at managing acute intoxication and withdrawal. It denotes a clearing of toxins from the body of the patient who is acutely intoxicated and/or dependent on substances of abuse. Detoxification seeks to minimize the physical harm caused by the abuse of substances. The Washington Circle Group (WCG), a body of experts organized to improve the quality and effectiveness of substance abuse prevention and treatment, defines detoxification as "a medical intervention that manages an individual safely through the process of acute withdrawal. The WCG makes an important distinction, however, in noting that "a detoxification program is not designed to resolve the longstanding psychological, social, and behavioral problems associated with alcohol and drug abuse."

Detoxification is generally accepted as a broad process with three essential components that may take place concurrently or as a series of steps:

- **Evaluation** entails testing for the presence of substances of abuse in the bloodstream, measuring their concentration, and screening for co-occurring mental and physical conditions. Evaluation also includes a comprehensive assessment of the patient's medical and psychological conditions and social situation to help determine the appropriate level of treatment following detoxification. Essentially, the evaluation serves as the basis for the initial substance abuse treatment plan once the patient has been withdrawn successfully.
- **Stabilization** includes the medical and psychosocial processes of assisting the patient through acute intoxication and withdrawal to the attainment of a medically stable, fully supported, substance-free state. This often is done with the assistance of medications, though in some approaches to detoxification no medication is used. Stabilization includes familiarizing patients with what to expect in the treatment milieu and their role in treatment and recovery. During this time practitioners also seek the involvement of the patient's family, employers, and other significant people when appropriate and with release of confidentiality.
- **Fostering the patient's entry into treatment** involves preparing the patient for entry into substance abuse treatment by stressing the importance of following through with the complete substance abuse treatment continuum of care. For patients who have demonstrated a pattern of completing detoxification services and then failing to engage in substance abuse treatment, a written treatment contract may encourage entrance into a continuum of substance abuse treatment and care. This contract, which is not legally binding, is voluntarily signed by patients when they are stable enough to do so at the beginning of treatment. In it, the patient agrees to participate in a continuing care plan, with details and contacts established prior to the completion of detoxification. All three components (evaluation,

stabilization, and fostering a patient's entry into treatment) involve treating the patient with compassion and understanding. Patients undergoing detoxification need to know that someone cares about them, respects them as individuals, and has hope for their future. Actions taken during detoxification will demonstrate to the patient that the provider's recommendations can be trusted and followed.

Management of Withdrawal without Medication

Detoxification is a set of interventions aimed at managing acute intoxication and withdrawal. Supervised detoxification may prevent potentially life-threatening complications that might appear if the patient were left untreated. At the same time, detoxification is a form of palliative care (reducing the intensity of a disorder) for those who want to become abstinent or who must observe mandatory abstinence as a result of hospitalization or legal involvement. Finally, for some patients it represents a point of first contact with the treatment system and the first step to recovery. Treatment/rehabilitation, on the other hand, involves a constellation of ongoing therapeutic services ultimately intended to promote recovery for substance abuse patients.

Social Detoxification

The management of an individual in alcohol withdrawal without medication is a difficult matter because the indications for this have not been established firmly through scientific studies or any evidence-based methods. Furthermore, the course of alcohol withdrawal is unpredictable and currently available techniques of screening and assessment do not allow us to predict with confidence who will or will not experience life-threatening complications. Severe alcohol withdrawal may be associated with seizures due to relative impairment of gamma-aminobutyric acid (GABA) and relative overactivity of N-methyl-D-aspartate (NMDA) systems (a subtype of the excitatory glutamate receptor system). The failure to treat incipient convulsions is a deviation from the established general standard of care.

Positive aspects of the nonmedication approach are that it is highly cost-effective and provides inexpensive access to detoxification for individuals seeking aid. Observation is generally better than no treatment, but people in moderate to severe withdrawal will be best served at a higher level of care. Young individuals in good health, with no history of previous withdrawal reactions, may be well served by management of withdrawal without medication. However, personnel supervising in this setting should possess assessment abilities and be able to summon help through the emergency medical system. Methods of withdrawal management without medication include frequent interpersonal support, provision of adequate fluids and food, attention to hygiene, adequate sleep, and the maintenance of a nonalcohol/nondrug environment.

Detoxification as Distinct from Substance Abuse Treatment

Social detoxification programs are defined as short-term, nonmedical treatment services for individuals with substance use disorders. A social detoxification program offers room, board, and interpersonal support to intoxicated individuals and individuals in substance use withdrawal. In actual practice, social detoxification programs vary greatly in their approach and scope. Some programs offer some medical and nursing onsite supervision, while others provide access to medical and nursing evaluation through clinics, urgent care programs, and emergency departments. Some social detoxification programs only offer basic room and board for a "cold turkey" detoxification, while other programs offer supervised use of medications. Sometimes medications are prescribed at the onset of withdrawal by healthcare professionals in an outpatient setting, while the staff in the social detoxification program supervises the administration of these medications. Whatever the particular situation might be, there should always be medical surveillance, including monitoring of vital signs, as part of every social detoxification program.

Experts agree that for alcohol, sedative-hypnotic, and opioid withdrawal syndromes, hospitalization (or some form of 24-hour medical care) is generally the preferred setting for detoxification, based on principles of safety and humanitarian concerns. When hospitalization cannot be provided, a setting that provides a high level of nursing and medical backup 24 hours a day, 7 days a week is desirable. It is also acknowledged that social detoxification programs are, for some communities, the only available resources for uninsured, homeless individuals. Social detoxification is preferable to detoxification in unsupervised settings such as the street, shelters, or jails. It is also a known fact that in some large urban areas, social detoxification programs have long-standing, excellent reputations of providing high-quality supervision and nurturance for their clients. Social detoxification programs are organized and funded by a variety of sources, including faith-based organizations, community charities, and municipal and other local governments.

The genesis of social detoxification is complex. Often, these programs grew out of community needs when no other alternatives were available. Early reports indicated that many individuals in alcohol withdrawal could be managed successfully without medications in a social detoxification setting. Subsequent reviews that have revisited the topic have reached similar conclusions. Critical analysis of these reports, however, indicates that some of the scientific issues were oversimplified and misleading. A number of these studies, in fact, excluded many seriously ill clients from their surveys prior to referral to social detoxification. Some of these surveys had a very high staff to client ratio during social detoxification, thus providing an unusually high level of psychological support. This level of staffing is not frequently found in social detoxification programs.

Studies indicate that for a substantial group of individuals, substance use withdrawal syndromes do not lead to fatal outcomes or even significant morbidity. Determining which individuals will have benign outcomes often is difficult, and in fact this determination prior to social detoxification referral frequently is not made. Some incorrect beliefs have sprung up in the context of social detoxification: Individuals undergoing opioid withdrawal often are considered to require hospitalization to alleviate suffering, while individuals undergoing alcohol withdrawal sometimes are, for a variety of reasons, denied hospital-level treatment for detoxification, even though alcohol withdrawal produces suffering and may have fatal consequences.

General Guidelines for Social Detoxification Programs

- Such programs should follow local governmental regulations regarding their licensing and inspection
- It is highly desirable that individuals entering social detoxification be assessed by primary care practitioners (physicians, physician assistants, nurse practitioners) with some experience in substance abuse treatment
- Such an assessment should determine whether the patient currently is intoxicated and the degree of intoxication, the type of withdrawal syndrome, severity of the withdrawal, information regarding past withdrawals, and the presence of co-occurring psychiatric, medical, and surgical conditions that might well require specialized care

- Particular attention should be paid to those individuals who have undergone multiple withdrawals in the past and for whom each withdrawal appears to be worse than previous ones—this is the so-called "kindling effect. Subjects with a history of severe withdrawals, multiple withdrawals, delirium tremens, or seizures are not good candidates for social detoxification programs
- All social detoxification programs should have an alcohol and drug free environment, have personnel who are familiar with the features of substance use withdrawal syndromes, have training in basic life support, and have access to an emergency medical system that can provide transportation to emergency departments and other sites of clinical care

Management of Withdrawal with Medications

Over the last 15 years several reviews and position papers have asserted that only a minority of patients with alcoholism will in fact go into significant alcohol withdrawal requiring medications. Identifying that significant minority sometimes is problematic, but there are signs and symptoms of impending problems that can alert the caretaker to seek medical attention. Deciding on whether to use medical management for the treatment of alcohol withdrawal requires that patients be separated into three groups. The first and most obvious group comprises those clients who have had a previous history of the most extreme forms of withdrawal, that of seizures and/or delirium. In general, the medication treatment of this group in early abstinence, whether or not they have had the initiation of withdrawal, should proceed as quickly as possible.

The second group of patients requiring immediate medication treatment includes those patients who are already in withdrawal and demonstrating moderate symptoms of withdrawal. The third group of patients includes those who may still be intoxicated and therefore have not had time to develop withdrawal symptoms or who have, at the time of admission, been abstinent for a few hours and have not developed signs or symptoms of withdrawal. A decision regarding medication for this group should be in part based on age, number of years of alcohol dependence, and the number of previously treated or untreated severe withdrawals (three or four appears to be a significant threshold in predicting future serious withdrawal). If there is an opportunity to observe the patient in the emergency department of the clinic or similar setting over the next 6–8 hours, then it is possible to delay a decision regarding treatment and periodically reevaluate a client of this category. If this is not possible, then the return of the patient to a setting in which there is some supervision by family, significant others, or in a social detoxification program is desirable.

Settings and Levels of Care for Detoxification

Because the choice of a treatment setting and intensity of treatment (level of care) are so important, the American Society of Addiction Medicine (ASAM) created the Patient Placement Criteria, Second Edition, Revised (PPC-2R), a consensus-based clinical tool for matching patients to the appropriate setting and level of care. The ASAM PPC-2R represents an effort to define how care settings may be matched to patient needs and special characteristics. These criteria currently define the most broadly accepted standard of care for the treatment of substance use disorders

The five "Adult Detoxification" placement levels of care are:

1. Level I-D: Ambulatory Detoxification Without Extended Onsite Monitoring (e.g., physician's office, home healthcare agency). This level of care is an organized outpatient service monitored at predetermined intervals.

2. Level II-D: Ambulatory Detoxification With Extended Onsite Monitoring (e.g., day hospital service). This level of care is monitored by appropriately credentialed and licensed nurses.

3. Level III.2-D: Clinically Managed Residential Detoxification (e.g., nonmedical or social detoxification setting). This level emphasizes peer and social support and is intended for patients whose intoxication and/or withdrawal is sufficient to warrant 24-hour support.

4. Level III.7-D: Medically Monitored Inpatient Detoxification (e.g., freestanding detoxification center). Unlike Level III.2.D, this level provides 24-hour medically supervised detoxification services.

5. Level IV-D: Medically Managed Intensive Inpatient Detoxification (e.g., psychiatric hospital inpatient center). This level provides 24-hour care in an acute care inpatient setting.

Challenges to Providing Effective Detoxification

It is an important challenge for detoxification service providers to find the most effective way to foster a patient's recovery. Effective detoxification includes not only the medical stabilization of the patient and the safe and humane withdrawal from drugs, including alcohol, but also entry into treatment. Successfully linking detoxification with substance abuse treatment reduces the "revolving door" phenomenon of repeated withdrawals, saves money in the medium and long run, and delivers the sound and humane level of care patients need. Studies show that detoxification and its linkage to the appropriate levels of treatment lead to increased recovery and decreased use of detoxification and treatment services in the future. In addition, recovery leads to reductions in crime, general healthcare costs, and expensive acute medical and surgical treatments consequent to untreated substance abuse. While detoxification is not treatment per se, its effectiveness can be measured, in part, by the patient's continued abstinence.

Another challenge to providing effective detoxification occurs when programs try to develop linkages to treatment services. A study conducted for the Substance Abuse and Mental Health Services Administration highlights the pitfalls of the service delivery system. According to the authors, each year at least 300,000 patients with substance use disorders or acute intoxication obtain inpatient detoxification in general hospitals while additional numbers obtain detoxification in other settings. Only about one-fifth of people discharged from acute care hospitals for detoxification receive substance abuse treatment during that hospitalization. Moreover, only 15 percent of people who are admitted through an emergency room for detoxification and then discharged receive any substance abuse treatment.

Reimbursement systems can present another challenge to providing effective detoxification services. Third-party payors sometimes prefer to manage payment for detoxification separately from other phases of addiction treatment, thus treating detoxification as if it occurred in isolation from addiction treatment. This "unbundling" of services has promoted the separation of all services into somewhat scattered segments. In other instances, some reimbursement and utilization policies dictate that only "detoxification" currently can be authorized, and "detoxification" for that policy or insurer does not cover the nonmedical counseling that is an integral part of substance abuse treatment. Many treatment programs have found substance abuse counselors to be of special help with resistant patients, especially for patients with severe underlying shame over the fact that their substance use is out of control. Yet some payors will not reimburse for nonmedical services such as those provided by these counselors, and therefore the use of such staff by a detoxification or treatment service may be impossible, in spite of the fact that they are widely perceived as useful for patients.

Chapter 58

Withdrawal from Alcohol

Chapter Contents

Section 58.1

Acute and Protracted Withdrawal

This section includes text excerpted from "Protracted Withdrawal," Substance Abuse and Mental Health Services Administration (SAMHSA), July 2, 2010. Reviewed April 2018.

Most clients in treatment for substance use disorders (SUDs) do not immediately feel better after stopping their substance use. In a pattern unique to each client, symptoms related to substance abuse may be felt for weeks, months, and sometimes years. Clients may be affected by less intense versions of the acute signs and symptoms of withdrawal as well as by other conditions such as impaired ability to check impulses, negative emotional states, sleep disturbances, and cravings. These symptoms may lead clients to seek relief by returning to substance use, feeding into the pattern of repeated relapse and return to treatment. SUD treatment providers can help clients avoid this cycle by helping them recognize and manage symptoms.

Some clients in recovery also experience symptoms from co-occurring substance use and mental disorders. The SUD treatment provider's challenge is to determine which of a client's abstinence symptoms are substance-use related and will resolve over time and which indicate a possible co-occurring disorder (COD) that calls for a thorough assessment by a mental health provider and concurrent care.

What Is Acute Withdrawal?

Acute withdrawal is usually referred to simply as "withdrawal." The American Society of Addiction Medicine (ASAM) defines withdrawal as "the onset of a predictable constellation of signs and symptoms following the abrupt discontinuation of, or rapid decrease in, the dosage of a psychoactive substance." Such signs and symptoms are generally the opposite of the intoxication effects of the particular substance. For example, pupils constrict during opioid intoxication and dilate during acute withdrawal. These signs and symptoms begin within hours or days after last use of the substance and gradually resolve. The length of time symptoms last depends on the particular substance used.

What Is Protracted Withdrawal?

Protracted withdrawal, strictly defined, is the presence of substance-specific signs and symptoms common to acute withdrawal but persisting beyond the generally expected acute withdrawal timeframes. A broader definition of protracted withdrawal and the one used in this advisory includes the experiencing of the above symptoms and of nonsubstance-specific signs and symptoms that persist, evolve, or appear well past the expected timeframe for acute withdrawal.

Despite clinical observation and clients' reports of symptoms experienced past the acute withdrawal stage, the research on protracted withdrawal (particularly for substances other than alcohol) is limited, and no consensus on the term or definition exists. These reasons have precluded the *Diagnostic and Statistical Manual of Mental Disorders (DSM–5)* from including a protracted withdrawal diagnosis for any psychoactive substance. For these reasons also, this advisory does not provide timeframes for protracted withdrawal as is done for acute withdrawal.

How Do Protracted Withdrawal Symptoms Develop?

Chronic substance use causes molecular, cellular, and neurocircuitry changes to the brain that affect emotions and behavior and that persist after acute withdrawal has ended. Adaptive changes in the central nervous system may lead to affective changes that persist for many weeks or longer beyond acute withdrawal. For example, repeated use of a substance causes the brain to respond more readily to its effects but less readily to naturally rewarding activities such as listening to music. This state, in which a person's ability to experience pleasure is decreased, is called anhedonia. Anhedonia was observed in individuals who had been abstinent from alcohol, opioids, and/or other drugs for a period and who had no identified CODs.

Their study examined whether anhedonia may be linked to psychosocial factors in the lives of people recovering from SUDs. They conclude that anhedonia appeared to be a symptom of protracted withdrawal that was unrelated to other clinical and psychosocial features. Martinotti and colleagues found that signs and symptoms, including anhedonia, lasted the duration of a year-long study of people recovering from alcohol use disorders. A variety of other symptoms have been attributed to protracted withdrawal, including anxiety, sleep difficulties, problems with short-term memory, persistent fatigue, difficulty concentrating and making decisions, alcohol or drug cravings, and impaired executive control (e.g., impulse control, solving problems).

Are Protracted Withdrawal Symptoms the Same for All Substances?

No. They are similar but not identical. Each psychoactive substance class has different effects on the brain. Protracted withdrawal from alcohol has been well documented. Common protracted withdrawal symptoms include anxiety, hostility, irritability, depression, mood instability, fatigue, insomnia, difficulties concentrating and thinking, reduced interest in sex, and unexplained physical complaints, especially of pain. Anecdotal literature and case studies going back several decades suggest that signs and symptoms may last 2 years or longer after the last use of alcohol. A review of seven sleep studies using polysomnographic recordings of the brain while people slept found evidence that sleep abnormalities can persist for 1–3 years after stopping alcohol consumption. These abnormalities include difficulty falling asleep, decreased total sleep time, and sleep apnea. Research on drug-specific protracted withdrawal signs and symptoms is scarce but indicates the following:

- **Opioids.** Symptoms such as anxiety, depression, and sleep disturbances can last for weeks or months following withdrawal from opioids. Other possible symptoms include fatigue, dysphoria (i.e., feeling down or emotionally blunted), and irritability. A small National Institutes of Health (NIH) study found that subjects who had been abstinent from opioids for a prolonged period showed decreased ability to focus on a task compared with subjects who had never used opioids. People in recovery from heroin dependence also show deficits in executive control functions that may persist for months beyond the period of acute withdrawal.
- **Methamphetamine.** A review noted that studies have shown that deficits in executive control functions resulting from amphetamine use also persist well into recovery from methamphetamine dependence.
- **Cocaine.** Fox and colleagues examined emotional regulation issues and problems with impulse control in newly abstinent individuals dependent on cocaine. Significant improvement in several aspects of emotional regulation (e.g., understanding and managing emotions, ability to develop emotional coping

strategies) was seen after 4 weeks of abstinence. However, impulse control had not improved after 4 weeks of abstinence.

- **Marijuana.** A review of 19 studies of marijuana withdrawal found that sleep difficulties and strange dreams persisted at least 45 days into abstinence (the longest duration of the studies).
- **Benzodiazepines.** Benzodiazepine protracted withdrawal may be difficult to diagnose because of difficulty distinguishing it from symptom rebound or symptom re-emergence. Protracted withdrawal symptoms typically wax and wane in intensity and are new to the client (i.e., they do not indicate symptom re-emergence). Clients also may have no symptoms for a time after stopping benzodiazepine use and then become extremely anxious. Psychological symptoms can mimic disorders such as agitated depression; generalized anxiety, panic, or obsessive-compulsive disorders; and schizophrenia. Fluctuating protracted withdrawal symptoms may last for months but gradually subside with prolonged abstinence.

Do All Clients Experience Protracted Withdrawal?

No. Some clients experience no symptoms after the acute withdrawal stage, whereas others have lingering symptoms. Still, others experience an initial clearing of symptoms for the first month or two of abstinence and then develop unpleasant symptoms again. The intensity of symptoms also differs among clients.

How Can Providers Help Clients through Protracted Withdrawal?

Clients affected by anhedonia and other symptoms of protracted withdrawal may want to alleviate those symptoms by returning to substance use at a time when they may have a weakened ability to resist such impulses. Treatment providers can improve their clients' chances for long-term recovery by educating clients about protracted withdrawal, offering support and understanding, monitoring them regularly, and intervening early with clients who seem headed for relapse:

- **Educate clients about protracted withdrawal and help them develop realistic attitudes toward recovery.** Remind clients that recovery is a process. Help clients understand that it is normal to feel not fully recovered within the first weeks and months of abstinence. Tell them about possible protracted withdrawal symptoms and reassure them that these symptoms will not last forever and can be managed. Advise clients on how to reduce or cope with symptoms and encourage them to focus on incremental improvements. Tell clients it takes time to undo the damage from substance use but in many cases, with long-term abstinence, substance-induced brain changes reverse.

- **Celebrate each accomplishment** (e.g., learning a new coping skill) and help clients not become discouraged if symptoms recur. Repeat encouragements at each meeting, especially with clients affected by memory and concentration impairments.
- **Assess for CODs.** The symptoms of protracted withdrawal can be similar to those of traumatic brain injury (TBI) and CODs. Carefully assess and reassess clients as recovery proceeds, including for depression and suicidal tendencies. An Advisory in development will provide information on assessing and addressing TBI in recovery. Appropriate treatment of a COD positively affects the course of treatment.
- **Ask about sleep problems.** Make a differential diagnosis to determine whether a client's sleep problems likely stem from protracted withdrawal or are the result of other causes. Such causes include poor sleep habits retained from a substance-using lifestyle, CODs, relapse to substance use, stress, or side effects of medication (including medication to treat SUDs). Educate clients about good sleep habits: adopting a regular sleep routine (going to bed and getting up at the same times), exercising early in the day, minimizing caffeine intake, eating well, and avoiding late afternoon naps. Use pharmacological treatments with caution to avoid use problems.
- **Advise clients to be active.** Encourage clients to engage in physical and mental exercises, which improve sleep, promote positive emotional states, reduce stress and nervousness, help clients avoid triggers, and distract clients' attention from symptoms. Assist clients in adopting habits that help them cope with memory and thinking problems (e.g., making to-do lists, establishing daily routines).
- **Advise clients to be patient.** Clients in early recovery may try to "make up for lost time" by overbooking and generally trying to do too much, increasing their overall stress levels and possibly

exacerbating symptoms. Tell clients that they are doing enough by focusing on their recovery and regaining their health.

- **Prescribe medications as needed to control symptoms past the acute withdrawal stage.** Inform clients recovering from alcohol addiction that treatment medications, such as acamprosate, might relieve some protracted withdrawal symptoms. Although acamprosate's mechanism of action is not well understood, it may reduce uncomfortable symptoms such as anxiety and sleep disturbances that clients feel after they have stopped drinking. Substance Abuse and Mental Health Services Administration (SAMHSA), Center for Substance Abuse Treatment (CSAT) Advisory on acamprosate provide more information. Consider methadone or buprenorphine replacement treatment for clients who find that protracted opioid withdrawal symptoms are too powerful and for whom the risk of relapse is high.
- **Encourage clients to join mutual support groups.** Tell clients that participation in mutual support groups such as Alcoholics Anonymous or Women in Sobriety is associated with long periods of recovery. Make clients aware of population-specific support groups (e.g., adolescents- or women-only groups). Direct clients in medicated-assisted treatment to support groups that accept the use of prescribed medications for substance abuse treatment. Tell clients that they may need to visit several groups over several weeks to find groups with which they feel comfortable.
- **Include interventions that help clients strengthen executive control functions.** Provide interventions such as cognitive–behavioral therapy to help clients manage problems with impulse control, solve problems, and make decisions.
- **Monitor clients for symptoms during continuing care.** Provide clients with opportunities to obtain professional guidance on such issues as lapses and relapses, stress, triggers, and activities to maintain abstinence. Monitoring can be through periodic office visits or by telephone or e-mails. Arrange for a transition to a case manager as needed.

Section 58.2

Complications of Alcohol Withdrawal

This section includes text excerpted from "Complications of Alcohol Withdrawal," National Institute on Alcohol Abuse and Alcoholism (NIAAA), February 2002. Reviewed April 2018.

Abrupt reduction or total cessation of long-term alcohol consumption produces a well-defined cluster of symptoms called acute alcohol withdrawal (AW). Although some patients experience relatively mild withdrawal symptoms, disease processes or events that accompany AW can cause significant illness and death. After acute withdrawal has subsided, a poorly defined syndrome of protracted withdrawal may ensue. The persistent alterations in physiology, mood, and behavior associated with protracted withdrawal may motivate the patient to relapse to heavy drinking. This section deals with the acute withdrawal syndrome and its complications, including seizures, delirium tremens, Wernicke-Korsakoff syndrome (WKS), neuropsychiatric disturbances, and cardiovascular complications as well as the protracted withdrawal syndrome. The findings discussed here is about alcohol-induced alterations of nervous system function that underlie these syndromes and their implications for the treatment of withdrawal.

Acute Alcohol Withdrawal Syndrome

Alcohol withdrawal is a distinctive clinical syndrome with potentially serious consequences. Symptoms begin as early as 6 hours after the initial decline from peak intoxication. Initial symptoms include tremor, anxiety, insomnia, restlessness, and nausea. Particularly in mildly alcohol-dependent persons, these symptoms may comprise the entire syndrome and may subside without treatment after a few days. More serious withdrawal symptoms occur in approximately 10 percent of patients. These symptoms include a low-grade fever, rapid breathing, tremor, and profuse sweating. Seizures may occur in more than 5 percent of untreated patients in acute alcohol withdrawal. Another severe complication is delirium tremens (DT's), which is characterized by hallucinations, mental confusion, and disorientation. The mortality rate among patients exhibiting DT's is 5–25 percent.

Seizures

Withdrawal seizures usually consist of generalized convulsions alternating with spasmodic muscular contractions (i.e., tonic-clonic seizures). Seizures that begin locally (e.g., with twitching of a limb) suggest the presence of a co-occurring disorder, which should be fully investigated. More than 90 percent of alcohol withdrawal seizures occur within 48 hours after the patient stops drinking. Fewer than 3 percent of such seizures may occur 5–20 days after the last drink. Clinical data suggest that the likelihood of having withdrawal seizures, as well as the severity of those seizures, increases with the number of past withdrawals. The correlation between the number of alcohol detoxifications and the development of alcohol withdrawal complications, including seizures, has been ascribed to cumulative long-term changes in brain excitability (i.e., the "kindling" hypothesis).

Delirium Tremens

DT's are a serious manifestation of alcohol dependence that develops 1–4 days after the onset of acute alcohol withdrawal in persons who have been drinking excessively for years. Signs of DT's include extreme hyperactivity of the autonomic nervous system, along with hallucinations. Women experiencing DT's appear to exhibit autonomic symptoms less frequently than men. Co-occurring medical problems may obscure the diagnosis and treatment of DT's or worsen the outcome. Such medical problems include altered blood chemistry, certain infections, and Wernicke syndrome.

Death may occur in up to 5 percent of patients with DT's. The risk of death is reduced, however, in patients receiving adequate medication and medical support. Alcoholics who are awaiting surgical or medical treatment often exhibit DT's when their alcohol consumption is abruptly interrupted by hospitalization. Therefore, hospital staff must remain vigilant for signs and symptoms of alcohol withdrawal, even in patients not known to be alcoholic. In addition, clinicians must learn to differentiate DT's from other possible causes of delirium.

The prediction of complicated alcohol withdrawal is an important part of alcoholism treatment to ensure that appropriate therapies may be planned in advance. Risk factors for prolonged or complicated alcohol withdrawal include lifetime or current long duration of alcohol consumption, lifetime prior detoxifications, prior seizures, prior episodes of DT's, and current intense craving for alcohol. Certain clinical and biochemical findings have been associated with high risk for the development of DT's, including specific alterations of blood chemistry;

elevated liver enzymes; and certain nervous system disturbances, including muscular incoordination.

Wernicke-Korsakoff Syndrome

The combination of Wernicke and Korsakoff syndromes is not a complication of AW but rather of a nutritional deficiency. Nevertheless, the syndromes usually occur during AW. Wernicke syndrome is a disorder of the nervous system caused by thiamine deficiency, and alcoholics account for most cases in the Western world. The syndrome is characterized by severe cognitive impairment and delirium, abnormal gait (i.e., ataxia), and paralysis of certain eye muscles. A majority of patients are profoundly disoriented, indifferent, and inattentive; some exhibit an agitated delirium related to alcohol withdrawal. Ocular signs improve within hours to days; ataxia and confusion improve within days to weeks. A majority of patients are left with an abnormal gaze, persistent ataxia, and a potentially disabling memory disorder known as Korsakoff syndrome. Although fewer than 5 percent of patients initially exhibit a depressed level of consciousness, the course in untreated patients may progress through stupor, coma, and death.

Nutritional status should be closely monitored during treatment of acute AW to prevent Wernicke-Korsakoff syndrome. Approximately 80 percent of alcoholic patients recovering from Wernicke syndrome exhibit the selective memory disturbance of Korsakoff syndrome. Symptoms of Korsakoff syndrome include severe amnesia for past events, along with impaired ability to commit current experience to memory. The patient often recites imaginary experiences to fill gaps in his or her memory. Although the patient may be apathetic, intellectual abilities other than memory are relatively preserved. Korsakoff syndrome can occur in the absence of alcohol use; however, the disease rarely follows Wernicke syndrome in nonalcoholics. This observation has led to speculation that the neurotoxicity of alcohol is an important contributing factor in the memory disorders of alcoholics.

Disturbances of Mood, Thought, and Perception

Withdrawing alcoholics exhibit psychiatric difficulties that may be related to the process of withdrawal itself or to co-occurring conditions. The major psychiatric problems associated with acute and protracted withdrawal are anxiety, depression, and sleep disturbance.

Less frequently, psychotic symptoms, including delusions and hallucinations, may be associated with withdrawal.

Anxiety

Anxiety disorders are manifested by extreme fear and anxiety, accompanied by heart palpitations; shallow, rapid breathing (i.e., hyperventilation); sweating; and dizziness. Alcohol has antianxiety properties that promote its use to self-medicate anxiety. However, prolonged alcohol use and especially acute AW states can increase anxiety levels. Marked signs of anxiety commonly appear between 12 and 48 hours after cessation of alcohol consumption. Hyperventilation may occur during acute withdrawal, leading to disturbed blood chemistry and resulting in symptoms that may be indistinguishable from those that occur in anxiety disorders. Some researchers have hypothesized that repeated AW may predispose alcoholics to certain anxiety disorders through the process of kindling.

Depression

Depressive symptoms often are observed in patients who are intoxicated or undergoing alcohol detoxification. As many as 15 percent of alcoholics are at risk for death by suicide, and recent consumption of alcohol appears to increase the danger of a fatal outcome from self-harm. This finding may be attributable to the release of behavioral inhibition associated with alcohol intoxication or with the depressive feeling states that accompany the decline from peak intoxication. Depressive disorders commonly emerge during AW; in addition to the depressive feeling states associated with alcohol consumption and withdrawal, the social, psychological, and physical problems associated with alcoholism may contribute to the development of depressive disorders.

Sleep Disturbances

Sleep disturbances—including frequent awakening, restless sleep, insomnia, and night terrors—are among the most common complaints of alcoholics. Sleep problems persist into AW, with pronounced insomnia and marked sleep fragmentation. In addition, alcoholics show an increased incidence of interrupted breathing during sleep compared with the general population. These sleep disturbances can cause daytime drowsiness, reducing the efficiency of performance of day-time tasks and increasing the risk of car crashes.

Hallucinations and Perceptual Disturbance

Visual, auditory, and tactile hallucinations are frequently experienced in acute, complicated AW or DT's. Hallucinations that are not connected with DT's occur in 3–10 percent of patients during severe AW from 12 hours to 7 days after cessation or reduction of alcohol consumption. In one study, 10 percent of 532 male patients admitted to a Veterans Affairs Hospital for AW developed hallucinations. Patients who hallucinated tended to be younger at the onset of their alcohol problems, consumed more alcohol per drinking occasion, developed more alcohol-related life problems, and had higher rates of other drug use than patients who did not hallucinate.

Cardiovascular Complications

The heart is a major site of alcohol-induced organ damage, including disturbances of heartbeat rhythm. For example, the "holiday heart syndrome" consists of episodes of abnormal cardiac rhythms following a bout of drinking. Because arrhythmia generally occurs after a binge, rather than during intoxication, AW may be a contributing factor to the occurrence of alcohol-related arrhythmia. Further study is required to elucidate the possible connection between AW and increased sudden cardiac death.

Protracted Withdrawal Syndrome

Data appear to indicate that a protracted withdrawal syndrome (PWS) may develop following AW and may persist for at least 1-year. Some manifestations of PWS include symptoms associated with AW that persist beyond their typical time course. These symptoms include tremor; sleep disruption; anxiety; depressive symptoms; and increased breathing rate, body temperature, blood pressure, and pulse. Other symptoms of PWS appear to oppose symptoms of AW. These symptoms of PWS include decreased energy, lassitude, and decreased overall metabolism. The significance of this cluster of symptoms has been debated. For example, PWS could reflect the brain's slow recovery from the reversible nerve cell damage common in alcoholism. Clinically, the symptoms of PWS are important, because they may predispose abstinent alcoholics to relapse in an attempt to alleviate the symptoms.

Neurobiology of Alcohol Withdrawal

Alcohol affects the way in which nerve cells communicate. For example, alcohol's sedating effect is related to an altered function of specific receptors in the brain. Receptors are specialized proteins on the surface of nerve cells that receive chemical signals from other cells. These signals are generally conveyed by chemical messengers released by nearby nerve cells (i.e., neurotransmitters). With long-term alcohol consumption, receptors affected by alcohol undergo adaptive changes in an attempt to maintain normal function. When alcohol consumption ceases, these changes are no longer adaptive and may contribute to the phenomena associated with AW. Two important brain communication systems affected by alcohol involve the neurotransmitters gamma-aminobutyric acid (GABA) and glutamate.

The GABA System

GABA is an inhibitory neurotransmitter that helps to regulate brain function by rendering nerve cells less sensitive to further signaling. Single doses of alcohol facilitate the inhibitory function of the GABA A receptor, contributing to alcohol's intoxicating effects. During withdrawal, brain GABA levels fall below normal and GABA activity declines. In addition, the sensitivity of GABA A receptors to chemical signals also may be reduced in recently detoxified alcoholic patients. The combination of reduced brain GABA levels and GABA A receptor sensitivity may be considered an adaptation to the presence of alcohol. In the absence of alcohol, the resulting decrease in inhibitory function may contribute to symptoms of nervous system hyperactivity associated with both acute and protracted AW.

The Glutamate System

The major excitatory neurotransmitter in the brain is glutamate, which communicates with three major subtypes of glutamate receptors. Among these, the N-methyl-D-aspartate (NMDA) receptor plays a role in memory, learning, and the generation of seizures. Alcohol inhibits the excitatory function of the NMDA receptor in laboratory studies at concentrations associated with mild to moderate alcohol intoxication in humans. As with the increased inhibitory function of the GABA A receptor, the decreased excitatory function of the NMDA receptor is consistent with alcohol's general sedative effect. Long-term alcohol administration produces an adaptive increase in the function of NMDA receptors. Acute AW activates glutamate systems. In turn, AW seizures are associated with increased NMDA receptor function. Persistent alterations in NMDA receptor function may potentiate the neurotoxic and seizure-inducing effects of increased glutamate release during withdrawal.

Reproductive Hormones and Alcohol Withdrawal

Declines in the levels of neurosteroids may contribute to AW. Neurosteroids are substances involved in the metabolism of reproductive hormones that also have potent and specific effects on various functions of the brain. Certain neurosteroids modulate the function of the GABA A receptor; plasma levels of these neurosteroids are decreased during AW. Because decreases in neurosteroids may contribute to AW symptoms, these compounds may have potential as medications for alleviating withdrawal. Ruusa and Bergman investigated the role of the male reproductive hormone testosterone on withdrawal symptoms. Long-term alcohol consumption causes failure of the reproductive system in men. In addition, testosterone levels decrease during alcohol consumption and increase after withdrawal. Low levels of testosterone during AW are associated with psychological symptoms, such as indecision, excessive worrying, fatigability, and lassitude during detoxification to determine whether a causal relationship exists.

Antiseizure Medications

For many years, seizures and other symptoms of AW have been treated with a class of sedating medications called benzodiazepines (e.g., Valium®). Several studies have demonstrated that the antiseizure medications Carbamazepine (Tegretol®) and valproic acid (Depakene®) are as effective as benzodiazepines for this purpose. Moreover, unlike the benzodiazepines, these antiseizure medications are not potential drugs of abuse. Alcohol withdrawal seizures and PWS have been linked to both GABA and NMDA dysregulation. Although the mechanisms of action of Carbamazepine and valproic acid are not entirely understood, both medications appear to increase GABA levels in the brain in patients with seizure disorders.

In addition, valproic acid at therapeutic levels appears to be effective at inhibiting seizures induced by the stimulatory effect of NMDA receptors. Laboratory studies suggest that valproic acid may inhibit GABA metabolism and activate GABA synthesis. In addition, data indicate that Carbamazepine decreases the flow of glutamate into slices of the hippocampus, a part of the brain involved in seizures. Therefore, Carbamazepine and valproic acid prevent alcohol withdrawal seizures and kindling. The antianxiety and mood-stabilizing actions of these anticonvulsants may enhance their efficacy in treating withdrawal symptoms. These actions also may help relieve the constellation of symptoms associated with PWS, perhaps resulting in fewer and milder relapses during the period following acute withdrawal.

Conclusion

AW and its complications are among the most visible consequences of alcoholism. Those syndromes arise directly from adaptations made within nerve cell communication systems that are targets of alcohol in the brain. Among its actions, alcohol acutely facilitates the activity of GABA A receptor function and blocks NMDA receptor activity. The adaptations within these systems contribute to withdrawal-related symptoms, seizures, and neurotoxicity. Repeated AW episodes appear to increase the risk of future AW seizures. Acute withdrawal symptoms and complications, including seizures, hallucinations, and DT's, represent medical emergencies. Some complications, including Wernicke-Korsakoff syndrome, may be permanently disabling. In addition, the distress associated with acute and protracted withdrawal presents an ongoing motivation to relapse to alcohol use in recently detoxified patients. Thus, the early stages of sobriety represent a period of risk at many levels. Available treatments suppress many symptoms and complications of AW.

Consequently, greater emphasis may now be placed on developing strategies to facilitate long-term sobriety. An important step in this direction may be the development of medications that lack the addiction potential of the benzodiazepines. The antiseizure medications meet these criteria and have the added capacity to suppress kindling. AW represents a period of significant clinical risk that requires attentive medical management. However, AW also provides an opportunity to initiate treatments that may lead to extended sobriety. As such, it is a critical component of the long-term treatment strategy for every patient with alcoholism.

Section 58.3

Repeated Alcohol Withdrawal: Sensitization and Implications for Relapse

This section includes text excerpted from "Alcohol Dependence, Withdrawal, and Relapse," National Institute on Alcohol Abuse and Alcoholism (NIAAA), April 23, 2009. Reviewed April 2018.

Repeated Alcohol Withdrawals

Given that alcoholism is a chronic relapsing disease, many alcohol-dependent people invariably experience multiple bouts of heavy drinking interspersed with periods of abstinence (i.e., withdrawal) of varying duration. A convergent body of preclinical and clinical evidence has demonstrated that a history of multiple detoxification/withdrawal experiences can result in increased sensitivity to the withdrawal syndrome—a process known as "kindling." For example, clinical studies have indicated that a history of multiple detoxifications increases a person's susceptibility to more severe and medically complicated withdrawals in the future. Similarly, animal studies have demonstrated sensitization of electrographic and behavioral measures of withdrawal seizure activity in mice following multiple withdrawals compared with animals tested after a single withdrawal episode, even if both groups of animals had been exposed to the same total amount of alcohol.

Most studies demonstrating this sensitization or "kindling" of alcohol withdrawal primarily have focused on the withdrawal related excessive activity (i.e., hyperexcitability) of the central nervous system (CNS), as indicated by seizure activity because this parameter is relatively easy to observe in experimental as well as clinical settings. However, researchers have been turning their attention to the evaluation of changes in withdrawal symptoms that extend beyond physical signs of withdrawal—that is, to those symptoms that fall within the domain of psychological distress and dysphoria. This new focus is clinically relevant because these symptoms (e.g., anxiety, negative affect, and altered reward set point) may serve as potent instigators driving motivation to drink. Sensitization resulting from repeated withdrawal cycles and leading to both more severe and more persistent symptoms, therefore, may constitute a significant motivational factor that underlies increased risk for relapse.

The development of alcohol dependence is a complex and dynamic process. Many neurobiological and environmental factors influence motivation to drink. At any given time, an individual's propensity to imbibe is thought to reflect a balance between alcohol's positive reinforcing (i.e., rewarding) effects, such as euphoria and reduction of anxiety (i.e., anxiolysis), and the drug's aversive effects, which typically are associated with negative consequences of alcohol consumption (e.g., hangover or withdrawal symptoms).

Memories associated with these rewarding and aversive qualities of alcohol, as well as learned associations between these internal states and related environmental stimuli or contexts, influence both the initiation and regulation of intake. These experiential factors, together with biological and environmental influences and social forces, are central to the formation of expectations about the consequences of alcohol use. These expectations, in turn, shape an individual's decision about engaging in drinking behavior. The nature of and extent to which these factors are operable in influencing decisions about drinking not only vary from one individual to another but also depend on the stage of addiction—that is, whether the drinker is at the stage of initial experience with alcohol, early problem drinking, or later excessive consumption associated with dependence. Although many people abuse alcohol without meeting the criteria for alcohol dependence, an individual must meet at least four of the following criteria: drinking more alcohol than intended, unsuccessful efforts to reduce alcohol drinking, giving up other activities in favor of drinking alcohol, spending a great deal of time obtaining and drinking alcohol, continuing to drink alcohol in spite of adverse physical and social effects, and the development of alcohol tolerance. This continued excessive alcohol consumption can lead to the development of dependence. Neuroadaptive changes that result from continued alcohol use and abuse (which manifest as tolerance and physiological dependence) are thought to be crucial in the transition from controlled alcohol use to more frequent and excessive, uncontrollable drinking. Indeed, for some dependent individuals, the fear that withdrawal symptoms might emerge if they attempt to stop or significantly curtail drinking may prominently contribute to the perpetuation of alcohol use and abuse.

Alcohol Withdrawal

When an alcohol-dependent individual abruptly terminates or substantially reduces his or her alcohol consumption, a characteristic withdrawal syndrome ensues. In general, alcohol acts to suppress central nervous system (CNS) activity, and, as with other CNS depressants, withdrawal symptoms associated with cessation of chronic alcohol use are opposite in nature to the effects of intoxication. Typical clinical features of alcohol withdrawal include the following:

- Signs of a heightened autonomic nervous system (The autonomic nervous system is that division of the nervous system which regulates the functions of the internal organs and controls essential and involuntary bodily functions, such as respiration, blood pressure, and heart rate, or digestion.) activation, such as rapid heartbeat (i.e., tachycardia), elevated blood pressure, excessive sweating (i.e., diaphoresis), and shaking (i.e., tremor)
- Excessive activity of the CNS (i.e., CNS hyperexcitability) that may culminate in motor seizures
- Hallucinations and delirium tremens in the most severe form of withdrawal

In addition to physical signs of withdrawal, a constellation of symptoms contributing to a state of distress and psychological discomfort constitute a significant component of the withdrawal syndrome. These symptoms include emotional changes such as irritability, agitation, anxiety, and dysphoria, as well as sleep disturbances, a sense of inability to experience pleasure (i.e., anhedonia), and frequent complaints about "achiness," which possibly may reflect a reduced threshold for pain sensitivity. Many of these signs and symptoms, including those that reflect a negative-affect state (e.g., anxiety, distress, and anhedonia) also have been demonstrated in animal studies involving various models of dependence.

Although many physical signs and symptoms of withdrawal typically abate within a few days, symptoms associated with psychological distress and dysphoria may linger for protracted periods of time. The persistence of these symptoms (e.g., anxiety, negative affect, altered reward set point manifesting as dysphoria and/or anhedonia) may constitute a significant motivational factor that leads to relapse to heavy drinking.

Studying Alcohol Relapse Behavior

Relapse may be defined as the resumption of alcohol drinking following a prolonged period of abstinence. Clinically, vulnerability to relapse commonly is associated with an intense craving or desire to drink. Although a precise definition for craving remains elusive, and there even is some debate about the role of craving in relapse, there is no question that relapse represents a prevalent and significant problem in alcoholism. In fact, given the high rate of recidivism in alcoholism, relapse clearly is a major impediment to treatment efforts. Consequently, substantial research efforts have been directed at modeling relapse behavior, as well as elucidating neural substrates and environmental circumstances that are associated with or promote excessive drinking.

Events that potently trigger relapse drinking fall into three general categories: exposure to small amounts of alcohol (i.e., alcohol-induced priming), exposure to alcohol-related (i.e., conditioned) cues or environmental contexts, and stress. Clinical laboratory studies have found that compared with control subjects, alcohol-dependent people are more sensitive to the ability of these stimuli and events to elicit craving and negative affect, which in turn presumably drives an increased desire to drink. The combination of these clinical laboratory procedures with neuroimaging techniques has proven to be a powerful tool allowing investigators to identify brain regions that are more strongly activated in alcohol-dependent subjects than in control subjects when they are exposed to these stimuli/events. Similar experimental procedures have been employed to evaluate the ability of pharmacotherapeutics to quell craving and temper the brain activation provoked by alcohol-related cues in humans.

More detailed insight regarding mechanisms underlying fundamental changes in brain function that occur as a consequence of dependence and which relate to enduring relapse vulnerability has been gained through research in animals. Several animal models have been used to study alcohol self-administration behavior and the issue of relapse. In one type of model, animals with a long history of daily access to alcohol are abruptly denied access to the drug. When alcohol is reintroduced after this period of "forced" (i.e., experimenter-induced) abstinence, the animals exhibit a transient increase in alcohol consumption. This alcohol deprivation effect has been demonstrated using both measures of voluntary alcohol consumption and operant procedures. In operant procedures, animals must first perform a certain response (e.g., press a lever) before they receive a stimulus (e.g., a small amount of alcohol). By modifying the required response (e.g., increasing the number of lever presses required before the alcohol is delivered) researchers can determine the motivational value of the stimulus for the animal. Another model frequently used to study alcohol (and other drug) relapse behavior involves operant reinstatement procedures. In this model, animals first are trained to respond for access to alcohol (i.e., to receive the reinforcement provided by alcohol). Then, the response-contingent reinforcement is interrupted with extinction training—that is, even if the animals perform the required response, they do not receive alcohol; as a result, the animals eventually reduce or even completely stop responding. When the animals then are exposed again to small alcohol doses, environmental stressors, or stimuli previously associated with the delivery of alcohol (i.e., conditioned cues), they resume responding (to varying degrees)—as if "seeking" alcohol reinforcement. This renewed alcohol-seeking behavior becomes even more robust when several of these relevant stimuli are presented in combination. Interestingly, this reinstatement of alcohol responding occurs even though the animals still do not receive alcohol reinforcement.

This experimental design can be further modified by the use of discriminative contextual cues. This means that certain contextual cues (e.g., a unique odor or testing environment) will indicate to the animal that responding will pay off with a delivery of alcohol reinforcement, whereas a different contextual cue is used to signal that responding will not result in access to alcohol. If the responding is extinguished in these animals (i.e., they cease to respond because they receive neither the alcohol-related cues nor alcohol), presentation of a discriminative cue that previously signaled alcohol availability will reinstate alcohol-seeking behavior. This renewed alcohol-seeking behavior can be observed even after a long period of time has elapsed since the animals last were given an opportunity to self-administer alcohol, suggesting that these contextual cues can serve as powerful triggers for relapse-like behavior. Additional studies found that re-exposure of the animals to the general environmental context in which they could self-administer alcohol not only enhanced subsequent alcohol responding but also modulated the ability of alcohol-conditioned cues to reinstate alcohol-seeking behavior.

Finally, and perhaps most importantly, animals used in all of these models generally have demonstrated sensitivity to treatment with various medications that have been shown to be clinically effective in preventing and/or retarding alcohol relapse. From a clinical standpoint, this is important because it underscores the value of these models in identifying and evaluating new treatment strategies that may be more effective in battling the problem of relapse.

Alcohol Dependence, Withdrawal, and Relapse

As mentioned earlier, alcohol addiction is a complex and dynamic process. Prolonged excessive alcohol consumption sets in motion a host of neuroadaptive changes in the brain's reward and stress systems. The development of alcohol dependence is thought to reflect an allostatic state—that is, a state in which the chronic presence of alcohol produces a constant challenge to regulatory systems that attempt (but ultimately fail) to defend the normal equilibrium of various internal processes (i.e., homeostatic set points). In the dependent individual, this allostatic state is fueled by progressive dysregulation of the brain's reward and stress systems beyond their normal homeostatic limits. These neuroadaptive changes associated with dependence and withdrawal are postulated to impact the rewarding effects of alcohol and, consequently, contribute to the transition from controlled alcohol use to more excessive, uncontrollable drinking. Manifestations of these perturbations in brain reward and stress systems also appear to mediate the myriad symptoms of alcohol withdrawal, as well as underlie persistent vulnerability to relapse.

As noted above, clinical laboratory studies have shown that alcohol-dependent people are more sensitive to relapse-provoking cues/stimuli compared with control subjects. By definition, alcohol-dependent subjects also are heavier drinkers and (too) often experience an insidious return to excessive levels of alcohol consumption once a "slip" occurs after abstinence. Not surprisingly, numerous rodent and primate models have been employed to examine the influence of dependence on relapse. Early studies using these animal models generally yielded equivocal findings, most likely because investigators used procedures that neither sufficiently established alcohol's positive reinforcing effects prior to dependence induction nor optimized the development of alcohol's negative reinforcing capacity (i.e., the animals did not have an opportunity to associate alcohol drinking with alleviation of withdrawal symptoms).

More studies that have incorporated these procedural considerations, however, have demonstrated increased alcohol responding and/or drinking in dependent compared with nondependent mice and rats. Moreover, in some studies, the enhanced alcohol consumption in dependent animals during withdrawal produced blood and brain alcohol levels that nearly reached levels attained during the initial chronic alcohol exposure which had produced the dependent state. Also, consistent with the findings of clinical studies, animals with a history of alcohol dependence exhibited exaggerated sensitivity to alcohol-related cues and various stressors that lead to enhanced alcohol-seeking behavior. In many instances, these effects were observed long after the animals had experienced chronic alcohol exposure.

Finally, experience with repeated cycles of chronic alcohol exposure and withdrawal not only led to an exacerbation of the physiological symptoms of withdrawal but also to enhanced susceptibility to relapse. Thus, a growing body of evidence indicates that alcohol dependence and withdrawal experiences significantly contribute to enhanced relapse vulnerability as well as favor sustained high levels of alcohol drinking once a "slip" occurs.

Treatment Implications

Relapse represents a major challenge to treatment efforts for people suffering from alcohol dependence. Till date, no therapeutic interventions can fully prevent relapse, sustain abstinence, or temper the amount of drinking when a "slip" occurs. For some people, loss of control over alcohol consumption can lead to alcohol dependence, rendering them more susceptible to relapse as well as more vulnerable to engaging in drinking behavior that often spirals out of control. Many of these people make numerous attempts to curtail their alcohol use, only to find themselves reverting to patterns of excessive consumption.

Significant advancements have been made in understanding the neurobiological underpinnings and environmental factors that influence motivation to drink as well as the consequences of excessive alcohol use. Given the diverse and widespread neuroadaptive changes that are set in motion as a consequence of chronic alcohol exposure and withdrawal, it perhaps is not surprising that no single pharmacological agent has proven to be fully successful in the treatment of alcoholism.

The challenge of choosing the most appropriate agent for the treatment of alcoholism is compounded by the complexity and heterogeneity of this relapsing disease as well as by the host of other variables (e.g., genotype, coexisting disorders, treatment regimens, and compliance) that must be considered in the context of treatment interventions. Further, the efficacy of treatment may depend on temporal factors, such as the stage of addiction (e.g., whether the patient seeks treatment or not) as well as drinking pattern (e.g., binge-like intake), especially when both amount and frequency of alcohol consumption is assessed to determine drinking behavior/phenotype.

Nevertheless, numerous pharmacotherapies have been employed to treat alcoholism, guided principally by advancing knowledge about alcohol's interactions with various components of the brain's reward and stress pathways. To date, two medications targeting these brain systems—naltrexone (Revia®) and acamprosate (Campral®)— have been approved by the Food and Drug Administration (FDA) for treatment of alcoholism. (6A third FDA-approved medication to treat alcohol dependence (disulfiram; Antabuse®) targets alcohol metabolism.) The efficacy of naltrexone and acamprosate in treating alcohol dependence and relapse is based on numerous clinical studies, although support is not universal. Naltrexone operates as an antagonist of certain receptors (principally μ and δ receptors) for brain-signaling molecules (i.e., neurotransmitters) called endogenous opiates that are involved in reward systems, whereas acamprosate is thought to modulate signal transmission involving another neurotransmitter called glutamate. It has been postulated that naltrexone may blunt the rewarding effects of alcohol, whereas acamprosate may attenuate adaptive changes during abstinence that favor relapse.

Chapter 59

Prescription Medicines Used for Alcohol Abuse Treatment

Prescribing Medications for Alcohol Dependence

Three oral medications (naltrexone, acamprosate, and disulfiram) and one injectable medication (extended-release injectable naltrexone) are currently approved for treating alcohol dependence. Topiramate, an oral medication used to treat epilepsy and migraine, has been shown to be effective in treating alcohol dependence, although it is not approved by the FDA for this indication. All of these medications have been shown to help patients reduce drinking, avoid relapse to heavy drinking, achieve and maintain abstinence, or gain a combination of these effects. As is true in treating any chronic illness, addressing patient adherence systematically will maximize the effectiveness of these medications.

When Should Medications Be Considered for Treating an Alcohol Use Disorder?

The drugs noted above have been shown to be effective adjuncts to the treatment of alcohol dependence. Thus, consider adding a medication whenever you're treating someone with active alcohol dependence

---

This chapter includes text excerpted from "Helping Patients Who Drink Too Much: A Clinician's Guide," National Institute on Alcohol Abuse and Alcoholism (NIAAA), October 2008. Reviewed April 2018.

or someone who has stopped drinking in the past few months but is experiencing problems such as craving or "slips." Patients who previously failed to respond to psychosocial approaches alone are particularly strong candidates for medication treatment.

Must Patients Agree to Abstain?

No matter which alcohol dependence medication is used, patients who have a goal of abstinence, or who can abstain even for a few days prior to starting the medication, are likely to have better outcomes. Still, it's best to determine individual goals with each patient. Some patients may not be willing to endorse abstinence as a goal, especially at first. If a patient with alcohol dependence agrees to reduce drinking substantially, it's best to engage him or her in that goal while continuing to note that abstinence remains the optimal outcome. A patient's willingness to abstain has important implications for the choice of medication. Most studies on effectiveness have required patients to abstain before starting treatment. A notable exception is topiramate, which was prescribed to study volunteers who were still drinking. Both oral and extended-release injection naltrexone also may be helpful in reducing heavy drinking and encouraging abstinence in patients who are still drinking.

However, its efficacy is much higher in patients who can abstain for 4–7 days before initiating treatment. Acamprosate, too, is only approved for use in patients who are abstinent at the start of treatment, and patients should be fully withdrawn before starting. Disulfiram is contraindicated in patients who wish to continue to drink, because a disulfiram–alcohol reaction occurs with any alcohol intake at all.

Which of the Medications Should Be Prescribed?

Which medication to use will depend on clinical judgment and patient preference. Each has a different mechanism of action. Some patients may respond better to one type of medication than another.

Naltrexone

Mechanism. Naltrexone blocks opioid receptors that are involved in the rewarding effects of drinking alcohol and the craving for alcohol. It's available in two forms: oral (Depade®, ReVia®), with once-daily dosing, and extended-release injectable (Vivitrol®), given as once-monthly injections.

Efficacy. Oral naltrexone reduces relapse to heavy drinking, defined as 4 or more drinks per day for women and 5 or more for men. It cuts the relapse risk during the first 3 months by about 36 percent (about 28% of patients taking naltrexone relapse versus about 43 percent of those taking a placebo). Thus, it is especially helpful for curbing consumption in patients who have drinking "slips." It is less effective in maintaining abstinence. In the single study available, extended-release injectable naltrexone resulted in a 25 percent reduction in the proportion of heavy drinking days compared with a placebo, with a higher rate of response in males and those with lead-in abstinence.

Topiramate

Mechanism. The precise mechanism of action is unclear. Topiramate is thought to work by increasing inhibitory (GABA) neurotransmission and reducing stimulatory (glutamate) neurotransmission. It is available in oral form and requires a slow upward titration of dose to minimize side effects.

Efficacy. Topiramate has been shown in two randomized controlled trials to significantly improve multiple drinking outcomes, compared with placebo. Over the course of a 14-week trial, topiramate significantly increased the proportion of volunteers with 28 consecutive days of abstinence or nonheavy drinking. In both studies, the differences between topiramate and placebo groups were still diverging at the end of the trial, suggesting that the maximum effect may not have been reached. The magnitude of topiramate's effect may be larger than that for naltrexone or acamprosate. Importantly, efficacy was established in volunteers who were drinking at the time of starting the medication.

Acamprosate

Mechanism. Acamprosate (Campral®) acts on the GABA and glutamate neurotransmitter systems and is thought to reduce symptoms of protracted abstinence such as insomnia, anxiety, restlessness, and dysphoria. It's available in oral form (three times daily dosing).

Efficacy. Acamprosate increases the proportion of dependent drinkers who maintain abstinence for several weeks to months, a result demonstrated in multiple European studies and confirmed by a meta-analysis of 17 clinical trials. The meta-analysis reported that 36 percent of patients taking acamprosate were continuously abstinent at 6 months, compared with 23 percent of those taking a placebo. Two large U.S. trials failed to confirm the efficacy of acamprosate, although secondary analyses in one of the studies suggested possible efficacy in patients who had a baseline goal of abstinence. A reason for the discrepancy between European and U.S. findings may be that patients in European trials had more severe dependence than patients in U.S. trials, a factor consistent with preclinical studies showing that acamprosate has a greater effect in animals with a prolonged history of dependence. In addition, before starting medication, most patients in European trials had been abstinent longer than patients in U.S. trials.

Disulfiram

Mechanism. Disulfiram (Antabuse®) interferes with degradation of alcohol, resulting in accumulation of acetaldehyde, which, in turn, produces a very unpleasant reaction including flushing, nausea, and palpitations if the patient drinks alcohol. It's available in oral form (once-daily dosing).

Efficacy. The utility and effectiveness of disulfiram are considered limited because compliance is generally poor when patients are given it to take at their own discretion. It is most effective when given in a monitored fashion, such as in a clinic or by a spouse. (If a spouse or other family member is the monitor, instruct both monitor and patient that the monitor should simply observe the patient taking the medication and call you if the patient stops taking it for 2 days.) Some patients will respond to self-administered disulfiram, however, especially if they're highly motivated to abstain. Others may use it episodically for high-risk situations, such as social occasions where alcohol is present.

How Long Should Medications Be Maintained?

The risk for relapse to alcohol dependence is very high in the first 6–12 months after initiating abstinence and gradually diminishes over several years. Therefore, a minimum initial period of 3 months of pharmacotherapy is recommended. Although an optimal treatment duration hasn't been established, it is reasonable to continue treatment for a year or longer if the patient responds to medication during this time when the risk of relapse is highest. After patients discontinue medications, they may need to be followed more closely and have pharmacotherapy reinstated if relapse occurs.

If One Medication Doesn't Work, Should Another Be Prescribed?

If there's no response to the first medication selected, you may wish to consider a second. This sequential approach appears to be common clinical practice, but currently there are no published studies examining its effectiveness. Similarly, there is not yet enough evidence to recommend a specific ordering of medications.

Is There Any Benefit to Combining Medications?

A large U.S. trial found no benefit to combining acamprosate and naltrexone. Naltrexone, disulfiram, and both in combination were compared with placebo in the treatment of alcohol dependence in patients with coexisting Axis I psychiatric disorders. Equivalently better outcomes were obtained with either medication, but combining them did not have any additional effect. At this time, there is no evidence supporting the combination of medications, but the number of studies examining this question is limited.

Should Patients Receiving Medications Also Receive Specialized Alcohol Counseling or a Referral to Mutual Help Groups?

Offering the full range of effective treatments will maximize patient choice and outcomes, as no single approach is universally successful or appealing to patients. The different approaches—medications for alcohol dependence, professional counseling, and mutual help groups—are complementary. They share the same goals while addressing different aspects of alcohol dependence: neurobiological, psychological, and social. The medications aren't prone to abuse, so they don't pose a conflict with other support strategies that emphasize abstinence. Almost all studies of medications for alcohol dependence have included some type of counseling, and it's recommended that all patients taking these medications receive at least brief medical counseling. Evidence is accumulating that weekly or biweekly brief (i.e., 15–20 minutes) counseling by a health professional combined with prescribing a medication is an effective treatment for many patients during early recovery. Medical counseling focuses on encouraging abstinence, adherence to the medication, and participation in community support groups.

Supporting Patients Who Take Medications for Alcohol

Dependence Pharmacotherapy for alcohol dependence is most effective when combined with some behavioral support, but this doesn't need to be specialized, intensive alcohol counseling. Nurses and physicians in general medical and mental health settings, as well as counselors, can offer brief but effective behavioral support that promotes recovery. Applying this medication management approach in such settings would greatly expand access to effective treatment, given that many patients with alcohol dependence either don't have access to specialty treatment or refuse a referral.

How Can General Medical and Mental Health Clinicians Support Patients Who Take Medication for Alcohol Dependence?

Managing the care of patients who take medication for alcohol dependence is similar to other disease management strategies, such as initiating insulin therapy in patients with diabetes mellitus. In the Combining Medications and Behavioral Interventions (COMBINE) clinical trial, physicians, nurses, and other healthcare professionals in outpatient settings delivered a series of brief behavioral support sessions for patients taking medications for alcohol dependence. The sessions promoted recovery by increasing adherence to the medication and supporting abstinence through education and referral to support groups.

What Are the Components of Medication Management Support?

Medication management support consists of brief, structured outpatient sessions conducted by a healthcare professional. The initial session starts by reviewing with the patient the medical evaluation results as well as the negative consequences of drinking. This information frames a discussion about the diagnosis of alcohol dependence, the recommendation for abstinence, and the rationale for medication. The clinician then provides information on the medication itself and adherence strategies and encourages participation in a mutual support group such as Alcoholics Anonymous (AA). In subsequent visits, the clinician assesses the patient's drinking, overall functioning, medication adherence, and any side effects from the medication. When a patient doesn't adhere to the medication regimen, it's important to evaluate the reasons and help the patient devise plans to address them.

Chapter 60

Treating Co-Occurring Drug and Alcohol Use Disorders

Chapter Contents

Section 60.1

Treatment of Co-Occurring Alcohol and Other Drug Use Disorders

This section includes text excerpted from "Treatment of Co-Occurring Alcohol and Other Drug Use Disorders," National Institute on Alcohol Abuse and Alcoholism (NIAAA), March 19, 2009. Reviewed April 2018.

Drug use disorders (DUDs) frequently co-occur with alcohol use disorders, affecting approximately 1.1 percent of the U.S. population. Compared with alcohol use disorders or DUDs alone, co-occurring disorders are associated with a greater severity of substance dependence; co-occurring psychiatric disorders also are common in this patient population. Many effective medications and behavioral treatments are available to treat alcohol dependence and drug dependence when these occur independent of one another. There is a paucity of research, however, specifically focused on the treatment of persons with co-occurring alcohol and other DUDs (AODUDs). The evidence to date on treating this patient population suggests that combining some of the behavioral and pharmacologic treatments that are effective in treating either drug or alcohol use disorders alone may be useful in the AODUD population as well.

An estimated 1.1 percent of the U.S. population has an alcohol use disorder with a co-occurring drug use disorder (DUD). This type of comorbidity is sometimes referred to as homotypic comorbidity or dual dependence. To be consistent with the theme of this issue, this section refers to people with this combination of disorders as having alcohol and other drug (AOD) use disorders (AODUDs). Many people with alcohol use disorders use other substances at some point in their lives. This section focuses on the following AOD combinations: alcohol and cocaine, alcohol and cannabis, opioids and cocaine, and alcohol and cocaine with methadone maintenance.

After a brief discussion of assessment, placement, and treatment matching, this section reviews the literature on evidence-based pharmacologic and behavioral treatment strategies for AOD dependence. It also presents evidence for using specific treatments for AODUDs and provides recommendations on how to implement these treatments.

Assessment, Placement, and Treatment Matching

In general, patients with AODUDs have a greater severity of substance dependence than patients with only an alcohol use disorder or a DUD. People with AODUDs are at least as likely to have co-occurring psychiatric disorders as those who have only DUDs and are more likely to have such disorders than those with only alcohol use disorders. In addition, people with AODUDs are more likely than those with either drug or alcohol use disorders alone to seek treatment. Thus, patients with AODUDs are perhaps best evaluated for treatment planning by a practitioner with specialized expertise in addictive disorders. Although many factors dictate the initial placement and treatment of the AODUD patient (e.g., co-occurring pregnancy or the need for medical detoxification), general guidelines are available. The American Society of Addiction Medicine (ASAM) has guidelines for placement and treatment matching (ASAM Patient Placement Criteria for the Treatment of Substance-Related Disorders 2001). The American Psychiatric Association (APA) also has guidelines for the treatment of substance use disorders (SUDs), which cover the issue of placement into various treatment settings. Treatment that integrates AODUDs and psychiatric care probably is optimal for most AODUD patients, particularly those with greater severity of psychiatric comorbidity. Effective integrated, dual-diagnosis programs emphasize the combination of multiple treatment modalities delivered in a format that acknowledges the limitations and nature of co-occurring psychiatric illness and is delivered by a staff skilled in the treatment of both addictive and psychiatric disorders.

Evidence-Based Treatments for Inpidual SUDs

Although a complete review of the behavioral and pharmacologic treatment literature for specific addictive disorders is beyond the scope of this article, this section provides a brief summary of the major treatment modalities that currently are in use. In general, an approach that combines behavioral and pharmacologic treatments is optimal for most patients. However, findings from studies of the pharmacotherapy of alcohol dependence have shown that some patients may do well when medication is combined with a minimal behavioral approach focusing on medication adherence. In addition, among alcohol-dependent patients, those with a goal of abstinence from alcohol likely have better treatment outcomes.

However, because some patients do not subscribe to such a goal, it often is necessary to negotiate a "harm reduction" approach with them, with the option of modifying the goal if their efforts to reduce their drinking substantially are not successful. In drug dependence treatment, behavioral therapies often are considered primary and medications secondary, except in the case of patients receiving opioid agonist maintenance therapy. (In opioid agonist therapy, patients receive a drug, such as methadone or buprenorphine, that is chemically similar to opioid drugs.)

Behavioral Therapies

Table 60.1 lists the research-based behavioral therapies for different SUDs, with a general description of the level of research evidence supporting each of the treatments. Because people with substance dependence often are ambivalent about changing their behavior, some experts consider motivational enhancement therapy (MET) to be an essential element of addictions treatment, although the evidence supporting its use may be strongest in the treatment of alcohol use disorders. MET aims to engage in treatment patients who are resistant to behavioral change and may be the most acceptable therapeutic approach when patients are new to treatment for AODUDs. MET can help to build a working alliance between the patient and practitioner and provide a foundation on which other useful therapies, including medications, may be added. Cognitive-behavioral therapy (CBT) and MET are effective in the treatment of cannabis dependence. Contingency management interventions also have proven to be effective in treating SUDs, including reducing both drug use and drinking in alcohol-dependent patients. (Contingency management is the systematic reinforcement of desired behaviors and the withholding of reinforcement or punishment of undesired behaviors.) In addition to the therapies shown in table 60.1, an intensive outreach counseling program may be helpful in reducing illicit drug use and returning to treatment patients who drop out from methadone maintenance.

Table 60.1. Summary of Research on Behavioral Therapies for Specific Substance Use Disorders

Behavioral Therapies	Alcohol	Cocaine	Opioid*	Marijuana
CBT	++ (A)	++ (A)		+ (B)
MET	++ (A)	+/– (B)	+/– (B)	+ (B)
CM	++ (A)	+ (A)	+ (A)	+ (B)
BI	++ (A)			
TSF	+ (A)	+/– (B)		
CET	+ (B)			
BCT	+ (B)			
CRA	++ (A)			

Notes: BCT = Brief Couples Therapy, BI = Brief Intervention, CBT = Cognitive-Behavioral Therapy, CET = Cue Exposure Therapy, CM = Contingency Management, CRA = Community Reinforcement Approach, MET = Motivational Enhancement Therapy, TSF= Twelve-Step Facilitation.

For level of evidence supporting the use of therapies: (–) indicates that the treatment appears not to be efficacious, (+/–) indicates conflicting results or preliminary evidence of efficacy, (+) indicates evidence of efficacy from randomized controlled trials, and (++) indicates evidence of efficacy from multiple trials and/or meta-analyses.

Evidence-based strength of recommendation taxonomy:

A. Recommendation based on consistent and good-quality patient-oriented evidence.

B. Recommendation based on inconsistent or limited-quality patient-oriented evidence.

C. Recommendation based on consensus, usual practice, opinion, disease-oriented evidence, or case series for studies of diagnosis, treatment, prevention, or screening.

**Behavioral treatments for opioid dependence likely are most effective when combined with pharmacotherapy.*

A variety of behavioral approaches have shown efficacy in the treatment of alcohol use disorders. BRENDA, which is an acronym for Biopsychosocial, Report, Empathy, Needs, Direct advice, and Assessment, has been used to provide a flexible, and practical, client-centered therapy for use in conjunction with pharmacotherapy. BRENDA, like MET, is a client-centered approach that, by building a working alliance with the patient, can act as a foundation for other treatments. BRENDA may enhance medication adherence in the treatment of alcohol dependence.

Volume 1 of the Project COMBINE monograph series, which describes combined behavioral intervention (CBI), provides detailed guidelines for a state-of-the-art counseling approach to the treatment of alcohol dependence that combines elements of CBT and MET.

Volume 2 describes medication management (MM), an intervention that was used in the COMBINE study as a minimal supportive approach to accompany medication therapy in alcohol-dependent patients. In this study, treatment with the opioid receptor antagonist naltrexone accompanied by MM was efficacious in achieving successful drinking outcomes. (Receptor antagonists block the binding of other substances (i.e., agonists) that trigger responses in the cell.) However, combining elements of multiple behavioral therapies (e.g., combining motivational interventions with CBT and clinical management) may be the most effective approach to the treatment of SUDs.

Pharmacotherapies

Table 60.2 summarizes the current research findings on the efficacy of pharmacologic treatments for SUDs. This section will review the relevant findings on treatments for alcohol, cocaine, opioid, and cannabis dependence.

Table 60.2. Summary of Research on Pharmacotherapies for Specific Substance Use Disorder

Research on Pharmacotherapies	Alcohol	Cocaine	Opioid*
Disulfiram	+/–* (B)	+(B)	
Naltrexone	++ (A)	+/– (B)	+/–* (B)
Acamprosate	++ (A)		
Topiramate	(+ (A))	+/– (B)	
Ondansetron	+/–** (C)	+/– (C)	
Sertraline/SSRI	+/–** (C)	– (C)	
Carbamazepine		– (C)	
Valproate		+/– (B)	
Tiagabine		+/– (B)	
Aripiprazole	– (C)		
Modafinil		(+ (B))	
Quetiapine	+/–** (C)		

Table 60.2. Continued

Research on Pharmacotherapies	Alcohol	Cocaine	Opioid*
Olanzapine	– (C)	– (C)	
Lithium	– (C)		
Baclofen	+/– (B)	+/– (B)	– (C)
Buprenorphine			++ (A)
Methadone			++ (A)

Notes: For level of evidence supporting the use of therapies: (–) indicates that the treatment appears to be ineffective, (+/–) indicates either conflicting results or preliminary/potential evidence of efficacy, (+) indicates support from randomized controlled trials, (++) indicates support for efficacy from multiple trials and/or meta-analyses.

**Effective in highly motivated patients that will adhere.*

*** May be effective in certain subtypes of alcohol dependence, or in dually-diagnosed individuals.*

Evidence-based strength of recommendation taxonomy:

A. Recommendation based on consistent and good-quality patient-oriented evidence.

B. Recommendation based on inconsistent or limited-quality patient-oriented evidence.

C. Recommendation based on consensus, usual practice, opinion, disease-oriented evidence, or case series for studies of diagnosis, treatment, prevention, or screening.

Alcohol dependence. Despite progress in pharmacotherapy research, medications approved to treat alcohol dependence are underutilized.

Disulfiram. This medication causes flushing, nausea, nervousness, and other unpleasant physiologic effects when combined with alcohol. It was approved by the U.S. Food and Drug Administration (FDA) in 1949, making it the first medication approved for treating alcohol dependence. Disulfiram was approved before implementation of the FDA requirement that a medication have demonstrated efficacy as well as safety. In a multicenter trial that included more than 600 male veterans, disulfiram failed to increase the likelihood of abstinence during a 1-year treatment period. However, among individuals who drank, a 250-mg dose of disulfiram reduced drinking days relative to a 1-mg dose of disulfiram or a placebo. Note though, the potentially serious adverse effects produced by the medication when combined with alcohol argue for its use in abstinence-oriented treatment rather than for harm reduction.

Patients who are likely to respond well to disulfiram treatment are older; have a longer drinking history; greater social stability, impulsivity, and motivation for recovery; attend Alcoholics Anonymous meetings; and are cognitively intact. When disulfiram ingestion in a clinical trial was supervised by an inpidual designated by the patient, the drug was shown to increase abstinent days and decrease overall drinking relative to a placebo. Based on these and other findings, the efficacy of disulfiram may depend upon supervised administration of the drug.

Naltrexone. Several meta-analyses support the efficacy of oral naltrexone (at a daily dosage of 50 mg) in the treatment of alcohol dependence. Naltrexone has been shown most consistently to be effective in reducing the risk of relapse to heavy drinking, with less consistent evidence that it reduces the percentage of drinking days or increases the likelihood of total abstinence.

One long-acting formulation of naltrexone has been shown to be effective in reducing heavy drinking among alcohol-dependent patients and may offer enhanced adherence, at least early in treatment, which can be a critical time in the process of recovery for AODUD patients. Based on the findings from that study, the FDA approved long-acting naltrexone for the treatment of alcohol dependence. A second injectable formulation of naltrexone reduced the number of drinking days and increased the likelihood of total abstinence compared with a placebo injection.

Acamprosate. Acamprosate is an amino acid derivative that affects the brain signaling molecules (i.e., neurotransmitters) γ-aminobutyric acid (GABA) and glutamate. The mechanism of action of acamprosate is shown in table 60.3.

Meta-analyses of European clinical trials have shown that acamprosate nearly doubles the likelihood of abstinence and reduces the risk of heavy drinking. Based on these studies, later age of onset of alcohol dependence, the absence of a family history of alcohol dependence, and the presence of physiologic dependence and higher levels of anxiety are associated with a beneficial response to acamprosate. Based on three pivotal trials from Europe, the FDA approved acamprosate to treat alcohol dependence. However, two studies of acamprosate conducted in the United States show the drug to be no better than placebo, when a standard, intent-to-treat analysis was used. (An intention-to-treat analysis is an analysis based on the initial treatment intent not on the treatment eventually administered. It is based on the assumption that, as in real life, sometimes patients do not all receive optimal treatment, even though that was the initial intention.)

Table 60.3. Mechanisms of Action of Medications Used to Treat Alcohol and Other Drug Use Disorders

Name	Main Mechanism	Pharmacologic Action
Disulfiram	Aversive therapy: consumption of alcohol within up to 2 weeks of ingesting the medication produces the disulfiram–ethanol reaction, consisting of flushing, palpitations, increased heart rate, decreased blood pressure, nausea/vomiting, sweating, dizziness, among other possible symptoms. Anticipating these effects averts drinking. Also may diminish the "high" produced by cocaine, reducing cocaine craving. It also directly reduces cocaine use independent of the patient's level of drinking.	For alcohol dependence: inhibits the action of the metabolic enzyme aldehyde dehydrogenase, resulting in a buildup of acetaldehyde during ethanol metabolism. May also indirectly modulate receptors for the neurotransmitter glutamate. For cocaine dependence: inhibits the function of the enzyme dopamine β-hydroxylase, thus inhibiting metabolism of the neurotransmitter dopamine, thereby increasing the unpleasant effects of cocaine. Also increases cocaine plasma concentrations.
Naltrexone	Attenuates the rewarding effects of alcohol in the brain and also may reduce the conditioned anticipation of those effects, as manifested in the urge to drink.	Is an opioid receptor antagonist; it blocks the effects of increased endogenous opioids (caused by alcohol) on dopaminergic transmission in the nucleus accumbens.
Acamprosate	Postulated to reduce relapse risk by reducing the urge to drink and the drive to experience the negative reinforcing effects of alcohol.	Essentially a modulator of glutamatergic transmission; has a complex mechanism of action that involves the modulation of certain glutamate (NMDA) receptors, calcium channels, and other downstream intracellular molecular events.
Topiramate	Postulated to reduce the rewarding effects of drinking and the conditioned anticipation of those effects, as manifested in the urge to drink.	Multiple pharmacologic effects; facilitates some chemical connections in the brain and inhibits others. Indirectly attenuates dopaminergic transmission in the nucleus accumbens in response to drinking and directly attenuates neuronal glutamatergic hyperexcitability in the absence of alcohol. Mechanism in reducing cocaine use is unknown but is perhaps related to its GABAergic and glutamatergic effects.

Table 60.3. Continued

Name	Main Mechanism	Pharmacologic Action
Modafinil	Attenuates the rewarding effects of cocaine, perhaps reducing the urge to use as well. Acts as a "functional partial agonist," meaning that it has stimulant-like effects but also reduces cocaine self-administration and euphoria.	Unknown mechanism of action; thought to have minimal abuse potential and limited euphoric effects.
Buprenorphine	Blocks the rewarding effects of opioids, reduces withdrawal and the urge to use the drugs.	Partial agonist at μ-opioid receptors, blocks κ-opioid receptors. Unknown mechanism in reducing cocaine use in opioid-dependent patients.
Methadone	Blocks the rewarding effects of opioids, reduces withdrawal and the urge to use the drugs.	Agonist at μ-opioid receptors; has unique pharmacokinetic and pharmacodynamic properties, including a long latency to peak blood concentrations (thereby minimizing its euphoric effects), a long half-life (reducing acute withdrawal symptoms), and opioid cross-tolerance (reducing euphoria from heroin and other short-acting opioids). Unknown mechanism in reducing cocaine use in opioid-dependent patients.

Note: An agonist is a substance that binds to a specific receptor and triggers a response in the cell.

Two studies of naltrexone plus acamprosate versus either agent alone for the treatment of alcohol dependence did not show a clear advantage of the combination. Kiefer and colleagues found that the combination treatment was superior to acamprosate alone but was not better than naltrexone alone. In the COMBINE study, treatment with the combination of naltrexone and acamprosate was no better than placebo treatment.

Anticonvulsant medications. Topiramate is the best studied of the anticonvulsant medications that have been evaluated for the treatment of alcohol dependence. It has been shown to be effective in reducing a variety of drinking outcomes among alcohol-dependent patients in both a single-site study and in a randomized, placebo-controlled, double-blind, multicenter trial. Studies of other anticonvulsants, including carbamazepine and valproate, also have shown some evidence of efficacy for the treatment of alcohol dependence and may be especially useful in patients with co-occurring bipolar disorders.

Other medications. A thorough discussion of serotonergic medications (e.g., selective serotonin reuptake inhibitors (SSRIs), ondansetron) and other medications (e.g., atypical antipsychotics, lithium) is beyond the scope of this review. At present, there is not sufficient evidence to recommend the use of these agents for the treatment of primary SUDs. Ongoing research may clearly define a role for such medications in treating SUDs, particularly in certain subgroups of alcohol-dependent patients and those with co-occurring psychiatric illness.

Lithium does not appear efficacious for the treatment of alcohol dependence and has not been adequately tested among patients with comorbid alcohol dependence and bipolar disorder. In a randomized, placebo-controlled clinical trial, baclofen, a GABAB receptor agonist, was shown to be safe and effective for the treatment of alcohol dependence. However, given the possibility of misuse and other complications from baclofen, which have been noted in the medical literature (e.g., withdrawal, psychosis, and delirium), more research with this medication is needed before it can be recommended as a safe and effective treatment for SUDs.

Cocaine dependence. Although many medications have been evaluated to treat cocaine dependence, few agents have shown efficacy. At present, disulfiram, tiagabine, topiramate, and modafinil are the most promising of the available treatments.

Disulfiram. Some of the initial research with disulfiram was conducted in study participants with alcohol and cocaine dependence and is discussed below. Disulfiram probably reduces cocaine use in cocaine-dependent individuals by producing an aversive reaction to the drug and also may reduce the euphoria produced by the drug, although some studies note an increase in subjective "highs." Disulfiram also may delay the high from cocaine, decreasing its reinforcement value.

Combined with associated increases in plasma concentrations of cocaine, patients may experience greater nervousness and increased cardiovascular strain, which are aversive. However, similar to what is seen in the treatment of alcohol dependence with disulfiram, adherence limits the utility of this medication in the treatment of cocaine dependence. Practical approaches to dealing with this problem include making access to a desired treatment (e.g., methadone for co-occurring opioid dependence) contingent on adherence or using social reinforcers (e.g., an agreement or contract between patient and spouse requiring adherence).

Tiagabine. A GABA reuptake inhibitor, tiagabine has yielded mixed results for the treatment of cocaine dependence. In 2005, a black-box warning was added to the label for tiagabine, warning physicians of new-onset seizures that were noted in some patients (without a history of epilepsy) taking the medication (Gabatril® package insert). (Tiagabine inhibits the reuptake of GABA by neurons, thus providing increased GABA availability.)

Modafinil. Of particular interest in the treatment of cocaine dependence is modafinil because it has a mild stimulant-like effect and produces a mild euphoria (the exact nature of which has been debated in the literature). The drug appears to blunt the desirable effects and the craving associated with cocaine use and reduces cocaine use in a human laboratory setting, with little or no abuse potential.

Naltrexone. Most of the findings concerning the effects of naltrexone on cocaine dependence come from studies of patients with co-occurring alcohol and cocaine dependence, although one study evaluated its use in patients with only cocaine dependence. This study evaluated the effects of naltrexone in a prospective, randomized trial that compared four groups receiving placebo or naltrexone (50 mg) combined with either relapse prevention therapy or standard drug counseling. The group that received naltrexone combined with relapse prevention treatment outperformed the other three groups, supporting its use, but only in combination with that specific psychosocial intervention.

Baclofen. Some evidence of efficacy in treating cocaine dependence also has been shown with the use of baclofen.

Other medications. Antipsychotic medications do not appear useful for treating cocaine dependence. A vaccine that causes patients to develop antibodies to cocaine in the blood is in development and has shown promise in treating cocaine dependence.

Opioid dependence. Opioid dependence in the United States is most often treated with behavioral treatment approaches combined with maintenance therapy with the opioid agonists methadone or buprenorphine. Considerable evidence supports the efficacy of these agents for opioid dependence treatment. Although some patients are able to maintain abstinence from opioids following detoxification through involvement in self-help groups such as Narcotics Anonymous (NA), many patients require treatment with opioid agonist medications, and some require maintenance treatment indefinitely. Methadone treatment of opioid dependence is available only through licensed methadone programs that monitor patients' drug and alcohol use and sometimes provide treatment for co-occurring psychiatric disorders.

Opioid antagonists, including naltrexone (which is FDA approved for this indication), also can be used to treat opioid dependence in patients who are able to transition from physiologic dependence to abstinence. To avoid precipitating acute withdrawal, a patient should be free of opioid use for a minimum of 7 days before being treated with an opioid antagonist. In a meta-analysis of naltrexone treatment of opioid dependence, retention in treatment was a significant moderator of a beneficial effect of the drug. This likely reflects the key problem of adherence to naltrexone that is seen in treatment populations. However, behavioral therapies such as contingency management appear to improve naltrexone adherence and treatment retention in this population. Patients should be warned that death by overdose can occur despite opioid receptor blockade by naltrexone or after treatment with naltrexone.

Baclofen, which has shown some promise in the treatment of alcohol and cocaine dependence, also has been evaluated as a maintenance treatment for opioid dependence In a 12-week, randomized, double-blind, placebo-controlled trial, baclofen was superior to placebo on treatment retention, opioid withdrawal symptoms, and depressive symptoms. However, there was no significant difference in terms of opioid use, alcohol use, opioid craving, or side effects.

***Cannabis* dependence.** There are no medications that have demonstrated efficacy for the treatment of cannabis dependence.

Treatment of AODUDS

As reviewed above, most studies have focused on the treatment of inpidual SUDs rather than co-occurring disorders. Although studies conducted specifically in AODUD populations are limited, the evidence to date suggests that approaches similar to those used to treat the

Table 60.4. Summary of Research on Treatments for AODUDs

	Alcohol/Cocaine	Alcohol/Opioid	Cocaine/Opioid
Disulfiram	+/– (B)	+/– (B)**	+ (B)
Naltrexone	+/– (B)	* (C)	* (C)
Buprenorphine			+ (B)
Methadone		+/– (C)	+ (B)
Desipramine			+ (B)
Topiramate	* (C)		
Baclofen	* (C)		
Tiagabine			+/– (B)
CBT	+ (B)		+ (B)
CM	+/– (B)	+ (B)	+ (B)
TSF	+/– (B)		

Notes: AODUDs = Alcohol and other drug use disorders, CBT = cognitive-behavioral therapy, CM = contingency management, TSF = twelve-step facilitation.

** = recommendation synthesized from studies performed in primarily alcohol or cocaine dependent subjects, not specifically in the dually dependent group*

*** = may only be effective when continued opioid agonist therapy is made contingent on disulfiram ingestion.*

For level of evidence supporting the use of therapies: (–) indicates that the treatment appears to be ineffective, (+/–) indicates conflicting results or preliminary evidence of efficacy, (+) indicates evidence of efficacy from randomized controlled trials, (++) indicates evidence of efficacy from multiple trials and/or meta-analyses.

Evidence-based strength of recommendation taxonomy:

A. Recommendation based on consistent and good-quality patient-oriented evidence.

B. Recommendation based on inconsistent or limited-quality patient-oriented evidence.

C. Recommendation based on consensus, usual practice, opinion, disease-oriented evidence, or case series for studies of diagnosis, treatment, prevention, or screening.

inpidual SUDs may be effective. As with the treatment of dependence on inpidual substances, behavioral therapies provide the "backbone" or main component of treatment for patients with AODUDs. In addition, because the studies evaluating pharmacotherapies in AODUD patients almost always include at least one behavioral therapy component, this review does not examine these types of therapy separately. Table 60.4 summarizes the evidence for various inpidual treatments for AODUDs.

Contingency management has been shown to increase treatment retention and improve outcomes across a spectrum of addictive disorders, irrespective of psychiatric severity. Hence, contingency management may serve effectively as a platform for the treatment of AODUDs. A review of treatments for alcoholic methadone patients suggested that making methadone treatment contingent on disulfiram ingestion may effectively reduce drinking and alcohol-related adverse outcomes. Along similar lines, contingency management using both prizes and vouchers has been shown to be beneficial for co-occurring opioid and cocaine/stimulant use disorders, as well as other co-occurring substance dependence disorders, including alcohol dependence.

Co-Occurring Alcohol and Cocaine Dependence

Similarities in the pathophysiology of cocaine and alcohol dependence suggest that these disorders may respond to the same medications. Carroll and colleagues examined the effects of disulfiram, CBT, and 12-step facilitation (TSF) on drinking and cocaine use in patients with these co-occurring disorders. Compared with no medication, disulfiram was efficacious in reducing the use of both drugs, and both CBT and TSF were superior to supportive counseling. In a 1-year follow-up, the effects of disulfiram on cocaine use persisted, but no effects were found on drinking behavior. Other studies of disulfiram in cocaine-dependent subjects have shown that co-occurring alcohol use and dependence, as well as female gender, may actually limit the efficacy of the medication.

Hersh and colleagues found no advantage for naltrexone (50 mg/day) over placebo in the treatment of people with co-occurring cocaine and alcohol use disorders. In a randomized, controlled trial in which alcohol- and cocaine-dependent subjects received either naltrexone (50 mg/day) or placebo, combined with either relapse prevention or drug counseling psychotherapy, Schmitz and colleagues also found no effects of the medication. In a small, open-label trial of oral naltrexone (150 mg/day), Oslin and colleagues found that patients with co-occurring alcohol and cocaine dependence reduced both their drinking and their cocaine use. A follow-up, randomized, placebo-controlled trial of a 150-mg daily oral dose of naltrexone, in which patients were stratified by gender, showed that the active treatment reduced cocaine and alcohol consumption among men but not among women. These findings suggest that, at least in men, a higher dose of naltrexone may be efficacious in treating patients with co-occurring cocaine and alcohol dependence.

In a 11-week comparison of disulfiram, naltrexone, or a combination of the two for the treatment of cocaine and alcohol dependence, study participants receiving disulfiram (alone or in combination) had higher rates of combined abstinence (to both alcohol and cocaine) than those on placebo. The combination of disulfiram and naltrexone was superior to either drug given alone, or placebo, on a secondary outcome measure (i.e., the achievement of 3 weeks of continuous abstinence). All the patients received concurrent CBT as a behavioral regimen. A study of 12 patients with co-occurring alcohol and cocaine dependence showed significant reductions in the use of both substances with the addition of naltrexone (50 mg/day) or disulfiram (400 mg/day) to CBT, compared with CBT alone.

Because topiramate (at a target dose of 300 mg/day) has demonstrated efficacy in studies of alcohol dependence and preliminary evidence of efficacy in studies of cocaine dependence (at a target dose of 200 mg/day), it may be an ideal candidate for the treatment of these disorders when they co-occur. Further, topiramate can be safely prescribed to patients taking buprenorphine or methadone, so it could be combined with other treatments for alcohol and drug dependence.

Although modafinil appears to be effective for reducing cocaine use in cocaine-dependent patients, a study showed that those with co-occurring alcohol dependence may not experience this benefit. Because alcohol use disorders may have a negative effect on outcomes for cocaine abuse treatment, particularly when patients continue to drink after initiating cocaine abuse treatment, addressing the use of both substances through combined treatment approaches may be optimal.

Co-Occurring Opioid and Cocaine Dependence

Buprenorphine appears dose-dependently to reduce cocaine use in opioid-dependent patients, although it does not appear to be any more effective than methadone for that purpose. The addition of desipramine to buprenorphine or methadone may augment or facilitate abstinence from cocaine and opioids in patients dependent on both substances. Interestingly, in a placebo-controlled study comparing desipramine alone or in combination with contingency management in buprenorphine-maintained patients, the combined group did significantly better than the other groups on measures of cocaine use.

High-dose tiagabine (24 mg/day), in addition to methadone, also was superior to placebo in reducing cocaine use in patients dependent on both opioids and cocaine. A double-blind, randomized, placebo-controlled trial of disulfiram in methadone-maintained patients with co-occurring dependence on cocaine found that disulfiram significantly decreased cocaine use in these patients. George and colleagues also found disulfiram to reduce cocaine use and increase the number of weeks of cocaine abstinence in buprenorphine-maintained patients with co-occurring cocaine dependence.

Two randomized controlled studies of bupropion in methadone-maintained patients have shown a possible role for the medication in the treatment of cocaine dependence. Margolin and colleagues compared bupropion with placebo in a 12-week study of 149 methadone-maintained patients with cocaine dependence. Although there was no overall difference in cocaine use between the two groups, a subgroup of patients that was depressed at the beginning of the study showed a significant reduction in cocaine use. Poling and colleagues conducted a 6-month trial of bupropion and contingency management in methadone-maintained patients with cocaine dependence.

These investigators found that bupropion combined with contingency management reduced cocaine use. Although in this population bupropion without contingency management has not been shown to be efficacious, combining the medication with contingency management may have a synergistic effect. No serious adverse events were reported in either study. However, as with cocaine, bupropion can lower the seizure threshold.

Co-Occurring Opioid and Alcohol Dependence

Preliminary research suggests that adequate dosing of methadone during maintenance treatment (achieved by increasing the dose until urine screens are negative for all opioids and benzodiazepines) may be effective in reducing both drug and alcohol use in patients with a co-occurring alcohol use disorder. As mentioned above, disulfiram appears to be efficacious in reducing drinking in this population but probably only when continued methadone maintenance is made contingent on disulfiram ingestion.

Naltrexone, in both the oral and long-acting injectable forms, has been shown to be effective in treating detoxified opioid-dependent patients and thus can be considered for use in highly motivated individuals. However, the high cost of the only long-acting naltrexone formulation available in the United States, combined with reports of patient deaths from opioid overdose stemming from efforts to overcome the blockade produced by naltrexone, require that practical and ethical concerns be evaluated before this approach can be recommended widely to treat opioid dependence. Nonetheless, the use of naltrexone for selected patients (e.g., physicians) with opioid dependence appears justified.

The use of naltrexone therapy in patients with alcohol dependence and a less severe form of co-occurring opioid use disorder (i.e., abuse rather than dependence, with no history of intravenous use) also may be a viable option because it does not present as great a risk of opioid overdose as may be present in patients with moderate to severe opioid dependence.

Treatment Recommendations for Patients with AODUDs

For patients with alcohol and cocaine dependence, disulfiram has better empirical support than any other medication. Less compelling evidence exists for the use of either naltrexone or topiramate, but these also should be considered for treatment of these co-occurring disorders. A daily dose of more than 50 mg of naltrexone is needed to treat these disorders but may not be efficacious for women with co-occurring alcohol and cocaine dependence. Topiramate has not yet been studied in AODUD patients, but its safety and efficacy have been demonstrated in patients with alcohol or cocaine dependence.

Although the optimal dosage has not yet been determined, preliminary findings suggest that 200–300 mg per day, increased gradually over 6–8 weeks, is required. Second-line therapies may be effective in patients with cocaine dependence but not alcohol dependence (i.e., modafinil and tiagabine) or vice versa (i.e., acamprosate). Baclofen also could be considered for use in select patients based on evidence of its efficacy in alcohol or cocaine dependence. In addition to an absence of data on the efficacy of these medications in co-occurring cocaine and alcohol dependence, it is unclear whether these medications should be used alone or combined with first-line or other second-line agents. There is limited evidence to support combining disulfiram and naltrexone to treat co-occurring alcohol and cocaine dependence; further research on the combination is needed before it can be recommended as offering an advantage over the use of either medication alone.

For alcohol-dependent patients on methadone maintenance, optimizing the dosage of methadone may help to reduce drinking. Stabilizing opioid withdrawal symptoms and illicit opioid use with methadone or buprenorphine in qualifying patients is an appropriate first step. For patients who continue to drink while receiving opioid maintenance therapy, the first-line alcohol treatments (with the exception of naltrexone) should be considered. Disulfiram may be the medication of choice for such patients, because they also may have a cocaine use disorder. To increase adherence to disulfiram treatment in this patient population, it is probably necessary to require that the patient submits to observed disulfiram ingestion as a condition of continued opioid agonist treatment. Topiramate may be an option in this population as well, though there are no published reports to guide this approach.

For patients dependent on opioids and cocaine, adequate dosing of buprenorphine and methadone may reduce use of both substances. This approach should be considered as a first-line therapy for such patients, as long as the severity of their opioid dependence warrants opioid agonist therapy. If monotherapy with buprenorphine or methadone is inadequate to control co-occurring cocaine use, adding disulfiram to either agonist treatment should be considered. Research also suggests that adding desipramine or high-dose tiagabine to an opioid agonist maintenance regimen can be helpful.

However, caution is necessary in prescribing medications to patients with co-occurring opioid and cocaine dependence as they may have significant medical comorbidity, including cardiac and liver disease. This strategy also has the potential to cause drug interactions. As is true for the treatment of patients with other combinations of AODUDs, pharmacotherapy in this patient group should be combined with behavioral therapies, such as contingency management, which may be particularly useful in combination with desipramine.

General Treatment Recommendations

Although the treatment literature is rapidly growing for inpidual SUDs, there is a paucity of systematic research on treatments for AODUDs. The existing literature shows that, as with DUDs alone, combined behavioral and psychopharmacological treatments for patients with AODUDs are likely to be optimal. At a minimum, patients should be encouraged to participate in a 12-step program and are likely to benefit from the addition of group or inpidual therapies that use motivational enhancement and cognitive-behavioral techniques. When available, the use of contingency management is likely to enhance outcomes for patients with AODUDs. The use of medications to improve outcomes in AODUD patients has shown initial promise, particularly for co-occurring alcohol and cocaine dependence.

Treatment planning for patients with AODUDs should include medical and psychiatric evaluations and integrated treatment to address co-occurring substance use and psychiatric disorders. Given the burden of psychopathology, patients with AODUDs often may require a higher level of care (e.g., inpatient rehabilitation, psychiatric partial hospital or intensive outpatient "dual diagnosis" programs) for initial stabilization. Medications with beneficial effects on drinking behavior and other drug use should be used in combination with behavioral interventions.

In short, treatment for patients with AODUDs should start with a motivational intervention, with a focus on developing a therapeutic alliance. In these efforts, the clinician should be mindful of the patient's stage of change and level of motivation, utilize empathic listening and expression, address the patient's goals and needs, emphasize and promote self-regulation skills, utilize multiple treatment modalities, actively address co-occurring medical and psychiatric illness, and promote adherence to the treatment program.

Section 60.2

Integrated Care for Co-Occurring Alcohol and Other Conditions

This section includes text excerpted from "Integrating Care for People with Co-Occurring Alcohol and Other Drug, Medical, and Mental Health Conditions," National Institute on Alcohol Abuse and Alcoholism (NIAAA), June 15, 2010. Reviewed April 2018.

Most people with alcohol and other drug (AOD) use disorders suffer from co-occurring disorders (CODs), including mental health and medical problems, which complicate treatment and may contribute to poorer outcomes. However, care for the patients' AOD, mental health, and medical problems primarily is provided in separate treatment systems, and integrated care addressing all of a patient's CODs in a coordinated fashion is the exception in most settings. A variety of barriers impede further integration of care for patients with CODs. These include differences in education and training of providers in the different fields, organizational factors, existing financing mechanisms, and the stigma still often associated with AOD use disorders and CODs. However, many programs are recognizing the disadvantages of separate treatment systems and are attempting to increase integrative approaches.

Although few studies have been done in this field, findings suggest that patients receiving integrated treatment may have improved outcomes. However, the optimal degree of integration to ensure that patients with all types and degrees of severity of CODs receive appropriate care still remains to be determined, and barriers to the implementation of integrative models, such as one proposed by the Institute of Medicine, remain.

It is widely recognized that the majority of patients with alcohol use problems also suffer from co-occurring mental health and medical problems. Co-occurring disorders (CODs) complicate the treatment process and, in many cases, contribute to poorer outcomes as well as higher service utilization and costs over time. In the past, clinicians within each treatment setting—alcohol treatment, mental health, and general medicine—frequently treated COD patients as they would patients with only one of these disorders; however, such treatment is not well suited to the special needs of patients with CODs.

Extensive research has documented the need to treat all conditions from which patients suffer and has identified many key components of the best practices for achieving this goal. Moreover, a growing body of research suggests that integrated approaches to treatment may improve the outcomes of patients with alcohol problems. Although optimally integrated care still is the exception in most treatment settings, interest in this approach is mounting, and many programs are attempting to incorporate integrated models of care.

Scope of the Problem

Prevalence of Co-Occurring AOD and Mental Health Problems

The high prevalence of co-occurring AOD problems and mental health conditions has been well documented in the addiction and psychiatric literatures. There are several excellent reviews of the epidemiologic research, and many studies of clinical samples, as well as large national and international population surveys, have been published. Lifetime prevalence of CODs among those seeking treatment for AOD disorders has been estimated at anywhere from one-quarter to well over one half.

For example, the National Comorbidity Survey (NCS), a general population survey of adults, found that 51.4 percent of those surveyed with a lifetime AOD disorder also reported a lifetime mental health disorder, whereas 50.9 percent of those with a mental health disorder reported having had an AOD disorder. The co-occurrence of AOD problems with mood and anxiety disorders is especially high. In a general population sample, the National Epidemiologic Survey on Alcohol and Related Conditions (NESARC) found that of those with at least one AOD disorder, 20 percent suffered from a mood disorder and 18 percent from an anxiety disorder in the same period.

Many studies determine the prevalence of CODs by examining clinical *Diagnostic and Statistical Manual of Mental Disorders, Fourth Edition (DSM-IV)* diagnoses or by assessing patients' scores on research instruments that are well validated and which typically assess type and severity of problems consistent with the criteria used to make DSM–IV diagnoses. The true prevalence of co-occurring AOD and mental health problems, however, probably is much higher than that documented in the literature, particularly when including lower severity, sub diagnostic threshold cases. In addition, co-occurrence of AOD use and more than one mental disorder is not unusual.

Chronology and Etiology of Co-Occurring AOD and Mental Health Problems

The chronology and etiology of CODs also are complex issues and often a contentious subject in the AOD treatment and psychiatry fields, because many of the factors that predispose patients to develop AOD use problems also are related to mental health problems. For example, on the one hand, AOD problems can stem from self-medication for mental health problems; on the other hand, they also can catalyze or exacerbate certain mental health problems (e.g., depression). The differences in how professional disciplines have perceived and addressed these complexities have contributed to the historical lack of treatment integration.

Regardless of the origin or order of problem development, however, the co-occurrence of AOD and mental health problems usually complicates the treatment process. In studies of treatment populations, psychiatric status has proven an important predictor of the course of AOD problems; in fact, it is one of the more salient and well-replicated variables associated with treatment seeking and lack of improvement. In longitudinal population studies, psychiatric problem severity predicts increases in alcohol consumption and adverse consequences of drinking over time. In addition to having poorer outcomes, AOD patients with psychiatric problems are at heightened risk of readmission.

Prevalence of Co-Occurring AOD Problems and Medical Conditions

Co-occurring AOD problems and general medical conditions have been less studied than co-occurring AOD and mental health problems. However, the literature suggests that people with AOD problems have a higher prevalence of health problems in general and of many specific conditions in particular, including human immunodeficiency virus (HIV) disease, infection with hepatitis B and C viruses, hypertension, asthma, chronic obstructive pulmonary disorder (COPD), arthritis, headache, acid-related disorders, and many pain conditions. The AOD field has begun to develop a framework for examining the specific AOD abuse-related medical conditions that could be targeted for integrated interventions. For example, COPD, depression, or hypertension patients could be targeted for alcohol screening (and brief treatment if appropriate) in primary care or disease management programs.

People with AOD disorders are at increased risk for many chronic medical conditions. As with mental health problems, clear etiologic relationships are not easy to establish. Thus, unhealthy alcohol use is implicated in the development of some conditions (e.g., cirrhosis), increased exposure to some diseases (e.g., HIV, hepatitis), or exacerbation of existing medical problems (e.g., diabetes). Conversely, alcohol use also may result from attempting to cope with overwhelming medical problems (e.g., chronic pain). In addition, it is clear that medical conditions and their sequelae frequently interfere with the alcohol treatment process (e.g., doctor's appointments may conflict with treatment program schedules or pain conditions may make it impossible to attend treatment) and impede recovery. Similarly, unhealthy AOD use can thwart medical treatments. For example, patients' AOD use may impede their ability to comply with treatment regimens. In addition, AOD use is contraindicated with many medications and can inhibit immune system functioning.

Integrating the Treatment of Co-Occurring AOD and Other Health Problems

Co-Occurring AOD and Mental Health Problems

Although AOD treatment occurs mainly in a separate system, it historically was located within the larger mental health treatment system. Until well into the 20th century, patients with alcohol problems—if they received treatment at all—received care from institutions and organizations charged with mental healthcare, such as asylums and sanatoria. (More often, alcohol problems were addressed within the criminal justice and, to a lesser extent, the social welfare systems.) The latter part of the 20th century saw the alcohol treatment field begin to separate from the mental health system in a variety of ways. Thus, programs were designed to specifically treat alcohol (and other drug) problems; the "disease model" of addictions and the attendant proliferation of the 12-step and self-help movements became more prominent, and research institutions dedicated to the formal study of AOD use problems, such as the National Institute on Alcohol Abuse and Alcoholism (NIAAA) and the National Institute of Drug Abuse (NIDA), were established.

Many researchers and clinicians in the addictions field welcomed the separation because of concern that AOD problems had been given short shrift under the mental health system. The two separate public systems of care became largely funded by the federal government via separate block grants, further reinforcing the separation of services. Unfortunately, however, the separation also created a system in which most programs and providers do not have the resources, training, or inclination to treat patients with CODs and instead reinforced differences in provider attitudes toward specific disorders and in overall treatment philosophy. Regrettably, this often resulted in patients being referred to another agency for treatment of the other disorder before they were eligible to be seen for their presenting problem, or in ignoring the co-occurring problem entirely.

Differences between the mental health and AOD fields in clinician beliefs, training, behavior, and ideology pose significant barriers to the effective treatment of COD patients. On the mental health side it often has been argued that AOD problems are symptoms of deeper psychological distress and that when those other disorders are properly treated, AOD problems will lessen or subside. This conceptualization reinforces a hierarchy in which AOD disorders and their treatment are seen as less legitimate and less deserving of attention and resources. At the same time, the AOD treatment field frequently is ideology-driven, and its disagreements with the mental health field on appropriate diagnosis and treatment often have been contentious.

Although AOD treatment programs may vary in other ways, the great majority have been influenced by the Alcoholics Anonymous (AA) tradition, and the major treatment model currently used in the United States, the "Minnesota Model," is based on the same 12-step principles.

Although AA and AA influenced programs have given much to the field, they have had a pervasive unitary influence, resistant to competing treatment models, even in the case of CODs. These programs traditionally have emphasized more confrontational approaches than mental health programs, which have emphasized more supportive techniques (or have simply not treated patients until they are "clean and sober"). Many AOD treatment providers themselves are in recovery and graduates of AA and AA influenced programs and adhere to a philosophy of abstinence. These treatment providers often frown on medications such as methadone or naltrexone for their patients, whereas medications are commonplace in mental health programs for psychiatric problems. This has significantly slowed the adoption of pharmacotherapeutic interventions for COD patients in many AOD treatment settings.

Screening and referral practices also differ. Historically, mental health providers have not routinely assessed patients for AOD misuse, and, by the same token, AOD treatment providers have not systematically screened for mental health problems. The reasons are many and in some cases may simply signify lack of training. However, too often assessment and diagnosis of CODs are ignored or delayed because the provider conceptualizes either the AOD or the mental health problem as "primary" and needing to be addressed before dealing with any other problems. Conversely, some clinicians may not feel equipped to treat patients with complex CODs, and prefer to refer them out to another agency for treatment. Both practices contribute to COD patients receiving suboptimal treatment.

Mental health and AOD treatment also have differed in their use of self-help groups. Whereas AOD treatment has a long tradition of relying on self-help, particularly 12 step-oriented groups, as a key therapeutic ingredient, they are much less commonly used in the psychiatric setting. Although the literature is mixed on whether COD patients are more or less likely than others to participate in 12-step meetings. In the past two decades, self-help groups that are rooted in traditional 12-step programs but have been adapted to meet the special needs of people with CODs have been growing in number, and evaluations point to positive direct and indirect effects on several key components of recovery for COD patients.

Clearly, reaching a consensus on treatment strategies that work for COD patients remains a challenge. However, this may be an opportune time to experiment with new treatment approaches. AOD treatment providers who see patients with CODs are becoming more open to trying new interventions (e.g., medications) for AOD disorders, as evidence for the effectiveness of these interventions is accumulating rapidly.

Co-Occurring AOD Problems and Medical Conditions

Historically, alcohol and general medical services have been even less integrated than AOD treatment and psychiatry. Except for medically supervised detoxification, medical and AOD treatment providers continue to operate separately, although evidence suggests that integration would contribute to better outcomes.

For a variety of reasons—including discomfort with or insufficient knowledge about AOD problems, inadequate clinical tools, time constraints, ignorance of treatment resources, and issues of professional jurisdiction—many primary care providers rarely screen for or discuss AOD use with their patients. Moreover, general medical practitioners only treat a small proportion of their patients' AOD use problems. Stigma and societal attitudes about addictions affect physicians as well as the general public. Accordingly, many treatment providers are uncomfortable about discussing AOD use with their patients, and few are trained in assessment and treatment. The proliferation of "carve outs"—arrangements whereby health plans contract with managed behavioral healthcare companies to provide AOD and mental healthcare services rather than reimbursing the providers—has reduced financial incentives for providers to treat patients rather than referring them. As a result of all these factors, general medical practitioners are not commonly considered the appropriate healthcare professional to handle treatment for AOD use problems.

The role of general medicine in AOD treatment may be changing, however, because of increased interest in moving identification and brief treatment for AOD problems into medical settings in general, and primary care in particular. Evidence supporting the effectiveness of such interventions is growing; moreover, several factors have been identified that can make such integrative practices more likely to succeed. These factors include the adoption of the drug and alcohol problem identification and treatment initiation measures set forth in the Healthcare Effectiveness Data and Information Set (HEDIS) of the National Committee for Quality Assurance (NCQA); the development of Current Procedural Technology (CPT) and Healthcare Common Procedure Coding System (HCPCS) codes that permit Medicare and Medicaid reimbursement for brief AOD treatments in medical settings; and NIAAA's Assessing Alcohol Problems.

The growing evidence supporting the efficacy and effectiveness of medications for AOD problems also may encourage physicians to treat such problems, although studies suggest that pharmacotherapies for treatment of AOD disorders are adopted more slowly than for other medical conditions. The extent of adoption of medications for AOD disorders also may be context related and depend on organizational policies and capacities. For example, adoption of a new medication is more likely in settings where other AOD medications already are being prescribed; therefore, AOD medications are more likely to be adopted in AOD treatment programs than in primary care.

Barriers to Integrating Care for Patients with CODs

AOD, mental health, and general medicine providers differ widely in education and training. Providers in medicine generally are physicians or advanced practice nurses and mental health clinicians who typically hold doctoral or masters level degrees. In contrast, the education and training among addiction treatment providers is more varied, ranging from medical or doctoral degrees to non-degreed peer counselors.

Organizational factors also pose significant barriers to the integration of care for patients with CODs. According to Ridgely and colleagues, "The system problems are at least as intractable as the chronic illnesses themselves." Most research indicates that people with CODs do not readily fit into either medical or traditional AOD treatment or psychiatry programs and that like patients with other chronic conditions they need ongoing services, possibly over several years.

This need for longterm services also is related to the issue of financing mechanisms for chronic care patients. On the whole, financing mechanisms currently are geared to acute rather than long-term treatment. Inclusion of reimbursement for long-term disease management of CODs might help lower hospitalization costs and improve outcomes. Related questions that should be addressed are whether treatment patterns and costs differ for different CODs and whether more coherent treatment policies could increase appropriate utilization of different treatment settings (i.e., primary care versus emergency departments versus inpatient care) and reduce costs.

Because of these complex organizational constraints, patients often are forced to navigate separate systems of care (sometimes both public and private), contacting different agencies or departments within large organizations (e.g., a health plan) and seeing multiple providers. Too often patients must coordinate their own care, even when appropriate linkages between providers and organizations are lacking. This can be especially challenging for patients experiencing cognitive and/or functional impairments related to their CODs, and, not surprisingly, many fail to follow through with one or more of their treatment regimens. Because of the stigma attached to co-occurring problems, many patients also experience considerable prejudice not only from society but from treatment providers, their own families, and even from themselves. Under these circumstances, it is difficult for patients to assume the role of proactive consumers, empowered to demand the highest quality, coordinated healthcare. As a result, many patients fall through the cracks in these fragmented systems of care, and treatment initiation, engagement and retention rates in this population are notoriously low.

Models of Treatment for Patients with CODs

Many programs now recognize the downside of separate systems for COD patients and are attempting to add integrative elements into their curricula. Currently, treatment models for patients with AOD problems and CODs broadly fall into four categories:

- **Serial treatment care** is received in sequential treatment episodes, in separate systems of care
- **Simultaneous/parallel care** is received for both/all disorders simultaneously, but in separate, noncoordinated systems
- **Coordinated/parallel care** for both/all disorders is received simultaneously in separate but well coordinated and closely linked systems, with established and formalized collaborative agreements.
- **Integrated care** for both/all disorders is provided by the same cross trained clinicians and in the same program, resulting in clinical integration of services.

Unfortunately, the evidence base for recommending one type or model of treatment over another is small. Controlled studies on integrated programs and services have been few, and the methodological challenges many, including small sample sizes. Moreover, most studies have focused on treatment for co-occurring AOD and mental health disorders, focusing particularly on patients with severe mental illness. A review of randomized clinical trials of psychosocial interventions to reduce AOD problems of severely mentally ill patients found no compelling evidence to recommend one type or model of treatment delivery over another, partly because none of the models have been studied extensively.

The review by Ley and colleagues did not detect strong effects of different treatments on AOD outcomes. Only a few studies have examined the integration of medical care and AOD treatment. Nevertheless, research has provided some evidence that integrated treatment may improve posttreatment outcomes or produce favorable outcomes compared with other types of services. One study of AOD treatment patients with CODs found that patients in programs with more services for CODs (e.g., more "dual diagnosis" groups, higher percentages of clinicians with training or certification in COD treatment, or a higher number of psychological services) more frequently used psychological services and had better psychological and AOD use outcomes at 6 months.

Another study examined the impact on patient outcomes of training psychiatric clinicians in the treatment of CODs, including comprehensive assessment, motivational interviewing, and relapse prevention techniques. These investigators found that patients assigned to COD trained clinicians had significantly better mental health outcomes at 18 months than did those who received usual mental health services. Other study findings have suggested that treatment components which increase integration of services for CODs may be beneficial. However, because many of these studies were of small samples, with most patients uninsured (often homeless) or on Medicaid, more research is needed "to compare outcome for nonhomeless clinical patients in well defined and monitored examples of integrated treatment and parallel treatment."

Fully Integrated Treatment: Is That the Goal?

In response to the growing evidence base for integrated care, one could argue that, ideally, all AOD treatment and mental health and medical programs should be fully clinically integrated—that is, all services should be provided simultaneously within the same organizations, by the same providers—and capable of treating patients with

CODs. However, complete clinical integration does not seem feasible for most programs in the short term, if only for logistical reasons, particularly with regard to integrating medical care and AOD treatment.

A survey estimates that only half of AOD programs nationwide offer dual AOD and mental health treatment, and even fewer offer integrated medical services. There is no evidence in the literature that mental health programs are more likely to coordinate services for patients with CODs. In fact, a survey of AOD and psychiatric treatment programs found that AOD programs were more likely to provide services for CODs than were psychiatric programs. Another strategy would be to incorporate specialty AOD and mental health services into general medical settings such as primary care. This approach could potentially reach far more patients in less stigmatized healthcare settings.

Another question is whether complete integration would even be desirable. For example, Minkoff suggested that full integration within programs actually might threaten choice, flexibility, and quality of treatment. Because COD patients are highly heterogeneous in their specific diagnoses and acuity, it is conceivable that integration and coordination of care across programs might be preferable to within program clinical integration. History suggests that in fully integrated programs, patients with AOD and severe co-occurring mental health disorders are likely to receive the most attention, whereas patients with single disorders or with sub diagnostic comorbidities are more likely to be excluded from treatment or their co-occurring problems not identified.

Although the evidence does not point to a single optimal level of integration, accrediting bodies, purchasers, and federal and state agencies can greatly facilitate integration of services by implementing certain overarching strategies, identified by the Institute of Medicine (IOM) Committee. The IOM report endorses a conceptual model that was developed by Friedmann and colleagues to illustrate the spectrum of care integration. In this model, according to Friedmann and colleagues, mechanisms for coordinating services range from "the ad hoc, market-based purchase of services from local providers to the complete control and coordination of a fully integrated, centralized service delivery system." It seems entirely plausible that more extensive and formalized integrative mechanisms would improve the quality of care for patients with CODs and would offer the best chance of improving their outcomes. It is worth noting however, that this model emerged from an examination of how service coordination affected service utilization of drug treatment patients; it did not specifically address services for CODs, and did not examine patient outcomes beyond utilization. Thus, much more research needs to be conducted comparing the organization of care for CODs.

The flow of confidential information poses a complex barrier to implementing integrated care for patients with CODs. Patient health information is carefully (and rightly) protected, and information about the treatment of AOD problems is particularly well guarded by federal and state regulations and organizational policies, such as 42 CFR, part 2 (Electronic Code of Federal Regulations (eCFR) 2009). Although preventing sensitive and potentially damaging patient information from falling into the wrong hands is essential, these regulations, originally designed to protect drug treatment patients from legal prosecution, have had the unintended consequence of inhibiting the coordination of healthcare across agencies and departments. The stringent requirements for obtaining consent to release information (especially challenging for some patients with CODs) may inhibit coordination of care, enhanced referral, consultation, and follow-up. For example, integration of care may be compromised if a provider in one program cannot determine if a patient has followed through with a referral, or if a patient has a health condition that is related to, could be exacerbated by, or requires medication which is contraindicated with AOD use. Moreover, these regulations and practices can serve to reinforce the stigma associated with AOD and mental health problems.

The IOM recommends that sharing of information between providers treating the same patient become more routine. Clinicians should discuss with each patient the importance of sharing diagnoses, medications, and other therapies between providers treating CODs to enable collaborative care between clinicians. The report acknowledges that information on mental health and AOD conditions is sensitive and that sharing this information often is governed by federal and state laws and individual organization practices. The report therefore calls on state and federal entities and organizations implementing additional information policies to re-examine their policies and practices on information sharing to ensure that they are not inappropriately interfering with coordinating care. The rapid development of health information technology (IT) and the growing adoption of electronic medical records further complicate these issues. Integrated health IT systems could potentially contribute significantly to the integration of care for patients with CODs and improve the quality of care, and the field must carefully weigh these potential benefits against privacy concerns. Several leading policy groups are considering this issue, which was included as one of the key strategic areas at the "National

Summit on Defining a Strategy for Behavioral Health Information Management and Its Role Within the Nationwide Health Information Infrastructure," convened in 2005 by the Substance Abuse and Mental Health Services Administration (SAMHSA). The summit concluded that "Legal issues should be clarified and in some cases changed to facilitate appropriate information sharing across service systems for care coordination and service improvement."

Chapter 61

Gaps in Clinical Prevention and Treatment for Alcohol Use Disorders (AUDs)

Heavy drinking causes significant morbidity, premature mortality, and other social and economic burdens on society, prompting numerous prevention and treatment efforts to avoid or ameliorate the prevalence of heavy drinking and its consequences. However, the impact on public health of current selective (i.e., clinical) prevention and treatment strategies is unclear. Screening and brief counseling for at-risk drinkers in ambulatory primary care have the strongest evidence for efficacy, and some evidence indicates this approach is cost-effective and reduces excess morbidity and dysfunction. Widespread implementation of screening and brief counseling of nondependent heavy drinkers outside of the medical context has the potential to have a large public health impact. For people with functional dependence, no appropriate treatment and prevention approaches currently exist, although such strategies might be able to prevent or reduce the morbidity and other harmful consequences associated with the condition before its eventual natural resolution.

This chapter includes text excerpted from "Gaps in Clinical Prevention and Treatment for Alcohol Use Disorders: Costs, Consequences, and Strategies," National Institute on Alcohol Abuse and Alcoholism (NIAAA), February 5, 2014. Reviewed April 2018.

For people with alcohol use disorders, particularly severe and recurrent dependence, treatment studies have shown improvement in the short term. However, there is no compelling evidence that treatment of alcohol use disorders has resulted in reductions in overall disease burden. More research is needed on ways to address functional alcohol dependence as well as severe and recurrent alcohol dependence.

Heavy drinking takes a high toll on society. This issue summarizes the disease burden and economic cost to society attributable to alcohol use, which provides a powerful incentive to develop and implement ways to reduce them. Therefore the focus is on the role of selective (i.e., clinical) prevention and treatment approaches for heavy drinkers and people with alcohol use disorders (AUDs) in reducing the burden associated with excessive alcohol use. As used here, selective, or clinical, prevention refers to strategies targeted at individuals at higher risk of experiencing adverse alcohol effects, such as screening and brief counseling of heavy drinkers in healthcare settings or internet-based screening and advice provided to college students.

The term "treatment" refers to services for alcohol dependence provided by a professional, such as a counselor, social worker, nurse, psychologist, or physician. Community peer-led support groups such as Alcoholics Anonymous are considered to be distinct from professional treatment services, much like a diabetes support group would be distinguished from endocrinology services. The focus is on the following three questions: Can selective prevention and treatment reduce the disease burden attributable to heavy drinking? Are some treatment approaches more cost-effective than others? Do gaps exist in the current continuum of care? After addressing these issues, the review suggests research priorities to help close existing gaps and reduce the burden of disease.

Selective Prevention and Treatment: Effectiveness, Cost Effectiveness, and Disease Burden

Screening and brief advice for at-risk (i.e., nondependent) drinkers, commonly known as screening and brief intervention (SBI), is effective at reducing drinking for a year or more and in many studies also has been shown to reduce alcohol-related harms, such as motor-vehicle crashes and driving violations. Its efficacy is supported by numerous randomized controlled trials and multiple meta-analyses; as a result, the U.S. Prevention Task Force has listed it as a Type B recommendation for medical prevention services. The evidence is strongest for nondependent heavy drinkers who present for primary care services in ambulatory settings. Unfortunately, a meta-analysis of studies of SBI in primary care settings failed to show significant reductions in subsequent healthcare utilization. The efficacy of SBI in other settings, such as emergency departments (EDs) or hospitals, has not been established, although several randomized controlled trials have been conducted. One explanation for the observed differences may be the patient populations analyzed. Thus, in most of the outpatient primary care studies, participants with alcohol dependence were excluded from the analysis, whereas that generally was not the case for studies conducted in EDs or hospital settings. Moreover, patients with alcohol dependence are much more commonly encountered in ED and hospital settings than in primary ambulatory care. At this time, SBI in primary care ambulatory settings for adults can be strongly recommended as highly efficacious, whereas SBI in EDs or hospitals cannot.

SBI also seems to be effective among select groups when delivered through internet-based or computerized applications. In particular, there is strong evidence that digital SBI can effectively reduce drinking and associated consequences among college students. It is not clear whether or to what extent this finding might generalize to other population subgroups, but it is certainly plausible that it could, provided the target population has easy access to computers and is computer literate. The same holds true for other methods, such as telephone-based SBI or use of the relatively new publication and website called Rethinking Drinking, which is published by the National Institute on Alcohol Abuse and Alcoholism (NIAAA).

Despite the evidence supporting its effectiveness, SBI is not yet being implemented widely. Widespread dissemination of information about recommended drinking limits and easy access to screening and brief counseling has the potential to make a significant public health impact. Because at-risk drinkers are much more numerous than alcohol-dependent people, at-risk drinking contributes a much greater disease burden than alcohol dependence. Accordingly, widespread implementation of SBI has the potential to reduce a greater proportion of disease burden than even very effective treatment, a concept known as the prevention paradox. Therefore, more research is needed to expand the implementation of SBI in the at-risk population and further increase its effectiveness.

Estimating the effectiveness and cost effectiveness of treatment is more complex. Most reviews conclude that treatment is effective at reducing drinking and associated consequences. Multiple behavioral treatment approaches—such as cognitive-behavioral therapy (CBT), motivational enhancement therapy (MET), 12-step facilitation, behavioral marital therapy, and community reinforcement—have similar and relatively high levels of short-term success in reducing drinking and associated consequences, at least when treatment is provided by the highly trained, motivated, and closely supervised clinicians participating in clinical efficacy trials. Why these technically diverse counseling techniques produce almost identical drinking outcomes is unclear. Three alternative explanations have been offered:

- The specific technique is less important than other, mostly unidentified, factors associated with psychotherapy.
- Each approach works via different mechanisms but produces similar results on average, much like different antidepressants acting through different mechanisms produce similar outcomes in the treatment of depression.
- Professional treatment only has a small effect in determining outcome compared with other, nontreatment factors, such as social control (e.g., driving-while-intoxicated laws, family pressure, or employer mandate), natural history of alcohol dependence, and the tendency to revert to usual levels of drinking following resolution of a crisis where drinking had peaked (i.e., regression to the mean).

This last explanation is supported by research demonstrating that changes in drinking habits begin weeks before treatment entry. Likewise, in another study of treatment of alcohol dependence that examined events leading to treatment seeking, the findings suggested that the change point occurred prior to treatment entry. Thus, it is unclear how much of the positive change can be attributed to the treatment processes themselves as opposed to other factors leading to and following treatment seeking.

What is clear, however, is that researchers and clinicians do not yet understand how or why some people change in response to treatment and others do not. To address this issue, NIAAA led the way at the National Institutes of Health (NIH) in shifting the focus of behavioral treatment research to identifying the mechanisms of behavior change rather than encouraging more comparisons of different psychotherapy approaches. The NIH subsequently developed a major initiative on basic behavioral research. This research initiative provides an opportunity to investigate many obvious questions. For example, what are the social forces that either support or impede positive health behavior change? What determines their impact, in terms of the response of the individual? Why and how do people begin to change, and what determines the resilience of that change? What is the basic science underlying behavior change, at all levels from genetic and genomic to cellular, organic, individual, and social interactions? Research elucidating the basic science of behavior change is an exciting and promising area that has the potential to substantially change the types of interventions that are available, making them more powerful, available, and cost-effective.

The lack of clarity about what causes a change in drinking behavior also results in uncertainty as to whether treatment of alcohol dependence reduces disease burden. The community prevalence of alcohol dependence, which is about 4 percent in any year, has not changed substantially to date. Earlier studies found a cost offset of treatment—that is, lower healthcare costs after treatment than before treatment. More studies, however, have found that heavy drinkers who are not in crisis underutilize healthcare, at least in an employed population, suggesting that the observed cost reduction is more a reflection of the natural history of drinking behavior and of a regression to the mean. In other words, people suffering from any disease tend to seek treatment when their condition is most severe. In the case of alcohol dependence, treatment seeking, therefore, would be preceded by an escalation of drinking, complications, and utilization of medical services and, consequently, high costs before treatment entry. Because chronic conditions such as alcohol dependence wax and wane, most people will tend to improve after a period of greater severity, even without effective treatment, so that subsequently reduced costs may not necessarily be associated with treatment.

Also, every patient's disease trajectory is different, so that when drinkers are assessed before and after treatment, some of them will be well at follow-up, whereas for others their condition will be more severe. The average severity, however, will be less following treatment, because for all patients studied, their disease severity at treatment entry will have been high. The most rigorous study of the cost effectiveness of alcoholism treatment, the COMBINE trial, found that treatment was cost-effective, especially pharmacotherapy with medical management. The interpretation of these findings is limited, however, by the study's highly rigorous trial design, intensive follow-up, and exclusion criteria, and it is unknown to what extent these findings generalize to community treatment programs and participants.

Another limitation when estimating the effects of treatment on public health is that relatively few affected people seek treatment. For example, among people who develop alcohol dependence at some point in their lives, only 12 percent seek treatment in a specialty treatment program. Among people who have AUDs and who perceive a need for treatment, almost two-thirds (i.e., 65%) fail to obtain it because they are not ready to stop drinking or feel they can handle it on their own. Other common reasons for the failure to seek treatment include practical barriers, such as lack of health insurance, the cost of treatment, and lack of transportation or access to treatment, which are reported by 59 percent of respondents, and stigma, which is reported by 31 percent. Thus, more people might seek treatment if it was less expensive, stigmatizing, and disruptive than most treatment approaches. Efforts to improve access, affordability, and attractiveness of treatment, especially for individuals with less severe AUDs should be encouraged.

Despite these limitations, some tentative conclusions can be drawn as to which approaches to treating alcohol dependence are more cost-effective. Studies found no significant difference in outcomes between residential and outpatient treatment and no clear relationship between the intensity of treatment and outcome. For example, medical management plus pharmacotherapy with naltrexone generated similar outcomes to more expensive counseling approaches, even when counseling was performed once weekly and on an outpatient basis.

These studies suggest that a more individualized, outpatient, and medically based approach may provide a cost-effective alternative to approaches favoring intensive psycho-education, which often are provided in residential settings. Treatment provided in residential rather than outpatient settings may add considerable expense without a commensurate improvement in outcomes. In addition, confidential treatment by their usual primary care physician involving only routine clinic visits may attract more people, thus expanding access to effective treatments.

Gaps in the Continuum of Care

There are several gaps in the continuum of care that deserve attention, affecting drinkers across the spectrum of alcohol involvement. Epidemiological research has demonstrated that alcohol involvement varies along a continuum ranging from asymptomatic heavy drinking (i.e., at-risk drinking), through functional alcohol dependence, and to severe and recurrent alcohol dependence. The continuum of care ideally should correspond to this epidemiology but does not at this time. Most studies and treatment approaches have focused on the more severe end of the spectrum—that is, people with severe, recurrent dependence. However, the vast majority of heavy drinkers either does not have alcohol dependence or has a relatively milder, self-limiting form. This spectrum of severity is similar to that for other chronic diseases, such as asthma. Likewise, examining treatment seekers in the current system of care yields similar results to studying hospitalized asthmatics: thus, heavy drinkers in treatment exhibit more severe dependence, more comorbidity, less response to treatment, and a less supportive social network compared with people who do not seek intensive treatment.

In contrast, people with functional alcohol dependence predominantly exhibit "internal" symptoms, such as impaired control; a persistent desire to cut down on their drinking but finding it hard to do; and alcohol use despite internal symptoms such as insomnia, nausea, or hangover. These individuals generally drink much less than more seriously affected people. Functional alcohol dependence typically resolves after a few years, mostly without requiring specialty treatment. Large gaps in services exist for people at both ends of the spectrum of dependence severity—that is, both for people at the milder end of the spectrum (i.e., at-risk drinkers and people with functional alcohol dependence) and for those at the most severe end (i.e., with recurrent, treatment-refractory dependence). There are few services for at-risk drinkers and people with functional alcohol dependence. In primary medical care, very few patients are screened and positive screening results addressed. Furthermore, functional alcohol dependence largely is ignored because although these individuals meet diagnostic criteria for dependence, they rarely seek treatment in the system. These gaps are significant from a public health perspective because the prevalence of at-risk drinking and functional dependence is much higher than that of more severe disorders and these conditions, therefore, account for the majority of excess morbidity, mortality, and associated costs attributable to alcohol consumption. Whether wider implementation of SBI would result in a reduction in disease burden is not known at this time. However, enhancement of these approaches, especially among young people and community-dwelling heavy drinkers not seeking medical care, might reduce disease burden, although the two populations require somewhat distinct approaches. More studies of secondary prevention efforts outside of medical settings therefore are needed.

SBI in primary care settings to identify people with AUDs at the milder end of the severity spectrum is effective and may be cost-effective, but many questions remain. For example, is it more cost-effective to target higher-risk groups (e.g., young people) for routine screening or is universal screening better overall? And when should screening occur (e.g., only during annual prevention visits or at every new patient visit) and how often should it be repeated? However, the biggest problem remains that effective selective prevention interventions such as SBI are not widely implemented. Although implementation has worked well in situations where additional grant funds were available, it still is unknown whether physicians will engage in this widely or how to best facilitate implementation. The Veterans Affairs health services system has been the most effective at implementing annual screening, but this system is unique in its structure and hierarchical nature. Implementation of such approaches in private healthcare organizations is much more complex and difficult. Therefore, more research is needed on low-cost ways to encourage wider adoption of SBI in primary care settings. Additional research should focus on SBI in other medical settings, especially mental health settings and medical specialties particularly affected by heavy drinking, such as gastroenterology (with patients with alcohol-related liver disease, gastritis, and pancreatitis) and otolaryngology (with patients with alcohol-related head and neck cancers).

Because so many hospitalized heavy drinkers have dependence, SBI is much less effective in this group and its effectiveness with patients in EDs or trauma centers also is unknown. Although some early studies showed positive results, subsequent research has yielded as many negative as positive findings. At present, efforts to implement SBI in these more acute-care settings therefore are premature, and more research is needed to determine if heavy drinkers encountered in such settings require more intensive services, linkage to ambulatory care services, or both.

People with functional alcohol dependence likely require more than brief counseling, but there is a major gap in research concerning optimal treatment strategies. At present, few, if any, services are available for this group because they fall between at-risk drinkers and those with severe recurrent alcohol dependence (who are most likely to enter the current specialty treatment system). Pharmacotherapy (e.g., anti-relapse medications) combined with medical management offers an attractive possible approach for this group, and evidence suggests that this combination yields comparable results to state-of-the-art counseling. Such an approach would allow most people with functional dependence to be treated in primary care and mental healthcare settings, similar to people with mild to moderate depression. More research, especially regarding effectiveness and implementation, is needed on this approach. Although most people with functional alcohol dependence eventually recover without any treatment, their period of illness is associated with less severe but still significant dysfunction, such as absenteeism, attending work or school while sick (i.e., presenteeism), and reduced productivity. Early identification and treatment could reduce or hopefully eliminate these costs to the affected individuals and society. Gaps in treatment also exist for people with severe recurrent alcohol dependence—the group that most people tend to think of when they think of "alcoholism." An exhaustive report examining the treatment system concluded that "Most of those who are providing addiction treatment are not medical professionals and are not equipped with the knowledge, skills or credentials necessary to provide the full range of evidence-based services to address addiction effectively," and that "Addiction treatment facilities and programs are not adequately regulated or held accountable for providing treatment consistent with medical standards and proven treatment practices." The current addiction treatment system first was conceptualized in the middle of the last century, and has changed little since. No other chronic disease is treated with brief stints in a program with limited follow-up care. Instead, for other chronic conditions patients are followed closely by physicians and other professionals over long periods of time, with the goal of minimizing symptoms and relapses, treating complications, and maximizing function. In these cases, care is provided indefinitely, often for life. Such a longitudinal-care approach also offers considerable promise in treating people with severe recurrent alcohol dependence. Several studies have found a highly significant positive effect for longitudinal care in people who have one or more medical complications of alcohol dependence, including two studies that found a significant reduction in 2-year mortality. Some findings also indicate that integrating treatment for substance use disorders into that for severe and persistent mental illness may be effective at reducing substance use, although no high-quality randomized controlled trials of this approach have been published. Pharmacotherapy for AUDs also may be effective in people with severe mental illnesses. Finally, the ongoing need for recovery support and maintenance should be addressed. Thus, more research is needed on the best long-term management strategies for recurrent alcohol dependence.

Conclusion

At this time no solid conclusions can be drawn as to whether current approaches to prevention of and treatment for AUDs reduce the disease burden attributable to heavy drinking, although these strategies have shown positive outcomes in the short term. SBI for at-risk drinkers in ambulatory primary care settings has the strongest evidence for efficacy, and some evidence supports its cost effectiveness and the associated reduction in excess morbidity and dysfunction. However, these benefits do not necessarily indicate that healthcare costs for these patients are reduced. Widespread implementation of SBI for nondependent heavy drinkers outside of the medical context has the potential to have a large public health impact. For heavy drinkers with more severe conditions (i.e., recurrent alcohol dependence), time-limited counseling may improve short-term recovery rates, but its long-term impact is less clear. Moreover, research findings have not been widely implemented. Scientifically based, medically anchored treatment approaches may provide a more attractive and cost-effective approach than the current intensive but time-limited treatment. More research is needed on ways to address functional alcohol dependence as well as severe and recurrent alcohol dependence.

Chapter 62

Counseling and Long-Term Support

The Substance Abuse and Mental Health Services Administration (SAMHSA) is working to build a behavioral health system that enables Americans to find effective treatments and services in their communities for mental and/or substance use disorders. While effective treatments exist, far too few people with behavioral health conditions receive the help they need. For instance, data from SAMHSA's National Survey on Drug Use and Health (NSDUH)—2014 show that in 2014, 15.7 million adults reported having a major depressive episode (MDE) in the past 12 months. Of those, about one-third of adults (33.2%) did not seek professional help during the previous 12 months. The 2014 NSDUH data also show that 21.2 million Americans ages 12 and older needed treatment for an illegal drug or alcohol use problem in 2014. However, only about 2.5 million people received the specialized treatment they needed in the previous 12 months.

While many Americans still go without needed behavioral health treatment, the United States health system is removing the barriers to accessing behavioral health services. As a result of the Affordable Care Act (ACA), a range of health plans are being required to cover essential benefits including mental health and substance abuse treatments. The

---

This chapter includes text excerpted from "Behavioral Health Treatments and Services," Substance Abuse and Mental Health Services Administration (SAMHSA), September 20, 2017.

Affordable Care Act (ACA) extends the impact of the Mental Health Parity and Addiction Equity Act (MHPAEA) so that many health plans must offer coverage for mental health or substance use disorders with at least an equal level of benefits as the plans offer for the treatment of physical health problems.

Treatments and Supportive Services

Individual paths to recovery differ, and packages of treatments and supportive services for mental and substance use disorders should be tailored to fit individual needs. For many people with behavioral health problems the most effective approach often involves a combination of counseling and medication. Supportive services, such as a case or care management, can also play an important role in promoting health and recovery.

Treatments and supportive services are provided in a variety of locations, including:

- Specialty community behavioral health centers
- Substance use disorder rehabilitation programs
- Independent providers
- Hospitals
- Community health centers
- Mutual support groups and peer-run organizations
- Community-based organizations
- Schools
- Jails and prisons
- At home through telebehavioral or home-based services
- Inpatient service providers
- Primary care programs with integrated behavioral health services
- And a variety of other community settings

Individual and Group Counseling

Individual and group counseling include a variety of treatments used to treat behavioral health problems. Counseling and more specialized psychotherapies seek to change behaviors, thoughts, emotions, and how people see and understand situations. Counseling is provided by trained clinicians such as psychologists, psychiatrists, social workers, and counselors.

Different clinicians have different orientations, or schools or thought, about how to provide these services. One common orientation is cognitive-behavioral; clinicians who use this approach provide cognitive-behavioral therapy (CBT). CBT helps people in treatment seek their own solutions to problems by addressing behaviors, thoughts, and feelings with systematic goal-oriented strategies. It is important to understand that even within CBT, as with other orientations, there is a great amount of variability and most clinicians borrow on strategies from many different orientations when they provide counseling or psychotherapy. Finding the right therapist and developing a productive relationship is important for treatment to be successful. Treatment success may be more important than choosing a therapist based on a particular orientation.

Counseling can take a number of forms depending on the type of therapy being used, the goals of the treatment, and other factors in the life of the person receiving therapy. Some courses of counseling last for months or even years, while others can be brief. One brief, goal-oriented strategy, which may be used by itself or as a part of a broader course of counseling is motivational enhancement therapy (MET). MET is based on principles of motivational psychology and designed to produce rapid, internally motivated change. Rather than directing an individual through recovery, practitioners make efforts to help to mobilize the person's own resources and build their own motivation to address a goal, such as reducing alcohol use. Counseling is usually provided on an individual basis, but can also be conducted with small groups of people addressing common issues.

Medication

Prescription medications also are an important resource for treating mental and substance use disorders. Medications for mental and substance use disorders provide significant relief for many people and help manage symptoms to the point where people can use other strategies to pursue recovery. Medications work better for some people than others, even if they have the same disorders.

Medication effectiveness can also change over time, so it is not uncommon for a person to find that the medication needs to be changed or adjusted even after it has been working. Medications also often have significant side effects. As a result, it is important for people receiving medications for behavioral health problems to have regular contact with the prescribing provider to ensure that the approach being used continues to be safe and effective. Medication tends to be most effective when it is used in combination with counseling or psychotherapy. There are many different types of medication for mental health problems, including anti-depressants, medication for attention issues, anti-anxiety medications, mood stabilizers, and antipsychotic medications. Medications are also increasingly being used to treat substance use disorders. This practice often referred to as Medication-Assisted Treatment (MAT), is the use of medications, in combination with counseling and behavioral therapies, to provide a whole-patient approach to the treatment of substance use disorders. Medications exist that can reduce the cravings and other symptoms associated with withdrawal from a substance, block the neurological pathways that produce the rewarding sensation caused by a substance, or induce negative feelings when a substance is taken.

Supportive Services

Supportive services are critical components of a behavioral health system and can help people meet their treatment goals. Supportive services take a variety of forms. Case or care management can coordinate behavioral health services with housing, employment, education, and other supports. Frequently, when individuals are involved in multiple public systems it is important for a single point of contact to coordinate care and engage all the system partners in service planning and delivery. For young people, this is often done through a wraparound process. For people with serious mental illnesses, this can be done through an Assertive Community Treatment (ACT) team.

Because people with mental and substance use disorders often have more physical health problems than the general population, assistance in coordinating care across behavioral and physical healthcare providers can be a valuable support. One important outcome for people with serious mental illnesses is employment, and supported employment services can be an important link to a job that not only supports independence but also provides important social interaction. People may face barriers like lack of transportation or child care, so the ability to provide some flexible supports can be the difference between wellness and failure to receive treatment. Another important set of services is recovery supports. In combination with treatment, recovery support services can enable individuals to build a life that supports recovery as they work to control symptoms through traditional treatments or peer-support groups. These types of services support the goals of community integration and social inclusion for people with mental and/or substance use disorders and their families. SAMHSA also encourages the use of peer support services, or services designed and delivered by people who have experienced a mental and/or substance use disorder and are in recovery.

Evidence-Based Treatments

Individual and group counseling, medication treatments, and supportive services are evidence-based treatments that can be offered by providers individually or jointly. Depending on the type of service, some or all of these can be offered in a variety of settings. SAMHSA also seeks to support the most effective treatment methods possible through its programs, this includes support of evidence-based programs and treatments. Evidence-based programs are programs that have been shown to have positive outcomes through high-quality research. In addition to working with grantees to identify and implement appropriate evidence-based programs, SAMHSA funds the National Registry of Evidence-based Programs and Practices (NREPP). NREPP provides descriptive information and expert ratings for evidence-based programs submitted by researchers and intervention developers across the nation. NREPP assists states and communities in identifying and selecting evidence-based programs that may meet their particular requirements through its library of rated programs.

Treatment for Co-Occurring Mental and Substance Use Disorders

People with a mental disorder are more likely to experience a substance use disorder and people with a substance use disorder are more likely to have a mental disorder when compared with the general population. According to the National Survey of Substance Abuse Treatment Services (N-SSATS), about 45 percent of Americans seeking substance use disorder treatment have been diagnosed as having a co-occurring mental and substance use disorder.

SAMHSA supports an integrated treatment approach to treating co-occurring mental and substance use disorders. Integrated treatment requires collaboration across disciplines. Integrated treatment planning addresses both mental health and substance abuse, each in the context of the other disorder. Treatment planning should be client-centered, addressing clients' goals and using treatment strategies that are acceptable to them.

Integrated treatment or treatment that addresses mental and substance use conditions at the same time is associated with lower costs and better outcomes such as:

- Reduced substance use
- Improved psychiatric symptoms and functioning
- Decreased hospitalization
- Increased housing stability
- Fewer arrests
- Improved quality of life

Cultural Competency in Mental Health and Substance Use Disorder Treatment

Culture is often thought of in terms of race or ethnicity, but culture also refers to other characteristics such as age, gender, geographical location, or sexual orientation and gender identity. Behavioral healthcare practitioners can bring about positive change by understanding the cultural context of their clients and by being willing and prepared to work within that context. This means incorporating community-based values, traditions, and customs into work plans and project evaluations.

The enhanced National Standards for Culturally and Linguistically Appropriate Services in Health and Healthcare (National CLAS Standards) are intended to advance health equity, improve quality, and help eliminate healthcare disparities. Implementing strategies to improve and ensure cultural and linguistic competence in behavioral healthcare systems by using the CLAS standards is a powerful way to address disparities and ensure all populations have equal access to services and supports.

Chapter 63

The Role of Mutual Help Groups in Alcohol Abuse Recovery

Alcohol use disorders (AUDs) are highly prevalent in the United States and often are chronic conditions that require ongoing episodes of care over many years to achieve full sustained remission. Despite substantial scientific advances in specialized care, professional resources alone have not been able to cope with the immense burden of disease attributable to alcohol. Perhaps in tacit recognition of this, peer-run mutual help groups (MHGs), such as Alcoholics Anonymous (AA), have emerged and proliferated in the past 75 years and continue to play an important role in recovery from AUDs.

Alcohol-related disorders are highly prevalent in the United States, with an estimated 30 percent of Americans meeting diagnostic criteria for an alcohol use disorder (AUD) at some point in their life. In addition, AUDs, especially alcohol dependence, often are chronic conditions that require numerous episodes of care over many years to achieve and maintain full remission. The professional healthcare system delivers a combination of pharmacological and behavioral interventions in an attempt to cope with the immense burden of disease attributable to alcohol.

This chapter includes text excerpted from "The Role of Mutual Help Groups in Extending the Framework of Treatment," National Institute on Alcohol Abuse and Alcoholism (NIAAA), April 10, 2011. Reviewed April 2018.

However, professional resources have struggled to keep these problems in check by themselves. Perhaps in tacit recognition of this, peer-run mutual help groups (MHGs), such as Alcoholics Anonymous (AA), have emerged and proliferated in the past 75 years, and despite considerable advances in pharmacological and behavioral treatments for AUDs, these community groups continue to play an important role in helping millions of Americans achieve recovery. Indeed, MHGs are the most commonly sought source of help for alcohol and drug use problems in the United States.

MHG Overview

MHGs—also known as self-help groups—are groups of two or more people who share an experience or problem and who come together to provide problem-specific help and support to one another. Members themselves run groups in rented venues, without professional involvement. And, unlike professional interventions, people can attend MHGs as intensively and for as long as they desire, without insurance approval or divulgence of personally identifying information. In contrast to professional treatments, people typically have access to MHGs at times when they are at higher risk of relapse, such as evenings and weekends, and many MHGs encourage members to contact each other by telephone between meetings whenever help is needed. Consequently, these organizations provide an adaptive, community-based system that is highly responsive to undulating relapse risk.

AA is by far the most widespread MHG in the United States, with over 53,000 groups and 1.2 million members. Other substance-specific 12-step MHGs, such as Narcotics Anonymous (NA), and Cocaine Anonymous (CA), are numerous and can be found in most states. However, dual diagnosis 12-step MHGs such as Double Trouble in Recovery (DTR), cognitive MHGs such as Women for Sobriety, and cognitive-behavioral MHGs such as SMART (Self-Management And Recovery Training) Recovery and Secular Organizations for Sobriety (SOS) are less common. In contrast to these groups, which all focus on abstinence from alcohol and drugs, one MHG, Moderation Management, focuses on limiting alcohol use to within safe limits and is designed to help a large number of nondependent "problem drinkers." In addition to these more typical MHGs, the Internet has given rise to online meetings, which some people may find helpful either as an adjunct to, or instead of, face to face meeting attendance.

Evidence for the Effectiveness of MHGs

Because of its longevity, size, and influence, the vast majority of MHG research has focused on AA and other substance focused 12-step groups, including some research on the dual diagnosis 12-step group DTR. Researchers rarely perform randomized controlled trials on MHGs, in large part because participation in them is self-initiated, voluntary, and anonymous, making them difficult to randomize or control. That said, researchers still can obtain information on the effectiveness of MHGs through prospective, longitudinal studies that control for major confounders. Along these lines, it is important to note that researchers often draw study samples from treated populations rather than from community-based MHG populations, which may limit the generalizability of findings and make it difficult to estimate the independent contribution of MHGs to outcomes.

One long-term prospective study took this potential confounder into account by comparing outcomes informally treated problem drinkers (i.e., AA attendees), and untreated problem drinkers over a 16-year follow-up period. At the 1- and 3-year follow-ups, half of the drinkers who self-selected into AA only were abstinent compared with about a quarter of those who self-selected into formal treatment. By the 8-year follow-up, 46 percent of those in formal treatment reached abstinence compared with 49 percent of the AA only group. Drinkers in the study who self-selected into both AA and formal treatment also were more likely than those in formal treatment only to be abstinent at years 1 and 3 (42% and 51% versus 21% and 26%) and, again, were not significantly different by year 8. Those who received formal treatment plus AA did not differ significantly from those in AA only across the follow-up in terms of abstinence rates. Additionally, a longer duration of AA attendance in the first 3 years independently predicted abstinence, as well as a lower likelihood of drinking problems at year 16. These findings indicate that for some people, MHG participation alone can serve as an effective intervention for AUDs.

Another naturalistic study of 3,018 male inpatients drawn from 15 U.S. Department of Veterans Affairs (VA) treatment programs found that after controlling for confounders, patients who attended only 12-step MHGs during a 1-year follow-up were more likely to be abstinent and free of alcohol dependence symptoms than patients who received only outpatient treatment. Patients in the MHG only group also were less likely to be depressed and had more friend resources after controlling for major confounders.

However, patients attending both MHGs and outpatient treatment had the best outcomes on these variables. A further 2-year follow-up of 2,319 men from the same sample used structural equation modeling to examine the causal links between AA involvement and substance use. Findings showed that AA involvement led to decreased alcohol consumption and fewer alcohol-related problems, after controlling for the level of patient motivation, comorbid psychopathology, and demographics. A mixed gender community outpatient study, which used a rigorously controlled, lagged design to enhance causal inferences, similarly found that participation in MHGs led to subsequent improvement in alcohol-related outcomes.

Questions sometimes arise as to whether MHGs are less suitable for certain populations. For example, because these groups focus purely on substance use and emphasize abstinence, some believe they may not appeal to people with dual diagnoses or people taking psychotropic or anti-relapse medications. In addition, it is believed by some that such groups may not resonate with atheists or agnostics because of their spiritual orientation, and that women and young people may not feel comfortable because they perceive MHGs to be male-dominated and composed largely of middle-aged and older adults. Whereas the available empirical evidence suggests that these populations can benefit from participation in traditional AA or NA meetings, the benefits may be enhanced if people attend groups tailored more specifically to their individual needs, as with youth-oriented meetings and DTR, which is aimed at people with dual diagnoses.

Cost Effectiveness of MHGs

Rising costs in healthcare make the question of cost effectiveness increasingly important. Research suggests that involvement in MHGs may reduce the need for more costly professional treatment services. A 3-year prospective study of problem drinkers, for example, found that those who chose to attend only AA had overall treatment costs that were 45 percent lower than costs for people who chose to attend outpatient treatment, but outcomes were similar for both groups. A large, multisite study of Veterans Affairs inpatient treatment programs that compared outcomes among substance dependent patients who received either cognitive-behavioral treatment (CBT) or professional 12-step treatment found even bigger savings for MHGs. During a 1-year follow-up, patients in 12-step treatment programs participated in substantially more community AA and NA meetings, whereas patients in CBT programs utilized significantly more professional mental health services. As a result, annual costs for CBT patients were 64 percent higher than for 12-step patients, amounting to an additional $4,729 per patient. Notably, the patients in the two types of programs did not differ at intake on demographic and clinical characteristics, and their 1-year outcomes were similar, except that patients treated in 12-step programs had significantly higher rates of abstinence than those treated in CBT programs (46% compared with 36%). In a subsequent 2-year follow-up of a matched sample, patients who received the 12-step treatment continued to show increased abstinence rates and higher levels of 12-step MHG participation. In addition, the CBT patients continued to rely more on professional services, resulting in 43 percent higher costs—an additional $2,440 per patient—during the second year posttreatment.

Mechanisms of Change in MHGs

Each MHG has its own implicit or explicit theory about how people achieve recovery. From AA's perspective, people recover from alcohol dependence through a "spiritual awakening" or "psychic change" resulting from a combination of factors that include working the 12-steps, having a sponsor, believing in a "higher power," and helping others. However, other theories also may explain how AA works. For example, the more implicit social component of AA meetings may promote therapeutic elements through group dynamics, such as the instillation of hope, vicarious learning and modeling, and altruism.

In addition, empirical research on the mechanisms of change in AA highlights important cognitive, behavioral, and social factors associated with AUD remission. For instance, several studies have found that the positive relationship between AA/ MHG involvement and substance use outcomes can be explained by an increase in people's social network and greater network support for abstinence. Other studies have found that people who participate in AA have improved self-efficacy and motivation for abstinence, which in turn appears to mediate the relationship between AA participation and better outcomes. In a study of DTR, Magura found that the relationship between DTR affiliation and abstinence was mediated by internal locus of control, which included internal motivation for change, coping skills, and self-efficacy.

MHGs such as AA also appear to mobilize the same change processes—such as coping, motivation, and self-efficacy—that are mobilized by many different types of professionally led treatment. Hence, the positive effects of AA and other MHGs may not be tied to the specific technical content the groups contain. Rather, their chief strength may lie in their ability to provide free, long-term, easy access to recovery related common therapeutic elements, the dose of which people can adaptively self-regulate according to their perceived need.

In summary, evidence suggests MHGs such as AA can help people make and maintain beneficial changes to their alcohol use while also helping to reduce healthcare costs by providing a free and responsive recovery support system. These groups may help people recover by providing an ongoing recovery specific social context that mobilizes active coping efforts, enhances self-efficacy, and continually remotivates people toward recovery. As such, MHGs appear to be a valuable resource that can serve as an important adjunct to, or, for some, an alternative to, professional care.

Facilitating Participation in MHGs

Given that MHG participation appears to be an effective and cost-effective public health resource, it is important to consider how clinicians can best facilitate patient participation in such groups. These clinicians surely include those working at specialty substance use disorder facilities, but it is primary care physicians, psychologists, psychiatrists, and emergency room staff who typically first come into contact with people who meet the criteria for an AUD. Indeed, most people with an AUD do not seek treatment at a specialty substance use disorder facility and, even when they do, they typically do not do so until 5 years after the onset of alcohol dependence. These statistics highlight how important it is that all types of healthcare providers routinely screen for AUDs and, when necessary, intervene.

One way to intervene is to facilitate patient participation in AA and other MHGs. To do that, clinicians—addiction specialists or not—can use strategies from 12-step facilitation (TSF) therapy. TSF is a professionally delivered intervention that is designed to educate patients about, and promote active engagement in Alcoholics Anonymous (AA). For example, clinicians using TSF might help connect patients with current MHG members or help them prepare to attend an MHG meeting by dispelling myths and providing information about what to expect. Clinicians also may monitor and discuss patients' reactions to meetings and explore potential barriers to attendance. And they can deliver TSF effectively to groups of patients as well as individuals.

When incorporating TSF strategies into practice, it is important for clinicians to keep an open mind about the utility of MHGs and have some degree of firsthand knowledge about groups such as AA. In fact, they may wish to attend local AA meetings that are open to the public and should become familiar with the times, locations, and various types of meetings available in their area, including meetings for beginners, for women only, or for young people. It also is useful for clinicians to develop a list of current and former patients who are willing to serve as AA contacts for new members.

There is evidence that primary care providers can successfully incorporate TSF strategies into their practice. In the Medical Management treatment condition of the COMBINE study, providers focused on educating patients about addiction, providing them with support and optimism for recovery, and encouraging them to comply with medication regimens. They also described MHGs, such as AA, to patients as a helpful way to maintain sobriety and gave them MHG pamphlets along with phone numbers, times, and locations of meetings. The providers emphasized that MHG participation was voluntary but encouraged patients to try the groups even if they were reluctant or had had a negative experience with such groups in the past. Providers also recommended that patients try several different meetings to find a good match. Although data on the efficacy of this approach among nonspecialty clinicians is not yet available, this study demonstrates the feasibility of implementing such approaches among addiction nonspecialists.

Clinicians Can Make a Difference in Patients' MHG Attendance

Several studies have demonstrated that clinicians can make a substantial difference in increasing the likelihood that patients will become and stay involved in MHGs. One early study found that when therapists had patients speak on the phone with current 12-step group members during an office visit and make arrangements to attend a specific meeting, every patient attended at least one meeting during the month following referral. In contrast, when therapists simply gave patients information about MHGs and encouraged them to attend a meeting, not one person attended. In the large, randomized controlled trial on alcohol dependence called Project MATCH, participants in a condition that included TSF attended AA at a significantly higher rate during treatment and within the first 3 months of follow-up than those receiving CBT and motivational enhancement therapy (MET).

Another randomized controlled trial compared standard 12-step group referral, in which patients were given a schedule of local meetings and simply encouraged to attend, to intensive referral, which included several additional components, such as introducing patients to current AA/Narcotics Anonymous members and addressing patient concerns about attendance. At the 6-month follow-up, similar numbers of patients in both conditions attended a similar number of 12-step meetings. However, those in the intensive referral condition became significantly more involved in several aspects of the 12-step program; for example, they were more likely to have a sponsor and to report having had a spiritual awakening. These patients also improved more on alcohol and drug addiction severity scores than did patients in the standard referral condition.

Evidence for the Beneficial Effects of TSF on Alcohol Use Outcomes Evidence for the Beneficial

Along with improving MHG attendance, studies show that TSF also positively influences patients' alcohol and drug use outcomes. In Project MATCH, for example, TSF was as effective as the more empirically supported CBT and MET at reducing the quantity and frequency of alcohol use posttreatment and at 1- and 3-year follow-ups. Moreover, TSF was superior to CBT and MET at increasing rates of continuous abstinence, such that 24 percent of the outpatients in the TSF condition were continuously abstinent throughout the year after treatment, compared with 15 percent and 14 percent in CBT and MET, respectively. Abstinence rates at 3 years continued to favor TSF, with 36 percent reporting abstinence, compared with 24 percent in CBT and 27 percent in MET.

Another study examined the incremental effects of incorporating TSF into an empirically supported cognitive-behavioral intervention, called Social Skills Training (SST).

The study compared SST alone with two other therapies that combined SST with TSF, but delivered them using two different therapeutic styles; one was more directive, spending 38 percent of session time discussing AA participation and encouraging AA attendance; the other was more client-centered, based on the principles of motivational interviewing. Patients in the directive TSF condition attended more AA meetings, became more involved in the AA program, and had a higher percentage of days abstinent than those receiving SST alone or the motivational interviewing-based TSF approach. Because the TSF motivational condition spent only 20 percent of session time discussing AA and SST alone spent only 8 percent of session time discussing AA, it suggests that more time spent focusing on AA and/or being more directive about attending

AA meetings may be optimal for enhancing AA participation and improving alcohol use outcomes. In yet another randomized study of alcohol-dependent outpatients, researchers attempted to increase social network support (NS) for abstinence by systematically encouraging patients to exploit the social aspects of AA. They compared this intervention with two other cognitive behavioral treatment interventions and found that study participants in the 12-step NS group were abstinent 20 percent more days than participants in the other conditions and were more involved in AA at 2-year follow-up. Furthermore, AA participation and the number of abstinent friends in the NS condition partially mediated this treatment effect.

Part Eight

Additional Help and Information

Chapter 64

Glossary of Terms Related to Alcohol Use and Abuse

abstinence: Not drinking any alcoholic beverage, including beer, wine, and hard liquor. It is recommended that all pregnant women abstain from alcohol to avoid fetal damage.

abuser: A person who uses alcohol or other drugs in ways that threaten his health or impair his social or economic functioning.

addiction: A state of dependence caused by habitual use of drugs, alcohol, or other substances. It is characterized by uncontrolled craving, tolerance, and symptoms of withdrawal when access is denied. Habitual use produces changes in body chemistry and treatment must be geared to a gradual reduction in dosage.

AIDS: Acquired immunodeficiency syndrome. Acquired—not inherited; immuno-relating to the body's immune system, which provides protection from disease-causing germs; deficiency-lack of immune response to germs; syndrome—a number of signs and symptoms indicating a particular disease or condition.

alcohol: A drink containing the substance ethanol.

alcohol dependence: A diagnosis of a maladaptive pattern of substance use as shown by three of the following criteria, noted in

---

This glossary contains terms excerpted from documents produced by several sources deemed reliable.

a 12-month period tolerance; withdrawal or use of alcohol to avoid withdrawal; use in larger amounts or for longer than intended; unsuccessful efforts to decrease or discontinue use or a persistent desire to do so; alcohol use as a major focus of time and life; abandonment of social, occupational, or recreational activities; continued use despite recognized psychological or physical consequences.

alcohol metabolism: Refers to the body's process of converting ingested alcohol to other compounds. Metabolism results in some substances becoming more or less toxic than those originally ingested. Metabolism involves a number of processes, one of which is oxidation. Through oxidation, alcohol is detoxified and removed from the blood, preventing the alcohol from accumulating and destroying cells and organs. A minute amount of alcohol escapes metabolism and is excreted unchanged in the breath and in urine. Until all the alcohol consumed has been metabolized, it is distributed throughout the body, affecting the brain and other tissues.

alcohol-related birth defects (ARBD): A term used to describe individuals with confirmed maternal alcohol use and one or more congenital defects, including heart, bone, kidney, vision, or hearing abnormalities.

alcohol-related neurodevelopmental disorder (ARND): A term used to describe individuals with confirmed maternal alcohol use, neurodevelopmental abnormalities, and a complex pattern of behavioral or cognitive abnormalities inconsistent with developmental level and not explained by genetic background or environment. Problems may include learning disabilities, school performance deficits, inadequate impulse control, social perceptual problems, language dysfunction, abstraction difficulties, mathematics deficiencies, and judgment, memory, and attention problems.

alcohol screening: A question-based method for identifying individuals with alcohol problems and assessing the severity of use.

alcohol use disorder (AUD): Problem drinking that becomes severe is given the medical diagnosis of "alcohol use disorder" or AUD.

Alcohol Use Disorders Identification Test (AUDIT): A simple ten-question test developed by the World Health Organization (WHO) to determine if a person's alcohol consumption is excessive. WHO designed the test for international use and it was validated in a six-country study. Questions 1–3 deal with alcohol consumption, 4–6 relate to alcohol dependence and 7–10 consider alcohol related problems. A score of eight or more in men (seven in women) indicates a strong likelihood of hazardous or harmful alcohol consumption. A score of 13 or more is suggestive of alcohol-related harm.

alcoholism: A treatable illness brought on by harmful dependence upon alcohol which is physically and psychologically addictive. As a disease, alcoholism is primary, chronic, progressive, and fatal.

binge drinking: Refers to the consumption of four or more drinks in about two hours. Binge drinking during pregnancy can result in fetal alcohol spectrum disorders (FASD).

birth defect: Physical or biochemical defect (for example, Down syndrome (DS), fetal alcohol syndrome (FAS), cleft palate) that is present at birth and may be inherited or environmentally induced.

blood alcohol concentration (BAC): The amount of alcohol in the bloodstream measured in percentages. A BAC of 0.10 percent means that a person has one part alcohol per 1,000 parts blood in the body.

brain disorder: It refers to conditions which cause impairing or debilitating behavior.

breathalyzer: It is a device used by police for measuring the amount of alcohol in a driver's breath.

brief intervention: Approximately one to four therapy sessions delivered to individuals with problem drinking and other problematic behaviors. The intervention may include advice to abstain from alcohol use or decrease alcohol consumption to below risk drinking levels, brief counseling, goal setting, and development of action plans.

CAGE: A screening tool for identifying risk drinkers. Each positive answer is scored as one point. A score of two or more points is considered evidence of possible risk drinking. The CAGE has been used effectively to identify alcoholic clients, but it may not be as sensitive as other brief scales with female populations. The acronym stands for:

C — Have you ever felt you ought to Cut Down on your drinking?

A — Have people ever annoyed you by criticizing your drinking?

G — Have you ever felt bad or guilty about your drinking?

E — Have you ever had a drink first thing in the morning to steady your nerves or get rid of a hangover (Eye-Opener)?

cirrhosis: It is a chronic disease of the liver marked by degeneration of cells, inflammation, and fibrous thickening of tissue. It is typically a result of alcoholism or hepatitis.

co-occurring: Simultaneous existence of a disorder (for example alcoholism) interacting with one or more independent disorders (such as depression, schizophrenia) or disabilities. The disorder/disability is of a type and severity that exacerbates the other conditions, complicates treatment, or interferes with functioning in age-appropriate social roles. In substance abuse, it is typically used to describe persons who have both mental illness and a substance abuse/dependence disorder.

cognitive-behavioral therapy (CBT): In the field of substance abuse treatment, CBT is an approach that includes self-management and relapse prevention strategies. It is designed to help individuals stop or reduce alcohol consumption by observing their drinking behavior, setting behavioral objectives, or training in skills to handle conflicts or stress without resorting to drinking.

coronary heart disease (CHD): CHD is a disease in which a waxy substance called plaque (plak) builds up inside the coronary arteries. These arteries supply oxygen-rich blood to your heart muscle.

counseling: A process of interpersonal communication by which a person with a need or problem is helped to understand his or her situation in order to determine and use viable solutions to meet the need or problem.

culture: It is broadly defined to include the customs and practices of a group of people. Diversity in cultures reflects differences in race, ethnicity, language, and nationality, and in shared values, norms, traditions, and customs. Street children may feel a part of more than one culture, e.g., that of their parents and several youth cultures (represented by the groups with whom they share common interests, beliefs and activities).

depression: Major depressive disorder is marked by a depressed mood or a loss of interest or pleasure in daily activities consistently for at least two weeks. This mood must represent a change from the person's normal mood; social, occupational, educational, or other important functioning must also be negatively impaired by the change in mood.

detoxification: The care provided to a dependent person during the period of reduction or stoppage of a dependence-producing substance with the aim of withdrawing the substance safely and effectively. A substance user might experience a difficult period of transition when he or she stops using a substance or reduces the amount of substance use after prolonged or excessive use.

diagnosis: The process of determining disease status through the study of symptom patterns and the factors responsible for producing them.

dopamine: It is a neurotransmitter that helps control the brain's reward and pleasure centers. Dopamine also helps regulate movement and emotional responses, and it enables us not only to see rewards, but to take action to move toward them.

dose: The amount of a substance that a person takes in a defined period.

drug: In medicine, the term refers to any substance with the potential to prevent or cure a disease or the potential to enhance physical or mental well-being. In pharmacology, the term "drug" refers to any chemical agent that alters the biochemical or physiological processes of body tissues or organisms. In common usage, the term often refers to illicit drugs, frequently used for nonmedical (e.g., recreational) reasons.

enabling: Allowing irresponsible and destructive behavior patterns to continue by taking responsibility for others, not allowing them to face the consequences of their own actions.

ethnicity, ethnic background: Refers to racial, national, tribal, religious, linguistic, or cultural origin or background.

ethyl alcohol: Ethanol is the member of the alcohol series of chemicals which is used in alcoholic beverages. It is less toxic than other members of this series, but it is a central nervous system depressant and has a high abuse potential.

fetal alcohol spectrum disorders (FASD): An umbrella term describing the range of effects that can occur in an individual whose mother drank alcohol during pregnancy. These effects may include physical, mental, behavioral, and/or learning disabilities with possible lifelong implications. The term FASD is not intended for use as a clinical diagnosis.

fetal alcohol syndrome (FAS): Describes individuals with documented prenatal exposure to alcohol and prenatal and postnatal growth retardation, characteristic facial features, and central nervous system problems.

gender: Widely shared ideas and expectations (norms) about women (girls) and men (boys). These include typical feminine and masculine characteristics, abilities, and expectations about how women and men should behave in various situations.

genetic disorders: Caused by a disturbance of one gene or several genes or chromosomes. They may be inherited or caused by environmental factors. Genetic disorders may cause various diseases and disorders.

heavy drinking: Refers to the consumption of five or more drinks on the same occasion on five or more days in the past month.

human immunodeficiency virus (HIV): It attacks the immune system and gradually destroys it. The body cannot defend itself against infections and this results in the condition known as AIDS.

intervention: An intervention is defined as an action or activity that helps in the prevention, modification, or treatment of problems related to substance use and other health problems.

intoxication: The state of being under the influence of one or more substances. There is a change in the person's wakefulness, alertness, thinking, perceptions, decision-making, emotional control, or behavior. The specific manifestations depend on the nature of the substance taken.

methadone: A drug used as a substitute to assist opioid (for example, heroin) users to stabilize their drug use and to move from injecting and other hazardous methods of taking drugs to (usually) oral forms of the drug. The drug is provided under supervised conditions as part of an intervention that may also involve counseling, primary healthcare, HIV treatment, and other services.

moderate drinking: Moderate drinking is defined as up to 4 alcoholic drinks for men and 8 for women in any single day, according to the National Institute on Alcohol Abuse and Alcoholism (NIAAA), and a maximum of 14 drinks for men and 7 drinks for women per week.

osteoporosis: It is a condition that weakens bones, making them fragile and more likely to break.

overdose: Deliberate or accidental consumption of a much larger dose than that habitually used by the individual. It leads to acute adverse physical or mental effects, which might have short- or long-lasting consequences. Overdose can lead to death. The amount of a substance that can cause death varies with the individual and the circumstances.

philtrum: The vertical groove between the nose and the middle part of the upper lip. Individuals diagnosed with fetal alcohol syndrome have a flattening of the philtrum.

posttraumatic stress disorder (PTSD): It is a psychiatric disorder that can occur following the experience or witnessing of a life-threatening events such as military combat, natural disasters, terrorist incidents, serious accidents, or physical or sexual assault in adult or childhood.

prenatal exposure to alcohol (PEA), prenatal alcohol exposure (PAE): Refers to the exposure of a fetus to alcohol through maternal drinking during pregnancy.

prevalence: The number of instances of the disorder in a given population at a designated time, for example the prevalence of fetal alcohol spectrum disorders is estimated to be at least ten per 1,000 live births.

prevention: The protection of health through personal and community efforts.

problem drinking: An individual with problem drinking has issues concerning alcohol use and may require treatment to manage the problem.

residential treatment: A living setting designed for individuals who have difficulty living with family or on their own due to alcohol abuse, alcoholism, physical problems, developmental disabilities, or mental illness. It provides adult supervision, therapy, and skills training in a large or small group setting.

standard drink: Because alcoholic beverages vary in alcohol concentration, drinks are designated by a standard drink conversion. One standard drink is 12 ounces (oz.) of beer, 5 oz. of wine, or 1.5 oz. of hard liquor. All have the same equivalency of 0.48 oz. of absolute alcohol.

substance abuse treatment: A therapeutic program, staffed by addiction professionals, for individuals with alcohol or drug problems. It may involve inpatient or outpatient care.

substance use disorder: It also known as alcohol/drug use disorder, is a condition in which the use of one or more substances leads to a clinically significant impairment or distress.

T-ACE: A screening tool for identifying pregnant women with alcohol problems. The tolerance question is scored as two points if the respondent reports needing more than two drinks to get high. A positive response to A, C, or E is scored as one point each. A score of two or more indicates likely drinking during pregnancy. The T-ACE has been found to be effective in identifying pregnant women who consumed sufficient amounts of alcohol to endanger a fetus. The acronym stands for:

T — **Tolerance:** How many drinks does it take you to feel high?

A — **Annoyed:** Have people annoyed you by criticizing your drinking?

C — **Cut Down:** Have you ever felt you ought to cut down on your drinking?

E — **Eye-Opener:** Have you ever had a drink first thing in the morning to steady your nerves or get rid of a hangover?

tolerance: A state in which the body's tissue cells adjust to the presence of a drug, a state in which the body becomes used to the presence of a drug in given amounts and eventually fails to respond to ordinarily effective dosages. Hence, increasingly larger doses are necessary to produce desired effects.

TWEAK: A screening tool for identifying pregnant women with alcohol problems. On the tolerance question, two points are given if a woman reports that she can consume more than five drinks without falling asleep or passing out. A positive response to the worry question yields two points and positive responses to the last three questions yield one point each. A score of two signals an at-risk drinker. TWEAK has been found to be highly sensitive in identifying women who are at-risk drinkers. The acronym stands for:

T — **Tolerance:** How many drinks can you hold?

W — **Worried:** Have close friends or relatives worried or complained about your drinking in the past?

E — **Eye-Opener:** Do you sometimes take a drink in the morning?

A — **Amnesia:** Has a friend or family member ever told you about things you said or did while you were drinking that you could not remember?

K(c)—**Cut Down:** Have you ever felt you ought to cut down on your drinking?

withdrawal: Symptoms that appear during the process of stopping the use of a drug that has been taken regularly.

Chapter 65

Directory of Support Groups for Alcohol-Related Concerns

Mutual-Help Groups

AA Online Intergroup
Website: www.aa-intergroup.org

Alcoholics Anonymous (AA)
P.O. Box 459
Grand Central Stn
New York, NY 10163
Phone: 212-870-3400
Website: www.aa.org

Moderation Management
2885 Sanford Ave.
S.W. 36026
Grandville, MI 49418
Website: www.moderation.org
E-mail: mm@moderation.org

SMART Recovery
7304 Mentor Ave.
Ste. F
Mentor, OH 44060
Toll-Free: 866-951-5357
Phone: 440-951-5357
Fax: 440-951-5358
Website: www.smartrecovery.org

Women for Sobriety, Inc.
P.O. Box 618
Quakertown, PA 18951
Phone: 215-536-8026
Fax: 215-538-9026
Website: www.
womenforsobriety.org
E-mail: contact@
womenforsobriety.org

Resources in this chapter were compiled from several sources deemed reliable; all contact information was verified and updated in April 2018.

Groups for Family and Friends

Adult Children of Alcoholics (ACA)
ACA World Service Organization (WSO)
P.O. Box 811
Lakewood, CA 90714
Phone: 310-534-1815
Website: www.adultchildren.org
E-mail: information@acawso.com

Al-Anon
1600 Corporate Landing Pkwy.
Virginia Beach, VA 23454-5617
Toll-Free: 888-425-2666
Phone: 757-563-1600
Fax: 757-563-1656
Website: www.al-anon.org
E-mail: wso@al-anon.org

Groups for People with Co-Occurring Disorders

Co-Anon Family Groups World Services
P. O. Box 3664
Gilbert, AZ 85299
Phone: 480-442-3869
Website: www.co-anon.org
E-mail: info@co-anon.org

Double Trouble in Recovery, Inc.
Brooklyn, NY 11224
Website: www.doubletroubleinrecovery.org

National Association for Children of Alcoholics (NACoA)
10920 Connecticut Ave.
Ste. 100
Kensington, MD 20895
Toll-Free: 888-55-4COAS (888-55-42627)
Phone: 301-468-0985
Fax: 301-468-0987
Website: www.nacoa.net
E-mail: nacoa@nacoa.org

Chapter 66

Directory of State Agencies for Substance Abuse Services

Alabama

Department of Mental Health
Division of Mental Health & Substance Abuse Services
100 N. Union St.
P.O. Box 301410
Montgomery, AL 36130-1410
Toll-Free: 800-367-0955
Phone: 334-242-3454
Fax: 334-242-0725
Website: www.mh.alabama.gov/sa

Alaska

Department of Health and Social Services
350 Main St. P.O. Box 110620
Ste. 214
Juneau, AK 99811
Phone: 907-465-3370
Fax: 907-465-2668
Website: dhss.alaska.gov

Resources in this chapter were compiled from several sources deemed reliable; all contact information was verified and updated in April 2018.

American Samoa

American Samoa Government
Department of Human and Social Services
Executive Office Bldg.
Pago Pago, AS 96799
Phone: 684-633-4116
Fax: 684-633-2269
Website: www.americansamoa.gov/services
E-mail: info@as.gov

Arizona

Department of Health Services
150 N. 18th Ave.
Phoenix, AZ 85007
Toll-Free: 800-867-5808
Phone: 602-542-1025
Fax: 602-364-0883
Website: www.azdhs.gov

Arkansas

Department of Human Services
305 S. Palm St.
P.O. Box 1437
Little Rock, AR 72203
Phone: 501-686-1001
TDD: 501-682-8820
Website: www.humanservices.arkansas.gov/about-dhs/dbhs

Colorado

Department of Human Services
1575 Sherman St.
Eighth Fl.
Denver, CO 80203-1714
Phone: 303-866-5700
Fax: 303-866-5563
Website: www.colorado.gov/pacific/cdhs/contact-us-5
E-mail: cdhs_communications@state.co.us

Connecticut

Department of Mental Health and Addiction Services (DMHAS)
410 Capitol Ave.
P.O. Box 341431
Hartford, CT 06134
Toll-Free: 800-446-7348
Phone: 860-418-7000
TTY: 860-418-6707
Website: www.ct.gov/dmhas

Delaware

Health and Social Services (DHHS)
Division of Substance Abuse and Mental Health (DSAMH)
1901 N. Du Pont Hwy.
Main Bldg.
New Castle, DE 19720
Toll-Free: 800-652-2929
Phone: 302-255-9399
Fax: 302-255-4428
Website: ww.dhss.delaware.gov/dhss/dsamh/contact.html

District of Columbia

Behavioral Health Addiction Prevention and Recovery Administration (APRA)
Department of Behavioral Health
64 New York Ave.
Third Fl.
Washington, DC 20002
Phone: 202-673-2200
TTY: 202-673-7500
Fax: 202-673-3433
Website: www.dbh.dc.gov
E-mail: dbh@dc.gov

Florida

Substance Abuse Program Office
Department of Children and Families
1317 Winewood Blvd.
Bldg. 1 Rm. 202
Tallahassee, FL 32399-0700
Toll-Free: 800-962-2873
Phone: 850-487-1111
Fax: 850-922-2993
Website: www.dcf.state.fl.us; www.myflfamilies.com

Georgia

Department of Behavioral Health & Developmental Disabilities
Office of Public Affairs
Two Peachtree St. N.W.
Fl. 24
Atlanta, GA 30303
Toll-Free: 888-785-6954
Phone: 404-657-5964
Fax: 770-408-5439
Website: mhddad.dhr.georgia.gov
E-mail: DBHDDconstituentservices@dbhdd.ga.gov

Guam

Behavioral Health and Wellness Center (GBHWC)
Department of Mental Health and Substance Abuse
790 Gov. Carlos G. Camacho Rd.
Tamuning, GU 96913
Toll-Free: 800-222-1222
Phone: 671-647-5440
Fax: 671-647-0250
Website: www.gbhwc.guam.gov
E-mail: care@gbhwc.guam.gov

Hawaii

Alcohol and Drug Abuse Division
Department of Health
601 Kamokila Blvd.
Rm. 360
Kapolei, HI 96707
Phone: 808-692-7506
Website: health.hawaii.gov/substance-abuse

Illinois

Department of Human Services
401 S. Clinton St.
Chicago, IL 60607
Toll-Free: 800-843-6154
Toll-Free TTY: 866-324-5553
Website: www.dhs.state.il.us/page.aspx?

Indiana

Division of Mental Health and Addiction
Family and Social Services Administration
402 W. Washington St.
Rm. W353
Indianapolis, IN 46204
Toll-Free: 800-457-8283
Phone: 317-232-7895
Fax: 317-233-3472
Website: www.in.gov/fssa/dmha/index.htm

Iowa

Department of Public Health
Lucas State Office Bldg.
321 E. 12th St.
Des Moines, IA 50319-0075
Toll-Free: 866-834-9671
Phone: 515-281-7689
Toll-Free TTY: 800-735-2942
Website: idph.iowa.gov

Kansas

Addiction and Prevention Services
Department of Social and Rehab Services
915 Harrison St.
Topeka, KS 66612
Phone: 785-296-6807
Website: www.srskansas.org/hcp/AAPSHome.htm

Kentucky

Division of Mental Health and Substance Abuse
275 E. Main St. 1E-B
Frankfort, KY 40621
Toll-Free: 800-372-2973
Phone: 502-564-4456
Toll-Free TTY: 800-627-4702
Fax: 502-564-9523
Website: chfs.ky.gov

Louisiana

Office for Addictive Disorders
Department of Health
628 N. Fourth St.
Baton Rouge, LA 70802
Toll-Free: 855-229-6848
Phone: 225-342-9500
Fax: 225-342-5568
Website: ldh.la.gov

Maine

Office of Substance Abuse and Mental Health Services
State House Station #11
Augusta, ME 04333-0011
Toll-Free: 800-499-0027
Phone: 207-287-2595
Toll-Free TTY: 800-606-0215
Fax: 207-287-4334
Website: www.maine.gov/dhhs/samhs

Maryland

Alcohol and Drug Abuse Administration
Department of Health and Mental Hygiene
201 W. Preston St.
Baltimore, MD 21201
Toll-Free: 877-463-3464
Phone: 410-767-6500
Website: health.maryland.gov/Pages/contactus.aspx

Massachusetts

Bureau of Substance Abuse Services (BSAS)
Department of Public Health
250 Washington St.
Boston, MA 02108
Toll-Free: 800-327-5050
Phone: 617-624–5111
Toll-Free TTY: 888-448-8321
Website: wwww.mass.gov/orgs/bureau-of-substance-addiction-services

Michigan

Department of Health and Human Services
333 S. Grand Ave.
P.O. Box 30195
Lansing, MI 48909
Toll-Free: 855-ASK-MICH (855-275-6424)
Phone: 517-373-3740
Website: www.michigan.gov/mdhhs/0,5885,7-339--352302--,00.html

Minnesota

Alcohol and Drug Abuse Division
Department of Human Services
P.O. Box 64977
Saint Paul, MN 55164-0977
Toll-Free: 866-333-2466
Phone: 651-431-2460
Fax: 651-431-7449
Website: mn.gov/dhs/general-public/about-dhs/contact-us/division-addresses.jsp

Mississippi

Bureau of Alcohol and Drug Abuse
Department of Mental Health
1101 Robert E. Lee Bldg.
239 N. Lamar St.
Jackson, MS 39201
Toll-Free: 877-210-8513
Phone: 601-359-1288
TDD: 601-359-6230
Fax: 601-359-6295
Website: www.dmh.state.ms.us/substance_abuse.htm

Missouri

Department of Mental Health
1706 E. Elm St.
P.O. Box 687
Jefferson City, MO 65102
Toll-Free: 800-364-9687
Phone: 573-751-4122
Fax: 573-751-8224
Website: dmh.mo.gov
E-mail: dmhmail@dmh.mo.gov

Montana

Addictive and Mental Disorders Division
Department of PH and HS
100 N. Park
Ste. 300
Helena, MT 59620-2905
Phone: 406-444-3964
Fax: 406-444-4435
Website: dphhs.mt.gov/amdd/Mentalhealthservices

Nebraska

Department of Health & Human Services
Division of Behavioral Health
State Office Bldg. Fl. 3
301 Centennial Mall S.
Lincoln, NE 68509
Phone: 402-471-7818
Fax: 402-471-7859
Website: dhhs.ne.gov/behavioral_health/Pages/beh_behindex.aspx

Nevada

Division of Public and Behavioral Health
Department of Health and Human Services
4150 Technology Way
Carson City, NV 89706
Phone: 775-684-4200
Fax: 775-684-4211
Website: dpbh.nv.gov
E-mail: dpbh@health.nv.gov

New Hampshire

Bureau of Drug and Alcohol Services
Department of Health and Human Services
105 Pleasant St.
Concord, NH 03301
Toll-Free: 800-804-0909
Phone: 603-271-6738
Website: www.dhhs.nh.gov/dcbcs/bdas/contact.htm

New Jersey

Department of Health
P. O. Box 360
Trenton, NJ 08625-0360
TTY: 609-292-6683
Website: www.nj.gov/health

New Mexico

Behavioral Health Services Division
Department of Health
1101 Fifth Ave., Ste. 250
San Rafael, CA 94901
Website: www.bhc.state.nm.us

New York

Office of Alcoholism and Substance Abuse Services (OASAS)
1450 Western Ave.
Albany, NY 12203
Phone: 518-473-3460
Website: www.oasas.ny.gov
E-mail: communications@oasas.ny.gov

North Carolina

Mental Health, Developmental Disabilities and Substance Abuse Services
2001 Mail Service Center
Raleigh, NC 27699-2001
Toll-Free: 800-662-7030
Phone: 919-733-7011
Website: www.ncdhhs.gov
E-mail: contactdmh@dhhs.nc.gov

North Dakota

Behavioral Health Division
Department of Human Services
1237 W. Divide Ave.
Ste. 1C
Bismarck, ND 58501-1208
Toll-Free: 800-755-2719
Phone: 701-328-8920
Fax: 701-328-8969
Website: www.nd.gov/dhs/services/mentalhealth
E-mail: dhsbhd@nd.gov

Ohio

Department of Mental Health & Addiction Services
The James A. Rhodes State Office Tower
30 E. Broad St. Fl. 8
Columbus, OH 43215-3430
Toll-Free: 877-275-6364
Phone: 614-466-2596
TTY: 614-752-9696
Website: mha.ohio.gov

Oklahoma

Department of Mental Health and Substance Abuse Services (ODMHSAS)
1200 N.E. 13th St.
P.O. Box 53277
Oklahoma City, OK 73152
Phone: 405-522-3908
Fax: 405-248-9321
Website: www.odmhsas.org

Oregon

Addictions and Mental Health Services (AMH)
Health Systems Division
500 Summer St. N.E.
Salem, OR 97301-1079
Toll-Free: 800-375-2863
Phone: 503-947-2340
Toll-Free TTY: 800-375-2863
Fax: 503-947-5461
Website: www.oregon.gov/oha/HSD/AMH/Pages/Contact-Us.aspx

Pennsylvania

Department of Drug and Alcohol Programs (DDAP)
One Penn Center
2601 N. Third St. Fl. 5
Harrisburg, PA 17110
Phone: 717-783-8200
Fax: 717-787-6285
Website: www.ddap.pa.gov

Puerto Rico

Mental Health and Anti-Addiction Services Administration
Carr. No. 2 Km 8.2
Bo. Juan Sánchez
Bayamon, PR 00960
Phone: 787-764-3670
Website: www.samhsa.gov/capt/about-capt/state-tribe-jurisdiction-contacts/puerto-rico

Rhode Island

Department of Behavioral Healthcare, Developmental Disabilities and Hospitals (BHDDH)
14 Harrington Rd.
Cranston, RI 02920
Phone: 401-462-3201
Website: www.bhddh.ri.gov

South Carolina

Department of Alcohol and Other Drug Abuse Services
1801 Main St.
Fl. 4
Columbia, SC 29201
Phone: 803-896-5555
Fax: 803-896-5557
Website: www.daodas.state.sc.us

South Dakota

DHS Division of Alcohol and Drug Abuse
3800 E. Hwy. 34 Hillsview Plaza
500 E. Capitol Ave.
Pierre, SD 57501
Phone: 605-773-3123
Fax: 605-773-7076
Website: dhs.sd.gov

Tennessee

Department of Mental Health and Substance Abuse Services
500 Deaderick St.
Nashville, TN 37243
Toll-Free: 855-CRISIS-1 (855-274-7471)
Phone: 615-532-6500
Website: www.tn.gov/behavioral-health.html
E-mail: OCA.TDMHSAS@tn.gov

Texas

DSHS Substance Abuse Services
P.O. Box 149347
Austin, TX 78714
Toll-Free: 888-963-7111
Phone: 512-776-2150
Toll-Free TDD: 800-735-2989
Fax: 512-206-5714
Website: www.dshs.state.tx.us/sa/default.shtm
E-mail: customer.service@dshs.texas.gov

Utah

Division of Substance Abuse and Mental Health
Department of Human Services
195 N. 1950 W.
Salt Lake City, UT 84116
Phone: 801-538-3939
Fax: 801-538-9892
Website: www.dsamh.utah.gov

Vermont

Alcohol and Drug Abuse Programs
Department of Health
108 Cherry St.
Burlington, VT 05402
Toll-Free: 800-464-4343
Phone: 802-863-7200
Fax: 802-865-7754
Website: healthvermont.gov/adap/adap.aspx
E-mail: vtadap@vdh.state.vt.us

Virgin Islands

Department of Health
3500 Estate Richmond
Christiansted, VI 00820-4370
Phone: 340-774-7700
Fax: 340-774-4701
Website: www.samhsa.gov/capt/about-capt/state-tribe-jurisdiction-contacts/u.s.-virgin-islands

Virginia

Department of Behavioral Health & Developmental Services
1220 Bank St.
Richmond, VA 23219
Phone: 804-786-3921
TDD: 804-371-8977
Fax: 804-371-6638
Website: www.dbhds.virginia.gov

Washington

Department of Social and Health Services
P.O. Box 45130
Olympia, WA 98504-5130
Toll-Free: 877-501-2233
Website: fortress.wa.gov/dshs

West Virginia

Bureau for Behavioral Health and Health Facilities (BBHHF)
350 Capitol St.
Rm. 350
Charleston, WV 25301
Phone: 304-558-0627
Fax: 304-558-1008
Website: dhhr.wv.gov/bhhf/Pages/default.aspx
E-mail: obhs@wvdhhr.org

Wisconsin

Bureau of Prevention, Treatment, and Recovery
Department of Health Services
1 W. Wilson St.
Madison, WI 53707
Phone: 608-266-1865
Toll-Free TTY: 800-947-3529
Website: www.dhs.wisconsin.gov

Wyoming

Behavioral Health Division
Department of Health
6101 Yellowstone Rd.
Ste. 220
Cheyenne, WY 82002
Toll-Free: 800-535-4006
Phone: 307-777-6494
Fax: 307-777-5849
Website: health.wyo.gov/behavioralhealth

Chapter 67

Directory of Organizations with Information about Alcohol Use and Abuse

Government Agencies That Provide Information about Alcohol Use and Abuse

Alcohol Policy Information System (APIS)
National Institute on Alcohol Abuse and Alcoholism (NIAAA)
Website: www.alcoholpolicy.niaaa.nih.gov

Center for Substance Abuse Treatment (CSAT)
Substance Abuse and Mental Health Services Administration (SAMHSA)
5600 Fishers Ln.
Rockville, MD 20857
Phone: 240-276-1660
Website: www.samhsa.gov/about-us/who-we-are/offices-centers/csat

---

Resources in this chapter were compiled from several sources deemed reliable; all contact information was verified and updated in April 2018.

Centers for Disease Control and Prevention (CDC)
1600 Clifton Rd.
Atlanta, GA 30329-4027
Toll-Free: 800-CDC-INFO
(800-232-4636)
Toll-Free TTY: 888-232-6348
Website: www.cdc.gov
E-mail: cdcinfo@cdc.gov

Division of Workplace Programs (DWP)
Substance Abuse and Mental Health Services Administration (SAMHSA)
Phone: 240-276-2600
Website: www.samhsa.gov/workplace
E-mail: dwp@samhsa.hhs.gov

National Heart, Lung, and Blood Institute (NHLBI)
Bldg. 31
31 Center Dr.
Bethesda, MD 20892
Phone: 301-592-8573
Website: www.nhlbi.nih.gov
E-mail: nhlbiinfo@nhlbi.nih.gov

National Highway Traffic Safety Administration (NHTSA)
1200 New Jersey Ave. S.E.
W. Bldg.
Washington, DC 20590
Toll-Free: 888-327-4236
Phone: 202-366-4000
Toll-Free TTY: 800-424-9153
Website: www.nhtsa.gov

National Institute of Allergy and Infectious Diseases (NIAID)
Office of Communications and Government Relations
5601 Fishers Ln. MSC 9806
Bethesda, MD 20892-9806
Toll-Free: 866-284-4107
Phone: 301-496-5717
Toll-Free TDD: 800-877-8339
Fax: 301-402-3573
Website: www.niaid.nih.gov
E-mail: ocpostoffice@niaid.nih.gov

National Institute of Arthritis and Musculoskeletal and Skin Diseases (NIAMS)
NIAMS Information Clearinghouse
Bethesda, MD 20892
Toll-Free: 877-22-NIAMS
(877-226-4267)
Phone: 301-495-4484
TTY: 301-565-2966
Fax: 301-718-6366
Website: www.niams.nih.gov
E-mail: NIAMSinfo@mail.nih.gov

National Institute of Diabetes and Digestive and Kidney Diseases (NIDDK)
Health Information Center
Toll-Free: 800-860-8747
Toll-Free TTY: 866-569-1162
Website: www.niddk.nih.gov
E-mail: healthinfo@niddk.nih.gov

National Institute of Environmental Health Sciences (NIEHS)
P.O. Box 12233
MD K3-16
Research Triangle Park, NC 27709-2233
Phone: 919-541-3345
Fax: 301-480-2978
Website: www.niehs.nih.gov
E-mail: webcenter@niehs.nih.gov

National Institute of Mental Health (NIMH)
Science Writing, Press, and Dissemination Branch
6001 Executive Blvd.
Rm. 6200 MSC 9663
Bethesda, MD 20892-9663
Toll-Free: 866-615-6464
Toll-Free TTY: 866-415-8051
TTY: 301-443-8431
Fax: 301-443-4279
Website: www.nimh.nih.gov
E-mail: nimhinfo@nih.gov

National Institute of Neurological Disorders and Stroke (NINDS)
NIH Neurological Institute
P.O. Box 5801
Bethesda, MD 20824
Toll-Free: 800-352-9424
Phone: 301-496-5751
Website: www.ninds.nih.gov

National Institute on Alcohol Abuse and Alcoholism (NIAAA)
Toll-Free: 888-MY-NIAAA (888-69-64222)
Phone: 301-443-3860
Website: www.niaaa.nih.gov
E-mail: niaaaweb-r@exchange.nih.gov

National Institute on Drug Abuse (NIDA)
Public Information and Liaison Branch
6001 Executive Blvd.
Rm. 5213 MSC 9561
Bethesda, MD 20892
Phone: 301-443-1124
Fax: 301-443-7397
Website: www.drugabuse.gov
E-mail: webmaster@nida.nih.gov

National Kidney & Urologic Diseases Information Clearinghouse (NKUDIC)
3 Information Way
Bethesda, MD 20892-3580
Toll-Free: 800-891-5390
Phone: 301-654-4415
Website: www.ninds.nih.gov/node/6854
E-mail: nkudic@info.niddk.nih.gov

Substance Abuse and Mental Health Services Administration (SAMHSA)
5600 Fishers Ln.
Rockville, MD 20857
Toll-Free: 877-SAMHSA-7
(877-726-4727)
Toll-Free TTY: 800-487-4889
Fax: 240-221-4292
Website: www.samhsa.gov

U.S. Food and Drug Administration (FDA)
10903 New Hampshire Ave.
Silver Spring, MD 20993
Toll-Free: 888-INFO-FDA
(888-463-6332)
Phone: 301-796-8240
Website: www.fda.gov

Private Agencies That Provide Information about Alcohol Use and Abuse

Adult Children of Alcoholics (ACA)
ACA World Service Organization (WSO)
P.O. Box 811
Lakewood, CA 90714
Phone: 310-534-1815
Website: www.adultchildren.org
E-mail: information@acawso.com

Alcohol Justice
24 Belvedere St.
San Rafael, CA 94901
Phone: 415-456-5692
Website: www.alcoholjustice.org

Alcoholics Anonymous (AA)
P.O. Box 459
Grand Central Stn
New York, NY 10163
Phone: 212-870-3400
Website: www.aa.org

Al-Anon
1600 Corporate Landing Pkwy.
Virginia Beach, VA 23454-5617
Toll-Free: 888-425-2666
Phone: 757-563-1600
Fax: 757-563-1656
Website: www.al-anon.org
E-mail: wso@al-anon.org

American Heart Association (AHA)
7272 Greenville Ave.
Dallas, TX 75231
Toll-Free: 800-AHA-USA
(800-242-8721)
Phone: 214-570-5978
Website: www.heart.org

American Liver Foundation (ALF)
National Office, 39 Bdwy.
Ste. 2700
New York, NY 10006
Toll-Free: 800-465-4837
Phone: 212-668-1000
Website: www.liverfoundation.org
E-mail: info@liverfoundation.org

Center of Alcohol Studies (CAS)
607 Allison Rd.
Piscataway, NJ 08854
Phone: 848-445-2190
Fax: 732-445-3500
Website: www.alcoholstudies.rutgers.edu

Center on Alcohol Marketing and Youth (CAMY)
Johns Hopkins Bloomberg School of Public Health
624 N. Bdwy.
Ste. 288
Baltimore, MD 21205
Website: www.camy.org

Co-Anon Family Groups World Services
P. O. Box 3664
Gilbert, AZ 85299
Phone: 480-442-3869
Website: www.co-anon.org
E-mail: info@co-anon.org

Higher Education Center for Alcohol and Other Drug Abuse and Violence Prevention
125 Stillman Hall
1947 College Rd.
Columbus, OH 43210
Phone: 614-292-5572
Website: www.hecaod.osu.edu
E-mail: hecaod@osu.edu

Mothers Against Drunk Driving (MADD)
511 E. John Carpenter Fwy
Irving, TX 75062
Toll-Free: 877-ASK-MADD (877-275-6233)
Website: www.madd.org
E-mail: media@madd.org

National Association for Children of Alcoholics (NACoA)
10920 Connecticut Ave.
Ste. 100
Kensington, MD 20895
Toll-Free: 888-55-4COAS (888-55-42627)
Phone: 301-468-0985
Fax: 301-468-0987
Website: www.nacoa.net
E-mail: nacoa@nacoa.org

National Association of Addiction Treatment Providers (NAATP)
The Chancery Bldg.
1120 Lincoln St., Ste. 1303
Denver, CO 80203
Toll-Free: 888-574-1008
Website: www.naatp.org
E-mail: info@naatp.org

National Center on Addiction and Substance Abuse (CASA)
633 Third Ave.
19th Fl.
New York, NY 10017-6706
Phone: 212-841-5200
Website: www.centeronaddiction.org

National Council on Alcoholism and Drug Dependence (NCADD)
217 Bdwy.
Ste. 712
New York, NY 10007
Toll-Free: 800-NCA-CALL (800-622-2255)
Phone: 212-269-7797
Fax: 212-269-7510
Website: www.ncadd.org
E-mail: national@ncadd.org

National Organization on Fetal Alcohol Syndrome (NOFAS)
1200 Eton Ct. N.W.
Third Fl.
Washington, DC 20007
Toll-Free: 800-66-NOFAS (800-66-66327)
Phone: 202-785-4585
Fax: 202-466-6456
Website: www.nofas.org
E-mail: information@nofas.org

SMART Recovery
7304 Mentor Ave., Ste. F
Mentor, OH 44060
Toll-Free: 866-951-5357
Phone: 440-951-5357
Fax: 440-951-5358
Website: www.smartrecovery.org

Students Against Destructive Decisions (SADD)
1440 G St.
Washington, DC 20005
Phone: 508-481-3568
Website: www.sadd.org

Women for Sobriety, Inc.
P.O. Box 618
Quakertown, PA 18951
Phone: 215-536-8026
Fax: 215-538-9026
Website: www.womenforsobriety.org
E-mail: contact@womenforsobriety.org

Index

Index

Page numbers followed by 'n' indicate a footnote. Page numbers in *italics* indicate a table or illustration.

A

D

E

G

I

M

N

O

P

Q

R

S